BUSINESS INFORMATION SOURCES

Third Edition

BUSINESS INFORMATION SOURCES

Third Edition

LORNA M. DANIELLS

UNIVERSITY OF CALIFORNIA PRESS

Berkeley   Los Angeles   Oxford

University of California Press
Berkeley and Los Angeles, California

University of California Press, Ltd.
Oxford, England

© 1993 by
The Regents of the University of California

Library of Congress Cataloging-in-Publication Data

Daniells, Lorna M.
    Business information sources / Lorna M. Daniells.—3rd ed.
        p.   cm.
    Includes bibliographical references and index.
    ISBN 0-520-08180-3
    1. Business—Bibliography.   2. Management—Bibliography.
  3. Reference books—Business—Bibliography.   4. Reference
books—Management—Bibliography.   I. Title.
    Z7164.C81D16   1993
    [HF5351]
    016.33—dc20   92-41827
                                                            CIP

Printed in the United States of America
9 8 7 6 5 4 3 2 1

CONTENTS

Chapter 9 BUSINESS IN AMERICAN SOCIETY, 215

Chapter 10 MANAGEMENT, 238

Chapter 19 HUMAN RESOURCES/PERSONNEL MANAGEMENT (INCLUDING INDUSTRIAL RELATIONS), 515

Chapter 20 PRODUCTION AND OPERATIONS MANAGEMENT, 552

Chapter 21 A BASIC BOOKSHELF, 582

PREFACE

This is a complete and thorough revision even though it may appear, at first glance, very much like the previous editions. I started from scratch once again, looking at all publications in light of the increasing quantity of business information published since 1985, in an effort to update the book without making it too much longer.

The purpose and scope remain the same. This book is intended as a guide to the vast and varied sources of business information for three types of users: (1) the practicing business person—to provide possible sources for solving particular business problems or to fill information needs and suggest books for professional reading; (2) the business student—as a general introduction to the literature of business; and (3) the librarian and information specialist—as a basic reference tool. In the business world, obtaining up-to-date information in an increasingly complex computerized age is imperative, yet many students and business persons either do not know what is available or how to find what they need. We have attempted here to help users find a selection of the better business books, periodicals, reference sources, and online databases.

Some general comments are necessary to set the scope and limitations of this volume. It is a selected, annotated list of business books and reference sources, with an emphasis on recent material in the English language. The selection was based on several factors: my experience as a business reference librarian; the accessibility of material, principally in Baker Library at the Harvard Business School but also in a few other Boston libraries; some personal preferences; and my endurance in what turned out to be a three-year concentrated project which has now become really too much for one person to accomplish alone. There is an admitted emphasis on books published in the United States, since these are the ones with which I am most familiar. Thus, because many good books necessarily are omitted, readers are urged to consult bibliographies mentioned throughout when researching any business topic.

Whereas this book focuses primarily on print sources, online databases play such an important role in this day of wide acceptance and usage that we hope we have also described here the most important business-related databases and CD-ROMs. They are covered along with other information on the same topic. In many instances, they are mentioned as the online counterpart of a print source rather than as a separate entry. For an alphabetical list of online sources mentioned, refer to the index under the heading "Computerized Information Services". Despite an effort to include the best of the databases, it is important to remind users that these are always changing and expanding, with new databases and CD-ROMs appearing almost daily. This book then should be used only as a point of departure in identifying business information online, with continuous monitoring of directories and other sources important for finding the most up-to-date information. Since speedy full-text access to journal articles is increasingly important, a new feature of this edition helps to identify the many magazines that are now available online in full text. See explanation at the end of this preface.

Chapter titles remain the same. Many older books have been eliminated to make room for more current ones; thus, with the exception of a few classics, much of the material described has been published within the past five years. More attention has been given to a few topics of recently developed interest and/or concern. For instance short sections have been added on the following: guides to economic and financial measures (Chapter 3); bonds and other fixed income securities; guides to reading the financial pages; guides to world stock exchanges; investment banking (in Chapter 8); competitive intelligence; leadership; managers (Chapter 10); health care marketing (Chapter 11); service industries (Chapter 18); job analysis (Chapter 19). In certain instances annotations are longer, and I hope this makes the book more useful.

Since it was not possible to read all the books cited or the many other volumes examined during the course of making these selections, the annotations, for the most part, are descriptive rather than critical. The fact that a value judgment may have been made in describing some books and not others should be of little significance in one's decision about which of several books to consult. Most of the books are of high quality, but the reader will want to look at several titles before deciding which will suit a particular need.

Two kinds of books are not covered in this work. Published proceedings of association conferences, with but a few exceptions, are not included even though they often contain useful information on new developments and new research. Business casebooks also are omitted unless they have a substantial percentage of text. An exception was made for books on strategic management which are often half text and half cases since the use of cases is especially important in developing strategic management skills.

This book is arranged roughly in two parts. Chapters 1 through 8 describe the basic kinds of business reference sources, such as bibliographies, indexes and abstracts, directories, statistical and financial sources, and data on current business and economic trends. With Chapter 9 the emphasis shifts to management and to each specific management function, so the arrangement of material is different. In this latter part, handbooks and basic textbooks are usually of greater importance, so their descriptions appear first, followed in each chapter by the reference works relating to the particular subject (bibliographies and abstracts, dictionaries, loose-leaf services, statistics, periodicals, directories, and names of associations). Chapter 21 lists a few important reference works indispensable for almost any small office library. A detailed subject index and an author/title index are at end.

Within each list of books I have attempted, where possible, to include examples of textbooks, books written especially for the practicing manager, and collections of readings. Textbooks, although written for course work, usually are intended also for management training programs and for general reading by business executives, although this fact is not mentioned in every instance. Selected readings are useful in amplifying concepts discussed in textbooks and in providing a broad and varied view of professional thinking not always found in a textbook.

Each book entry contains essential bibliographic data including pagination of books and pamphlets. We feel it is helpful for users to know the length of each book as an aid in assessing its value to them, since a work of over 700 pages presumably treats a topic in greater depth than does one under 100 pages. Special notice is made when a book contains a bibliography, a glossary, or has suggested reading lists. Usually only the U.S. publisher is given for each book unless it was originally published in another country, in which case the foreign publisher is cited along with the U.S. publisher when that was known. Where the title page of a book lists several cities as the location for a publisher, only the first location is given in the bibliographical citation.

Frequency of periodicals and serials is noted after the name of the publisher unless that information is included in the title. When a publication varies from the usual monthly, quarterly, etc., this information is provided in abbreviated form: for example "5/wk." refers to a daily newspaper consisting of five issues per week; "10/yr." refers to a journal published 10 times each year. The annotations for periodicals were usually based on an examination of 1991 or occasionally 1990 issues. Readers are cautioned that dates of issue for special annual issues or ranked lists in periodicals often vary from year to year. Notation is made at end of the annotation for each periodical when its articles are indexed in one of the better known commercial indexes or online databases, since this is important to many researchers. In addition an attempt was made to note which periodicals are also available online in full text. The names of these indexes and databases are cited as abbreviations (for example, "BPI" for *Business Periodicals Index*), and they are explained at the end of the preface. For other abbreviations consult the index.

Once again I have decided, after careful consideration, *not* to give prices, although I realize this disappoints some users. An exception is made for some very expensive publications when the price was easily found. Prices change so frequently that, even if checked at the last moment before publication (a lengthy chore), they would soon be out of date and inaccurate. Prices ARE included, however, in Chapter 21's "Basic Bookshelf."

To find current prices of American books and handbooks consult *Books in Print,* described in Chapter 1. Note especially whether the book is available also in a paperback edition, because that will obviously cost less than a cloth bound edition. Prices of periodicals and newspapers can be found by checking in one of the directories cited in the "Directories of Periodicals" section of Chapter 7. For locating directories that contain prices of government documents, market research reports, etc., consult the index to this book. Prices of highly specialized, expensive sources such as directories, financial manuals, and loose-leaf legal services can usually be obtained by a direct inquiry to the publisher.

Most of the books listed can be purchased through any bookstore, from a book agent, or directly from the publisher. Periodicals can be obtained through a subscription agent. These firms may also be willing to check a few prices for you. Complete names and addresses of American book publishers are listed in a volume of *Books in Print* and in several other annuals found in most libraries or bookstores. Potential buyers abroad will find that many of the better known publishers of business books (Irwin, McGraw-Hill, Prentice-Hall, for example) have branch offices in larger foreign cities.

Users will find at least one inconsistency in some entries. In a few instances I have listed handbooks under title but in most cases these are entered under the name of the editor. Also many journals are listed by title but some are cited instead under the issuing agency or firm. Cataloging experts seem to favor title entries, but I have vacillated. If this has caused problems for users, check for any title wanted in the index.

However much an author tries to avoid errors and inaccuracies, some are bound to appear in a work as comprehensive as this. I hope they are few and I will appreciate having them called to my attention along with any serious omissions or suggestions for improvement. The intent has been to provide information believed to be accurate as of May 1992. It is unfortunate that publishers make changes almost daily, and this possibility should be kept in mind as one searches for the publications listed here.

It has been a source of great personal satisfaction to realize, through the many complimentary comments and letters received about the usefulness of my book (as well as receipt of the prestigious Professional Award given by Special Libraries Association), that I have indeed achieved my longtime ambition to publish a bibliographical work that has made a significant professional contribution in the business information field. I hope this latest revision will prove to be even more helpful and well received.

ACKNOWLEDGMENTS

Many publishers were helpful in answering inquiries about their publications or about upcoming editions of their books. My special thanks go to two publishers: to Gale Research, Inc., for permission to use their *Encyclopedia of Associations* to find addresses for many of the associations cited, and to BiblioData and Ruth M. Orenstein for letting me use a 1991 edition of *FullText Sources Online* in checking for vendors with full-text databases covering articles in specific periodicals and newspapers. Other libraries were cordial in making their facilities available. Of special help was the wonderfully friendly staff at Harvard's John F. Kennedy School of Government Library for permitting me to use their OCLC machine on a regular basis.

The two previous editions of my book would never have been published without the complete support of the Harvard Business School while I was head of Baker Library's Reference Department. Now that I am retired, this latest edition has been accomplished on my own. I would be remiss, however, if I did not express appreciation to Dean John H. McArthur for making it possible for me to continue having access to Baker Library books and serials before they were cataloged. This has made my work more efficient, and I am deeply grateful. Members of the Library staff have been supportive. Those who need a special note of appreciation include Claire Abernathy, Mark Blumberg, Michael Curry, Terri Lewis, Erika McCaffrey, and the other reference librarians. Your cheerfulness and patience despite my frequent questions concerning serials and book orders meant a lot to me, but more than that, your making me feel I still "belonged" did more for my morale than you will ever know. Thank you very, very much!

Cambridge, Massachusetts
September 1992

ABBREVIATIONS USED
FOR PERIODICAL INDEXES

ABI/I   *ABI/INFORM* database
ASTI   *Applied Science & Technology Index*
BPI   *Business Periodicals Index*
PAIS   *PAIS International in Print*
PTS/F&S   *Predicasts F&S Indexes*
RG   *Readers' Guide to Periodical Literature*
SSI   *Social Sciences Index*
TI   *Trade and Industry Index* database

IMPORTANT DATABASE VENDORS

Throughout my book, when I have mentioned which indexes cover articles in a specific periodical, I have also cited which of the five important database vendors listed below offer full-text coverage of that periodical. It is important to note, however, that users must also know which specific database to use, and my citations do not provide this information. They give only an abbreviation for the name of the vendor as noted below. Therefore, any user wanting to access a specific periodical on a full-text database must check in another source to get the name of the database to use and the time period for which it is available in full text. One of these sources is the semiannual *Fulltext Sources Online,* described at the end of the section on "Computerized Information Services" in Chapter 2.

BRS   BRS Information Technologies, McLean, VA.
DATA-STAR   D-S Marketing, Ltd., London, England.
DIALOG   Dialog Information Services, Palo Alto, CA.
DOW JONES   Dow Jones News/Retrieval, Princeton, NJ.
MEAD/NEXIS   Mead Data Central, Dayton, OH.

1

METHODS OF LOCATING FACTS

**TYPES OF LIBRARIES – Business Services of Public Librar-
ies – University Libraries – Company Libraries – Other Special Libraries and Information Sources – Directories of Libraries and Information Centers – ENCYCLOPEDIC SOURCES OF
INFORMATION – Almanacs and Yearbooks – Encyclopedias –
Dictionaries (General) – Business Dictionaries – Comprehensive Booklists**

Since this book is to serve as a guide to business information, it must
first indicate where to go to look for material that may provide answers to an
information need. Therefore Chapter 1 will discuss briefly the kinds of libraries and information centers of use to businessmen, and then it will describe
several broad encyclopedic sources that are often good first places to check on
almost any topic.

TYPES OF LIBRARIES

The *American Library Directory* listed 34,613 public, academic and special
libraries in the United States and Canada in 1990. This is an awesome figure
when one contemplates what vast storehouses of information must then be
available for anyone to use. These libraries come in all sizes and varieties–
some are general, serving all people and covering all subjects; others concentrate on a particular subject or are limited to a specialized clientele. An
understanding of these differences can be useful.

BUSINESS SERVICES OF PUBLIC LIBRARIES

Today public libraries in almost every city with manufacturing and commercial interests have well-rounded collections of the books and reference tools
that are most useful to the business person. Some are in special departments
of the main library, occasionally combined with materials on economics or

the social sciences; others are in separate branches located near the business and financial district. The emphasis in these libraries is on *current* information—a large part of it in nonbook sources such as company and city directories, financial manuals, statistical sources, tax and other legal services, online databases, and current journals. Any person who makes the initial effort to visit the local business library, introduce him/herself to the reference librarian, and ask for guidance in unraveling the mysteries of its systems and procedures, will be amply rewarded by discovering the proverbial gold mine of information that can be of immense value to him in his work. He or she will discover a staff that is eager and ready to help, sources never dreamed of, useful guides, bibliographies or booklists the library prepares, and new surprises on almost every visit. Not only will much of the material needed be immediately accessible, but the business person will find also that librarians have at their fingertips a whole network of other information sources either via the telephone or through a cooperative system among libraries called "interlibrary loan" whereby books not located in one library may be borrowed by mail or messenger service for use in any other library. And all of this service is usually free of charge! Once this contact with a business library is established, assistance in answering specific inquiries for data or statistics is often no farther away than one's telephone, since public libraries also offer prompt and efficient telephone service. Several of the largest, best known business libraries in the United States are located in Brooklyn, Cleveland, and Newark, but there are many others in cities such as Boston, Dallas, Detroit, Los Angeles, Minneapolis, Philadelphia, and Toronto in Canada, to name just a few. It should not be inferred, however, that only large cities have good business libraries. On the contrary, many small cities with industrial interests have excellent library facilities, adequately financed and staffed with enthusiastic and service-minded librarians.

UNIVERSITY LIBRARIES

Every accredited business school has a good collection of materials needed to support its teaching program. The scope of its library reflects the nature of the courses, the extent of its research activities, and also whether it is a school for management or business administration exclusively or is combined with schools in such related departments as economics or public administration. Many of these libraries are located within the main university library building, while others, particularly the large ones, are in separate buildings or even on separate campuses. Business school collections tend to be more extensive than those in public libraries and to emphasize both the importance of maintaining a good collection of current materials and of preserving the essential retrospective, scholarly and theoretical publications that any first-rate permanent research collection must have. Several of the leading business school libraries are the Baker Library (Harvard), Dewey Library (MIT), Jackson Library (Stanford), Lippincott Library (University of Pennsylvania), Watson Library (Columbia), Management Library (UCLA), and Management and

Economics Library (University of Indiana). These and the many other business and management school libraries are necessarily concerned primarily with their own students, faculty and graduates, but they do arrange in varying degrees to assist any business person who has a serious need. Those libraries that are part of state universities make their facilities freely available to everyone as far as is possible; some of those in private universities have found it necessary to charge an annual fee for continuous use of their facilities by local businessmen. Thus, it is usually wise to exhaust the resources of a public library first before turning to college and university libraries.

COMPANY LIBRARIES

Many large progressive business firms have well-established libraries to serve their organizations. These specialized libraries are found not only in various manufacturing concerns but also in financial firms such as banks, insurance companies, and investment management firms; service firms such as those of accountants, consultants, market research, and advertising specialists; and businesses such as publishing, transportation, engineering, and technical and scientific companies. The executive who works for one of these firms is fortunate indeed because he or she has all informational needs taken care of quickly and thoroughly by staffs of well trained information specialists who concentrate their entire effort in the executive's behalf. These specialized librarians make it their business to know the information needs and interests of each individual in the company. They compile tailor-made bibliographies, do in-depth indexing and abstracting (often by using a variety of databases), route journals, alert individuals to new developments and publications, maintain clipping files for up-to-date subject retrieval and perform many other related tasks. Since their book collections are often relatively small and highly concentrated from a subject point of view, company librarians are experienced in knowing where to go or whom to telephone for speedy answers to questions, and they will usually take over the responsibility for research themselves rather than expect the executive to search. Although company libraries are usually not open to the general public, it is important to know of their existence and, for the lucky business person who is employed by a company with a library, it is obviously the first and usually the only one required to satisfy all usual information needs.

OTHER SPECIAL LIBRARIES AND INFORMATION SOURCES

The federal government is a prime source of information and advice. Many of its departments maintain libraries to collect materials in the area with which each is concerned. Although these libraries are most accessible to people living in the Washington, DC, area, there are other services of government agencies that anyone can take advantage of. The many excellent statistical publications of such agencies as the Department of Commerce and its Bureau of the Census, the Department of Agriculture, and the Bureau of Labor Statistics are well known, and several are discussed elsewhere in this book.

Periodic catalogs of government publications help to locate the wide range of material available either free or at a modest cost. These are described in Chapter 2. If one does not find answers to problems through published documents one can always write or telephone the agency involved or contact its regional office if there is one. A good example of one federal agency whose sole purpose is to give both financial assistance and management advice to small business persons is the Small Business Administration. Anyone can obtain a list on request of their various published management aids or bibliographies. Many state and municipal agencies and groups are also useful information sources that the business person can tap. State departments of commerce and development, local chambers of commerce, for instance, can often supply information on local economic conditions, plans, and trends. For information on particular industries or professions, many large trade and professional associations maintain excellent libraries. Although these are often restricted to use only by their own members, the librarians are usually willing to answer legitimate outside inquiries. A few associations publish short factbooks that are available free or at a nominal cost. Several examples of associations with good research and library facilities are the American Bankers Association, American Council of Life Insurance, American Institute of Certified Public Accountants, American Petroleum Institute, Motor Vehicle Manufacturers Association, and National Association of Realtors. An excellent directory of associations (which includes statements on the scope of each association and the names of its publications) is described in Chapter 7.

DIRECTORIES OF LIBRARIES AND INFORMATION CENTERS

The following directories will suggest many other libraries and information centers, both those located in individual cities and those covering specific subject specialties.

American Library Directory. New York: R. R. Bowker. 2 volumes (annual). Online counterpart is *ALD Online;* also on CD-ROM.

> This is a geographic list of libraries in the United States and Canada, including for each the names of top personnel, total number of volumes (books, periodicals, microforms, audio-visual materials), budget and expenditure figures, specific subject interests, special collections, automation information. It covers public libraries, college and university libraries, and many of the best known special libraries (corporate, association, government, etc.). At end of volume 2 are lists of related organizations such as library schools, networks and consortia, state library agencies.

Directory of Special Libraries and Information Centers. Detroit, MI: Gale Research, Inc. 3 volumes (biennial).

> Vol. 1, in two volumes, is a comprehensive guide to U.S. and Canadian "special libraries, research libraries, information centers, archives, and data centers maintained by government agencies, business, industry, newspapers, educational institutions, nonprofit organizations, and societies in the fields of science and engineering, medicine, law, art, religion, the social sciences, and humanities." For each, the data include: when founded; subject specialty; special collections; number of staff and

names of top people; holdings in total books, bound periodicals, microfilms, microfiche etc.; publications; computerized information services; networks/consortia; services offered (whether library is open to the public, whether it accepts interlibrary loans, etc.). Vol. 2 contains "Geographic and Personnel Indexes." Vol. 3 is a periodic supplement listing "New Special Libraries." Gale has also published a three-volume *Subject Directory of Special Libraries and Information Centers* (11th ed., 1988) which rearranges the information in the directory above under 27 subject sections. Of these, vol. 1 covers "Business, Government, and Law Libraries".

Special Libraries Association. New York Chapter. *Special Libraries Directory of Greater New York.* 17th ed. New York: 1989. 179 pp.

New York City has more good business, financial, and other specialized libraries than any other metropolitan area. This is a descriptive directory, arranged by broad subject. Several other SLA chapters with recently published directories are those in Boston, Philadelphia, and Texas. Directories are also available for a few SLA subject divisions. SLA itself publishes a directory of individuals who are members, called "Who's Who in Special Libraries." It contains indexes by SLA chapter and division, and by company/business.

ENCYCLOPEDIC SOURCES OF INFORMATION

With a brief description of various libraries as background, we can now turn to the principal task at hand, which in the first part of this book is to describe different kinds of reference works used for finding information. Probably most familiar to the largest number of people regardless of age or interest are compilations such as almanacs and encyclopedias, so full of material on almost any topic that they often answer one's need for concise data without recourse to other more specialized publications. Dictionaries are in constant use for checking word meanings or spelling. Lastly, while not as well known to the general public, comprehensive booklists are used daily by librarians for identifying books their clients request or those they want to order.

ALMANACS AND YEARBOOKS

Almanacs

The one-volume almanacs listed below are almost portable reference libraries and are well worth the modest paperback price for persons who like to keep a copy at hand either on an office desk or at home for the whole family. *The World Almanac* is perhaps the best known but the *Information Please Almanac* is also a comprehensive and useful source. Both are worldwide in scope, revised annually, and can answer all sorts of factual and statistical questions about nations, states, people, dates, events of the year, education, sports, the arts, awards, weather, geography, business, government, and on and on. *Whitaker's* is the British counterpart of *The World Almanac,* concentrating on factual data, organizations, and events in Commonwealth countries but also including a section on other countries.

Information Please Almanac: Atlas & Yearbook. Boston: Houghton Mifflin.

The World Almanac and Book of Facts. New York: Pharos Books (annual).

Whitaker's Almanack. London: J. Whitaker & Sons (annual). Distributed in U.S. by Gale Research, Inc., Detroit, MI.

Business Almanacs

The Business One Irwin Business and Investment Almanac. Ed. by Sumner N. Levine. Homewood, IL: Business One Irwin (annual).

A compilation of useful data, most of it taken from published sources and covering the following categories: a daily chronology of business events during the previous year; industry surveys; financial statement ratios (from FTC); general business and economic indicators; bank mergers; government budget data; largest companies (from *Fortune*, etc.); capital sources for small business; stock market information (includes how to read stock market quotations, stock market averages, guide to SEC corporate filings, a glossary, how to understand financial statements); tracing obsolete securities; bond and money market instruments; options and futures; taxes; investing in specific items such as real estate; computer services; future employment opportunities; U.S. demographics; employee benefits; the European community; and lastly business information directory (including sources of state information such as directories, international information sources, and a bibliography). This will be an especially useful volume for those libraries that do not have many of the separately published sources from which much of this data is taken.

Louis Rukeyser's Business Almanac. New rev. ed., with Louis Rukeyser, editor-in-chief. New York: Simon & Schuster, 1991. 587 pp.

This is very different from the almanac above, it being a compendium of some statistical data plus analysis and commentary on important aspects of the American economy. The material is arranged in 7 parts: people in business; money and wealth; government's role; the business of business; the money game (stocks, bonds, etc.); industries in America (very short sections on each of over 50 industries, including some information on leading companies); two ranked lists of largest companies (from *Fortune*). Some of the information here can be found in more detail or better treated in several other sources, but this almanac can still be of interest if it is revised more frequently than it has been in the past.

Yearbooks

Yearbooks differ from almanacs in that they usually give fuller information but concentrate either on a broad subject area, a country, or current trends and events (as in the case of yearly supplements to encyclopedias). One good example of a yearbook covering the governments of the world is:

Statesman's Year-Book. New York: St. Martin's Press.

This yearbook is in two sections, with the larger devoted to providing concise, descriptive data and a few statistics on "countries of the world." For each it usually includes history, area and population, constitution and government, defense, economy, energy and natural resources, industry and trade, communications, diplomatic representatives, and a few books of reference. The first section contains factual data about important international organizations.

Europa World Year Book gives much the same type of information, and it is also worldwide in scope despite the title. It is more strictly a list of names, organizations, etc., for each country and is especially useful for that information. A description of this important yearbook is included in both Chapters 5 and 16.

Yearbooks published for individual countries permit a more detailed review of the economic, social, and political developments in that country. Following are typical yearbooks for three countries:

Canada Year Book. Ottawa: Minister of Supply and Services (biennial).

India: A Reference Annual. New Delhi: Ministry of Information and Broadcasting.

Japan Economic Almanac. Tokyo: The Japan Economic Journal.

Although these usually include brief statistics, many governments also publish separate statistical yearbooks, a few examples of which are mentioned in Chapter 5. That same chapter also contains examples of several country guides, of interest primarily to executives intending to travel or live in those countries.

ENCYCLOPEDIAS

While almanacs and yearbooks serve a vital function in providing factual data, there are times when one wants to delve into a subject in somewhat more depth, so one will turn instead to an encyclopedia. Here can be found excellent, signed articles on every imaginable subject and on important personalities, each written in a concise but easy-to-understand style. Useful features include frequent illustrations, plates, diagrams, and maps. Good, short bibliographies accompany most entries for persons interested in pursuing a topic. A detailed index volume as well as yearbook supplements provide up-to-date information on current trends and events.

Even though only two of the leading encyclopedias are described in this book, it is important to realize that there are other good encyclopedias on the market today. Most libraries purchase more than one set so that they can be compared for completeness and accuracy on any topic. Persons considering which encyclopedia to purchase for either business or home use would be advised to consult with a professional librarian who can supply the name of a current article or book giving comparative evaluations.

The Encyclopedia Americana. International ed. Danbury, CT: Grolier, Inc., 30 volumes.

A top-ranking general encyclopedia with special emphasis on the sciences, social sciences, and humanities. There are good illustrations, plates, diagrams, maps. Bibliographies accompany the long articles (which are signed), and glossaries are sometimes included for technical or difficult terms. A detailed index appears as Vol. 30. This encyclopedia is continuously revised, and there is also an *Americana Annual* that contains the year's major political, economic, scientific, and cultural developments.

The New Encyclopaedia Britannica. 15th ed. Chicago: 1985. 32 volumes.

This newest edition of the oldest, perhaps most widely known, encyclopedia offers a completely new concept in encyclopedias based on a division of its 32 volumes into 3 sections. Readers are expected to turn first to the "Micropaedia" (12 volumes) because it serves both as a ready reference and as an index. This section contains over 120,000 short, factual articles and includes references to topics to be found in the "Macropaedia." The Macropaedia (17 volumes) contains over 4,200 major articles written by experts and treating each subject in much greater depth. Bibliographies accompany all articles for persons wanting to study a topic further. There are maps with articles on countries and their leading cities; many illustrations, plates, diagrams appear throughout. The last section is a one-volume "Propaedia," a systematic outline of the whole of human knowledge. Volumes 31–32 are an index. Thus the new encyclopedia is an exciting departure, designed to serve two functions: a reference function for quick answers and basic facts; an educational function, with longer articles that discuss and interpret the more important subjects. The annual *Britannica Book of the Year* provides an update for the events of the previous year. It is arranged by subject and also has a section giving one-page current figures on the economy of each of "The Nations of the World."

For convenience and ready reference, two large, one-volume encyclopedias contain excellent, concise data of wide general interest, with good illustrations and biographical facts about prominent persons. These are:

The Concise Columbia Encyclopedia. 2d ed. New York: Columbia University Press, 1989. 920 pp.

The Random House Encyclopedia. 3d ed. New York: Random House, 1990. 2,781 pp. plus an atlas (130 pp.).

DICTIONARIES (GENERAL)

English-language dictionaries serve an important function when one needs to check the meaning, spelling, or pronunciation of words, terms, or phrases. It is not essential to own an unabridged dictionary, but it is preferable to use one if it is available. The best known unabridged dictionary is:

Webster's Third New International Dictionary of the English Language, Unabridged. Springfield, MA: Merriam-Webster.

There are many abridged collegiate and desk dictionaries and it may be wise to look at a number before deciding which one to purchase for one's personal use. Noting the number of definitions and checking a sample in each may be helpful as well as looking for added features such as illustrations, a gazetteer, a style manual, a pronunciation key, lists of signs and symbols, weights and measures, colleges and universities, or a biography section. Paperback editions are often not as complete as clothbound dictionaries, but they are inexpensive, handy, and may serve the purpose. If searching for a "Webster's," care should be taken not to select one of the several imitations that can now legally use this name. (The one published by G. & C. Merriam is the official "Webster.") Several good collegiate dictionaries are listed below. The dates and pages are included only for comparative purposes; these volumes are updated at regular intervals, and you will obviously want to purchase the latest edition available.

Random House Webster's College Dictionary. New York: Random House, 1991. 1,568 pp.

Webster's Ninth New Collegiate Dictionary. Springfield, MA: Merriam-Webster, 1989. 1,563 pp. Also on CD-ROM.

Webster's New World Dictionary. 3d college ed. New York: Simon & Schuster, 1988. 1,574 pp.

Thesaurus

Anyone who wants to write or speak effectively should have a personal copy of a good thesaurus and use it often. Unlike a dictionary, a thesaurus arranges words and phrases according to the ideas they express. Thus they are excellent for: finding the most appropriate word when we know what we mean but can't think of how to say it; when we are looking for a better way of expressing a thought; when we find ourselves using one term to excess and wish to find another. They are also a good means of enriching vocabulary. The index in a thesaurus is the key to its effective use since the words and phrases are classified. The following thesaurus has been a useful household/office/library item for many years:

Roget's International Thesaurus. 4th ed. rev. by Robert L. Chapman. New York: T.Y. Crowell, 1977. 1,317 pp. Paperback published in 1984 by Harper & Row.

BUSINESS DICTIONARIES

Most business dictionaries concentrate on just one area of business, such as accounting, finance, investment management, or marketing. These are described with other reference material on each subject, and they can all be located by checking in the index to this book under "Dictionaries." Of special interest are the several good economic dictionaries (those of most interest to business) listed in Chapter 3 and a few on management in Chapter 10.

There is no one dictionary that stands out as being *the* best in an area as broad as the entire field of business, and surely no dictionary under 500 pages can hope to cover all important terms and concepts on every aspect, even though most of them have two columns per page. Thus it is helpful to have access to more than just one business/management dictionary and also to consider using one of the more specialized dictionaries when the term you seek relates to one functional area such as finance. Of the five dictionaries described here, you will notice that four combine business with related topics (economics, finance, management); one has an international focus.

Ammer, Christine, and Dean S. Ammer. *Dictionary of Business and Economics.* Expanded and enlarged ed. New York: Free Press, 1986. 517 pp.

These authors have focused rather successfully on covering the whole range of important business and economics terms. An effort was made to write simple yet clear definitions and to include helpful examples with some.

Friedman, Jack P. *Dictionary of Business Terms.* New York: Barron's, 1987. 650 pp. paper.

A useful, recent dictionary of more than 6,000 key business terms intended for anyone who needs to understand business terminology. It was prepared with the help of 17 contributing editors who each focused on one or more functional area of business. The definitions are concise but meaningful, and there is frequent use of cross-references to related terms. Abbreviations and compound interest tables are at end.

Johannsen, Hano, and G. Terry Page. *International Dictionary of Management.* 4th ed. East Brunswick, NJ: Nichols/GP Publishing, 1990. 359 pp. Published also in London by Kogan Page.

This is a good dictionary covering the whole area of business and management, with its more than 6,000 concisely defined terms, techniques, and concepts of use and interest worldwide. Occasionally it notes U.K. and/or U.S. usage of a term, and often contains cross references. At end is a directory of associations, trade unions, and other organizations referred to in the dictionary; also a list of world currencies and time zones.

Rosenberg, Jerry M. *Dictionary of Business and Management.* 2d ed. New York: Wiley, 1983. 631 pp.

Rosenberg's dictionary contains concise definitions for approximately 10,000 business and management terms in current usage, with some abbreviations, acronyms, associations, etc., and occasional cross-references. Useful supplementary data in an appendix includes units of measurement, interest tables, foreign exchange, relevant quotations, list of graduate business schools, summary of major U.S. business and economic events, 1776–1983. A third edition is announced for publication in 1992, but it will be shorter (384 pp.) and contain fewer definitions (7,500).

Terry, John V. *Dictionary for Business & Finance.* Fayetteville: University of Arkansas Press, 1989. 497 pp. paper.

A recent paperback dictionary, this is the effort of a finance professor who was not satisfied with the dictionaries combining major terms in both business and finance. He includes terms in such related areas as investing, insurance, real estate, accounting, banking, etc., but not in as much depth as a dictionary focusing on just one of these topics. Useful appendices explain ratios, formulas, job titles, real estate and financial abbreviations.

Glossaries

A glossary is a short list of difficult terms usually limited to a particular area of knowledge and included in some textbooks to help the reader understand concepts and terminology used in the book. These can be helpful as one studies in particular functional areas of business and so, when a textbook we cite includes a glossary, this fact is noted in the annotation. See, for example, the books on real estate principles and practices in Chapter 15—almost all of them contain glossaries.

Dictionaries of Acronyms and Abbreviations

Acronyms, Initialisms & Abbreviations Dictionary. Detroit, MI: Gale Research, Inc. 3 volumes in 5 (annual).

Vol. 1 (in 3 parts) contains not only acronyms, initialisms, and abbreviations but also contractions, alphabetic symbols, and similar condensed appellations. It covers a wide range of subjects and is kept up to date by vol. 2, *New Acronyms, Initialisms*

& Abbreviations, published as two interim supplements. Vol. 3 is a *Reverse Acronyms, Initialisms & Abbreviations Dictionary.*

De Sola, Ralph. *Abbreviations Dictionary.* Augmented International 7th ed. New York: Elsevier, 1986. 1,240 pp.

As an alternative to the first volume above, this less expensive dictionary covers abbreviations, acronyms, appellations, contractions, geographic equivalents, initialisms, nicknames, and much more. Among the many useful supplementary lists in back are: abbreviations for airlines, railroads, steamship lines, airports, nations, capitals of the world, and states in the U.S.; also the Greek alphabet, Roman numerals, international conversions, signs and symbols, superlatives, weather symbols, birthstones, wedding anniversaries.

COMPREHENSIVE BOOKLISTS

Several comprehensive, periodic lists of all in-print books (*not* government publications, services, or pamphlets) are published by commercial publishing firms and university presses. These are excellent for identifying titles and prices of all books on a particular subject or by an individual author. Every library, regardless of size, and most bookstores will have at least one of these bibliographies. If it is not in evidence, you should feel free to ask for it, because librarians and bookstore personnel usually keep these close by for checking purposes. Note that these booklists cover all areas of knowledge and not just business. Bibliographies and booklists focusing on business are described in Chapter 2; directories needed to identify periodicals and newspapers are in Chapter 7.

United States

Books in Print. New York: R. R. Bowker. 8 volumes (annual); and *Subject Guide to Books in Print.* 5 volumes (annual). Also available online and on CD-ROM discs.

These volumes list more than 850,000 titles available from over 33,000 U.S. publishers, with three volumes of *Books in Print* indexing the books by author, and three volumes by title. The two other volumes consist of "Books Out of Print and Out of Stock Indefinitely," and a publishers' index. For each book the information includes publisher, publication date, paging (usually), and price. *Subject Guide to Books in Print* is a companion series that lists all of these books (except for fiction) by specific subject, and so it is a good source if you want to know what recent books have been published in the U.S. on any one topic (corporate mergers, franchises, or public speaking, for example). A midyear author/title/subject *Books in Print Supplement* (2 volumes) gives updated information with price and other major changes, out-of-print titles, and new and forthcoming books. For paperback books only, consult their *Paperbound Books in Print,* semiannual, in 3 volumes.

Since Bowker now has all of this information on computer tapes, they are able to produce separate annual volumes devoted to specific subject areas such as medicine and healthcare, religion, science and technology. There are also volumes covering children's books, and large-print books. Bowker also publishes the monthly *American Book Publishing Record,* a continuing list of newly published U.S. books from nongovernmental publishers. This is of use primarily to librarians for order checking. Each issue is arranged by the Dewey Decimal classification, with author/title/subject indexes but no cumulation.

Among Bowker's other more specialized publication lists is an annual comprehensive bibliography of spoken word audiocassettes called *On Cassette*. It is described in the Chapter 2 section on "Microforms and Cassettes."

Cumulative Book Index. Bronx, NY: H.W. Wilson (monthly, except August, with quarterly and annual cumulations). Available also online in *WILSON-LINE,* and on CD-ROM as *WILSONDISC.*

This is a continuing worldwide author/title/subject index of English-language books, including publication date and price for each.

Forthcoming Books. New York: R. R. Bowker (bimonthly). Available also on CD-ROM discs.

Occasionally one needs to know about books that are in press and about to be published. This lists, by title, author, and subject, not only books to be published in the U.S. in the coming five months but also updated information on books published since the previous summer. There is also a list of publishers at end.

Paperbound Books in Print. New York: R. R. Bowker (semiannual).

Provides continuing, complete coverage for current, in-print paperback books, and forthcoming books, arranged by subject, and with an author index.

Great Britain

Whitaker's Books in Print. London: J. Whitaker & Sons Ltd. 4 volumes (annual). Also available online and on CD-ROM.

This is an author/title/subject index to more than 484,000 books in print and for sale in the United Kingdom, from over 16,000 publishers, including books published worldwide in the English language and available in Western Europe. A monthly that updates this list is available on microfiche.

A related annual is *Whitaker's Book List* which is an alphabetical author/title list and some subjects (when that is part of the title) for all books published in the U.K. during the previous year. This is a cumulation of two current publications useful for checking recent books: *The Bookseller,* a weekly which includes in each issue a list called "Publications of the Week"; and *Whitaker's Books of the Month & Books to Come,* a monthly author/title/subject list of new books published in the U.K. and those announced by publishers as being forthcoming. This monthly also includes English language titles published in Western Europe and those published elsewhere in the world which are available in the U.K.

Periodic booklists are compiled in other countries. Persons interested in checking these can consult with a librarian about their availability.

2

BASIC TIME-SAVING SOURCES

Bibliographies of Business Literature – Indexes and Abstracts – Government Publications – Doctoral Dissertations – Computerized Information Services – Microforms and Cassettes – Handbooks – Loose-leaf Services

There are many aids available to help one locate useful business information. A familiarity with some of these can be advantageous in carrying out a successful library search with the least expenditure of time. This chapter discusses several of the principal kinds of time-saving sources.

BIBLIOGRAPHIES OF BUSINESS LITERATURE

In undertaking any literature or statistical search the first step is to determine whether or not the information needed is already available. For statistics this is a matter of using basic bibliographies of statistics (mentioned in Chapters 4 and 5) and also database directories (listed later in this chapter). For literature searches, this can be ascertained by checking in card catalogs, in books, and in indexes (both those that are in hard copy and those that are online), looking for recent bibliographies that may cover the subject. Today more and more bibliographies are being compiled on a wide range of subjects. Those that are annotated are preferable because the descriptive notes often indicate which citations are most pertinent.

Every chapter in this book includes the names of bibliographies on specific topics. In the section below are a few that cover all business literature or business reference sources and also several examples of booklists and bibliographies prepared by libraries or other organizations. A few lists on management in general are in Chapter 10, while the basic bibliographies of economic literature are included in Chapter 3.

Bibliographies of Books

Bibliographic Guide to Business and Economics. Boston: G. K. Hall. 3 volumes (annual).

This guide will be of most use to librarians as a bibliographical checklist because it is a comprehensive author/title/subject listing of all business and economics materials cataloged during one year by the Library of Congress and the Research Libraries of the New York Public Library, both of which have extensive collections. It was begun in 1975 and contains complete bibliographical citations but no annotations. Inconvenient to use for long-term coverage of one author or subject because there is no cumulative volume.

Business Administration Reading Lists and Course Outlines. Durham, NC: Eno River Press, 1990. 14 volumes.

Of interest primarily to academic persons and graduate students, this is a series of paper-bound volumes giving the required reading lists and course outlines for a sampling of individual courses (both undergraduate and graduate) at selected universities. Each volume concentrates on one of the following business functional areas: accounting; marketing; corporate finance and investments; financial theory, institutions, and money markets; international business; international banking and finance; organizational behavior; industrial relations and human resources management; quantitative methods, research design and computer applications in business; business, government, and society; business policy and strategy; risk, decision making, and bargaining; entrepreneurship, small business, and venture capital; management communication. Universities represented (none of them completely) include Columbia, Massachusetts Institute of Technology, New York University, University of Michigan, University of Pennsylvania. This series will need to be updated periodically in order to be of continuing interest. The complete set cost $225 in 1991 ($20 per volume).

Companion series are published in the following two subject areas: *Economics* (1990, 25 volumes); *Political Science* (1989, 13 volumes).

Directions. Bridgewater, NJ: Baker & Taylor Books (monthly).

Baker & Taylor is one of several book distributors offering a wide range of customized book fulfillment programs for all types of libraries. This is their monthly list of book selections from their "approval program," a service which assists libraries by automatically shipping books according to individual arrangements with each library. Thus this is a useful continuing list of new books, arranged by over 130 subjects. Those topics of most interest to business are: accounting and finance; business administration; economics; financial economics; industrial economics; industrial engineering; international economics; labor economics; transportation. Although used primarily by librarians for checking, this can be an interesting short list for anyone who wants to keep informed about new books on specific subjects. There is no cumulation.

University Research in Business and Economics. Morgantown, WV: Published for the Association for University Business and Economic Research by the Bureau of Business Research, West Virginia University (annual).

A more specialized bibliography, this is a useful two-part list (by subject and by name of university) of the books, bulletins and other series, working papers, and selected articles in journals published by each AUBER-member business school.

An author index is at end. Slow in publishing, with the latest edition published in 1991 covering only the year 1989.

Booklists Compiled by Libraries and Organizations

To keep informed about newly published business books, it is worthwhile to review, on a regular basis, one or more of the various booklists, checklists, or bibliographies compiled by many libraries and organizations. These may be periodic lists of selected books added to the business section of a public library or those in a business school library, a company library, or an association or government agency library. Public libraries almost always have guides or lists distributed free or at a small cost to users. Those lists prepared by specialized institutions and organizations are not always available to outsiders, but this is well worth investigating if an especially pertinent list is found.

A number of business schools prepare good lists of their current acquisitions, but unfortunately these usually are available only on a limited basis outside the school. There are several exceptions. The University of Chicago publishes a short list of "Books Received" (arranged by subject) that appears in each issue of its *Journal of Business*. Indiana University includes an annotated "Book Notes" in frequent issues of *Business Horizons*. Baker Library of the Harvard Business School offers the following two periodic bibliographies on a subscription basis:

Baker Library. *Recent Additions*. Boston: Baker Library, Harvard Business School (monthly).

A monthly, numbered list (not annotated) of most of the books and substantial pamphlets added to Baker Library. The books in each issue are arranged within 16 broad subject headings, and then by title. Information given for each book includes author, publisher, paging, price (when known), call number in Baker Library, whether it contains a bibliography. A few new serials and title changes are listed at the front.

Harvard Business School Core Collection: An Author, Title, and Subject Guide. Boston: Harvard Business School Press (annual).

This is a computer-produced list of a selection of around 3,400 English-language business books collected on open shelves in Baker Library's Reading Room to encourage HBS students to browse among a relatively small group of recent books. Books are added to the collection on a continuing basis, but the collection is kept at about the same number through periodic weeding. This list is not meant as a purchasing guide for other libraries, but it does attempt to include a few representative titles in each subject field. It is a numbered list, arranged by subject and then by title. The information about each book includes publisher, date, paging, price when known, whether it contains a bibliography, Baker Library's call number, the LC and ISBN numbers. There are separate sections covering books on international business, also arranged by subject, and business books pertaining to a particular region. The four indexes are by: country, detailed subject, author, title. It is unfortunate that the indexes do not give complete citations; the author index, for example, cites only the item number, making it necessary to check the number to find out what the title is. A directory of publishers is at end.

In former days many public libraries compiled and reproduced series of short bibliographies for their users, with each issue focusing on a different business topic of current interest. Today library budget cuts have forced elimination of many of these. One useful series still being published as of 1991 is:

Brooklyn Public Library. *Service to Business & Industry.* Brooklyn, NY (10/yr.).

> Useful folded two-page annotated lists on subjects of current interest, with some each year compiled by the Business Library and others by the Science and Industry Division. Several topics covered in 1990 by the Business Library were: "Retirement," "Selling to the Government," "Starting a Small Business."

Book Reviews

Checking critical book reviews on a continuing basis can also be a way of keeping informed about recent books on business subjects, although it usually takes up to a year for a review to appear in one of the professional journals. When attempting to find the review of a particular book, try using one of the Wilson indexes (see next section). Their *Business Periodicals Index,* for example, has a separate listing in each issue, arranged by author, of the reviews appearing in journals which that index covers. If you do not find the reviews you want there, you can try using one of the two general indexes of book reviews found in most large public or university libraries, but be warned that these do not cover the business field well. They are: *Book Review Digest* (H.W. Wilson Co.; 10/yr.; also available online as *WILSONLINE* and on CD-ROM as *WILSONDISC*) and *Book Review Index* (Gale Research, Inc.; bimonthly; also available online). The first is the more useful for its helpful excerpts from reviews; the latter merely identifies the source, but it does cover more journals.

For each of the periodicals described throughout this book, notice is made when that publication contains book reviews. Some of these book review sections are better and more thorough than others. Several of the more useful ones appear in: *Academy of Management Review; Accounting Review; Administrative Science Quarterly; The Executive; Industrial and Labor Relations Review; Journal of Economic Literature; Personnel Psychology.*

Two quarterly reviews of business books are:

Business Book Review. Barrington, IL: Corporate Support Services (quarterly).

> Each issue describes about 15 business books which the editor feels are most important. For each, it summarizes the contents, gives an evaluation, the audience/ intentions, and reading suggestions.

Business Library Review: An International Journal. New York: Gordon and Breach Science Publishers (quarterly).

> This is a recently published quarterly (1990) taking the place of *The Wall Street Review of Books* and *Economics and Business: An International Bibliography.* Each issue contains reviews of individual business/economic books, comparative analyses of several works on the same subject, and at the end a list of further selected titles

with one-sentence annotations. Occasionally it may also contain a review of a presentation in electronic format. The first few issues focus on books published more than five years ago; it is hoped they will eventually include more recent business books.

Bibliographies of Business Information

The Basic Business Library: Core Resources. Ed. by Bernard S. Schlessinger. 2d ed. Phoenix, AZ: Oryx Press, 1989. 278 pp.

Second edition of a useful three-part bibliography. Part 1 is an annotated core list of printed business reference sources, arranged by title with a subject index. Part 2 is a descriptive list of literature on business libraries and business reference, primarily those appearing as articles in periodicals from 1976 to 1987. Part 3 contains an essay on organization of materials in business libraries, as well as descriptive lists of online business databases, investment sources, government information, and business periodicals essential for the smaller business library.

Brown, Barbara E., ed. *Canadian Business and Economics: A Guide to Sources of Information.* rev. ed. Ottawa: Canadian Library Association, 1984. 469 pp. A new edition is scheduled for publication late in 1991.

This is a useful annotated guide to books, reference publications, and services on Canadian business and economics. The text is in both English and French; the arrangement is by broad subject, then by more precise subject. There are author/ title indexes. Although this edition has been revised to cover changes only as of early 1981, the new edition will incorporate more recent material.

Encyclopedia of Business Information Sources. Detroit: Gale Research, Inc. (biennial, with an interim supplement).

A useful listing of information sources on detailed subjects, industries, and business topics, running from the "Abrasives Industry" to the "Zinc Industry." For each of its some 21,000 citations it covers, where applicable, the names of abstracting and indexing services, almanacs and yearbooks, bibliographies, biographical sources, directories, encyclopedias and dictionaries, financial ratios, handbooks and manuals, online databases, periodicals and newsletters, price sources, research centers and institutes, statistics sources, trade associations, and professional societies.

Companion volumes are *Encyclopedia of Geographic Information Sources: U.S. Volume* (4th ed., 1987, 437 pp.) and *Encyclopedia of Geographic Information Sources: International Volume* (1988, 479 pp.), each described elsewhere in this book.

Freed, Melvyn N., and Virgil P. Diodato. *Business Information Desk Reference: Where to Find Answers to Business Questions.* New York: Macmillan, 1991. 513 pp.

As the subtitle indicates, this is a new type of reference guide in that it uses a question-and-answer format for finding published business information. Section C is arranged by subject, listing "where should I go to find. . ." (each topic), and then citing one or more possible sources. Section D then contains descriptive listings of the printed sources, arranged by type of source such as "directories". Sections E and F do the same for online databases. Sections A and B provide brief guidelines for finding and evaluating business information; sections G and H are directories of selected business and trade organizations and federal departments and agencies. Appendixes contain additional online databases and directories of publishers.

Grant, Mary M., and Riva Berleant-Schiller, comps. *Directory of Business and Financial Services.* 8th ed. New York: Special Libraries Association, 1984. 189 pp.

This directory is now out of date, but a 9th edition is in progress by two different compilers (Charles J. Popovich and M. Rita Costello). Its possible title is "Information Services Directory for Business Intelligence," and a tentative publication date is 1993. Like the present directory, this will describe business, economic, and financial service (loose-leaf, online, as well as newsletters), and it will presumably also have similar indexes by subject, by geographic area covered, and by name of publisher.

Lavin, Michael R. *Business Information: How to Find It, How to Use It.* 2d ed. Phoenix, AZ: Oryx Press, 1991. 448 pp.

Just published is Lavin's recently revised and expanded book combining useful "descriptions of major business publications and databases with explanations of concepts essential for using them effectively." This makes it a good source not only for the beginner, but also as a refresher for the more knowledgeable, or as a text for a library school course on business information. Three of its five parts cover: information about companies (including directories, investment information, investment advice); statistical information; special topics (information on states and local areas, marketing information, business law sources, taxation, and accounting). Lavin does not attempt to cover each major topic completely. Instead he selects only a few basic sources on each subject. His annotations are longer than in most bibliographies, and his explanations of such topics as how to read financial listings, what is GNP, etc., are good. Short bibliographies at end of each chapter list books recommended for additional reading.

One major topic Lavin does not cover at all is foreign business information sources, and so it is good to know that a reference book is in progress to fill this gap. The two compilers are Michael Halperin and Ruth A. Pagell, both librarians at the Wharton School. Their purpose is somewhat similar to Lavin's in focusing on a selection of major business publications, databases, and concepts containing foreign company, industry, financial, marketing, statistical, etc., information. The publisher will also be Oryx Press and publication is tentatively scheduled for 1993.

Strauss, Diane W. *Handbook of Business Information: A Guide for Librarians, Students, and Researchers.* Englewood, CO: Libraries Unlimited, 1988. 537 pp.

Strauss's reference book is similar in purpose to Lavin's, it being a useful guide for beginners and librarians, combining descriptions of key business reference works with explanations of basic business concepts and the vocabulary one needs in using those business sources she describes. Chapters 1–8 cover business information according to format (bibliographies, directories, statistics, and so forth); chapters 9–18 focus on specific fields such as accounting, marketing. Appendixes list business acronyms, government departments, periodic censuses, free vertical file material. Like Lavin, it describes only a limited number of sources on each subject covered, and it does not attempt to cover certain broad areas such as foreign business information sources. Its annotations are also longer than in most bibliographies, and its explanations of such terms as "price-earnings ratios" and "market share" are well written. Although these two books are similar in purpose, they are both useful and different enough that each is worth consulting. Lavin's is more recent but Strauss is beginning work on a revision. Both authors are business information specialists who also teach courses on the subject in library schools.

Several business school libraries compile very short subject reference guides meant as handy pickups on topics of special interest to their students. Those prepared by the Business Library at the University of California, Berkeley, are the attractive, annotated four-page *Berkeley Business Guides* series. Other business school libraries prepare useful lists primarily for internal use, such as those at the Horn Library at Babson College, the Dewey Library at MIT, and the Management Library of the University of Rochester.

Library School Course Lists

The syllabuses prepared for teaching library school courses on business information sources can be useful for identifying those important business reference works that all prospective information specialists should know about. These are usually typed lists (not annotated), revised annually, and arranged in 15 or so units according to the sequence of the course, e.g. general reference, directories, statistics, finance, and investment. These courses are usually taught by practicing librarians. An example is listed below:

Teich, Peggy. *LIS 616: Business, Economics, and Statistical Sources.* New York: Pratt Institute, Dept. of Library and Information Science, 1991. 73 pp. (This is probably revised each year; in 1991 it could be purchased from the publisher for $19.95).

INDEXES AND ABSTRACTS

On many occasions a book is not what is needed since the subject being researched is either too new a development or too specific a topic for full-length treatment. In such cases one may turn to periodical indexes and abstracting services, both those that are in hard copy and those that can be accessed online. These are valuable sources for current information on a wide variety of subjects.

Several indexes and abstracts covering specific topics such as economics, operations research, and personnel administration are described elsewhere in this book with other material on these subjects. Most of the indexes described below focus on U.S. periodicals or foreign journals in the English language, and all but one are published in the United States. Files of *Business Periodicals Index* and *PAIS International in Print* will be found in most libraries of average size. Larger public and university libraries will probably have most of the other American indexes, and they are likely also to offer computer search services for those persons wanting to access the various online bibliographical databases.

As a matter of fact, many more librarians and other information specialists now use the online or CD-ROM versions of indexes with much more regularity than they do the paper copy. Therefore it is important to know something about the better known databases and why many prefer to search for articles online. Four basic reasons are: (1) current articles are entered into the system much faster which means they are much more up to date; (2) one can search by much more specific topics or key words, or can also ask only for articles on one subject as it related to another (e.g. articles on mergers as they relate just to the petroleum industry); (3) many databases now contain brief abstracts or annotations about the articles, which helps one to decide quickly which articles to eliminate and which ones to read completely; and (4) more and more databases are available in full text which makes for easy access especially when the periodical concerned is not in a library nearby. The disadvantages of searching for articles online is primarily the cost involved, which is still high enough that not all libraries can afford to have a wide selection of databases.

For a complete listing of "Abstracting and Indexing Services" on all subjects as well as on business, refer to the latest annual volume of *Ulrich's International Periodicals Directory*. To discover which index will best suit a particular need, consider checking the list of periodicals covered in each (this is usually found at the front of any bound volume). As an aid in learning which of the 9 most important American periodical indexes cover articles in any one magazine, note that this fact is mentioned with the description of each magazine in this book; for example there is a notation with the entry for *Fortune* which says: "Indexed in ABI/I, BPI, PTS/F&S, PAIS, TI; also full text on DATA-STAR, DIALOG, DOW JONES, MEAD/NEXIS." The first are the abbreviated titles of indexes cited below; these abbreviations are explained both below and at the front of this book. The full text citations identify five important vendors offering full text coverage of that magazine; see also the note at the beginning of the book explaining that you need also to get the names of the specific databases which this book does not provide.

ABI/INFORM database **(ABI/I)**. Available also on CD-ROM and magnetic tape.

This is probably the most used business database, covering approximately 800 English-language journals in the broad area of business/management. About half of these periodicals have complete coverage of all feature articles (with some 250 now available in full text), and the rest have selected coverage; about 20% are published outside the U.S. *ABI/INFORM* is a registered trademark of UMI/Data Courier.

Applied Science & Technology Index (ASTI). New York: H.W. Wilson (monthly, except July, with periodic cumulations). Online counterpart is *WILSONLINE;* also on CD-ROM as *WILSONDISC.*

Subject index to approximately 400 selected journals in the fields of aeronautics and space science, chemistry, computer technology and applications, construction industry, energy resources and research, engineering, fire and fire prevention, food and food industry, geology, machinery, mathematics, metallurgy, minerology, oceanography, petroleum and gas, physics, plastics, textile industry and fabrics, transportation, and related industrial and mechanical arts. An author listing of book reviews appearing in the indexed journals is at end of each issue.

Business Periodicals Index (BPI). New York: H.W. Wilson (monthly, except July, with periodic cumulations). Online counterpart is *WILSONLINE.* There are two CD-ROM products: *WILSONDISC: BPI,* and *Wilson Business Abstracts* which contains abstracts of articles.

For many years this has been the best known index for its overall coverage of some 345 selected, English-language periodicals in the fields of business and management, including accounting, advertising and marketing, banking, building and buildings, communications, computer technology and applications, economics, finance and investments, industrial relations, insurance, international business, labor, management, personnel administration, occupational health and safety, public relations, public utilities, real estate, regulation of industry, industries such as the chemical industry, paper and pulp. An author listing of books reviewed in the indexed journals is at end of each issue.

Canadian Business Index. Toronto: Micromedia Ltd. (monthly, with annual cumulations). Online counterpart is called *CBI.* Available also on CD-ROM.

An index to over 200 English-language Canadian periodicals and a few newspapers covering business, administrative studies, industry, economics, and related fields. It indexes by subject, corporate and personal authors. The newspapers included are the *Financial Post, Financial Times,* and *Globe and Mail.*

Engineering Index Monthly. New York: Engineering Information, Inc. (monthly, with annual cumulations). Online counterpart is *Compendex;* also available on CD-ROM.

Abstracts of the world's significant engineering literature, by subject and author, and encompassing all important engineering and related disciplines. The annual volume is called *Engineering Index Annual.*

National Newspaper Index. Available also on CD-ROM.

An online database containing citations to articles and news appearing in the *New York Times,* the *Wall Street Journal,* as well as in the *Christian Science Monitor, Los Angeles Times,* and *Washington Post.*

Full text of news items and feature stories in these newspapers as well as in other regional newspapers such as the *Boston Globe,* the *Chicago Tribune,* the *San Francisco Chronicle,* and *The Times* (London) are part of Mead Data Central's *NEXIS* databases.

PAIS International in Print (PAIS). New York: Public Affairs Information Service, Inc. (monthly, with three cumulated issues and an annual bound volume). Online counterpart is *PAIS International Online;* also available on CD-ROM.

A selective subject index focusing on business, economic and social conditions, public policy and administration, and international relations. The important differences in this index are that: (1) it selectively indexes journals, to cover only those articles pertinent to its subject coverage (e.g. business topics emphasize socio-economic aspects rather than business operation); (2) it covers not only periodical articles but also selected books, pamphlets, government documents, reports of public and private agencies; (3) it contains citations published in 5 languages besides English (French, German, Italian, Portuguese, Spanish). This is a successor to the long-time *PAIS Bulletin,* and it incorporates the *PAIS Foreign Language Index.*

Predicasts F & S Index United States (PTS/F&S). Cleveland, OH: Predicasts, Inc. (weekly, with monthly, quarterly and annual cumulations). Online counterpart is *PTS F&S Indexes;* also on CD-ROM.

This is the best periodical index to use when searching for current information on U.S. companies, products and industries in a wide selection of trade magazines, business-oriented newspapers, and other financial publications. The subject/product section in each issue lists articles (or data in articles), arranged by a modified 7-digit SIC industry code, and it also covers basic economic indicators. These industry articles focus on indexing data about new products, new capacities, end use, sales, and so forth. The company section in each issue indexes articles or parts of articles on current developments in specific U.S. companies relating to such topics as management, products and processes, marketing information. See next entry for the companion indexes covering foreign industries and companies. As of 1991, these three indexes are also available on CD-ROM as *F & S Plus TEXT,* but only to nonprofit organizations. It consists of one-or-two line summaries from the *F & S Indexes* plus *PROMT* abstracts or full text when available, all on two monthly disks—one covering the U.S. and the other all foreign countries/industries/companies.

Predicasts F & S Index Europe and **Predicasts F & S Index International (PTS/ F&S).** Cleveland, OH: Predicasts, Inc. (monthlies with annual cumulations). Online counterpart is *PTS F&S Indexes;* also on CD-ROM.

These are companion indexes to the one above, covering articles or data in articles on foreign companies, products, and industries. They are similar in arrangement and scope except that these indexes have a third section arranging the articles by region and country.

Readers' Guide to Periodical Literature (RG). New York: H.W. Wilson (semimonthly, with periodic cumulations). Also available online via *WILSON-LINE;* and on CD-ROM as *WILSONDISC.*

An author and subject index to selected U.S. general interest and nontechnical periodicals. Book reviews in these journals are listed at end.

Social Sciences Index (SSI). New York: H.W. Wilson (quarterly, with annual cumulations). Also available online via *WILSONLINE,* and on CD-ROM as *WILSONDISC.*

A subject and author index to articles in over 300 English-language periodicals that cover the fields of anthropology, community health and medicine, economics, geography, international relations, law, criminology, political science, psychology and psychiatry, public administration, sociology and social work, and related subjects. Book reviews that appeared in the journals indexed are listed at end of each issue.

Trade and Industry Index database (TI).

This database is especially good for its indexing and abstracting more than 300 trade and industry journals while selectively covering the business/industry articles that appear in over 1,300 additional publications. It also indexes and abstracts over 100 local and regional business publications, plus PR Newswire press releases. Related to this database is *Trade and Industry ASAP,* which provides selective full text and indexing for articles in some 600 business/industry journals, plus the PR Newswire press releases. Also available on CD-ROM.

Several more specialized indexes are:

Conference Board. *Cumulative Index.* New York (annual).

A subject index to the studies, pamphlets, and articles that this business research firm has published in the areas of consumer research, corporate relations, economic and business environment, human resources, management functions. It covers primarily material published during the past five years.

Current Contents: Social & Behavioral Sciences. Philadelphia, PA: Institute for Scientific Information (weekly).

A pocket-sized weekly that reproduces tables of contents from about 1,300 periodicals worldwide in the social and behavioral sciences. It covers 13 disciplines, including short sections for "economics and business" and for "management" journals. The other disciplines include sociology, social issues, psychology, public health & social medicine, education, geography, political science, law, and information sciences. Each issue has a title word index and an author/address directory. Subscribers receive a semiannual list of journals covered and a triannual cumulative journal index. Full text of articles not easily accessible in one's library can be obtained by using ISI's document delivery service. Monitoring tables of contents can be a useful means of keeping up on what is being written in current issues of journals, but if one wants to monitor only business/management periodicals, this is an expensive way of doing it at $360 per year as of 1991.

Social Sciences Citation Index. Philadelphia, PA: Institute for Scientific Information (3/yr., with last issue an annual cumulation in 6 volumes). Also available online as *Social SciSearch,* and on CD-ROM.

This international, multidisciplinary index covers all articles from over 1,400 social and behavioral sciences journals and selected articles relevant to the social sciences appearing in over 3,300 science journals. The *SSCI* is made up of four separate indexes which cover the same material in different ways: (1) the "Source Index" provides access by author and gives complete bibliographic information; (2) the "Permuterm Subject Index" indexes the same articles by important words appearing in each title; (3) the "Corporate Index" is an index arranged by each author's organizational affiliation; (4) the "Citation Index" is an important section based on the concept that an author's references to previously published materials indicate subject relationships; it is a good means of locating other publications on the same topic. Thus it provides access by authors of cited publications (these can be abstracts, book reviews, editorials, letters, or a book, article, technical paper, etc.). Multi-year cumulations are published for retrospective searching. ISI publications are all computer-produced, making it possible for them to offer various individualized alerting services in any area of interest.

Newspaper Indexes

New York Times Index. New York (semimonthly, with quarterly and annual cumulations).

An excellent and very detailed index, arranged alphabetically and including many helpful cross-references. Indexing is based on the Late City Edition. Articles and news from the *Times* can be accessed online in the *National Newspaper Index.* A full-text online index is available in *The New York Times.*

Wall Street Journal Index. Ann Arbor, MI: University Microfilms International (monthly, with quarterly and annual cumulations).

Each issue of this useful index is in two parts: corporate news and general news. Indexing is based on the three-star Eastern Edition. There are often short descriptions of an entry. The annual cumulation is in two volumes: volume 1 indexes corporate news and, at the end the green pages are an annual index to articles in *Barron's;* volume 2 indexes general news. At the end of this second volume are short lists of articles in a series, special reports, plus tables giving daily Dow Jones Averages for the year. Articles and news in this financial newspaper can also be accessed online in the *National Newspaper Index;* full text can be found as part of the *Dow Jones Text-Search Services* database.

Financial Times. *Index.* London: Research Publications Ltd. (monthly, with annual cumulations).

Begun in 1981, this is a detailed index, formerly in three parts, but now all in one alphabet to cover information on companies, organizations, subjects, countries, and personalities that have appeared in this excellent British financial newspaper. The indexing is based on the final London Edition. Full text of this newspaper can be accessed on the database *Financial Times Fulltext.*

GOVERNMENT PUBLICATIONS

The publications of various governments are excellent sources for authoritative studies and official information on all sorts of subjects. The many departments, bureaus, ministries, agencies, and committees publish a wide variety of reports, statistical publications, bibliographies, periodicals, etc., and much of this is of vital importance to business persons. The U.S. government probably stands at the top in total volume of publications. Since its various departments and bureaus shift their responsibilities frequently, it is especially important to have well-indexed, easily understood manuals, bibliographies, and catalogs of publications. This section describes a few of the most important lists and catalogs as well as two indexes covering current legislation and congressional news. Examples of the catalogs of other governments are also listed. Bibliographies and catalogs that describe the many U.S. government statistical publications are described in Chapter 4; directories of U.S. government agencies and of congressmen are in Chapter 7.

Census Catalog & Guide. Washington, DC: U.S. Government Printing Office (annual).

Here is an example of a useful annual descriptive catalog of statistics and other publications of an important bureau within the federal government. The listings are arranged by type of census (agriculture, business, etc.), and there are series, title, and subject indexes at end. Symbols with each entry note whether the item is available as a print report, or online as fiche, tape, diskette, or CD-ROM.

CIS/Index. Washington, DC: Congressional Information Service (monthly, with annual cumulations). Also available online and on CD-ROM.

A wealth of information of potential interest to business is contained in congressional documents and, prior to the publication of this monthly, it has been difficult to identify. This is a comprehensive subject index and abstract for the "working papers" of Congress, comprising committee hearings, reports, prints, as well as publications of joint committees and subcommittees, executive reports, Senate treaty documents, and special publications. Each monthly issue is in two parts: index; abstracts. The extensive indexes cover not only all subjects, but also titles, names, bill numbers, publication numbers, and there are helpful cross-references. The three volume cumulation is called *CIS/Annual,* with 2 volumes containing the indexes and the abstracts,

and the third devoted to "Legislative Histories" of U.S. public laws, allowing researchers to trace the development of a law from its first consideration through to its arrival
on the President's desk. Every four years there is a 4-volume cumulated index, the
latest published in 1991 covering the years 1983–1986.

CIS offers a "Microfiche Library" providing copies of all the publications covered. They also publish other useful indexes and microfiche collections of congressional publications which can usually be found in the documents divisions of large
university or public libraries.

U.S. Superintendent of Documents. *Monthly Catalog of United States Government Publications.* Washington, DC: U.S. Government Printing Office.
Available online as *GPO Monthly Catalog;* also on CD-ROM.

This is a continuing list of federal government publications, most of which are free
or available at a moderate cost. It is arranged alphabetically by agency, with an
index in each issue and a separate semiannual cumulated index. A separate *Serials
Supplement* is issued annually.

Persons searching only government publications for sale can use a microfiche
GPO catalog called *Sales Publications Reference File,* updated bimonthly; this is also
available online as *GPO Publications Reference File.* In addition a free catalog of
"Government Periodicals and Subscription Services" is available from the GPO as
Price List 36.

Foreign Government Publications

The governments of other countries also publish detailed catalogs. Those for
Canada and Great Britain are especially noteworthy for identifying their
many excellent statistical publications.

Government of Canada Publications: Quarterly Catalogue. Ottawa: Canadian
Government Publishing Centre (quarterly, with annual cumulations).

A bilingual (French and English) catalog of parliamentary publications and all
department publications, with an index in each issue.

Great Britain. H.M. Stationery Office. *HMSO Monthly Catalogue.* London
(monthly, with annual cumulations). Available online as HMSO; also on
CD-ROM.

Each issue of this catalog of British government publications is in three parts:
parliamentary publications; publications arranged by name of government department; Northern Ireland HMSO publications. An index is in each issue.

Congressional Legislation and News

Commerce Clearing House. *Congressional Index.* Chicago. 2 volumes, loose-
leaf. (biennial).

Published for every two-session Congress, this loose-leaf service provides quick
access to the status of all legislation pending in Congress by listing and indexing all
Public Bills and Resolutions and reporting their progress from introduction to final
disposition.

Congressional Quarterly Weekly Report. Washington, DC: Congressional
Quarterly, Inc. (weekly).

This excellent weekly service provides up-to-date news on all activities of Congress, the federal government, and politics. It includes status of legislation, House and Senate roll call votes, presidential messages, and much more. There is a quarterly cumulated index and an annual *Congressional Quarterly Almanac,* which is a compendium of legislation for one session of Congress, including a list of Public Laws, lobby registrations, political reports. A review of government and politics for one presidential term is published every four years as *Congress and the Nation.* CQ also publishes an annual *Washington Information Directory* which is a directory guide to federal departments and agencies, congressional committees, and nongovernmental organizations located in the capital. At end are lists of foreign embassies, U.S. ambassadors, labor unions, state officers, mayors, etc.

United States Code Congressional and Administrative News. St. Paul, MN: West Publishing Co. (monthly, with annual cumulations).

Texts of all Public Laws enacted by Congress are arranged by Public Law number, with a subject index that cumulates in each monthly issue. It also includes legislative history, proclamations, executive orders, popular names of acts.

DOCTORAL DISSERTATIONS

Often overlooked as a source for finding in-depth, original research on all subjects, including business and economics, are the many unpublished dissertations required for completion of a doctoral degree at all universities. These are easily identifiable by subject and author, and many are readily accessible by checking one or both of the two publications noted below (these directories can also be searched online). University Microfilms International is a firm that specializes in making available unpublished research and out-of-print books via microfilm or paper (xerographic) copy. The prices for purchasing any single dissertation from UMI are reasonable: in 1990 a microform copy cost $32.50 ($20 for academic purposes), and a paper copy was $57.50 ($29.50 for academics), all plus shipping charges. Outside the U.S. and Canada the higher prices noted above apply.

American Doctoral Dissertations. Ann Arbor, MI: Compiled for the Association of Research Libraries by University Microfilms International (annual). Available online as *Dissertation Abstracts Online* and also on CD-ROM.

A complete listing of all doctoral dissertations accepted at American and Canadian universities. It is arranged by broad subject classifications and, under each heading, alphabetically by name of university. Includes an author index. Publication is slow, with the latest volume, as of 1992, covering only 1990/91. However, this is all now available online.

Dissertation Abstracts International. Section A: The Humanities and Social Science. Ann Arbor, MI: University Microfilms International (monthly). Available online as *Dissertation Abstracts Online,* and also on CD-ROM.

This monthly contains informative abstracts of those dissertations submitted to UMI by nearly 500 cooperating institutions in the U.S. and Canada, so it provides a good cross section but is not a complete listing as is the preceding annual. These abstracts are arranged in the same broad subject categories, but each issue also has a detailed "Keyword Title Index" and an annual cumulative index as well. UMI publishes a companion abstracting service called *Section B: The Sciences.* Section C covers

Worldwide theses (quarterly). A separate quarterly lists *Masters Abstracts International*. These are all included in the online service.

In addition there is a complete retrospective series of indexes in hard-copy of all dissertations, arranged by subject, and noting which ones are abstracted in *DAI*. This is called *Comprehensive Dissertation Index*. The first series, in 37 volumes, covers the years 1861–1972, with volumes 25–26 devoted to "Business and Economics"; a ten-year cumulation covers 1973–1982, in 38 volumes; since then there have been annuals of 5 volumes each. A file of these various volumes can probably be found in large libraries, for those who do not wish to access the data online.

In the United Kingdom there is an annual list of British theses called *Index to Theses, with Abstracts, Accepted for Higher Degrees by the Universities of Great Britain and Ireland*, published annually in London by ASLIB (Association of Special Libraries and Information Bureaus) and the Council for National Academic Awards. These theses are available only on interlibrary loan within the United Kingdom through the Lending Division of the British Library at Spa, Wetherby, West Yorkshire, England.

Specialized Dissertation and Theses Lists

Two general, annual lists in the business/economics areas are:

Journal of Business of the University of Chicago (January). "Doctoral Dissertations Accepted" during the previous academic year.

Economic Journal (March). "Thesis Titles for Degrees in the United Kingdom," arranged by subject.

Several lists covering specific subjects are in:

American Journal of Agricultural Economics (May). "Ph.D. Recipients by Subject," and also by institution.

Industrial & Labor Relations Review. "Research in Progress" is described in each issue; this covers all kinds of research, not only dissertations.

Journal of Economic History (June). "Summaries of Doctoral Dissertations."

Journal of International Business Studies. A few "Dissertations Abstracts" are in most issues.

Stonier Graduate School of Banking, *Cumulative Catalog of Theses.* An annual cumulating list that describes those banking theses written by Stonier Graduate School students and selected for deposit in the American Bankers Association library in Washington, DC.

COMPUTERIZED INFORMATION SERVICES

Recent rapid advances in computer technology have resulted in the development of much more efficient and faster methods of storing and retrieving information, and this has revolutionized the whole information business. In operation today are computer-based search services using well-established machine-readable files to provide: (1) indexing and abstracting of articles, books, etc., on a much greater scale than was ever previously possible and so flexible that they can meet almost any individual request in a matter of minutes; (2) access to in-depth statistics that can be easily adapted to meet widely varying specifications, both historical statistics and those which produce forecasts based on a variety of alternatives; (3) mailing lists and other directories of companies variously arranged according to such factors as geographic locations, type of business, and size of company; (4) full-text retrieval of newspaper and periodical articles, court decisions, etc.

The newest trend of real significance is the marketing of many databases on CD-ROM (Compact Disk-Read Only Memory). Complete databases can now be stored on compact disks and used via a personal computer for immediate viewing without the need for a telephone line and without the per-minute charge required by database vendors. The advantages of CD-ROMs for users are: figures can be manipulated to fit a particular need, and any data can be downloaded into one's own files. Several advantages for libraries are: CD-ROMs are less expensive for libraries that make heavy use of any one database; the disks are usually more user-friendly; and the user does his/her own searching. Disadvantages include the fact that the data is "frozen," with no new material added until a new disk is received (usually once a month); also only one person can use the disk and the work station at any one time. (CD-ROMs can be networked for multiple use, but the technology has not been perfected as of 1991). The advantages have far outweighed the disadvantages, however, and this trend toward making available more and more data on compact disks is bound to grow.

Online search services are offered by commercial search firms, by regional information centers, and by large university and public libraries, all of which own or lease their own computer terminals. Online searching is also extensively used by information specialists in large companies where there are frequent and often urgent requests from company executives and researchers for complete and up-to-date answers to informational questions as quickly as possible.

With the correct equipment, with a link to the host computer (which is usually many miles away), and with a previously arranged per-hour fee (different for each database), any searcher can access the hundreds of databases that are currently available. Most potential users of bibliographical databases have found it worth the expense to attend training sessions on how to search first the system and then each file before they begin using one. These are held periodically in various cities and are usually only one day long.

We have chosen in this book to mention specific databases when describing other kinds of information on the same subject, rather than to list them all here. Therefore this section may seem rather short considering the importance of the topic. As you use the book you will see that, for most reference works, the note about availability of an online counterpart appears with the bibliographical citation; in some instances the note is at the end of the annotation. We make no claim of completeness, especially for statistical databases, and we strongly urge readers to use the directories of online services described below—these are *so* important for everyone to monitor on a regular basis in order to keep up to date both on new databases and on the enhancement of existing files. Here we will only briefly mention four basic kinds of online business information, with a few examples for each.

Kinds of Business Databases

The term "database" is usually defined as any organized collection of data or information in a particular subject area or bearing some relationship to each other. These collections are processed in computer-readable form by publishers or other organizations for electronic publishing and/or electronic distribution. Several of the best-known and oldest companies (called "vendors" or "online service companies") providing online interactive access to many of the bibliographic and factual databases are: (1) DIALOG Information Services, Inc. (part of Knight-Ridder Inc., Palo Alto, CA) which offers the largest number of databases in a wide range of subject areas—over 500 as of 1991; (2) BRS Information Technologies (a division of Maxwell, Inc., McLean, VA), with more than 150 databases; (3) DATA-STAR (Data-Star Marketing Ltd., London), which focuses on marketing about 180 databases especially to European customers; and (4) Mead Data Central *NEXIS* (Dayton, OH), with its many full-text databases for newspapers, magazines, and other sources. The directories on online databases listed below provide names of other important vendors. It should be noted here that some of the popular business databases are available from more than one vendor—for example, *ABI/INFORM* is available through all four of the vendors noted above.

The *Directory of Online Databases* (see description below) identifies five major types of database. Two are called "reference" databases, these being either (1) bibliographic, or (2) referral (sometimes called "directory" databases). The other three types are called "source" databases, and these can be either (1) numeric, (2) textual-numeric ("dictionary" or handbook-type databases), or (3) full text. ("Sources" databases are those containing complete information—for example, economic or financial statistics, statistics combined with text, or full text of an article or document). Two other source categories noted are: software (computer programs that can be downloaded) and images (such as maps and other illustrations).

I prefer to describe the basic kinds of databases more informally as (a) bibliographic; (b) directory; (c) statistical and financial; and (d) full text (the first two are reference databases; the third is numeric; the last can be any of these although most are probably reference-type databases).

(a) Bibliographic Databases

As the term indicates, these are online indexes, abstracts or bibliographies of books, articles in periodicals or newspapers, government reports, dissertations, etc. It is this category of database that is used most frequently by librarians. Several examples (noted elsewhere in this book) are: *ABI/INFORM* for abstracts of articles appearing in basic business/management journals: *Dissertation Abstracts Online* for details of American and Canadian dissertations; *PTS/PROMT* for abstracts of articles on a wide range of industries.

(b) Directory Databases

The computer has made it possible instantly to provide lists of companies, cards, or mailing-list labels that take into account a wide variety of marketing or financial factors. Probably the most extensive directory database is *Dun's Market Identifiers Online* service, which offers over 40 searchable fields (plus other special features) for each of some 7,000,000 U.S. companies. These are great time-savers for purchasing and marketing people. Chapter 7 cites several other directories whose data is also available online or on CD-ROM, including such specialized directories as the *Encyclopedia of Associations* and *Ulrich's International Periodicals Directory*.

(c) Statistical and Financial Databases

Numeric databases are probably used more by end-users (usually business/ economic professionals and researchers) than by librarians for in-depth and complex searches not only because the databases are often more expensive but also because they occasionally call for some background in quantitative methods. These end-users are already familiar with their own data and with what they hope to find, and they also understand how to manipulate the figures in order to get the correct mix of data that will best meet their particular needs. Librarians are able to retrieve statistics asked for but as yet are usually not experienced about interpreting the data. This lack is being addressed by many through further training and experience.

Statistical and financial databases can be divided into those produced by the government and other nonprofit organizations and those that come from commercial firms (and so are usually much more expensive). The various economic and financial time series, for instance, are often taken from government statistics—the Bureau of the Census tapes, for example, and the Bureau of Labor Statistics data banks on labor, employment, and prices. Other examples are: the data banks for International Monetary Fund statistics on international finance and balance of payments; economic statistics on European countries of the OECD; the Statistics Canada *CANSIM* database.

Commercial firms also produce large and varied data banks which are sold to the public or to client companies. Well-known econometric firms such as DRI/McGraw-Hill, Data Products Division, for example, often take statistics and/or financial data from a wide range of databases, both governmental and nongovernmental, while feeding their own statistics into the system and, from all this, generate their own specialized data banks which include forecasts and alternative scenarios. DRI produces or sells over 100 different databases, and companies pay high fees to use this statistical material and to take advantage of other services and advice offered. Important commercially produced databases also provide easy access to financial data from corporate reports, investment services, current newspaper securities prices, etc. *Compustat* (and its CD-ROM *Compustat PC-Plus*) and *Value Line Datafile* are two examples.

For the names of these and several others see the "Computerized Financial Data" section in Chapter 8.

(d) Full Text

These are databases that provide the full text of articles or documents in the sources they cover. Two examples are: *Business Dateline,* providing full text for articles and news on regional business trends and activities appearing in 160 U.S. and Canadian regional business periodicals and about 25 local newspapers, and *Investext,* complete text of investment research reports on companies and industries prepared by investment banking and financial research firms. Full text databases are growing rapidly in number and are of great importance for making available to a wide audience the complete articles in journals or newspapers not easily located by the potential user in paper copy. There is now a directory devoted exclusively to listing periodicals, newspapers, and newsletters available online in full text. See description of *Fulltext Sources Online* in "Directories" section below.

Directories of Computer Information Systems

Many organizations offer computerized information systems and services, and these can be identified by using one or more of several published directories. It is important once again to emphasize here the need to monitor these directories on a continuing basis in order to keep up with the many changes and new developments in online systems that are occurring almost daily. Another useful way of keeping on top of these developing systems is to read one or more of the online information systems journals, such as the monthly *Online* which has a regular "Database Updates" feature as well as news of European databases.

Two of the directories below also describe various information services that are not computerized.

Computer-Readable Databases. Detroit: Gale Research, Inc. (annual). Also available online.

Originally compiled by Martha E. Williams in 1975, this "directory and data sourcebook" has grown from describing about 300 databases to the 1991 edition which covers more than 6,000 publicly available databases worldwide. The information for each includes basic facts, subject coverage, data elements, database availability, print/microform products, contact person. There are separate lists of database producers and database vendors, with addresses. Three indexes cover: CD-ROM products, subjects, and a master index.

Directory of Online Databases. Detroit: Gale Research, Inc. (semiannual).

Formerly published by Cuadra/Elsevier Associates, this is a directory of nearly 5,000 databases that are available for interactive access by users, from remote computer terminals and microcomputers. For each database, it cites the type, subject, producer, full name of service (vendor), language, country coverage, time span, frequency of up-dating. It also briefly describes the contents, the conditions of use (if any). It is well indexed: by subject, producer, online service, telecommunications network, and there is also a master index.

A companion service is *Directory of Portable Databases* (semiannual) which describes CD-ROM products, diskettes, magnetic tapes, and so forth. Both directories are also available online.

Fulltext Sources Online. Ed. by Ruth M. Orenstein. Needham Heights, MA: BiblioData (PO Box 61). (semiannual).

Another continuously updated directory, this one focuses on those periodicals, newspapers, newsletters that are available online in full text. For each periodical, it lists the vendors and their specific databases that are full text, the time period for which the periodical is available in full text, frequency of update, and time lag. It also cites which databases index all articles in an issue of the periodical, and which cover only selected articles in full text. Geographic and subject indexes are at end.

Throughout this book, when a periodical I cite is also available online in full text, I mention this fact, but only by noting which of five important vendors to consult. (That information is taken, with permission, from this directory). It is important to note, however, that users must know which specific database to use, and my citations do not provide this information. Therefore, you must check yourself either in this directory or in some other source if you want to access a periodical on a full-text database. The vendor abbreviations I use in my citations are: BRS, DATA-STAR, DIALOG, DOW JONES, and MEAD/NEXIS.

Information Industry Directory. Detroit: Gale Research, Inc. 2 volumes (annual). Also available on diskette and magnetic tape.

Formerly called the *Encyclopedia of Information Systems and Services,* this is the most comprehensive, international descriptive guide to "data base producers and their products, online host services and timesharing companies, CD-ROM publishers and service companies, videotext/teletext information services, transactional services, library and information networks, bibliographic utilities, library management systems, information retrieval software, mailing list services, fee-based information on demand services, document delivery sources, data collection and analysis centers and firms, and related consultants, service companies, professional and trade associations, publishers, and research activities." Volume 1 is arranged alphabetically by name of organization or service. For each entry the data includes, where available, a description of the system or service, when founded, president, number of staff, scope, input sources, holdings and storage media, publications, microform products and services, computer-based products and services, clientele/availability, contact person. Volume 2 contains a master index, 31 indexes grouped by type of activity or function, and indexes for databases, publications, microforms, software, personal name, geographic location, subject.

Information Sources. Washington, DC: Information Industry Association (annual).

The IIA is an association of companies involved in the generation, processing, distribution, and use of information. This is a directory of member firms, usually giving for each a description, key contacts, products, services, telex, fax, and electronic mail numbers. The green pages at end contain a directory of individual members. There are indexes by geographic location, products/services, and key principal.

For a descriptive directory of the vast amount of statistical data available from the Bureau of the Census in machine-readable form, see their annual *Census Catalog & Guide* cited in the last section of Chapter 4.

MICROFORMS AND CASSETTES

Micropublishing and microcopying provide a new form of information that has many advantages, probably the greatest being a saving of large blocks of shelf space, which is a perennial problem in most libraries. The two principal types of microforms are microfilm and microfiche.

Microfilms are films of published works that are stored on reels. The material can be read by putting the reel onto a special microfilm reader that projects an enlarged image of the page on a screen in front of the viewer. Hand-operated levers are used to turn from page to page and to sharpen the focus. Those reading machines that are combined reader/printers have the advantage of making it possible to copy any page needed for one's personal file simply by pushing a copy button. Most libraries today have large and growing collections of microfilm—principally for back files of important newspapers, for many lesser-used periodicals, and for such materials as doctoral dissertations purchased from University Microfilms International.

A newer form of microcopying used today with increasing frequency is the microfiche. These are 4 × 6 sheets of film containing photographically reduced pages of books, documents, serial publications, and other works. Most of these sheets (or cards) contain about 70 pages each, but there have been successful efforts at much greater photographic reductions, making it feasible to reproduce complete sets of works on just one small sheet. Documents on microfiche are read by placing the card into a special fiche reader and manipulating it by hand until the pages wanted appear on the viewing screen. These machines are easy to operate, and some have combined features of reader and printer.

Many U.S. government reports and studies are now available on microfiche as are back files of periodicals and scholarly collections. A good example of a large body of material now being distributed on microfiche is U.S. corporate disclosure documents, such as annual reports, 10-K reports, and prospectuses (discussed in Chapter 7). The micropublishing business has grown so dramatically in the past few years that there are now a number of complete catalogs listing the various publications available in these new formats. Reading certain types of books and serial publications on a screen has become common practice in most libraries, and, eventually, with the aid of portable lap-sized readers, the same will be true in homes and offices as well.

A somewhat different development in nonbook information sources is the audiocassette tape. These can be speeches, articles, seminars, or interviews, as well as books (both fiction and nonfiction), and plays. Audio tapes have many uses for the business person because they can be played at the listener's convenience either at home, in a car, or even while jogging. They can relate to business and finance, or cover a wide range of nonbusiness but interesting topics. One comprehensive bibliography of spoken word audiocassettes is:

On Cassette: A Comprehensive Bibliography of Spoken Word Audiocassettes. New York: R. R. Bowker (annual).

> This is a descriptive list of over 44,500 audio cassettes available from over 400 producers. The listing by title usually includes for each a brief description, name of reader, publisher/producer, running time, price and rental price. The subject index includes a wide range of topics including "Business, Economics, and Personal Finance," "Personal Growth and Achievement," and all sorts of other subjects, including some fiction. Other indexes are for: authors/readers/performers or producers-distributors, with titles published by each.
>
> One can also contact individual producers for lists they may have. Audio-Forum (in Guilford, CT), for example, has a descriptive brochure on the "Personal Development Audio and Video Cassettes" it publishes.

HANDBOOKS

Business handbooks are often excellent first places to check for good, short introductions to the concepts, procedures, and techniques of specific management functions, such as accounting, finance, investment management, marketing, personnel, public relations, and purchasing. These useful compendiums are comprehensive yet concise; most chapters are written by experts; many include glossaries, bibliographies, directories, statistics, and legal forms. In addition, they are well organized and well indexed for easy access to the precise facts or explanations needed, since they are meant more as handy reference volumes than as books to be read from cover to cover.

Individual handbooks are described in Chapters 9 through 20 along with the basic books in each subject area. They can also be located by consulting the index under "Handbooks."

LOOSE-LEAF SERVICES

The increased complexities and frequent changes in federal and state laws regulating business make it imperative for the business person to have an efficient, up-to-date method for keeping informed about all legal matters that affect his/her day-to-day operations and decisions. Topical law reports provide such a service by bringing together all the laws, regulations, rules, orders, and decisions (along with explanations and interpretations) on a specific topic, arranged in loose-leaf volumes that are constantly revised and thoroughly indexed for quick and easy access. Their weekly or biweekly supplementary packets of newly revised, prepunched pages include instructions for removing all pages that have become obsolete.

The two principal business law and tax service publishers are Commerce Clearing House (Chicago) and Prentice-Hall, Inc. (Englewood Cliffs, NJ). The Bureau of National Affairs (Washington, DC) is another excellent publisher, perhaps best known for its personnel and labor information services. Today each of these firms maintains a large and expert staff to prepare these complex and highly specialized services. They are important reference works, widely used and highly regarded by lawyers, accountants, governmental officials, and business persons, and files of the most important ones can usually be found in large business or law libraries or in libraries specializing in each subject area.

There is a great similarity in the arrangement of CCH and P-H services, and a general explanation may be helpful. First, every service contains an introductory section explaining its scope and giving instructions on how to use it. Second, each service contains several indexes and tables that are detailed and easy to use. There is a topical, or master, index; a current index (for the most recent changes); an index of court cases; and a "Finding List" (for locating the paragraph number that corresponds to the official section number of the statute, regulation, or ruling). With tax services there is also a "Citator Table" that lists federal tax decisions and refers to other decisions that have cited them. Supplementary data of value often includes official forms, special pamphlets with texts and explanations of new bills and statutes, reports or studies undertaken by congressional committees, and brief summaries of current news accompanying the packages of revised pages.

In using any CCH or P-H service it is important to understand that the numbers in the index refer to a paragraph numbering system (at the bottom of each page) rather than to a page number (at the top of each page). This is essential in publications such as these where pages are continually changing but paragraph numbers remain constant.

Descriptions of individual loose-leaf services are scattered throughout this book with other material on each subject. The index lists these under both publisher and title. Brochures containing complete lists of all services are available directly from each publisher. CCH also has a separate pamphlet explaining how to use its services, called *Today's Tax and Business Law–And How to Find It.*

3

U.S. BUSINESS AND ECONOMIC TRENDS

Newspapers and News Weeklies – Business and Economic Periodicals – Current Economic Trends and Forecasts – Regional Statistics and Periodicals – ECONOMICS LITERATURE – Introductory Economics Texts – Managerial Economics – Industrial Organization – Economic Bibliographies and Indexes – Economic Dictionaries – Directories of Economists and Associations – Business Research – Business Cycles and Forecasting Methods – Guides to Economic and Financial Measures

Urgent social, economic, and financial problems within the United States and throughout the world make it more important than ever to keep well informed in areas beyond the day-to-day operations of a business. This chapter concentrates on publications that provide daily and weekly news of national and world events, current analyses of business and the U.S. economy, regional trends, and economic forecasts. (See Chapter 5 for similar publications devoted to foreign economic trends.) For those who want a refresher in basic economics there are several introductory economics texts, a few economics reference works, and recent books on managerial economics, industrial organization, business research methods, and forecasting methods and techniques. The chapter ends with several useful guides to economic and financial measures. It should be emphasized that no effort has been made in this book to cover economics sources completely since one can already find full-length bibliographies devoted to this broad subject. Here you will find listed only a few publications that may be of background interest to the business person.

NEWSPAPERS AND NEWS WEEKLIES

To keep abreast of current domestic and international events the business man or woman will want to read or skim several daily newspapers. Besides the indispensable *Wall Street Journal,* this may include the *New York Times* with its excellent business and finance section, and perhaps *The Times* of London for current foreign opinion. (All three newspapers publish detailed periodic indexes, and articles can also be searched online, often in full text–see Chapter 2 for notes about newspaper and other online indexes.) The knowledgeable business person will also want to have access to a good metropolitan daily like the *Chicago Tribune,* the *Los Angeles Times,* the *Washington Post,* and, of course, a local paper as well. The *Journal of Commerce and Commercial* (New York) is another important daily newspaper with general business and industrial news, but it is especially important for its coverage of commodities, commerce, and shipping.

Regular reading of either *Newsweek* or *Time* magazine is essential for a quick, weekly summary of national and international news and also for news about business, science, medicine, religion, sports, the arts, and other current topics. Both magazines are published in New York. *U.S. News & World Report* (Washington, DC) concentrates on popular, short articles about current economic, social, and political topics.

Several weekly "confidential" advisory letters are available for those who like a concise analysis and appraisal of political, economic, and financial trends, with possible implications for business and the economy. These are usually quite expensive but have strong followings. Probably the most popular is *Kiplinger Washington Letter* published in Washington, DC.

BUSINESS AND ECONOMIC PERIODICALS

Here is a list of the most important general business and economic periodicals. For those journals oriented more toward management, for example *California Management Review* or the *Harvard Business Review,* refer to Chapter 10. Those covering finance, marketing, personnel, and other management functions are included in chapters on each subject. A selection of trade journals is listed in Chapter 6; directories of business and economic periodicals are described in Chapter 7.

Across the Board. New York: Conference Board (10/yr.)

> The general interest articles in this journal cover a wide range of topics of interest to business managers. Regular columns include notes on emerging trends, new findings, global news, comments of executives, and usually a few book reviews. Indexed in ABI/I, BPI, PAIS, PTS/F&S, TI.

Business (UK). London: Business People Publications Ltd. (monthly).

> Begun in 1986, this is a glossy monthly, usually of more than 100 pages per issue, covering articles on a wide range of topics of interest especially to British managers. Includes profiles of people, cities, companies, industries. Special annual features include: "The Hot 100" which is a list of Britain's fast growth companies (April); "The Business 1000" (extra issue in November), ranking the largest British companies; "Europe's Business Billionaires," a ranked list of over 40 persons (December). Includes a few book reviews. Indexed in ABI/I, PAIS.

Business Economics. Cleveland: National Association of Business Economists (quarterly).

Short but authoritative articles in a wide area of applied business, some of which are papers presented at NABE meetings. A section in each issue called "The Business Economist at Work" contains regular departments on such topics as specific economic indicators, statistics, abstracts of current articles, and one or more book reviews. Indexed in ABI/I, BPI, PAIS, TI; full text on BRS, DATA-STAR, DIALOG.

Business Week. New York: McGraw-Hill.

This is probably the most useful and widely read business news magazine, with its short, concisely written articles covering new business trends and developments in management, markets, industries and technology, companies, people, international business, the economy, the environment, government, etc. Usually one longer article is featured in each issue as well as regular columns, a page for their "Business Week Index" (important economic and monetary indicators), a page of "Investment Figures of the Week," one book review, and an "index of companies" covered in that issue. Annually or quarterly, 9 different "Scoreboard" lists of leading companies provide useful current financial statistics for each, some not ranked but arranged by industry. They cover: U.S. banks; corporate performance; executive compensation; global companies; international banks; investment outlook factors; mutual funds; patent granting companies; research & development expenditures. For further descriptions of these special company lists, including dates they appeared in *Business Week,* see section on "Concise Statistical Data and Stock Prices" in Chapter 8.

Other interesting annual features in *BW* are: "Industry Outlook" (mid-January issue), consisting of one-page profiles of 24 key industries; "The Business Week 1000" (a bonus issue in mid-April), ranking the top 1,000 U.S. companies, and also including the ranking arranged by about 40 industries; "Hot Growth Companies: Annual Ranking of the 100 Best Small Corporations" (third or fourth May issue); "Innovation" (a bonus issue in mid-June); "Mid-Year Outlook" (last June); "The Corporate Elite" (late November), consisting of brief biographical facts (in tabular format) about the CEOs of BW's 1,000 companies; "Where to Invest in (year)" (a combined last December/first January issue). *BW* is indexed in ABI/I, BPI, PTS/F&S, PAIS, RG; also full text on DIALOG, DOW JONES, MEAD/NEXIS.

The Economist. London and New York (weekly).

This longtime highly respected British weekly covers feature articles and news of worldwide interest both on world politics and current affairs, and on business, finance, and science. The current affairs section includes surveys from each geographic region, with the "American Survey" providing a good picture of recent events and news about the American scene from the British view. A section on "books and arts" is at end. Each issue has two pages of statistical tables giving "Economic and Financial Indicators." Indexed in BPI, PTS/F&S, PAIS, TI; full text on BRS, DATA-STAR, DIALOG, DOW JONES, MEAD/NEXIS.

Fortune. New York: Time Magazine Company Inc. (biweekly).

Must reading for all executives, this well-known magazine contains concise and interestingly written articles on all aspects of business and management. Typical of current issues are articles on U.S. or foreign corporate performance of specific companies, innovation, money and markets, the economy, politics and policy, technology, executive life. Often contains one book review. An index to companies covered is now in each issue. Indexed in ABI/I, BPI, PTS/F&S, PAIS, TI; full text on DIALOG, DOW JONES, MEAD/NEXIS.

Fortune's famous lists of largest companies appear in the following issues each year (with the U.S. lists eventually also published and sold as a separate pamphlet): "The Fortune 500" (second April issue) ranks the 500 largest U.S. industrial corporations; "Fortune's Service 500" (first June) ranks companies in the various service industries; "The Fortune Global 500" (last July) ranks the largest industrial corporations in the world; "The Fortune Global Service 500" (last August) ranks the top worldwide service companies in the same service categories as is in the domestic list noted above. Other useful annual features include: "Deals of the Year" and "The Best & Worst Stocks of (the year)" both in last January issue; "America's Most Admired Corporations" (first February issue); "The National Business Hall of Fame" (first March); "CEO Pay Sweepstakes" (mid-June), an annual ranking of the CEOs in 200 major companies arranged by compensation received; "The List of Billionaires" (first September issue), a ranked list of billionaires worldwide, with background on the source of wealth for each; "America's 100 Fastest-Growing Companies" (first October), a ranked list of public companies by growth over a three-year period; "Best Cities for Business" (first November).

Industry Week. Cleveland, OH: Penton Publishing Co. (semimonthly).

Billed as the "industry management magazine," this consists of short, practical articles of current interest to managers on a wide range of topics. Includes also regular departments with news about economic trends, emerging technologies, Washington, and more. About every other issue contains a few book reviews. "Economic Trends" is a page of tables/charts. The mid-November issue has an "Annual CEO Survey." Indexed in ABI/I, BPI, PTS/F&S, TI; full text on BRS, DATA-STAR, DIALOG, DOW JONES, MEAD/NEXIS.

Journal of Business. Chicago: University of Chicago Press (quarterly).

This excellent academic journal, edited by the Faculty of the Graduate School of Business and the Department of Economics at the University of Chicago, is devoted to professional and academic thinking and research in business. Its articles consist of original research on business and economic theory and methodology, with many of the studies using quantitative techniques. Each issue contains a topical list of new books received and a list of new faculty appointments at university schools of business. The January issue includes a subject list of business-related doctoral dissertations accepted at American universities during the previous year. Indexed in ABI/I, BPI, PAIS, PTS/F&S.

Nation's Business. Washington, DC: United States Chamber of Commerce (monthly).

Popular articles representing the business viewpoint (and that of the Chamber of Commerce) on business, economic, and political topics, government activity, and other areas of interest to business persons. Most issues include an interesting article about a top executive called "Lessons of Leadership"; also continuing departments such as small business update, franchising, a report from Washington. Indexed in ABI/I, BPI, PTS/F&S, RG, TI; full text on BRS, DATA-STAR, DIALOG, DOW JONES, MEAD/NEXIS.

Quarterly Review of Economics and Business. Urbana-Champaign: Bureau of Economic and Business Research, University of Illinois.

This is the official publication of the Midwest Economics Association, and its articles report on research and interpretive comments on economic and business questions. Indexed in ABI/I, BPI, PAIS; full text on BRS, DATA-STAR, DIALOG, DOW JONES.

Review of Economics and Statistics. Amsterdam: Published for the Department of Economics, Harvard University, by Elsevier Science Publishers B.V. (North Holland) (quarterly).

Another academic review containing empirical studies on economics, finance, and statistical methods. Indexed in ABI/I, BPI, PAIS.

Periodicals Containing Key Indicators

A few general business periodicals contain a regular feature providing charts and statistics giving current business and economic indicators. See, for example:

Barron's: "Pulse of Industry and Trade" and "Economic Indicators."

Business Week: "Business Week Index."

Economist: "Economic and Financial Indicators."

Forbes: "The Forbes Index."

Industry Week: "Economic Trends" including business barometers.

New York Times Sunday Business Section: "Data Bank" and "The Stock Market Last Week."

Purchasing World: "Business Datatrak" and "PW Predicts."

CURRENT ECONOMIC TRENDS AND FORECASTS

In today's fast-paced, complex and turbulent environment, corporate planners and researchers are spending more and more time analyzing trends and issues that may have an impact on the firm's future in general or that may relate more specifically to such factors as market demand or product development. This means they are closely following current business and economic statistics as a basis for making their estimates and projections. They are also watching for and using reputable published forecasts and projections prepared by research organizations or government agencies, some of them available online.

The basic sources of current U.S. business and economic statistics, including important economic and financial indicators, are described in Chapter 4 (foreign statistics are in Chapter 5). Discussions of important business barometers and indicators as forecasting tools (GNP, prices, employment, construction, for example) can be found in several useful "Guides to Economic and Financial Measures," described at the end of this chapter. In this section we cover two good general sources for forecasts of leading economic indicators and for industries, as well as several guides to market studies that usually contain an outlook for the industry under study and sometimes market share for leading brands. We also suggest here various types of publications that often contain short-range forecasts.

Predicasts Forecasts. Cleveland: Predicasts, Inc. (quarterly with annual cumulations). Online counterpart is *PTS U.S. Forecasts.*

This is a very useful first place to check when looking for short- and long-range forecasts not only for the leading economic indicators but also for statistics on specific U.S. industries and products (arranged by a modified 7-digit SIC number). Accompanying each forecast is the date and page reference of the current journal from which the statistics were taken so it is a valuable source. A companion service, *Worldcasts,* covers foreign countries and industries and is described in Chapter 6.

U.S. Industrial Outlook. Washington, DC: U.S. Government Printing Office for the U.S. International Trade Administration (annual).

A handy and inexpensive annual compilation which should be of interest to anyone wanting recent trends and an outlook (about five years) for 350 of the nation's most important four-digit manufacturing and service industries. The short narrative for each industry contains a discussion of the current situation, short and long-term prospects, international competitiveness, and often a list of additional sources of information. Includes statistical tables for historical trends and short-range forecasts for product and industry data and for foreign trade. A short list of major trade events is at front.

Among the more specialized forecasts is one the U.S. Bureau of Economic Analysis publishes from time to time that projects regional economic activity and population. The latest as of 1991 is *BEA Regional Projections to 2040* (Washington, DC: 1990, 3 volumes). This set gives projections of total personal income, of per capita personal income, total population, earnings, and employment (by industry groups) for selected years from 1995 to 2040: for states (vol.1), for metropolitan statistical areas (vol.2), and for BEA economic areas (vol.3). Some statistics from this projection, with forecasts to the year 2000, are printed as articles with statistics in the May, October, and November 1990 issues of the *Survey of Current Business.* Yet another specialized source is "Metro Market Projections," in the annual "Survey of Media Markets" of *Sales & Marketing Management* (extra October issue). It forecasts percent change over the coming five years for population, effective buying income, total retail sales, and buying power index, for each U.S. state, county, and metropolitan area.

Forecasts in Market Research Reports

Many commercial research firms and some publishers prepare and publish market studies on a specific industry or product which provide potentially useful data on current trends as well as prospects for the future of that industry. It is unfortunate that the majority of these reports are too expensive to be found in a public or university library (many are priced over $1,000). These studies have a sale usually limited to companies or organizations specializing or expanding into the product area involved, and their libraries are not often open to the public. Despite this, it is helpful to know about several directories of these reports which can be found in many business libraries. The most useful for its coverage of U.S. market research is *Findex* (see description in "Marketing Reports on Industries and Locations" section of Chapter 18).

Short-Range Forecasts

One can find frequent outlook-for-the-year articles in all sorts of business and trade journals, as well as a number of brief annual outlook publications prepared by universities, banks, or other organizations. Several examples are:

Colorado Business/Economic Outlook Forum. Denver: College of Business
and Administration, University of Colorado (annual).
Consists of statistical tables and diagrams showing historical trends and short-range
outlook for major Colorado business and economic indicators, plus brief text.

Conference on the Economic Outlook. *The Economic Outlook for (coming
year): Papers.* Ann Arbor: Department of Economics, University of Michigan (annual).
Among the papers presented each year at this Conference are two: one devoted to a
discussion of the U.S. economic outlook, and the other on outlook for the Michigan
economy. The rest of the papers cover a variety of related topics. Most include
statistical tables and charts.

First Interstate Bancorp. *Forecast.* Los Angeles (annual).
Brief outlook for the national and international economy, for financial institutions,
and for "First Interstate Territory." Contains statistics and graphs, including major
economic indicators for the coming two years.

Journal of Business Forecasting: Methods & Systems. Flushing, NY: Graceway Publishing Co. (quarterly).
Section 2 of each issue is called "business and economic outlook." This consists of
four short-term forecasts, with brief text. These continuing forecasts are: "international economic outlook" (a table giving three basic outlook figures for each country, including % change in inflation); "consensus forecasts of financial institutions"
(four-part tables giving the short range forecasts for 13 economic and financial
indicators as estimated by the economists in 12 banks, 2 insurance companies, and 7
security dealers and money managers); the "Kent Model Forecast" (also giving
selected economic and financial indicators); "corporate earnings outlook—a consensus forecast" with earnings forecasts for industries. The first half of this journal
contains about six short articles, a software review, and a book review.

Mellon Bank. Economics Department. *Mellon Economic Briefing.* Pittsburgh
(monthly).
Four-page briefings on the U.S. economy, including one table giving outlook figures
on GNP, business indicators, and interest rates.

Standard & Poor's Corporation. *Trends & Projections.* New York (monthly).
Issued as part of S&P's *Industry Surveys,* this contains brief text and some charts on
the economic outlook. One of its 6 pages gives short-range forecasts of GNP and
other key "Economic Indicators".

University of California, Los Angeles. *UCLA Business Forecasting Project.* Los
Angeles: John E. Anderson Graduate School of Management, UCLA. 2
volumes (annual).
This is published in two short unbound and unnumbered volumes: one titled *The
UCLA National Business Forecast* and the other *The UCLA Business Forecast for
California.* They each contain short articles and useful tables and charts based on
figures from the WEFA Group (Wharton Econometric Forecasting Associates) data
banks. Those statistical tables in the 1991 volumes cover basic economic indicators
usually from 1985 to 1994.

Some trade journals publish annual forecast issues that contain short analyses
of the prospects for that industry and for the economy during the coming year.

These often appear in a December or January issue. Several are noted in Chapter 6 on "Industry Statistics." Three examples are: *Electronics* "World Market Forecast" (January issue); *Oil & Gas Journal* has both a "Forecast/ Review Issue" (last January issue) and a "Midyear Forecast/Review" (last July); and *Pulp & Paper* "Outlook" (January).

Future Bibliography

Future Survey Annual. Bethesda, MD: World Future Society.

An abstract of books, articles and reports concerning forecasts, trends, and ideas about the future. These are arranged within 17 sections to cover such topics as the environment, the U.S. economy, work, families and education, communications, science and technology, and "methods to shape the future." This is an annual cumulation of their monthly abstracting service, *Future Survey,* which is usually arranged in about five sections, with subjects varying according to the material being abstracted.

REGIONAL STATISTICS AND PERIODICALS

The Census Bureau statistics described in Chapter 4 include excellent figures for regions, states, counties, MSAs, and cities although they are often quite old. A good monthly abstracting service for locating government statistical sources by region is cited with the bibliographical guides at the end of this section. Marketing guides mentioned in Chapter 18 are also good sources for regional estimates of such important market indicators as population, effective buying income, households, and retail sales. Following are several other types of publications that provide useful regional information:

State Statistical Abstracts

Every state in the United States publishes a statistical abstract, almanac, or economic data book covering statistics for the state, its counties, and its cities, as compiled from a variety of sources. These are usually published either by a state agency or a business school bureau of business research. They are occasionally patterned after the *Statistical Abstract of the United States,* are quite comprehensive, and give the sources for the statistics at the foot of each table. A complete list of these abstracts is at the end of each volume of the *Statistical Abstract* and also in several of the bibliographical guides noted in the section below. Several examples of state statistical abstracts are:

Florida Statistical Abstract. Gainesville: Published for the Bureau of Economic and Business Research, College of Business Administration, University of Florida, by University Press of Florida (annual).

Nebraska Statistical Handbook. Lincoln: Nebraska Department of Economic Development (biennial).

New York State Statistical Yearbook. Albany: Nelson A. Rockefeller Institute of Government, State University of New York in cooperation with the New York State Division of the Budget (biennial).

Local Statistical Reviews

A few local newspapers publish useful statistical reviews of the economy and of the cities within their metropolitan area. See, for example, the *Union Tribune's Annual Review of San Diego Business* (Union-Tribune Publishing Company).

Regional Periodicals

Each of the 12 district banks of the Federal Reserve System publishes a periodic *Economic Review* or *Quarterly Review* devoted to banking, economic and financial topics of interest to that geographic district, often with statistics relating to the district. These reviews are good sources for current regional data on the economy. The Federal Reserve Bank of Philadelphia publishes a semiannual *Fed in Print,* a useful subject index to these reviews and other Fed publications. The Federal Reserve Bank of Boston also publishes a monthly *New England Economic Indicators.*

The bureaus of business research at a number of business schools publish bulletins that are especially good for regional data. Several of these are:

Arkansas Business and Economic Review. Fayetteville: Bureau of Business and Economic Research, University of Arkansas (quarterly).

Georgia Business and Economic Conditions. Athens: Selig Center for Economic Growth, College of Business Administration, University of Georgia (bimonthly).

Illinois Business Review. Champaign/Urbana: Bureau of Economic and Business Research, University of Illinois (bimonthly).

Indiana Business Review. Bloomington: Business Research Center, School of Business, Indiana University (bimonthly).

Pennsylvania Business Survey. University Park: Division of Research, The Smeal College of Business Administration, Pennsylvania State University (monthly).

Commercially published magazines can also be found that cover U.S. regions and metropolitan areas. These usually contain interesting articles and current news of practical interest to the local business community. They also usually include one or more annual ranked lists of local firms in various types of business. Several examples of this type of business magazine are noted below. These can all be accessed full text on the databases noted in "Bibliographical Guides" below, and most of these examples are also available online in *PAIS International Online* and in TI.

Boston Business Journal. Boston: P & L Publications, Inc. (weekly).
This weekly contains an annual supplement called "The Book of Lists," which contains over 50 ranked lists of the top 25 firms in various industry categories, the top hospitals, schools, etc., in the Greater Boston area. It can be purchased separately.

California Business. Los Angeles: California Business News, Inc. (monthly).

Colorado Business Magazine. Englewood, CO: Wiesner, Inc. (monthly).

Crain's Chicago Business. New York: Crain Communications Inc. (weekly). The publisher offers similar weeklies focusing on business in Cleveland, Detroit, and New York. They each have an extra issue in December called "Top Business Lists," which contains ranked lists of all kinds of companies in that metropolitan area. Occasional ranked lists are also in some other issues. The Chicago weekly also includes a useful annual "Metro Chicago Market Facts" issue (part 2 of first July issue) which has data on metro Chicago population, employment, housing, regional buying power, banking, taxation, tourism, and more.

San Francisco Business. San Francisco Chamber of Commerce (monthly).

In former days, the research departments of some large banks (both U.S. and foreign) prepared useful brief letters or bulletins analyzing current financial and economic trends in the area. Very few banks do this today. Following are the names of two:

Business Review. San Francisco: Wells Fargo Bank (quarterly).

California Business Conditions. Los Angeles: Security Pacific Corporation (quarterly).

Other sources for information about states and cities are state agencies such as a Department of Commerce and Development, a Department of Labor and Industry, and local organizations such as chambers of commerce.

City Rating Guides

Boyer, Richard, and David Savageau. *Places Rated Almanac.* [New ed.]. New York: Prentice-Hall, 1989. 421 pp.

This is one of several guides useful for evaluating best places to live or work according to a variety of measures. It rates and ranks 333 U.S. metro areas according to 9 factors that influence the quality of life: living costs, job outlook, crime, health care and environment, transportation, education, the arts, recreation, and climate. Each section contains brief text, profiles, graphs, ranked lists. At end, "Putting It All Together" includes a table by metro area giving the ranked numbers in each of the 9 categories.

Two somewhat similar books, with rankings based on older data, are: *The Book of American City Rankings* by John T. Marlin and James S. Avery (NY: Facts on File Publications, 1983, 396, [2] pp.) with over 250 ranked lists, and brief text; and *Finding Your Best Place to Live in America* by Thomas F. Bowman et al (NY: Red Lion Books, 1982, 337 pp. paper), also arranged by topic and covering 80 major areas. For a book focusing on foreign cities see *Book of World City Rankings* by John T. Marlin et al (NY: Free Press, 1986, 604 pp.). The major portion of this latter book contains profiles of foreign cities arranged geographically; part 2 has comparable tables for various aspects of 8 broad factors.

Thomas, G. Scott. *The Rating Guide to Life in America's Small Cities.* Buffalo, NY: Prometheus Books, 1990. 538 pp. (paper).

Designed to help persons evaluate 219 micropolitan alternatives to metropolitan areas, this covers: climate/environment, diversions, economics, education, sophistication, health care, housing, public safety, transportation, and urban proximity for small cities of from 15,000 to 50,000 residents. Four states did not qualify for inclusion.

For an annual *Metro Insights* (DRI/McGraw-Hill) and other profiles and statistics on U.S. metropolitan areas, see the "Marketing Guides" section in Chapter 18.

Bibliographical Guides for Regional Data

American Statistics Index. Bethesda, MD: Congressional Information Service (monthly, with annual cumulations). Online counterpart is *ASI;* also on CD-ROM.

The complete description of this comprehensive guide to U.S. government statistics is in Chapter 4. We repeat it here to emphasize that it will help identify the many government statistical sources providing figures by state, county, MSA, and city. It can be accessed online; an added order service can supply microfiche copies of any report not easily located in a library nearby.

Business Dateline database.

This is a full-text database covering articles and news on regional business trends and activities, local industries, companies, their products, executives, appearing in some 160 U.S. and Canadian regional business periodicals and about 25 local newspapers. Included are most of the regional magazines noted above. This database is also available on CD-ROM as *Business Dateline OnDisc.*

Encyclopedia of Geographic Information Sources: U.S. Volume. 4th ed. Detroit: Gale Research, Inc., 1987. 437 pp.

For all states and for over 300 cities, this lists the following kinds of information, when applicable, for each location: general works, abstracting and indexing services, almanacs and yearbooks, bibliographies, biographical sources, directories, encyclopedias and dictionaries, gazetteers and guides, government publications, guides to doing business, handbooks and manuals, newsletters, newspapers and periodicals, organizations, research centers and institutions, statistical sources, and other sources of information. It is a good place to start when researching a particular region, state, or city. Gale publishes a companion volume, *Encyclopedia of Geographic Information Sources: International Volume* (4th ed., 1988) covering similar sources of information for foreign countries and cities. It is more fully described in the "Bibliographies and Indexes" section of Chapter 5.

PTS PROMT database.

PROMT is a much-used broad database covering worldwide market and technology information appearing in articles. It is important to mention here because it also includes abstracts and often full text for articles in almost 200 U.S. and Canadian regional magazines and daily newspapers. For a more complete description, see listing at the beginning of Chapter 6.

Statistical Reference Index. Bethesda, MD: Congressional Information Service (monthly with annual cumulations).

A companion guide to the first index above, also repeated here to point out that it contains two sections in each issue describing sources of regional statistics: (1) abstracts of state government statistical publications, including statistical yearbooks and economic outlooks, as well as those on agriculture, labor, education, health, crime, taxes, and vital statistics, etc.; (2) regional statistics available from universities, such as business and economic reviews, forecasts. A set of microfiche cards for most of these publications can be purchased from CIS.

State and Local Statistics Sources: A Subject Guide to Statistical Data on States, Cities, and Locales. Ed. by M. Balachandran and S. Balachandran. Detroit: Gale Research, Inc, 1990. 1,124 pp. Published biennially.

This is a comprehensive finding guide for sources of regional statistics, with the arrangement, under each state, alphabetical by approximately 52 major subjects. Included are the names of regional sources on: banks and banking, climate, cost of living, elections, finance, labor force, real estate, taxation, and much more. Lists of data centers, databases, and source publications are at end. This might be a useful starting point if one is researching a special location in the U.S.

Trade and Industry Index database (TI).

Included in this database are indexes and abstracts for articles in over 100 local and regional business publications. As the title indicates it also indexes and abstracts articles in many trade and industry journals. See listing in Chapter 6 for a complete annotation.

PAIS International in Print (see Chapter 2) occasionally indexes articles and a few reports or books under the name of a state or city. The annual *Business One Irwin Business and Investment Almanac* (see Chapter 1) contains a "State Information Guide" section, arranged by state, which lists a few regional publications about states and cities, state industry and business directories, addresses of information offices.

ECONOMICS LITERATURE

The large body of materials being written in the area of economics has already been well documented in several full-length bibliographies. Here we will mention only four introductory texts on economics, a few recent books on managerial economics and industrial organization, several important bibliographies, indexes, dictionaries, directories, a book on business research methods, a selection of sources on forecasting methods and techniques, and finally four useful guides that explain economic and financial measures. For the names of a few books on international economics see Chapter 16.

INTRODUCTORY ECONOMICS TEXTS

Bach, George L. *Economics: Analysis, Decision Making, and Policy.* 11th ed. Englewood Cliffs, NJ: Prentice-Hall, 1987. 752 pp.

Professor Bach still aims his popular introductory text toward kindling a real interest in economics among serious students by emphasizing key concepts, principles, and models and by helping students to apply these analytical tools themselves to big and little real-world problems. The 47 chapters are divided into 8 parts which cover: foundations; national income, employment, and inflation; markets, the price system, and the allocation of resources; the distribution of factor and personal income; economics, politics, and the public choice; international economics in a shrinking world; economic growth—causes and consequences; the changing economic world. There is effective use of two-color type, with charts, boxed notes, and some diagrams; one or more case incidents are with most chapters. This substantially revised edition was written with the assistance of four other economists. It must be revised soon to continue to be of use.

Heilbroner, Robert L., and James K. Galbraith. *The Economic Problem.* 9th ed. Englewood Cliffs, NJ: Prentice-Hall, 1990. 716 pp.

This latest revision of a well-established economics text strengthens the international focus. The material is presented in 6 major parts to cover: economic history and background; some basic economics (explanation of such concepts as supply/demand), macroeconomics, microeconomics, microeconomic challenges, the rest of the world. The text is visually attractive, with effective use of two-colors, frequent charts and graphs as well as boxed notes, and summaries of key concepts with each chapter. A glossary is at end. As an alternative, these two authors have also prepared two paperbacks covering micro- and macroeconomics in separate volumes. These are: *Understanding Macroeconomics* (9th ed., 1990, 498 pp.) and *Understanding Microeconomics* (9th ed., 1990, 449 pp.).

For persons who want a short, useful nontextbook-type book, Heilbroner (with Lester C. Thurow) has written *Economics Explained* (Updated ed. New York: Simon & Schuster, 1987, 250 pp., paper). They say this book is for people in the real world—to teach them about "the economics they ought to know—not to get rich, and not to have a particular point of view, but simply to be effective investors, educated business persons, informed workers, or just good citizens." In addition Professor Heilbroner has written a good, nontechnical historical account in *The Making of Economic Society* (7th ed., Prentice-Hall, 1985, 268 pp., paper).

McConnell, Campbell R., and Stanley L. Brue. *Economics: Principles, Problems, and Policies.* 11th ed. New York: McGraw-Hill, 1990. 866, [67] pp. Twelfth edition to be published in 1992.

Along with Samuelson (see next book), this text is considered one of the best introductions to economics, with straightforward and logical writing. Extensively revised, its basic purpose remains "to introduce the beginning economics student to those principles essential to an understanding of fundamental economic problems and the policy alternatives society may utilize to contend with these problems." There are 42 chapters arranged in 7 parts: introduction to economics and the economy; national income, employment, and fiscal policy; money, banking, monetary policy; problems and controversies in macroeconomics; the economics of the firm and resource allocation; current economic problems; international economics and the world economy. This latest edition makes good use of color in diagrams, charts, and section headings. Useful summaries, questions, bibliographical references are at end of chapters. A glossary and index are separately paged at end.

Samuelson, Paul A., and William D. Nordhaus. *Economics.* 14th ed. New York: McGraw-Hill, 1992. 784 pp.

With the 1985 edition, Professor Samuelson took on a coauthor to help in writing what has always been one of the best known and most popular introductions to the principles of modern economics, the aim of which is to offer a clear, accurate, up-to-date, and interesting basic economics text. Now completely revised once again, it is in 7 parts to cover: basic concepts; microeconomics (supply, demand, and product markets); wages, rent, and profits—the distribution of income; efficiency, equity and government; fundamental concepts of macroeconomics; aggregate supply and macroeconomic policy; international trade and the world economy. Throughout the text there is a "careful layering" of the material so that the more advanced discussions appear either in appendixes or in specially designated sections. This means the text can be used at all levels of proficiency, and the individual reader can go as far as s/he wishes and stop. There is effective use of graphs, and helpful two-color type; a useful glossary is at end.

MANAGERIAL ECONOMICS

Coyne, Thomas J., ed. *Readings in Managerial Economics.* 4th ed., Plano, TX: Business Publications, 1985. 574 pp.

A selection of readings to cover the most important concepts of managerial economics, arranged in 7 parts: introduction; demand; costs, production and productivity; pricing; financial management; risk, uncertainty, and factors to consider when making business decisions; forecasting.

Related to this is Professor Coyne's upper-level, undergraduate text entitled *Managerial Economics: Analysis and Cases* (5th ed., Business Publications, 1984, 680 pp.), which is arranged for the most part in the same sections as is the book of readings.

Hirschey, Mark, and James L. Pappas. *Fundamentals of Managerial Economics.* 4th ed. Chicago: Dryden Press, 1991. 713 pp.

This is a good introduction to those aspects of economic theory and analysis that are important in managerial decision making. It focuses on the economics—not on the mathematics—of the management decision process, and the emphasis is on practical applications. Its five parts cover: overview; demand analysis; production and cost analysis; market structure analysis and estimation; long-term investment decision making. Useful nonnumerical "Managerial Applications" boxes appear in each chapter showing current examples of how managerial economics is actually used in real-world situations. "Math Analysis for Managers" is at end of Chapter 2. Selected references are at end of chapters; appendixes contain interest factor tables.

A more comprehensive and rigorous text (requiring a working knowledge of calculus) has been published, with Professor Pappas as lead author; its title is *Managerial Economics* (6th ed., Dryden Press, 1990, 826 pp.).

McGuigan, James R., and R. Charles Moyer. *Managerial Economics.* 4th ed. St. Paul, MN: West Publishing Co., 1986. 714 pp.

Latest edition of a standard, comprehensive text dealing with the application of economic theory to the decision-making problems faced by both private and public enterprise. "The major emphasis is to provide the theory and tools essential to the analysis and solution of those problems which have significant economic consequences, both for the firm and society at large." Its basic sections cover: tools of analysis; demand and forecasting; production and cost; pricing; long-term investment decisions; regulation of private enterprise. Short glossaries of new terms are at the start of each chapter, and bibliographies conclude them. Statistical tables are at end of book. The authors presume a background in economics and say that prior work in statistics and quantitative methods is recommended.

Naylor, Thomas H., John M. Vernon, and Kenneth L. Wertz. *Managerial Economics: Corporate Economics and Strategy.* New York: McGraw-Hill, 1983. 443 pp.

"The major premise of this book is that the single most important application of microeconomics to practical business problems is in strategic planning." Thus part 3 applies microeconomics to the firm's competitive environment and part 5 applies it to strategic planning models and to the policies of corporate economics. Part 2 focuses on basic elements of microeconomics; part 4 covers capital budgeting and risk analysis. Emphasis is placed throughout on practical examples; bibliographies are at end of chapters. High-school algebra is required and some elementary statistics would be helpful.

Seo, K. K. *Managerial Economics: Text, Problems and Short Cases.* 6th ed. Homewood, IL: Irwin, 1984. 720 pp.

Latest edition of a text aimed primarily at intermediate-level undergraduates and first-year graduate students in economics and business administration. A few problems, case incidents, and short bibliographies appear at end of chapters; tables and charts are at end of book.

Two alternative intermediate-level texts also meant to present basic theoretical and analytical tools of economics useful in managerial decision making are: *Managerial Economics: Applied Microeconomics for Decision Making* by S. Charles Maurice, Christopher R. Thomas and Charles W. Smithson (4th ed., Irwin, 1991, 768 pp.); or *Managerial Economics: Analysis and Strategy* by Evan J. Douglas (3d ed., Prentice-Hall, 1987, 648 pp.).

Periodicals

Managerial and Decision Economics. Chichester, West Sussex, Eng.: J. Wiley & Sons Ltd. (quarterly).

Billed as "the international journal of research and progress in management economics," this journal aims to publish research findings and to focus on their development and applications. Articles cover a wide range of specific topics using economics as an aid in such areas as advertising, competitive strategy, diversification, financial decisions, forecasting, innovation. Indexed in ABI/I.

INDUSTRIAL ORGANIZATION

Adams, Walter, ed. *The Structure of American Industry.* 8th ed. New York: Macmillan, 1990. 386 pp.

A collection of "case studies" examining the structure, conduct, performance, and public policy of 11 American industries. Each industry is well covered by an academic authority (including Scherer and Shepherd) and each includes bibliographical notes and suggested readings. Industries covered are: agriculture, petroleum, steel, automobile, beer, computer, motion picture, airline, telecommunications, banking, weapons industries. There is also a chapter on conglomerates, and on public policy in a free enterprise economy. Where relevant, the authors have made international comparisons with industries in Japan and the EEC.

Caves, Richard. *American Industry: Structure, Conduct, Performance.* 6th ed. Englewood Cliffs, NJ: Prentice-Hall, 1987. 124 pp. paper.

Not an in-depth text but rather an excellent, concise introduction to the central problems of industrial organization written by a leading specialist, and using as a framework the three concepts in the sub-title. Professor Caves says his book shows you how to apply the basic concepts of price theory to industries in the American economy; it summarizes what economists have discovered by applying these concepts to American industries; and it reviews government policies toward business. Useful suggestions for additional reading are at end. This volume is in the helpful "Foundation of Modern Economics Series," each one of which is a concise paperback survey of a major branch of economics written by a respected academic authority.

Clarkson, Kenneth W., and Roger L. Miller. *Industrial Organization: Theory, Evidence, and Public Policy.* New York: McGraw-Hill, 1982. 518 pp.

This text "has interwoven both the standard industrial organization theory and hundreds of accompanying empirical studies with recent developments in the theory of firm behavior and market outcomes." The authors begin by examining the firm and market structure, and models of industries and markets. They then focus on specific aspects of firm behavior and market outcomes (such as price discrimination, administered prices, mergers and vertical integration, barriers to entry, and more). A final section looks at public policy (including antitrust and trade regulation policies). A one-semester course in microeconomics is presumed.

Greer, Douglas F. *Industrial Organization and Public Policy.* 2d ed. New York: Macmillan, 1984. 572 pp.

The purpose of Greer's undergraduate text is to give the reader a broad understanding of markets and their regulation. The four parts cover: structure (product differentiation, concentration, barriers to entry); conduct (price and production behavior, for example); performance (end results as determined by such variables as efficiency, profit and policy, technological change); and a beginning introductory section. The book tries to blend theory, empiricism and policy; some background in economics and high-school algebra is helpful.

Scherer, F. M., and David Ross. *Industrial Market Structure and Economic Performance.* 3d ed. Boston: Houghton Miffin, 1990. 713 pp.

Like most other texts on industrial organization, the organizational thrust of this one centers on a structure/conduct/performance trichotomy. Chapters 3–5 describe the structure of industry in the U.S. and abroad; chapters 6–17 then undertake an extended analysis of conduct in the pricing, product policy, and technological innovations spheres; chapter 18 assesses the quality of the resulting performance. Extensive bibliographical footnotes appear throughout. This is another good undergraduate text.

Shepherd, William G. *The Economics of Industrial Organization.* 3d ed. Englewood Cliffs, NJ: Prentice-Hall, 1990. 566 pp.

This is a basic text on how enterprises function under varying conditions of competition and market power. It is arranged in 7 parts to cover: basic concepts; market structure; performance; determinants of market structure; behavior and related topics; industry case studies; public policies. Shepherd says some technical details have been consigned to footnotes and appendixes to keep his text as lucid as possible. A general bibliography of research papers and monographs is at the end of chapter 2. For a more detailed study of public policy see his book *Public Policies Toward Business* described in chapter 9.

ECONOMIC BIBLIOGRAPHIES AND INDEXES

See also Chapter 2 for several bibliographies of books covering both business and economics.

Economic Books: Current Selections. Compiled by the Department of Economics and University Library System of the University of Pittsburgh. Pittsburgh (quarterly).

A useful, annotated list of English-language economic books classified by subject and coded by budget size of college or university library for which each book is recommended. Several sections of potential interest to business are: international economics (including trade theory and relations, balance of payment, international investment and foreign aid); administration; business finance and investment; marketing; industrial organization and public policy; economics of technological change; industry studies. Sections at end cover selected reference works, bibliographies, textbooks, working papers.

Economic Literature Index.

This is an online bibliographical service corresponding to the *Index of Economic Articles in Journals and Collective Volumes* and *The Journal of Economic Literature* (see descriptions in this section). It is also available on CD-ROM.

Index of Economic Articles in Journals and Collective Volumes. Nashville, TN: American Economic Association. 2 volumes (annual). Online counterpart is *Economic Literature Index*.

A classified list, with author index, of English-language articles in major professional economics journals and in collective volumes. Vols. 1–7 are for the years 1886–1965; since then each volume covers articles written in just one year, with Vol. 30, for 1988, the latest published in 1992.

Journal of Economic Literature. Nashville, TN: American Economic Association (quarterly). Online counterpart is *Economic Literature Index*.

This is an excellent, bibliographical quarterly. Each issue includes: an annotated list of new books classified by subject (including a few on "administration" and on "industrial organization"); a subject index of articles in current periodicals; selected abstracts of the more significant articles arranged by subject; tables of contents for current economics journals. Critical book reviews are at the beginning of each issue.

Sources of Information in the Social Sciences: A Guide to the Literature. 3d ed. comp. by William H. Webb and Associates. Chicago: American Library Association, 1986. 777 pp.

A monumental work, essential as an excellent compilation of the older (prior to 1986) basic books and reference sources in the social sciences as a whole and in it 8 subfields: history; geography; economics and business administration; sociology; anthropology; psychology; education; political science. The lists of basic books on each topic are preceded by short introductions; the reference guides are usually annotated and cover bibliographies, abstracts and indexes, directories, dictionaries, encyclopedias, handbooks, almanacs, yearbooks, statistical sources, atlases, services, professional journals, organizations, sources of current information, databases.

ECONOMIC DICTIONARIES

We make no attempt here to cover completely the many good economic dictionaries found in most university libraries and used often by economics students and researchers. The dictionaries below are those which may be of most interest to business students and practitioners. The 1986 edition of Ammer's *Dictionary of Business and Economics* is described in Chapter 1.

Encyclopedia of Economics. Ed. by Douglas Greenwald. New York: McGraw-Hill, 1982. 1,070 pp.

For the lay person who wants more in-depth definitions of 310 important economic terms including related fields of econometrics and statistics, here is an authoritative encyclopedia bringing together the expertise of over 170 well-qualified contributors.

The articles, arranged alphabetically, vary in degrees of complexity; each contains references for further research. Subject and name indexes are at end, as well as an interesting time table of economic events, technological and financial developments, and economic thought from 8000 B.C. to 1981.

Garwood, Alfred N., and Louise L. Hornor. *Dictionary of U.S. Government Statistical Terms.* Palo Alto, CA: Information Publications, 1991. 247 pp. paper.

A guide for the non-specialist data user to the terms found in such diverse government publications as the *Statistical Abstract,* the *Survey of Current Business,* and Census Bureau products.

McGraw-Hill Dictionary of Modern Economics. Comp. by Douglas Greenwald & Associates. 3d ed. New York: McGraw-Hill, 1983. 632 pp.

This is the economics dictionary I have usually turned to first because I like the practical, well-written definitions, the fact that they are usually more than one sentence long, and that, in many instances, at least one bibliographical citation is provided for users who need a more detailed explanation. It also seems to cover a wider range of terms, theories, and techniques of interest to business persons as well as to economists. Over 200 organizations and associations are described at end, but this information is now out of date.

Moffat, Donald W. *Economics Dictionary.* 2d ed. New York: Elsevier, 1983. 331 pp.

Moffat says his dictionary "is intended as a companion for all who listen to the news, read newspapers or trade journals, or study economics or related business subjects." Definitions vary in length according to need, and there are many helpful cross-references.

The New Palgrave: A Dictionary of Economics. Ed. by John Eatwell et al. London: Macmillan Press Ltd.; New York: Stockton Press, 1987. 4 volumes (about 3,500 pp.).

Originally published in 1894 and revised several times since, this is a basic and comprehensive dictionary covering economic thought and theory. Its nearly 2,000 entries (many over 3 double-column pages in length), are written by one of some 900 expert contributors. Included are biographies of the more important economists. Suggestions for further reading are with most entries.

Pearce, David W., and Robert Shaw. *The MIT Dictionary of Modern Economics.* 4th ed. Cambridge, MA: MIT Press, 1992. 474 pp.

An up-to-date dictionary of economic words, phrases, and concepts that a first-year economics student might need, with some business terms also included, as well as biographical information on celebrated economists and descriptions of international institutions. This dictionary has always had somewhat of a British flavor since most of the contributing authors have been Scottish economists.

DIRECTORIES OF ECONOMISTS AND ASSOCIATIONS

American Economic Association (1313 21st Avenue South, Nashville, TN. 37212). *Survey of Members.*

This directory is revised periodically and usually appears as an issue of the *American Economic Review* (e.g. December 1989). It includes biographical information about each member.

Association for University Business and Economic Research. *Membership Directory*. Indianapolis: Indiana Business Research Center, Indiana University (annual).

A directory of bureaus of business and economic research and divisions of research at American universities, giving (for full members) names of directors and other officers, number of secretarial staff, names of publications. Lesser information is usually given for associate member universities.

National Association of Business Economists (28790 Chagrin Blvd., Suite 300, Cleveland, OH 44122). *Membership Directory*.

Published each year as the March issue of *Business Economics*.

BUSINESS RESEARCH

Business research can play an important role in effective decision making. We list here just one recent textbook on business research methods and one periodical reporting on business research. For several useful books on marketing research refer to Chapter 18.

Books

Zikmund, William G. *Business Research Methods*. 3d ed. Chicago: Dryden Press, 1991. 742 pp.

This undergraduate text introduces students to the basic tools of business research by explaining the various research techniques and methodologies. Its organization follows the logic of the business research process: introduction; beginning stages (including a chapter on secondary data, with a bibliography of selected secondary sources); research methods for collecting primary data; measurement concepts; sampling fieldwork; data analysis and presentation; ethical issues in business research. Numerous real-world examples are used throughout the book along with boxed features called "Research Insights" and "Statistical Tutor," this latter intended for quick reviews of basic statistical concepts to make the quantitative aspects easier to understand. At end are 18 short cases, statistical tables, and a glossary.

Periodicals

Journal of Applied Business Research. Littleton, CO (quarterly).

Publishes refereed articles (both theoretical and applied) relating to research results in the areas of accounting, economics, entrepreneurship, finance, information systems, management, marketing. In each issue the articles are arranged by these headings.

BUSINESS CYCLES AND FORECASTING METHODS

A few books on strategic and long-range planning are described in Chapter 10.

Handbooks

Makridakis, Spyros, and Steven C. Wheelwright, eds. *The Handbook of Forecasting: A Manager's Guide*. 2d ed. New York: Wiley, 1987. 638 pp.

Makridakis and Wheelwright are academicians who are also forecasting specialists. In this updated handbook they have brought together a wide range of experts to provide managers with a useful guide to the important aspects and issues of forecasting. It is arranged within four main parts to cover: the role and application of forecasting in organizations (exploring such functions as sales, operations and control, finance, strategic planning); approaches to forecasting (6 chapters describing major techniques); forecasting challenges (13 chapters on critical issues such as recessions, country political risk, raw material availability); managing the forecasting function. There are bibliographies with each chapter; a glossary and detailed subject index are at end for ease in finding information.

Books

Armstrong, J. Scott. *Long-Range Forecasting: From Crystal Ball to Computer.* 2d ed. New York: Wiley, 1985. 687 pp.

Unlike other guides to forecasting methods, this book is written with a delightful sense of humor. Thus it is interesting, enjoyable, and yet informative and persuasive. It is still written for "doers" (forecasters, practicing managers, academicians, students); it is easy to follow and is sprinkled with anecdotes and a few cartoons, as well as data from a wide reading of the research literature. Armstrong describes five types of forecasting methods and processes, and ends by commenting on future trends and research. In his appendix he has reprinted the lengthy list of references (with annotations and ratings based on his evaluation of relevance and usefulness) that was in the 1978 edition, and he has added an "Updated Bibliography" to describe research published roughly from 1978 through 1984. The appendix also contains a glossary.

Granger, C. W. J. *Forecasting in Business and Economics.* 2d ed. Boston: Academic Press, 1989. 279 pp.

For persons interested in a textbook for a course on the title subject, this has been revised to include newly evolving practical techniques in forecasting as of 1989. Included are chapters on leading indicators, population and technological forecasting, world models, as well as on specific forecasting techniques. An empirical project, involving actual forecasts, runs throughout the text. Further readings are with chapters; some basic statistical concepts are in an appendix.

Hanke, John E., and Arthur G. Reitsch. *Business Forecasting.* 3d ed. Boston: Allyn and Bacon, 1989. 530 pp. Fourth edition published in 1992.

This book presents the basic statistical techniques useful for preparing individual business forecasts and long-range plans in connection with company decision making. The authors say they have tried to write in a straightforward style, and they make extensive use of practical examples. They start with three chapters as introduction and background. Then they cover in turn: averaging and smoothing techniques; casual forecasting techniques (correlation, regression analysis, multiple regression); techniques involving time series analysis; and finally judgmental elements in forecasting. Short case incidents and bibliographies are with chapters; glossaries are with some chapters. Statistical tables are in appendixes.

Kress, George. *Practical Techniques of Business Forecasting: Fundamentals and Applications for Marketing, Production, and Financial Managers.* Westport, CT: Quorum Books, 1985. 257 pp.

Although this is an older book that will not cover some of the newer techniques, still it is a useful discussion of business forecasting at the company level. It is written both for business managers and business school students to give them the basic information they need in an easy-to-understand style and assuming only limited knowledge of quantitative methods. Professor Kress describes those forecasting techniques most commonly used to make forecasts at a micro level, explaining how each works and when each should be used. He also covers methods of acquiring needed data in a chapter that describes some important external secondary data sources.

Makridakis, Spyros, and Steven C. Wheelwright. *Forecasting Methods for Management.* 5th ed. New York: Wiley, 1989. 470 pp.

Substantially revised and reflecting the newest developments as of 1989, this latest edition addresses a broad set of managerial concerns through down-to-earth descriptions of forecasting, the possibilities and limitations, and the role of forecasting in the management process. It starts with an introduction to the role and importance of forecasting in management. Then it discusses in turn: quantitative forecasting methods; management judgment in forecasting; and lastly, it describes forecasting applications for short-, medium-, and long-term horizons. Selected references for further reading are at end of chapters.

These two professors have collaborated on several other works. Their *Handbook of Forecasting* (1987) is described above. Their earlier book, written with Victor E. McGee, is *Forecasting: Methods and Applications* (2d ed., Wiley, 1983, 923 pp.).

Sherman, Howard J. *The Business Cycle: Growth and Crisis Under Capitalism.* Princeton, NJ: Princeton University Press, 1991. 447 pp.

Unlike other texts on the subject, this one "attempts to place the instability of the business cycle at the center of macroeconomic understanding, a position that is exactly contrary to the present view in macroeconomics." Professor Sherman arranges it in three parts: overview; the basic model—demand and supply over the cycle; more realistic approximations. Cycle tables and bibliography are at end.

Stewart, Hugh B. *Recollecting the Future: A View of Business, Technology, and Innovation in the Next 30 Years.* Homewood, IL: Dow Jones-Irwin, 1989. 356 pp.

Stewart hopes he can provide here a nontechnical digest of forecasting methods and conclusions of interest both to business people and to general readers. He explains concepts and methods in simple language and relates the concepts to practical situations, without resorting to "sometimes dry and mathematical background." The four parts cover: the patterns of growth; the long economic wave and reason for it; the future according to RECALL (a mythical growth analysis company); the lessons from RECALL. Appendixes contain some mathematical background information. A list of references is at end.

Valentine, Lloyd M., and Dennis F. Ellis. *Business Cycles & Forecasting.* 8th ed. Cincinnati: South-Western, 1991. 586 pp.

A standard upper level or graduate text covering: business fluctuations; national income analysis; business cycle theories; forecasting economic activity; proposals for achieving economic growth and stability. Suggested reading lists are at end of chapters.

Periodicals

Futures. London: Butterworth-Heinemann Ltd. (10/yr.).

This international journal contains scholarly articles on forecasting methods and practice and on long-range planning and policy making; also news of upcoming meetings, book reviews. Indexed in ABI/I, SSI, TI; full text on BRS, DATA-STAR, DIALOG, MEAD/NEXIS.

Futures Research Quarterly. Bethesda, MD: World Future Society.

A worldwide refereed magazine seeking high quality articles on futures research, both theoretical and practical.

Futurist. Bethesda, MD: World Future Society (bimonthly).

Meant for the general public, this journal has short, popularly written articles on forecasts, trends, and ideas about the future. Includes book reviews. Indexed in ABI/I, F&S, RG, SSI; full-text on BRS, DATA-STAR, DIALOG, DOW JONES, MEAD/NEXIS.

International Journal of Forecasting. Amsterdam: Elsevier Science Publisher B.V. (quarterly).

An international journal publishing refereed papers on all aspects and types of forecasting, with "strong emphasis on empirical studies, evaluation activities, implementation research and ways of improving the practice of forecasting." Includes book reviews, a software review section, and "Research on Forecasting," which critiques papers published elsewhere. Indexed in ABI/I, PAIS.

An international bimonthly with a similar focus of providing refereed papers on both the theory and practice of forecasting is *Journal of Forecasting* (Chicester, Eng., and New York: Wiley).

Journal of Business Forecasting: Methods & Systems. Flushing, NY: Graceway Publishing Co. (quarterly).

A forum for the exchange of ideas about the methods and systems used in business and technological forecasting. Each issue is in two parts, with the first consisting of about six short articles geared to interests of business managers whose responsibilities include evaluating forecasts. Part 2, called "business and economic outlook," contains four continuing short-term forecasts, with brief text. These are described in this chapter's section on "Current Economic Trends and Forecasts." Each issue usually also has a software review section and a book review.

Technological Forecasting and Social Change. New York: Elsevier Science Publishing Co. (8/yr.).

Another international journal, this one for scholarly articles dealing with the methodology and practice of technological forecasting as a planning tool; also for analysis of the interaction of technology with the social, behavioral, and environmental aspects in integrative planning. Includes book reviews. Indexed in BPI, PTS/F&S.

Directories

The Futures Research Directory: Individuals. 1991/92. Bethesda, MD: World Future Society, 1991. 246 pp.

Latest edition of a directory of nearly 1,200 individuals professionally involved in the study of the future. Data on each person includes (besides address and phone number) specialization, education, recent employment, recent publications. Geographic and subject indexes are at end.

GUIDES TO ECONOMIC AND FINANCIAL MEASURES

For several helpful guides to reading stock and other financial quotations appearing in newspapers, refer to the section on "Guides to Reading the Financial Pages" in Chapter 8.

Carnes, W. Stansbury, and Stephen D. Slifer. *The Atlas of Economic Indicators: A Visual Guide to Market Forces and the Federal Reserve.* New York: HarperBusiness, 1991. 232 pp.

The authors, senior economists on Wall Street, have produced here an easy-to-understand, visual guide to the most significant economic indicators and why they are important to investors. Each of 17 indicators (such as GNP, employment) are well explained in separate chapters, and the authors make frequent good use of charts, graphs, and other visual aids. The book begins with an introductory overview and ends with three chapters on Federal Reserve operations.

Fabozzi, Frank J., and Harry I. Greenfield, eds. *The Handbook of Economic and Financial Measures.* Homewood, IL: Dow Jones-Irwin, 1984. 517 pp.

This useful compilation provides good explanations of the background, construction, and uses of those major measures of economic and financial activity that are most likely to appear regularly in current journals or daily newspapers. Each chapter is written by a professional economist, and they are arranged in 6 parts to cover: measures of aggregate economic activity (such as GNP, capital spending, construction activity, unemployment, leading economic indicators); indicators for government deficit and trade balance; money supply and capital market conditions (flow of funds, stock market indicators, etc.); inflation; firms and consumers; forecasting.

Frumkin, Norman. *Guide to Economic Indicators.* Armonk, NY: M. E. Sharpe, 1990. 242 pp.

Written for people with no special background in economics, this contains concise descriptions of over 50 economic indicators, arranged alphabetically from "average hourly earnings index" to "value of the dollar indexes." Includes a few references from primary data sources with each indicator.

Lehmann, Michael B. *The Dow Jones-Irwin Guide to Using the Wall Street Journal.* 3d ed. Homewood, IL: Dow Jones-Irwin, 1990. 382 pp.

More specialized than Fabozzi/Greenfield above, this is a useful nontechnical guide to understanding the ups and downs of the American business economy by explaining the key statistical series that appear in the *Wall Street Journal.* Lehmann describes each series in the context of the business cycle and explains the relationship of each to the overall picture. Included are discussions of such economic figures as money supply, housing starts, GNP, industrial production, consumer price index, leading economic indicators, business capital expenditures, international transactions; also such investment tables as stock and bond price quotations and how to read them, the Dow Jones Industrial Averages, interest rates, money market funds. His book is full of useful explanatory charts, graphs, and tables reprinted from the *Journal;* an appendix contains listings of the statistical series according to chapter arrangement and according to the *Journal's* publication schedule.

Sommers, Albert T. *The U.S. Economy Demystified: What the Major Economic Statistics Mean and Their Significance for Business.* Lexington, MA: Lexington Books, 1985. 137 pp.

Sommers (chief economist for the Conference Board) says his book is for the sophisticated business person and the individual consumer or investor who seeks a compact, digestible guide in order to better understand where the U.S. economy is now (judging from its statistical condition) and where it is likely to go. He starts by laying out the essentials of the U.S. statistical system and then he proceeds to explain: the nature of the business cycle, the influences of economic policy, the U.S. in its world context, and the evidence of performance with respect to inflation. This is a lucid, well-written book.

4

BASIC U.S. STATISTICAL SOURCES

Comprehensive Statistical Compilations – Basic Specialized Sources – Census Statistics – Standard Industrial Classification Scheme – Foreign Trade Statistics – Monthly Statistical Periodicals – Statistics on Government Finance – Guides to Statistics

Statistics are such an absolute necessity to business that three chapters in this book are devoted to describing the most important published sources available from such organizations as government agencies, trade associations, universities, corporations, publishers, and private organizations. In addition, other statistical publications are scattered throughout this book: banking and monetary statistics in Chapter 14; corporate and investment statistics in Chapter 8; industrial research expenditures in Chapter 20; insurance and real estate statistics in Chapter 15; labor statistics in Chapter 19; marketing statistics in Chapter 18; plant and equipment expenditures in Chapter 14; and U.S. regional trends and statistics in Chapter 3.

It is important to note here that much of this vast statistical data is now also available in machine-readable form, especially that relating to business and economic trends, forecasting, financial and company data, and statistics important for tracking market potential. Throughout this book I have tried to mention which of the most important data is also available online (as of 1991). But this whole field is developing so rapidly that readers are urged to make frequent use of one or more of the "directories of computer information services" described in Chapter 2.

This first of the three statistics chapters describes those publications that one will usually turn to first because they are so comprehensive and so basic for locating U.S. business and economic statistics. At the end of the chapter are several bibliographical guides to suggest other useful works. Chapter 5 concentrates on the important international and foreign statistics and foreign economic trends, including also indexes and bibliographies. Chapter 6 covers sources that provide data on specific industries, including compilations of operating ratios for industries. Fundamental to all of this vast statistical data is knowing how to use it. There are many books devoted entirely to the study of the techniques, tools, and theories of statistical analysis in decision making, and a selection of these appears in Chapter 17.

COMPREHENSIVE STATISTICAL COMPILATIONS

The following publications form the backbone of any statistical reference collection and are often the compilations to use first if one is not familiar with a more specialized source that may contain the data needed.

Predicasts Basebook. Cleveland, OH: Predicasts, Inc. (annual). Online counterpart is *PTS U.S. Time Series.*

A comprehensive, loose-leaf volume containing approximately 27,700 time series, arranged by a modified 7-digit SIC number, and including also statistics for economic indicators. The industry statistics often include production, shipments, consumption, employment, exports/imports, wholesale price, plant and equipment expenditures, payroll, each for a 14-year period. The published source and an annual growth rate is included for each citation. This data is also available online via the PTS system which includes quarterly updated figures and additional series not in the print volume.

Standard & Poor's Corp. *Statistical Service.* New York. 1 volume (looseleaf, with monthly supplements).

Excellent for its coverage of current and basic statistics arranged in the following areas: banking and finance; production indexes and labor statistics; price indexes (commodities, producer indexes, and cost of living); income and trade; building and building materials; energy, electric power and fuels; metals; transportation; textiles, chemicals, paper; agricultural products; security price index record (excellent source for S&P's stock price indexes, Dow Jones averages). One must check in each of its three parts to get a complete run of any statistics in this service: the "basic statistics" sections (arranged by subjects listed above); the white current statistics issue giving latest annual figures; the yellow monthly issue for latest figures covering the current year.

U.S. Bureau of the Census. *Statistical Abstract of the United States.* Washington, DC: U.S. Government Printing Office (annual).

This is probably *the* most important U.S. statistical reference work because it serves both as a prime source for U.S. industrial, social, political, and economic statistics and also as a bibliographical guide. Source notes are at the foot of each table; a useful "Guide to Sources of Statistics" (at end) lists important statistical publications arranged by subject; there is also a "Guide to State Statistical Abstracts," and a "Guide to Foreign Statistical Abstracts."

Although the figures in the *Statistical Abstract* usually cover just one or a few years, the Bureau also publishes a useful historical supplement called *Historical Statistics of the United States: Colonial Times to 1970* (1975, 2 volumes). There are also two other supplementary volumes: *County and City Data Book, 1988* (GPO, 1988, 797, 126 pp.) and *State and Metropolitan Area Data Book* (GPO, 4th ed., 1991, 388 pp.). This latter compilation (published triennially) contains statistics from the census and a few other government sources for each state, MSA and for consolidated areas as well. Beginning in 1992 Bernan Press in Lanham, PA, is publishing a *County and City Extra: Annual Metro, City and County Data Book* intended to keep the census publication giving county and city data up to date between its editions. This is available also as the *County and City Plus CD-ROM*.

BASIC SPECIALIZED SOURCES

Board of Governors of the Federal Reserve System. *Industrial Production.* 1986 Revision. Washington, DC: 1986. 697 pp.

The major portion of this volume contains retrospective statistics for the 1985 revised industrial production index (with 1977=100). Monthly averages are given from 1954–1985 for major industry groups and for industry subtotals. Separate tables cover figures that are both seasonally adjusted and not seasonally adjusted. At front is a summary of the 1985 revision, a discussion of the methodology, the structure and series composition, a bibliography, and a glossary. More recent statistics can be found in the Board's monthly *Federal Reserve Bulletin* and in their monthly Statistical Release No. G17, with title *Industrial Production and Capacity Utilization.* In 1990 the index base year changed to 1987=100, and so current issues of these sources use the revised figures.

CENDATA database.

This is a numeric database for selected census statistics, primarily from the various current summary reports (not part of the regular census-taking program), and also from such sources as the *County Business Patterns,* some of the *Current Industrial Reports,* population estimates, and much more. A complete list of statistical reports included in *CENDATA* is at the front of the annual *Census Catalog & Guide.* Check this catalog also to identify the many census sources also on microfiche, magnetic tape, diskettes, or on CD-ROM.

CRB Commodity Year Book. New York: Commodity Research Bureau (annual).

A useful statistical compilation covering about 100 commodities, plus interest rates, stock index, currencies, and futures markets. Data for each commodity usually includes production, prices, futures (where applicable), sometimes consumption, stocks, export/import. A current *Commodity Year Book Statistical Abstract Service* (3/yr.) is also available which updates statistics in the yearbook.

Dun's Census of American Business. Parsippany, NJ: Dun & Bradstreet, Inc. (annual).

Based on Dun's extensive files of some 8.4 million U.S. businesses, this directory counts the number of establishments (which often total more than just the number of companies) in each SIC industry—by sales volume and employee size groups. This data is given for three geographic levels: the NATIONAL sections give figures both for primary and secondary 4-digit figures ("primary" describes the main activity of the establishment while "secondary" covers activities that contribute at least 10% of the establishment's revenue); the STATE sections give number of establishments for primary 4-digit industries as well as figures by employee size and sales-volume range but only for 9 broad SIC categories; the COUNTY sections have overall totals for each county by employee size and sales volume range but with no industry data. At end are 2-digit industry and state totals based on statistics in the *Million Dollar Directory.* Statistics are updated as of June each year, and so data is more current than in *County Business Patterns* (see listing under U.S. Bureau of the

Census) for states by SIC industry; but it does not give the SIC figures broken down by county as does *CBP*. Both sources are potentially useful for market studies that investigate such questions as where to locate a firm or branch; how large a local market exists for a product or service; how to define sales territories, and so forth.

Predicasts Forecasts. Cleveland, OH: Predicasts, Inc. (quarterly with annual cumulations). Online counterpart is *PTS U.S. Forecasts.*

This much-used quarterly service gives short- and long-range forecast statistics both for basic economic indicators and for individual industries/products (arranged by a modified 7-digit SIC number). Accompanying each forecast is the date and page reference of the current journal, government report, or special study from which the statistics are taken. At end are alphabetical lists of SIC industries and of published sources.

A companion forecasting service, covering foreign countries and industries, is called *Worldcasts* (see description in Chapter 5).

U.S. Bureau of Economic Analysis, Department of Commerce. *Business Statistics.* Washington, DC: U.S. Government Printing Office (biennial).

An historical record of the basic business series (about 2,100) that can be found currently in the important monthly *Survey of Current Business*. Published as a supplement to the *Survey,* this contains annual averages, beginning with the year 1967, and monthly figures for the most recent years. An appendix has pre-1985 monthly or quarterly statistics for over 300 series (blue pages); also quarterly historical data for "National Income and Product Accounts" series and U.S. international transactions (yellow pages). Includes source references and good explanatory notes.

U.S. Bureau of Economic Analysis, Department of Commerce. *Survey of Current Business:* "U.S. National Income and Product Accounts: Revised Estimates". (annual, July issue).

The monthly *Survey* itself is described with other statistical periodicals. This special issue is important enough to list by itself, since it is the prime source of U.S. national income and account statistics. Figures in this annual issue cover: gross national product and national income (including GNP, GNP in constant dollars, GNP by major type of product; national income by type of income; gross domestic product; auto and truck output; farm and housing sector output); personal income and outlay (including personal consumption expenditures by type of product); government receipts and expenditures (including expenditures by type and function); foreign transactions; saving and investment; product income and employment by industry (includes corporate profits both before and after taxes, by industry); fixed-weighted price indexes and implicit price deflators. These statistics usually cover a four-year period; the most recent totals are in each monthly issue of the *Survey.* For historical statistics see another supplement to the Survey called *The National Income & Product Accounts of the United States, 1929–82; Statistical Tables* (Washington, DC: U.S. Government Printing Office, 1986, 425 pp.).

U.S. Bureau of the Census. *County Business Patterns.* Washington, DC: U.S. Government Printing Office (annual, with separate numbers for each state and a U.S. summary volume). Also available on CD-ROM and on magnetic tape.

This is a very useful annual compilation of mid-March employment and first quarter and annual payroll statistics by state, county, detailed industry, and employment-size class. For each 4-digit SIC industry this gives county totals, in number of employees, payrolls, and number of establishments by employment size class. Includes finance, insurance, and real estate SIC categories that are not covered in the census itself. Like *Dun's Census* (see listing above) this can be of value for analyzing market potential in a particular geographic location and for other business uses. *CBP*, however, is based on a more comprehensive survey of establishments; it gives a county breakdown by 4-digit industry (which *Dun's* does not), but the figures are not always as up to date (latest published in 1991 contain figures only for 1989).

U.S. Industrial Outlook. Washington, DC: U.S. Government Printing Office for the U.S. International Trade Administration (annual).

A handy and inexpensive compilation on recent trends and outlook (about five years) for 350 of the nation's most important 4-digit manufacturing and service industries. The short narrative for each industry contains a discussion of the current situation, short and long-term prospects, international competitiveness, and often a list of additional sources of information. Includes statistical tables for historical trends and short-range forecasts for product and industry data and for foreign trade. This is a popular and very useful source for current industry trends and prospects.

U.S. Internal Revenue Service. *Statistics of Income: Corporation Income Tax Returns.* Washington, DC: U.S. Government Printing Office (annual).

Balance sheet and income statement statistics taken from a sample of corporate income tax returns. Includes tables by major industry, by asset size, etc. The IRS also prepares an annual *Source Book: Statistics of Income for Active Corporation Income Tax Returns,* which are worksheet tables forming the basis of the report above. This is in two parts (one giving statistics based on firms both with and without net income, and the other for returns with net income only); balance sheet and income statement statistics are reported by four-digit SIC number and then by size of total assets.

A companion annual is *Statistics of Income: Individual Income Tax Returns,* which includes statistics on individual returns filed and sources of income (with some tables by size of income), exemptions and itemized deductions, and tax computations. A quarterly *SOI Bulletin* provides preliminary statistics for these annuals as well as for other SOI-related data. This is helpful since the figures in the annuals are so slow in being published (1988 statistics were the latest published as of 1992). Other useful tables in the *SOI Bulletin* cover: "Partnership Returns" and "Sole Proprietorship Returns" (both published annually in the summer issue); "Estimates of Personal Wealth, 1986" (spring 1990); "Domestic Corporations Controlled by Foreign Persons" (summer 1990); "Foreign Recipients of U.S. Income, 1988" (winter 1990–91).

U.S. President. *Economic Report of the President. Transmitted to the Congress, February (each year); Together with the Annual Report of the Council of Economic Advisers.* Washington, DC: U.S. Government Printing Office (annual).

The Annual Report of the Council of Economic Advisers comprises the major portion of this publication. It discusses economic policy and outlook, economic trends, with over 100 pages of statistical tables covering such basic economic indications as national income, employment, production, prices, corporate profits, government finance, agriculture, international transactions.

CENSUS STATISTICS

The Bureau of the Census is by far the largest publisher of comprehensive statistical data of importance to American business. Its periodic census reports can be of immense value to anyone needing detailed economic, statistical, and marketing data because much of it is arranged by state, county, metropolitan statistical area (MSA), city, and some of it is also by census tracts, blocks, Congressional districts, and standard industrial classification (SIC) industries. The economic censuses in particular (retail, wholesale, service industries, construction, manufactures, mineral industries, and transportation) are a major source of essential facts about business.

The one problem is that these census enumerations are often quite out of date. The economic censuses, the agriculture, and government censuses are all taken only every five years in the years ending with the numbers 2 and 7; the censuses of population and of housing are taken only every 10 years in the year ending with the number zero. Therefore, although census data is of great value, it is often necessary to look elsewhere for more recent statistics even though these may not be given in such great detail.

The Census Bureau publishes much more than just the census reports noted below. A few statistical publications are described elsewhere in this chapter as, for example, their useful annual *County Business Patterns*. For an annual descriptive listing of all census publications see their *Census Catalog & Guide* or the more specialized *Guide to the 1987 Economic Censuses and Related Statistics* (1990, 130 pp.). These, as well as the *American Statistics Index* which also describes census statistical reports, are described at the end of this chapter. Further it is important to note here that, although the Census Bureau publishes only their most widely used censuses and statistical surveys, much more information is available on computer tapes and other nonprint sources. Since much of this material is available in more than one media format, it is useful to know that both the census guides above include symbols with each item to identify in which formats each is available—printed copy, computer tape, microfiche, CD-ROM, diskette, or the online service called *CENDATA*. This mass of material now available in computerized formats provides almost limitless possibilities for subject cross-classifications or area tabulations, any of which can be processed (except for confidential records) according to a customer's individual specifications.

Economic Censuses

The descriptive information for the economic censuses below is based on examination of data in the 1987 census.

Census of Construction Industries (CC).

The construction industry consists of building and heavy construction contractors, special trade contractors, and land subdividers and developers. The "Industry Series" (27 separate industry reports plus a U.S. Summary) provides detailed statistics on number of construction establishments, number of employees, payroll, hours worked, value of construction work done, cost of materials, rental costs, capital expenditures, depreciable assets, and more—all by state and some statistics by size classification. The "Geographic Area Series" groups the statistics according to 9 census geographic divisions. Its "Subject Series," consists of just one report on the *Legal Form of Organization and Type of Operation.* The Census Bureau also publishes *Current Construction Reports,* not part of the five-year enumerations but useful just the same for current monthly or quarterly statistics on such topics as "Housing Starts," "Housing Completions," "Value of New Construction Put in Place."

Census of Financial Industries (FC).

Not as yet in existence, this is planned as a useful new part of the economic census program, to be conducted for the first time in 1992. It will cover statistics on business establishments in the important banking/insurance/finance sector which has not as yet been tabulated in any census source except for the annual *County Business Patterns,* that giving number of establishments by employment size for each 4-digit SIC industry (see listing in previous section).

Census of Manufactures (MC).

Business persons probably use this census more than any of the others since it reports on approximately 450 manufacturing industries in every state, including for each: number of establishments, payroll, value of shipments, cost of materials, new capital expenditures, inventories, production hours worked, value added by manufacture; also material consumed by kind, and some of this data by employment-size class. The "Industry Series" consists of 83 reports; the "Geographic Area Series" has reports for each state, including statistics by MSAs. There are 7 reports in its "Subject Series" including *Concentration Ratios in Manufacturing,"* and *Location of Manufacturing Plants* (both available only on computer tape or CD-ROM).

In the years between each census the Bureau publishes an *Annual Survey of Manufactures,* which gives census-type data based on a sample survey. In addition, the Bureau publishes a continuing series of over 100 monthly, quarterly or annual *Current Industrial Reports.* These contain detailed statistics on about 5,000 manufactured products that account for 40% of all U.S. manufactured output, giving production, shipments, and inventories for specific products or industries to the 7-digit SIC number. Included are such industries as apparel, chemicals, metal products, machinery.

Census of Mineral Industries (MIC).

This census covers establishments in 31 industries in metal and coal mining, oil and gas extraction, and mining and quarrying of nonmetallic minerals. Its "Industry Series" consists of 12 reports for these groups of industries. The data is similar to that in the *Census of Manufactures.* There are also a "Geographic Area Series" (99 reports) giving the statistics by states and three "Subject Series" reports.

Census of Retail Trade (RC).

Another important census for the business researcher, this provides statistics for states, counties, and MSAs for approximately 100 different kinds of retail enterprises. The "Geographic Area Series" (52 reports) includes data on number of establishments, employment, payroll, sales, and number of proprietorships and partnerships, by kind of business. The other reports in this census are: "Nonemployer Statistics Series" (four geographic reports); "Subject Series" (four reports including one on *Merchandise Line Sales*); "Zip Code Statistics Series" (available only on tape or CD-ROM). For selected current statistics, not part of the regular census, there is a

"Current Business Reports" series, two of which are *Revised Monthly Retail Trade: Sales and Inventories* and *Annual Retail Trade*.

Census of Service Industries (SC).

Consists of similar tabulations as the retail census for more than 100 service businesses such as hotels, laundries, auto repair shops, amusement and recreation services, law firms, engineering firms. The reports are: "Geographic Area Series" (52 reports); "Subject Series" (four reports); "Nonemployer Statistics Series" (four geographic reports); "Zip Code Statistics Series" (available only on tape or CD-ROM). Selected current statistics, not part of the regular census, are in their "Current Business Reports" series, with title *Service Annual Survey*.

Census of Transportation (TC).

This census does not cover all types of transportation. Rather it is in three parts: one covering establishment-based statistics on selected transportation industries (motor freight transportation and warehousing, water transportation, and transportation services); *Truck Inventory and Use Survey;* "Subject Series." For titles and a short description see listing in Chapter 6.

Census of Wholesale Trade (WC).

Statistics for nearly 100 types of wholesale businesses are published in the following series: "Geographic Area Series" (52 reports) and "Subject Series," four parts including one on *Commodity Line Sales*. As with the retail and service censuses, the Census Bureau also publishes several "Current Business Reports," not part of the regular census but covering selected current statistics. The titles are *Revised Monthly Wholesale Trade: Sales and Inventories* and *Annual Wholesale Trade*.

Enterprise Statistics (ES).

After the economic censuses are completed each five years, the data are regrouped to show various economic characteristics of the owning or controlling firms. There are three reports in the 1987 Enterprise Statistics series: *Large Companies,* which collects data for companies with 500 or more employees; *Auxiliary Establishments,* supplying information on separately operated central administrative offices and other auxiliary establishments for states and the U.S. in general; *Company Summary,* with the data arranged by enterprise industrial classifications.

Other Periodic Censuses

The descriptions of the censuses of population and housing noted below are based on an examination of the 1980 census, since the 1990 censuses were not as yet available. This means that the geographic statistics contain data arranged by SMSA (Standard Metropolitan Statistical Area) and related SCSA (Standard Consolidated Statistical Area) rather than for the newer designations which are MSA (Metropolitan Statistical Area), related CMSA (Consolidated Metropolitan Statistical Area), and PMSA (Primary Metropolitan Statistical Area).

Census of Agriculture (AC).

This census provides complete information about farms, farming, ranching, and related activities. It is now taken in the years ending with the numbers 2 and 7, but was formerly taken in the years ending with 4 and 9. For a description of its volumes see the listing in the "Agriculture and Food" section of Chapter 6.

Census of Government (CG).

Although not of as much continuing interest to business researchers, this is an important source for detailed statistics on government finance. The census is taken in the years ending with the numbers 2 and 7. The titles of its volumes are listed later in this chapter in the section for "Statistics on Government Finance."

Census of Housing (HC).

Very detailed tabulations on the number and characteristics of houses. Includes volumes for metropolitan housing characteristics and also "Subject Reports" on such topics as mobile homes, condominium housing, and mover households. The titles of each volume are listed in Chapter 15 under "Housing and Real Estate Statistics."

Census of Population (PC).

Detailed characteristics of the population for states, counties, cities, and towns appear in a series of reports covering: *Characteristics of the Population: Number of Inhabitants* (PC80-1-A); *Characteristics of the Population: General Population Characteristics* (PC80-1-B) giving data by age, sex, race, etc.; *General Social and Economic Characteristics* (PC80-1-C), statistics on education, occupation, income, poverty status, etc.; *Detailed Population Characteristics* (PC80-1-D). There are also separate "Subjects Reports" (PC80-2) and "Supplementary Reports" (PC80-S1).

In addition, the Bureau publishes several series of short *Current Population Reports,* the most useful of which are: *Current Population Reports: Consumer Income* (Series P-60); *Current Population Reports: Population Estimates and Projections* (Series P-25).

Census of Population and Housing (PHC).

The joint population/housing reports are in four series to cover: *Block Statistics* (PHC80-1), housing and some population data for individual city blocks; *Census Tracts* (PHC80-2), reports giving socioeconomic data by census tract; *Summary Characteristics for Governmental Units and Standard Metropolitan Statistical Areas* (PHC80-3); statistics by *Congressional Districts of the 98th Congress* (PHC80-4); and two supplementary reports.

STANDARD INDUSTRIAL CLASSIFICATION SCHEME

To facilitate the collection and presentation of statistical data on so many industries, the federal government some years ago developed a standard industrial classification (SIC) scheme, which is a four-digit classification of all manufacturing and nonmanufacturing industries. Not only are all the census industry statistics arranged by this scheme, but it has also been widely adopted by many nongovernment sources for use in such publications as market guides, directories of companies, and indexes. Following is the name of the manual that is an important guide to the kinds of establishments included within each SIC number:

U.S. Office of Management and Budget, Executive Office of the President.

Standard Industrial Classification Manual. Washington, DC: U.S. Government Printing Office, 1987. 705 pp.

If you need only a short numeric index of SIC codes, look in any of the first three directories described in Chapter 7.

FOREIGN TRADE STATISTICS

The Bureau of the Census publishes a Foreign Trade (FT) series consisting of a number of monthlies and annuals containing detailed export and import statistics. Two useful annuals are:

FT 447: *U.S. Exports: Harmonized Schedule B Commodity by Country.*

FT 247: *U.S. Imports for Consumption: Harmonized TSUSA Commodity by Country of Origin.*

These give quantity and value for very specific exports (imports), the first by Schedule B commodity classification numbers and by country of destination, and the second by harmonized TSUSA commodities by country of origin.

An important monthly is:

FT 925: *U.S. Merchandise Trade. Exports, General Imports, and Imports for Consumption: SITC Commodity by Country.*

As the title indicates, this gives monthly dollar value for both exports and imports by a 5-digit product classification scheme, for the current month and for the year to date. Table 1 has the figures arranged by SITC commodity groupings; table 2, by SITC commodity groupings and by country; table 3 covers value of re-exports by SITC groupings by country. FT 925 began publication in 1989, replacing the former FT 135 and FT 410.

The Census Bureau publishes other numbers in its FT Series. Several are available only on microfiche, such as the following monthlies:

EM-575: *U.S. Exports for Consumption and General Exports by SIC-Based 1, 2, and 3-Digit Product Code Summaries and 4-Digit Codes by World Area of Destination.*

IM-175: *U.S. Imports for Consumption and General Imports by SIC-Based 1, 2, and 3-Digit Product Code Summaries and 4-Digit Codes by World Area of Origin.*

For a more complete descriptive listing of numbers in the FT Series, consult the annual *Census Catalog & Guide* described in the last section of this chapter.

The following CD-ROM may be useful as an easy way to find census and other foreign trade statistics:

National Trade Data Base (NTDB).

This new CD-ROM (1990) consists of a compilation of U.S. import and export statistics and related international trade data taken from publications of such U.S. government agencies as the Bureau of Economic Analysis, Bureau of the Census, Foreign Agricultural Services, International Trade Administration, International Trade Commission.

Classification Schemes

The Bureau of the Census has published the following two commodity classification schemes intended to facilitate reporting export and import statistics:

Schedule A: A Statistical Classification of Commodities Imported into the United States (GPO, 1960, 1,034 pp., and *Revisions,* 1964).

Schedule B: Statistical Classification of Domestic and Foreign Commodities Exported from the United States (GPO, 1991, 2 volumes).

For an alphabetical index to HTSUSA commodities consult the *Harmonized Tariff Schedule of the United States Annotated,* published by the U.S. International Trade Commission. There is also a cross-classification volume called *U.S. Foreign Trade Statistics: Classifications and Cross-Classifications, 1980* (GPO, 1981, 1 volume, various pagings). This brings together the basic schedules of commodity and geographic trade classifications used in compiling U.S. foreign trade statistics, including the TSUSA (for imports), Schedule B (for exports), Schedule A cross classification to the TSUSA, and Schedule E, which has been converted on a one-for-one basis to Schedule B.

The United Nations developed its own statistical classification to make possible international comparisons of commodity trade statistics. The best known is the SITC. Two published volumes are:

Standard International Trade Classification. Revision 3. New York: United Nations, 1986. 1 volume (various pagings). (Statistical Papers, Series M, No.34/Rev.3). Contains comparative HS and SITC Rev. 2 numbers.

Commodity Indexes for the Standard International Trade Classification, Rev.2. New York: United Nations, 1981. 2 volumes. (Statistical Papers, Series M, No.38/Rev.). This is the earlier revision, with a useful alphabetical index in volume 2.

For persons who need only an abbreviated (3-digit rather than 5-digit) SITC classification, see the listing in the "Abstracts" volume of the annual *Index to International Statistics.* This gives both the SITC Revision 2 and Revision 3. It also contains two other classification schemes used in international trade: the ISIC (International Standard Industrial Classification), a 4-digit classification of industrial enterprises according to primary type of economic activity; and NACE (Nomenclature Générale des Activités Économiques des Communautés, or General Industrial Classification of Economic Activity Within the European Community), a 3-digit scheme used for the same purpose within the European Community.

MONTHLY STATISTICAL PERIODICALS

The most important of many government periodicals for current American business statistics are described below along with two non-governmental monthlies.

Board of Governors of the Federal Reserve System. *Federal Reserve Bulletin.* Washington, DC (monthly).

This is the best single source for finding current U.S. banking and monetary statistics, including federal finance, interest rates on money and capital markets, stock market indexes, new security issues, mortgage markets, flow of funds, consumer installment credit, interest and exchange rates; also some international financial statistics and basic U.S. business statistics including the well-known Federal Reserve

Board's index of industrial production. The articles in each issue cover recent developments and are indexed in ABI/I, BPI, PAIS, PTS/F&S; full text on MEAD/ NEXIS. There are also announcements, statements to Congress, news of legal developments.

Federal Reserve Bank of St. Louis. *National Economic Trends* and *Monetary Trends.* St. Louis (monthlies).

For persons interested in tables and charts giving compounded annual rates of change (monthly) for both basic economic and financial indicators, these are two useful monthlies. The first covers such indicators as employment, consumer and producer price indexes, industrial production, personal income, retail sales, GNP and several other national income and product figures. The second includes rates of change for money stock, deposits, commercial bank loans and investments, federal government expenditures. Their *Annual U.S. Economic Data* covers annual rates of change over a 20-year period for both the monetary and economic indicators. A companion monthly, *International Economic Conditions,* is described in Chapter 5.

U.S. Bureau of Economic Analysis, Department of Commerce. *Business Cycle Indicators.* In their monthly *Survey of Current Business.*

Beginning in 1990, the yellow pages in the *Survey* contain the latest monthly estimates for over 250 business cycle series, in both chart and table format. These cover: cyclical indicators (composite indexes, employment/unemployment, production and income, consumption/trade/orders/deliveries, fixed capital investment, prices/costs/ profits, inventories, money and credit), and "other important economic measures" (savings, prices/wages/productivity, labor force and employment, government activities, U.S. international transactions, international comparisons for 7 leading countries). These tables were formerly published in the now-ceased monthly called *Business Conditions Digest.*

U.S. Bureau of Economic Analysis, Department of Commerce. *Survey of Current Business.* Washington, DC: U.S. Government Printing Office (monthly).

This is the most important single source for current U.S. business statistics. It covers (green pages): general business indicators; commodity prices; construction and real estate; domestic trade; labor force, employment and earnings; finance; foreign trade of the U.S.; transportation and communication; chemicals and allied products; food and kindred products/tobacco; leather and products; lumber and products; metals and manufactures; petroleum, coal and products; pulp, paper and paper products; rubber and products; stone, clay and glass products; textile products; transportation equipment. Starting in 1990 each issue also contains monthly statistics and charts for "Business Cycle Indicators" (yellow pages), described more fully in a separate listing above. Besides these regularly quoted statistics, special statistical reports appear at intervals. The best known is the annual "National Income and Product Accounts" issue (July, as well as some continuing figures in each issue). Other special statistical reports include: "State Personal Income" (quarterly); "U.S. International Transactions" (quarterly); "Capital Expenditures of Majority-Owned Foreign Affiliates of U.S. Companies" (March and September); "County and Metropolitan Area Personal Income" (April); "U.S. Business Enterprises Acquired or Established by Foreign Direct Investors in (year)" (May); "U.S. Multinational Companies: Operations in (year)" (June); "Foreign Direct Investment in the U.S." and "U.S. Direct Investment Abroad" (both in the August issue); "U.S. International

Sales and Purchases of Services" (September); "Pollution Abatement and Control Expenditures" (November in 1990). In addition every year or so there is a useful table giving "Annual Input-Output Accounts of the U.S. Economy," with the latest as of 1991 covering 1985 in the issue for January 1990. Articles in the *Survey* are indexed in ABI/I, BPI, PAIS, TI; full text on BRS, DATA-STAR, DIALOG, DOW JONES, MEAD/NEXIS.

An important biennial supplement, *Business Statistics,* provides a historical record of the statistics quoted in each monthly issue. In addition to all this, the BEA also publishes historical or annual figures on some of the same subjects as are in current issues of the *Survey.* Several examples are: *Fixed Reproducible Tangible Wealth in the United States, 1925–85; State Personal Income, 1929–87;* and annuals for *Foreign Direct Investment in the United States: Operations of U.S. Affiliates of Foreign Companies; Local Area Personal Income* (5 volumes, with the latest published in 1991 covering the years 1984–89); *U.S. Direct Investment Abroad: Operations of U.S. Parent Companies and Their Foreign Affiliates.*

U.S. Bureau of Labor Statistics. *Monthly Labor Review.* Washington, DC: U.S. Government Printing Office.

Indispensable for its current statistics covering employment, hours, earnings, consumer and producer price indexes, productivity, compensation and collective bargaining data, injury and illness, with some international comparison data. The articles in this review (usually they are studies by BLS researchers, with statistics) are indexed in ABI/I, BPI, PAIS, SSI, TI; full text on BRS, DATA-STAR, DIALOG, DOW JONES, MEAD/NEXIS. Useful features in most issues include: research summaries; major labor agreements expiring the following month; recent developments in industrial relations; significant decisions in labor cases; technical notes; one or two book reviews, and often a subject listing of selected books and articles received by the BLS. For a short statement about the many other useful BLS statistical publications, see under "Labor Statistics" in Chapter 19.

U.S. Council of Economic Advisers. *Economic Indicators.* Washington, DC: U.S. Government Printing Office (monthly).

A good source for statistical tables and charts of basic economic indicators. Includes total output, income and spending; employment, unemployment and wages; production and business activity; prices; money, credit and security markets; federal finance; international statistics. In each issue the data is usually quoted for about 10 years and monthly for the past year.

STATISTICS ON GOVERNMENT FINANCE

In this section are the names of several good sources for statistics on government finance. Although economics and business researchers may not use them as often as other statistics, all researchers should be aware of their existence.

Municipal Year Book. Washington, DC: International City Management Association.

An authoritative source book for urban data and developments. There are 6 sections, with section A discussing management trends and issues, and section B, intergovernmental dimension. Section C, "Staffing and Compensation," gives salaries for 21 specific types of municipal and county officials, but only by broad geographic area and population size of city. Section D has tabular profiles of individual cities and counties, with data for each including the forms of government, population estimate, general revenues, expenditures, city employment and payroll. Section E consists of directories of associations, agencies, names of municipal officials (by city), and names of county officials. Section F is a useful descriptive bibliography, including books, reports, bibliographies, reference sources, and online data services, including such specific topics as fire protection, housing, personnel and labor relations.

Tax Foundation. *Facts & Figures on Government Finance.* Baltimore: Johns Hopkins University Press (annual).

Useful statistics on fiscal activities of federal, state, and local governments; also selected basic economic statistics. Includes a glossary.

U.S. Bureau of the Census. *Census of Governments.* Washington, DC. 6 volumes.

This provides the most detailed statistics on U.S. government finance, with the census taken every five years in the years ending with the numbers 2 and 7. Volume titles in the 1987 census are: Vol. 1, "Governmental Organization" (2 reports); vol. 2, "Taxable Property Values"; vol. 3, "Public Employment" (4 reports); vol 4, "Governmental Finances" (6 reports, including finances of school districts, special districts, county governments, municipal and township governments); vol. 5, "Topical Studies" (4 reports including historical statistics, and state payments to local governments); vol. 6, "Guide to the 1987 Census of Governments."

U.S. Office of Management and Budget, Executive Office of the President. *Budget of the United States Government.* Washington, DC: U.S. Government Printing Office (annual).

An overview of the president's budget proposals, with summary statistical tables including federal programs by function, agency and account, budget receipts by source, offsetting receipts by type, estimates of tax expenditures by function; also some historical tables. A glossary of budget terms is at end.

U.S. Treasury Department. *Treasury Bulletin.* Washington, DC: U.S. Government Printing Office (quarterly).

Up-to-date statistics on: federal fiscal operations (including budget receipts and outlays); federal obligations; account of the U.S. Treasury; federal debt; Treasury financing operations; public debt operations; U.S. savings bonds and notes; ownership of federal securities; market yields on Treasury securities; Federal agencies' financial reports; international financial statistics; capital movements; foreign currency positions; Exchange Stabilization Fund; special reports (trust funds, U.S. currency and coin outstanding and in circulation).

GUIDES TO STATISTICS

American Statistics Index. Bethesda, MD: Congressional Information Service (monthly in two parts, with annual cumulations). Online counterpart is *ASI;* also on CD-ROM as *Statistical Masterfile.*

If you are not sure where to find specific statistics published by the federal government, this may be the best first place to check. It is a comprehensive, descriptive guide and index to the statistics published by all government agencies, congressional committees and statistics-producing programs. Each issue is in two parts: the "Abstracts" section which is arranged by issuing agency and gives full description of the statistics in each publication, including time period covered, geographical breakdown; the "Index" section which provides access by detailed subjects and names, by categories (such as breakdown by age and sex, commodity or industry, by geographic areas such as city, county, MSA, state), and by titles and report numbers. During the current year the index sections cumulate so that one need check only in the most recent monthly plus any quarterly. As of 1991, three volumes of a *Cumulative Index* have been published covering 1974–79, 1980–84, and 1985–89.

This is an expensive service but can probably be found in most large public or university libraries. It is also available online, and on CD-ROM. Microfiche copies of almost every report in *ASI* are available from CIS on a subscription basis. A companion index covering nongovernment statistics is described below under the title *Statistical Reference Index;* a monthly index to international statistics is described in Chapter 5 (see *Index to International Statistics*).

Encyclopedia of Business Information Sources. Detroit, MI: Gale Research, Inc. (biennial, with an interim supplement).

A useful bibliographical guide to information sources on detailed subjects and industries from "Abrasives" to "Zinc Industry." For each topic it usually gives, when applicable, the names of abstracting and indexing services, almanacs and yearbooks, bibliographies, biographical sources, directories, encyclopedias and dictionaries, financial ratios, handbooks and manuals, online databases, periodicals and newsletters, price sources, research centers and institutes, statistical sources, trade association and professional societies, and other sources on each topic.

Encyclopedia of Geographic Information Sources: U.S. Volume. 4th ed. Detroit: Gale Research, Inc., 1987. 437 pp.

For all states and for over 300 cities, this lists the following kinds of information, when applicable, for each location: general works, abstracting and indexing services, almanacs and yearbooks, bibliographies, biographical sources, directories, encyclopedias and dictionaries, gazetteers and guides, government publications, guides to doing business, handbooks and manuals, newsletters, newspapers and periodicals, organizations, research centers and institutions, statistical sources, and other sources of information. It is a good place to start when researching a particular region, state, or city.

Predicasts Forecasts. Cleveland, OH: Predicasts, Inc. (quarterly, with annual cumulations). Online counterpart is *PTS U.S. Forecasts.*

This quarterly statistical service (described earlier in this chapter) can also be used as an index of current forecasting statistical sources, since it gives the date and page reference of the current journal, government report, or special study from which the statistics were taken.

Statistical Reference Index. Bethesda, MD: Congressional Information Service (monthly in two parts, with annual cumulations). Available also on CD-ROM as *Statistical Masterfile.*

A good, comprehensive, selective guide to American statistical publications available from sources other than the U.S. government, such as: trade, professional and other nonprofit associations and institutes; business organizations; commercial publishers (including trade journals); independent research centers; state government agencies, universities and allied research centers. It is a companion service to the *American Statistics Index* (above), with each issue also in two parts: the "Abstracts" section, arranged by issuing organizations and giving descriptions of the statistics in each publication (level of detail, time periods covered, geographic breakdown, and page locations); the "Index" section which provides access by subject, by geographic location, and by names; by categories (geographic, economic, demographic); by issuing sources; by title. Like *ASI*, its index cumulates so that one need check only in the most recent monthly of the current year plus any quarterly. Note that this service includes descriptions of state government agency statistics such as those of agriculture, education, finance, labor. Also like *ASI*, this is an expensive service which may be found only in large public or university libraries. A microfiche reproduction service is offered by the publisher for most of the source material.

Statistics Sources. Detroit, MI: Gale Research, Inc. 2 volumes (annual).

Likely to be found in most large libraries is this finding guide to general U.S. and international statistics on industrial, business, social, educational, financial, and other topics. It is arranged alphabetically by topic, running from "Abortions" to "Zinc." Under each subject or country, publications are cited where statistics can be found. At front of volume 1 is a "selected bibliography of key statistical sources" and a list of federal statistical telephone and online database contacts. At end of volume 2 is a list of source publications and sources of nonpublished statistical data. A companion volume is *State and Local Statistics Sources: A Subject Guide to Statistical Data on States, Cities, and Locales*, 1990. It is arranged by state and then by approximately 52 subjects.

U.S. Bureau of the Census. *Census Catalog & Guide.* Washington, DC: U.S. Government Printing Office (annual).

A descriptive list of census publications, arranged by major subject field, with a detailed subject index at end. This includes not only printed reports, but also those available as computer tapes, microfiche, databases, diskettes, compact discs, and maps. Symbols with each item note in which of these formats each report is available. Their current *Monthly Product Announcements* lists new publications.

A more specialized descriptive listing is *Guide to the 1987 Economic Censuses and Related Statistics* (Washington, DC: 1990, 130 pp.). This also contains symbols with each item to identify in which of the various print and nonprint formats each report is available.

U.S. Bureau of the Census. *Statistical Abstract of the United States.* Washington, DC: U.S. Government Printing Office (annual).

The "Guide to Sources of Statistics" at end of this annual is a subject listing of important primary and some secondary sources of statistical information published by the federal government. There is also a "Guide to State Statistical Abstracts," and a "Guide to Foreign Statistical Abstracts."

5

FOREIGN STATISTICS AND ECONOMIC TRENDS

**Foreign Economic Conditions – Forecasts of Foreign Econo-
mies – Basic International Statistics – Financial Statistics and
Balance of Payments – Foreign Trade Statistics – National
Income Statistics – Production Statistics – Social Statistics –
Regional Economic and Financial Data – Bibliographies and
Indexes**

This chapter concentrates on basic publications covering foreign economic statistics and foreign economic trends. The various foreign tax and
trade guides and reference data for exporters can be found in Chapter 16 with
books and other material on international management. These trade guides
contain useful summaries of the various factors affecting trade and investment
in each country, including information on the government, laws dealing with
finance, labor, licensing, taxation. A few sources for foreign labor statistics
are in Chapter 19. Financial manuals covering foreign companies are in Chapter 8, and directories of foreign companies are in Chapter 7.

FOREIGN ECONOMIC CONDITIONS

Business International database.

Based on the Dialog File description, this is a full-text database providing information on 57 countries, with the principal focus on political and economic trends,
market analysis, and corporate strategies. It includes case examples of successful
firms and their use of innovative financial tools and techniques. The information is
taken from a variety of Business International Corporation sources, including country reports, regional overviews, weekly newsletters, business guides, and investment
profiles. Some of this country data is probably taken from quarterly country profiles
noted in the next citation.

Economist Intelligence Unit. *Country Reports.* London (quarterly).

The EIU (since 1987 a division of Business International) publishes 92 separate,
concise, quarterly reports covering political and economic trends and short-term
prospects on 165 countries. They each usually discuss: the outlook, a review of the

political scene, economic policy, domestic policy, foreign trade and payments, business news. In each issue statistical tables give indicators of economic activity, foreign trade statistics, and a few graphs. What formerly was issued as an annual supplement with each country is now published as a separate series of *Country Profiles* for the same countries. These profiles provide resumés of the politics, economy, and industries of the country plus six-year retrospective statistical tables for basic macroeconomic indicators.

Among the many other useful EIU publications are the following: (1) *Economic Prospects Series,* a series of country reports providing news on recent developments and five-year forecasts for the future; (2) *European Trends* (quarterly), a review of key issues and developments in the European Community; (3) *Marketing in Europe* (monthly), which studies markets for specific consumer products in Europe, including statistics for food/drink/tobacco, for clothing/furniture/leisure goods, for chemists' goods/household goods/domestic appliances; (4) *Multinational Business* (quarterly), with news and analysis ranging from economic and political conditions to aspects of governmental policies relevant to multinational companies; (5) *Retail Business* (monthly), which deals with consumer goods markets and retail trade in the United Kingdom, often including reports on specific consumer products, with statistics; (6) *World Outlook,* a one-volume annual forecast of political and economic trends in 165 countries; *World Commodity Outlook,* two annual forecasts, one covering "Industrial Raw Materials" (20 commodities such as aluminum and zinc) and the other, "Food, Feedstuffs & Beverages"); *World Commodity Forecasts* (bimonthly); (7) bimonthlies for *Textile Outlook International* and *Travel & Tourism Analyst;* (8) quarterlies for *Europe's Automotive Components Business; European Motor Business; International Motor Business; Japanese Motor Business; International Tourism Reports; Paper & Packaging Analyst; Rubber Trends;* (9) special "Research Reports," each devoted to a single important topic and providing in-depth analyses of major issue and strategies. Most of these various EIU publications are quite expensive, but you may be able to locate some of them in a large business on economics library. Contact either the EIU or Business International for a complete list of publications and information on prices.

Europa World Year Book. London: Europa Publications. 2 volumes (annual). Distributed in the U.S. by Gale Research, Inc.

This is an international reference work rather than an economic review, but it is packed so full of useful data that it deserves mention here as well as in Chapter 16. Vol. 1 covers information on international organizations and Europe, as well as countries from Afghanistan to Jordan; vol. 2 is devoted to all other countries, from Kenya to Zimbabwe. The data provided for each country usually includes: recent history, economic affairs, basic economic statistics, constitution, government, political parties, diplomatic representation, judicial system, religion; also lists of leading newspapers, periodicals, publishers, radio and TV, banks, insurance companies, trade and industrial organizations, trade fairs, railroads, shipping firms, tour organizations.

Europa also publishes 6 regional yearbooks: *Africa South of the Sahara; The Far East and Australasia; The Middle East and North Africa; South America, Central America and the Caribbean; The USA and Canada; Western Europe.* These give much the same sort of directory information as well as concise data about geography, government, basic economic statistics, and a "Who's Who" of prominent people in the countries covered by each yearbook.

Organization for Economic Cooperation and Development. *OECD Economic Surveys.* Paris (annuals).

Separate annual reviews for each of the 25 OECD countries, providing a discussion of recent trends and prospects, and economic policies. A "statistical annex" in each survey usually contains statistics for basic economic indicators, such as national accounts, labor market indicators, foreign trade, balance of payments, money supply and counterparts, financial markets—sometimes for a 10-year period—plus a folded table of international comparisons.

Several important OECD statistical volumes are described in the following sections of this chapter.

United Nations. Department of International Economic and Social Affairs. *World Economic Survey.* New York: (annual).

An annual analysis of major current trends, emerging issues, and policies in the world economy, including trends in output, international trade, international finance, and special issues which vary from year to year. Statistical tables at end include rate of growth, unemployment, balance of payments.

The UN is organized into separate "Economic and Social Commissions" for various geographic regions (Africa, Asia and the Pacific, Europe, Latin America), and each publishes various periodic economic bulletins or economic and social surveys reviewing and analyzing developments in countries of the region. Some of the more important UN statistical publications are described later in this chapter. For a quarterly index of UN documents see last section of this chapter.

U.S. International Trade Administration, Department of Commerce. *Foreign Economic Trends and Their Implications for the United States.* Washington, DC: U.S. Government Printing Office (semiannual or annual series of reports).

This continuing series of brief reports for over 100 countries covers the current economic situation, trends, and their implications for U.S. business operating overseas. Compiled by the various U.S. embassies abroad, each includes a table of "Key Economic Indicators." Not all of the reports are up to date.

U.S. International Trade Administration, Department of Commerce. *Overseas Business Reports.* Washington, DC: U.S. Government Printing Office.

A series of useful reports on over 100 countries, with many of the recent ones titled "Marketing in (name of country)." These usually contain brief information on industry trends in the country, foreign trade outlook, transportation and utilities, distribution and sales channels, advertising and market research, banks and credit, trade regulations, "investment in" information (forms of business organization, industrial property, taxation, labor), guidance for business travelers, sources of economic and commercial information. Some of these country reports are rather old since they are revised only once every three to seven years.

Country Guides

Following is an example of a series of annual guides containing profiles and current data of interest to executives traveling in foreign countries. Two other types of country information of interest to business are described elsewhere: (1) yearbooks—some covering all countries such as the *Statesman's Year-Book,* and others on individual countries (see Chapter 1 for several examples); (2) tax and trade guides for specific countries, providing brief but useful facts about each and meant primarily for companies doing business in that country (see Chapter 16).

Asia & Pacific Review. Saffron Walden, Essex, Eng.: World of Information. Distributed in U.S. by Hunter Publishing Company, Edison, NJ (annual).

This is one of a series of five annual guides that contains short country-by-country profiles of major developments and current affairs, plus a "Business Guide" section for each country that gives basic data such as climate, time, national and city transport, car hire, hotels, banks, holidays, working hours, telecommunication, sources of business information, and much more. The companion guides are: *Africa Review; Europe Review; Latin America & Caribbean Review; Middle East Review.*

FORECASTS OF FOREIGN ECONOMIES

In today's highly competitive and often hostile world, it is essential that international companies watch for emerging trends and developments, potential political and financial risks, etc., in the countries in which they invest or operate. They must anticipate new competition, new technologies, new markets that may come from either their own or other countries. Thus corporate planners and researchers eagerly study and weigh any serious effort to predict what lies ahead in relation to foreign economies, finance, politics, regulations, industries, products, innovations, etc. Most of the comprehensive services providing forecasts for foreign economies are expensive and so not usually found in a public or university library. Many of the books pertain to forecasts in just one country. Of the two expensive services noted below, *Worldcasts* is more likely to be found in a few libraries. Noted here also are a bibliography, forecasting data in market research reports, and several short-term periodic outlook publications. A useful but very expensive political risk forecast service covering individual countries is mentioned in the "Political and Financial Risk Assessment" section of Chapter 16. Described there also are several books on political risk assessment and two country risk rankings that appear in periodicals.

Economist Intelligence Unit. *Global Forecasting Service.* New York: Business International (quarterly).

A series of quarterly medium-term forecasts covering political, economic, and business environmental trends in 55 countries (two main reports of about 24 to 30 pages for each country plus two 10- to 12-page updates). The reports focus on key factors affecting the outlook for the country, and they include important indicators, with supporting historical data and an alternative scenario. Received with this is a quarterly *Global Outlook* including a detailed macroeconomic forecast for the world economy. Regional Overviews are also available for Western Europe, Asia Pacific, Middle East, and Latin America. This is an expensive service intended primarily for large multinational companies rather than for libraries. One can subscribe on a country-by-country basis, with each country's subscription costing from $330 up to $600 (as of 1991), depending on how many countries are ordered. The EIU is a division of Business International.

Worldcasts. Cleveland, OH: Predicasts, Inc. 8 volumes (quarterly). Online counterpart is *PTS Forecasts.*

Although also expensive ($450 per volume), this publication differs from the one above and is more likely to be found in a large university or corporate library. Like its companion service *Predicasts Forecasts* which covers the U.S., this useful index consists of short- and long-range forecasts both for leading foreign economic indicators and for detailed (modified 7-digit SIC) industries outside the United States. Its 8 volumes are in two parts:

World-Regional-Casts (4 volumes covering: West Europe; East Europe, USSR, Africa, Middle East; North America, Canada, Central and South America; Asia and Oceania).

World-Product-Casts (4 volumes covering: General Economics, Utilities, Trade and Services; Agriculture, Mining, Food, Textiles, Wood and Paper; Chemicals, Energy, Rubber, Plastics, Leather, Stone, Clay and Glass; Metals, Metal Products, Nonelectrical Machinery, Electrical Machinery, Electronics, Transportation Equipment, Instruments.).

One may subscribe to individual volumes. Since, like its companion service, this gives the name, date, and page of the current journal from which the statistics were taken, it is useful not only for its statistical forecasts but also as an index of articles containing forecast information.

Bibliographies

World Index of Economic Forecasts. 3d ed. Ed. by Robert Fildes and Thana Chrissanthaki. New York: Stockton Press, 1988. 563 pp.

Section 3 of this five-part index contains data about the kinds and components of forecasts available from more than 300 organizations in some 100 countries. For each organization it outlines their macroeconomic forecasts, has a checklist of financial forecasts, and other specialist forecasts, as well as providing the names of the organization's publications, and name of the contact person. Section 4 has a much shorter list of organizations undertaking surveys of business activity, investment plans and consumer purchasing intentions; section 5 is a list of official social and economic development plans, arranged by country. Section 1 is an introductory review on macroeconomic forecasts and surveys, while section 2 contains several indexes need to locate the specifics of data provided by the organizations.

Worldcasts (see above) can also be used as a bibliographic source for forecast articles on countries and specific foreign industries.

Market Research Reports

Market research reports for specific industries or products usually provide an outlook for that industry along with a discussion of current trends. These reports are often expensive, but corporate libraries may have those on subjects in which they have a special interest. A directory covering market research reports on foreign industries is *Marketsearch* described in the last section of this chapter.

Short-Term Outlook

Economist Intelligence Unit. *World Outlook.* London (annual).

Short summaries of political and economic trends and short-range forecasts for over 165 countries.

The EIU *Country Reports* and *Country Profiles* series (see description at beginning of chapter) includes some data on prospects for each country reviewed, and their two *World Commodity Outlook* annuals contain forecasts for raw materials and commodities.

International Monetary Fund. *World Economic Outlook.* Washington, DC (semiannual).

This is a semiannual survey conducted by the IMF staff which summarizes the current situation and gives short-term prospects for the world economy. It covers not only key issues of policy but also recent developments as they pertain to both industrial countries and developing countries. Charts and tables appear throughout the text. A "Statistical Appendix" contains useful tables for output, inflation, financial policies, trade, and so forth, usually for a 10-year period and for both industrial and developing countries or regions.

The following two sources focus on recent trends and prospects for the European economy and those industries important to the European Communities:

Commission of the European Communities. *Panorama of EC Industry.* Luxembourg (annual).

Begun in 1989, this useful annual is patterned somewhat after the *U.S. Industrial Outlook* in that it describes about 180 specific industries important in the European Communities, including both manufacturing and services industries. For each it usually discusses the current situation, production, consumption, trade, employment, structural features, and a short- and medium-range outlook. Industry highlights and interesting special features are at front. The industries are arranged by a NACE coding system.

Organization for Economic Cooperation and Development. *OECD Economic Outlook.* Paris (semiannual).

Surveys recent trends and policies and assesses short-term prospects for the economies of each OECD country. Includes useful statistical tables in a section called "Detailed Projections and other Background Information." Indexed in ABI/I, TI. An annual volume of *Historical Statistics* accompanies the mid-year issue each year. The data in this annual gives % rates of change to show the movements of major economic variables over a 30-year period.

An example of a useful periodic outlook for the economy in one country is *Economic Outlook,* a monthly prepared by the Centre for Economic Forecasting at the London Business School (published by Gower Publishing in Aldershot, Hampshire, England). This consists each year of three "major" forecasts and nine intermediate forecast releases, primarily for the U.K. economy but including some international data.

BASIC INTERNATIONAL STATISTICS

Demographic Yearbook. New York: United Nations.

A yearbook covering statistics on population, births, deaths, life expectancy, marriages, divorces, for more than 200 countries. There are also special topic tables with the subjects covered varying in each yearbook.

International Bank for Reconstruction and Development. *World Tables.* Baltimore, MD: Johns Hopkins University Press (annual). Also available on diskettes.

For those who need historical statistics, this contains a time series taken from the data files of the World Bank. Statistics for 139 member countries in the 1991 volume cover a time span of 21 years. The country tables give population, use and origin of resources (GNP and GDP), domestic prices/inflators, manufacturing activity, monetary holdings, government deficit or surplus, foreign trade, balance of payments, external debt, social indicators. There are also topical tables, arranging the statistics by such topics as GDP and then by country. This data, back to 1950, is also available on computer tapes.

The World Bank publishes an annual *World Debt Tables: External Debt of Developing Countries,* with volume 1 providing recent developments in international lending to developing countries, and summary debt tables for 107 countries; volume 2, "Country Tables," contains external debt tables for the 107 countries.

B. R. Mitchell has also prepared several compilations of historical statistics: *European Historical Statistics, 1750–1975* (2d rev. ed., New York: Facts on File, 1980, 868 pp.); *International Historical Statistics: Africa and Asia* (New York University Press, 1982, 761 pp.); *Second Abstract of British Historical Statistics* (Cambridge, Eng.: University Press, 1971, 227 pp.).

International Marketing Data and Statistics. London: Euromonitor Publications, Ltd. (annual).

Comparative statistical data for some 150 non-European countries arranged in 24 sections covering: demographic trends and forecasts; economic indicators; finance and banking; foreign trade; employment; production; energy resources and output; defense; consumer expenditure patterns; retailing; advertising; consumer market sizes; consumer prices and costs; households and facilities; health and living standards; literacy and education; agricultural resources; communications; transportation; tourism and travel; cultural indicators. Regional comparisons are at end. Latest figures in most categories are several years behind the date of the volume. A companion volume for similar data on European countries is *European Marketing Data and Statistics.*

United Nations. *Statistical Yearbook.* New York.

This is a basic reference work for internationally comparable statistics on UN countries, with the tables often covering a 10-year period. The sections are: world summary; general socio-economic statistics (population and manpower, national accounts, wages/prices and consumption, balance of payment, finance, health, education, culture, science and technology, development assistance, industrial property); statistics of basic economic activity (agriculture, forestry, fishing, industrial production, mining and quarrying, manufacturing, energy, external trade, transport, communications, international tourism). This yearbook is slow in publishing, with the one covering 1987 the latest received in 1991. Some current statistics can be found in the UN's useful *Monthly Bulletin of Statistics.* The UN also publishes a little annual statistical pocket book called *World Statistics in Brief,* for persons who need only the most important facts relating to UN countries.

World Competitiveness Report. Lausanne, Switzerland: IMD International and World Economic Forum (annual).

"A multi-dimensional analysis of how national environments are conducive or detrimental to the domestic and global competitiveness of enterprises operating in those countries." Over 100 pages of statistical tables contain 326 criteria arranged by 10 subject factors, such as market orientation, financial dynamics, human resources—

all for 34 countries (24 OECD countries and 10 "newly industralized economies"). Graphic presentations of 10 factors, arranged by country, are at end.

Basic Regional Statistical Publications

Here are a few of the more important regional statistical sources. Also useful are the many helpful publications covering individual countries such as statistical yearbooks and monthlies and statistical publications of banks. These are highlighted later in this chapter in the section for "Regional Economic and Financial Data."

Asia and the Pacific Area

Pacific Economic Community Statistics. Tokyo: Japan Member Committee of the Pacific Basin Economic Council (biennial).

Statistical tables and graphs, for PEC countries, usually for four selected years. They are arranged in the following categories: macro data, trade, agriculture/fisheries/ forestry, mining, energy manufacturing, transportation, tourism, communication, education and culture, investment and assistance, balance of payments. PEC countries include Pacific Island countries, 11 Latin American countries, the U.S. and Canada.

United Nations. Economic and Social Commission for Asia and the Pacific. *Statistical Yearbook for Asia and the Pacific.* Bangkok, Thailand. Order from the UN.

Statistics are by country, often for an 11-year period, and they cover population, national accounts, agriculture/forestry/fishing, industry, energy, consumption, transport and communication, external trade, wages/prices, consumption, finance, and social statistics. A list of principal sources by country is at end.

Europe

European Marketing Data and Statistics. London: Euromonitor Publications, Ltd. (annual).

For 30 countries of Western and Eastern Europe, this contains statistics similar to those in its companion volume, *International Marketing Data and Statistics,* which is described above. These statistics are usually several years old, with the volume published in 1991 usually containing figures no more recent than 1987 or 1988.

Federal Reserve Bank of St. Louis. *International Economic Conditions.* St. Louis, MO (quarterly).

Statistical tables cover compounded annual rates of change during a 20-year period in 11 industrial countries for money supply, consumer prices, wholesale prices, GNP or GDP, manufacturing, employment, industrial production and foreign trade. European countries included are: Belgium, France, Germany, Italy, Netherlands, Sweden, Switzerland, the United Kingdom; other countries are Canada, Japan, and the United States.

Organization for Economic Cooperation and Development. *Main Economic Indicators.* Paris (monthly). Data is also available on magnetic tape and on diskettes.

Current basic economic and financial indicators, both in table and chart form, for each of the 24 OECD countries. Part 1 of two parts is arranged by the following subjects: national accounts, industrial production, deliveries/stocks/orders, construction, internal trade, labor, wages, prices, domestic and foreign finance, interest rates, foreign trade, and balance of payments. Part 2 has the tables arranged by each of the OECD countries. On an irregular basis, the OECD also publishes historical tables over a 20-year period in its *Main Economic Indicator: Historical Statistics*.

Statistical Office of the European Communities. *Eurostatistics*. Luxembourg (monthly). Available also on diskettes.

General statistics for short-term economic analysis in the 10 European Community countries and in the U.S. and Japan. Included, usually for a five-year period (with the latest year given by month), are figures for: national accounts, employment and unemployment, industrial production, opinions in industry, industrial products, retail sales, agricultural products, external trade, consumer prices, producer prices of agricultural products, wages and salaries, financial statistics, balance of payments. Part 2 contains the tables by country, with figures usually for the past three years. The titles of all Eurostat publications are in three languages (French, German and English).

Two annuals, providing general statistics, are: *Basic Statistics of the Community* (a pocket-sized brief review of general statistics in all fields) and *Eurostat Review* (a 10-year compilation of the more important statistics for each member country and for five other countries as comparison). In addition, the Commission of the European Communities publishes a quarterly review of the economic situation in the *European Economy*, which has two separately published supplements, Series A, "Recent Economic Trends" and Series B, "Business Survey Results," both published 11 issues per year.

United Nations. Economic Commission for Europe. *Statistical Indicators of Short Term Economic Changes in ECE Countries*. New York (monthly).

Country-by-country economic indicators for each ECE country, to show current monthly trends.

U.S. Central Intelligence Agency. *Handbook of Economic Statistics*. Washington, DC: (annual).

Formerly this focused on historical statistics for Communist countries but, with political changes in Eastern Europe, it now has been revamped to provide basic statistics for OECD countries, the USSR and Eastern Europe, and a few other countries. The statistical tables include figures on OECD country trends, Soviet economic performance, production of agricultural products, minerals and metals, chemicals and manufacturing goods, energy, foreign trade and aid, environmental topics. The data covers selected years from 1960, with the latest 6 years quoted annually.

Latin America

United Nations. Economic Commission for Latin America and the Caribbean. *Anuario Estadistico de America Latina y el Caribe: Statistical Yearbook for Latin America and the Caribbean*. Santiago, Chile.

A two-part yearbook. Part 2 gives country statistics for population, national accounts, domestic prices, balance of payment, external trade, natural resources and production of goods, employment, social conditions. Part 1 covers indicators of economic and social development in Latin America and the Caribbean including economic growth, capital formation, and financing.

University of California, Los Angeles. Latin American Center. *Statistical Abstract of Latin America.* Los Angeles (annual).

A useful compilation of over 900 pages containing statistics in the following broad areas: geography and land tenure; transportation and communication; population/health/education; church/state/crime; working conditions/migration/housing; industry/mining/energy; sea and land harvests; foreign trade; financial flows; national accounts/government policy and finances; prices. A guide to data is at end.

FINANCIAL STATISTICS AND BALANCE OF PAYMENTS

Board of Governors of the Federal Reserve System. *Federal Reserve Bulletin.* Washington, DC: U.S. Government Printing Office (monthly).

Each issue of this important financial bulletin has a short section for "International Statistics." It includes: summary data on international transactions and foreign trade; liabilities and claims on foreigners reported by banks and by nonbanking enterprises; foreign securities holdings and transactions; interest and exchange rates.

International Financial Statistics. Washington, DC: International Monetary Fund (monthly, with yearbook issue). Data is also on computer tapes, and on CD-ROM.

An essential source for current financial statistics. For each country the statistics include: exchange rate, fund position, international liquidity, money and banking statistics, nonbank financial institutions, interest rates, prices and production, international transactions, government finance, national accounts, population. Daily exchange rates, international reserves, interest rates, changes in money, etc., are given in comparative tables at front. The yearbook issue covers annual statistics for 30 years. About once a year there is a new issue of their "Supplement Series," each on a different topic and each providing detailed historical data supplementing financial or economic statistics appearing in the *IFS.* Two recent titles are: No.14: "Supplement on International Liquidity" (1987); No.15: "Supplement on Trade Statistics" (1988).

International Monetary Fund. *Balance of Payments Statistics.* Washington, DC. 2 parts, with monthly supplements. Data is also on computer tapes.

Part 1 gives 8-year detailed balance of payments figures for some 146 countries, including statistics for goods, services and income; unrequited transfers; capital account; reserves (including special drawing rights). Notes to the tables accompany each country section. Part 2 contains world totals for balance of payments components and aggregates.

International Monetary Fund. *Government Finance Statistics Yearbook.* Washington, DC Data is also on computer tapes.

For each of 125 countries this presents detailed statistical tables on central government revenue, expenditure, lending, financing and debt, as well as tables for derivation of principal central government aggregates from national sources. For state and local government finance within each country, there are parallel tables but in much less detail. At front are comparison tables arranged by topic rather than by country.

Organization for Economic Cooperation and Development. *OECD Financial Statistics.* Paris. Data also available on magnetic tape and on diskette.

This publication has three separately published parts. Part 1, *Financial Statistics*

Monthly, is itself in two parts and covers international and foreign bond issues, international bank loans, as well as domestic financial markets for each OECD country (security issues, borrowing and lending flows, and interest rates); part 2, *Financial Accounts of OECD Countries* (annual) has flow-of-funds and balance-sheet accounting for 20 countries, broken down by sector and financial instruments; part 3, *Non-Financial Enterprises Financial Statements* (annual), has balance sheets, statements of accounts and uses of funds for a representative sample of private nonfinancial companies in 12 OECD countries.

Statistical Office of the European Communities. *Balance of Payments.* Luxembourg. 2 parts (annual).

The "Geographical Breakdowns" volume is in two sections: country tables and tables for selected items. The data in the 1987 issue covers the years 1981–1985. There is also a "Global Data" volume, with the data covering a 10-year period. This is slow in publishing.

U.S. Bureau of Economic Analysis, Department of Commerce. *Survey of Current Business.* Washington DC: U.S. Government Printing Office (monthly).

Besides being very useful for current domestic statistics this important monthly contains feature articles with statistics on topics of interest to international business. These are: (1) "U.S. International Transactions" (quarterly); (2) "Capital Expenditures of Majority-Owned Foreign Affiliates of U.S. Companies" (March and September); (3) "U.S. Business Enterprises Acquired or Established by Foreign Direct Investors in (year)" (May); (4) "U.S. Multinational Companies: Operations in (year)" (June); (5) "Foreign Direct Investment in the U.S." and "U.S. Direct Investment Abroad" (both in the August issue); (6) "U.S. International Sales and Purchases of Services" (September). In addition, the BEA publishes historical or annual figures on some of these same subjects, e.g. *Foreign Direct Investment in the United States: Operations of U.S. Affiliates of Foreign Companies* and *U.S. Direct Investment Abroad: Operations of U.S. Parent Companies and Their Foreign Affiliates.*

World Currency Yearbook. Brooklyn, NY: International Currency Analysis.

This consists of complete descriptions of 147 currencies, including a discussion of the history, transferability, currency developments, currency varieties, currency administration, as well as statistics over four or five years for each on currency in circulation, official exchange rates, free or black market rates. There is also a section on the Eurocurrency market. One of three tables at end of 1988–89 volume is called "Destruction of Paper Money, 1950–1987," which gives, by country, % decline in purchasing power and % increase in cost-of-living.

World Financial Markets. New York: Morgan Guaranty Trust Co. (monthly).

An excellent bank letter on international financial and monetary developments. The "Statistical Appendix" in each issue contains tables on exchange rates, government bond index and yield, Eurocurrency deposit rates.

Individual foreign governments and foreign banks also publish useful financial statistics. An excellent statistical monthly covering the U.K. is *Financial Statistics* compiled by Great Britain's Central Statistical Office (London: H.M. Stationery Office), while a CSO annual is *United Kingdom Balance of Payments.* Several other examples are given with "Regional Economic and Financial Data," later in this chapter.

FOREIGN TRADE STATISTICS

United Nations trade statistics are arranged by an SITC commodity number, which provides internationally comparable categories for the economic analysis of trade. This scheme is explained in United Nations Statistical Office, *Statistical Papers, Series M, No.38, Rev.: Commodity Indexes for the Standard International Trade Classification, Revision 2* (New York: 1981, 2 volumes). Vol. 1 is a list by revised SITC number and describes the commodities included under each number; Vol. 2 is an alphabetical item index. See also *Statistical Papers, Series M, No.34/Rev.3: Standard International Trade Classification, Revision 3* (United Nations, 1986, 1 volume, various pagings). The original SITC system was begun in 1950, and the second revision was approved in 1975. A *Correlation Between the United States and International Standard Industrial Classification* was issued as a *Technical Paper* of the U.S. Office of Federal Statistical Policy and Standards, U.S. Department of Commerce, October 1979, 101 pp.

Direction of Trade Statistics. Washington, DC: International Monetary Fund and International Bank for Reconstruction and Development (monthly and annual). Data is also on computer tapes.

Gives monthly and annual totals for value of exports and imports in U.S. dollars and arranged by country.

Food and Agriculture Organization of the United Nations. *FAO Trade Yearbook.* Rome.

Export and import statistics of food and agricultural commodities arranged by SITC number and then by country for a 6-year period. Summary data also by country.

Handbook of International Trade and Development Statistics. New York: United Nations (annual).

This is a basic collection of statistical data on world trade and development brought together for the use of the UN Conference on Trade and Development and for any other interested persons. It includes: statistics on value, growth, and shares of world trade in current prices for selected years from 1950; volume, unit value, and terms of trade indexes for developed and developing countries; network of world trade; export and import structure by commodities and country; balance of payments; and basic indicators of development. 1988 figures are the latest published as of early 1992.

Organization for Economic Cooperation and Development. *Monthly Statistics of Foreign Trade (Series A).* Paris. Data is also on diskette and magnetic tape.

Current summary foreign trade statistics for each OECD country broken down by country of origin and destination, and volume and average value indexes. Series B of the OECD's foreign trade data is *Trade by Country* (annual, only on microfiche), with single year trade statistics for each OECD country. Series C is an annual *Foreign Trade by Commodities*, covering single year's trade by commodity (available both in paper copy and on microfiche).

Statistical Office of the European Communities. *Monthly External Trade Bulletin.* Luxembourg.

Monthly external trade statistics for 10 European Communities countries, arranged by SITC commodities. For historical statistics, see their *External Trade-Statistical Yearbook.*

UNCTAD Commodity Yearbook. New York: United Nations.

Compiled as background material for discussions and negotiations at the annual United Nations Conference on Trade and Development, this provides export/import statistics, by country, for selected agricultural primary commodities and minerals, ores and metals; occasionally it gives consumption figures. The tables often cover statistics for selected years from 1970.

United Nations. Statistical Office. *International Trade Statistics Yearbook.* New York. 2 volumes.

Vol. 1 contains detailed annual export and import statistics, usually over a four-year period, for each of more than 150 countries, with the commodity figures under each country given by SITC commodity code. Vol. 2 arranges the data (usually for a five-year period) by SITC commodity code. Volumes are slow in being published; latest volume received in 1992 covers figures only through 1988. Some current quarterly statistics are in its *Commodity Trade Statistics* (published irregularly as the UN's *Statistical Papers, Series D*).

The UN also publishes a *Yearbook of International Commodity Statistics* which focuses on foreign trade statistics for agricultural primary commodities (food and beverages, raw materials), and for minerals, ores and metals (the latter also contains production figures) for each country. The tables are annual, usually for a 13-year period. This yearbook is sponsored by the United Nations Conference on Trade and Development.

NATIONAL INCOME STATISTICS

Organization for Economic Cooperation and Development. *National Accounts.* Paris. 2 volumes (annual). Data is also on diskette and magnetic tape.

Vol. 2 contains the "detailed tables" for national accounts over about a 13-year period, by country, for each of the 24 OECD-member countries plus the U.S. Included are GDP by kind of economic activity and consumption expenditures by type and purpose. Vol. 1 has "Main Aggregates" and comparative tables for 25 countries. There is also a *Quarterly National Accounts* providing the latest figures.

Statistical Office of the European Communities. *National Accounts ESA: Detailed Tables by Branch.* Luxembourg (annual).

Contains both country tables and comparative tables for national income in the Euro-12 countries. Data usually covers an 18-year time period. There is also a volume called *National Accounts ESA: Aggregates.*

United Nations. Statistical Office. *National Accounts Statistics.* New York (annual). 1 volume in 2.

This is the most comprehensive source for national account statistics. For each of 168 countries and areas, the detailed statistics include GDP, private final consumption expenditures by type and purpose, capital transactions of the nation, general government income and outlay account; cost components of value added, and more. Some tables cover as much as a 15-year period. This volume is slow in publishing, with data for 1988 the latest published as of 1992. Another unnumbered volume is: *National Accounts Statistics: Analysis of Main Aggregates.* Related volumes are: *National Accounts Statistics: Government Accounts and Tables, 1983* (1986, 398 pp.) and *Study of Input-Output Tables, 1970–1980* (1987, 321 pp).

Some individual foreign countries also publish national income studies, for example, Great Britain, Central Statistical Office, *United Kingdom National Accounts* (annual) and Japan Economic Planning Agency, *Annual Report on National Accounts* (Tokyo).

PRODUCTION STATISTICS

Food and Agriculture Organization of the United Nations. *FAO Yearbook: Production.* Rome.

Annual data on: land, population, index of agricultural production, crops, livestock, food supply, means of production, prices. Statistics usually cover the most recent three years and a three-year average prior to that.

The *FAO Quarterly Bulletin of Statistics* gives current production, trade, and prices. The FAO *Commodity Review and Outlook* (annual) summarizes production and trade developments of major agricultural commodities and includes some statistics.

Organization for Economic Cooperation and Development. *Industrial Structure Statistics.* Paris (annual). Data is also on diskette and magnetic tape.

This contains industrial statistics and exports/imports arranged by industry and by country. Includes production, value added, number of establishments, investment, employment, wages/salaries. Statistics in section 1 (covering three years and arranged by ISIC industries) are derived from industry surveys and foreign trade data; section 2 data, arranged within similar categories, is based on national accounts disaggregates. Sources of data are at the end. The OECD also publishes a quarterly *Indicators of Industrial Activity,* in two parts, with the first containing indicators, and the second, qualitative business tendency survey data by country.

Statistical Office of the European Communities. *Industrial Trends.* Luxembourg (monthly).

Part 2 contains current indexes of industrial production, as well as turnover, producer price indexes, number of employees—arranged by industry and then by country. Part 1 gives statistics on basic indicators both in table and graphic format. Their *Industry Statistics Yearbook* provides retrospective statistics about industries, annually for selected years since 1970. Eurostat also publishes a quarterly *Industrial Production* which has industrial production statistics arranged by the NACE industry scheme. Another annual is their *Agriculture: Statistical Yearbook* which includes statistics on production of specific crops and animals as well as prices, land use, etc., with brief data at end on forestry and fisheries.

United Nations. *Industrial Statistics Yearbook.* New York. 2 volumes (annual).

Vol. 1, "General Industrial Statistics," gives five-year industry data for each country, usually including number of establishments, average number of employees, wages, salaries, and hours, quantity of electricity consumed, output and value added in producers' prices, gross fixed capital formation, value of stocks, index numbers of industrial production. Vol. 2 contains detailed "Commodity Production Statistics" for a 10-year period on over 500 industrial commodities and under each, by country. The coding of commodities is based on the ISIC (International Standard Industrial Classification). For information about this classification scheme refer to UN Statistical Office, *Statistical Papers, Series M, No. 4, Revised 2: International Standard Industrial Classification of all Economic Activity* (ISIC). (1968, 48 pp.).

SOCIAL STATISTICS

United Nations Educational, Scientific and Cultural Organization (UNESCO). *Statistical Yearbook. (Annuaire Statistique).* Paris.

Detailed statistical tables, by country, for education (including educational expenditures); science and technology; culture and communication (including libraries, museums, archival institutions, book production, newspapers and other periodicals, cultural paper, film and cinema, radio and TV broadcasting).

The Central Statistical Office of Great Britain publishes an annual *Social Trends* (London: H.M. Stationery Office) which consists of U.K. statistics, charts, and explanatory text on population, households and families, education, employment, income and wealth, expenditure and resources, health and personal social services, housing, transport and the environment, leisure, participation, law enforcement.

REGIONAL ECONOMIC AND FINANCIAL DATA

It is impossible to cover all of the important sources for economic and financial data on every country. This section only mentions several kinds of information that will be useful and includes a few titles primarily as examples. To find other information, the bibliographies at the end of this chapter will be helpful. Use of a large public or university library may be of value in searching for books on countries, as well as for finding lists of foreign government publications, lists of publications of the various regional organizations such as the UN, names of foreign trade associations (several directories are listed in Chapter 7), names of foreign trade journals, indexes to foreign journal articles, etc. Consulting a reference librarian may also be beneficial in tracing specific data.

Statistical Yearbooks of Foreign Governments

Many countries publish excellent statistical annuals, similar to the one published in this country, which abstract the more important statistics and sometimes include bibliographical sources at the foot of each table. Several examples from different parts of the world are:

Brazil. Fundaçao Instituto Brasileiro de Geografia e Estatística. *Anuário Estatístico do Brasil.* Rio De Janeiro.

Great Britain. Central Statistical Office. *Annual Abstract of Statistics.* London: H.M. Stationery Office. (Includes index of sources by subject).

Japan. Statistics Bureau. *Japan Statistical Yearbook.* Tokyo.

Switzerland. Bundesamt für Statistik. *Statistisches Jahrbuch Der Schweiz.* Zurich: Verlag Neue Zürcher Zeitung.

Yearbooks published for individual countries are useful for their reviews of economic, social and political developments in that country. Several examples are given in Chapter 2.

Monthly and Quarterly Statistical Publications

The governments of some countries also publish good periodic reviews that provide current monthly or quarterly statistics. Several examples are:

Australian Bureau of Statistics. *Monthly Summary of Statistics, Australia.* Belconnen, Australia.

Belgium. Institut National de Statistique. *Statistiques Industrielle.* Brussels (monthly).

France. Institut National de la Statistique et des Études Économiques. *Bulletin Mensuel de Statistique.* Paris (monthly).

Great Britain. Central Statistical Office. *Monthly Digest of Statistics.* London: H.M. Stationery Office.

The Central Statistical Office publishes other useful current statistical publications including *Economic Trends* (monthly, with an annual supplement) and *Financial Statistics* (monthly).

Statistical Publications of Nongovernment Organizations

Few statistical sources in this category are general in scope yet devoted to statistics in a single country. Following is one example:

Conference Board of Canada. *Handbook of Canadian Consumer Markets.* Ottawa (biennial).

Statistical Publications of Banks

Many banks publish bulletins or bank letters that are either partially or entirely statistical reviews. Several examples are:

Bank of Canada Review. Ottawa (monthly). Entirely statistical.

Bank of England. *Quarterly Bulletin.* London.

Bank of Japan. *Economic Statistics Monthly* and *Economic Statistics Annual.* Tokyo.

Banque Nationale de Belgique. *Bulletin.* Brussels (monthly). Entirely statistical.

Deutsche Bundesbank. *Monthly Report.* Frankfurt am Main.

South African Reserve Bank. *Quarterly Bulletin.* Pretoria.

Swiss Bank Corporation. *Economic and Financial Prospects.* Basel (bimonthly).

Bank Letters

Below are examples of short bank letters, which analyze current financial and economic trends.

Banco Nacional De México. *Review of the Economic Situation of Mexico.* Mexico City (monthly).

Bank Leumi le-Israel B.M. *Leumi Review.* Tel-Aviv (irregular).

Bank of Montreal. *Business Review.* Montreal (monthly).

Barclays Bank. *Barclays Economic Review.* London (quarterly).

Kansallis-Osake-Pankki. *Economic Review*. Helsinki (semiannual).

Skandinaviska Enskilda Banken. *Quarterly Review*. Stockholm.

Data on Foreign Companies

Foreign financial manuals are described in Chapter 8. Directories of foreign companies are included in Chapter 7.

Foreign Business and Economic Trends

It is just as important for the business executive to keep abreast of foreign and international events/trends as it is to be informed about domestic affairs. This is especially true for the person who is involved in the foreign operations of his or her firm or who travels/lives abroad in connection with business. This person will surely want to have available on a daily basis *The Times* of London, *The Financial Times*, the *Wall Street Journal/Europe* (or the *Asian Wall Street Journal* as the case may be), and a good metropolitan newspaper such as *Le Monde* (Paris), or the *Frankfurter Allgemeine Zeitung*. S/he will also want to have access to *The Economist* and to one or more of the various foreign business/management magazines such as *L'Expansion* (see Chapter 10).

Canadian and British Statistics

Whereas we say we cannot cover statistical sources for every country, we would be remiss if we did not make two brief exceptions. The Canadian government's agency called "Statistics Canada" is a prolific publisher of useful statistics of all sorts and particularly for industry data. They publish an annual review called *Canada Year Book*, an annual compilation of basic economic statistics called *Market Research Handbook*, and many more specialized statistical publications. Current and historical time series statistics can be accessed online and on CD-ROM via *CANSIM* (*Canadian Socio-Economic Information Management System*). Specific Canadian government statistical publications can be identified by using the annual bibliography *Statistics Canada Catalogue*. The numerous statistical publications of the United Kingdom can be identified by using the annual *Guide to Official Statistics* (Great Britain, Central Statistical Office), starting first with their *Annual Abstracts of Statistics*. To identify the many nongovernment statistical sources for each country, check in the bibliographies and indexes noted at the end of this chapter; look also under the names of each country in the index to this book which cites a few other sources for statistics.

BIBLIOGRAPHIES AND INDEXES

BISSE: Business Information Sources & Services for Europe. Ed. by Henri Broms [et al]. Helsinki, Finland: Published for the European Business Schools' Librarians' Group by the Helsinki School of Economics, 1989. 290 pp. Distributed in the UK by Cranfield Case Clearing House.

This list is arranged by European country and, for each country, it identifies the most important business directories, organizations publishing statistical and forecasting services, business research organizations, periodicals and newspapers, online databases, major book publishers, booksellers, and business information centers. Usually gives one-line annotations for the sources listed. To be of continuing use, this directory must be updated in the near future.

Encyclopedia of Geographic Information Sources: International Volume. 4th ed. Detroit: Gale Research, Inc., 1988. 479 pp.

For each of 75 foreign countries and for over 80 foreign cities, this lists basic information sources such as statistical publications, directories, yearbooks, guides for doing business, periodicals (including the various economic reviews of the country), bibliographies, gazetteers, online databases. Multinational and regional publications are at the front. This is a good place to start when researching a particular foreign country or city. Gale publishes a companion volume, *Encyclopedia of Geographic Information Sources: U.S. Volume* (4th ed., 1987, 437 pp.) which is described in Chapter 3.

European Directory of Marketing Information Sources. 2d ed., London: Euromonitor Publications Ltd., 1990. 400 pp.

A directory of European official and non-official business and marketing source material, arranged in the following 9 sections (within which the sources are listed alphabetically by country): official sources and publications (government and statistical sources); libraries and information services; leading marketing research companies; private research publishers; information databases; abstracts and indexes; major business and marketing journals; leading associations; European business contacts (chambers of commerce, embassies and consulates, etc.). A tenth section in the European volume contains profiles for each country. A companion volume, giving essentially the same type of information for non-European countries is *International Directory of Marketing Information Sources* (1988, 362 pp.).

Several other of the more general directories published by Euromonitor are: *The Compendium of Marketing Information Sources* (1989, 400 pp.) for descriptions of U.K. marketing data and business information sources; *European Directory of Non-Official Statistics Sources* (1988, 281 pp.); and its companion *International Directory of Non-Official Statistical Sources* (1990, 200 pp.).

Halperin, Michael, and Ruth A. Pagell. *Foreign Business Information: How to Find It; How to Use It.* Phoenix, AZ: Oryx Press. Scheduled for publication in 1993.

This work in progress promises to be a useful source that may serve as a companion volume to Michael R. Lavin's *Business Information* (see description in Chapter 2) by covering foreign business information sources. It will not only describe selected major foreign business publications and databases but it will also contain explanations of business concepts essential to using them effectively. Included will be chapters covering sources on foreign companies, industries; also financial, marketing, statistical information, and much more. The title noted above is tentative.

Index to International Statistics. Bethesda, MD: Congressional Information Service (monthly in two parts, with annual cumulations). Available also on CD-ROM as *Statistical Masterfile*.

A descriptive guide and index to statistical publications (in English) compiled by about 95 of the world's major international governmental organizations (IGOs), such as those of the UN, OECD, EC, OAS. Thus it is excellent for locating statistics on individual countries, but it does *not* cover statistical publications of individual governments. Each issue is in two parts: one provides descriptive abstracts arranged by issuing agency; the other is a detailed index by country, subject, name of organization, and by categories such as age and sex. Microfiche copies of about 95% of the publications abstracted are available from CIS on a subscription basis. For two companion services describing American statistical publications see Chapter 4.

Joint Library of the International Monetary Fund and the World Bank (International Bank for Reconstruction and Development). *Biblio List Updates in Print.* Washington, DC (monthly).

A current awareness service for articles and working papers recently added to the Joint Library on aspects of economic development and finance of potential interest to the staff. Each issue is in two parts: by subject and by regions and countries. This is based on their online information system called *JOLIS.*

Kurian, George T. *Sourcebook of Global Statistics.* New York: Facts on File Publications, 1985. 413 pp.

A descriptive list of over 200 statistical publications from international, national, and important trade organizations, providing for each: bibliographical data, tables of contents, new features, evaluation, price, whether it is also available on tape or in a database. A subject index is at end. This can be useful if one realizes that the facts are based on out-of-date information.

Marketsearch: International Directory of Published Market Research. London: Arlington Management Publications, Ltd. in association with the British Overseas Trade Board (annual, with semiannual supplement). U.S. orders: MacFarlane & Co., Atlanta, Georgia 30318.

More than 18,000 published market research studies are identified in this directory which covers over 150 countries. The directory section itself (part 2) is arranged according to the British Standard Industrial Classification scheme. There is an alphabetical products/services index at front, with author and source indexes; a list of reports (publishers) by name of publisher is at end. For each report, it gives title, countries covered, brief statement of products/services covered, number of pages, date, source, and price.

PAIS International in Print (PAIS). New York: Public Affairs Information Service (monthly, with three cumulated issues and an annual bound volume). Online counterpart is *PAIS International Online;* also available on CD-ROM.

This indexing service incorporates the former *PAIS Foreign Language Index,* and so it includes selected books and articles published in French, German, Italian, Portuguese, Spanish as well as those written in English. For a complete description of this selected index, see description in Chapter 2.

Predicasts F & S Index Europe and **Predicasts F & S Index International.** Cleveland, OH: Predicasts, Inc. (monthlies, cumulating quarterly and annually). Online counterpart is *PTS F&S Indexes.*

These two periodic indexes are useful for locating articles or parts of articles on foreign companies and foreign industries that have appeared in many foreign and domestic financial publications, business-oriented newspapers, trade magazines, and special reports. Each is arranged in three parts: (1) by a modified 7-digit SIC industry or product; (2) by region and country (the first index covering European countries and the second, all other foreign countries); (3) by company. Under each industry or company, the indexing usually covers: organizations and institutions, management procedures, products and processes, resources and resource use, marketing information, financial data, government expenditures. As of 1991 these indexes are also available on CD-ROM as *F & S Plus TEXT,* but only to nonprofit organizations. A companion index devoted to U.S. industries and companies is *Predicasts F & S Index United States.*

Worldcasts. Cleveland, OH: Predicasts, Inc. 8 volumes (quarterly). Online counterpart is *PTS Forecasts.*

Not only is this a comprehensive source for short- and long-range forecasts both on foreign countries and foreign industries but it is also useful as a bibliographical guide since it gives the date and page reference of the current journal from which the statistics were taken. Its 8 quarterly volumes are in two parts: *World-Regional-Casts* and *World-Products-Casts.* For the titles of each volume consult the description in the "Forecasts" section of this chapter. An expensive service, and so not found in many libraries.

More Specialized Bibliographies

Great Britain. Central Statistical Office. *Guide to Official Statistics.* London: H.M. Stationery Office (annual)

A useful descriptive guide to official U.K. statistical publications. The HMSO publishes *HMSO Annual Catalogue* and *HMSO Monthly Catalogue* covering all types of government documents. HMSO publications can also be searched online and on CD-ROM. Other countries have similar publications: for example, there is an annual *Statistics Canada Catalogue,* which is a descriptive list arranged by broad topic, and also a quarterly *Government of Canada Publications* (these can also be searched online and on CD-ROM).

United Nations. *UNDOC: Current Index. United Nations Documents.* New York (quarterly, with annual cumulation on fiche).

A continuing checklist of all UN documents and publications received in the Dag Hammarskjold Library at UN headquarters in New York, except for restricted material. It is arranged by document symbol (which is by issuing body), and subject, author (both personal and corporate), and title indexes are included.

A useful annotated guide to publications and services on Canadian business and economics by Barbara E. Brown is described in Chapter 2.

6

INDUSTRY STATISTICS

Guides to Industry Data – Industry Financial and Operating
Ratios – Aerospace Industry – Agriculture and Food – Appli-
ance Industry – Automobiles and Trucks – Brewing and Distill-
ing – Chemicals and Plastics – Commodities and Financial
Futures; Grain Statistics – Construction Industry – Drug In-
dustry – Electric and Gas Utilities – Electronics – Energy –
Machinery Industry – Metals and Minerals – Paper and Allied
Products – Petroleum – Publishing Industry – Rubber and
Shoes – Textiles and Apparel – Tobacco and Cigars – Trans-
portation and Equipment – Commodity and Consumer Prices

This chapter contains a selection of references to illustrate the wide
variety of sources for statistical data on specific industries. These include
government agencies, trade associations, commercial organizations, publishers, and trade journals. No attempt is made here to cover each industry
completely; the statistical publications described are, for the most part, a few
of those that were easily accessible in Baker Library. Statistical issues in trade
journals often vary widely from year to year. The issues examined were
usually those published in 1990 or 1991. There are many other good trade
journals not mentioned here only because they did not contain statistics.
Industry statistical sources in other chapters include: department, discount
and food stores, franchise businesses, restaurants and hotels, in Chapter 18;
and insurance and real estate in Chapter 15. Financial surveys for industries
(Chapter 8) usually also include some basic industry statistics.

GUIDES TO INDUSTRY DATA

When undertaking a statistical search on a U.S. industry, if your need seems
to be a simple one, you may want to start with one or more of the comprehensive publications listed in Chapter 4, such as the *Statistical Abstract,* the *Statisti-*

cal Service of Standard & Poor's, or the Census Bureau volumes. (Note particularly the detailed industry figures in the *Census of Manufactures*).

But if you soon realize these do not provide the data you want, then try one or more of the following:

1. The useful abstracts/indexes of the publisher Congressional Information Service which are described at the end of Chapter 4:
   American Statistics Index (for identifying sources of government statistics)
   Statistical Reference Index (for U.S. nongovernment statistics)
   Index to International Statistics (for foreign intergovernmental statistics)

2. The Predicasts indexes for articles and parts of articles on SIC industries and products:
   Predicasts F & S Index United States and its companion indexes (see Chapter 2)
   Predicasts Forecasts for outlook articles on SIC industries (see Chapter 4)
   PROMT (see listing below)

3. Other "Guides to Statistics" in Chapter 4.

4. Foreign industry data sources described in Chapter 5, such as:
   Panorama of EC Industry
   Section on "Production Statistics"
   Worldcasts

5. Directories of market research reports (the reports are usually very expensive) described in Chapter 18, one of which is:
   Findex

6. Two further guides to industry data:

PROMT. Cleveland, OH: Predicasts, Inc. (monthly, with quarterly and annual cumulations). Online counterpart is *PTS PROMT;* also on CD-ROM.
PROMT is an acronym for "Predicasts Overview of Markets and Technology." It is a useful continuing source for abstracts and some full-text items about industries, companies, products, and markets as reported in major business and trade journals, U.S. and Canadian regional business magazines, and other literature. The indexing is arranged within 28 major industry sections, with further industry subdivisions under each major industry. The articles selected for indexing usually cover such topics as competitive activities, new products and technologies, market size and share, financial trends, acquisitions, contracts, joint ventures, new facilities, foreign trade, regulation. A cumulative index lists abstracts by product, country, company name, type of information. Subscription is high ($975 in 1991), but most people use the very popular online counterpart. Some PROMT abstracts are included in the new CD-ROM *F & S Plus TEXT* which, as of 1991, is available as two monthly disks, but only to nonprofit organizations. For persons needing industry-specific data only, there is a related monthly called *Predi-Briefs* which sells the abstracts for any one of the 28 major industries separately.

Trade and Industry Index database (TI).
This has been an increasingly important business database for its indexing and selectively abstracting more than 300 trade and industry journals while selectively covering the business/industry articles that appear in nearly 1,200 additional publications. It also indexes and abstracts over 100 local and regional business publications, plus PR Newswire press releases. Related to this database is *Trade and Industry ASAP,* providing selective full text and indexing for articles from over 200 journals, and also the PR Newswire press releases.

7. Two guides to special issues of trade journals, now out of date, but perhaps of some use as a point of departure are:

Guide to Special Issues and Indexes of Periodicals. 3d ed. by Miriam Uhlan. New York: Special Libraries Association, 1985. 160 pp. 4th ed., 1993.

This is the latest edition of a guide to special issues (statistical outlooks and reviews, directory issues, and other annual or continuing feature articles) in over 1,300 U.S. and Canadian trade, consumer, and technical periodicals. It is arranged alphabetically by name of journal, and there is a subject index. Data for each journal includes note as to whether it is indexed or abstracted in a computerized database, and whether it has an editorial and/or advertiser index.

Sicignano, Robert and Doris Prichard, comps. *Special Issues Index: Specialized Contents of Business, Industrial, and Consumer Journals.* Westport, CT: Greenwood Press, 1982. 309 pp.

An alphabetical list of over 1,300 periodicals, giving for each the names of the special issues (and dates) in four categories: buyer's guides/directories; statistical summaries; convention and show reports; review/preview issues. A subject index is at end.

Looking through current issues of trade journals can also be of value in searching for industry data, since these usually include articles of interest, news of the industry and of people, and regular columns on such topics as new equipment, new products, new literature, and coming events. For the names of trade journals, check one of the periodicals directories in Chapter 7. For example, *Standard Rate & Data Service: Business Publication Rates and Data* lists trade journals by industry. Within the information it provides for some of these journals, one can sometimes find titles of upcoming "special feature issues" which may give more up-to-date information about special issues than is found in the two rather old guides described above.

8. Trade Associations

If all else fails, try telephoning or writing to a relevant trade association (see Chapter 7 for several directories of associations). Someone in the industry may be helpful in tracking statistics for that industry.

INDUSTRY FINANCIAL AND OPERATING RATIOS

This section describes the best known sources for financial and operating ratios. Many trade associations, especially those in wholesaling and retailing, compile operating ratios. Some trade journals include operating statistics in their annual statistical issues. Several ratio studies for department and food stores are described in Chapter 18. Others can be located by using the bibliography of sources of composite financial data at the end of Robert Morris Associates *Annual Statement Studies* (see listing below).

Dun & Bradstreet Information Services. *Industry Norms & Key Business Ratios.* Desk-Top Edition. New York (annual). Available also on diskette.

This is a useful annual giving balance sheet, income statement statistics and financial ratios for over 800 lines of business, arranged by 4-digit SIC industries. Consult D&B for a more detailed asset/geographical breakdown of this data.

Dun and Bradstreet International publishes a periodic *Key Business Ratios* (4th ed., High Wycombe, Bucks, Eng., 1990) which contains over 700 pages of British financial ratios and % figures for some 378 SIC industries in the U.K.

Financial Research Associates. *Financial Studies of the Small Business.* Orlando, FL (annual).

Financial and operating ratios for about 50 lines of small business (those with capitalization under $1,000,000)—retail, wholesale, services, contractors and professional services, and manufacturers—by asset size categories and some figures by sales volume. Includes also tables based on the 25% most profitable, and a five-year trend by category.

Robert Morris Associates. *Annual Statement Studies.* Philadelphia.

This useful annual contains financial and operating ratios for more than 360 lines of business (by 4-digit SIC number)—manufacturers, wholesalers, retailers, services, and contractors—all based on information obtained from member banks of RMA. It is in 6 parts: Parts 1–4 cover balance sheet and income statement composites and also selected ratios, all by company size groups; part 5 is a finance industry supplement for small loan and sales finance ratios. Part 6 is a bibliography of sources of composite financial data.

Troy, Leo. *Almanac of Business and Industrial Financial Ratios.* Englewood Cliffs, NJ: Prentice-Hall (annual).

Financial and operating ratios for about 160 industries, with figures for each covering 22 financial categories in 12 asset group sizes. These are arranged by a 4-digit industry classification similar to the SIC, and there is an alphabetical index of the industries at the end.

A similar and alternate source is *IRS Corporate Financial Ratios* (5th ed., Lincolnshire, IL: Schonfeld & Associates, 1991). This is also classified by over 180 industries; it contains more key ratios (70) but for fewer asset size groups (4). It does not have an alphabetical industry index. Statistics for both are based on figures from IRS returns and, since the IRS is slow in making the data available, the statistics when published are usually about three years old.

U.S. Bureau of the Census. *Quarterly Financial Report for Manufacturing, Mining, and Trade Corporations.* Washington, DC: U.S. Government Printing Office.

This has quarterly income statement and balance sheet data as well as selected financial and operating ratios classified by industry (22 manufacturing industries) and by asset size, with totals only given for mining, retail and wholesale trade.

AEROSPACE INDUSTRY

Aerospace Facts & Figures. Washington, DC: Aerospace Industries Association of America (annual).

A useful statistical annual for U.S. aircraft production, missile and space programs, air transportation, research and development, foreign trade, employment, and finance. Includes brief explanatory text and a glossary. The AIA also publishes a short *Year-end Review and Forecast.*

Air Transport. Washington, DC: Air Transport Association of America (annual).

This is a slim statistical brochure of about 20 pages giving figures on the U.S. scheduled airline industry, including passenger travel, traffic and operations data, revenues and expenses, and some data on specific airlines.

Air Transport World. Stamford, CT: Penton Publishing Inc. (monthly).

This is "the magazine of world airline management." Its useful "Annual World Airline Report" (June) includes world airline statistics by geographic regions (giving number of passengers, freight tonnage, number of employees, number of aircraft); also short profiles of airlines, data on U.S. majors, nationals, cargo carriers, regional/specialty carriers, a ranked list of "the world's top 25 airlines." A "Forecast" article appears in January. Current "Facts & Figures" in each issue includes statistics on specific carriers. Indexed in ABI/I, BPI, PTS, TI; also full text on BRS, DATA-STAR, DIALOG, DOW JONES, MEAD/NEXIS.

Association of European Airlines. *Yearbook.* Brussels.

The "Statistical Appendices" in each Yearbook cover tables on the passenger and cargo traffic, capacity, revenue and operation of specific AEA airlines by geographic area, each for a period of three years. The Yearbook itself discusses current developments, AEA airlines' performance and outlook. It includes a "digest of statistics," which has ranked lists of AEA companies according to such factors as passengers carried, revenue, freight.

Aviation Week & Space Technology. New York: McGraw-Hill.

Their annual "Aerospace Forecast & Inventory" issue (mid-March) contains articles, charts, and some statistics on growth trends (in chart format) for the aerospace industry, including military aircraft, air transport, space technology, avionics, business flying, as well as detailed specifications tables. Indexed in ABI/I, ASTI, BPI, PTS/F&S, TI; full text on DIALOG, DOW JONES, MEAD/NEXIS.

General Aviation Manufacturers Association. *General Aviation Statistical Databook.* Washington, DC (annual).

This consists of some 27 pages of statistics on U.S. general aviation shipments, fleet and flight activity, pilots, airports, and aeronautical facilities.

International Air Transport Association. *World Air Transport Statistics.* Geneva (annual).

Traffic, operating and other industry statistics for IATA members, including ranking lists of top 50 member-airlines and operating data for individual airlines. Among other current publications of the IATA are: *Scheduled Passenger Traffic Forecast* (annual), and *Freight Traffic Forecast* (annual), the first providing five-year forecasts of scheduled international passenger traffic and the second, the same for charter international freight traffic; *IATA Quarterly,* a concise analysis of the economic and financial airline industry; *North Atlantic Passenger Traffic Report* (quarterly). Most IATA publications are also available on diskettes.

International Civil Aviation Organization. *Civil Aviation Statistics of the World.* Montreal, Quebec, Can. (annual). Published also in French, Russian, and Spanish editions.

Presents the most widely used statistical information on civil aviation activities—worldwide data on aircraft, pilots, safety, fleets, traffic, finance, airport traffic. Among other ICAO publications is an irregularly published *Digest of Statistics,* with each issue providing statistics on a particular aspect, e.g. finance.

U.S. Dept. of Transportation. *Air Carrier Financial Statistics Quarterly.* Washington, DC.

Income and balance sheet statistics for specific large certified air carriers, prepared by the Research and Special Programs Administration of the DOT. A companion volume giving detailed traffic statistics for large air carriers is *Air Carrier Traffic Statistics Monthly.* Traffic statistics for small certified air carriers and commuter air carriers are reported in their quarterly *Air Carrier Scheduled Service Traffic Statistics.*

U.S. Federal Aviation Administration. *FAA Statistical Handbook of Aviation.* Washington, DC: U.S. Government Printing Office (annual).

Provides a convenient source for historical statistics on the national airspace system, airports, airport activity, U.S. civil air carrier fleet, U.S. air carrier operating data, U.S. civil airmen, general aviation aircraft, aircraft accidents, aeronautical production, and imports/exports. Among other FAA publications is their annual *FAA Aviation Forecasts* which forecasts aviation activity at FAA facilities for the coming 12 years.

AGRICULTURE AND FOOD

See also in this chapter: "Brewing and Distilling"; "Commodities and Financial Futures; Grain Statistics"; "Textiles and Apparel"; and "Tobacco and Cigars."

U.S. Bureau of the Census. *Census of Agriculture.* Washington, DC: U.S. Government Printing Office (quinquennial). Data from vol. 1 is on CD-ROM.

An excellent source of detailed statistics on farms, farming, ranching, and related activities, but the data is often old. Volume 1, "Geographic Area Series," consists of separate reports for each state and U.S. territory, with statistics by county for number of farms, land in farms, land use, irrigation, production and value of specific crops, livestock, poultry, value of farm products sold, expenses, and operator characteristics; also state-level data tabulating size of farm, tenure of operator, type of organization, age and principal occupation of operator, and SIC. The other volumes are: vol.2 "Subject Series," 4 volumes including one on *Ranking of States and Counties;* vol.3, "Related Surveys"; vol.4, "1988 Census of Horticulture Specialties."

This agriculture census is now taken in the years ending with 2 and 7 to coincide with the economic censuses; it was formerly taken in the years ending with 4 and 9.

U.S. Department of Agriculture. *Agricultural Statistics.* Washington, DC U.S. Government Printing Office (annual).

An annual compilation (about 500 pages) of the most important USDA statistics on agricultural production, supplies, consumption, facilities, costs, and returns, with sources for statistics at foot of each table.

The Economic Research Service of the DOA publishes a series of periodic "Situation and Outlook" reports that include current statistics. Those on commodities are: *Aquaculture; Cotton and Wool; Dairy; Feed; Fruit and Tree Nuts; Livestock and Poultry; Oil Crops; Rice; Sugar and Sweetener; Tobacco; Vegetables and Specialties; Wheat.* The titles of each begin: *Situation and Outlook Report . . .;* they vary in frequency, usually 2, 4 or 8 issues per year. The ERS publishes several other more general reports in this series, such as *Agricultural Income and Finance* (quarterly);

Agriculture and Trade (five annuals covering each of five regions of the world); *Agriculture Exports* (quarterly).

The Department publishes many other publications that include statistics. One of the more general monthlies is *Agricultural Outlook* (for sale by the GPO), with about half of each issue containing current agricultural developments and outlook and the other half a useful selection of recent agricultural "statistical indicators" covering current tables on farm prices, producer and consumer prices, farm-retail price speads, livestock and products, crops and products, world agriculture, U.S. agricultural trade, farm income, food expenditures, transportation, indicators.

The monthly *Bibliography of Agriculture* (Phoenix, AZ: Oryx Press) is a detailed subject index to the literature of agriculture and allied sciences, based on the indexing records prepared by the U.S. National Agricultural Library for its *AGRICOLA* computer data files. One can also go directly to the online *AGRICOLA* for citations wanted, or use the CD-ROM version.

Food Engineering. Radnor, PA: Chilton Co. (monthly).

This monthly is billed as "the source on processing, packaging, and product development." Each year a "State of the Food Industry" issue (June) contains trends in the food industry and in 11 categories of foods, e.g. breakfast foods, bakery products, usually including a table for shipments or sales. Other annual features include a "New Food Plant Construction Survey (November) and an "Annual Salary Survey" (December). Indexed in ASTI, PTS/F&S, TI; full text on BRS, DATA-STAR, DIALOG, MEAD/NEXIS.

The IFMA Encyclopedia of the Foodservice Industry. 6th ed. Chicago: International Foodservice Manufacturers Association, 1988. 1 volume (loose-leaf).

A useful compendium of facts and data on the foodservice industry drawn from a variety of sources. Included are statistical sections with brief text covering: an historical overview; consumer demographics and trends; foodservice industry segments and definitions (including statistics and ranked lists on such segments as convenience stores); chain/multi-unit operators; industry personnel; foodservice distribution; food categories and manufacturers/brokers (including statistics on per capita consumption of specific foods, ranked lists of top food companies, food consumed away from home, etc.); packaging and labeling. Directory data covers: associations/ groups, and publications; government sources and information; information resources. A subject/topic index and an index of reference sources are at end.

The Food and Agriculture Organization of the United Nations publishes many periodic statistical studies covering agricultural commodities in all UN countries. A few of the more general FAO sources are included in Chapter 5.

Beverage Industry (see also "Brewing and Distilling")

Beverage Industry. Cleveland: Edgell Communications Inc. (monthly).

This journal publishes a separate *Annual Manual,* with the first of its six parts reviewing major segments of the beverage industry. Includes a table giving soft drink consumption by company and brand, and trends in beer, distilled spirits, bottled water, juice, sweeteners, advertising, vending, packaging, equipment and more. The other parts cover: new products/services; a manual of operations; a directory of beverage companies, including a list of brand names; associations and exhibitions; a buyer's guide. The January 1991 issue has statistics on "Beer (coming year)", with production by brewer and brand. A pull out section with the March 1991 issue is "Annual Soft Drink Report." Indexed in PTS/F&S, TI; full text on DATA-STAR, DIALOG.

Beverage World. Great Neck, NY: Keller International Publishing Co. (monthly).

The May issue is the "Beverage Market Index" issue, with regional comparisons of sales (in gallons, per capita, wholesale and retail dollars) for soft drinks, beer, spirits, wine, fruit juices and fruit drinks, bottled water. A ranked list of the "Beverage World Top 50" is in the July issue. A "Buyers Guide" is in the December issue. Each issue contains "Statistical Insight." Published separately is an annual *Beverage World Databank* which is in three parts: a product/equipment directory; marketing data such as are in the May and July issues; desk reference sources such as directories of brokers, manufacturers reps., brand names, associations, conventions, government agencies. Received with this is a monthly newsletter called *Beverage World Periscope.* Indexed in ABI/I, BPI, PAIS, PTS, TI; also full text on BRS, DATA-STAR, DIALOG, DOW JONES, MEAD/NEXIS.

Coffee Annual. New York: George Gordon Paton & Co.

Short articles on the industry which vary each year plus statistics, including volume of green coffee roasted in the U.S., U.S. and worldwide foreign trade, world coffee supply and distribution, total production of green coffee. Contains also a chronology of events for the year.

International Tea Committee. *Annual Bulletin of Statistics.* London.

This contains tea production, consumption, stocks, foreign trade, prices—by country and often for more than 10 years; also statistics on instant tea, tea duties, and a directory of companies. Some current figures are in their *Monthly Statistical Summary.*

Tea & Coffee Trade Journal. New York: Lockwood Trade Journal Co. (monthly).

There are no special issues in this international trade journal but it does contain frequent articles discussing current trends in the coffee or tea industries in specific countries. Indexed in PTS/F&S, TI: also full text on BRS, DATA-STAR, DIALOG, MEAD/NEXIS.

Canned Foods

Almanac of the Canning, Freezing, Preserving Industries. Westminster, MD: E.E. Judge & Sons (annual).

The raw products section gives harvested acreage, production, total values, etc., for specific crops by state. Also given are U.S. canned and frozen fruit and vegetable pack statistics, data from the census, international trade, and world packs. Other information in this almanac includes names of associations, food laws and regulations, labeling and packaging, grading, quality grade standards, a "Buyer's Guide." This publisher also has a *Directory of the Canning, Freezing, Preserving Industries* (biennial).

Frozen Foods

American Frozen Food Institute. *Frozen Food Pack Statistics.* McLean, VA (annual).

Pack statistics for the various frozen food categories.

Specific Food Products

American Meat Institute. *Meat Facts*. Washington, DC (annual).

A statistical summary of the U.S. meat industry, with tables and graphs covering past trends, and the current situation in the livestock and meat sector. Includes a ranked list of top meat companies. The AMI also publishes an annual *Meat Industry Financial and Operating Survey* (expensive for non-members) that contains operating and financial figures for the meat packing industry.

International Sugar Organization. *Sugar Year Book*. London.

Gives sugar production, consumption, foreign trade by country. Some current figures are in their *Monthly Statistical Bulletin*.

APPLIANCE INDUSTRY

Appliance. Oak Brook, IL: Dana Chase Publications (monthly).

The April issue each year contains a 10-year "Annual Statistical Review," giving manufacturer shipments or factory sales for specific consumer electronic products, electric housewares, plumbing appliances/fixtures, commercial equipment. The January issue gives "Annual Appliance Industry Forecasts" which includes short term projections of specific appliances. The January issue also has an "Appliance Industry Purchasing Directory." One page of current "Statistics" is in each issue. Indexed in PTS, TI; full text on BRS, DATA-STAR, and DIALOG.

Association of Home Appliance Manufacturers. *Major Home Appliance Industry Factbook*. Chicago (annual).

Tables, charts, and brief text on the U.S. major home appliance industry. Includes data on manufacturing, shipments, distribution, ownership, consumer value.

Dealerscope Merchandising. Philadelphia: North American Publishing Co. (monthly).

This is billed as "the marketing magazine for consumer electronics and major appliance retailing." Of special interest is its two-part "Annual Statistical & Marketing Report" (March and April issues) with part 1 covering consumer electronics and electronic highlights and part 2, major appliances. "The Dealerscope 400" (May) is a compendium of facts on the industry; December issue contains a directory. Indexed in ABI/I, BPI, PTS/PROMT.

The Bureau of the Census series of *Current Industrial Reports* includes separate annual statistical reports giving production for "electric housewares and fans" (MA-36E), "major household appliances" (MA-36F), "radio receivers and television sets, phonographs and record players, speakers and related equipment" (MA-36M).

AUTOMOBILES AND TRUCKS

American Trucking Associations. *American Trucking Trends*. Washington, DC (annual).

Graphs and some statistics on truck and trailer registration and sales, employment, financial state of the industry, taxes, operating statistics. A glossary is at end.

Automotive Executive. McLean, VA: National Automobile Dealers Association (monthly).

The August issue each year is a reference guide for automobile and truck dealers. The first part contains: "NADA Data: Economic Impact of America's New Car & Truck Dealers" (formerly published separately by the NADA). This gives brief statistics and graphs, with explanatory text, profiling franchised new car dealerships, including dealership sales, used-vehicle department, service and parts, employment and payrolls, advertising, consumer credit; with lesser data on franchised new truck dealers. The rest of this issue is a "Dealer Business Guide," covering directories of: aftermarket/accessories; business management; sales support; service/parts/body shop; index of suppliers. A "Forecast Special Section" is in the December issue.

Automotive News. Detroit, MI: Crain Communications (weekly).

A special "Market Data Book" appears as an extra issue, usually in late May. This is full of useful statistics on: U.S. car and truck production; sales and registrations; specifications; prices; equipment installation; product profiles (of the world's leading cars, with brief data and pictures of each); dealer statistics. At end is a directory of automobile companies, which lists officers; a list of associations; pictures of top executives, giving title only. Each issue of this trade journal has two tables, one giving U.S. and Canadian car and truck production, and the other, customer and dealer incentives. The second issue each month has statistics on sales of cars, imported cars, and trucks; other issues have occasional statistics which vary. The second February issue contains a section called "Face of the Dealer," which consists of profiles of leading car dealers in the U.S. and Canada, arranged by city. Indexed in BPI, PTS, TI; also full text on DATA-STAR, DIALOG, MEAD/NEXIS.

Edmund's New Car Prices. Concord, MA: Edmund Publications Corporation (3/yr).

A current source for car prices is useful in any kind of library because so many people need the information at one time or another. This is one such guide to prices of new cars. There are two companion guides: *Edmund's Used Car Prices* (4/yr.) and *Edmund's Import Car Prices* (2/yr.).

A more general guide to the whole topic of the economics of buying and owning a new car is *The Complete Car Cost Guide* (San Jose, CA: IntelliChoice Inc.; annual). For each model car, it gives concise data on purchase price, ownership costs, warranty/maintenance information, repair frequency, and more.

International Road Federation. *World Road Statistics.* Geneva (annual).

The statistics here on motor vehicles (by country) include production, registration, vehicles in use, foreign trade; there is also data on road networks, traffic, motor fuels, road accidents, taxation, road expenditures. Explanations of tables are in English, French and German.

Motor Vehicle Manufacturers Association of the United States. *MVMA Motor Vehicle Facts & Figures.* Detroit, MI (annual).

This annual contains statistics on automobile, truck, and bus production; sales and registrations; ownership and usage; economic and social impact (employment, highways, pollution control, taxes, etc.).

The MVMA also publishes annual *World Motor Vehicle Data,* providing auto and truck production statistics, foreign trade, registration—all by country.

Society of Motor Manufacturers and Traders, Ltd. *Motor Industry of Great Britain: World Automotive Statistics.* London (annual).

Car and commercial vehicle production, new registrations, vehicles in use, both in the United Kingdom and overseas, as well as detailed statistics for overseas trade.

Descriptions of motor-related organizations are at end. For the most recent statistics, see their *Monthly Statistical Review.*

Another useful statistical annual for an important automobile producing country is *Motor Vehicle Statistics of Japan* (Tokyo and Washington, D.C.: Japan Automobile Manufacturers Association).

Ward's Automotive Yearbook. Detroit, MI: Ward's Communications.

The last half of this useful yearbook consists of statistics on: U.S. vehicle production (including production by make and by line); retail sales; registrations; also Canadian statistics. This is followed by a section called "World Outlook," which includes some country statistics plus recent trends in individual companies in the country. The first half has sections covering: industry trends; materials usage; manufacturing equipment; suppliers; engines and drivetrains; electronics; and recent trends for specific domestic vehicle manufacturers, with pictures of some car models.

Ward's also publishes: *Ward's Automotive Reports,* a weekly containing current statistics (indexed in PTS); *Ward's Auto World,* a monthly management magazine (indexed in BPI, PTS, TI; also full text on BRS, DATA-STAR, DIALOG, Dow Jones, MEAD/NEXIS); *Ward's Automotive International,* an expensive monthly newsletter with a global view.

World Automotive Market. New York: Automobile International (annual).

Vehicle production for 34 countries, registrations, world trade in new motor vehicles, and U.S. exports of automotive products.

The Economist Intelligence Unit issues four expensive research quarterlies analyzing trends in the automobile industry. These are: *European Motor Business; Europe's Automotive Components Business; International Motor Business;* and *Japanese Motor Business.*

BREWING AND DISTILLING

Beer Institute. *The Brewing Industry in the United States: Brewers Almanac.* Washington, DC (annual).

Statistics cover production and withdrawals, shipments and sales, foreign trade, taxes.

For sales and per capita consumption in Canadian provinces see the *Annual Statistical Bulletin* of the Brewers Association of Canada.

Beer Statistics News. West Nyack, NY: Beer Marketer's Insights, Inc. (monthly).

This gives one month's statistics for shipments of leading brands by region and by state, compared with the same month last year; also total barrels, year to date, and market share.

Jobson's Liquor Handbook. New York: Jobson Publishing Corporation (annual).

The largest section of this useful annual covers the markets for distilled spirits, by type. The rest covers: national trends and statistics, advertising and promotion, supplier performance data, distilling operations and industry data, national market data, international consumption, other beverages.

A companion volume is *Jobson's Wine Marketing Handbook.*

For current statistics see the annual "Statistical Study" of the weekly *Modern Brewery Age* (Norfolk, CT: Business Journals, Inc.) which appears in the mid-March issue of the "Magazine Section."

CHEMICALS AND PLASTICS

Chemical & Engineering News. Washington, DC: American Chemical Society (weekly).

The most important of its several annual statistical issues is "Facts & Figures for the Chemical Industry" (late June issue) containing useful statistics on important chemical products production, finances, (including capital spending, R&D spending, financial figures for specific companies), employment, foreign trade, foreign chemical industry trends (with statistics for specific companies or regions); also ranked lists of top 50 chemicals and of top 100 chemical companies, with comparative financial data. Other annual statistical articles include: industrial "R & D Spending" (third January issue); "Federal R&D Budget" (third February); "Top 50 Chemical Products" (early April); "Top 100 Chemical Producers" (first May); "Salary Survey" for chemists (first or second July issue); "Facts & Figures for Chemical R&D" (third August); "Employment Outlook" (third October); "World Chemical Outlook" (mid-December); "Capital Spending" preview (late December). In addition there are quarterly figures for "Chemical Companies Earnings" in mid-May, August, November and February issues. Indexed in ASTI, BPI, PTS, TI; full text on DIALOG, DOW JONES, MEAD/NEXIS.

Chemical Marketing Reporter. New York: Schnell Publishing Co. (weekly).

This weekly newspaper is especially important for its continuing list of "Chemical Prices." It also covers news of the industry and of specific chemical products. Indexed in BPI, PTS; full text on BRS, DATA-STAR, DIALOG, Dow Jones, MEAD/NEXIS.

Chemical Week. New York: Chemical Week Associates.

An important trade journal on the chemical process industry. Special annual features include: "Forecast" (first January issue); "The CW 300" (first May issue), which consists of financial statistics for leading chemical process companies arranged by type of chemical produced (there are similar quarterly statistical tables in first issues of March, June, September, and December); an annual "Executive Pay" survey giving salary statistics for top chemical company executives (first August); "Buyers' Guide," a separately numbered issue published in late October. Each issue contains a one-page "Economic Trends" with varying data, such as leading economic indicators or production report. Once a month, in mid-month, it consists of a "Monthly Stock Report." Indexed in ABI/I, BPI, PTS, TI; full text on DIALOG, MEAD/NEXIS. A companion weekly focusing on news and articles about the chemical process industry in other countries is *Chemical Week International.* An early January issue is a "World Forecast Issue."

Modern Plastics. New York: McGraw-Hill (13/yr.).

The January issue of this plastics trade journal contains an annual report on "Resins," with sales statistics for specific plastic resins by process and market; also capacities and some figures for Canadian resin sales. Another special report, on "Additives," (September) discusses current trends for about 12 specific products, with sources for further information. A one-page "Barometer" in each issue gives varying statistics such as prices, foreign trade. A useful separate *Modern Plastics*

Encyclopedia (issued in mid-October each year) is a reference guide on plastic materials, processing techniques, equipment and components; also a buyers' guide, list of plastics companies, and list of trade names. The journal is indexed in ABI/I, ASTI, PTS, TI.

Rauch Guide to the U.S. Plastics Industry. Bridgewater, NJ: Rauch Associates, 1990. 275 pp. $189.

An economic analysis of the plastics industry, including production, products, and uses; sales by product line for over 500 leading U.S. plastics companies; also sources of information.

James A. Rauch has published several other guides for specific industries, each revised periodically and each now quite expensive to purchase. These are on "The U.S. Adhesive and Sealants Industry" (1989, 250 pp., $215), "The U.S. Ink Industry" (1991, 175 pp., $207), "The U.S. Packaging Industry" (1989, 325 pp. $225), "The U.S. Paint Industry" (8th ed., 1990, 210 pp., $195). They were all formerly published as "The Kline Guides".

Society of the Plastics Industry. *Facts & Figures of the Plastics Industry.* Washington, DC (annual).

Statistics, usually including, for each type of plastic, figures on production, sales and captive use, domestic consumption by end-use, distribution by major market, typical applications, names of manufacturers.

Current statistics are in the *Monthly Statistical Report—Resins.* The SPI also publishes an annual *Financial and Operating Ratios: Plastics Processing Companies.*

U.S. Bureau of the Census. *Current Industrial Reports. Series M-28A: Inorganic Chemicals.* Washington, DC (annual).

This gives production statistics for many inorganic chemicals. In addition monthly figures are available online in *CENDATA.* The U.S. International Trade Commission publishes an annual for *Synthetic Organic Chemicals: United States Production and Sales.* Several other reports in the Census Bureau's *Current Industrial Reports* series cover: inorganic fertilizer materials; industrial gases; paint, varnish, and lacquer products; pharmaceutical preparations, except biologicals.

The Economist Intelligence Unit publishes *Chemical Outlook International,* an expensive bimonthly analysis of key chemical issues, trends, and developments.

COMMODITIES AND FINANCIAL FUTURES; GRAIN STATISTICS

Chicago Board of Trade. *Statistical Annual Supplement.* Chicago.

Most of the data on CBT commodities and futures is available only on diskettes. This is a short volume containing fundamental trade and market data only. Includes: daily futures contracts; delivery totals for wheat, corn, soybeans, oats, and some financial futures; options exercised/assigned; cash prices; miscellaneous data.

Chicago Mercantile Exchange. *Yearbook.* Chicago.

Daily price range, volume, and open interest for: agricultural products futures (live cattle, feeder cattle, live hogs, frozen pork bellies, random length lumber); 7 major foreign currencies; interest rate products (Eurodollars, Treasury Bills); the S&P 500 stock index. General CME statistics are at front. At end are such tables as daily cash market price range for financial instruments such as Treasury Bills, London

Eurodeposits, daily close for foreign currencies, daily S&P 500 composite price index, Nikkei 225 stock price index, DJ 30 industrials, NYSE daily volume.

Among other statistical annuals of specialized commodity exchanges are: *Annual Statistical Report* of the Kansas City Board of Trade for futures prices and options on wheat and other commodities traded on this exchange, as well as Value Line futures; *Statistical Annual* of the Coffee, Sugar & Cocoa Exchange, Inc., of New York City, which gives trading and futures prices for sugar, coffee, and cocoa.

Commodity Exchange, Inc. *Statistical Yearbook.* New York. 2 volumes.

These are unnumbered volumes, one covering "Metals Data" and the other "Options Data." The former gives daily futures prices and trading statistics (as well as open interest, stocks and deliveries) for gold, silver, copper, aluminum. The latter gives similar data for gold, silver, and copper options trading.

Commodity Research Bureau. *Futures Chart Service.* Chicago. Two separate weeklies.

This charting service is now divided into two weeklies: one is called *Futures Chart Service: Agricultural* and the other, *Futures Chart Service: Financial.* The former gives weekly futures price charts for actively traded agricultural commodity contracts, such as coffee, cotton, wheat; the latter provides the same for currencies, precious metals, energy products such as oil, Treasury instruments, Eurodollars, interest rates, stock indexes. Current charts are in a weekly *CRB Futures-Chart Service.* The CRB also publishes a semimonthly *Easy Update Charts.* Their useful statistical *CRB Commodity Year Book* (see listing in Chapter 4) contains some futures prices in its coverage of statistics on about 100 commodities.

There are other futures charting services such as *Commodity Price Charts* (Cedar Fall, IA, weekly) which contains over 530 charts and studies on more than 45 markets.

Feedstuffs. Minnetonka, MN: Miller Publishing Co. (weekly, with extra issue in July).

Called "the weekly newspaper for agribusiness," each issue includes a page of prices and futures for specific feed ingredients; also some cash market prices. Its annual "Reference Guide" (extra July issue) is in four sections: feed marketing (with national, regional, and state marketing statistics on the feed, grain, and feeding industries, as well as animal production and consumption); "Animal Management," an analysis of animal nutrition and health; "Feed Milling" manual; "Buyers Guide," including directories of companies and of associations. This weekly is indexed in PTS, TI.

Futures. Cedar Falls, IA (monthly, except semimonthly in January and November).

This monthly covers articles on all types of futures trading, both commodities and options. It is listed here for its extra issue in November called "Reference Guide to Futures/Options Market." This includes a list of futures and options exchanges and "trading facts and figures," giving summary trading statistics for individual futures contracts on each exchange—both U.S. and foreign. The rest is primarily a directory listing futures/options firms by categories, country government sources, related organizations. At the end is an index of articles printed in *Futures* during the previous year. The regular January issue contains an "Economic Outlook"; the extra January issue is a "Trader's Calendar & Record Keeper". This monthly is indexed in ABI/I, BPI, PAIS; full text on BPS, DATA-STAR, DIALOG, MEAD/NEXIS.

New York Futures Exchange. *Data and Statistics.* New York (annual).
Statistical summary of trading data in tables and graphs. Includes daily (for one year) high/low/close for NYSE Composite Index price data, NYSE Composite Index futures price data, CRB index of futures daily price data, and NYFE U.S. Treasury bond futures contracts; also monthly options on CRB futures contracts.

The daily newspaper *Journal of Commerce and Commercial* (New York) contains, in each issue, a current futures trading/open interest and sales table for basic commodities and a few financial instruments, arranged by individual commodities exchanges; also New York oil futures. Current spot prices given include specific chemicals, metals, commodities such as the most important grains, foods, textiles; also good coverage of daily petroleum prices.

CONSTRUCTION INDUSTRY

For housing and real estate statistics see Chapter 15.

The Blue Book of Major Homebuilders. Lexington, MA: F. W. Dodge Statistical Services, McGraw-Hill (annual).
Called the "Who's who in the housing industry," this contains information about nearly 3,000 U.S. homebuilders, arranged by region and state. For each firm that returned the survey, the data usually includes names of key personnel, operating areas, production volume by type of construction, gross revenue, average value of construction, average rents and home sales prices, construction methods, money and land requirements. A ranked list of the "Top 100 Blue Book Builders" is at front.

Construction Review. Washington, DC: International Trade Administration, U.S. Department of Commerce (bimonthly). Purchase from U.S. Government Printing Office.
A useful bimonthly source for current statistics on: construction put in place; housing; building permits; nonresidential construction, cost, prices and interest rates, construction materials; contract construction employment. A feature article or two on the industry is in each issue. Indexed in BPI, PAIS, PTS; full text on DIALOG.

ENR: Engineering News-Record. New York: McGraw-Hill (weekly).
A trade journal for the construction industry. A "Quarterly Cost Report" (usually the fourth issues in March, June, September, December) contains construction materials price movement, highway bid price indexes, and other varying statistics such as construction and building cost indexes, history from the early 1990s, ENR cost indexes in 22 cities, hourly union pay scale by occupation by city, water and power construction costs. Ranked lists and other special annual features include: "Forecast" issue (last January issue); "The Top 500 Design Firms" ranked by billings ranges (early April); "The Top 400 Contractors" (last May); "Top 100 CM Firms" (construction management firms; first June); "The Top 250 International Contractors" (first July); "The Top 200 International Design Firms" (first August); "The Top 600 Specialty Contractors" arranged by specialty (last August). In each issue one can find a page of "Materials Prices," and a page of "Market Trends" giving cost indexes, contract awards, new plans, and other varying current statistics. Indexed in ABI/I, ASTI, BPI, PTS, TI; also full text on DIALOG, DOW JONES, MEAD/NEXIS.

Professional Builder & Remodeler. Newton, MA: Cahners Publishing Co. (18/yr.).

The July issue each year contains "The 400: Annual Report of Housing's Giants," which ranks 400 firms by dollar volume and gives a brief description of the operating plans for each. That same issue contains a "Salary & Bonus Survey" for executive compensation. Two other annual features are: "The Giant 100" (March) ranks housing starts leaders with facts about each; "Annual Consumer Survey" (December). Two-page "Indicators" are in each issue. Indexed in BPI, TI; full text on BRS, DATA-STAR, DIALOG, Dow Jones.

U.S. Bureau of the Census. *Census of Construction Industries.* Washington, DC: U.S. Government Printing Office (quinquennial, in years ending with 2 and 7). Available also on fiche, tapes, compact discs, diskettes.

This 1987 census is a detailed enumeration of U.S. statistics on construction establishments operating as building contractors, heavy construction contractors, special trade contractors, land developers and subdividers. Statistics include number of establishments, value of construction work, number of employees, payrolls, hours worked, selected operating costs, capital expenditures, inventories, assets, depreciation. There are 28 reports in the "Industry Series" and 10 in the "Geographic Area Series". In addition there is a "Subject Report" on "Legal Form of Organization and Type of Operations."

The Bureau of the Census also publishes a number of series of *Current Construction Reports* on such subjects as: *Housing Completions* (monthly); *Housing Starts* (monthly); *Housing Units Authorized by Building Permits* (monthly) with data for states, selected Metropolitan Statistical Areas and individual places; *Value of New Construction Put in Place* (monthly).

DRUG INDUSTRY

For statistics on drugstores and products sold in drugstores see Chapter 18.

PMA Statistical Fact Book. Washington, DC: Pharmaceutical Manufacturers Association (loose-leaf, annual?).

Statistics and explanatory text on the U.S. pharmaceutical industry, including sales, earnings, foreign trade, employment, R&D. The 1988 volume has a section also covering "today's health environment" with statistics on health expenditures, number of personnel and facilities. A list of sources for pharmaceutical data is at end. The PMA also publishes an *Annual Survey Report* that contains sales (by dosage-form and product class) and R&D expenditures by product class, function, etc., based on a survey of PMA members.

ELECTRIC AND GAS UTILITIES

American Gas Association. *Gas Facts.* Arlington, VA (annual).

A comprehensive statistical record of the gas utility industry, with a glossary and a conversion table at end. Includes statistics on energy reserves, natural gas supply, distribution and transmission, energy consumption, customers, sales, revenues, prices, appliances and housing data, finance, personnel data. Once every 10 years the AGA publishes historical statistics, the latest of which is *Historical Statistics of the Gas Utility Industry, 1976–1985* (1987, 242 pp.). Among their other statistical publications is an annual *Gas Consumption in the United States,* which includes forecasts for four years; *Commercial Gas Market Survey* (annual); a two-page *Gas Stats: Monthly Gas Utility Statistical Report;* and *Gas Stats: Quarterly Report of Gas Industry Operations.*

Edison Electric Institute. *Statistical Yearbook of the Electric Utility Industry.* Washington, DC.

Statistical categories include national and state statistics on: generating capacity; electric power supply; generation; fuel; energy; energy sales; customers; revenues; financial; economics and other data. A glossary is at end. Each summer the EEI publishes an "Advance Release" of this data.

Electric Light & Power. Tulsa: PennWell Publishing Company (monthly).

This monthly news magazine is called the "voice of the electric utility industry." Among its several feature articles are: "Forecast" issue (January), with statistics projecting capital spending; "Annual Top 100 Electric Utilities Operating Report" (June), a ranked list; "The Top 100 Electric Utilities Operating Performance" (August) ranking companies by peak rate/fuel consumption, and also including tables on peak demand and capability, type of generation, etc.; "Annual Utility of the Year Report" (November) featuring one company each year. Indexed in TI; also full text on MEAD/NEXIS.

Electrical World. New York: McGraw-Hill (monthly).

A long-time trade journal for the electric utility industry. Annual features include: "Annual New-Plant Construction Survey" (January issue); "Annual Statistical Report" (April) which contains such statistics as construction spending, installed capacity of utility generating plants by state and type, electric customers, electric energy sales, electric revenues, annual average use and bill, investor-owned electric utility balance sheet and income figures; "Annual Buyers' Guide" (June); "Annual Industry Forecast" (October). Indexed in ABI/I, ASTI, BPI, PTS, TI.

Moody's Public Utility Manual. New York: Moody's Investors Service. 2 volumes (annual, with semiweekly supplements). Also available online and on CD-ROM.

An important financial manual covering all major types of American public utility companies. Center blue pages in each bound volume include: Moody's averages, statistics on the electric light and power industry, comparative data for independent electric operating companies, discussion of U.S. governmental activities, statistics on the gas utilities industry, the telephone industry; also a directory of public utilities by state and city, a list of securities offerings during the past year, a five-year chronological list of maturing public utility bonds and notes, and more.

National Propane Gas Association. *LP-Gas Market Facts.* Lisle, IL (annual).

This annual factbook gives LP-gas production, storage, sales, foreign trade, equipment, appliances, and utilization.

U.S. Energy Information Administration. *Electric Power Annual.* Washington, DC: U.S. Government Printing Office.

Useful statistics on the U.S. electric power industry, including generating capability, net generation, fossil-fuel statistics, electricity/sales/revenues/average revenue per kilowatthour sold, financial statistics, environmental statistics, and electric power transactions. Some figures are given by region and by state. A glossary is at end. Their *Electric Power Monthly* provides current statistics; the *Electric Power Quarterly* gives statistics on electric utilities at the plant level.

Among the EIA's many other statistical publications are two covering natural gas: *Natural Gas Annual* (2 volumes) and *Natural Gas Monthly*.

U.S. Energy Information Administration. *Financial Statistics of Selected Electric Utilities*. Washington, DC: U.S. Government Printing Office (annual).

Detailed financial and operating data for each of some 179 major privately-owned electric utilities; with statistics also for almost 500 major publicly-owned electric utilities, and summary data for 6 federally owned electric utilities and almost 900 electric cooperatives. The EIA publishes other financial statistics including *Financial Statistics of Selected Investor-Owned Electric Utilities* and *Statistics of Interstate Natural Gas Pipeline Companies*.

ELECTRONICS

See also "Appliance Industry."

Electronic Business. Newton, MA: Cahners Publishing Company (semi-monthly except monthly in December).

Intended "for the management team in electronics, computer and systems companies," this business magazine has current news, trends, figures and forecasts for the industry. Among its many annual features (including a number of ranked lists) are: "Outlook" (first January issue); "Top 100 Electronics Exporters" (first March); "Annual Survey of Electronics CEOs" (last March); "Top 50 Semiconductor Companies" (second April); "Most Profitable Companies" (second May); "Midyear Outlook" (second June); "The Electronic Business 200" U.S. companies (second July); "Top 100 U.S. R&D Spenders" (first August); "Top 50 Japanese Electronic Companies" (second October); "Electronic Business International 100" (second November). "Business Barometer" data is in first issue of each month. This journal is indexed in ABI/I, BPI, PTS, TI; also full text on BRS, DATA-STAR, DIALOG, DOW JONES, MEAD/NEXIS.

Electronic Industries Association. *Electronic Market Data Book*. Washington, DC (annual).

Useful statistics, charts, and explanatory text covering consumer electronics, communications equipment, computers and industrial electronics (including artificial intelligence, medical electronics), electronic components, government electronics, electronic-related products and services, general information. The Consumer Electronics Group of the EIA also publishes a separate short *U.S. Consumer Electronics Industry In Review* which contains industry facts and figures.

Electronic News. New York: Chilton Company (weekly).

A weekly newspaper for current news and trends of interest to the industry's management, including special sections devoted to computers and communications, components, military & aerospace, design/text/manufacturing, distribution/purchasing/VARs, and financial news. This latter section contains current stock prices quoted on the AMEX, NYSE, and OTC. A useful annual "Looking at the Leaders" issue (first September) is a descriptive list of electronics companies, usually giving for each, officers, major facilities, a summary and forecast, electronic sales, and total sales. A ranked list of the leading 50 U.S. and about 23 foreign electronic companies is at the front. Indexed in BPI, PTS, TI; also full text on BRS, DATA-STAR, DIALOG, DOW JONES, MEAD/NEXIS.

Electronics. Cleveland: Penton Publishing Company (monthly).

The first January issue of this established trade journal contains a "World Market Forecast" discussing trends but not including statistics. Other features include: "State of the Semiconductor Industry" (July); "Company of the Year" (December). Indexed in ASTI, PTS, TI; also full-text on BRS, DATA-STAR, DIALOG, DOW JONES, MEAD/NEXIS.

Fairchild's Electronics Industry Financial Directory. New York: Fairchild Fashion Group (annual).

This is a good financial manual covering electronic companies, usually listing for each the names of officers, directors, divisions, subsidiaries, areas of work, sales and earnings, revenues by line of business, income account, balance sheet data, number of employees, plant footage, common stock equity, stock exchange, ticker symbol. A ranked list of top U.S. and foreign companies is at front. If this manual is not readily accessible to you, try the "Looking at the Leaders" issue of *Electronic News* (first September issue each year) for more information about leading companies than is found in a directory.

Japan Electronics Almanac. Tokyo: Dempa Publications, Inc. (annual).

This is a comprehensive review (written in English) of the Japanese electronics industry and its leading companies. The major portion consists of brief text with statistics and a few graphs. It is arranged in 24 chapters to cover such topics as consumer electronics, electronic components and devices, computers, telecommunication equipment, factory automation-related equipment, electronic equipment for medical use. A much shorter second part contains one-to-two page profiles of leading Japanese electronics companies, often including a sales breakdown by principal products and geographic region, and the names of overseas affiliates.

Video Data Book. Washington, DC: Warren Publishing, Inc. (annual).

This is an annual compilation of key statistics on the consumer electronics industry. Each section consists of news items about the industry for the past fiscal year, arranged chronologically week by week, probably with much of the information taken from *Television Digest.* Interspersed are statistical tables. The sections cover: market share tables; international trade and statistics; surveys and studies; weekly sales to dealers; product statistics; company financial data; mergers and acquisitions; broadcast and cable.

The Bureau of the Census series of *Current Industrial Reports* includes separate annual statistical reports giving production for "communication equipment, including telephones and other electronic systems and equipment" (MA36P); "computers and office and accounting machines" (MA35R); "semiconductors, printed circuit boards, and other electronic components" (MA36Q).

ENERGY

See also sections in this chapter for specific kinds of energy: electric and gas utilities; metals and minerals (for sources on coal); petroleum.

Financial Post. *Survey of Mines and Energy Resources.* Toronto, Ontario, Can. (annual).

This Canadian financial manual includes data on over 3,000 mining and energy companies operating in Canada, including oil, gas, and minerals as well as hydroelectric power generating companies.

Great Britain. Dept. of Energy. *Digest of United Kingdom Energy Statistics.* London: H.M. Stationery Office (annual).

Provides useful statistics for energy in the U.K.

United Nations. *Energy Statistics Yearbook.* New York.

Country-by-country production, trade, consumption, by type of energy. Some current statistics are in the UN's *Monthly Bulletin of Statistics.*

Similar annuals are *Energy Statistics of OECD Countries* (published by the Organization for Economic Cooperation and Development), and *Energy Statistical Yearbook* published by the Statistical Office of the European Communities.

U.S. Energy Information Administration. *Monthly Energy Review.* Washington, DC.

A good source for current U.S. statistics, with each issue providing tables and charts on the following: energy summary; energy consumption; petroleum; natural gas; oil and gas resource development; coal; electric utilities; nuclear; price; international data. A glossary is at end.

Among the many other statistical publications of the EIA are: *Annual Energy Review; International Energy Annual; Annual Energy Outlook; International Energy Outlook.* These latter two annuals give detailed projections of energy supply and demand to 2010. For abstracts of articles on all types of energy and related topics, see *Energy Information Abstracts* described in Chapter 9.

MACHINERY INDUSTRY

American Machinist. Cleveland, OH: Penton Publishing Inc. (monthly).

This is called "the magazine of manufacturing technology," and it consists of short articles and news on metalworking and machine tools. The February 1991 issue contains a survey on "Which Nations Buy the Most Machine Tools." There are two directory issues: "Metalworking Buyers' Guide" (April) and "Outsourcing Services Directory" (June). Indexed in ASTI, PTS, TI; full text on BRS, DATA-STAR, DIALOG.

Every five years the publisher conducts an "American Machinist Inventory of Metalworking Equipment," which is then summarized in a November issue (see November 1989 issue, pp.91–110 for a summary of the 14th Inventory). It gives estimates of the number of machine tools and related equipment in actual use in U.S. factories, with the data compiled by: 150 kinds of machine types, four equipment age groups, SIC of user plant, location of user plant, and size of user plant based on number of employees. The complete figures collected in the 1989 Inventory are stored in a database. Contact the publisher for details on their customized search service.

Economic Handbook of the Machine Tool Industry. McLean, VA: Association for Manufacturing Technology (annual).

Useful statistics on the machine tool industry in general and on shipments and orders, foreign trade, employment and earnings, finance, machine tools in use. Primarily U.S. figures, with one section on the world machine tool industry. Explanation of terms is at end.

The *Current Industrial Reports* series of the Bureau of the Census includes a number of separate annual or quarterly reports giving production for specific kinds of machinery and equipment such as farm and lawn, mining, construction, metalworking, robotics.

METALS AND MINERALS

Aluminum Association. *Aluminum Statistical Review for (year).* Washington, DC (annual).

Contains U.S. shipments, markets, supply, U.S. foreign trade statistics; also world statistics. An *Historical Supplement* is published every five years; some current statistics are in their monthly *Aluminum Situation.*

American Bureau of Metal Statistics. *Non-Ferrous Metal Data.* New York (annual).

Worldwide statistics for copper, lead, zinc, aluminum, gold, silver, and other nonferrous metals. This is expensive for nonmembers ($290 as of 1990).

American Iron and Steel Institute. *Annual Statistical Report.* Washington, DC.

Financial and economic statistics, employment and wages, shipments of steel mill products, foreign trade, raw steel production, basic materials (pig iron, coal, scrap, etc.), Canadian statistics, and a few world statistics.

American Iron Ore Association. *Iron Ore.* Cleveland, OH (annual).

Production, shipments, consumption, foreign trade for iron ore in the United States and Canada; also grade names and analyses and a directory of reporting companies.

American Metal Market. New York (5/wk.).

An important newspaper for news and current prices of specific metals, including special tables for prices of specific scrap iron and steel and nonferrous scrap; also AMM closing prices, and London Metal Exchange prices. Indexed in PTS/PROMT, TI; also full text on BRS, DATA-STAR, DIALOG, DOW JONES.

British Geological Survey. *World Mineral Statistics.* Keyworth, Nottingham, Eng. (annual).

This covers over 65 economically important and internationally traded mineral commodities. For each it gives statistics on production, exports, imports over a five-year period. The BGS also publishes an annual volume that focuses on U.K. statistics called *United Kingdom Minerals Yearbook.*

Canadian Minerals Yearbook. Ottawa: Energy, Mines & Resources Canada.

Chapters focus on each of over 60 minerals and metals important to the Canadian economy, giving information somewhat similar to that in the U.S. *Minerals Yearbook* noted below. 1988 volume is latest received in 1990, but there is also a series of preprints for each chapter called *Annual Mineral Reviews.*

Copper Development Association. *Annual Data.* Greenwich, CT.

An annual brochure that has 20-year statistics on the supply and consumption of copper and copper alloys in the U.S. Included are tables for production and foreign trade of primary and secondary copper, consumption of metals by brass mills, foundries and others, supply of products in five end-use market areas.

E/MJ: Engineering and Mining Journal. Chicago: Maclean Hunter Publishing Co. (monthly).

Now incorporating *International Mining, E/MJ* gives worldwide coverage to the mining and processing industry. The two-part "Annual Commodities Survey & Outlook" issues (March and April) contain one-to-four pages of text with some statistics on each of over 20 minerals, usually discussing recent trends, production, demand/supply, prices, outlook, consumption. Two other annual features are: "Annual Project Survey" (January), which lists new projects by type of metal, region, and then by company name; "Buyers Guide" (September). Book reviews are in some issues. Indexed in ASTI, TI; also full text on MEAD/NEXIS.

This journal also publishes separately a useful directory called *E&MJ International Directory of Mining*.

Financial Post. *Survey of Mines and Energy Resources*. Toronto, Ontario, Can.: Maclean Hunter Ltd. (annual).

A Canadian financial manual covering data on over 3,000 mining and energy companies operating in Canada. A few statistics are at end.

Financial Times Mining International Year Book. Harlow, Essex, Eng: Longman Group UK Ltd. and Chicago: St. James Press.

Financial data for the world's principal mining and metals/minerals companies, usually including for each, officers, subsidiaries, property and operations, capital, financial results. At end is a descriptive list of associations, as well as geographic, product, and company indexes.

Foundry Management & Technology. Cleveland, OH: Penton Publishing Co. (monthly).

This trade journal is intended to cover articles and news of interest to personnel in foundries and metalworking departments of manufacturing firms. The January issue has an annual "Outlook" article that includes some casting shipment statistics, based on an annual industry survey. The February 1991 issue has an article on capital spending plans. "Data Book for Metalcasters" (December) is a technical reference source for the foundry industry. Indexed in TI; also full text on BRS, DATA-STAR, DIALOG, DOW JONES, MEAD/NEXIS.

This journal publishes a separate *Metal Casting Industry Census Guide* (triennial) which contains an analysis of the top 20 foundry market areas (of the total 96 areas), including size of foundries (by number of employees), types of metals cast, kinds of melting equipment, departments operated, casting methods. There are also state and Canadian province totals for this same information.

International Iron and Steel Institute. *Steel Statistical Yearbook*. Brussels.

This yearbook provides a cross-section of steel industry statistics, covering production, deliveries, trade, consumption, raw materials—often by country and for a 10-year span.

Iron Age. Wheaton, IL: Hitchcock Publishing (monthly).

Here is a long-time trade magazine covering the primary metals industry. Several features include: "Iron Age's Guide to Steel Prices, Production Level" (May); "Capital Spending Survey" (September); quarterly "Steel Earnings" (in issues for March, June, September, December). Each issue includes two pages of "Materials Prices" for both nonferrous and ferrous materials, as well as "Market Indicators." Indexed in ABI/I, BPI, PTS, TI; also full text on BRS, DATA-STAR, DIALOG.

Metal Bulletin's Prices & Data Book. Worcester Park, Surrey, Eng.: Metal Bulletin Books, Ltd. (annual).

Now published in one volume rather than two, the "prices" section gives country-by-country prices (usually weekly for one year) for iron and steel and for specific nonferrous metals. Prices are taken from their twice-weekly *Metal Bulletin*. The "statistics" section contains production and occasionally consumption for steel and other metals, annually from 1965; the "memoranda" section includes such miscellaneous information as lists of associations by country, country trading organizations, brands, tariff, specifications, ports.

Metal Statistics. New York: American Metal Market, Fairchild Publications (annual).

A useful statistical annual. For each metal this gives U.S. consumption, production, stocks, foreign trade, prices, world production; also industry highlights or profiles for each metal. At end are metal working statistics, a short directory section, and a conversion table.

Metallgesellschaft AG. *Metallstatistik.* Frankfurt am Main, Germany (annual).

Worldwide nonferrous metals statistics for an 11-year period.

Mining Annual Review and **Metals & Minerals Annual Review.** London: Mining Journal, Ltd. two annuals.

The first of these two annual reviews surveys the international minerals industry, with the first part containing country-by-country reviews of recent mining, mineral developments, often with a paragraph or two on those minerals of special importance to the country. The second half has 6 technical articles, and a short buyers' guide. The other annual, *Metals & Minerals Annual Review,* focuses on more than 60 specific minerals/metals, usually discussing for each, supply/demand, price trends, end use, outlook. It often includes several paragraphs relating to the leading countries that produce the mineral. Each of these reviews contains indexes to the mining and manufacturing companies in both volumes. Both are published by the *Mining Journal,* a long-time British trade weekly.

National Coal Association. *Coal Data.* Washington, DC (annual).

Parts 2 and 3 of this annual contain statistics on coal industry production and coal distribution and consumption, including a ranked list of the 50 largest bituminous coal and lignite mining companies. Parts 1 and 4 focus on energy statistics and energy resources and reserves. Appendices and a glossary are at end.

A companion annual is *International Coal* providing worldwide statistics in three parts: world energy statistics; U.S. coal in world trade; coal statistics for selected countries. Still further NCA publications are: *Coal Distribution Statistics* (annual); *Coal Transportation Statistics* (annual); *International Coal Review* (monthly) for current statistics on coal trade.

United Kingdom Iron and Steel Statistics Bureau. *Iron and Steel Industry: Annual Statistics for the United Kingdom.* Croydon, Eng.

This annual gives U.K. production and consumption of raw materials, energy, cokemaking, ironmaking, steelmaking, steel products, foundries, prices, manpower; also U.K. trade. There is also a monthly supplement.

Among this bureau's other statistical publications is: *International Steel Statistics: Summary Tables* (annual, with a companion service available in individual books for 23 specific countries). It contains worldwide statistics for iron ore, pig iron, crude steel, selected finished steel products. Two quarterlies are: *World Trade Steel* and *World Trade–Stainless, High Speed & Other Alloy Steel.*

U.S. Bureau of Mines. *Minerals Yearbook.* Washington, DC: U.S. Government Printing Office. 3 volumes.

Vol. 1, "Metals and Minerals," contains chapters on all metallic and industrial mineral commodities important to the U.S. economy. The discussion and statistics for each include production, consumption and uses, prices, foreign trade, world

capacity, world review, technology. Vol. 2, "Area Reports: Domestic," consists of
chapters on the mineral industries of each state and territory. Vol. 3, "Area Reports: International," gives the latest mineral data for more than 150 foreign countries. Preprints are issued as each chapter is completed and these are eventually
superseded by the three bound volumes.

The Bureau of Mines issues several other useful statistical compilations. Their
Mineral Industry Surveys are a series of periodic (monthly, quarterly, or annual)
statistical releases giving production, consumption, stocks, etc., for more than 100
individual minerals and metals, with the data usually eventually appearing in the
Minerals Yearbook above. The bureau's annual *Mineral Commodity Summaries*
consists of two-page up-to-date summaries on some 86 individual nonfuel mineral
commodities, briefly discussing production and use, salient statistics, recycling, tariff, government stockpile, events/trends/issues, world mine production, reserves and
reserve base, world resources. An older volume that provides good background data
on over 70 mineral commodities is *Mineral Facts and Problems* (quinquennial, with
1985 edition published as Bureau of Mines *Bulletin* 675, 956 pp.).

The *Current Industrial Reports* series of the Bureau of the Census includes
quarterly or annual production statistics reports on primary metals (such as
iron and steel foundries, steel mill products, nonferrous castings, steel mill
shapes and forms) and a few intermediate metal products such as closures for
containers.

PAPER AND ALLIED PRODUCTS

American Paper Institute. *Statistics of Paper, Paperboard & Wood Pulp*. New
York (annual).

Production and related output, regional statistics, inputs and related data (labor and
materials required, capital expenditures, R&D), financial figures and price indexes.

Several other API publications are: *Paper, Paperboard, and Wood Pulp* (a
monthly statistical summary); *Paper, Paperboard, Wood Pulp Capacity* with statistics for the latest two years and additional data for the coming three years. The
American Paper Institute is an important source for paper statistics, but these
publications may not be found in many libraries because the subscription cost has
risen to $325 as of 1990.

PPI: Pulp & Paper International. San Francisco: Miller Freeman Publications
(monthly).

This international trade journal focuses primarily on the paper industry outside the
U.S. Its July issue is an "Annual Review," consisting of a country-by-country review
of paper, board, and pulp trends, with statistics on production and foreign trade. At
front are summary tables. Each issue also includes a brief country-by-country analysis of current "Worldwide News." The January issue contains a "Preview" of the
coming year, and it also has an article on capital investments. A ranked list of the
world's top companies called "PPI Top 150" is in the September issue. Indexed in
PTS, TI; also full text on BRS, DATA-STAR, DIALOG, MEAD/NEXIS.

Paperboard Packaging. Cleveland, OH: Edgell Communications, Inc.
(monthly).

Focusing on the paperboard converting industry, this journal includes several short
annual features: "Forecast" issue (January); report on a salary survey (March);

"The (year) Census Report" (July), with graphs on corrugated container and folding carton industry. One page of statistics is in each issue giving containerboard and boxboard updates. Indexed in PTS, TI; full text on DATA-STAR, DIALOG.

Pulp & Paper. San Francisco: Miller Freeman Publications (monthly, except semimonthly in November).

Pulp & Paper absorbed the *Paper Trade Journal* in late 1986. It focuses primarily on the pulp, paper, and paperboard industry in North America. The January issue contains a useful "Outlook" article and one also on "Capital Spending," both with statistics. The extra issue in November is a "Buyer's Guide" issue. A continuing feature is one page of statistics on paper and paperboard production and foreign trade called the "Month in Statistics."

Each year this journal publishes a separate "Pulp & Paper North American Factbook," consisting of more than 400 pages of useful tables and brief text providing: an overview of the industry in the U.S. and Canada; data on paper and paperboard grades; fiber sources and other industry products; a world review; a glossary; sources of industry information; and North American company profiles that include, for each, production facilities, sales and earnings, total production capacity. The journal is indexed in BPI, PTS, TI; also full text on BRS, DATA-STAR, DIALOG, DOW JONES, MEAD/NEXIS.

The Bureau of the Census publishes an annual *Current Industrial Report* that gives production statistics for *Pulp, Paper and Board* (Series MA-26A). The Economist Intelligence Unit publishes *Paper & Packaging Analyst,* an expensive quarterly providing research information and forecasts for major paper and packaging markets and end uses, with emphasis on the EC and the U.K.

PETROLEUM

For statistics on the gas utility industry see "Electric and Gas Utilities" in this chapter.

American Petroleum Institute. *Basic Petroleum Data Book: Petroleum Industry Statistics.* Washington, DC (3/yr.).

Detailed statistics in 15 sections to cover: energy; crude oil reserves; exploration and drilling; production; financial; prices; demand; refining; import; export; offshore; transportation; natural gas; OPEC; miscellaneous.

The API also publishes a *Monthly Statistical Report* and *Weekly Statistical Bulletin.*

British Petroleum Co., Ltd. *BP Statistical Review of World Energy.* London (annual).

A short annual brochure (about 36 pages) giving colorful charts and worldwide statistics on oil reserves, production, consumption, prices, trade, and also brief statistics on natural gas, coal, nuclear energy, hydro-electricity, and primary energy.

The statistical half of the *Oil Economists' Handbook* (4th ed., London: Elsevier Applied Science Publisher, 1986) grew out of this statistical review and contains useful historical statistics on oil and energy. The latter half of the handbook is a dictionary of terms and a chronology of events.

Canadian Petroleum Association. *Statistical Handbook.* Calgary, Alberta, Can. 1 volume (loose-leaf with update sheets).

Canadian statistics on exploration, drilling, reserves, production, expenditures/revenue, prices, demand/consumption, refining, gas plants, pipelines, imports/exports.

DeGolyer and MacNaughton. *Twentieth Century Petroleum Statistics.* Dallas, TX (annual).

Worldwide statistics and charts, arranged by country and covering crude oil production, reserves, prices, refined products demand, refining capacity; also more detailed statistics for U.S. petroleum including wells drilled, drilling costs, natural gas.

Financial Times Oil and Gas International Year Book. Harlow, Essex, Eng.: Longman Group U.K. Ltd., and Chicago: St. James Press.

Financial details for leading oil companies of the world, including data on subsidiaries, property and exploration, production and reserves, capital, financial results. At end are some statistics; also lists of associations and brokers/traders, and geographic and company indexes.

International Energy Agency. *Oil and Gas Information.* Paris (annual).

Formerly published by the OECD as *Annual Oil and Gas Statistics,* this is a two-part statistical volume. Part 1 is an overview of world oil and gas market developments, with time series going back to the early 1970s, not only for OECD countries but also for developing countries, centrally planned and other countries. Part 2 contains OECD country-by-country tables covering a 10-year time span, for oil and gas supply and consumption, and detailed export/import figures for the past three years. For current statistics see *Quarterly Oil Statistics and Energy Balances* (Paris: OECD), published quarterly for the OECD by the International Energy Agency. For each OECD country, it gives statistics (for three years) on supply and demand, including figures for specific products such as gasoline, LPG, kerosene; detailed export/import tables are at the end.

International Petroleum Encyclopedia. Tulsa, OK: PennWell Publishing Co., 1990. 392 pp.

A useful compendium, with the major portion briefly discussing country-by-country trends and developments, occasionally with maps and other illustrations. "Special Features" appearing throughout (yellow pages) include such tables as worldwide production, consumption, refining, each table by country; and also a list of leading oil and gas companies, a directory of government agencies, and more.

NPN: National Petroleum News. Des Plaines, IL: Hunter Publishing Ltd. Partnership (monthly, with extra unnumbered issue in June).

This is a trade journal for persons interested in news and trends in the marketing and distribution of petroleum and related products. Brief statistics in each issue give average gasoline prices. The January issue has a short "outlook" article. The extra "Factbook" issue (published in June each year) contains useful statistics on capital spending, distribution, imports, international activities, prices, branded retail outlets, gasoline market share, tires/batteries/accessories (TBA) aftermarket, financial data for leading companies; also refining capacities, a directory of associations, names of marketing management personnel. The journal is indexed in BPI, PTS, TI: also full text on BRS, DATA-STAR, DIALOG, DOW JONES, MEAD/NEXIS.

Oil & Gas Journal. Tulsa, OK: PennWell Publishing Co. (weekly).

Almost every other issue of this important trade journal has a special feature article with some statistics. The "Forecast/Review" issue (last January) includes statistics on U.S. oil production, forecast of supply and demand, well forecast by state, rotary-rig activity by state; also a section on technology. The "Midyear Forecast/

Review Report" is in the last July issue. Among the other special feature articles/issues are: "Pipeline Construction Report" (mid February); "Capital Spending Report" (third February); "Annual Refining Report" (third March); "Worldwide Construction Report" (mid-April and mid-October); "Annual Production Report" (third April); "Offshore Report" (first May); "Annual Pipeline Report" (first August); "Annual Petrochemical Report" (second September); the "OGJ 300," a ranked list of the top 300 U.S. public oil and gas companies (last September); "Pipeline Economics Report" (last November); "Annual API Report" on the changing outlook for petroleum (second November); "Worldwide Report" (last December), with country-by-country statistics on estimated reserves, oil production, oil refining. Two pages of current statistics are in each issue. This journal is indexed in ASTI, BPI, PTS, TI; also full text on BRS, DATA-STAR, DIALOG, DOW JONES, MEAD/NEXIS. The special feature articles noted above, and other special features as well, are reprinted each year in an annual called *Oil & Gas Journal Data Book* (Tulsa: PennWell Books). This is a useful reference source with statistics and other tables used throughout.

Oil Economists' Handbook. By Gilbert Jenkins. 5th ed. London and New York: Elsevier Applied Science, 1989. 2 volumes.

Volume 1 contains worldwide historical "Statistics" over a long period of time, on oil and energy prices, energy reserves, production, trade, consumption, oil refining, oil production and sales, petrochemicals, oil market share; also weather analysis, shipping routes, rates, exchange rates, oil quality data and conversion factors. Most of volume 2 consists of a dictionary, but there is also a chronology of events from 1776–1988, and a directory of government organizations compiling and supplying energy and oil statistics. Volume 1 statistics grew out of British Petroleum Company's *BP Statistical Review of World Energy* cited above.

Oil Industry Outlook. By Robert J. Beck. Tulsa, OK: PennWell Books (annual).

This annual guide was developed to provide a review of recent, significant trends and an outlook for the future as an aid for those making decisions about the future of the petroleum industry. Sections cover: demand and supply (both worldwide and for the U.S.), capital expenditures, exploration/drilling/production, refining and petrochemicals, transportation, natural gas, other energy resources. The text discusses recent trends and outlook; the statistical tables, which are interspersed, are historical trends covering figures for anywhere from 5 to 20 or more years. The author is Economics Editor of *Oil & Gas Journal*.

Oilweek. Calgary, Alberta, Can.: Maclean Hunter Canadian Publishing (weekly).

Trade journal for the Canadian petroleum industry. The "Annual Review and Forecast" (third February issue) contains brief text with statistics for Canadian oil production, consumption, drilling activity, revenues and expenditures, and more. There is also a "First Quarter Review and Forecast" article (mid-April); one for the midyear (fourth July); one for the fall (fourth October); a list of the "Top 100 Oil and Gas Companies" ranked by Canadian production and reserves (mid-June issue). In each issue are current drilling statistics, a list of new locations in Canada, and well completions. Indexed in PTS, TI; full text on BRS, DATA-STAR, DIALOG, MEAD/NEXIS.

Organization of the Petroleum Exporting Countries. *Annual Statistical Bulletin.* Vienna, Austria.

A concise yet comprehensive statistical record, with some graphs, of the oil and natural gas industries in OPEC countries and the rest of the world. Contains data on exploration and reserves, production, consumption, refining, prices, export/imports, transportation (pipelines, etc.), and financial data for 7 major oil companies.

Petroleum Independent. Washington, DC: Petroleum Independent Publishers (monthly, except bimonthly in May/June and November/December).

Since this is the official publication of the Independent Petroleum Association of America, it covers articles and news of interest primarily to independent oil and gas producers. Each year the September issue is on "The Oil & Gas Producing Industry in Your State". The first part consists of two-page, state-by-state summaries. The rest gives summary statistics for: exploration, drilling, financial statistics, number of producing wells, prices, miscellaneous. Each issue contains three pages of "Trends & Statistics." Indexed in TI; also full text on BRS, DATA-STAR, DIALOG.

Pipeline & Gas Journal. Houston: Oildom Company of Texas, Inc. (monthly).

A trade journal covering "international pipeline & gas utility operations, design & maintenance." Its 1991 issues contain a "quarterly stock index" in the issues for February, May, August, and November. Its special features include: "Buyers Guide" (May issue); "P&GJ 500 Report" (September), ranking the leading U.S. companies involved in the transportation of energy through pipelines by three types of pipelines; "North American Report" (January), and "International Pipeline Report" (August). The publisher noted above took over publication in early 1991 and incorporated the journal *Pipeline*; consequently there may be changes in special features in the future. Indexed in ASTI, PTS, TI; full text on DATA-STAR, DIALOG.

Platt's Oil Price Handbook and Oilmanac. New York: McGraw-Hill (annual). Also available online as *DRI/Platt's Oil Prices.*

A complete record of prices for specific kinds of oil and gas at various locations. Includes worldwide crude and product specifications. This is compiled by Platt's Oilgram Price Report.

U.S. Energy Information Administration. *Petroleum Marketing Annual.* Washington, DC. Available also on magnetic tape.

Covers monthly figures for three years on: crude oil prices, sales prices and volume for petroleum products, first sales of petroleum products for consumption. The price and sales data, by state, is for motor gasoline, distillates, residuals, aviation fuels, kerosene, and propane. At front are summary statistics; at end is an annual report on sales of fuel oil and kerosene. For the most recent figures see their *Petroleum Marketing Monthly.*

U.S. Energy Information Administration. *Petroleum Supply Annual.* Washington, DC 2 volumes. Available also on magnetic tape.

Provides useful statistics on U.S. supply and disposition of crude oil and petroleum products, production, natural gas processing, refinery operations, exports/imports, stocks, movements (transportation). Volume 2 has final data for each month of the year replacing their *Petroleum Supply Monthly* which can be used for the most current statistics.

U.S. Energy Information Administration. *Statistics of Interstate Natural Gas Pipeline Companies.* Washington, DC (annual).

Financial and operating information on all major interstate natural gas companies operating in the United States.

World Oil. Houston, TX: Gulf Publishing Co. (monthly).

Another long-time trade journal for persons interested in gas and oil exploration, drilling, and production. Its two most useful annual features are: "Annual Forecast-Review" (February), which includes statistics on drilling, rig activity, number of U.S. producing wells, estimated reserves of crude oil, production by country, explorative and producer expenditures by company; and "International Outlook" issue (August), which discusses trends in exploration, drilling, and production by region and country. The October issue has an "Annual Reed Rig Census." Two pages of current statistics called "Industry at a Glance" are in each issue. Indexed in ASTI, BPI, TI; also full text on BRS, DATA-STAR, DIALOG, DOW JONES, MEAD/NEXIS.

PUBLISHING INDUSTRY

Book Industry Study Group. *Book Industry Trends.* New York (annual).

Chapter 2, the major portion of this annual, contains publishing data for each of 30 market segments (such as trade books, religious books, book clubs, mail order publications, professional books). For each it gives total sales, sales to wholesalers and jobbers, sales by wholesalers and jobbers, domestic sales by type of buyer (such as library, school, direct to consumer). Shorter chapters cover library acquisition data (statistics by type of library and four types of books), publishers' average unit cost, manufacturers' expenditures. The first chapter is a summary. The BISG also publishes *Trends Update,* an irregularly published newsletter with some statistics which vary from issue to issue.

Publishers Weekly. New York: Cahners Publishing Co.

The best known weekly journal for the book trade. Their "Facts & Figures for (year)" (first March issue) gives production of books by category of book, and also lists of titles that sell the most copies, also by category. Indexed in BPI, RG.

RUBBER AND SHOES

Footwear Industries of America. *Footwear Manual.* Washington, DC. (annual).

Sections in this annual cover statistics for both rubber and nonrubber footwear on: manufacturing, labor, plant openings and closings, foreign trade. Total market statistics at front include footwear retail sales. Many of the tables are taken from government statistical sources. Brief current statistics are in their quarterly *Statistical Reporter.*

FN: Footwear News. New York: Fairchild Publications (weekly).

A weekly newspaper for the shoe trade industry. Each issue has an "FN Stock Index" containing current statistics on shoe company stocks; also a short table for hide and skin prices. Indexed in TI; also full text on BRS, DATA-STAR, DIALOG, DOW JONES, MEAD/NEXIS.

International Rubber Study Group. *Rubber Statistical Bulletin.* Wembley, Eng. (monthly).

Worldwide statistics (usually production, consumption, foreign trade) for natural rubber, natural rubber latex, synthetic rubber, current rubber positions, major sectors, and end products.

Rubber & Plastics News. Akron, OH: Crain Communications Inc. (biweekly).

Billed as "the rubber industry's international newspaper," this is a biweekly for rubber products manufacturers and related products such as tires, rubber and plastic footwear. The first January issue contains a short "Review" of the previous year, and the last January has "Forecasts" for the coming year. Useful "Rubber Industry Rankings" are in the first July issue. Some issues contain an "Industry Overview" with one page of rubber and plastics statistics; frequent issues have a "Producer Price Index" table for rubber related products. In December each year there is a rubber industry directory called "Rubbicana." Indexed in PTS/PROMT; also full text on DATA-STAR and DIALOG.

Rubber Manufacturers Association. *Rubber Consumption Monthly Report.* Washington, DC. $200.

Monthly production, foreign trade, stocks, and apparent consumption for both natural and synthetic rubber. The RMA no longer publishes its *Rubber Industry Facts,* and this current report plus its *Monthly Tire Report* are probably too expensive for most libraries to have.

Rubber World. Akron, OH: Lippincott & Peto, Inc. (monthly).

The focus of this monthly has changed in recent years toward the technical services aspect of the rubber industry, and there are no special statistical issues. A short "business briefs" section in each issue often includes one short statistical table or other news about corporations. The publisher issues a separate annual "Blue Book" which contains technical information on materials, ingredients, and machinery for the rubber industry. Indexed in PTS, TI; also full text on BRS, DATA-STAR, and DIALOG.

Tire Business. Akron, OH: Crain Communications, Inc. (biweekly).

This is "the tire industry's international newspaper." Its annual "Market Data Book" (a mid-November issue) contains tire shipments for specific kinds of vehicles, top selling sizes, ranked lists of top dealerships, the world's 50 largest tire makers, largest retreaders, worldwide directory of tire manufacturers (with facts about each), most popular private brand shares, dealers' associations, and more. Other feature issues are: "Forecast" (first January); "Global Tire Report" (mid-August) which lists tire plants by region and country, and also contains the directory of worldwide tire manufacturers. Indexed in PTS/PROMT; also full text on DATA-STAR, DIALOG.

The Bureau of the Census publishes a monthly and annual *Current Industrial Report* giving production statistics for specific kinds of "Footwear" (M-31A); and annuals, "Rubber" (MA-30A), and "Rubber Mechanical Products" (MA-30C). The Economist Intelligence Unit publishes *Rubber Trends,* an expensive quarterly that reports on market developments, current position, and future prospects of the rubber industry.

TEXTILES AND APPAREL

ATI: America's Textile International. Atlanta: Billian Publishing (monthly).

This trade journal incorporates the publications *Modern Textiles, Textile Industries, Fiber World,* and *Knitting/Apparel.* Annual features include: "Hall of Fame" issue (January); "ATI's Top Ten Industry Leaders" (April); "International Buyers' Guide" (July). Each issue contains feature articles and sections covering "dyeing and finishing," "knitting/apparel", "fiber world;" also a page of "Textile Barometers," and statistics in a short section called "yarn market." Indexed in TI.

American Apparel Manufacturers Association. *Focus: An Economic Profile of the Apparel Industry.* Arlington, VA. (biennial).

Statistics collected from other sources for general economic facts, employment and earnings, apparel production and prices, corporate investment, consumer demand, imports and exports.

Cotton: World Statistics. Washington, DC: International Cotton Advisory Committee (quarterly).

Consists of world and country tables for supply and use (including production, consumption, and foreign trade). This is received with *Cotton: Review of the World Situation,* (bimonthly) which discusses recent trends and prospects.

Fairchild's Textile & Apparel Financial Directory. New York: Book Division, Fairchild Fashion Group (annual).

A financial manual which usually provides, for each leading textile and apparel company, the names of officers and directors, business activities, trademarks and/or brand names, plant locations, divisions and subsidiaries, sales and earnings, common stock equity, income account, assets and liabilities, ticker symbol, stock exchange, FAX number. A few industry statistics are at front; indexes of trademarks and of subsidiaries are at end.

Fiber Organon. New York: Fiber Economics Business (monthly).

This is the basic source for current statistics on shipments and foreign trade for both artificial and synthetic manufacturered fibers. Special statistical tables appear annually in many issues, e.g. "Capacity Utilization Review" (January), "Per Capita Consumption Review" (May), "Worldwide Manufactured Fiber Survey" (June), "Manufactured Fiber, Cotton & Wool End Use Survey" (September), "U.S. Production of Hosiery" (October), "Worldwide Natural Fiber Survey" (December). A "Worldwide Directory of Manufacturered Fiber Products," arranged by country, is in the June issue; a "Directory of American Fiber Manufacturers" appears in the November issue.

International Textile Manufacturers Federation. *International Cotton Industry Statistics.* Zurich (annual).

Consists of graphs and some statistics covering productive capacity and machinery utilization for spinning and weaving machinery, and raw materials consumption for textile-producing countries.

Kurt Salmon Association. *The KSA Perspective: Textile Profile for (year).* New York (annual).

Brief text with a "Textile Performance Profile" table giving financial statistics for 26 public textile companies, and a ranked list by sales. A similar annual is *The KSA Perspective: Apparel Profile for (year).*

National Association of Hosiery Manufacturers. *Hosiery Statistics.* Charlotte, NC. (annual).

Charts and annual tables for production and shipments by specific kinds of hosiery; also foreign trade, plants, employment, and other data.

National Cotton Council of America. *Cotton Counts Its Customers.* Memphis, TN. (annual).

A statistical report that measures the quantity of cotton and competing materials consumed in final uses in the U.S. Section I summarizes end-use consumption in 92 major product classifications; Section II is a detailed tabulation of statistical data for each end-use within the major product classifications.

The National Cotton Council also publishes an annual *Economic Outlook for U.S. Cotton* which contains an extensive statistical appendix for world and U.S. fiber data, U.S. mill consumption and capacity, cotton supply/offtake, U.S. cotton volume and value, raw cotton exports, fiber prices, cottonseed product data, production cost; also basic economic indicators of importance to the textile industry.

Textile Hi-Lights. Washington, DC: American Textile Manufacturers Institute (quarterly).

This gives statistics and charts for U.S. textile production and related data; also prices, resources, international trade.

Textile Outlook International. London: Economist Intelligence Unit (bi-monthly).

This is an expensive ($615) periodic analysis of worldwide trends in textile trade, manufacturing, and markets including upstream activities (fibers and yarns) and downstream activities (end uses, apparel, and distribution). Usually two country profiles are in each issue. The EIU is now a division of Business International.

Textile World. Chicago: Maclean Hunter Publishing Co. (monthly).

The January issue contains an outlook article; the July issue is a "Buyer's Guide." Each issue contains one page of "Activity Indicators." Indexed in ABI/I, ASTI, BPI, PTS, TI.

The Economic Research Service of the Department of Agriculture publishes a useful quarterly *Cotton and Wool Situation and Outlook Report.* The Bureau of the Census issues a number of separate reports in its *Current Industrial Reports* series that contain production statistics for specific types of apparel and textile mill products. *Textile Month,* a monthly trade journal published in the U.K., is billed as "The International Textile Journal" (Timperley, Altrincham, Cheshire, Eng.: World Textile Publications, Ltd.)

TOBACCO AND CIGARS

Cigar Association of America. *Statistical Record.* Washington, DC (looseleaf, with periodic supplements).

A comprehensive statistical volume covering U.S. cigar production and consumption, cigar leaf tobacco production, U.S. international trade, taxation, U.S. Census statistics, etc.

U.S. Agricultural Marketing Service. *Annual Report on Tobacco Statistics.* Washington, DC.

This annual report covers tobacco production, value, prices, stocks, manufactured products, tax rates, foreign trade. The Economic Research Service of the DOA publishes a quarterly *Tobacco Situation and Outlook Report* which has current statistics and trends.

TRANSPORTATION AND EQUIPMENT

See also "Aerospace Industry" and "Automobiles and Trucks" in this chapter. Books, bibliographies, financial manuals, and periodicals on traffic and transportation are described in Chapter 20.

Association of American Railroads. Economics and Finance Department. *Railroad Facts*. Washington, DC.

Handy, pocket-sized annual containing statistics on financial results, traffic, train and car miles, operating averages, plant and equipment, employment and compensation, a Railroad Cost Recovery Index, Rail Cost Adjustment Factor, fuel consumption and costs, loss, and damage.

The AAR publishes other statistics: *Analysis of Class 1 Railroads* (annual); *Railroad Revenues, Expenses and Income, Class 1 Railroads in the United States* (quarterly); *Railroad Ten-Year Trends* (annual, with volume published in 1990 covering the years 1980-1989).

British Road Federation. *Basic Road Statistics*. London (annual).

British statistics on motor vehicles, road traffic, accidents, road transport, road mileage.

Eno Foundation for Transportation. *Transportation in America: A Statistical Analysis of Transportation in the United States*. Washington, DC. (annual, with updates in July and November).

A brief statistical analysis to illustrate the importance of transportation to the United States, and to point out trends in the field. Most of the data is taken from other sources. A *Historical Compendium, 1939–1985* was published in 1989 (64 pp.).

International Road Federation. *World Road Statistics*. Lausanne, Switzerland, and Washington, DC (annual).

Country statistics for: road networks; production and export of motor vehicles; first registrations; vehicles in use; road traffic; accidents; motor fuels; road expenditures; data on taxes. The volume published in 1989 covers figures for 1984–1988.

International Road Transport Union. *World Transport Data*. Geneva (quinquennial).

This gathers together the most recent official statistics for air, rail, motor road vehicles, inland waterways, in 165 countries.

International Union of Railways. Statistics Bureau. *International Railway Statistics*. Paris (annual).

Statistical data for specific railroads of the world, including lines and tracks, rolling stock, technical operating results, financial results.

Railway Age. New York: Simmons-Boardman (monthly).

An "Outlook" article appears in the January issue, and one on "Railroads at Midyear" in June. In each issue the "Market Indicators" page contains carloading statistics, and the "Market Outlook" page has statistics on freight cars and locomotives ordered. Indexed in BPI, PAIS, PTS/F&S; full text on BRS, DATA-STAR, DIALOG, DOW JONES.

U.S. Bureau of the Census. *Census of Transportation.* Washington, DC: U.S. Government Printing Office (quinquennial, in years ending with 2 and 7).

The 1987 census consists of three parts. One is the *Geographic Area Series: Selected Transportation Establishment Industries, Summary* which gives, for each state and for some MSAs, number of establishments, revenue, payroll, employment by various transportation classifications in the following three selected industries: motor freight transportation and warehousing, water transportation, transportation services. The second is their *Truck Inventory and Use Survey,* with releases for each state and also a U.S. summary. This contains tables for number of trucks, and for truck miles, arranged by such categories as major use, body type, annual miles, range of operation, vehicle size, weight, length, products carried, engine type and size, truck type, and axle arrangement. The third part is *Subject Series: Miscellaneous Subjects* which gives statistics for states and some MSAs by revenue and employment size, and by number of establishments operated.

U.S. Department of Transportation. Research and Special Programs Administration. *National Transportation Statistics: Annual Report.* Washington, DC: U.S. Government Printing Office.

This is a selection of statistics from varied government and private sources on major modes of transportation, with data including cost, inventory and performance for both passenger and cargo operations. Supplemental statistics include data on energy in transportation, and transportation and the economy. Source information by subject and a glossary are at end.

U.S. Federal Highway Administration. *Highway Statistics.* Washington, DC: U.S. Government Printing Office (annual).

Brings together statistics in three areas of highway transportation: highway use (ownership and operating of motor vehicles); highway finance (receipts and expenditures for highways by public agencies); the highway plant (the extent, characteristics, and performance of the public highways, roads and streets in the nation). The volume covering 1990 is the latest published as of 1992.

U.S. Interstate Commerce Commission. Bureau of Accounts. *Transport Statistics in the United States.* Washington, DC. 2 parts (annual).

Formerly published in 6 parts, this now contains financial and operating data for only two modes of transportation: part 1, railroads; part 2, motor carriers. It is rather slow in being published, with 1988 data the latest as of 1991. The ICC publishes several quarterly statistical publications.

COMMODITY AND CONSUMER PRICES

Commodity Prices

Commodity prices can be found in some of the statistical volumes mentioned in this chapter. Current prices of important commodities as well as futures prices can also be found in daily newspapers. One of the best newspapers for spot and/or futures prices of important foods, grains, textiles, chemicals, metals, etc., is the *Journal of Commerce and Commercial.* See also the commodities pages in the *Wall Street Journal,* and the *Financial Times* (London). A few trade journals or newspapers quote current prices in each issue for commodities of particular interest to their industry. See, for example, *Chemical Market-*

ing Reporter for prices of many chemicals and *American Metal Market* for metals prices. Price data is also given in statistical publications of several government agencies, for example, the U.S. Bureau of Labor Statistics, *Producer Price Indexes* (monthly, with annual supplements), and the U.S. Agricultural Statistics Board, *Agricultural Prices* (monthly).

Bibliographies

Friedman, Catherine, ed. *Commodity Prices.* 2d ed. Detroit: Gale Research, Inc., 1991. 630 pp.

A source book and index providing references to wholesale, retail, and other price quotations for more than 10,000 agricultural, commercial, industrial, and consumer products. It is arranged alphabetically by specific commodity name, and it usually gives for each the price source, price frequency, effective markets, type of price, time period covered. At end is a list of almost 200 publications that regularly report prices.

Consumer Prices

Although consumer prices are an important economic indicator rather than an industrial indicator, it seems logical to discuss a few of the sources for statistics in this section on pricing. The Consumer Price Index (CPI) is one of the most commonly cited indicators of inflation. It is a monthly measure of the average change in price of a fixed list of goods and services purchased by urban families and individuals. Although the consumer price index is often called the "cost of living index," it is important to note that there is a difference, since the CPI measures only price changes and none of the other important factors affecting living costs. Users should also note that, although the CPI does include figures for 15 U.S. metro areas, these indexes do *not* measure differences in the level of prices among these several cities; they measure only the average in prices for each area as compared with base period of the index.

The principal source for the CPI is the second citation below.

American Chamber of Commerce Researchers Association. *Cost of Living Index.* Louisville, KY. (quarterly).

Here is a useful continuing source for living costs in selected U.S. cities. It consists of a comparative index for over 50 items in 6 broad categories of products and services in each of almost 300 participating U.S. urban areas. (The 6 categories are: grocery items, housing, utilities, transportation, health care, miscellaneous goods and services). Section 1, "Urban Area Index Data," gives comparative index weights for each of the 6 broad categories in each city. Section 2, "Average Prices," reports the dollar and cents average price of 27 grocery products and over 30 nonfood items in the same cities.

U.S. Bureau of Labor Statistics. *CPI Detailed Report.* Washington, DC (monthly).

This reports on changes in the Consumer Price Index, by expenditure categories, commodities, and services, for the U.S. as a whole and for 15 metro areas across the country. The expenditure categories cover: specific food and beverage items; housing (including rent, fuel and utilities); specific kinds of apparel and upkeep; transportation (including new and used automobiles); medical care; entertainment; other goods and services (tobacco and smoking products, personal care, personal and educational expenses). The extensive CPI tables are given both for "all urban consumers" (CPI-U) and for "urban wage earners and clerical workers" (CPI-W). These CPI figures are also quoted in other BLS publications such as the *Monthly Labor Review* and the historical *Handbook of Labor Statistics*.

Worldwide Cost of Living

Foreign consumer price indexes are included in the several foreign labor statistical sources mentioned in Chapter 19. Worldwide comparative cost of living figures can be found in the following:

Business International. *Executive Cost of Living Survey—BI/COL.* New York (semiannual).

For each of 111 cities in over 70 countries, these reports (usually about 8 pages in length) give costs/price information on some 160 key products and services regularly used by the international executive and his/her family. These include specific foods and beverages, household supplies, items of personal care, clothing, recreation and entertainment, transportation, housing, domestic help, hotel and restaurants prices, educational costs. Weighted indexes compare cost of living in one city with another. This is an expensive service intended primarily for large companies with executives living abroad. The reports for each city can be purchased separately, with the cost varying (from $380 to over $12,000 in 1991) depending on the number of cities purchased.

Monthly Bulletin of Statistics. New York: United Nations.

Two issues each year (usually March and September) contain a special table for "Retail Price Indexes Relating to Living Expenditures of United Nations Officials." This consists of a living-cost index by country, with New York City the base city equaling 100. It also gives exchange rates.

Union Bank of Switzerland. *Prices and Earnings Around the Globe.* Zurich (triennial).

This informative little brochure discusses and compares purchasing power in 48 cities of the world and includes tables giving comparative purchasing power and prices for food, clothing, household appliances, apartment rents, restaurants and hotels, automobile purchase prices and maintenance cost, public transportation. An appendix gives comparative earnings and working hours for 12 categories of workers.

U.S. Department of State Indexes of Living Costs Abroad, Quarters Allowances and Hardship Differentials. Washington, DC. (quarterly).

An index similar to the one above published by the UN, but using Washington, DC, as the base city equaling 100.

Purchasing Power of the Dollar

Purchasing power of the dollar is a reciprocal of the price index and can be computed either from the producer (formerly "wholesale") or the consumer price index depending upon whether one wants prices at the primary market level or the consumer level. These indexes are both compiled by the Bureau of Labor Statistics. To obtain the purchasing power figure, divide the price index number for the base period by the price index number for the date to be compared and express the result in dollars and cents. Most basic statistical sources that give CPI and PPI tables also include figures for purchasing power. See, for example, current issues of the *Monthly Labor Review* or the *Survey of Current Business;* for historical figures see the *Statistical Abstract of the United States* or *Standard and Poor's Statistical Service,* as well as the biennial supplement to the *Survey* called *Business Statistics.*

It is also possible to find purchasing power of the British pound. Current figures are in two monthly publications of Great Britain's Central Statistical Office: their *Economic Trends* and their *Monthly Digest of Statistics.* A long-term historical table is in any issue of Barclay Bank's quarterly *Barclays Economic Review.*

Inflation Rate

The inflation rate most often quoted in published sources is the % change in the Consumer Price Index (U), from year to year. This figure can be found in several current sources: in the Bureau of Labor Statistics monthly *CPI Detailed Report,* table 16 (comparing only one year from previous year); the annual *Economic Report of the President,* table B62, with figures from 1929; *Economic Indicators* of the U.S. Council of Economic Advisers, changes in CPI(U) from 1979; and the Tax Foundation's biennial *Facts and Figures on Government Finance,* table 8, figures from 1950 to date. Some international sources contain statistics. See, for example, the International Monetary Fund's annual *World Economic Outlook,* table A8, which contains inflation figures from 1970 for regions of the world and for a few countries.

7

LOCATING INFORMATION ON COMPANIES, ORGANIZATIONS, AND INDIVIDUALS

Basic U.S. Company Directories – Basic International and Foreign Directories – U.S. Regional, State, and Local Directories – Directories of Industries – Directories of Trade Names – Directories of Associations – Directories of Consultants – Directories of Foundations and Corporate Philanthropy – Directories of Government Organizations – Directories of Periodicals and Newspapers – Directories of Research Centers – Biographical Dictionaries – Guides to Directories

Directories are another important time-saving source when one seeks brief data on companies, organizations, or individuals. They are used for varied purposes: to find out who manufactures a specific product; to check companies located in a particular area; to verify company names, addresses, and telephone numbers; and to identify company officers or directors. This chapter describes a selection of basic business directories, those for specific industries or geographic locations and those covering government agencies, organizations, periodicals, and individuals. Company directories that include financial information are described in Chapter 8, as are the best known lists of largest companies. Several bibliographies of company histories and biographies of businessmen are mentioned in Chapter 9. Many other specialized directories are scattered throughout this book with other material on each subject, for example, accountants, advertising agencies, banks, brokers, department stores, franchising companies, insurance companies, investment managers, labor unions, mailing lists, market research agencies, online services, public relations firms, real estate companies, and venture capital companies. See index for page citations.

It is assumed that all directories give addresses and that most include the company's telephone number, and so these facts are usually not given with each entry in this chapter.

BASIC U.S. COMPANY DIRECTORIES

Million Dollar Directory: Leading Public and Private Companies. Parsippany, NJ: Dun & Bradstreet Information Services. 5 volumes (annual). Available also online, on CD-ROM, and selected data on magnetic tape and as mailing labels.

The first three (unnumbered) volumes contain approximately 160,000 U.S. public and private businesses with an indicated worth of over $500,000. For each firm it usually gives officers and directors, line of business, Standard Industrial Classification (SIC) code, approximate sales and number of employees, stock exchange abbreviation, stock ticker symbol, division names and functions, principal bank, accounting firms, legal counsel where available. The other two volumes are *Series Cross-Reference by Geography,* indexing the companies by location, and *Series Cross-Reference by Industry,* indexing the companies by SIC code. Published separately is a *Master Index* (paper) which indexes these and several other basic D&B directories. In addition a one-volume *Top 50,000 Companies* gives the same information but for only 50,000 companies, including the geographic and subject (SIC) indexes in the same volume.

The information from these and from other Dun's directories is also available on magnetic tape, and as mailing labels, which makes a variety of personalized services possible. For example *Dun's Market Identifiers* is a database providing up to 40 business facts or identifiers for each of over 6.7 million public and private U.S. business establishments and more than 5 million of their executives. Thus one can purchase customized directory data by geographic location, number of employees, sales volume, line of business, and much more. For further information contact D&B.

Standard & Poor's Register of Corporations, Directors and Executives. New York: Standard & Poor's Corp. 3 volumes (annual, with three cumulated supplements). Also available online and on CD-ROM.

Another basic directory, the first volume of which describes more than 55,000 U.S. and some Canadian or international companies, about 45,000 of which are private. For each it usually gives officers, line of business, SIC codes, sales range, number of employees, the company's accounting firm, primary bank and law firm, stock exchange symbol. Includes some subsidiaries listed separately from the parent company. Vol. 2 is a listing of over 70,000 executives and directors, with brief data about each. Vol. 3 contains the following indexes and lists: index of companies by SIC code; by geographic location; list of companies added for the first time; list of individuals included for the first time; corporate family indexes (cross-reference index for subsidiaries listed in vol. 1, and a listing of ultimate parent company); an obituary section.

Standard Directory of Advertisers. Wilmette, IL: National Register Publishing Co. 2 volumes (annual, and 5 cumulating supplements).

Volume 1 is a directory of more than 25,000 U.S. companies that advertise nationally, and it is arranged by 50 product classifications. For each company it usually gives year founded, phone and fax, officers, products, occasionally divisions/subsidiaries, approximate sales and number of employees, the SIC number, advertising agency (with name of account executive), advertising appropriations, media used. At front is an alphabetical index, ranked lists of top advertisers and ad agencies, a list of associations giving functions of each. Volume 2 contains an index of over 62,000 trade names, a list of companies by SIC, an index by name of individual officers. Published separately is a "Geographic Index" of the companies.

Two companion volumes are described elsewhere in this book: *Standard Directory of International Advertisers & Agencies* and *Standard Directory of Advertising Agencies*.

The "100 Leading National Advertisers" issue of *Advertising Age* (last September issue) contains profiles of the 100 leaders, which include facts and figures about the marketing operation of each company, how their leading product lines and brands rank nationally, what share of market they hold, advertising expenditures by media, the names of marketing personnel and advertising agency account executives, both for parent company and for principal divisions.

Thomas Register of American Manufacturers. New York: Thomas Publishing Co. 26 volumes (annual). Available also online and on CD-ROM.

If you need to find the name of a U.S. manufacturing firm or want to know who makes a specific product, this is the best place to look after an unsuccessful check of the first two directories above. Vols. 1–16 list over 145,000 U.S. manufacturers by specific product or service, with a product index in vol. 16; vols. 17–18 contain the list of companies arranged alphabetically usually giving, for each, the address, phone/fax/telex/twx (when available), branch offices, subsidiaries, products, asset ratings, and occasionally, principal officers. An "American Trademark Index" (yellow pages) is at back of vol. 18. Vols. 19–26 are the "Catalogs File," useful for their descriptions of products made by nearly 2,000 of these companies. Vol. 26 includes an "Inbound Traffic Guide," a handbook of intermodal facilities and services.

U.S. Industrial Directory. Stamford, CT: Cahners Publications. 3 volumes (annual).

This gives information similar to that in *Thomas* above but is not as comprehensive. Vol. 1 contains a telephone/address section which is an alphabetical list of some 52,000 industrial suppliers usually giving for each: address, phone, product. There is also a "Literature Section" describing suppliers' catalogs, brochures, and related literature. Vols. 2-3 are a listing by individual products.

Ward's Business Directory of U.S. Private and Public Companies. Detroit: Gale Research, Inc. 5 volumes (annual). Costs $1,150 in 1992 ($675 for vol. 5 only). Also available online and on CD-ROM.

Volumes 1–3 contain data on more than 130,000 private and public companies, including for each, when available: year founded, description of products/services offered, approximate sales, number of employees, SIC codes, one or more officers, fax number, stock exchange, ticker symbol, whether private, public, or a subsidiary. Volume 4 lists the companies by location (zip code), but it gives less information about each. This fourth volume also contains ranked lists of the 1,000 largest privately held companies, the largest public companies, the largest employers, and an analysis by revenue per employee of the nation's top firms. Volume 5 is especially useful for its ranked list (by sales) of the companies within each four-digit SIC category.

Probably the most comprehensive list of U.S. business enterprises is *Dun's Business Identification Service*. This consists of a set of microfiche cards, revised twice a year, and containing, for about 12,500,000 businesses (including 650,000 in Canada and 2 million elsewhere in the world, either set of which can be purchased separately), the address and branch locations. This is not found in many libraries because the cost for commercial firms is so high ($1,095 in 1991, just for the domestic microfiches); yet it is a useful source for locating headquarters and branches of companies. Another comprehensive list of U.S. and Canadian business firms, arranged geographically, is the four-volume, bimonthly *Reference Book* compiled by Dun & Bradstreet for customers of its *Business Information Reports,* a longtime, highly regarded credit rating service. This is not available to libraries, but persons employed by companies or organizations that are subscribers will find the *Reference Book* a very detailed listing of firms, by state and then by city, and giving for each the SIC number, an abbreviation for line of business, a code for estimated financial strength and for composite credit appraisal. The list for Canada is in the back of vol. 4. Since there is no index, one must know the city where each firm is located to use this publication.

"Who Owns Whom" Directories

This type of directory is useful for finding the relationships of companies. They are usually arranged in two or more parts, with one listing parent companies and giving names of their subsidiaries/divisions/affiliates, and the other an index arranged by subsidiary.

America's Corporate Families. Parsippany, NJ: Dun & Bradstreet Information Services. 2 volumes (annual).

The first volume of this directory gives details about approximately 11,000 U.S. "ultimate parent companies," with over 55,000 of their divisions and subsidiaries. The data for each parent company is similar to that in Dun's *Million Dollar Directory,* and it also gives telex and twx; lesser information about each subsidiary usually includes line of business, SIC number, approximate sales, number of employees, names of chief executives. Three indexes are by SIC, geographic location, cross-references. Volume 2 is *America's Corporate Families and International Affiliates.* This has two parts: a list of about 11,000 Canadian and foreign subsidiaries of some 1,500 U.S. parent companies; and 6,500 U.S. subsidiaries of over 2,400 foreign and Canadian parents.

Directory of Corporate Affiliations. Wilmette, IL: National Register Publishing Co. 2 volumes (annual, with bimonthly supplements). Online counterpart is *Corporate Affiliations;* also available on CD-ROM.

Volume 1 lists nearly 5,000 major American parent companies with over 50,000 subsidiaries, divisions or affiliates. For each parent it usually gives: year founded, line of business, SIC, phone/telex/fax, approximate assets, earnings, liabilities, net worth, number of employees, top officers and directors, stock exchange, ticker symbol, subsidiaries, divisions, and/or major affiliates. At front is an alphabetical cross reference index, and a list of mergers, acquisitions, and names changes. Volume 2 contains the indexes: by SIC, by geographic location, by individual officer, by specific job junctions. A short periodical supplement is called *Corporate Action.*

A companion volume is *International Directory of Corporate Affiliations* (annual; also available on CD-ROM). Its three sections consist of: an alphabetical cross-reference index; key details on approximately 1,750 major foreign parent companies, and their 40,000 U.S. and foreign holdings; a list of U.S. parent companies with their foreign interests. Volume 2 contains the indexes: by SIC, by geographic location, by trade names, by individual officer. At front of volume 1 are lists of foreign consulates, U.S. embassies, chambers of commerce, major international holidays,. foreign currency exchange, and a list of mergers, acquisitions, and name changes.

Who Owns Whom: North America. High Wycombe, Bucks, Eng.: Dun & Bradstreet, Ltd. (annual). Also available online.

Sections 1–2 are directories of U.S. and Canadian parent companies listing their subsidiaries and associate companies outside the United States (or Canada). Section 3 is a directory of foreign parent companies listing their subsidiaries in the U.S. and Canada. It contains only the address and phone number for each parent company. Includes a detailed index for subsidiaries and associates.

Companion volumes for Australasia and Far East, Continental Europe, and the United Kingdom and Ireland are noted below.

Other Lists of Companies

Exporting and importing companies are described in the "Directories" section of Chapter 16. Check in the index for reference to other more specialized directories such as those for accounting firms, advertising agencies, banks, brokers, department stores, franchising companies, health care companies, insurance companies, investment managers, labor unions, mailing lists, market research agencies, online services, public relations firms, real estate companies, venture capital companies.

Directory of American Firms Operating in Foreign Countries. 12th ed. New York: World Trade Academy Press, 1991. 3 volumes.

Just newly revised again, this is a useful directory of some 2,600 American companies with 19,000 subsidiaries and affiliates in 127 foreign countries. Vol. 1 is an alphabetical list of these companies, giving address, occasionally fax number, president or CEO, foreign operations officer and personnel director (when available), products or services, number of employees, foreign countries of operation. Vols. 2–3 list these companies by country, with local address and principal products.

A companion volume is the *Directory of Foreign Firms Operating in the United States* (6th ed., 1989, 680 pp.) in three parts: a list of 1600 foreign firms (with 2,500 American affiliates), arranged by country; an alphabetical list of foreign parent companies with the name of the corresponding American subsidiary; an alphabetical list of American subsidiaries, branches, and affiliates. To be useful, these must be revised frequently.

Directory of Foreign Manufacturers in the United States. By Jeffery S. Arpan and David A. Ricks. 4th ed. comp. by Virginia M. Mason. Atlanta: Georgia State University Business Press, 1990. 437 pp.

For each of approximately 6,000 foreign manufacturers in the U.S., this gives name of parent company, product made, and SIC number. Indexes are for: U.S. companies by state; parent companies; parent companies by country; companies by SIC products.

Directory of Leading Private Companies, Including Corporate Affiliations. Wilmette, IL: National Register Publishing Company (annual).

This is a directory of approximately 7,000 private parent companies in the U.S. and their 15,000 divisions or subsidiaries. Information about each parent usually includes, when available: description of the business, when founded, fax, assets, liabilities, net worth, sales range, number of employees, SIC codes, officers, number of manufacturing facilities, number of U.S. offices, computer system/hardware used, outside service firms, divisions and subsidiaries. There are four indexes: alphabetical (including subsidiaries); by SIC code; by geographic area; an index of officers by function/responsibility.

Dun's Directory of Service Companies. Parsippany, NJ: Dun & Bradstreet Information Services (annual).

A new (as of 1989) companion volume to the *Million Dollar Directory,* this one covers approximately 50,000 of the largest U.S. service companies (both public and private), including those that are hotels and other lodgings, personal services, auto repair, motion pictures, amusement/recreation, health, legal, social services. Most of these service companies are NOT also in the *MDD.* The arrangement is similar and so is the information usually given about each company; also there are geographic and SIC indexes.

Dun's Industrial Guide: The Metalworking Directory. Parsippany, NJ: Dun & Bradstreet Information Services. 3 volumes.

A comprehensive yet specialized directory covering some 71,000 U.S. plants and distributors in the metalworking field, including those manufacturing companies classified in SIC numbers 24–25, 33–39, and wholesalers in SIC 50. It is especially useful for details on specific plant operations since the listing (in volume 1) is arranged by geographic location. Data given for each plant includes principal manufacturing processes performed, principal products purchased and forms in which purchased, key executive in charge of general plant management, production, engineering, purchasing (when available). Slight varying data is given for metals distributors. Volume 2 contains indexes, by 4-digit SIC industries (yellow pages) and alphabetically by plant (blue pages). Volume 3, "Statistical Summary," tabulates the number of plants by employee size categories, by 4-digit SIC on a national level (grey pages), by each state (yellow pages), and by county (white pages).

Everybody's Business. Ed. by Milton Moskowitz et al. New York: Doubleday Currency, 1990. 732 pp. paper.

Subtitled "a field guide to the 400 leading companies in America," this is more than a simple directory. Rather it is a compilation of interesting company profiles, each of from two-to-three pages in length. They are written to provide a nontechnical picture of the company and whether or not it would be a good place to work. Besides assessing it for employment, each profile usually consists of a history of products/services, a few statistics, brief facts about top managers, names of brands and services, whether it has demonstrated social concerns, its stock performance, global presence, rankings within the industry. Scattered throughout are ranked lists of the top 10 in a wide variety of categories. This interesting compilation is arranged by industry, with a company index at end. It should be revised more frequently than in the past if it is to continue its usefulness.

Marketing Economics Institute. *Marketing Economics Key Plants.* Jamacia Estates, NY. 2 volumes (annual).

A directory of 40,000 plants with 100 or more employees. One volume is a geographic listing by state and county; within each county the plants are arranged by SIC number. The other volume lists these same companies by SIC and, within each industry, by state and county. Since this lists plants rather than just companies it is a potentially useful marketing tool. The data given is only address, phone, SIC code, employment range.

National Fax Directory. Detroit: Gale Research Inc. for General Information, Inc. (annual).

For persons who need a fax number and cannot find it in one of the general directories described in this chapter, here is a directory providing both alphabetical and subject access to major fax users in the U.S. The alphabetical section gives address, voice phone number, as well as the fax number. The subject section arranges the listing of companies into 150 subject headings.

Several good lists of largest companies, ranked either by sales or by assets, are described in two sections of Chapter 8, one describing those that rank U.S. companies and the other, largest foreign companies. Although of real interest and value for comparative company information these are technically not directories since they generally do not give addresses.

BASIC INTERNATIONAL AND FOREIGN DIRECTORIES

Major Companies of Europe. London: Graham & Trotman. 3 volumes (annual). Distributed in the U.S. by Gale Research, Inc.

This directory contains the following data on more than 7,000 Western European companies and subsidiaries in the Continental EEC (vol. 1), in the United Kingdom (vol. 2), and in Western Europe outside the EEC (vol. 3): officers, principal activities, subsidiaries, telex and fax, a few financial figures, number of employees, principal banks, contact information. Volumes 1 and 3 are arranged by country, and each volume contains three indexes. A companion three-volume set covers *Medium Companies of Europe*. These directories are useful but quite expensive: the first set cost $1,250 in 1991 and the second, $1,080. Volumes can be purchased separately.

Marconi's International Register. Larchmont, NY: Telegraphic Cable & Radio Registrations (annual).

Of possible use for persons who need the postal address, cable address, telex, answer back code, fax numbers, or telephone number of the principal firms of the world that have international contacts. This alphabetical list also briefly states the nature of each business. In the back are: an international trade index, listing companies by industry and then by country; a list of attorneys by specialty and country; a cable address index. Telex, fax, and cable address can sometimes be found in other directories.

Principal International Businesses. New York: Dun & Bradstreet Information Services (annual). Available also on magnetic tape.

Probably the most comprehensive foreign directory, section 1 lists approximately 55,000 leading companies, arranged alphabetically by 143 countries. For each it notes chief officer, line of business, cable/telex, SIC number, year founded, approximate sales and number of employees, whether company exports or imports, and whether it is a subsidiary. Sections 2 and 3 are indexed by SIC (yellow pages) and by company (blue).

D&B and its international affiliates publish many other directories of key businesses or the largest companies in specific countries, such as Austria, Canada, Italy. These are listed at the front of this international directory. Contact D&B for more information about their foreign regional directories.

Standard Directory of International Advertisers & Agencies. Wilmette, IL: National Register Publishing Co. (annual).

This is the international counterpart of two directories that give information on U.S. advertisers and agencies. For each foreign advertiser this provides (when available) address, telephone/telex/fax, officers, type of business, SIC numbers, approximate sales and number of employees, subsidiaries, advertising agency, advertising appropriations (in some cases), media used. For each foreign agency it usually includes address, telephone/telex/fax, officers, specialization, branch offices, account executives, sometimes names of clients, approximate annual billings. These two sections are arranged alphabetically, with geographic and subject (SIC) indexes. There is also an index of trade names, lists of consulates, U.S. embassies, international associations, chambers of commerce, mergers/acquisitions/name changes. The U.S. companion volumes are *Standard Directory of Advertisers* and *Standard Directory of Advertising Agencies.*

Who Owns Whom: Continental Europe. High Wycombe, Bucks, Eng.: Dun & Bradstreet Ltd. 2 volumes (annual). Available also online.

Vol. 1 is in two parts, with the first part a list of parent companies arranged by European country and including the names of subsidiaries and associates for each. The second part is a list of foreign parent companies, with continental subsidiaries and associates. Vol. 2 contains the alphabetical index.

Companion volumes cover: Australasia and Far East; North America; United Kingdom and Republic of Ireland. These are also included in the online database.

Dun & Bradstreet publishes several regional directories in connection with their international credit rating service. Two of these are *International Market Guide–Continental Europe* (annual, with two intervening supplements) and *International Market Guide–Latin America* (semiannual). There are also similar reference books for a few specific countries, e.g. Argentina, Canada. These directories list firms by geographic location and give for each a trade classification code as well as financial strength and a composite credit appraisal. Contact D&B for more information since these are available only to subscribers of their credit rating service.

In addition D&B publishes several database directories of foreign companies similar to their domestic *Dun's Market Identifiers.* One is *Canadian Dun's Market Identifiers* providing 23 directory-type facts for some 350,000 public and private Canadian companies. The other two are: *European Dun's Market Identifiers,* covering 1.8 million companies in more than 25 European countries, and *International Dun's Market Identifiers,* a file of facts about 2.2 million international companies from 150 countries. Contact D&B for more information about accessing these directories.

Canadian Directories

See also *Who Owns Whom: North American Edition* and *Standard & Poor's Register* in first section of this chapter.

Canadian Trade Index. Toronto: Canadian Manufacturers' Association. 2 volumes (annual).

Volume 2 contains an alphabetical list of over 16,500 Canadian manufacturing companies (green pages), usually giving for each the principal products manufactured, officers, phone/fax numbers, branch offices or plants, a code for sales and company size ranges, sometimes telex. That volume also lists the companies by geographic location (yellow pages) and it has a classified list of products distributed in Canada. Volume 1 consists of a classified list of products manufactured in Canada, and a list of trade marks, trade names or brands (yellow pages).

Dun and Bradstreet Canada, Ltd. *Canadian Key Business Directory.* Mississauga, Ontario, Can. (annual). Available in the U.S. from D&B.

Covers over 20,000 Canadian businesses, and for each it usually gives top officers, line of business, SIC, sales range, number of employees. There are geographic and 4-digit SIC industry indexes. This data is also available on magnetic tape, diskettes, and as mailing labels.

D&B's *Canadian Dun's Business Identification Service* is a microfiche service giving brief data on more than 650,000 Canadian establishments.

National List of Advertisers. Toronto: Maclean Hunter Canadian Publishing. (annual).

Section 1 contains the top national advertisers in Canadian media, showing personnel (often including marketing and sales executives), products, advertising agency (with account director), approximate budget appropriation, and media used. This is followed by sections covering: a brand name index; a list of Canadian advertising agencies with accounts handled; a category index; a direct marketing/advertising services directory.

British Directories

Britain's Privately Owned Companies. Bristol, Eng.: Jordan & Sons. 2 volumes (annual).

Volume 1 ranks "The Top 2,000" private companies by sales turnover, and also includes other financial statistics for each company. Volume 2 ranks "The Second 2,000." At front of each volume are 12 comparison tables for the top 20 companies.

Dun & Bradstreet, Ltd. *Key British Enterprises.* London. 2 volumes (annual).

This is a guide to some 50,000 leading British-based companies. For each it usually gives the nature of business, reference to parent company, location of branches, sales turnover range, number of employees, telex, trade names, capital or sales turnover range, names of officers. Includes an index of companies by SIC code, a list of products and services, a geographic index of companies listed by trade.

Dun & Bradstreet (Australia) Pty, Ltd., publishes *The Australian Key Business Directory,* (annual, 2 volumes) containing some 18,000 public and private businesses.

The Hambro Corporate Register. London: Hemmington Scott Publishing Ltd. (semiannual).

Billed as "the Who's Who of Corporate Britain," this is a two-part directory. The first half gives corporate details for 2,000 of Britain's quoted companies including, for each, names of directors, directors' pay, number of employees and employee pay. The last half is a directory of some 16,000 officers, directors, and advisers including brief biographical facts. At end are lists of various kinds of professional advisers such as auditors and lawyers, noting the clients of each.

United Kingdom Kompass Register. East Grinstead, West Sussex, Eng.: Reed Information Services Ltd. 3 volumes (annual). Also available online and on CD-ROM.

Volume 2, "Company Information," is a geographic directory of British companies, usually giving for each the nature of the business, officers, annual turnover and company registration number, number of employees, telex and fax numbers, office hours, trade names, sales office, year established. It also has an alphabetic index, and a list of trade names. Volume 1 is a classified list of specific "Products and Services"; volume 3, "Financial Data," is an alphabetical list of some 30,000 companies, giving dates of incorporation, brief financial statistics, and whether part of another company. This annual is published in association with the Confederation of British Industry.

Who Owns Whom: United Kingdom & Republic of Ireland. High Wycombe, Bucks, Eng.: Dun & Bradstreet Ltd. 2 volumes (annual). Also available online.

Vol. 1 has separate lists of U.K. and Irish parent companies, foreign parent (with related company in the U.K.) and consortia companies, showing subsidiaries for each. Vol. 2 is the index of subsidiaries and associate companies listed in vol. 1.

Directories of Other Foreign Companies

Directories are published for almost every country of any importance. Several firms publish more than just one directory. For example, there are Kompass directories for about 42 countries, each following the same format but written in the language of the country. Dun & Bradstreet publishes directories of key businesses in specific European countries and a few other countries such as Australia and Israel. There are many, many other directories; most can be located by referring to one of the "Guides to Directories" described at the end of this chapter. Several examples of country directories are:

Dun's Latin America's Top 25,000. Parsippany, NJ: Dun & Bradstreet Information Services (annual).

Japan Trade Directory. Tokyo: Japan External Trade Organization (annual).

Kompass Deutschland: Register of Selected German Industry and Commerce. Freiberg im Breisgau: Kompass Deutschland Verlag-u. Vertriebsgesellschaft mbH. 3 volumes (annual). All of the Kompass directories for European countries are also available online and on CD-ROM.

Major Companies of the Arab World. London: Graham & Trotman (annual). Distributed in U.S. by Gale Research, Inc.

Swedish Export Directory. Stockholm: Swedish Trade Council (annual).

U.S. REGIONAL, STATE, AND LOCAL DIRECTORIES

There are directories of manufacturing companies for every state. Most of them are arranged by geographic location (giving top officers, SIC number, products, number of employees), and they usually have both alphabetical and product indexes. A complete list of these is included in several of the "Guides to Directories" at the end of this chapter. They are published by a variety of organizations as is shown by the several examples below:

California Manufacturers Register. Sponsored by the California Manufacturers Association. Newport Beach, CA: DPC Database Publishing Co. (annual).

Classified Directory of Wisconsin Manufacturers. Madison, WI: WMC Service Corp. (annual).

Directory of New England Manufacturers. Boston: G.D. Hall (annual).

Directory of Texas Manufacturers. Austin: Bureau of Business Research, University of Texas at Austin. 2 volumes (annual).

MacRae's State Industrial Directory: Pennsylvania. New York: MacRae's Blue Book, Inc. (annual).

MacRae's Blue Book Inc. publishes directories similar to the Pennsylvania directory above for many states. Another firm, Manufacturers' News, Inc. (Evanston, IL), offers a service which makes available for purchase any or all of the state, regional, and a few county directories published by a variety of publishers. They also have an "On-Line Directory System" service. Of course you can also purchase directories from the individual publisher.

Directories for Local Areas

(1) Chamber of Commerce Publications

The chambers of commerce in a number of cities publish periodic lists of the industrial firms in their metropolitan areas. Two examples are: the annual *Business Firms Directory* of the Greater Philadelphia Chamber of Commerce; and *St. Louis Commerce,* "RCGA Roster" Issue (published as the April issue each year by the St. Louis Regional Commerce & Growth Association).

(2) City Directories

City directories are useful for checking names, addresses, and telephone numbers of residents and business firms. The *Minneapolis City Directory* is typical of some 1,400 city or suburban directories published periodically by R. L. Polk & Company. It is arranged in four parts: a buyers guide and classified subject directory; an alphabetical list of the names of residents (with occupations and marital status) and names of businesses (giving the nature of the business and chief officers); a directory of householders and businesses arranged by the name of the street or avenue; a numerical telephone directory. Public libraries in major cities may have a selection of these city directories in their business reference collection; not all of the directories are up to date.

(3) Telephone Directories

The classified sections of telephone directories are useful for identifying local firms in any industry, and the alphabetical sections for checking name, address, or telephone number. Most public libraries have a selection of telephone books for the region; many large libraries have a good collection covering all important U.S. and some foreign cities.

DIRECTORIES OF INDUSTRIES

Directories for many industries are published by either a trade association or a commercial publisher. These usually include names of officers and products;

some also give data such as subsidiaries, capacity, or trade names. For a complete list arranged by industry, consult the "Guides to Directories" at the end of this chapter. Several examples of trade directories for U.S. and Canadian companies are:

American Electronics Association. *Directory.* Santa Clara, CA (annual).

This is a directory of over 3,500 AEA member-firms, with geographic and product indexes. For each company it gives officers, products, when established, number of employees, stock exchange and ticker symbol (if public), other manufacturing or sales sites, fax/telex/twx. At end is a separate listing of associate members such as banks, accounting and law firms. At front are lists of local AEA council members.

Association of Iron and Steel Engineers. *Directory: Iron and Steel Plants.* Pittsburgh, PA. (annual).

Covers both U.S. and Canadian integrated and specialty steel producers, nonferrous specialty producers, selected foreign steel producers, suppliers, and major associations. Data for each company usually includes personnel, products, equipment, annual capacity, number of employees, railroad and shipping facilities. Each section has its own geographic index.

Corporate Technology Directory. Woburn, MA: Corporate Technology Information Services. 4 volumes (annual).

Volumes 2–4 of this directory cover data on over 35,000 U.S. companies that manufacture or develop high technology products, including operating units of larger corporations. The information given for each usually includes when the company was established, line of business, phone/telex/fax, sales range, number of employees, top executives, whether private or public, or minority owned, SIC numbers, ticker symbol (if public). Volume 1 contains the indexes: business indexes (by company name, by geographic location, by non-U.S. parent company) and product indexes (by product or technology, by "who makes what" which is the Corp Tech Code Index).

Davison's Textile Blue Book. Ridgewood, NJ: Davison Publishing Co. (annual).

A geographic list of U.S. and Canadian mills, dyers, finishers, with separate lists for converters, types of yarn dealers, cotton merchants and agents, brokers, dealers of specific kinds of textiles, testing and research laboratories, schools, designers, associations. For each company this usually gives officers, manufacturing and equipment data, phone/fax/telex or twx. At end is an advertisers buyers' guide.

Lockwood-Post's Directory of the Pulp, Paper and Allied Trades. San Francisco: Miller Freeman Publications (annual).

A directory of U.S. and Canadian pulp and paper manufacturing and converting industries, paper and paper products, paper merchants and distributors, paper stock buyers and sellers, and mill equipment and supplies sources. For each company it usually gives officers, products, paper mill stock preparation, steam/power, water treatment, telephone/fax/telex. Includes also lists of mill officials, rag and paper stock users, watermarks and brands, trade associations, and more. A buyers' guide is at end.

Thomas Grocery Register. New York: Thomas Publishing Co. 3 volumes (annual).

For both the U.S. and Canada, this covers manufacturers and processors of food, nonfood products, equipment, supplies, and industry-related machinery, importers, and services. Vol. 2 is arranged by specific products and services, and under each product, alphabetically by state and city. Vol. 3 is a listing by company for over 60,000 firms, usually giving address, phone/telex or twx, type of business, asset category, whether firm is a subsidiary. Lists of brand names and trade associations appears in this volume. Vol. 1 covers "sales and distribution services" and includes names of supermarket chains, convenience stores, wholesalers and distributors, institutional/food service users, brokers, manufacturers agents, exporters, warehouses.

Some trade journals publish annual "Buyers' Guide" issues, usually just giving names and addresses of companies. Two examples are:

Chemical Week. "Buyers' Guide" issue. Published in October.

Textile World. "Buyer's Guide for Machinery, Equipment & Supplies." Published as July issue.

DIRECTORIES OF TRADE NAMES

Trade names and brand names are given in a number of the directories above, with an especially long list in *Thomas Register of American Manufacturers.* There is also a separate guide to consumer brand names:

Brands and Their Companies. Detroit: Gale Research, Inc. 2 volumes, and an interim supplement. (annual). Available also online.

This is a guide to over 230,000 consumer brand names, with the yellow pages in volume 2 consisting of a list of about 43,000 companies that manufacture or import the brands. Gale publishes a companion set called *Companies and Their Brands* (2 volumes, annual) which is a directory of the companies giving brands and trade names of each.

Kompass publishes a biennial directory of *U.K. Trade Names* (East Grinstead, West Sussex, Eng.).

DIRECTORIES OF ASSOCIATIONS

Since trade associations are such valuable sources for statistics and other information about industries it is especially important to have access to a good, up-to-date directory.

Encyclopedia of Associations. Detroit: Gale Research, Inc. 3 volumes in 5. (annual). Also available online, and on CD-ROM.

Volume 1 (in three parts) is the most essential of these 5 volumes, since it is a comprehensive list of 22,000 national and international nonprofit organizations headquartered in the U.S. These are arranged in the following broad categories: trade, business and commercial; agricultural and commodity exchanges; legal, governmental, public administration and military; scientific, engineering and technical; educational; cultural; social welfare; health and medical; public affairs; fraternal, foreign interest, nationality and ethnic; religious; veterans', hereditary and patriotic; hobby and avocational; athletic and sports; labor unions, associations and federations; chambers of commerce, and trade and tourism; Greek and non-Greek letter societies, associations, and federations; fan clubs. For each association this directory usually provides year founded, name of chief officer, brief statement of activities, number of members, publications, computerized services offered, tele-communications services (fax, telex, electronic mail, etc.), approximate annual bud-get, dates of meetings. Part 3 of volume 1 is a "name and key word index." The other volumes are: vol. 2, "Geographic and Executive Indexes" to volume 1; vol. 3, "Supplement," containing descriptions of new associations.

Two companion publications are: *Regional, State, and Local Organizations* (5 volumes, annual) which is a guide to more than 47,000 regional associations, ar-ranged by five broad U.S. geographic regions; *International Organizations* (2 vol-umes, and supplement; annual) which describes more than 9,700 international non-profit organizations based outside the U.S.

It should be noted here that some of the addresses for associations that appear throughout the latter part of my book are taken, with permission, from volume 1 of this useful directory.

National Trade and Professional Associations of the United States. Washing-ton, DC: Columbia Books, Inc. (annual).

An alphabetical list of more than 6,400 national trade associations, labor unions, professional/scientific/technical societies, and other national organizations. For each it gives chief officer, approximate number of members, annual budget, historical note, names of publications, date of annual meeting. Five indexes are at end: subject, geographic, budget size, name of top officer, acronym. A companion an-nual is *Major State and Regional Associations of the United States*, giving similar information on over 5,000 selected regional associations.

Two other directories covering organizations and agencies as well as some associations are:

Business Organizations, Agencies, and Publications Directory. 5th ed. Detroit: Gale Research, Inc., 1990. 1,231 pp.

Here is a descriptive directory that covers much more than just the major trade and business organizations, but we include it here as a directory that may be found in smaller libraries which do not have separate directories for each of the organiza-tional types it covers. These are: U.S. and international organizations (associations, labor unions, commodity and stock exchanges, chambers of commerce, better busi-ness bureaus), government agencies and programs (including diplomatic offices in the U.S. and abroad, regional planning and development agencies as well as federal and state agencies), facilities and services (franchise companies, hotel-motel sys-tems, conference and convention centers, visitors bureaus, world trade centers, foreign trade zones, trade shows, awards/honors/prizes, banks, S&Ls), research and educational facilities (including graduate schools of business, research establish-ments and centers), publications and information services (publishers, directories, periodicals, newspapers, news syndicates, computer-readable databases, informa-tion-on-demand, business libraries and information centers). At the front it cites the various Gale and other directories from which this material was selected. A master name and keyword index is at end.

Yearbook of International Organizations, Vol. 1: Organization Descriptions and Index. Munich & New York: Published for the Union of International Associations by K.G. Saur. Also available on CD-ROM.

An excellent, comprehensive directory of over 27,000 international organizations of all types, usually giving for each: year founded, aim, structure, top officer, con-sultative status, activities, events, publications, countries in which there are members. It is arranged in 13 sections with a detailed index at front containing organization names (in all working languages), subject keywords, initials. There are two other volumes which are less essential to have: vol. 2 is a geographical volume, and vol. 3, a subject volume.

Regional Association Directories

Directory of Associations in Canada. Toronto: Micromedia (annual).

An alphabetical list, noting address and chief officer, with a subject index.

Directory of European Industrial & Trade Associations. 5th ed. Beckenham, Kent, Eng.: CBD Research Ltd., 1991. 418 pp. (Distributed in the U.S. by Gale Research Inc., Detroit, MI.)

This directory of European associations (excluding Great Britain and the Irish Republic) is arranged alphabetically, with a subject index, and an abbreviations index at end. Information for each association varies, but often includes year founded, subject area, number of members, conferences, publications, telephone/fax/telex, any former names.

A companion volume is *Directory of British Associations & Associations in Ireland* (biennial), covering about 7,000 national associations including trade unions and chambers of commerce. Another directory is *Pan-European Associations* (2d ed., 1992. 207 pp.) covering nearly 2,000 multinational organizations in both Eastern and Western Europe.

DIRECTORIES OF CONSULTANTS

ACME, Inc. *Directory of Members.* New York (annual).

A short directory of about 50 members of this association of management consulting firms, with a one-page description of the services offered by each. ACME (formerly the Association of Consulting Management Engineers) also publishes a useful *Management Consulting: ACME Annotated Bibliography of Selected Resource Materials,* with 1988 the latest edition published as of 1991. It covers books, articles, dissertations.

Consultants & Consulting Organizations Directory. Detroit: Gale Research Inc. 2 volumes (annual). Also available online.

This is a comprehensive directory of more than 17,000 U.S. and Canadian consulting firms and independent consultants which offer all types of consultation to business, industry, and government. Volume 1 arranges the descriptive listings into 14 broad subject sections such as "business and finance," "management," "marketing and sales." For each firm it usually gives: principal officers, number of staff, when founded, branch offices, type of service offered, and, when applicable, recent publications, seminars and workshops, computer and special services, telecommunication access. Volume 2 contains four indexes: geographic, by consulting activities, personal name, firm name. The supplement is called *New Consultants.*

Beginning in 1992, Gale is publishing a new European counterpart titled *European Consultants Directory.* It will describe more than 7,000 consulting firms, with the arrangement by over 30 European countries and then by broad subject categories.

The Directory of Management Consultants. 3d ed. Fitzwilliam, NH: Kennedy Publications (biennial).

For persons interested in information about management consultants only, this is probably the best and most convenient directory to use. For each of some 1,300 firms, it describes types of services offered, tells when founded, key officers, number of staff, branches, revenue range, geographical area served. There are indexes by type of service, industries served, geographic location, key person. At front are tips for clients and reviews of selected management consulting books, taken from the publisher's monthly *Consultants News*.

This publisher offers three other useful directories: *The Directory of Executive Recruiters* (annual), which describes over 2,100 executive recruiting firms in the U.S., Canada, and Mexico and for each usually includes functions/industries covered, minimum salary considered, and key contact; *The Directory of Outplacement Firms* (6th ed., 1990, 432 pp.), a descriptive list both of firms offering corporation-sponsored outplacement only and those that also offer services to individuals. At end of both of these directories is an annotated list of "the best books" on job changing.

Dun's Consultants Directory. Parsippany, NJ: Dun & Bradstreet Information Services (annual).

An alternative to the second directory above by Gale, this one identifies 25,000 commercial consulting firms. For each firm it usually provides address, phone number, year started, short business description, other locations (where applicable), officer/directors, approximate sales, and number of employees. Indexes are by geographical location (yellow pages), subject specialty (blue pages), and location of consultant branch offices (green pages).

Institute of Management Consultants. *Directory of Members.* New York (annual).

This is a directory of individuals who are IMC members, giving for each the address and area of expertise; also a separate list of associate members with address only. Includes indexes by geographic location and specialty.

The *Directory of Management Consultants in the U.K.* (5th ed., London: TFPL Publishing, 1988, 406 pp.), provides pertinent data about some 800 firms operating in the U.K.

DIRECTORIES OF FOUNDATIONS AND CORPORATE PHILANTHROPY

Corporate 500: The Directory of Corporate Philanthropy. San Francisco: Public Management Institute (annual, with supplement).

Profiles of companies that have corporate contribution programs of at least $500,000. Each usually includes a business profile, eligibility, analysis of funding policies, contributions profile, application process, list of sample grants, contact person. This is a large volume, with over 500 pages just for many indexes, including those by funding area, principal business, geographic areas of giving, contact person, grant recipients by state.

Foundation Directory. New York: Foundation Center (annual). Also available online.

A directory of U.S. foundations with assets of $1 million and over, arranged by state. The data for each foundation usually includes: date of incorporation, donors, purpose and activities, financial statistics (total assets, gifts, expenditures, grants), types of support, limitations, publications, officers, directors and trustees, number of staff, grant application information. Indexes are by: name of foundation; location; donor/officer/trustee; subject; types of support. An introduction has useful statistical tables and ranked lists of the 100 largest foundations by assets and by total giving. There is also a short glossary and an annotated list of the publications and services of the Center. Among their other publications are: *Foundation Grants Index* (annual and quarterly, and also available online); *National Data Book of Foundations* (1991), a comprehensive guide to the many smaller grantmaking foundations important for local financing.

DIRECTORIES OF GOVERNMENT ORGANIZATIONS

Book of the States. Lexington, KY: Council of State Governments (biennial).

Authoritative source for information on the structure, functions, finances, and personnel of each state, documenting significant trends and changes. Includes chapters on elections, management and administration, selected state activities, issues, and services (such as labor, health), and one called "State Pages" that gives names of elected executive branch officials, legislative heads, Supreme Court judges, statistics on population, state motto, flower, bird, and so forth. Three supplements identify: "state elective officials and the legislature;" "state legislative leadership, committees and staff;" and "administrative officials classified by function."

Congressional Staff Directory. Mt. Vernon, VA: Staff Directories, Ltd. (semi-annual). Also available on CD-ROM.

This is especially useful for its emphasis on listing staffs of congressional members, of committees and subcommittees, independent agencies, and the executive office, all with phone numbers. Included also are brief biographical facts about members of congress, a section containing over 3,200 staff biographies, a list of counties and cities giving their districts and the representative for each. A useful keyword subject index and varying colors of paper for each section make this easy to use.

U.S. Congress. *Official Congressional Directory.* Washington, DC: U.S. Government Printing Office (biennial).

Contains biographical data about each member of Congress; also the composition of each congressional committee, as well as top officers and staff of all federal departments, independent agencies, the executive office; also names of foreign and U.S. diplomats, press representatives which are not listed in the congressional directory above. Since this has changed to a biennial, the data is not always current.

United States Government Manual. Washington, DC: Office of the Federal Register, National Archives and Records Adminstration (annual). Purchase from U.S. Government Printing Office.

This is an indispensable official handbook of the federal government that describes the purposes and programs of each government agency and lists top personnel for each. Appendixes include names of terminated and/or transferred agencies, abbreviations and acronyms, and an alphabetical list of agencies appearing in the *Code of Federal Regulations*.

DIRECTORIES OF PERIODICALS AND NEWSPAPERS

Gale Directory of Publications and Broadcast Media. Detroit: Gale Research Inc. 3 volumes (annual). And interim update.

Volumes 1–2 are a geographic listing of U.S., Puerto Rican, and Canadian newspapers, magazines, journals, radio stations, TV stations and cable systems. For each print publication it usually gives: phone and fax, year founded, frequency, subjects covered, printing method, size, key personnel, ISSN, circulation, subscription and advertising rates. For broadcast media it usually gives network affiliation, owner, key personnel, operating hours, cities served, ADI (Area of Dominant Influence), wattage, advertising rates. Volume 3 contains 17 cross-reference indexes including one for "trade, technical, and professional publications" which is further divided by specific subjects. There is also a master name and keyword index, and maps for each state or Canadian province. This reference work has been in existence for over 100 years as a directory of newspapers and periodicals called *Ayer Directory of Publications*.

A companion directory is *Gale International Directory of Publications* (1st ed., 1989, 573 pp.) which gives country-by-country coverage to more than 4,800 newspapers and general interest magazines in over 100 countries.

Standard Periodical Directory. New York: Oxbridge Communications, Inc. (annual).

Probably the best first place to check if you know that the periodical you seek is published in the U.S. or Canada, this is a subject listing of about 75,000 journals, newsletters, directories, yearbooks. The data given for each is similar to that in the directory above; an alphabetical index is at end. One of its over 200 subject sections covers house organs.

Standard Rate & Data Service: Business Publication Rates and Data. Wilmette, IL. 3 parts (monthly).

Part 1 is the most important because it lists U.S. trade journals by industry groupings, and there is an alphabetical index. Usually the data given includes: publisher's editorial profile, personnel, representatives and/or branch offices, subscription rate, analysis of circulation, as well as varying advertising rates and specifications. Occasionally one can find with entries for some trade journals the titles of "special feature issues" for the coming year often noting which issues contain statistics, ranked lists, etc. Part 2 contains listings of U.S. healthcare publications, and classified advertising media; part 3 has listings of international publications, international healthcare publications, card decks, classified advertising media.

SRDS publishes companion monthlies for *Consumer Magazine and Agri-Media Rates & Data* and *Newspaper Rates & Data;* a semiannual *Community Publication Rates & Data* (this profiles weekly newspapers and shopping guides); an annual *Newspaper Circulation Analysis;* also monthlies for other advertising media such as radio and television. Similar volumes covering all media for Great Britain and for Canada are published by Maclean Hunter Ltd. These are titled *British Rates and Data* (monthly) and *Canadian Advertising Rates and Data* (monthly). In addition, publishers in 6 European countries each have similar directories written in the language of each country. Those countries covered are: Austria, France, Germany, Italy, Mexico, and Switzerland.

Ulrich's International Periodicals Directory. New York: R. R. Bowker. 3 volumes (annual). Online counterpart is *Bowker's International Serials Database;* CD-ROM product is *Ulrich's Plus.*

Especially good for its coverage of foreign as well as domestic periodicals and, since 1988, expanded to include also irregular serials and annuals (formerly published separately). Volumes 1–2 describe over 118,000 titles arranged by over 600 subject headings, with the section covering "business & economics" containing 23 subject subsections. For each title, the usual data given is: editor, language in which written, phone/fax/telex, subscription rate, circulation, special features, ISSN number (Inter-

national Standard Serial Number). It is also useful for noting whether each periodical: contains book reviews; has its own index or is indexed in an indexing service; is
refereed; is also available online; any title changes. Volume 3 comprises the following indexes: refereed serials, those available online or on CD-ROM; serials online
arranged by vendor; cessations; by ISSN number; publications of international organizations. *Ulrich's Update* is a quarterly supplement listing new titles, title changes,
and cessations.

Willings Press Guide. East Grinstead, West Sussex, Eng.: Reed Information
Services, Ltd. (annual).

An alphabetical guide to periodicals and newspapers published in the United Kingdom, as well as to the principal publications of Australasia, Europe, the Far East,
Middle East, and U.S., arranged by country. At end are a classified index, a geographic index of U.K. newspapers, a list of periodicals publishers, and a list of
services and supplies.

A more specialized directory is:

Editor & Publisher. *International Year Book.* New York.

Comprehensive source for data on newspapers in the U.S., Canada, and other
foreign countries; also lists of news and syndicate services, equipment and supplies,
newspaper services, and organizations. For each newspaper it includes names of
personnel, circulation, price, special editions and supplements, advertising rates,
specifications, equipment.

Newsletters

Since many business and financial newsletters are not listed in periodical directories, it is helpful to know that there are now several specialized directories
devoted just to describing newsletters. Most cover all subjects and not just
business/finance; most include some current periodic data sources such as
Moody's Bond Survey which we may not think of as strictly newsletters. Of the
two directories described below, Oxbridge covers more citations, but the descriptions of each item in it are usually not as specific as those in the Gale book
(at least this is true of the sources cited in the investment sections of each). For a
guide that profiles only investment newsletters, including performance evaluations for each, see *The Hulbert Guide to Financial Newsletters* described in the
"Weekly Investment Advisory Services" section of Chapter 8.

Newsletters in Print. Detroit: Gale Research, Inc. (annual). Also available
online.

This is a descriptive guide to more than 10,000 U.S. and Canadian newsletters and
similar serial publications that are currently in print or online. It is arranged in 33
subject sections of which 6 pertain to newsletters in the business and industry areas.
For each entry it usually gives the editor, a good description, intended audience,
editorial policies, when first published, frequency, size, circulation, price, ISSN,
whether there are illustrations, former titles (if any), whether available also online.
An appendix contains separate listings of online newsletters and free newsletters.
Three indexes are by: titles and keywords; detailed subjects; publishers.

Oxbridge Directory of Newsletters. New York: Oxbridge Communications,
Inc. (biennial).

Another comprehensive list of over 21,000 U.S. and Canadian newsletters, also arranged by subject, and with an alphabetical index. It covers a wide range including over 800 newsletters for investors and also a section listing house organs (internal magazines published by companies). For each publication it usually gives editor, frequency, price, year established, description of editorial content, distribution of readership, as well as such facts as length of issue, use of color, circulation, whether permits list rental, or is available in another format such as on microfilm.

DIRECTORIES OF RESEARCH CENTERS

A directory of industrial research laboratories is described in Chapter 20.

Research Centers Directory. Detroit: Gale Research, Inc., (annual, and interim supplement). Also available online.

A directory of over 12,000 research institutes, centers, operating foundations, laboratories, bureaus, experiment stations, and other university-related or nonprofit research facilities in the United States and Canada. It is arranged in 17 broad subject sections, including "Business and Economics," "Labor and Industrial Relations." For each this provides data on when the center was established, research activities and fields, sources of support, number of staff, names of directors, publications and services, meetings/educational activities, library facilities, phone and fax. The interim supplement is called *New Research Centers*.

Several related directories published by Gale are: *Government Research Directory* (6th ed., 1991, 1,200 pp.); *International Research Centers Directory* (6th ed., 1991, 1,327 pp.), which is arranged by country and lists both governmental and nongovernmental research organizations; *Research Services Directory* (4th ed., 1989, 841 pp.) listing contract or fee-for-service research and development companies in the U.S.

The World of Learning. London: Europa Publications. (annual).

For every country, this comprehensive directory lists academies, learned societies, research institutes, libraries and archives, museums and art galleries, universities and colleges, schools of art and music—stating purpose, officers, publications. A section on international organizations is at the front.

BIOGRAPHICAL DICTIONARIES

Collections of biographies are called biographical dictionaries. The various "Who's Who" usually follow a standard format for giving important facts about prominent individuals: when and where born, parents, education, marital status, names of children, career (itemized in chronological order), career-related activities, civic activities, political activities, nonprofessional directorships, military record, decorations and awards, political affiliation, religion, lodges, clubs, publications, home and office addresses.

Directories of directors (see section below) give much less information, usually only the current position and other organizations with which each director is associated. A troublesome problem in searching for biographical information about business persons is that only top executives can be found in most biographical dictionaries. For the executive in middle management it is often more difficult to find published biographical data; one must check the more specialized directories and consider other possibilities, such as association membership lists and local newspapers. Section 3 of the Financial Times *Index,* for example, indexes news about personalities; the indexes of the *New York Times* and *Wall Street Journal* may also contain news of executives.

Ingham, John W. *Biographical Dictionary of American Business Leaders.* Westport, CT: Greenwood Press, 1983. 4 volumes.

> Of interest more for historical purposes, this contains full-length biographical sketches of 835 American business leaders who lived from colonial times to the early 1980s, and whom the author felt were historically the most significant. Bibliographical citations follow each entry for persons who want further information. A more recent companion volume is *Contemporary American Business Leaders: A Biographical Dictionary* by Ingham and Lynne B. Feldman (Westport, CT: Greenwood Press, 1990, 788 pp.) which covers business leaders whose contributions have occurred since World War II.

Who's Who in America. Wilmette, IL: Marquis Who's Who. 2 volumes (biennial). Full-text online counterpart is *Marquis Who's Who.*

> Biographical data on prominent living Americans, including only the most important business executives.
>
> A companion series, *Who Was Who in America,* contains biographical sketches of prominent Americans who are now deceased. Among the other Marquis directories is *Who's Who of American Women* (biennial), and a series of four regional "Who's Whos" for men and women whose achievements are better known in one particular region of the U.S. These are *Who's Who in the East* (which covers also the eastern part of Canada; *Who's Who in the Midwest; Who's Who in the South and Southwest; Who's Who in the West.* There is also an annual index to Marquis *Who's Who* books.

Who's Who in Finance and Industry. Wilmette, IL: Marquis Who's Who (biennial). Also available online in *Lotus One Source.*

> Yet another Marquis directory, this one focuses on career sketches of leading North American business persons and others noteworthy in the fields of finance and industry.

For the names of specialized "Who's Who"s in consulting, economics, insurance, or securities, refer to the chapters covering each of these subjects.

International

Who's Who in the World. Wilmette, IL: Marquis Who's Who (biennial).

> This contains biographical sketches for approximately 28,000 internationally noteworthy persons in every sphere of human activity and in almost every country. It has a good representation of business leaders—better than a similar publication called *International Who's Who* (London: Europa; annual) which covers only 18,000 biographies. On the other hand the latter sometimes has more detail about each person and is revised annually.

A more specialized biographical dictionary is:

European Business and Industry. Herrsching nr. Munich: Who's Who Edition GmbH. 2 volumes (annual).

> Volume 1 contains biographies of leading personalities in European management; volume 2 has one-page company profiles arranged by broad subject. Most of the profiles seem to be written by the company involved.

Some biographical dictionaries cover prominent persons in specific countries, and a selection of the most important of these can usually be found in large public or university libraries. Two examples are:

Who's Who. New York: St. Martin's Press (annual).

Biographical data on prominent living British men and women, with a few leaders of other nations included. A companion series for deceased British persons is *Who Was Who.*

Who's Who in Canadian Business. Toronto: Trans-Canada Press (annual).

Brief biographical information about leading Canadian business persons. At end is a ranked list of the "Canadian Business 500" companies as taken from the June issue of *Canadian Business.* This publisher also has a companion annual called *Who's Who in Canadian Finance,* with a ranked list of the "Service 250" companies at end.

Directories of Corporate Officers and Directors

The various "directories of directors" do not contain complete biographical profiles, but they do give useful facts about a much larger number of corporate and organization executives and directors than can usually be found in most publications above. One or both of the first two described below will surely be found in most libraries.

Reference Book of Corporate Managements. Parsippany, NJ.: Dun & Bradstreet Information Services. 4 volumes (annual). Also available on CD-ROM.

Subtitled "America's Corporate Leaders," this is a directory of top executives and directors in some 12,000 leading U.S. companies. Volumes 1–3 are arranged by name of company. For each top executive covered, one can usually find his/her year of birth (but not place), colleges attended and degrees awarded, marital status, military service, present position, previous positions. At the end of most company listings are the names and titles of additional officers and directors who are not profiled. Volume 4 is a "cross-reference volume" containing: an alphabetical roster of companies (white pages), a company index by geographical location (yellow pages), a company index by SIC industry (blue pages), an alphabetical index of individual officers and directors (white pages).

Standard & Poor's Register of Corporations, Directors and Executives. Vol. 2: Directors and Executives. New York: Standard & Poor's Corp. (annual). Available also online as *Standard & Poor's Register-Biographical* and on CD-ROM.

Covers approximately 70,000 individuals who serve as officers, directors, trustees, partners. The arrangement (unlike the annual above) is alphabetical by name of the person. For each it usually gives date and place of birth, colleges attended and degrees awarded, principal business affiliation (but not previous employment), fraternal memberships, business address, and occasionally home address. The other two volumes of this directory are described earlier in this chapter.

Following are examples of "directory of directors" volumes for two metropolitan regions in the United States and for two foreign countries:

Directory of Directors in the City of Boston and Vicinity. Boston: Bankers Service Co. (annual).

An alphabetical list of executives, directors, and trustees in the greater Boston area, giving for each the person's business address and other affiliations. At end is a useful list of leading firms and organizations in Greater Boston, with names of officers or trustees.

Directory of Directors in the City of New York and Tri-State Area. Southport, CT: Directory of Directors Co. (annual).

This directory covers executives, directors, etc., in New York City and suburbs, New Jersey, and Connecticut. For each person one can find the business address, sometimes the home address, and also the companies with which the individual is affiliated. A company/organization list, with officers, is at end.

Directory of Directors. East Grinstead, West Sussex, Eng.: Reed Information Services Ltd. 2 volumes (annual).

Volume 1 is a directory of some 60,000 directors who control Britain's major companies, both public and private. For each it gives company affiliation, and other organizations with which s/he is affiliated. Volume 2 contains key financial data and facts about 16,000 major British companies.

Financial Post. *Directory of Directors.* Toronto (annual).

Section 1 is a list of executives and directors of Canadian companies, with their positions and directorships; section 2 (blue pages) is an alphabetical list of companies, giving officers, phone, and fax numbers.

GUIDES TO DIRECTORIES

Directories In Print. Detroit: Gale Research, Inc. 2 volumes (annual with interim supplement).

This is a useful annotated guide to over 14,000 directories arranged within 26 broad subject categories and covering a wide range of business and industrial directories, professional and scientific rosters, entertainment, recreation and cultural directories, directory databases and other nonprint products. For each directory one can usually find: a note about coverage, language used, arrangement, indexes, frequency, editor, price, whether advertising is accepted, whether also in computer readable format, phone/telex/fax. It now includes more than 4,000 foreign directories that were formerly described in *International Directories in Print.*

A companion directory is *City & State Directories in Print* which focuses on describing U.S. regional and local directories.

Guide to American Directories. Coral Springs, FL: B. Klein Publications (biennial).

Another useful directory, this one contains approximately 8,000 major U.S. industrial, professional, and mercantile directories, and a few foreign ones. It is arranged by subject and includes a description and price for each directory. Under the heading "Manufacturers" is a listing of industrial directories for each state. An alphabetical index is at end.

8

INVESTMENT SOURCES

U.S. INVESTMENT INFORMATION SOURCES – Comprehensive Investment Services – Industry Surveys – Concise Statistical Data and Stock Prices – Bonds and Other Fixed Income Securities – Charting Services – Dividends – Stock Price Indexes – Weekly Investment Advisory Services – Corporate Reports – Brokerage House Reports – Computerized Financial Data – Securities and Exchange Commission Publications – Capital Changes Services – New Securities Offerings – Stock Exchange Publications – Lists of Largest U.S. Companies – Credit Rating Services – Investment Companies – Guides to Reading the Financial Pages – Guides to Financial Services and Statistics – Indexes to Financial Publications – Investment Newspapers and Periodicals – FOREIGN INVESTMENT INFORMATION SOURCES – International Investment Services – Foreign Corporate Annual Reports – European Sources – United Kingdom Sources – Canadian Sources – Japanese Sources – Online Financial Services Covering Foreign Companies – Lists of Largest Foreign Companies – Guides to World Stock Exchanges – Bibliographies and Indexes on Foreign Companies and Industries – INVESTMENT MANAGEMENT BOOKS – General Books on Investments – Security Analysis and Portfolio Management – The Stock Market and Investment Management Guides – Bond and Money Markets – Options Market – Commodity and Financial Futures Markets – Investment Banking – Law and Securities Regulations – Bibliographies of Investment Books – Investment Dictionaries – Investment Management Journals – Directories of the Securities Industry – Securities Industry Associations

Of equal importance with statistical data are the various investment sources, both for their current evaluations of industries and for their detailed analyses of companies. Probably no business activity is as well supplied with advisory and statistical publications as the investment field. And in no other area is the presence of a good business/financial library more imperative, since most investment services are far too expensive for the individual pocketbook.

Many serious investors today are making use of personal computers or online financial services to monitor their investments and to watch for significant trends that may help improve their investment return. On the other hand these same persons also remain regular and frequent library users. Although they almost always head for the same few services they have learned to trust, they will be the first to warn would-be investors that no *one* service is infallible—that it is important to become thoroughly familiar with several services as well as with corporate records, articles in leading journals, etc., before making an investment decision.

This chapter describes a selection of published investment information—financial manuals, advisory services, statistical data, corporate reports, online services, indexes, and journals. It concentrates primarily on data about U.S. companies, although a short section describes several basic foreign investment sources. This is followed by descriptions of a few good books on investment management, security analysis, the stock and commodity markets.

U.S. INVESTMENT INFORMATION SOURCES

COMPREHENSIVE INVESTMENT SERVICES

There are two broad types of investment services: financial manuals and investment advisory services. The first two publications below are the most comprehensive and best known financial manuals, providing straight factual information on American companies as taken from published information. *Value Line,* on the other hand, contains not only massive statistical data taken from published sources but also brief investment advice, and so it is considered an investment advisory service.

Moody's Investors Service. *Moody's Manuals.* New York. 8 volumes (annual with semiweekly or weekly supplementary "News Reports"). Also available online and on CD-ROM.

The titles of these 8 separate financial manuals are:
Moody's Bank & Finance Manual (4 volumes)
Moody's Industrial Manual (2 volumes)
Moody's International Manual
Moody's Municipal & Government Manual (3 volumes)
Moody's OTC Industrial Manual
Moody's OTC Unlisted Manual
Moody's Public Utility Manual (2 volumes)
Moody's Transportation Manual
Moody's Complete Corporate Index (3/yr.)

Seven of these manuals contain important financial information about companies listed on U.S. exchanges or over-the-counter; the *International Manual* covers leading foreign companies. Using the *Industrial Manual* as an example, the information given for those companies in the section for full coverage ("Corporate Visibility–Plus") usually includes such data as capital structure, brief corporate history, complete list of subsidiaries and plant locations, business and properties, names of officers and directors, CEO's letter to stockholders, sometimes a "Management Discussion and Analysis," report of the independent public accountant, and other material from the annual report; also 7-year income, balance sheet, and financial and operating statistics, number of stockholders and employees. There are four separate sections to each volume, and so one needs to use the index to find the description of any one company. Besides the section giving data about companies that pay for full coverage (called "Corporate Visibility–Plus"), there are three other sections, in descending order, for companies with "Corporate Visibility–Select," "Corporate Visibility," and lastly, "Standard," providing the least information about companies who have not paid the special fee for better coverage. The center blue pages in vol. 1 contain Moody's averages on yields, Moody's Commodity Price Index (monthly from 1928), list of industrial stock splits for two years, stock purchase warrants, and other useful information; also an index of companies by industry and by location. (This statistical data varies with each type of manual.)

Moody's Complete Corporate Index makes it easy to determine in which of these manuals one can find any one company. Back volumes of the manuals are available on microfiche. Moody's offers several online and CD-ROM products, including *Moody's Company Data* which contains more than 160 searchable fields about 10,000 U.S. public companies, and *Moody's International Plus* for business and financial information on more than 5,000 non-U.S. based companies operating in over 100 countries.

Standard & Poor's Corp. *Standard Corporation Descriptions*. New York. 6 volumes. (loose-leaf with bimonthly supplements). Also available online as *Standard & Poor's Corporate Descriptions,* and on CD-ROM.

This is an excellent financial service comparable to Moody's above, covering over 12,000 companies having listed and unlisted securities. Its scope and subject matter are similar, but its arrangement of all types of companies in 6 loose-leaf volumes makes for easier updating. It includes CUSIP numbers. There is a well-indexed *Daily News Section* (also available online).

Standard & Poor's Corp. *Stock Reports*. New York (loose-leaf, with semi-weekly supplements).

These stock reports are really three separate services with the following titles:

Standard ASE Stock Reports (4 volumes)

Standard NYSE Stock Reports (4 volumes)

Standard OTC Stock Reports (4 volumes), and a supplement *OTC Profiles* (3/yr.)

Each two-page company report gives a business summary, recent developments, income, balance sheet and per share data, capitalization, dividends, etc. A supplement to the *OTC Stock Reports* provides concise data on over 900 companies less actively traded than those in the full report.

For persons interested in similar concise data on 800 of the more obscure, often undervalued OTC companies you may want to try using a quarterly similar in format to these S & P reports called *The Market Guide* which is described in the section for "Concise Statistical Data."

Value Line Investment Survey. New York (loose-leaf in several volumes, with weekly additions). Online counterpart is *Value Line Datafile.*

This popular investment advisory service continuously analyzes and reports on 1,700 companies in about 95 industries. The statistics, charts, and brief explanatory text are reviewed and updated, industry by industry, on a rotating basis so that the information on each company in every industry is revised quarterly. It packs a lot of useful data into its one-page per company, including: a 10-year statistical history of 23 key investment factors plus estimates three to five years into the future; quarterly sales, EPS, and dividends; such unique features as Value Line ratings (on timeliness, safety, and Beta), projected price appreciation, dividend yield expected, insider decisions to buy or sell; review of latest developments and future prospects. Brief information about the industry is at the beginning of each industry section. Received with this service is: a weekly "Summary & Index" which includes rankings of timely stocks, best/worst performers, highest/lowest PEs, and more; a weekly "Selection & Opinion" which usually gives views on business and a financial outlook, advice on investment policy, data on one recommended stock, Value Line stock price averages, etc.; a "Quarterly Economic Review" issue.

Other services include: *Value Line Convertibles,* a weekly statistical evaluation of convertibles and warrants (also available online); *Value Line Options,* a similar weekly for listed options.

Walker's Manual of Western Corporations. San Mateo, CA. 2 volumes (annual, with quarterly supplements).

A financial manual for corporations headquartered in the 13 western states. Geographic, corporate name, and subject (SIC) indexes are in both volumes.

INDUSTRY SURVEYS

Standard & Poor's Corp. *Analyst's Handbook.* New York (annual, with monthly supplements).

Composite corporate per share data, from 1959 to date, for approximately 90 industries (those represented in the S & P 500 Index). Statistics and percentages cover 14 components, including sales, operating profit, depreciation, earnings, dividends, prices, etc. Six years of this data is also given for industrial and transportation groups, arranged in income account and balance sheet format.

Standard & Poor's Corp. *Industry Surveys.* New York (loose-leaf; updated weekly).

This is a valuable source for basic data on 20 industries, with financial comparisons of the leading companies in each industry. For each industry there is a "Basic Analysis" (around 50 pages) revised annually, and a short "Current Analysis" (about 5 pages) published several times each year. Received with this is a four-page monthly on "Trends & Projections," which includes tables of economic and industry indicators, and a monthly "Earnings Supplement," giving concise, up-to-date revenue, income, and profitability data on over 1,000 leading companies arranged by these 20 industries.

Forbes. "Annual Report on American Industry" (appears as the first January issue each year).

While this cannot be compared with the preceding surveys, it is still a useful issue that contains short sections on 20 major industries. Within each industry a table of performance yardsticks ranks the leading companies in profitability (five-year average % return on equity, and return on total capital), and in growth (sales and earnings per share); also total figures for sales, net income, and profit margin. The issue also contains three ranked lists of the over 1,100 companies covered: by sales and profit growth; by stock market performance; by return on equity (profitability).

A number of the larger brokerage houses publish services or reports that give industry and comparative company data. Articles in financial journals such as *Forbes* occasionally discuss the outlook for an industry. Each issue of *The Wall Street Transcript* contains "A TWST Roundtable Discussion" on one specific industry with analysts discussing the industry—its performance, growth, outlook, and other pertinent topics. These are followed by critiques on the performance of several CEOs of major companies in the industry. Several financial manuals report on companies in just one industry, for example, *Fairchild's Electronics Industry Financial Directory*. (These are described under the name of the industry in Chapter 5).

CONCISE STATISTICAL DATA AND STOCK PRICES

Stock market price quotations in newspapers are not well explained. For the beginner who needs help in understanding abbreviations, symbols, and figures, several books containing simple explanations are described later in this chapter in the section on "Guides to Reading the Financial Page." These include a book that identifies the company abbreviations used in newspaper stock price tables as well as the stock trading or ticker symbol.

The most up-to-date stock and bond price information will be found in daily newspapers such as *Investor's Business Daily,* the *Wall Street Journal,* and the *New York Times.* The weekly *Barron's* also has a convenient tabulation of security prices. Several other useful, concise sources are listed below.

Bank & Quotation Record. Daytona Beach, FL: National News Service (monthly).

A monthly summary of price ranges for stocks and bonds listed on the American and New York stock exchanges as well as the Boston, Midwest, Pacific, Philadelphia, and Toronto exchanges, and NASDAQ OTC securities; also data on U.S. government securities, municipal bonds, foreign government and corporate bonds, mutual funds, commercial paper, stock market indexes, foreign exchange rates, etc.

Barron's. New York: Dow Jones & Co. (weekly).

Extensive statistics are in each issue covering the markets, indicators, and indexes. These tables include: weekly stock and bond price quotations for the NYSE, AMEX, NASDAQ, with fewer companies covered for other North American exchanges and for the more important exchanges overseas; also tables for mutual funds, option trading, government securities, commodity futures, foreign exchange rates; Dow Jones and other market indexes, Dow Jones Industry Group statistics; economic and financial indicators such as money supply, money rates, the "pulse of industry and trade," and more.

Business Week. New York: McGraw-Hill.

Annually or quarterly this important weekly publishes lists of companies (some are not ranked lists) that provide useful current financial data for larger companies. These are:

"Bank Scoreboard" (annual, third or fourth April issue). A ranked list of the top 100 American banks showing how they performed and including also assets, deposits, loans, market value. And "International Bank Scoreboard" (first July).

"Corporate Scoreboard" (quarterly, third issues in March, May, August, November). This lists 900 companies in 64 industries (24 key industries and their subdivisions) and gives sales, profits, and margins for each.

"Executive Compensation Scoreboard" (first May). Compensation and pay-performance analysis of the top two executives in the largest U.S. companies, arranged by 36 industries.

"The Global 1000" (mid-July). A ranked list of foreign companies by each of 27 countries giving, for each, market value, price per share, price/book value, P/E ratio, % yield, sales, profits, assets, return on equity.

"Investment Outlook Scoreboard" (combined last December/first January issue). An alphabetical list of about 900 companies, with recent stock price, book value per share, dividend rate, shares outstanding, shares held by institutions, EPS, EPS estimates for coming year.

"Mutual Fund Scoreboard" (mid-February). An alphabetical list of over 600 mutual funds giving, for each, rating, asset size, fees, objective, current and historical results, portfolio data, risk.

"Patent Scoreboard" (first August). Just begun in 1992, this is a new ranking of nearly 200 companies by number of patents granted.

"R & D Scoreboard" (in a bonus issue each year, e.g., October 25, 1991). For over 900 U.S. companies, this gives sales, profits, and R&D expenses, with the companies ranked within about 40 industries. There is a separate ranked list of the top 200 foreign companies by R&D expenses.

Business Week also publishes an annual "The Business Week 1000" (a mid-April bonus issue). This is not a "scoreboard" list, but it does rank the top 1,000 U.S. companies and, for each, gives market value, sales, profits, assets, valuation, dividends, shares, EPS. The issue also ranks these 1,000 companies within over 40 industries.

FW: Financial World. New York (semimonthly).

Usually once a month this financial magazine contains a statistical section called "Independent Appraisal of Stocks" which contains current financial data in tabular form on about 1,300 listed stocks one month and over 800 OTC stocks the next month. About twice a year the appraisal covers almost 1,000 mutual funds. For stocks, these tables give: ticker symbol, FW rating, recent price range, sales, EPS, profitability, dividends, common stock outstanding. For mutual funds, it gives performance and risk ratings, assets, total return, charges.

Hoover's Handbook of American Business. Austin, TX: The Reference Press (annual). Also available online.

The one-page profiles in this Handbook differ somewhat from those in the *Moody's Handbooks* noted below although a 10-year table gives some of the same financial figures. These profiles contain a concise statement of the nature of the business, its history and the products and services it delivers; also a list of major products, sales (occasionally by major product line or continent in which the company operates), names of officers, number of employees, ranking in the *Fortune, Business Week,* and *Forbes* annual ranked lists, names of competitors, and a Hoover's rating. Its four indexes are by: industry, location of headquarters, names of executives cited, company/products. At front are over 35 ranked lists of companies in this handbook and those in specific industries as taken from other sources. There is also a glossary.

A new companion volume is *Hoover's Handbook of World Business*. This consists, not only of one-page profiles on 165 important foreign companies, but also one-page profiles on 61 foreign countries. Over 40 ranked lists are at front, many taken from other sources. At end are lists of the companies included in several foreign stock indexes, such as the Nikkei Index (Japanese companies) and the FT-SE 100 Index (U.K. companies).

Insiders' Chronicle. Bethesda, MD: American Banker-Bond Buyer (weekly).

A 15-page financial news weekly that lists recent corporate insider trading sales and purchases for both listed and OTC stocks, and intents to sell "144 letter stock" (restricted securities recently filed on SEC Form 144). For each company it gives date of trade, price, name and title of the insider, his holding, whether stock was bought or sold. At front is a list of the largest trades. The publisher also issues a quarterly supplement, called *Summary of Insider Transactions* that cumulates the weekly lists of insider trading for a three-month period. Indexed in TI.

Not connected with this weekly is an online service called *Insider Trading Monitor* which provides information on the stock trades of some 100,000 corporate insiders.

The Market Guide. Select Over the Counter Edition. Glen Head, NY: The Market Guide, Inc. 3 volumes (quarterly). Also available online.

This consists of one-page profiles on 800 lesser-known, often undervalued over-the-counter companies, many not covered in other sources. For each company it usually gives a brief description of operations, equity and debt distribution, income and balance sheet statistics, financial data (such as stock price, EPS), officers and directors, number of employees, ticker symbol, market makers. At front of each issue are lists of the companies arranged by geographic location and by industry. Its online counterpart, *Market Guide Database,* covers 6,200 companies traded on the NYSE and ASE as well as over-the-counter.

Moody's Handbook of Common Stocks. New York: Moody's Investors Service (quarterly).

A popular handbook, with each issue containing price charts and concise financial statistics (one page each) for over 900 listed stocks of high investor interest. The data given includes gross revenues, working capital, EPS, P/E ratio, price range, capitalization, dividends (some of these figures are for a 10-year period). Also included is a brief background, recent developments, prospects, officers, number of stockholders, ticker symbol, date of annual meeting, institutional holdings, yield.

Moody's Handbook of Nasdaq Stocks. New York: Moody's Investors Service (quarterly).

Here is a companion to the quarterly handbook above, for almost 600 NASDAQ stocks of high investor interest.

National Quotation Bureau. *The National Bond Summary* and *The National Stock Summary.* Jersey City, NJ (monthlies, with semiannual cumulations).

Useful for their summaries of wants and offering prices. The stock summary covers over-the-counter and inactive listed securities, cumulating for a 6-month period. It also gives, for each stock, par value, capital changes, new issues, shares outstanding, transfer agent. The bond summary gives monthly bond market quotations which have appeared in the National Daily Quotation Services or were supplied by dealers.

Standard & Poor's Corp. *Bond Guide.* New York (monthly).

Financial data in tabular format on a broad list of American corporate bonds including convertibles and a few foreign bonds. Gives S & P bond quality ratings and also ratings on selected municipals.

Standard & Poor's Corp. *Daily Stock Price Record.* New York. Three separate quarterly services.

These three sets of volumes (one for each market: NYSE, AMEX, and OTC) provide a daily and weekly record of the volume, high/low, and closing prices for each stock. Daily market indicators, such as the Dow Jones averages, are at front of each volume. Also available on microfiche.

Standard & Poor's Corp. *Stock Guide.* New York (monthly).

Concise data in tabular format for about 5,100 common and preferred stocks, giving for each the S & P ratings, ticker symbol, par value, stock price range, capitalization, financial position, annual and interim earnings per share, dividends, sales for the month, P/E ratio. At end is a separate table with figures for over 700 mutual fund issues.

BONDS AND OTHER FIXED INCOME SECURITIES

Here we describe a few current sources for data on debt securities (such as corporate bonds, government and municipal bonds, money market instruments). See the previous section for the names of several publications that contain current bond as well as stock price quotations. For a description of two handbooks and several books on fixed income securities, see the section on "Bonds and Money Markets" near the end of this chapter.

Bond Buyer. *Yearbook.* New York: American Banker-Bond Buyer.

A useful statistical compendium giving facts and figures on municipal bond financing. The 1990 volume contains tables on: new-issue volume for 10 years (including municipal financing by state, lists of largest issues); interest rate trends; rankings of underwriters; ranked list of municipal bond holdings in 500 largest banks; sector reports for taxable issues, education, electric power, health care, housing, industrial development, solid waste/pollution, and more.

Their daily newspaper called *The Bond Buyer* is an important source for specialists who monitor municipal bonds each day, but it is too expensive to be found in most libraries ($1,750 in 1991).

BondWeek. New York: Institutional Investor.

This is a short newsletter which calls itself "the newsweekly of fixed income and credit markets." Each issue includes a table of rating changes. Periodic supplements contain lists on such topics as quarterly debt financing.

First Boston Corp. *Handbook of Securities of the United States Government and Federal Agencies and Related Money Market Instruments.* New York (biennial).

A handy reference volume for information about government securities meant for students and market participants. Contains simple explanations of the public debt, securities of government-sponsored agencies and international institutions, money market instruments, the government securities market.

Moody's Bond Record: Corporates, Convertibles, Governments, Municipals.
New York: Moody's Investors Service (monthly).

For over 56,000 fixed income issues, this contains (for corporate bonds): the CUSIP number, call price, interest dates, call dates, price range, yield, yield to maturity, Moody's rating, when it was issued, amount outstanding. Varying information is given about other types of bonds including convertible bonds, industrial development bonds; also preferred stock and commercial paper ratings. Their *Annual Bond Record* has corporate and government bond rating changes for the previous year.

Moody's Bond Survey. New York: Moody's Investors Service (weekly).

Good for its coverage of current information and tables on fixed income securities including: recent rating activity; recent corporate bond offerings; description of a few prospective issues; prospective offerings-shelf registrations (SEC Rule 415) for bonds and preferred stocks; brief analyses of shelf registrations for a few industrial, public utilities, financial institutions, transportation companies; rating activity on municipal securities, recent municipal bond offerings; a few international ratings changes or offerings; and more. An overview at the front of each issue includes a credit market update, and a few statistics on money market rates, short-term financings, Moody's yield spreads, and yield averages.

Moody's Municipal & Government Manual. New York: Moody's Investors Service. 3 volumes (annual, with semiweekly supplements).

This is the basic financial manual for details on federal, state, and municipal finances and obligations, usually including, for each, assessed value, tax rates, tax collections, receipts and disbursements or revenues and expenses, schedule of bonded debt, bond rating, etc. A general section at front discusses interest-bearing debt of the U.S. government, securities and financial contingencies of the U.S. government, government and finances, basic internal and external economic and financial data, loan trusts. The center blue pages contain Moody's government and municipal bond yield averages monthly for more than 40 years; also analysis of state highway fund operations, per capita personal income by state, and more.

Salomon Brothers. *Analytical Record of Yields and Yield Spreads.* New York (loose-leaf).

Gives historical yield and yield spread tables, often beginning as far back as 1945, for: U.S. government securities and agencies; corporates and mortgages; municipals; short-term market rates (yield on Treasury bills, bankers' acceptances, federal agencies, finance paper, commercial paper, certificates of deposit, Libor); preferred stocks.

Current statistics are in their *Bond Market Roundup* (weekly). For other current information see their *Comments on Credit* (weekly); *Relative Values in the Bond Market* (annual); *Total Rate-of-Return Indexes* (monthly).

Standard & Poor's Corp. *Bond Guide.* New York (monthly).

Financial data in tabular format on a broad list of American corporate bonds, including separate lists of convertibles and a few foreign bonds. Gives S&P debt ratings and also ratings on selected municipals (this latter being a sampling of what can be found in *Standard & Poor's Municipal Bond Book*).

Standard & Poor's CreditWeek. New York: Standard & Poor's Corporation.

Another useful weekly focusing on ratings, trends, and an outlook for fixed income securities. Each issue usually includes: a table of rating actions for the past week by type of fixed income; a section on "Credit Watch" which spotlights issuers facing change in credit quality; rating analyses which analyze factors underlying specific rating actions; ratings updates for specific bonds; credit comments; a few statistics in a section on "Credit Trends."

A companion bimonthly containing many of the same sections is *Standard & Poor's CreditWeek International.* A supplement received with this is *Standard & Poor's CreditWeek: International Ratings Guide* with tables giving recent new and revised ratings for international fixed income securities by sector and by country.

For persons with a serious interest in the municipal securities market, there is a quarterly newsletter, *Municipal Market Development,* published by the Public Securities Association ($125). It contains summary data on the market, a list of recent municipal research reports, and ranked lists of the top 50 or 100 managers in each sector (such as long-term issues) in terms of dollar volume and number of issues.

CHARTING SERVICES

O'Neil Database. Los Angeles: W. O'Neil & Co. 2 oversized volumes (weekly and quarterly).

An expensive but excellent charting service covering 2,500 listed and OTC companies arranged by 200 industry groups. Vol.1 has datagraphs for the strongest performing groups and vol.2, the weakest performing groups. Included are industrial companies as well as those in banking, insurance, utilities, food, and transportation. Each company datagraph is packed full of more data than is found in other charting services. This includes: earnings for 9 years and a forecast for the coming year; Beta and Alpha; notes of new developments; reference to recent brokerage reports; insider transactions; % change in backlog; list of investment advisers. It even gives citations for recent major articles in four journals and several regional newspapers, and locations of security analysts' meetings. Explanation of the 122 items contained in each graph are at end of each volume. At front are a number of useful ranked lists of companies, including largest 100 in the S & P 500 Index, outstanding growth stocks, 100 high income stocks, largest in earnings, amount spent on R & D, and more. There are also charts for those economic and monetary indicators of interest to the stock market, and market averages.

O'Neil Canadian Database is a biweekly companion service featuring datagraphs on the Toronto Stock Exchange 300 Index stocks.

Securities Research Corp. *The SRC Blue Book of 5-Trend Cycli-Graphs* (quarterly) and *The SRC Red Book of 5-Trend Security Charts.* (monthly). Boston.

The first of these two services provides a 12-year graphic presentation of prices, earnings, and dividends for 1,108 leading listed stocks on a quarterly basis; the second covers a 21-month period on a weekly basis and also includes quarterly and annual figures. A companion monthly, *The SRC Brown Book of 5-Trend O-T-C Charts,* gives a 20-month earnings and dividends chart for over 1,000 leading NASDAQ OTC stocks, while *The SRC Orange Book of 5-Trend Long-Term O-T-C Charts* (quarterly) provides a 12-year trend. For historical data there is a *SRC Green Book of 5-Trend 35-Year Charts,* with the 1992 edition showing long-term graphs covering the years 1957–1992.

Standard & Poor's Corp. *Trendline Chart Services.* New York.

Three separate publications comprise this comprehensive charting service: *Daily Action Stock Charts* (published weekly), which shows daily trends for the past 12 months on over 700 popular and active NYSE and some AMEX stocks; *Current Market Perspectives* (monthly) giving weekly price/volume charts on over 1,400 widely traded listed stocks arranged by industry and covering up to four years; *OTC Chart Manual* (bimonthly) with charts on over 800 actively traded OTC stocks for up to four years. Additional data and features are included with each of these services.

A few other well known charting services are often described in advertisements one can find in *Barron's* and sometimes in the *Wall Street Journal.* Useful price charts can also be found in several financial services mentioned elsewhere in this chapter, such as *Moody's Handbook of Common Stocks,* and *Value Line Investment Survey.*

DIVIDENDS

Both Moody's and Standard & Poor's have separate publications covering declarations and payments of cash and stock dividends, stock splits, stockholders' rights issued, tax status of dividends. These are: *Moody's Dividend Record* (semiweekly, with cumulated issues and an annual) and Standard & Poor's *Quarterly Dividend Record* (with annual cumulation; there are separate daily and weekly services). Recent dividend statistics can be found in several other financial sources; see the descriptive notes with publications in the section above on "Concise Statistical Data."

STOCK PRICE INDEXES

The best known stock price averages and indexes are the Dow Jones averages and the Standard & Poor's indexes. They are quoted over a long period of time in the following publications:

The Business One Irwin Investor's Handbook. Ed. by Phyllis S. Pierce. Homewood, IL: Business One Irwin (annual).

Dow Jones & Company compiles the most widely quoted averages, and they cover not only industrial stocks but also transportation and public utility stocks. This annual *Handbook* gives: daily closing DJ averages for the two most recent years; monthly closing averages for about 20 years; quarterly earnings, dividends, price-earnings ratios for over 30 years; weekly "Barron's Confidence Index" for 8 years; also the trading record for one current year (sales, high/low, last price) for NYSE, AMEX stocks and bonds, NASDAQ OTC stocks; trading data for mutual funds and U.S. government bonds and notes; a few foreign market prices; and stock market indexes. At front is a list of the companies comprising the several DJ averages; also a chronological table of changes in the DJIA companies from 1932 to date (including stock splits).

Current DJ averages are quoted in several financial journals and newspapers, especially in *Barron's* and the *Wall Street Journal.* The daily figures in the *Journal* always contain an inset listing the names of the companies used in calculating the averages. Retrospective statistics can be found in *The Dow Jones Averages, 1885–1990,* edited by Phyllis S. Pierce (Homewood, IL: Business One Irwin, 1991, 1 volume, about 400 pp.). Recent daily summaries of DJ averages back to 1982 can be accessed online via *Historical Dow Jones Averages.* The following publication also gives both current and historical figures.

Standard & Poor's Corp. *Security Price Index Record.* New York (Published annually as a section of S & P's *Statistical Service* and also available separately).

Standard & Poor's price indexes include weekly figures on over 100 industries for a 10-year period and monthly averages prior to that; daily indexes for industries, railroads, public utilities, and the composite 500 stocks, from 1930 to date; daily NYSE sales, from 1922; weekly bond indexes by rating; long-term municipal and government bond price and yield indexes; and Dow Jones averages from 1913. Included is a list of the companies comprising the various S&P indexes, as well as the names in each of the over 100 industries. The most recent monthly issue of the *Statistical Service* includes recent stock price indexes up to within the past month, and the most current figures are in their weekly advisory service, *The Outlook.*

There are other lesser-known but still useful stock price indexes: The American Stock Exchange "Market Value Index," the New York Stock Exchange "Common Stock Indexes," "NASDAQ Composite Index," "Value Line Composite Index," and "Wilshire 5000 Equity Index." These are quoted currently in such weeklies and dailies as *Barron's, Investor's Business Daily,* Standard & Poor's *Outlook,* and the *Wall Street Journal.*

Descriptive Guides

Berlin, Howard M. *The Handbook of Financial Market Indexes, Averages, and Indicators.* Homewood, IL: Dow Jones-Irwin, 1990. 262 pp.

Here is a useful compilation for persons wanting explanations on more than 200 financial market barometers, such as those noted above. Five of its eight chapters focus separately on those U.S. measures that are: stock averages and indexes; notes and bonds; commodities; mutual funds and money market funds; money and the dollar. Another chapter describes foreign stock indexes, arranged by 23 countries and including such indexes as the Nikkei Stock Averages in Japan and the Financial Times-Stock Exchange 100 Share Index in the U.K. For each index it includes the names of companies that are components. These component lists are useful to have despite the fact that there may be slight changes in names over time. A final chapter briefly describes 7 financial benchmarks on the lighter side, such as "Superbowl Indicators."

For persons who do not have access to the book by Berlin, one can find short but helpful discussions and explanations of the more important indexes/averages in most investment textbooks. See, for example, *Investment Analysis and Portfolio Management* by Frank K. Reilly (3d ed., Dryden, 1989, chapter 4 on "Security-Market Indicator Series"); *Management of Investments* by Jack C. Francis (2d ed., McGraw-Hill, 1988, chapter 9, "Market Averages and Indexes"). There is also a short section on "Market Averages" in the useful *Encyclopedia of Banking and Finance.*

WEEKLY INVESTMENT ADVISORY SERVICES

Here we list just two of the many investment advisory services plus a descriptive guide to more than 100 similar financial newsletters.

Standard & Poor's Corp. *The Outlook.* New York.

Analyzes and projects business and stock market trends. Includes brief data on individual securities, with purchase/sell recommendations; also current S & P stock market indexes. A mid-June issue contains a "Midyear Forecast."

United & Babson Investment Report. Wellesley Hills, MA: Babson-United Investment Advisors.

Commentary on the current business, financial, and economic situation, with specific buy/sell advice, information on companies, commodity price forecasts, and so forth. The first issue each month contains a "Supervised List of Common Stocks"; a midmonth issue has a tabular summary of "Current Views of Economic Authorities Briefly Interpreted" which represents the thinking of 7 economic and financial publishers about general business conditions, the stock market, etc.

Guides

The Hulbert Guide to Financial Newsletters. By Mark Hulbert. 4th ed. New York: New York Institute of Finance, 1991. 450 pp. paper.

Mr. Hulbert is a recognized expert who has concentrated his research on objectively monitoring investment newsletter performance and reporting on this in his *Hulbert Financial Digest.* Here he has prepared two-to-four-page profiles of more than 100 newsletters including for each, a sample page, a performance evaluation, and performance charts. The latter is a graph showing the % gain or loss on recommended investments over short and long-term periods, and the amount of risk associated with the recommendations made.

CORPORATE REPORTS

With all these important investment works, one must not overlook the fact that corporate financial reports and other disclosure documents are excellent sources for current financial statistics and for other detailed information about the operations of publicly traded companies. These documents include not only annual reports to stockholders but also the various reports that U.S. companies are required to file with the Securities and Exchange Commission: an Annual Report to SEC (called the 10-K); Quarterly Financial Report (10-Q); Report of Unscheduled Material Events or Corporate Changes (8-K); 10-C, which is similar to 8-K for OTC companies; Proxy Statement; Registration Statements; Prospectus; and a report required of registered investment companies (N-SAR). *Listing Application* statements, required by the NYSE and AMEX before listing a security on one of those exchanges, also contain useful information.

Today many more libraries keep relatively complete collections of these disclosure documents due primarily to the availability of this data on microfiche. (Readers unfamiliar with the use of microfiche may want to refer to the short, general note on microforms in Chapter 2 of this book). Disclosure Inc., a commercial firm located in Bethesda, Maryland, is a distributor for these reports, and they offer a variety of tailor-made "package" subscriptions to reports for all NYSE, AMEX, OTC, and investment companies, and to foreign companies as well. Although this service is expensive, many libraries now maintain full or partial subscriptions not only because of the importance of the material but because microfiche files are significant space savers as well as savers of library staff time that would otherwise be spent in requesting and processing reports on each company separately. Consequently, the libraries in most banks, accounting, and investment firms and in many large public and university libraries have good collections of corporate reports. These reports can also be consulted on microfiche in the SEC office in Washington, D.C., and in their New York, Chicago, and Los Angeles regional offices. Other regional SEC offices usually have paper copies of recent reports for those companies headquartered in their particular region. An individual can order a copy of any report from the SEC or can subscribe to a series of reports through Disclosure, Inc. For a note about the availability of foreign corporate reports, see the section later in this chapter on "Foreign Investment Information Sources."

There are a growing number of online services useful for obtaining financial facts appearing in disclosure documents. Several of the best known databases are described in the section below covering "Computerized Financial Data." Check also the notes with individual investment services and sources listed in this chapter, such as the *Moody's Manuals,* for names of their online counterparts.

Beginners who need a simple explanation of balance sheet terminology used in company annual reports may want to request a periodically revised brochure available free from Merrill Lynch Pierce Fenner & Smith entitled *How to Read A Financial Report* (5th ed., New York: 1984, 30 pp.). This and several other simple books are described in the "Financial Statement Analysis" section of Chapter 12. Disclosure, Inc., prepares *A Guide to SEC Corporate filings* (25 pp.) which is reprinted in the annual *Business One Irwin Business and Investment Almanac.* There are also explanations about the documents filed with the SEC in most investment textbooks. Disclosure also publishes an annual alphabetical list of *SEC Filing Companies,* giving, for each, a code for stock exchange, ticker symbol, SIC industry, and Disclosure I.D. number.

BROKERAGE HOUSE REPORTS

In the investment world a large number of reports and analyses on a wide variety of companies and industries exist, which are prepared by research departments of major investment houses and until very recently usually available only to customers. Most public and university libraries have not attempted to collect these reports because there are so many and because the information becomes obsolete so quickly. But today there is an online database that makes it possible to obtain a good selection of these research reports quickly and in full text. This database, *Investext,* is described below, along with a weekly that includes analysts' discussions of industries and their leading companies, a few brokerage reports, and speeches of company executives. Noted after these is a directory, useful for identifying many recent company-specific investment research reports. Also *Findex* (see description in Chapter 18) lists a small selection of company reports prepared by investment research firms, but these can only be purchased at a relatively high price per report, and are often rather out of date.

INVESTEXT online service.

This database provides complete text for over 200,000 investment research reports on some 11,000 U.S. and foreign publicly traded companies and on 53 industries, prepared by almost 200 investment banking and financial research firms worldwide. These are useful for tracking competitive data on companies, and sometimes include market share figures. The most recent of these reports are also available on CD-ROM as part of *Lotus One: CD/Corporate.* A related database is *INVESTEXT Plus,* covering not only the investment research reports noted above but also complete text of current company documents filed with the SEC, taken from *SEC Online* database.

The Wall Street Transcript. New York (weekly). Full text also available online.

This weekly is full of all sorts of useful current information about American companies and industries, including: roundtable discussions of leading analysts on one or two industries or topics (per issue), with profiles of top CEOs voted best in these industries, and insider trading tables for companies studied in these industries; speeches of company officials before financial analysts groups and some interviews with CEOs; profiles of money managers; a few brokers reports; recent news about companies by analysts in a feature called "Wall Street Roundup"; a "Technical Corner"; the "Current Art Scene" (for evaluations of art work). A cumulated index is in each issue.

Directory

Nelson's Guide to Institutional Research. Port Chester, NY: Nelson Publications (10/yr.).

Sections 1 and 2 of each issue are lists of company-specific investment research reports about American and foreign companies. For each report it gives: name of research firm, analyst, date, and paging. Section 3 lists the research reports by originating research firm; section 4 covers the industry reports. "Keeping Track" at front lists job changes of analysts; some positions available/wanted are scattered throughout.

For a directory of companies that contains the names of investment firms researching that company, see *Nelson's Directory of Investment Research* described in the section covering "Directories of the Securities Industry" at the end of this chapter.

COMPUTERIZED FINANCIAL DATA

The growth and development of new computer-based financial data continues at such a fast pace that computer terminals are now a standard piece of equipment in all large corporate financial offices, in securities firms, and on the floor of stock exchanges; they are also used daily in universities and other organizations where any sort of financial research is being conducted. Not only has this current method of obtaining financial information relieved professional investment researchers from time-consuming calculations while speeding up the retrieval of data and increasing its accuracy, but it also makes possible much more complex manipulation or selection from masses of financial statistical information. The cost for individual users is still high; companies are now resigned to the fact that savings in time and effort make computer searching well worth the price they pay. But whether each of us uses them or not, and most of us do, we have all benefited greatly from the publication in hard copy of a growing number of computer-developed tabulations, reports, and research articles.

We are describing below only a very few of the most important databases providing comprehensive current (and sometimes historical) financial data on U.S. companies. See also the section in this chapter for "Online Financial Services Covering Foreign Companies." Several of the other databases which we have noted elsewhere in this chapter (within the descriptions of their hardcopy counterpart) are: *DUNSPRINT* (for credit reports and other information on companies); *Moody's Company Data; Standard & Poor's Corporate Descriptions; Value Line Data File.* More specialized databases noted in other chapters include: *Insider Trading Monitor* (for facts about insider trading of company stocks); *M&A Data Base* (for data on mergers, acquisitions, buyouts, divestitures, and so forth); *M&A Filings* (for abstracts of M&A documents released by the SEC).

For descriptions of these and many other computer services, as well as for new ones that will surely be developed, readers are urged to refer frequently to one or more of the directories describing computerized databases and information storage and retrieval systems, in Chapter 2.

COMPUSTAT PC-Plus. New York: Standard & Poor's Corporation.

COMPUSTAT is the first and probably best known numeric database providing a vast range of financial, statistical, and marketing data on over 13,000 companies, including: 7,000 active publicly traded companies, 200 Class A utilities, 150 leading U.S. bank holding companies, 500 Canadian companies, and over 5,000 inactive companies; also wholly owned subsidiaries that issue preferred stock or carry debt, and more than 5,000 companies deleted from the database because of merger, bankruptcy, etc. Now this data is also available on CD-ROM as *COMPUSTAT PC-Plus.* It contains up to 500 pieces of information for each company. This information is primarily financial time series items, such as income statement, balance sheet, and statement of cash flows data, with the data available on an annual basis for the past 20 years and on a quarterly basis for the past 10 years. Also included is information on 200 industry composites, 100 Standard & Poor's industry indices, and business and geographic segments. Frequent users of company financial statistics usually subscribe to the complete *COMPUSTAT* on magnetic tape with its 9 separate files described in most database directories such as those noted in Chapter 2, but many companies and libraries also now have this useful CD-ROM product.

Dow Jones Quotes. Princeton, NJ: Dow Jones & Company.

For those who want to get a current or recent past stock price quotation online rather than in a newspaper, Dow Jones offers several pertinent databases. The most important are: (1) *Dow Jones Current Quotes* for current stock price quotations on the New York, American, Pacific, and Midwest stock exchanges, and NASDAQ OTC companies; also bonds, mutual funds, U.S. Treasury issues and options; (2) *Dow Jones Real-Time Quotes* provides current prices without the 15 minute delay of the previous database; (3) *Dow Jones Historical Quotes* gives daily volume and prices for common and preferred stocks for one year; monthly summaries back to 1979; quarterly summaries back to 1978; (4) *Dow Jones Futures & Index Quotes,* for current and historical quotations for commodities and financial futures traded on North American exchanges, and daily values for more than 100 selected indexes; (5) *Dow Jones Mutual Funds Reports,* which gives performance statistics, assets and background information on mutual funds. These Dow Jones databases are all part of *Dow Jones News Retrieval,* which consists of more than 50 databases not only providing securities price quotes and averages but also other company and industry information.

Laser D/SEC and **Compact D/SEC.** Bethesda, MD: Disclosure, Inc.
These are Disclosure's two most important compact disks. *Laser D/SEC* provides instant access to the full text of documents filed with the SEC by more than 12,000 public companies. These include the 10-K, 10-Q, 10-F, 8-K, Proxy Statement, Registration Statement, Annual Report. Perhaps found in more libraries is their *Compact D/SEC* which has less information but is still useful for its instant access to selected data abstracted from the SEC filings (including items from the balance sheet, income statement (for five years), cash flow; also price/earnings and ratio data, full text of President's Letter, Management Discussions, financial footnotes. Stock ownership information from the *Disclosure/Spectrum Ownership Database* can be accessed for an added fee.
    Other Disclosure disks include: *Compact D/Canada; Compact D/Europe; Laser D/Banking,* covering over 700 financial institutions; *Laser D/International.*

Lotus One Source. *CD/Corporate: U.S. Public Companies.* Cambridge, MA: Lotus Development Corporation.
Lotus One Source is a collection of useful business/financial information taken from many leading databases and delivered on compact disks, with Lotus software. Of these, their *CD/Corporate: U.S. Public Companies* is most likely to be found in libraries that have any sort of online financial service. Its popularity is due to the fact that it is actually a collection of data taken from 8 other databases and made available as a quick and easy means of finding a wide variety of facts on more than 10,000 U.S. public companies, 50 industries, and 80,000 officers and directors. It includes: financial statement data on over 10,000 companies (from *Moody's Investors Service* database); full text of investment analysts reports on companies and industries (from *Investext*); short reports on OTC and other smaller traded companies (from the *Market Guide* database); historical stock price and trading data (from Muller Data Corporation's *Securities Pricing* database); current news and securities quotes (from *Dow Jones News Retrieval* service); abstracts of articles on companies and industries (from *ABI/Inform* and *PTS/Promt* databases); biographies of key executives and directors (from Macmillan's *Who's Who in Finance and Industry* database).
    As of 1991, other CD products of Lotus One Source are: *CD/Corporate: SEC Filings,* full text of SEC documents on about 5,000 companies (Annual Reports, 10-Ks, 10-Qs, 20-Fs, Proxy Statements); *CD/ Corporate: U.S. Private +,* a directory product containing summary information on private companies, subsidiaries, and

major divisions; *CD/Corporate: International Public Companies,* with financial data on over 7,000 public companies worldwide; *CD/Corporate: U.K. Private +,* information on over 130,000 U.K. public and private companies; *CD/Corporate: M & A* and *European M & A,* both covering corporate mergers, acquisitions, and other major transactions, in the U.S. and in the U.K. and Europe; *CD/Banking,* which covers financial information on banks, S&Ls, and bank holding companies; *CD/Insurance,* with a disk for data both on property/casualty and on life/health insurance companies; *CD/Investment,* with separate disks devoted to data on "U.S. Equities," "International Equities," "U.S. Research," "Russell Profiles," and "Fixed Income."

PTS Annual Reports Abstracts. Cleveland, OH: Predicasts, Inc,

Information from annual reports and 10-K statements of more than 4,000 publicly held U.S. companies and a few international companies whose securities are traded on a U.S. exchange.

SEC Online. Hauppauge NY: SEC Online, Inc.

Complete text, without illustrations, of documents filed with the SEC, including 10-K's, 10-Q's, ARS, Proxies, for companies listed on the NYSE, AMEX, and also NASDAQ and OTC companies. A CD-ROM product is being planned.

SECURITIES AND EXCHANGE COMMISSION PUBLICATIONS

U.S. Securities and Exchange Commission. *Annual Report.* Washington, DC: U.S. Government Printing Office.

The text portion notes current developments and important changes in securities laws. The statistical appendix includes financial statistics for the broker-dealer business and other statistics for the securities industry; volume of securities listed on exchanges; pending reorganization proceedings for bankrupt companies.

Other SEC publications include: *Official Summary of Security Transactions and Holdings,* a monthly summary of security transactions and holdings reported by officers, directors, and other "insiders"; an annual *Directory of Companies Required to File Annual Reports with the Securities and Exchange Commission Under the Securities Exchange Act of 1934.*

Commerce Clearing House publishes a loose-leaf weekly *SEC Docket,* which reproduces the texts of SEC rulings, opinions, and other official acts.

CAPITAL CHANGES SERVICES

Commerce Clearing House. *Capital Changes Reporter.* Chicago. 6 volumes.

This service records the capital histories of companies. It is arranged alphabetically by company and the information for each, given chronologically, includes date of incorporation, stock rights, stock splits, stock dividends, exchanges of securities in recapitalization, reorganizing, mergers, and consolidations, etc. Vol. 6 contains historical tables on taxability of dividends, list of worthless securities, investors' tax guide.

Prentice-Hall, Inc. *Capital Adjustments.* Englewood Cliffs, NJ. 4 volumes (weekly).

A service similar to the one above but with a different arrangement. Vols. 1 and 2 are loose-leaf and contain current capital adjustments since 1980. In the back of the second volume are supplementary data on the taxable status of dividends, amortized convertible bond premiums, list of worthless securities, etc. The other two volumes are permanent volumes for the historical record of stock dividends, stock rights, reorganizations prior to 1980.

Predicasts F & S Index of Corporate Change. Cleveland, OH: Predicasts, Inc. (quarterly, with annual cumulations). Available also online in *PTS F&S Indexes.*

This is a continuing guide to information in newspapers and periodicals on mergers, acquisitions, and other organizational changes that affect corporate identity. It is in three sections, the principal one of which lists companies by SIC industries, briefly citing the corporate change involved and giving the date of the newspaper or periodical article. Section 1 is an alphabetical company index; Section 3 contains special tabulations of name changes, new companies, reorganizations, bankruptcies, liquidations, subsidiary changes, foreign operations, joint ventures. An index of sources is at front of each volume.

Persons researching obsolete companies may want to use the Financial Stock Guide Service's *Directory of Obsolete Securities* (Jersey City, NJ: Financial Information, Inc.). This is an annual list of companies whose identity has been lost as a result of name change, merger, acquisition, dissolution, reorganization, bankruptcy, charter cancellation, or related capital change.

The Financial Post publishes an annual *Survey of Predecessor and Defunct Companies* in Canada (Toronto), recording more than 60 years of changes in Canadian public corporations. For a "Register of Defunct and Other Companies" in the U.K. see the *London Stock Exchange Yearbook* described in the "U.K. Sources" section of this chapter.

NEW SECURITIES OFFERINGS

Corporate Finance: The IDD Review of Investment Banking. New York: Investment Dealer's Digest (semiannual).

Formerly called the *Directory of Corporate Financing,* this is a two-part source, with part 2 consisting of a list of recent U.S. corporate securities offerings arranged alphabetically by issuer (company), with details as to offering date, amount (for stocks this is the number of shares, price, and $ amount), character of the issue (e.g. debt, preferred, common), and underwriter. It identifies IPOs and Rule 415 Shelf Registrations. Part 1 contains three-page highlights of deals in each of over 20 industry segments. Current issues of *Investment Dealers' Digest* (weekly) contain continuing lists of securities issues in registration (identifying IPOs and Shelf Listings), those registered during previous week, and a weekly review of offerings by underwriters. Every five or ten years IDD publishes an historical record—see, for example their *Five-Year Directory of Corporate Financing, 1980–1984* (1985, 180 pp., paper).

Going Public: The IPO Reporter. New York: Investment Dealers' Digest (weekly).

Each issue provides information on initial public offerings, including the following; recent IPO filings; recent IPO's; upcoming offerings; "The IPO 100." There are supplementary reports, occasional special reports, a monthly list of IPO's finalized during the month with data about the deal (including date, terms, price, expenses), facts about the company, and names of professionals involved. About 6 profiles are in each issue, and these are indexed in a cumulating index of IPO issues in registration. A glossary is at end.

Standard & Poor's Emerging & Special Situations. New York: Standard & Poor's Corporation (monthly).

Designed for investors interested in emerging growth companies, new issues and special situations. Each issue usually consists of: a short OTC new issue market review; roster of completed offerings and major upcoming offerings; spotlight recommendations for a few stocks with best prospects for capital appreciation; prospective new issues highlighted (about 8 per issue); portfolio updates, downgrades, and deletions; list of current purchase recommendations; reports on emerging growth companies and new issues (concise data about one or more companies reprinted from S&P's *Stock Report* series).

STOCK EXCHANGE PUBLICATIONS

For descriptive guides to U.S. and foreign stock exchanges, see the section on "Guides to World Stock Exchanges" later in this chapter.

American Stock Exchange. *Fact Book: Equities and Options.* New York (annual).

Statistical profile of AMEX, including equities volume, membership, monthly AMEX "market indices," options statistics, trading statistics on listed stocks (including ticker symbol, list of companies by SIC code, historical highlights, descriptive list of publications.

Among their other publications: *Weekly Bulletin,* contains changes in AMEX membership, new listings, listing removals, rule changes, dividends, dates of stockholders meetings, etc.; a monthly one-sheet *Amex Indices;* a monthly *Amex Stats;* and an *Annual Report.*

American Stock Exchange. *Stocks & Bonds.* New York: F. E. Fitch (annual).

For each company on AMEX this gives ticker symbol, option symbol, par value, CUSIP number (Committee on Uniform Security Identification Procedures); also lists of U.S. government obligations, stock purchase warrants, and more.

Two companion volumes are *Stocks and Bonds on the New York Stock Exchange* (annual); and *NASDAQ Symbol Book* (annual).

For a separate directory of CUSIP numbers, see *The CUSIP Directory: Corporate* described in the "Directories" section at the end of this chapter.

Chicago Board Options Exchange. *Market Statistics.* Chicago (annual).

Although a slim little brochure, this has useful statistics on trading activity for equity options, index options, treasury bond and note options, interest rate composites, as well as historical trading statistics.

Commerce Clearing House. *New York Stock Exchange Guide.* Chicago. 3 volumes.

This is the official guide prepared by CCH for the NYSE and covering: directory of members; constitution and rules; laws and regulations. The CCH publishes similar guides for the American Stock Exchange (2 volumes) and for the Boston, Midwest, Pacific, Philadelphia exchanges; also the Chicago Board Options Exchange, the New York Mercantile Exchange, the Coffee, Sugar & Cocoa Exchange, the New York Futures Exchange.

London Stock Exchange. *Quality of Markets Monthly Fact Sheet.* London.

Current statistics covering: daily market movements (including FT-SE 100 and other indexes); total market turnover, and turnover for Irish equities, listed U.K. equities, individual FT-SE 100 Share Index companies, overseas equities; futures and options; new issues.

The London Stock Exchange also publishes a periodic *The FT-SE 100 Share Index* which contains tables giving daily values of the FT-SE 100 Index, the FT 30 Index, and the FT All Share Index from March 1984 up to the year in which the latest volume was published. It includes a list of the 100 companies comprising the Index. The FT-SE (Financial Times-Stock Exchange) Index is one of the most widely used indicators of performance in the U.K. equity market. This Index is also available on the *Financial Times Currency & Share Index* database, and the most recent figures are in current issues of the *Financial Times* newspaper.

National Association of Securities Dealers. *Fact Book.* Washington, DC (annual).

Similar to the stock exchange fact books, this contains NASDAQ trading, including annual data on trading volume for each company (with NASDAQ symbol), NASDAQ market-maker data, NASDAQ market index figures for over 10 years. The NASD also publishes an *Annual Report.*

New York Stock Exchange. *Fact Book.* New York (annual).

Statistics on market activity, listed companies, bonds, futures, options, securities market credit, shareholders, etc. Includes a historical section which, among other statistics, gives the "NYSE Common Stock Index" annually since 1939.

A separate brochure contains the NYSE *Common Stock Indexes* (1988) weekly closing price index from 1939 to May 1964 and daily from June 1964 to 1988, with updated sheets published for more recent years. Two other publications of the NYSE are: *Weekly Bulletin,* noting changes in NYSE membership, new listings, stockholders meetings, etc.; *Annual Report.*

Tokyo Stock Exchange. *Fact Book.* Tokyo (annual).

For persons needing statistics and brief text about the Tokyo Stock Exchange, this is a useful fact book written in English. It includes: stock price trends (including the Tokyo Stock Price Index called TOPIX); trading and clearing statistics; margin transactions; data on the bond market; futures and options markets; listed companies (including a ranked list of the 30 leading domestic companies on the TSE); data on shareowners; securities companies; capital markets; and more. At end are historical tables, and separate lists of TSE domestic and foreign companies. Among other publications is a *TSE Monthly Statistical Report,* and a periodic source giving the stock price index called *TOPIX.*

LISTS OF LARGEST U.S. COMPANIES

Ranked lists of largest companies are of interest to many because they show how one leading company compares with another; also they often include (in a concise tabular format) financial data other than sales (or assets) which is the figure used in making most rankings. The first four ranked lists below are the most comprehensive and best known. Several ranked lists of largest foreign companies are described in the "Foreign Investment Information Sources" section of this chapter. For a few "ranked lists of fastest growing companies," see that section near the end of Chapter 10. There are many other more specialized lists, a few of which are mentioned elsewhere in this book and can be found by checking in the index under "Corporations, Ranked Lists of Largest." To find the many others, use the bibliographic guide described below.

Dun's Business Rankings. Parsippany, NJ: Dun & Bradstreet Information Services (annual).

Comparative rankings of some 8,000 U.S. companies, both public and private, with each ranking given both by sales size (blue pages) and by employee size (yellow pages). Perhaps the most useful is the section ranking companies by two- and sometimes three- digit SIC industries. Other sections rank companies by: sales size; employee size; state; public companies; private companies. Besides sales and employee size, data in each table includes number of employees at this location, primary SIC code, stock ticker symbol. An alphabetical list of companies is at front; a division cross-reference index and a list of business executives by function are at end.

The Fortune 500. New York: Fortune Directories (annual).

Each year *Fortune* magazine publishes four widely-used ranked lists of companies. These are:

"The Fortune 500" (last April issue). This is a ranked list of the largest U.S. industrial corporations, with the listing also by each of 27 industries. Beginning with the 1992 issue, this also ranks the companies by state, and it ranks the top 50 companies by 12 measures of performance.

"The Fortune Service 500" (first June). Separate ranked lists of: 100 diversified service companies, 100 commercial banks, 100 diversified financial companies, 50 largest (each) savings institutions, life insurance companies, retailing companies, transportation companies, utilities.

"The Fortune Global 500" (last July). This ranks the top industrial companies in the world, with added lists by country for the top 10 countries, by industry; also the world's 100 biggest commercial banks.

"The Fortune Global Service 500" (last August). Separate ranked lists of top worldwide service companies in the same categories as those in the domestic list above, and also including lists for the 10 countries having the most companies.

These companies are all ranked by: sales, profits, assets, stockholders' equity, market value, profits as % of sales/assets/stockholders' equity, EPS, total return to investors.

Each year the publisher offers a reprint of the U.S. rankings called *The (year) Directory of U.S. Corporations.* These ranked lists are also available online in full text on the database called *FORTUNE.*

Moody's Industry Review. New York: Moody's Investors Service. 1 volume (loose-leaf).

For each of about 140 industry groups this provides a ranked list of the leading companies in that industry according to 12 key financial, operating, and investment criteria; also comparative financial statistics such as stock price range, earnings per share for the 15 or so leaders. About 4,000 companies are covered in all and an alphabetical list is at front. This is a useful source for ranked lists because it covers many industries and is updated twice a year on a rotating basis.

Ward's Business Directory of U.S. Private and Public Companies. Detroit: Gale Research, Inc. Volume 5 (annual). This volume alone is $655.

Volume 5 of this comprehensive directory ranks over 133,000 public and private companies by sales within 4-digit SIC industries. This makes it a useful source for persons needing ranked lists of top U.S. companies in specific industries. In addition to this, there are ranked lists at the front of volume 4 for the 1,000 largest privately held companies, the 1,000 largest public companies, and the 1,000 largest employers. For a more complete description of this directory see the listing in Chapter 7.

The Business Week 1,000. (annual, in the mid-April "Special Bonus Issue").

A useful annual ranking of the top 1,000 U.S. companies by stock market value, with other financial figures for each company: sales, profits, assets, valuation, dividends, shares outstanding, EPS. A separate ranking of the companies is arranged by industry. This issue also contains a ranking of "The Top 100 Deals" of the previous year, and profiles of 25 executives to watch.

Forbes. "Annual Directory of America's Largest Corporations." (last April issue each year).

This annual issue ranks the 500 largest U.S. corporations by sales, by profits, by assets, and by stock market value. A separate alphabetical list of these 500 companies gives the rankings in each of these four categories. Also in this issue is: a list within each industry, ranking the top companies in the industry by productivity (profits, sales, and assets per employee); "The Forbes 500s on Wall Street" which is an alphabetical list of the companies giving, for each, recent figures for stock price, stock performance, P/E ratio, earnings (including EPS and EPS estimated by analysts for the coming year), dividend yield, and payout.

Bibliography

Business Rankings Annual. Detroit: Gale Research, Inc.

Here is a useful bibliographic guide to more than 8,000 ranked lists of companies and other subjects that appear in over 1,000 periodicals, newspapers, financial services, statistical annuals, and other sources. It is arranged by specific subject, and the data about each usually includes the criteria for the ranking, the names of the top 5 or 10 in the ranking, the source (including date and page). At the end is an index by subject and ranked company, and a separate bibliography of the sources (such as *Fortune*). It is compiled each year by the Business Library Staff at the Brooklyn Public Library.

A companion volume has just been announced for publication in 1992 called *European Business Rankings Annual.*

A shorter paperback compilation of those U.S. rankings in most demand (about 2,000) is *Business Book of Lists* (Detroit: Visible Ink Press, 1991, 535 pp.) It is arranged within 13 broad subject chapters; there is no index.

CREDIT RATING SERVICES

Dun & Bradstreet, Inc. *Business Information Reports.* New York. Also available online as *DUNSPRINT.*

Since the mid-nineteenth century D & B has offered a confidential service for information about companies as a basis for credit, insurance, marketing and other

business decisions. The reports prepared on each of some 9 million business establishments include information on top personnel, finance, how the company pays its
bills, banking relations, operations, history, any special events, any court record.
D & B publishes, with this service, a four-volume *Reference Book* (bimonthly)
which is a detailed geographic list of about 3 million U.S. and Canadian business
firms of all types, giving for each the SIC number, an abbreviation for line of
business, a code for estimated financial strength and for composite credit appraisal.
DUNSPRINT is its online counterpart for high-volume subscribers. A companion
credit rating service for foreign companies is *International Report*. For further information, prospective subscribers should contact Dun & Bradstreet.

INVESTMENT COMPANIES

Handbook for No-Load Fund Investors. Hastings-on-Hudson, NY (annual).
This handbook explains what no-load funds are and how to invest in them. A
directory section contains important facts about each of over 1,100 funds, including
ordering information; there are also performance tables and brief industry statistics.

Investment Company Institute. *Directory of Mutual Funds*. Washington, DC
(annual).
If one needs only brief information about more than 3,000 funds, this may be worth
checking. The funds are organized by 22 different investment objectives. The data
for each, arranged in a tabular format, includes: year begun, total assets, minimum
initial and subsequent investment, fees, investment adviser, where to buy shares.
Introductory information about mutual funds is at the front.

Investment Company Institute. *Mutual Fund Fact Book*. Washington, D.C.
(annual).
The text briefly describes and explains the industry while a statistical appendix
includes figures on mutual fund assets, total sales, redemption, statistics on money
market funds, institutional investors, and so forth.

Morningstar Mutual Funds. Chicago: Morningstar, Inc. 1 volume (loose-leaf
biweekly). Also available on CD-ROM as *Morningstar Mutual Funds
OnDisc*.
An expensive ($395) but very useful loose-leaf financial advisory service somewhat
reminiscent of *Value Line* because each issue consists of one-page statistical profiles
of the important mutual funds, packed full of information, and also the fact that
sections are revised on a rotating basis. For each fund, one can find: a description
and analysis, basic operating facts such as minimum and subsequent investment,
fund manager, fees; several years of statistics for total return, income, capital gains,
performance/risk (including Alpha and Beta); 13-year historical financial statistics,
portfolio holdings for largest equities, sector weightings; % loan, yield, total assets,
NAV, Morningstar rating (one-to-five stars).
   Some potential subscribers may opt to purchase instead their annual *Mutual Fund
Sourcebook* (2 volumes, $225), which is a year-end reference guide to more than
1,000 equity funds and 1,000 fixed-income funds. It contains much the same information about each fund as of the end of each year, except that it does not include the
analyses and Morningstar ratings. Two other related publications are: *Morningstar
Closed-End Funds* (a biweekly covering more than 200 of the most actively traded
closed-end funds) and *Mutual Fund Performance Report* (a monthly source for
performance results on over 2,300 mutual funds).

Mutual Fund Directory. New York: Investment Dealers' Digest, Inc. (semi-annual).

Background information and statistics about each mutual fund, with sections for load funds, no-loads, institutional funds, contractual plans; also indexes of name changes/mergers, money market funds, managed municipal bond funds. For each fund it usually gives investment objective, shares outstanding, asset value, total assets, number of shareholders, minimum initial purchase, management fee, fund manager, a 10-year statistical record, officers, a Lipper analytical ranking, CUSIP number, and more.

Mutual Fund Profiles. New York: Standard & Poor's Corporation and Lipper Analytical Services (quarterly).

This consists of half-page statistical profiles of more than 750 mutual funds. Each profile gives investment policy, performance evaluation, portfolio composition, top holdings, NASDAQ symbol, when first offered, minimum investment, charges, portfolio manager, net asset value (NAV), total assets, volatility, Lipper rating, and a five-year statistical trend. Ranked list of top performers is at end, and also an index grouping firms by investment objective and by the fund administrator/advisor. Additional taxable funds and munibond funds are listed after the profiles.

United Mutual Fund Selector. Boston: United Business Service Co. (semi-monthly).

A short newsletter, giving performance comparisons and other information, including data on specific recommended funds.

Wiesenberger Investment Companies Service. *Investment Companies.* New York: Wiesenberger Financial Services (annual).

This is a long-time basic source for factual information on mutual funds and other types of investment companies. Part 3 contains statistics and other information on individual open-end investment companies, including money market funds, tax-exempt municipal bond funds, unit trusts; part 4 covers closed-end investment companies and mutual fund management companies. For each of the larger, older U.S. companies it usually gives objective, special services, 11-year statistical history, names of directors, facts such as sales charge, investment adviser, and value of shares over a 10-year period. Lesser information about smaller companies. Part 1 provides general background information; part 2 discusses investment companies in use, and it has a glossary. In addition part 3 contains: "Mutual Funds Panorama," a tabular listing of mutual funds registered in the U.S. (this is also available as a separate publication); a historical table for "Wiesenberger Mutual Fund Indexes"; a table on "price volatility of mutual fund shares," and more. This is a large volume with double-column pages. Current tables on management performance of many specific funds, arranged by objective of the fund, is in their monthly *Management Results.*

Annual or quarterly issues of several financial periodicals contain current lists of mutual funds, usually including for each, net assets, performance, expenses (and more as cited below). See, for example:

Barron's. "Lipper Mutual Funds Quarterly" (usually in second issues for February, May, August, and November).

An alphabetical list of over 2,000 funds, giving also objectives, fees, name of manager.

Business Week. "The Best Mutual Funds" (annual, 2 parts in last February issues).

The table of over 700 funds is called "Mutual Fund Scoreboard." It also gives for each the objective, rating, fees, portfolio data, risk; part 2 covers income funds (bond funds).

FW: Financial World. "Mutual Fund Annual" (first February issue).

Ranks the 100 best mutual funds by fund objective. Some current figures are in their "Mutual Fund Quarterly Review" (e.g. first issues in May, August). These latter issues also contain an "Independent Appraisal of Mutual Funds," tabular data on over 900 funds including assets, total return, charges, risk, and past performance ranks.

Forbes. "Annual Mutual Fund Survey" (first September issue).

Includes performance ratings on over 1,000 funds, with data on best buys.

Money. "The Money Rankings" (annual, February).

For 1,000 funds, it also gives portfolio analysis, Lipper market-phase rating, risk-adjusted grade. A mid-year report (August) lists a smaller number of funds.

Financial information on leading investment companies can be found in volume 2 of the annual *Moody's Bank & Financial Manual*. Brief data on prices can be found in the monthly *Bank & Quotation Record* and in S&P's *Stock Guide*. The most recent prices are in such newspapers as *Investor's Business Daily*, *The New York Times*, and the *Wall Street Journal*.

GUIDES TO READING THE FINANCIAL PAGES

For several helpful guides to the more general topic of understanding basic U.S. economic and financial measures, see section on "Guides to Economic and Financial Measures" in Chapter 3.

Warfield, Gerald. *The Investor's Guide to Stock Quotations and Other Financial Listings*. 3d ed. New York: Harper & Row, 1990. 254 pp.

Highly recommended for the beginner who wants to understand how to read the bewildering array of stock and other financial quotations and abbreviations appearing in newspaper financial sections. Enlarged photographic reproductions of specific tables appear throughout with easy to understand explanations of how to read and interpret each figure given. It is arranged in five parts to cover "how to read": stock market quotations; corporate, municipal, and government bond quotations; mutual funds and money market funds; option quotations; futures quotations. At end are: a table of dollar/decimal equivalents of fractions used in securities quotes; explanation for bond ratings; a short glossary. Warfield has also written another book for beginners called *How to Read and Understand Financial News* (Harper & Row, 1986, 214 pp.). It gives simple explanations of various securities, options, futures, etc., and of a few economic and financial measures.

Wuman, Richard S. et al. *The Wall Street Journal Guide to Understanding Money & Markets*. New York: Access Press, 1990. 119 pp. paper.

An even simpler guide, this primer uses the *Wall Street Journal* as a focal point in explaining the important financial terms, charts, and tables that are in each issue. There is little text except for the simple explanations, but it is full of useful illustrations, charts, and reproductions of financial tables. The sections cover: stocks, bonds, mutual funds, futures, options, and money.

Jarrell, Howard R. *Common Stock Newspaper Abbreviations and Trading Symbols.* Metuchen, NJ: Scarecrow Press, 1989. 413 pp.

This more specialized book fills a void by identifying listed and over-the-counter companies according to Associated Press abbreviations used in newspaper stock price tables (see part 2) and their stock trading or ticker symbol (part 3). Part 1 lists the companies alphabetically, giving for each the newspaper abbreviation, trading symbol, and the exchange on which the company is traded.

For persons who prefer a shorter explanation on "Reading the Financial Pages," consider using chapters that appear in several investment texts on this topic. See, for example, *Investments* by H. E. Dougall and F. J. Corrigan (11th ed., Prentice-Hall, 1984, pp. 227–230); *Techniques of Financial Analysis* by E. A. Helfert (7th ed., 1991, pp. 418–427); *Understanding Wall Street* by J. Little and L. Rhodes (3d ed., Blue Ridge Summit, PA: Liberty Hall Press, 1991, pp. 53–72); or *The Business One Irwin Business and Investment Almanac* (annual) in its sections on stocks, bonds, and so forth.

GUIDES TO FINANCIAL SERVICES AND STATISTICS

Chapman, Karen J. *Investment Statistics Locator.* Phoenix, AZ: Oryx Press, 1988. 182 pp.

This indexes, by specific subject/topic, the commodity, securities, and other investment statistics found in 22 standard reference sources, including several Moody's and S & P publications. It is of potential use especially for new or non-business information specialists, but only if it is revised periodically because this type of source is so quickly outdated.

Downes, John and Jordan E. Goodman. *Barron's Finance and Investment Handbook.* 3d ed. New York: Barron's, 1990. 1,234 pp.

A useful compendium especially for persons who do not have access to the information it contains in other sources. Part 1 of its 5 parts contains concise profiles of 30 key investment alternatives, such as annuities and money market funds. Parts 2 and 3 explain how to read corporate annual reports and the financial pages of newspapers. Part 4 is a "Dictionary of Finance and Investment" (about 400 pages; also published separately and described elsewhere in this chapter). Part 5 presents such "ready reference" lists as: sources for information and assistance (including names of finance and investment publications); major financial institutions (banks, stock exchanges, etc.); directory of mutual funds; summary of futures and options contracts; historical data on stock market indexes and on economic indicators; addresses of companies traded on each of the principal exchanges; stock symbols for over 6,000 companies. An appendix includes a good, short annotated list of key financial and investment books, currencies of the world, abbreviations and acronyms.

Grant, Mary M. and Riva Berleant-Schiller, comps. *Directory of Business and Financial Services.* 8th ed. New York: Special Libraries Association, 1984. 189 pp.

This directory is now out of date, but a 9th edition is in progress by two different compilers (Charles J. Popovich and M. Rita Costello). Its possible title is "Information Services Directory for Business Intelligence," and a tentative publication date is 1993. Like the present directory, this will describe business, economic, and financial services (loose-leaf, online, as well as newsletters), and it will presumably also have similar indexes by subject, by geographic area covered, and by name of publisher.

Most of the better textbooks on investment management include short, informative chapters discussing basic sources of investment information. These usually describe reference books both for industries and for companies and sometimes also cover useful sources of information about the current economy. The chapters often include sample pages from important investment manuals so one can visualize the kinds of data included in that particular service. Two texts with the longest chapters are: *Investment Analysis and Portfolio Management* by J. B. Cohen et al. and *Management of Investments* by J. C. Francis. Others are in texts by Reilly (example of an annotated list) and Alexander and Sharpe (short but with a good outline by category or frequency of publication). Levine's *The Financial Analyst's Handbook* has chapters describing published sources of value to analysts, and online databases. For complete citations to these and similar books see the section describing "Investment Management Books" in this chapter.

INDEXES TO FINANCIAL PUBLICATIONS

Predicasts F & S Index United States. Cleveland, OH: Predicasts, Inc. (weekly, cumulated monthly and annually). Online counterpart is *PTS F&S Indexes.*

This is the best periodical index to use when searching for current information on U.S. companies, products and industries in a wide selection of trade magazines, business-oriented newspapers, and other financial publications. The subject/product section in each issue lists articles (or data in articles), arranged by a modified 7-digit SIC industry code, and it also covers basic economic indicators. The company section indexes articles and parts of articles on current developments in specific U.S. companies relating to such topics as management, products and processes, marketing information. As of 1991, this index is also available on CD-ROM as *F & S Plus TEXT,* but only to nonprofit organizations. Companion indexes for articles on foreign industries and companies are described elsewhere in this chapter.

The *Wall Street Journal* has its own monthly index, with annual cumulations. Each issue is in two parts: corporate news; general news.

For an unannotated bibliography of finance that includes listings of many articles on specific investment topics (such as valuation of common stocks, options, hedging instruments), refer to *A Bibliography of Finance* by Richard Brealey and Helen Edwards (Cambridge, MA: MIT Press, 1991, 822 pp.), described in the "Finance Bibliographies" section of Chapter 14.

INVESTMENT NEWSPAPERS AND PERIODICALS

The general periodicals on finance, corporate finance, and banking are in Chapter 14. This section describes those financial periodicals and newspapers that are of most interest to investors both for their practical articles, their stock market quotations, and other statistical features. The *Financial Analysts Journal* and *Journal of Portfolio Management* are described in the "Investment Management Journals" section of this chapter.

Barron's. New York: Dow Jones & Co. (weekly).

This is an indispensable "national business and financial weekly" with excellent articles on prospects for industries and individual companies, and on a wide range of other business and financial topics of interest to investors. Among the several continuing features are: a short list of research reports by investment firms, data on a few IPOs, short list of insider transactions, and recent data from current corporate reports. Extensive statistics in each issue include: stock and bond price quotations for the NYSE, AMEX, and NASDAQ, and lesser companies covered for other North American exchanges and the more important exchanges overseas; tables for mutual funds, option trading, government securities, commodity futures, foreign exchange rates; Dow Jones and other market indexes, Dow Jones Industry Group statistics; economic and financial indicators such as money supply, money rates, the "pulse of industry and trade," and more. An index to companies cited is at the front of each issue. Once a month there are "short interest" tables, usually the third issue covering NYSE and AMEX companies and the fourth or last, NASDAQ companies. A quarterly survey of mutual fund performance for over 2,000 funds, called "Lipper Mutual Funds Quarterly," usually is in the second issue in February, May, August, and November. This weekly is indexed in ABI/I, BPI, PTS/F&S, TI; also full text on DOW JONES. An annual index is in the *Wall Street Journal Index,* volume 1 (the green pages).

Equities. New York: OTC Review, Inc. (monthly).

Formerly called *The OTC Review,* this contains articles and news about middle-market and emerging NASDAQ companies and people. Periodic issues contain lists of companies on the NYSE, AMEX, and NASDAQ based on specific factors such as most profitable companies (May 1991), dividends (June), fastest-growing American companies (August). The "NASDAQ 1000" (annual in September) is a ranked list arranged by market value, with a separate alphabetical list giving the rankings of each company according to four financial criteria; another annual list is for "Emerging Growth Funds" (November). Each issue has an index of companies cited in articles. Indexed in PTS/F&S.

FW: Financial World. New York (biweekly).

Articles often analyze general investment situations, prospects for industries and for individual companies. Each issue contains a "Financial Week/Merrill Lynch Index," as well as an index of the companies cited in the issue. About once a month there is a statistical section giving an "Independent Appraisal of Stocks," with one month covering about 1,300 listed stocks and the next, over 800 OTC stocks, and less often the table is devoted to current facts about almost 1,000 mutual funds. Special annual features include: "Mutual Fund Annual" (first February issue), with rankings of 100 best funds by category; "International Issue" (first March) with ranked lists of "The FW Foreign 500," "The 100 Largest Foreign Financial Companies," the "50 Cheap Foreign Growth Companies"; "The Reliability 500" (last April), a ranking by performance for the most valuable U.S. corporations; a short ranked list of 100 CEO salaries, "Executive Compensation" (last April); "Midyear Forecast" (first June); "America's Fastest Growing Companies" (first August); "Ranking America's Biggest Banks" (second August); "The Compensation 500" (last October 1991), a table giving salary facts for 500 CEOs, with the ranking by recommended (decrease) increase of 1991 salary over 1990; "The Performance 1,000" (last October), ranked list of the 50 most successful U.S. corporations and the 50 least successful; "Forecast" (combined last December, first January issue), containing a two-page outlook for each of about 25 industries, with statistics on the leading companies. The dates of these annual features is based on an inspection of 1991 issue. FW is indexed in ABI/I, BPI, PTS/F&S; also full text on BRS, DATA-STAR, DIALOG, DOW JONES, MEAD/NEXIS.

Forbes. New York (biweekly).

Short, readable articles of interest to business and financial executives, including prospects for industries and individual companies and brief sketches of individuals. Each issue contains regular columns, a "Forbes Index," a "Statistical Spotlight," the Forbes/Wall Street Review, an index to companies cited, and a page called "Thoughts on the Business of Life" (interesting/amusing quotes on a chosen topic). Their two most important annual issues are described elsewhere in this chapter: an "Annual Report on American Industry" (first January issue) and "Annual Directory Issue" (last April). Other useful annual features include: "Performance Ratings on 666 Mutual Funds" (first February); "Annual Mutual Fund Survey" with performance ratings on over 1,000 funds plus best buys (first September); "What 800 CEOs Made Last Year" (last May), giving also other brief information about each CEO; "The Forbes International 500 Survey" (third week in July), consisting of ranked lists of the 500 largest foreign companies by country (including other financial data for each), 100 largest foreign investments in U.S., 100 largest U.S. multinationals, 100 U.S.-trading foreign stocks, 100 cheapest foreign stocks; "The World's Billionaires," with profiles of each (last July); "The 400 Richest People in America" (last October), with profiles of each; "The 200 Best Small Companies in America," a ranked list (mid-November); the "Largest Private Companies in the U.S.", a ranked list (first December). This periodical is indexed in ABI/I, BPI, PTS/F&S, RG, TI; also full text on DATA-STAR, DIALOG, DOW JONES, MEAD/NEXIS.

Institutional Investor. New York (monthly).

A practical journal of interest to money managers. Its articles are on such topics as money management, banks, pensions, corporate finance, mergers and acquisitions, investor relations, portfolio strategy, and profiles of specific money managers. Almost every issue contains one or more useful annual features. Based on an inspection of the 1991 issues, these include: "Forecast" (January issue); "Deals of the Year" (January), ranking noteworthy financings of the past year; "Underwriting Sweepstakes" (February), ranking the top corporate underwriters by category of underwriting, the leaders in international bond financing, and municipal underwriters; "Midyear Financing Sweepstakes" (September); "The (year) All-British Research Team" (February) and "The (year) All American Research Team" (October), one ranking over 100 British analysts in 16 firms and the other over 400 U.S. analysts in 34 firms that have done the most outstanding work during the past year; "The (year) M & A Sweepstakes" (March), ranking the top M & A advisers and deals concerning U.S.-based companies; "Ranking America's Biggest Brokers" (April); "Ranking America's Largest Money Managers" (July); "The World's Largest Banks" (July); "America's Best IR Officers" (August), profiling the best investor relations officers; "The Best Annual Reports" (September). Specialized directories are often in issues including: "The (year) Pension Directory" (January), which contains key information on 500 large corporate employee benefit funds, on their managers, and on public pension funds (by state); "The (year) Foreign Exchange Directory" (February), listing key forex persons at major banks; "The (year) Public Finance Directory" (May), a directory of leading public finance underwriters; "The (year) M & A Directory" (November), listing leading M & A specialists; "The (year) Real Estate Directory" (December), giving corporate executives in charge of real estate. This journal is indexed in ABI/I, BPI, PAIS, TI; also in full text on BRS, DATA-STAR, DIALOG, MEAD/NEXIS.

This important journal has an "International Edition" (also published monthly), containing some of the same material but concentrating more on articles of interest to international money managers. Annual features include: "The (year) All-British Research Team (February); "The (year) International Financing Sweepstakes" (February), and the "Six Month International Financing Sweepstakes" (September); "Country Credit Ratings" (March and October), which ranks countries for their risk potential; "The European M & A Sweepstakes" (March), ranking the top M & A advisers and deals concerning European-based companies; "Ranking the World's Largest Banks" (July); the "World's Best Hotels" (October). Specialized directories in issues include: "The (year) Foreign Exchange Directory" (February); "The International Stock Exchange Directory" (April), giving brief facts on each of 81 stock exchanges in 55 countries; "The (year) International Investment Manager Directory" (October); "The (year) British Pension Directory (November); "The (year) Trade Finance Directory" December).

Investment Dealers' Digest. New York (weekly).

A weekly news magazine for the securities industry, with over half of each issue devoted to the following useful current lists relating to corporate financings: securities in registration and those registered during the previous week (including shelf and initial offers), weekly review of offerings by underwriter, a calendar of securities offerings, also a short table of "swaps and caps." Special features include a "Full Year Rankings" (first January issue), with quarterly rankings in the second issues for April, July, October. These consist of sections on: "Domestic Corporate Financing" (ranking underwriters by type of issue; also ranking IPOs, and other kinds of issues); "International Corporate Financing" (Eurobonds, etc.); "Municipal Financing." Other special issues are: the "M & A Rankings" (second January), with another M&A ranking in mid-July; "Private Placement Rankings" (second May and first September issues); "Deals of the Year" (last December). Indexed in PTS/ PROMT; full text on DATA-STAR, DIALOG, MEAD/NEXIS.

IDD also publishes two separate semiannual directories described elsewhere in this chapter: *Corporate Finance* and *Mutual Fund Directory*.

Investor's Business Daily. Los Angeles.

Begun in 1984 as an alternative to the *Wall Street Journal,* this is a financial newspaper, with many of the same financial tables but also with differences. It is primarily statistical although, beginning in September 1991, it does have three articles on the first page: one on a national issue or important company; one a profile on an important decision maker; one on a top economic or business story. There are also news items throughout. The tables of listed and OTC stock prices include the following figures not in the *WSJ:* EPS rank, relative price strength, industry group relative strength (on Mondays only), % change in volume, dividend % yield (every Friday); also companies in boldface have had a new price high or are up 1 point or more, while companies underlined are those with a new price low or are down 1 point or more. Stock charts are given for stocks that have hit new price highs. Tables are also given for the most important companies on regional exchanges and on overseas exchanges. Other data includes: tables on preferred stocks; company earnings news; Dow Jones and other stock price index charts, including "Investor's Business Daily 6000"; mutual fund performance, futures options, futures prices and charts; stock and index options, foreign exchange rates, issues in registration for about one month; data on bonds, government securities, money rates (including Libor). Each issue includes a detailed financial chart for one company as taken from the *O'Neil Database.*

Wall Street Journal. New York: Dow Jones & Co. (daily).

This is the leading U.S. daily financial newspaper, indispensable for all business persons. It is arranged in three sections. The first covers important news stories, interesting front-page feature articles, and a page each on international news, politics and policy, leisure and arts; section 2, "Marketplace," focuses on stories and news of companies and how they compete, consumers, marketing, technology, and more. It also contains an index of companies cited in the issue. Section 3, "Money & Investing," is full of useful tables including: daily stock market quotations for NYSE, AMEX, NASDAQ companies (giving, along with prices, the stock symbol, dividend % yield, PE ratio; also companies in boldface have had price changes of 5% or more, while companies underlined have had a large change in volume); selected stocks are listed on regional exchanges and on overseas exchanges; listed options, mutual funds, bond quotations; also commodity futures and cash prices, Treasury and government issues, money rates and interest rate instruments (including Libor), Dow Jones averages and other stock market indexes, foreign exchange rates. About 8 issues throughout the year contain a fourth, Special Report section, such as the one on "World Business" (appearing around September 24 each year) which includes ranked lists of the world's largest public companies, insurers, banks and securities firms, plus an "International Country Risk Guide" in the September 20, 1991 issue. This *Journal* is available online via *National Newspaper Index,* and its statistics are on *Dow Jones News Retrieval;* also full text of articles and news is on DOW JONES. It has its own index noted separately in this chapter.

For a book explaining the key statistical series in the *Wall Street Journal* see *The Dow Jones-Irwin Guide to Using the Wall Street Journal* by M.B. Lehmann (3d ed. Homewood, IL: Dow Jones-Irwin, 1990, 382 pp.).

FOREIGN INVESTMENT INFORMATION SOURCES

This section does not attempt to cover foreign investment sources completely; it does mention a few of the best known international, European, and Japanese services and several covering British and Canadian companies.

INTERNATIONAL INVESTMENT SERVICES

Disclosure/Worldscope Industrial Company Profiles. Bridgeport, CT: Worldscope/Disclosure Partners. 5 unnumbered volumes (annual). Available also on magnetic tape and CD-ROM.

This relative new service (1987) consists of one-page financial facts about more than 3,000 leading industrial companies in 24 countries and in 18 industries. Tables for each company cover (for a 6-year period): financial statement statistics; financial ratios and growth rates; per share data and investment ratios; also top officers, selected data in U.S. dollars, five-year annual growth rate, and averages of financial ratios. One volume is a "Users' Guide," containing an index as well as industry averages, company rankings (worldwide, within each country, and within industries). The other four volumes provide the profiles for companies in: Asia, Africa, Australia; North America (2 volumes); Europe.

A companion service is *Disclosure/Worldscope Financial and Service Company Profiles* (3 volumes) covering more than 1,000 financial and service companies in 24 countries, with similar data given for each company. One of the three volumes is a "Users' Guide," and the other two contain the company profiles.

Extel Card Services. London: Extel Financial Ltd.

Extel offers for the United Kingdom and for several other countries comprehensive company financial data services similar to those available on U.S. companies from Moody's and Standard & Poor's, but in a different format. The format is described in the following section covering United Kingdom sources. It is important to list here because it offers international *Extel Card* services for 8 other countries or regions: *Australian Card Service* (about 200 leading companies in Australia and New Zealand); *European Card Service* (over 600 companies); *Hong Kong Card Service* (100 companies); *Japanese Card Service* (100 companies); *Malaysian Card Service* (all companies on the Kuala Lumpur Stock Exchange); *North American Card Service* (500 companies in the U.S. and Canada); *Singapore Card Service* (all companies on the Singapore Stock Exchange); *Thai Card Service* (all companies on the Bangkok Stock Exchange).

Moody's International Manual. New York: Moody's Investors Service. 2 volumes (annual, with a biweekly *News Report*). Available also online and on CD-ROM.

Begun in 1981, this gives important financial and business information on over 5,000 major foreign corporations in more than 100 countries. It is arranged by country, with an alphabetical index at front and indexes by industry/product and by country in the center blue pages of each volume. One can usually find more complete information about those companies who pay for "ultra coverage," including a table for capital structure, history, business and properties, subsidiaries, officers and directors, letter to stockholders, 7 years of balance sheet, income figures, and financial & operating ratios. At the beginning of each country section is brief data on the country—a profile, loan data and bond descriptions, finance/currency/banking, resources/production/services, international transactions. The center blue pages in volume 1 contain useful statistical tables such as: stock exchange indexes for the principal foreign exchanges; stock splits; money market rates and exchange rates for countries; Moody's Daily Commodity Price Index (monthly since 1928); a 10- or 15-year run of selected world statistics for consumer prices, national income and gross domestic product, international reserves, foreign trade, motor vehicle registrations, world shipbuilding, and more. Moody's publishes a separate *Moody's Complete Corporate Index* which lists all companies in each of the Moody's Manuals. Back volumes of Moody's are available on microfiche. There are several online products, and the CD-Rom is *Moody's International plus*.

Stopford, John. *Directory of Multinationals.* 4th ed. New York: Stockton Press, 1992. 2 volumes. $595.

Useful financial profiles of 450 major multinational enterprises controlling important direct investments in the world. For each it gives names of directors, a profile of
the structure, products, background and current situation, major shareholders, principal subsidiaries and affiliates; also five-year financial statistics often including sales
for principal products as % of total sales, and net sales for each pertinent geographic
region.

For persons needing a reference service covering international bonds (including Eurobonds), Extel Financial, Ltd., offers an *International Bonds Service*.
This gives details on some 13,000 international bonds in 16 countries, with
weekly updated "News Sheets." Its online counterpart is *EXBOND*.

FOREIGN CORPORATE ANNUAL REPORTS

Disclosure, Inc., in Bethesda, MD, offers a microfiche service for annual reports from over 7,000 international corporations in more than 40 countries,
called *Microfiche D/International* (also available on CD-ROM as *Laser D/
International*). Subscribers can either get the complete file of reports, or they
can take advantage of a variety of options. Paper copies can also be requested.

A British firm, The ICC Information Group Ltd., produces a database
called *ICC International Annual Reports* which consists of the complete text of
Annual Reports and Accounts prepared by 500 European quoted companies
and all U.K.-quoted companies.

EUROPEAN SOURCES

Extel Card Services: European Card Service. London: Extel Financial Ltd.
This is a card service similar to their service for British companies which is described
in the following section on United Kingdom sources. It covers information on over
600 leading European companies from 15 countries. See also the next section for
mention of Extel's online services.

Besides the *Financial Times* newspaper which has good coverage of news
about European companies, now there is also a *Wall Street Journal Europe*.

UNITED KINGDOM SOURCES

Extel Card Services: The U.K. Listed Companies Service and **The Unlisted
Securities Market Service** (USM). London: Extel Financial Ltd.
Extel is the principal publisher of company financial data in the U.K., and they also
offer services for other European and Asian companies. Their services are similar in
data covered to those available on U.S. companies from Moody's and Standard &
Poor's, but they are published in a different format. The services usually consist of two
sets of what they call "cards" but which are in fact sheets of paper: one is a folded
white "Annual Card" that contains the same basic facts and statistics usually found in
U.S. financial manuals; the other is a colored "News Card" issued daily as there is
significant news to report, with this news cumulative. The two services listed above
are for British companies, with the Listed Companies Service providing data on
approximately 2,500 companies listed on the International Stock Exchange of the
U.K. and the Republic of Ireland. The USM Service contains cards for all companies
traded on the USM and the Irish Smaller Companies Market (updated semiannually).

A third British card service is *The Unquoted Companies Service* covering 1,700 of the larger unquoted companies. Subscribers to all the Extel services are offered a number of options, such as getting only the annual cards, or only those in a specific industry. The data in the various services are also available online via *EXSTAT;* statistics on securities is on *EXSHARE;* international bond statistics is on *EXBOND.*

Among Extel's more specialized services are: *Extel Handbook of Market Leaders* (described below); *Extel Professional Advisers to New Issues,* an annual record of major new issues for the previous year and a separate section providing details of their financial advisers, stockbrokers, solicitors, accountants; and *Extel Takeovers, Offers, and New Issues* (monthly), a record listing of all capital events during the year for U.K. Listed and USM companies.

The Hambro Company Guide. London: Hemmington Scott Publishing Ltd. (quarterly).

Most of each issue contains brief profiles (usually four or five per page) of all U.K. quoted companies, including those that are USM companies (Unlisted Securities Market), or Third Market, or OTC companies. For each, it usually provides a statement of activities, names of directors, financial advisers, balance sheet and profit and loss statistics for five years, and occasionally other figures such as EPS, ROCE (return on capital employed), debt to equity, and a share price graph. At the front are data and rankings of types of financial advisers, short reports, profiles of investment management groups, and indexes according to type of quoted company noted above and several other categories. At end are lists of professional advisers and their clients, including auditors, lawyers, property advisers, stockbrokers.

Handbook of Market Leaders. London: Extel Financial, Ltd. (semiannual).

One-page concise information (including charts) for each of the 674 leading British companies comprising the FT-Actuaries All Share Index. This is the British equivalent of the *Stock Market Encyclopedia of the S & P "500".* A companion volume is *Extel Secondary Markets Handbook* covering all USM and Irish Smaller Market Companies (annual).

London Stock Exchange Official Yearbook. London: Macmillan Publishers Ltd. (Published in U.S. by Stockton Press, New York City).

A basic financial manual for officially listed British companies and public corporations. At front is general information on: The LSE; the securities market in the U.K. (including a list of LSE companies arranged by industry); trading, settlement, and transfer; taxation; trustees; British, Commonwealth, Provincial and foreign government securities. At end is a "Register of Defunct and Other Companies" (which is no longer published separately).

Macmillan's Unquoted Companies. Comp. by ICC Business Publications Ltd. Basingstocke, Hant. Eng.: Macmillan. 2 volumes (annual).

Short profiles of Britain's top 20,000 unquoted companies (about 14 profiles per page). For each it usually gives: address, phone and fax numbers, principal activities, SIC numbers, directors, financial facts for a three-year period. At front of volume 1 are rankings of top 100 companies by sales, profits, and average employee remuneration. At end of volume 2 are industry and geographic indexes.

Newspapers and Periodicals

Financial Times. London (daily). Also available online, and on CD-ROM as of 1992.

An important British newspaper that provides worldwide coverage for business, financial, and economic news, including news of companies and some general news. Its section on "Companies and Markets" includes the following tables: London Share Service tables (arranged by industry and giving current stock quotes); some stock quotes on other exchanges around the world; FT Managed Funds Service tables (insurance, unit trusts, offshore and overseas funds); also stock price indexes, the "FT-Actuaries Share Indices," London traded options; money rates (including Libor), financial futures, world commodity prices, foreign exchange rates, and more. An annual "European 500" (e.g., January 13, 1992, and also published separately) consists of ranked lists both of Europe's top 500 companies and the top U.K. 500.

A separately published *Monthly Index to the Financial Times* (which cumulates annually) began in 1981. In addition there are several databases for information from this newspaper: *Financial Times Company Information Database* for abstracts of company and business news items; *Financial Times Currency and Share Index Database,* a time series for statistics on stocks, indexes, and so forth; and *Financial Times Fulltext* for complete text of all articles. The Financial Times Business Information Ltd. publishes a *Guide to Financial Times Statistics* (6th ed., 1991, about 60 pp.) which is helpful for its explanations of the statistics and indexes covered (with sample pages) as well as on how this newspaper handles company news.

Investors Chronicle. London: F. T. Business Information Ltd. (weekly).

Incorporating the *Stock Exchange Gazette* and the British *Financial World,* this is a useful financial weekly covering news about British companies, the London markets, international investment, and more. Each issue contains three profile sections for "Company Results" describing for investors a selection of British companies, European companies, and smaller companies. Each issue also lists new issues, mergers and acquisitions (takeover bids and rights issues), a page of brokers' tips, and a page of statistics (economic indicators and some stock market data). An index of companies covered is in each issue. Indexed in PTS/F&S, PAIS; also available online.

CANADIAN SOURCES

Financial Post. *Survey of Industrials.* Toronto, Ontario, Can.: Financial Post Information Service (annual).

This is the basic financial manual for more than 2,000 Canadian public industrial companies and for mutual funds. For each company it usually gives stock symbol, CUSIP number, fax number, details of operations, management, subsidiaries, financial data. Data on mutual funds is in a short section at end. A companion financial manual is their annual *Survey of Mines and Energy Resources.* The *Financial Post* itself is a weekly newspaper and the most important current source for news about Canadian business, investments, and public affairs. Each issue includes weekly stock price quotes covering all four of the Canadian stock exchanges in a single list. Every summer this newspaper publishes a separate report called *The Financial Post 500,* an annual ranked list of Canada's largest companies. It includes a separate ranking by industry; also lists of private companies, banks, and "the next 200." They also publish an annual *Ten Year Price Range* of listed stocks, and an annual *Canadian Bond Prices.* All of this data including articles in the newspaper is available in full text online in *FP ONLINE.*

Several other annual ranked lists of largest Canadian companies, besides the one noted above, are: (1) "The Canadian Business Corporate 500" in the monthly magazine *Canadian Business* (June issue), which also ranks the next 250, the subsidiaries 100, the finance 100; (2) the "Investors' 500" in the weekly *Financial Times of Canada* (a mid-June issue), ranking the companies by market value; (3) "The Top 1000" in the Globe and Mail's monthly *Report on Business Magazine* (July issue) which reports on corporate performance in Canada by ranking the companies by profit; also including separate rankings by industry, and a list of the top 300 private Canadian companies. Each of these rankings also gives other financial figures for each company.

JAPANESE SOURCES

Daiwa Securities Co. Ltd. *Analysts' Guide.* Tokyo (annual).
Written in both Japanese and English, this consists of one-page statistical tables containing five-year tabular financial data and stock prices for companies listed on the Tokyo Stock Exchange. Ranked lists of top 100 companies by various categories are at front.

Diamond's Japan Business Directory. Tokyo: Diamond Lead Co. (annual).
A comprehensive financial manual for Japanese companies, written in English. It is arranged by industry, with a company index at front. A list of brands and trade names and a list of organizations are at end.

Japan Company Handbook: First Section. Tokyo: Toyo Keizai Inc. (quarterly).
One-page concise data on 1,264 First Section companies on the Tokyo, Osaka, and Nagoya stock exchanges, arranged by industry. Another volume is *Japan Company Handbook: Second Section,* which contains similar data about 759 companies listed on the Second Section, plus separate half-page data on 370 over-the-counter, 252 unlisted, and 61 local market companies. A companion handbook is *Asian Company Handbook,* with brief data on 1,000 leading Asian companies.

Manual of Securities Statistics. Tokyo: Nomura Securities Co. (annual).
Key statistics on the stock market, including number of companies on the TSE, stock price indexes (including Nikkei stock averages), trading volume on all exchanges, market value on TSE, number of shareholders, security financings. Separate sections cover: investment trusts; bonds; foreign securities; futures & options; miscellaneous data.

Morningstar Japan. Chicago. 1 volume (loose-leaf, biweekly).
For potential investors, here is a useful (but expensive—$395) financial advisory service covering 700 leading Japanese companies. Its one-page profiles are filled with facts and figures including: description of company's operation, summary of activities, sales, capacity, ownership %, key employee statistics, dividends, stock price graph, growth rates, balance sheet statistics, 11-year historical operating and financial figures; also P/E, yield, recent stock price, Alpha, Beta, earnings forecast. It is arranged by industry and revised on a rotating basis. With each issue is a Summary Section containing an updated index, which gives a recent stock price, P/E, and EPS; also stock and industry rankings, statistics on the economy and on the market.

Tokyo Stock Market Quarterly Review. Tokyo: Daiwa Institute of Research Ltd.

Written in English and arranged by a Daiwa industry classification code, this is a continuing source for current financial statistics on Japanese companies. For each company it usually provides: current price (in yen), market value, rates of return, turnover ratio, risk, P/E ratio, dividend yield, adjusted EPS, per share data, return on equity. At front are useful tables and charts including: Tokyo Stock Price Index (TOPIX) and Nikkei Stock Averages (back to 1979), futures indices, comparative data on world stock markets, charts for Japan's main economic indicators, tables listing leading companies by industry giving financial statistics for each, and ranked lists of the 50 top stocks by rate of return, turnover ratio, and market value.

Newspapers

Asian Wall Street Journal. Hong Kong: Dow Jones & Co. (weekly). Also available online.

An important weekly newspaper that covers current financial and business news not only for Japan but for all of Asia. Includes securities quotes for Asian-Pacific companies, commodity prices, Asian stock market indexes, foreign exchange. Indexed in PTS/F&S; full text on DOW JONES.

ONLINE FINANCIAL SERVICES COVERING FOREIGN COMPANIES

Today more and more financial data on European and other foreign companies is available online, and this trend is bound to continue. Persons who need quick access to company financial figures and the latest corporate developments should monitor the several database directories and journals (such as *Online*) in order to keep up with the introduction of new databases and the enhancement of existing files covering foreign companies. Several of the best known or most useful are:

CIFARBASE. Princeton, NJ: Center for International Financial Analysis and Research.

This provides financial data on 7,000 leading companies in 48 countries.

DATASTREAM Company Accounts. London: Datastream International, Ltd.

Covers financial data on U.K. companies (both quoted companies, USM-quoted companies, and unquoted companies) as well as selected companies in other countries.

EXSTAT and **EXSHARE.** London: Extel Financial, Ltd.

The online counterpart of several print sources of data on British companies and securities information. See section covering British company sources in this chapter.

ICC International Annual Reports. Hampton, Middlesex, Eng.: ICC Online Databases, Ltd.

Provides full text of Annual Reports and Accounts for 500 European quoted companies, and for all U.K. quoted companies.

LASER D/INTERNATIONAL. Bethesda, MD: Disclosure, Inc.

International annual reports on CD-ROM.

Moody's International plus. New York: Moody's Investors Service, Inc.

This is the CD-ROM counterpart to *Moody's International Manual,* with information on more than 5,000 major foreign companies in some 100 countries.

NIKKEI FINANCIAL FILE. Tokyo: Nihon Keizai Shimbun, Inc.

Consists of about 7 different financial statistical databases, and includes some 287 items of financial company data both on listed and non-listed Japanese companies. For further description consult one of the directories of databases.

LISTS OF LARGEST FOREIGN COMPANIES

Britain's Top Privately Owned Companies. Bristol, Eng: Jordan & Sons Ltd., 1990. 2 volumes (annual).

Volume 1 is a ranking of the top 2,000 private companies, by sales, with additional financial figures given, plus employment statistics for each. Volume 2 covers rankings for the next 2,000 companies (2,001–4,000). Each volume has an alphabetic list of companies giving address, nature of business, top executive, phone number, and an index by industry/region. At the front of volume 1 are comparison tables of the top 20 companies by various criteria such as pre-tax profits.

Europe's 15,000 Largest Companies. London: ELC International (annual).

The main part of this directory ranks the 10,000 largest European (except for the U.K.) industrial companies by sales, also giving other financial figures such as profits, employees, equity capital, year established, plus % figures for some of the data. After this are ranked lists of: 3,750 largest trading companies; largest service companies (in separate lists of banks, insurance, transport companies, ad agencies, hotels & restaurants, miscellaneous). At front are lists of Europe's largest companies ranked by sales, by profits, profitability, employees, and the 100 largest companies arranged by country. An alphabetical index is at end.

ELC also publishes ranked lists of: *UK's 10,000 Largest Companies* (1990); *Asia's 7,500 Largest Companies* (1991); *Denmark's 20,000 Largest Companies* (1991); *Scotland's 8,500 Largest Businesses* (1991).

Le Nouvel Economiste 5000. Paris (annual, published as an extra issue in December of the weekly *Le Nouvel Economiste*).

A special issue of this journal which contains: a ranked list of the 500 largest worldwide companies; the 1,000 largest French companies; the 5,000 largest French and European companies, each arranged by industry; the 100 largest banks of the world; over 200 of the largest French bank trust companies; the largest insurance companies in Europe and in France; the top companies by geographic region in France.

The Times 1000. London: Times Books Ltd. (annual).

This ranks and gives financial statistics for the top 1,000 U.K. Industrial companies, with separate rankings for banks and other kinds of financial companies. There are also ranked lists for the 500 leading European companies, the 100 American, 50 Japanese, 30 Canadian, 20 Australian, 30 South African, 20 Republic of Ireland companies, leading companies in South East Asia, 50 South American companies. At front are the top 50 world companies and the largest takeovers.

Bibliography

European Business Rankings Annual. Detroit: Gale Research, Inc.

Just announced for publication in summer 1992 is a new companion to Gale's bibliographic guide to U.S. rankings called *Business Rankings Annual*. This new one names the top 10 in approximately 2,250 European rankings of companies as well as other subjects. It is arranged by subject, with appropriate indexes, and it was compiled at the Manchester (Eng.) Business School.

GUIDES TO WORLD STOCK EXCHANGES

Directory of World Stock Exchanges. Compiled by The Economist. Baltimore: Johns Hopkins University Press, 1988. 469 pp.

This provides concise data on the stock exchanges in 44 countries. For each it usually describes: organization; background information; types of market; systems of quotation for securities; ordering and settlement procedures; price publication procedure; takeover & mergers procedures; special rules for foreign investors; taxation; transaction charges/commissions/fees; turnover of exchange; technical publications and information sources; history. Includes also officers, telephone/telex, trading hours, and for most exchanges there is one page of statistical tables for securities listed and share price indexes.

The European Bond Markets: An Overview Analysis for Issuers and Investors. Prepared by the European Bond Commission. Chicago: Probus Publishing Company, 1989. 620 pp.

Included here even though it does not cover stock exchanges, each chapter of this analysis describes the bond market in one of 13 European countries. The topics covered for each are: composition; types of securities; issuers; investors; methods of issuance; new issue volume; methods of trading; market practices; yield calculations; taxation; interest rate history; intermarket spreads; sources of reference. This should be updated periodically as the other guides are if it is to continue its usefulness.

The G.T. Guide to World Equity Markets. London: Euromoney Publications PLC and G.T. Management PLC (annual).

The focus in this useful guide is on the equity market in each country rather than on the stock exchange, and so some of the data is the same and yet some different. It covers 36 developed markets, 6 emerging markets, and 4 Eastern European markets. For each country the data covered usually includes: introduction; market performance; the stock market (history, names, hours); market size (including ranked list of the largest quoted companies, and trading volume); types of shares; investors; operations (including trading system, list of brokers, settlement and transfer); taxation and regulations; report/research (including titles of financial publications); and other information.

The (year) Handbook of World Stock and Commodity Exchanges. Oxford: B. Blackwell (annual).

Noteworthy for its inclusion of commodity exchanges as well as stock exchanges. Part 2 consists of brief descriptions of each exchange, arranged alphabetically by over 60 countries. The concise data given (from 1 to 5 pages according to the importance of the exchange) for each is usually: principal officers; brief history; structure; trading hours; number of companies listed; market capitalization; main indices; types of securities traded; trading system; settling and clearing; commission rates; taxation and regulations affecting foreign investors; investor protection details; prospective developments (futures contracts if a futures exchange; options contracts). Part 1 (about 100 pages) contains short articles usually on recent developments in specific exchanges. At end are a glossary, list of abbreviations, and indexes to personnel and commodities.

For persons who do not have access to one of the directories above but do have access to *Institutional Investor* International Edition you will find in the April 1991 issue an "International Stock Exchange Directory" which contains key facts on 81 leading stock exchanges in 55 countries.

BIBLIOGRAPHIES AND INDEXES ON FOREIGN COMPANIES AND INDUSTRIES

Business International. *Publications Index.* New York (annual).

An annual index to BI publications available to subscribers and arranged by country. It includes publications of the Economist Intelligence Unit which is now a division of BI. A further description of this index is in Chapter 16.

Financial Times. *Monthly Index.* Reading, Eng: Research Publications Ltd. (with an annual cumulation). Also available online.

Begun in 1981, this is a detailed, descriptive index to the *Financial Times,* with the indexing based on the final London edition. Its back volumes are available on microfilm. Several databases also useful for obtaining information from this newspaper are: *Financial Times Fulltext* for complete text of all articles; *Financial Times Company Information Database* for abstracts of company and business news items: *Financial Times Currency and Share Index* database, a time series for statistics on stocks, indexes, and other tables appearing in daily issues.

Predicasts F & S Index Europe and **Predicasts F & S Index International.** Cleveland, OH: Predicasts, Inc. (monthlies with annual cumulations). On-line counterpart is *PTS F & S Indexes.*

These two periodic indexes are useful for locating articles or parts of articles on foreign companies and foreign industries that have appeared in many foreign and domestic financial publications, business-oriented newspapers, trade magazines, and special reports. Each is arranged in three parts: (1) by a modified 7-digit SIC industry or product; (2) by region and country (the first index covering European countries and the second, all other foreign countries); (3) by company. Under each industry or company, the indexing usually covers: organizations and institutions, management procedures, products & processes, resources and resource use, marketing information, financial data, government expenditures. As of 1991 these indexes are also available on CD-ROM as *F & S Plus TEXT,* but only to nonprofit organizations. A companion index devoted to U.S. industries and companies is *Predicasts F & S Index United States.*

Research Index. Dorchester, Dorset, Eng.: Business Surveys, Ltd. (fortnightly, with quarterly industry and company indexes).

This indexes news of financial interest on industries and companies, appearing in over 100 British business and trade journals as well as several newspapers. Each issue is in two parts: by industry/subject; by company. Quarterly cumulations of the industry/company indexes are available for an added price. The abbreviated type of entry is similar to that used in the Predicasts indexes above, with an asterisk noting company citations that are longer than one page. It has disadvantages, however, for it is not as comprehensive, it does not cover indepth articles, and the indexes cumulate only quarterly.

Reuter TEXTLINE database. London: Reuter Ltd.

Useful for news, comments, and often complete text (all in English) of articles from
an extensive range of financial and business newspapers and journals published in
foreign countries. Covers not only company and industries developments but also
news of products, markets, economics, public affairs.

INVESTMENT MANAGEMENT BOOKS

Many recent investment management texts tend to be more analytical than
descriptive which perhaps makes them of more interest to students and theorists than to potential investors. The several investment guides and books on
the stock market will be of more practical interest to the individual investor,
but there is no attempt here to include any of the many "how-to-get-rich"
books that are often well publicized but are of little real value. Books and
reference sources on corporate finance and banking (including books on the
mathematics of finance) are covered in Chapter 14; books on real estate
investing are in Chapter 15.

GENERAL BOOKS ON INVESTMENTS

Handbooks

Friedman, Jack P., ed. *Encyclopedia of Investments.* 2d ed. Boston: Warren,
Gorham & Lamont, 1990. 964 pp. And periodic updates.

This comprehensive work provides a single source for background information
about 48 different kinds of investment vehicles, including not only stocks and bonds
but also financial futures, mutual funds, real estate, stamps, paintings, gemstones,
and other collectibles. Each chapter, written by an expert, has a standard format in
discussing basic characteristics, attractive features, potential risks, tax consequences, representative types of investors, important factors in buying or selling, a
glossary, and suggested readings. At end is a separate section on "Investment Strategy," with articles providing a framework for assembling and assessing a portfolio.

The Financial Analyst's Handbook. Ed. by Sumner N. Levine. 2d ed. Homewood, IL: Dow Jones-Irwin, 1988. 1,870 pp.

A comprehensive handbook covering financial analysis and portfolio management
and intended for financial analysts, money managers, and financial executives. Its 56
chapters (each written by expert contributors) are arranged within 9 parts: background; economic analysis, company and industry analysis; equity investment analysis; fixed income investing; portfolio theory and practice; quantitative aids; information sources (consisting of a useful annotated list of "Published Sources of Value to
Analysts," by Susan S. DiMattia, pp.1717–1741, and a chapter describing pertinent
online databases); legal and ethical standards. Many chapters contain references to
other sources.

The Handbook of International Investing. Carl Beidleman, ed. Chicago:
Probus Publishing Company, 1987. 897 pp.

Designed to provide both the inexperienced and experienced investor with an understanding of the process of investment in international securities and to inform them
about the returns and risks. Its 33 chapters by 39 expert contributors (both scholars

and practitioners) are arranged in the following sections: international investment assessment; managing risk in an international portfolio; instruments available to international investors; opportunities for yield enhancement in international markets; investors in international portfolios; peripheral issues; summary.

Books

Alexander, Gordon J., and William F. Sharpe, *Fundamentals of Investments.* Englewood Cliffs, NJ: Prentice-Hall, 1989. 678 pp.

An advanced undergraduate text which aims to provide an understanding of the investment environment and process. It is organized into 6 parts: introduction; the investment environment (including explanations of the security markets, determining security prices, taxes, inflation); modern portfolio theory (with a chapter discussing the capital asset pricing model); common stocks; fixed income securities; alternative investments (investment companies, options, futures, international involvement). "Sources of Investment Information" are described in Chapter 14, including an outline by type or frequency. A glossary is at end. The authors presume some knowledge of economics, statistics, and accounting.

For persons who prefer a graduate text that is somewhat more rigorous, theoretical, and technical, see their *Investment,* with Professor Sharpe as lead author (4th ed., Prentice-Hall, 1990, 833 pp.).

Amling, Frederick. *Investment: An Introduction to Analysis and Management.* 6th ed. Englewood Cliffs, NJ: Prentice-Hall, 1989. 780 pp.

Revised and reorganized in this latest edition to reflect the many dramatic changes in the investment process, this introduction is designed to bring theory and principles to the practical decision-making process. It is arranged in 7 parts, the first three of which cover an overview of investments, investment alternatives available, and their markets and brokers. With this as background Amling then explains fundamental and technical analysis, including chapters on an economic analysis, industry analysis, and 7 chapters on specific aspects of company analysis. The last part studies problems of portfolio management, theory, and performance. A short appendix to chapter 1 covers "Sources of Investment Information." Self-correcting problems with solutions are at end of each chapters, as well as suggested reading lists.

Cohen, Jerome B., Edward D. Zinbarg and Arthur Zeikel. *Investment Analysis and Portfolio Management.* 5th ed. Homewood, IL: Irwin, 1987. 738 pp.

Another good introduction to investment intended to provide the investor with a sound framework and with the new theory presented in what the authors hope is readable English rather than in mathematical terms. They have arranged the text in five parts: an introduction; portfolio theory; investment timing; security analysis (8 chapters dealing with a variety of techniques for analyzing financial statements and for judging the merits of specific stocks, bonds, options, and also tangible assets such as real estate); portfolio management (including a chapter on international investing). Especially helpful is chapter 3, "Sources of Investment Information," which discusses basic sources of published information, but only as of 1987. "Suggested Readings" are with chapters.

Ellis, Charles D., ed. (James R. Vertin, collaborator). *Classics: An Investor's Anthology.* Homewood, IL: Dow Jones-Irwin, 1989. 759 pp.

An "investor's treasure chest" of writings by the industry's leading thinkers, the selections in this book are arranged in five chronological sections according to when they appeared in print. Some are from journal articles while others are from books, memos, or pamphlets. Among the leading investment thinkers represented are David L. Babson, Philip Fisher, Benjamin Graham, Gerald M. Loeb. In 1991 Ellis published a new collection of writings going further back in time and including more documents from the international community. This is called *Classics II; Another Investor's Anthology* (Business One Irwin, 1991, 626 pp.). It is arranged according to 6 broad topics such as "investment policy," and "markets and exchanges."

Fabozzi, Frank J., and T. Dessa Fabozzi, eds. *Current Topics in Investment Management.* New York: Harper & Row, 1990. 348 pp. paper.

A rather different book of 20 readings in that most are written by practitioners and none have appeared in academic journals. Since it is intended to supplement an investment management text, it focuses on topics the editors feel are not adequately covered in some texts, such as asset allocation and policy setting, stock index futures and their use in portfolio management, mortgage-backed securities, interest-rate risk control tools, and more. They are arranged in two parts, one covering equity and the other fixed income portfolio management. This is a volume in "The Institutional Investor Series in Finance."

Francis, Jack C. *Management of Investments.* 2d ed. New York: McGraw-Hill, 1988. 826, [16] pp.

The purpose of this text is to introduce the student or layperson to both traditional and modern theories of investment in a manner that is easy to understand and enjoyable to study. In this substantially revised edition, Professor Francis uses his first three sections to provide the basics, the setting, and an introduction to financial analysis. This latter section includes chapters describing "sources of financial information" and "market averages and indexes." He then studies in turn: the factors that contribute to total risk; valuation theory, security analysis, the behavior of stock prices; other investments; portfolio management. Annotated lists of further references are with chapters; a glossary is in the appendix. Slightly more mathematical background is needed for his text on *Investments: Analysis and Management* (4th ed., McGraw-Hill, 1986, 935, [16] pp.). Another book he coauthored with Gordon J. Alexander is *Portfolio Analysis* (3d ed., Prentice-Hall, 1986, 306 pp.).

Reilly, Frank K. *Investment Analysis and Portfolio Management.* 3d ed. Chicago: Dryden Press, 1989. 1,026, [35] pp.

Reilly says his text intends to be rigorous and empirical without being overly quantitative. Its five parts deal with: the investment background (including chapters on "security-market indicator series" and "sources of information on investments"); modern developments in investment theory; analysis and valuation of securities (contains chapters on industry, company, and technical analysis); extensions and applications of asset pricing and portfolio models (including a chapter on investment companies); analysis of alternative investments (options, warrants, commodity and financial futures). Most chapters include a discussion of how investment practice or theory is influenced by the globalization of investments. A code of ethics and interest tables are at end.

Just published is a new beginning text called *Essentials of Investment* by Zvi Bodie, Alex Kane, and Alan J. Marcus (Irwin, 1992, 639, [83] pp.). It is arranged in 6 sections and incorporates useful explanations of the various statistics in such sources as the *Wall Street Journal.*

SECURITY ANALYSIS AND PORTFOLIO MANAGEMENT

Fabozzi, Frank J., and Frank G. Zarb, eds. *Handbook of Financial Markets: Securities, Options, Futures.* 2d ed. Homewood, IL: Dow Jones-Irwin, 1986. 785 pp.

Intended for both experienced and novice investors, this handbook provides broad knowledge of the three types of financial markets in the subtitle. Over 500 pages are devoted to the securities markets, with sections on the environment, structure, instruments, and private financial intermediaries. This is followed by 7 chapters each on the options market and on the futures markets. Each of its 39 chapters is written by an expert.

Elton, Edwin J., and Martin J. Gruber. *Modern Portfolio Theory and Investment Analysis.* 4th ed. New York: Wiley, 1991. 736 pp.

A text by two New York University business school professors designed both for business school students and for practicing security analysts and portfolio managers. The first and longest part discusses modern portfolio theory. The other three parts deal with: a discussion of models of equilibrium in the capital markets; security analysis and portfolio theory; evaluating the investment process. Mathematical proofs involving more than simple algebra are relegated to footnotes and appendixes; bibliographies are with chapters.

Fischer, Donald E., and Ronald J. Jordan. *Security Analysis and Portfolio Management.* 5th ed. Englewood Cliffs, NJ: Prentice-Hall, 1991. 768 pp.

The authors (a professor and an accountant) have tried to make this introductory text comprehensive, readable, understandable, and as nonmathematical as possible (simple algebra and some elementary statistics are explained in lay terms). An innovation is their use of a continuing illustration of the application of techniques for security analysis and portfolio management to a real stock and a real portfolio—using as an example the food service industry and McDonald's Corporation. There are 7 basic parts: the investment environment; framework of risk and return; common-stock analysis; bond analysis; options and futures; technical analysis and the efficient market theory; portfolio analysis, selection, and management. Mathematical tables are at end.

Graham, Benjamin. *Graham and Dodd's Security Analysis: Principles and Techniques.* 5th ed. by Sidney Cottle, Roger F. Murray and Frank E. Block. New York: McGraw-Hill, 1988. 656 pp.

Ever since its first edition (1934) this has been the "bible" for security analysts, and it is still required reading especially for its analysis of the fundamentalist approach. Now three eminently qualified collaborators have published a restatement of Graham and Dodd principles updating the techniques used in their application for today's greatly changed investment environment. There are five parts: financial analysis and approach; analysis of financial statements; analysis of fixed-income securities; valuation of common stocks and contingent claims; impact of security analysis.

Walmsley, Julian. *The New Financial Instruments: An Investor's Guide.* New York: Wiley, 1988. 454 pp.

This is a guide to the most important new financial instruments, stating why they are useful to specific investors or borrowers and what the risks and benefits are. Parts 1–2 give background and basics; part 3 looks at three major tools for hedging risk and adding value to financial instruments (futures, options, swaps); part 4 describes the new instruments individually. Appendixes and "useful readings" are at end.

THE STOCK MARKET AND INVESTMENT MANAGEMENT GUIDES

Dun & Bradstreet Guide to Your Investments. New York: Harper & Row (annual).

A handy and continuously revised guide for beginning investors, probably of more use as a reference source than as a book to be read from cover to cover. It consists of short, easy to understand chapters providing simple explanations on various types of investments (stocks, bonds, real estate, commodities, futures, etc.), on retirement planning, how to invest like a pro, taxes, your portfolio, and so forth. Checklists, statistics, and other illustrations are used throughout; at end is a glossary. Sources for further information are with many sections. Contents varies somewhat from year to year.

Edwards, Robert D., and John Magee. *Technical Analysis of Stock Trends.* 5th ed. Boston: John Magee, Inc., 1983. 494 pp.

A classic text on the title subject. This 1983 printing is exactly the same as the 1966 edition except for the addition of several charts on pp. 475–482. It is written for the informed layman and Wall Street professional and is in two parts: technical theory and trading tactics. The many chart examples for specific companies are usually based on stock trading data for the 1940s, but the authors feel these are still valid as illustrations of important technical phenomena.

Engel, Louis, and Brendan Boyd. *How to Buy Stocks.* 7th rev. ed. New York: Bantam Books, 1984. 331 pp. paper.

One of the best simple books on fundamentals of investing in stocks and bonds for the beginning investor. This latest edition was updated by Mr. Boyd to conform to 1984 regulatory conditions and shifting market moods. There are new chapters added, one on computerized stock selection and the other on alternative investment vehicles that have emerged in recent years. A useful annotated list of books for "Further Reading" is at end.

Graham, Benjamin. *The Intelligent Investor: A Book of Practical Counsel.* 4th rev. ed., with a new preface and appendix by Warren E. Buffett. New York: Harper & Row, 1985. 340 pp.

Latest edition of a classic guide to the principles of sound investing, with the main objective "to guide the reader against areas of possible substantial error and to develop policies with which he will be comfortable." Graham is often called "the father of fundamental analysis," and his book is still required reading. This is a reissue of the 1973 edition with a new preface and appendix.

Little, Jeffrey, and Lucien Rhodes. *Understanding Wall Street.* 3d ed. Blue Ridge Summit, PA: Liberty Hall Press, 1991. 259 pp. paper.

Perhaps another simple guide is not needed, but this has been a popular paperback, and is one I often suggest for persons who know little or nothing about the stock market. The authors start by explaining in easy-to-understand terms what a share of stock is, how Wall Street works, how to read a financial statement as well as reading the financial page of a newspaper. They then briefly explain procedures for investing and trading, the principal types of investments (stocks, bonds, etc.), principles of technical analysis and, lastly, stock options. Illustrative charts and graphs are used throughout; a glossary is at end.

Lorie, James H. et al. *The Stock Market: Theories and Evidence.* 2d ed. Homewood, IL: Dow Jones-Irwin, 1985. 192 pp.

A useful book that "attempts to organize, summarize, translate into simple language, and interpret the voluminous theoretical and scientific literature" on the stock market. Included are explanations of stock prices and rate of return on stocks, stock market indexes, dividends, earnings, portfolio theory, options, and more. A short note on investment counseling and a glossary are at end.

Malkiel, Burton G. *A Random Walk Down Wall Street.* 5th ed. New York: Norton, 1990. 440 pp.

Here is a much-read, straightforward and nontechnical guide for the individual investor and student who seeks a better understanding of the complex world of finance and practical advice on investment opportunities and strategies, primarily about common stocks. Malkiel starts with some background on stocks and their value. This is followed by a useful explanation and comparison of the two methods used by investment pros—fundamental analysis and technical analysis. Part 3 then describes the new investment technology (modern portfolio and capital-asset pricing theory and the Beta concept). Part 4 pulls the whole thing together as a short how-to-do-it guide for random walkers and other investors. This last section, especially, has been extensively revised to keep pace with the many financial innovations, the changed investment climate, and various financial instruments. It contains a new chapter providing a life-cycle guide to personal investing. A bibliography is at end.

Pring, Martin J. *Technical Analysis Explained: The Successful Investor's Guide to Spotting Investment Trends and Turning Points.* 2d ed. New York: McGraw-Hill, 1985. 410 pp.

This is an excellent book on the more useful facets of technical analysis of the market. Part 1 examines various trend determination techniques such as the Dow Theory, price patterns, trendlines, moving averages. Part 2 analyzes market structure from the viewpoint of price, time, volume, breadth. Part 3 deals with the important subject of interest rates and their relation to movements of equity prices, and part 4 with speculation and other aspects of market behavior. A fifth part (added in this new edition) covers the application of technical analysis to specific financial markets including gold, currencies, commodities. At the end are charts for historical Dow Jones averages, a short glossary, and a bibliography.

Rugg, Donald D. *New Strategies for Mutual Fund Investing.* Homewood, IL: Dow Jones-Irwin, 1989. 272 pp.

A simple guide to mutual funds written for the small investor who wants a wise investment program for maximum return and safety. The author explains the basics of no-load stock and money market funds, how to time investment decisions, how to improve performance during down markets, and how to manage your portfolio over time.

Stocks, Bonds, Options, Futures: Investments and Their Markets. Ed. by Stuart R. Veale. New York: New York Institute of Finance, 1987. 332 pp.

Prepared by the staff of the NYIF, this is an easy-to-understand guide to today's securities markets written for entry-level professionals. Besides covering the title subjects, there are also chapters on underwriting (raising capital), exchange markets, OTC securities market, order processing, government regulations, taxation. The NYIF has published other guides including *How the Bond Market Works* (1988, 278 pp., paper) which is described in the section following, and another on *How the Stock Market Works* by John M. Dalton (1988, 292 pp., paper) which is a simple explanation of the title subject and includes a glossary of about 100 pages at the end.

Successful Investing: A Complete Guide to Your Financial Future. Ed. by Carolyn M. Finnegan. 4th ed., rev. and updated. New York: Simon and Schuster, 1987. 529 pp. paper.

Written by the staff of Babson-United Investment Advisors, Inc., this is designed to give the novice a foundation of knowledge for successful investing. It starts with a section on "the art of prudent investing," and from this proceeds in an orderly progression to discussing: your investment alternatives; how to make your choices; mastering the strategies and tactics; taking care of the housekeeping; investments and your financial plan. A glossary is at end.

Teweles, Richard J., and Edward S. Bradley. *The Stock Market.* 5th ed. New York: Wiley, 1987. 526 pp. A new edition will be published in 1992.

This study on how the stock market operates and functions is a thoroughly revised and updated edition of a book originally written by George L. Leffler in 1951. It is still arranged in the same five parts: fundamental information; work of the stock exchanges; work of the securities houses; regulations; investing practices and special instruments. Two chapters of special interest to information specialists are: chapter 4 with its helpful explanation of how to understand and use data on the financial page of a newspaper; chapter 24 discussing the chief sources of published information and security ratings. A glossary is at end.

For descriptions of several guides to reading stock and other financial quotations appearing in newspapers, see section on "Guides to Reading the Financial Pages" found elsewhere in this chapter. For books on "Personal Finance" see under that heading in Chapter 14.

BOND AND MONEY MARKETS

Handbooks

Darst, David M. *The Handbook of the Bond and Money Markets.* New York: McGraw-Hill, 1981. 461 pp.

A well-written handbook intended both for professional and lay investors who want a helpful analysis of the fixed-income securities market (both long-term and short-term issues), its participants, and investment techniques. It covers a broad range of subjects such as the analysis of debt statistics and the flow-of-funds account of the Federal Reserve System, the causes and effects of inflation and deflation, the history and calculation methods of major economic and price level indicators, and much more. Useful statistical tables and charts appear throughout. For those wanting further information, an excellent final chapter reviews important periodicals, books, articles, or other sources on the fixed-income securities markets, grouped according to chapters in the book. This is now rather old but still of value for background information.

Fabozzi, Frank J., T. Dessa Fabozzi and Irving M. Pollack, eds. *The Handbook of Fixed Income Securities.* 3d ed. Homewood, IL: Business One Irvin, 1991. 1,419 pp.

Much more up to date and more comprehensive is this third edition of a useful handbook. It is designed to provide extensive coverage not only of fixed income products but also of investment management strategies. The 60 chapters, each by a subject expert, are divided into 9 parts. Parts 2–4 cover the myriad of fixed income products. The other major parts are devoted to: options and futures; bonds with inbedded options; fixed income portfolio management strategies; interest rate swaps, caps, floors and compound options; modeling; and forecasting. This handbook is written for both novice investors and for professional money managers.

Books

Fabozzi, Frank J., and T. Dessa Fabozzi. *Bond Markets, Analysis and Strategies.* Englewood Cliffs, NJ: Prentice-Hall, 1989. 347 pp.

A practical overview of the fixed income market, including coverage of the securities available in the market (Treasury securities, agency securities, corporate, municipal, and international bonds, mortgages, and mortgage-backed securities; also interest rate futures and options). Besides giving their investment characteristics, it discusses the latest techniques for valuing them, and portfolio strategies for using them. Professor Fabozzi has written widely in the area of fixed income; see, for example, his handbook described above.

New York Institute of Finance. *How the Bond Market Works.* New York: 1988. 278 pp. paper.

Authoritative yet easy to understand descriptions of the workings of the bond market, which is a large market even though not as well known as the stock market. Contains information on the various types of fixed income securities, a short chapter on the Fed, on primary dealers, and on the secondary market. A glossary of over 60 pages is at the end.

An alternative nontechnical guide is *Getting Started in Bonds* by Michael C. Thomsett (New York: Wiley, 1991, 239 pp.).

Stigum, Marcia. *The Money Market.* 3d. ed. Homewood, IL: Dow Jones-Irwin, 1990. 1,252 pp.

Newly revised to cover the many changes since 1983, this is an excellent, comprehensive guide to the U.S. and Eurodollar money market in three parts. Part 1 describes in simple terms some fundamentals such as what instruments are traded, how yields on them are calculated, how banks under the control of the Federal Reserve System create our money supply. Part 2 focuses on the major players (operations of both domestic and Euro-banks, treasury and federal agencies, market dealers, investors) while part 3 covers individual markets (Treasury bonds, options, Euros, interest-rate swaps, certificates of deposit, bankers' acceptances, commercial paper, money market funds, etc.). Terms are explained when introduced, but there is also a glossary at the end. Readers who need data on key money market formulas and examples should refer to the author's *The Money Market Calculations: Yields, Break-Evens and Arbitrage* (2d ed., Dow Jones-Irwin, 1989, 200 pp.) written in collaboration with John Mann. A more specialized book by Stigum is *The Repo and Reverse Markets* (Dow Jones-Irwin, 1989, 375 pp.).

OPTIONS MARKET

For a handbook/overview on both the options and futures markets in Europe, see *European Options and Futures Markets* edited by Stuart K. McLean, described in the next section.

Ansbacher, Max G. *The New Options Market.* Rev. ed. New York: Walker and Company, 1987. 280 pp. paper.

In this book, an experienced stockbroker attempts "to give the intelligent investor everything he needs to know to start a profitable investment program in America's newest and most exciting form of investing." Written in understandable language, Ansbacher describes each of the various option strategies, such as calls and puts, spreads, straddles, and combinations—giving advantages and disadvantages, and specific strategy rules. He also covers implementation of the trades, taxation, and record keeping. Supplementary data and tables, as well as a glossary are at end.

Gastineau, Gary L. *The Options Manual.* 3d ed. New York: McGraw-Hill, 1988. 440 pp.

This excellent book for the intelligent investor tries to be comprehensive and to make the wealth of material on options both understandable and useful. Gastineau's overall focus is on the effect of options on the risk characteristics of a portfolio and on option evaluation. Starting first with background on the history and structure of options markets, he proceeds to study: use of options—investment positions and strategies; tax treatment; evaluation of the option contract; the application of option valuation techniques to other markets and instruments; an index of listed stock option premiums; who makes money in the options market?; systematic application of option strategies; and portfolio insurance. A useful bibliography of books (annotated), of articles, and exchange publications, plus a glossary are included in an appendix. Beginners may want to request several of the helpful booklets prepared by the exchanges which Gastineau recommends as good elementary introductions to options trading.

McMillan, Lawrence G. *Options as a Strategic Investment: A Comprehensive Analysis of Listed Option Strategies.* 2d ed. New York: New York Institutte of Finance, 1986. 684 pp.

A good, advanced book on options strategy—which strategies work in which situations and why. Chapters follow a logical sequence with one part devoted to call option strategies and another to put option strategies. A whole new section is added to this latest edition on index and other nonequity options, and there are other revisions to update and reflect changes. There is also a section discussing "additional considerations," with chapters on arbitrage and mathematical applications. A glossary is at end along with other supplementary material. In the first edition, McMillan recommended prior familiarity with the same brochures mentioned in the note above for Gastineau's book.

Walker, Joseph A. *How the Options Markets Work.* New York: New York Institute of Finance, 1991. 229 pp. paper.

Options are not for everyone, but a working knowledge of them is important. This is an informative, readable guide to options and options markets for those who need to understand them. At end is a list of companies having listed equity options, and a glossary.

COMMODITY AND FINANCIAL FUTURES MARKETS

Sources for statistics on commodities and commodity and financial futures are included in Chapter 6.

Handbooks

Kaufman, Perry J. *Handbook of Futures Markets: Commodity, Financial, Stock Index, Options.* New York: Wiley, 1984. 1 volume (various pagings).

One of two comprehensive handbooks published in 1984 (and so now rather dated), this one is designed as a learning manual and reference guide to the futures market, concentrating "on techniques, analysis, calculation and explanation." Its 49 chapters written by over 50 contributing authors are arranged in the following sections: the markets and their operation; market influences; use of the markets (includes chapters on hedging, commodity spreads and options); forecasting methods and tools; risk and money management; the commodities. This last section comprises about one-third of the book, with 25 chapters on each important commodity such as wheat, coffee, copper, interest-rate futures. At end is a glossary and a lengthy bibliography which is arranged by subject.

McLean, Stuart K., ed. *The European Options and Futures Markets.* Chicago: Probus Publishing Company, 1991. 1,086 pp.

Here is a new "overview and analysis for money managers and traders" which is sponsored by the European Bond Commission of the European Federation of Financial Analyst Societies, with chapters written by members. It describes differences and similarities of the options and futures markets in each of 14 European countries, with each following a standardized format covering: organization, history, overview of products, detailed contract specification, taxation, regulations, quote vendors, sources of information. A glossary is included. In 1989 the EBC prepared a similar book on *The European Bond Markets* (Probus Publishing Co., 1989, 620 pp.). It offers an overview and analysis of the bond markets in 13 European countries, and it also follows a standard format.

Rothstein, Nancy H., and James M. Little, eds. *The Handbook of Financial Futures: A Guide for Investors and Professional Financial Managers.* New York: McGraw-Hill, 1984. 638 pp.

The purpose of this second comprehensive handbook (see Kaufman above) "is to explain and illustrate important concepts and methods for the use and analysis of financial futures for hedging and trading purposes," and it is intended for both the novice and the sophisticated user of the financial futures markets. Its 22 chapters (over half of which are written by practicing authorities other than the editors) are arranged within five sections: the mechanics of financial futures markets; speculation and hedging—concepts and applications; market analysis; regulatory, accounting and tax implications; references (a directory of financial futures exchanges; contract specifications). A glossary and bibliography are at end.

Books

Babcock, Bruce. *The Dow Jones-Irwin Guide to Trading Systems.* Homewood, IL: Dow Jones-Irwin, 1989. 316 pp.

For the neophyte as well as the experienced commodity trader, this book takes a step-by-step approach through commodity trading basics, the process of creating your own system, how to evaluate those created by others, and what new computer technology is available.

Fink, Robert E., and Robert B. Feduniak. *Futures Trading: Concepts and Strategies.* New York: New York Institute of Finance, 1988. 685 pp.

This book covers the basics of the futures market and the futures industry, and it is written both for professionals and for active traders by one of each. It is in 6 parts, beginning with an introduction to concepts, terms, and the futures industry. From this the authors progress to an examination of commercial applications (including hedging); market analysis and trading; chapters on each market (interest rate futures, currency futures, stock index futures, agricultural commodities, metals, and energy futures). They end by discussing the role of options in the futures markets. A short bibliography is at end.

Herbst, Anthony F. *Commodity Futures: Markets, Methods of Analysis, and Management of Risk.* New York: Wiley, 1986. 289 pp.

Professor Herbst intends his book to be an easy-to-understand, yet technically sound, comprehensive treatment of futures for persons who may be unfamiliar with the futures markets. He starts by providing fundamental knowledge on the basics, and on such topics as hedging, speculation, money management. Then he focuses on specific types of futures—financial, currency, index, agricultural commodities, metals, and so forth. A last chapter covers commodity options.

Powers, Mark J., and Mark G. Castelino. *Inside the Financial Futures Markets.* 3d ed. New York: Wiley, 1991. 390 pp.

The purpose of this book is to introduce, explain, and illustrate basic concepts of trading interest rate futures contracts, the economic purpose of the trading, and its operational characteristics. The authors start with an introduction to futures trading, followed by discussions of: price analysis; cash and futures markets for debt instruments; foreign exchange futures, stock index futures, and options; hedging; and arbitrage. An appendix contains contract specifications for major U.S. exchanges, and money market formulas.

Schwager, Jack D. *A Complete Guide to the Futures Markets: Fundamental Analysis, Technical Analysis, Trading, Spreads, and Options.* New York: Wiley, 1984. 741 pp.

Of handbook proportions, this is a nontechnical (now rather old) book for the intelligent layperson "who is already familiar with the basic concepts of futures trading and is interested in a broad-based but more substantive and detailed discussion of analytical techniques." Its 38 chapters are divided into 7 parts to cover the important facets noted in the subtitle. Included is a useful guide to regression analysis, a chapter on classical chart analysis with many sample charts, and a section providing practical trading guidelines.

Teweles, Richard J., and Frank J. Jones. *The Futures Game: Who Wins? Who Loses? Why?* 2d ed. New York: McGraw-Hill, 1987. 649 pp.

Here is a comprehensive, updated reference work that brings together what is known about futures and options trading and mixes this with the authors' practical experience. The first two sections introduce the basics and explain how the futures game is played (included are chapters on the fundamental approach and the technical approach). The next two sections discuss the state of the art in understanding why losers lose and winners win and the role of the broker in building and servicing a clientele. The last section covers the various markets—what one needs to know about each important commodity and about financial futures. A lengthy bibliography is at end.

Wasendorf, Russell R. (Pat Stahl, collaborator). *Commodities Trading: The Essential Primer.* Homewood, IL: Dow Jones-Irwin, 1985. 197 pp.

A short, simple guide for the beginning investor or experienced trader that covers: the evolution of commodity trading; outline of technical and fundamental market analysis techniques; rules and regulations; practical suggestions for trading profitably.

Three other useful guides are: *Winning in the Futures Market: A Money-Making Guide to Trading, Hedging and Speculating* by George Angell (Rev. ed., Chicago: Probus Publishing, 1990, 310 pp. paper) which is shorter than Teweles above but is still a good introduction both for the novice or the seasoned trader; *Commodity Options: A User's Guide to Speculating and Hedging* by Terry S. Mayer (New York Institute of Finance, 1983, 350 pp.), a guide to understanding the investment aspects of option trading; and a more specialized *Handbook of Stock Index Futures and Options* ed. by Frank J. Fabozzi and Gregory M. Kipnis (Homewood IL: Dow Jones-Irwin, 1989, 446 pp.) written for both novices and professional money managers.

Bibliographies and Periodicals

Chicago. Board of Trade. *Commodity Futures Trading: Bibliography.* Chicago (annual).

A list (not annotated) of books and articles arranged by topic. There was a base volume covering sources published 1967–1974; since then this has been an annual and cites only the literature published during each year.

Daigler, Robert T. "Futures Bibliography." In each issue of *Journal of Futures Markets.*

Beginning with the Summer 1982 issue, this journal contains a continuing bibliography of articles, books, and other items relating to futures markets and futures trading. It does not attempt to include articles in trade journals and the financial press that might be in the bibliography above, and the topics covered vary from issue to issue.

Futures. Cedar Falls, IA (monthly, except semimonthly in January and November).

Billed as "the magazine of commodities & options," this journal consists of short articles on commodity/options markets, trading techniques, commercial tactics, trade trends, with regular columns on such topics as software review and option strategy. Includes a table of mutual funds, and some issues have book reviews. An extra issue each November is "Reference Guide to Futures/Options Markets," which is a directory of commission merchants, brokers, advisors, services, publishers, etc. (giving names of officers); also lists of exchanges around the world, with officers and brief facts, list of government sources, associations, and an index of articles printed in *Futures* during the previous year. The regular January issue contains an "Economic Outlook"; the extra January issue is a "Trader's Calendar & Record Keeper." This monthly is indexed in ABI/I, BPI, PAIS; full text on BRS, DATA-STAR, DIALOG, MEAD/NEXIS.

Journal of Futures Markets. New York: Wiley (quarterly).

A new journal (1981) with professional articles focusing on research results and discussions of ideas on a wide range of issues affecting all aspects of futures. A continuing "Futures Bibliography" is in frequent issues beginning with Summer 1982. This quarterly is published in affiliation with the Center for the Study of Futures Markets, Columbia Business School. Indexed in ABI/I, BPI, PAIS.

Two other publications are: *Futures and Options World* (Surrey Eng.: Metal Bulletin Journals, Ltd.; monthly), a source for international news, analyses and comments; and *Review of Futures Markets* (Chicago: Board of Trade; 3/ yr.), which publishes the proceedings of the various research seminars held by the Board of Trade as well as special research studies or papers.

Directories

Guide to World Commodity Markets: Physical, Futures & Options Trading. 6th ed. London: Kogan Page, 1990. 569 pp.

Part 3, the longest part of this book, is a directory of world commodity markets, arranged by country. For each it usually gives: hours of trading, contract details, membership, date established, volume of trading. Part 1 contains two articles on futures trading; part 2, annual country-by-country production, consumption, and foreign trade statistics, usually over a 10-year period, for each of 19 major commodities traded (coffee, copper, gold, grains, etc.); part 4 is a directory of commodity market trading members, and of some of the major commodity exchanges. Appendices include a glossary, a conversion table, and a list of world time zones. This guide is revised every two or three years.

See note for *Futures* above which publishes an annual guide including a directory of commodity exchanges and related services.

INVESTMENT BANKING

Handbooks

The Library of Investment Banking. Ed. by Robert L. Kuhn. Homewood, IL: Dow Jones-Irwin, 1990. 7 volumes.

This is a new, comprehensive, multi-volume handbook, with over 200 chapters written by leading investment bankers and academicians for investment bankers and other interested persons. It describes and discusses what goes on in investment banking, stressing processes and procedures as well as concepts and principles. The emphasis is on practice—what actually happens when deals get made and financing gets done. The volumes cover: investing and risk management; capital raising and financial structure; corporate and municipal securities; mergers, acquisitions, and leveraged buyouts; mortgage and asset securitization; international finance and investment; index to all volumes. Bibliographical citations are with many chapters.

Williamson, J. Peter, ed. *The Investment Banking Handbook.* New York: Wiley, 1988. 574 pp.

A useful handbook describing the more important aspects and activities of investment banking, with each chapter written from the experience of expert investment bankers or academic persons. The 32 chapters are arranged within 8 parts to cover: investment banking today (including a historical sketch); raising capital; transactional activities (including chapters on leveraged buyouts and mergers and acquisitions); specialized financial instruments; tax-exempt financing; border activities; commercial banks and investment banking; investment banking outside the U.S. (chapters cover Japan, the U.K., and Canada). An appendix contains a ranked list of the 75 leading managers of underwritten offerings as of 1986/87.

Books

Bloch, Ernest. *Inside Investment Banking.* 2d ed. Homewood, IL: Dow Jones-Irwin, 1989. 415 pp.

In this readable textbook on investment banking, Professor Bloch first discusses the market making function (including chapters on the stock market crash of 1987, market making by innovation, and how markets change). He then covers in turn: the market for corporate control (mergers and acquisitions and insider trading problems); new issues flotation (including the nuts and bolts of IPOs); and lastly, policy issues (including shelf registrations). A glossary and suggestions for further reading are at end.

Hayes, Samuel L., III, and Philip M. Hubbard. *Investment Banking: A Tale of Three Cities.* Boston: Harvard Business School Press, 1990. 424 pp.

A well-researched book about investment banking, its evolution and global strategies in the public market settings of London, New York, and Tokyo. Starting with chapters on the origins of investment banking and the history of Eurobonds, the authors then turn to a study of the contemporary securities marketplace principally in the U.K., the U.S., and Japan. They also profile three different firms—their evolution, strategies, and tactics for international expansion. These firms are Salomon Brothers, Nomura Securities, and Credit Suisse First Boston, a joint venture between a European Bank and a U.S. wholesale investment bank. Statistical appendices give vendor statistics on the Euromarkets, the domestic U.S. markets, and domestic Japanese markets, including some ranked lists of firms over several years.

Rappaport, Stephen P. *Management on Wall Street: Making Securities Firms Work.* Homewood, IL: Dow Jones-Irwin, 1988. 330 pp.

In five parts, Rappaport looks at how to make securities firms work, starting with a discussion of the retail and institutional securities business and its administrative dimension; then going beyond capital, commitment, and capability to cover motivation and other personnel practices, top management and strategy, recruitment and personnel development, and finally, a look briefly into the future. A selected bibliography of management books is at end.

For persons who want a picture of the back office operations and data processing functions of a securities firm, see *Securities Operations: A Guide to Operations and Information Systems in the Securities Industry* by Michael T. Reddy (New York Institute of Finance, 1990, 487 pp.).

LAW AND SECURITIES REGULATIONS

Loss, Louis, *Fundamentals of Securities Regulation.* 2d ed. Boston: Little, Brown, 1988. 1,175 pp. Updated with annual supplements.

Professor Loss has designed this book both as a teaching tool and an update of the fundamentals of his earlier comprehensive study of government regulation of securities primarily in the United States, which was published in the 1960s. This is an excellent, though lengthy, book which studies the basics of the entire field. Appendixes include a table of cases and citations to SEC Releases.

Another book on the SEC, while not devoted to laws and regulations, may also be worth mentioning here as a short introduction on the nature, origin, and workings of the SEC, particularly as it relates to the accounting profession. This is *An Introduction to the SEC,* by K. Fred Skousen (5th ed., Cincinnati: South-Western, 1991, 180, pp., paper).

Legal Services

Commerce Clearing House. *Federal Securities Law Reporter.* Chicago. 7 volumes (loose-leaf, with weekly supplements).

A comprehensive loose-leaf service covering federal regulations of securities—laws, regulations, forms, rulings, and court decisions. Volume 1 is devoted to the Securities Act of 1933, and has a topical index. Volumes 2–6 cover other securities laws, forms, regulations concerning investment companies, public utility holding companies, accounting and auditing releases and bulletins, and much more. The last unnumbered volume contains current cases, rulings, and decisions, and a topical index to new developments.

CCH publishes a separate one-volume service for *SEC Accounting Rules,* which provides detailed information on the latest accounting requirements of the SEC, with text of Regulations S-X and S-K, and other pertinent bulletins, releases, and forms. There is also a separate four-volume *Blue Sky Law Reporter* (4 volumes) covering state securities laws, regulations, and decisions; a *Commodity Futures Law Reporter* (2 volumes); a *Mutual Funds Guide* (2 volumes).

Prentice-Hall, Inc. *Securities Regulation.* Englewood Cliffs, NJ. 5 volumes (loose-leaf, with biweekly updates).

Provides complete coverage on all laws administered by the SEC.

BIBLIOGRAPHIES OF INVESTMENT BOOKS

There are a number of recent descriptive lists of important investment information sources but no good separately published list of investment books more recent than 1973. One needs to check the bibliographies in recent investment texts or suggested readings at end of their chapters. For instance the suggestions in Francis' *Management of Investments* are useful because they are annotated; the bibliography in Engel and Boyd's *How to Buy Stocks* is also annotated, but it is now quite old.

INVESTMENT DICTIONARIES

Downes, John, and Jordan E. Goodman. *Dictionary of Finance and Investment Terms.* 3d ed. New York: Barron's, 1991. 537 pp. paper.

This is the finance/investment dictionary I usually turn to first because its definitions are well-written, easy to understand, and sometimes include useful examples. This latest edition defines more than 3,000 terms including new terminology as well as updated definitions for the "traditional language." There are ample cross-references; abbreviations and acronyms are at the end. This useful dictionary also appears as part 4 of the authors' *Barron's Finance and Investment Handbook* (3d ed., Barron's, 1990, pp.163–565).

Pessin, Allan H., and Joseph A. Ross. *The Complete Words of Wall Street.* Homewood, IL: Business One Irwin, 1991. 799 pp.

Here is the culmination of three much shorter dictionaries the authors published beginning in 1983 with *Words of Wall Street.* Now the dictionary has grown into a comprehensive collection of Wall Street words, phrases, and jargon, defined in an easy-to-understand language. The authors are both experienced Wall Street professionals. Mr. Pessin has also recently published *The Illustrated Encyclopedia of the Securities Industry* (New York: New York Institute of Finance, 1988, 530 pp.), an encyclopedic dictionary which often included illustrative examples to help in the explanation of terms.

Rosenberg, Jerry M. *The Investor's Dictionary.* New York: Wiley, 1986. 513 pp.

Professor Rosenberg focuses here on investment terminology, defining about 8,000 terms, abbreviations, and acronyms. His several dictionaries are similar in style and format, with concise definitions adequate in most instances. A new and much shorter edition will be published in 1992 with the title *Dictionary of Investing* (384 pp.).

Scott, David L. *Wall Street Words.* Boston: Houghton Mifflin, 1988. 404 pp.

A dictionary of over 3,600 investment terms both for the individual investor and the investment professional. It is based on terminology encountered in financial broadcasts and in a few financial journals, and so it includes new terms and meanings. A few entries are supplemented with "case study" paragraphs providing further explanatory data or examples. There are also 87 "tips" from 32 experts scattered throughout.

Thomsett, Michael C., comp. *Investment and Securities Dictionary.* Jefferson, NC: McFarland & Company, 1986. 328 pp.

Yet another dictionary, this one provides a summary of more than 2,000 terms and phrases. Useful tables and illustrative examples appear throughout. At end is a guide to major sections of a prospectus, and a bond classification list. Too old to be counted on especially for its data on associations, laws, etc.

Valentine, Stuart. *International Dictionary of the Securities Industry.* 2d ed. London: Macmillan Press, 1989. 228 pp.

This dictionary has simple definitions for the beginner covering foreign as well as English terms and attempting to explain the differences between English and American usage. Includes entries for various stock exchanges, associations, commissions and other organizations in the securities industry worldwide.

INVESTMENT MANAGEMENT JOURNALS

Here are four excellent journals covering the theory and management of investments. For other recommended investment periodicals that focus on articles about industries, companies, stock market techniques, financial news, and stock prices, see the "Investment Newspapers and Periodicals" section of this chapter. See also the last section in chapter 19 for a biweekly newspaper of corporate and institutional investing called *Pensions & Investments.*

Financial Analysts Journal. New York: Financial Analysts Federation (bi-monthly).

Authoritative articles covering both theory and practical problems in relation to new developments in investment management, security analysis, accounting, etc. Includes news about securities laws and regulations, and pension funds. One or two book reviews are in most issues. Indexed in ABI/I, BPI.

Institutional Investor. New York: Institutional Investor (monthly).

A practical journal of interest to money managers, corporate finance officers, and related specialists. Its articles are on such topics as money management, corporate financing, pension fund management, investing and Wall Street, investor relations, with occasional articles on firms and CEOs. For a listing of the various useful rankings, guides, directories appearing annually in specific issues, check the description of this periodical in the "Investment Newspapers and Periodicals" section of this chapter. Indexed in AI, ABI/I, BPI, PAIS, TI: also full text on BRS, DATA-STAR, DIALOG, MEAD/NEXIS. A companion monthly is their *Institutional Investor, International Edition* which has a few of the same articles but also useful articles of interest to international money managers.

Journal of Portfolio Management. New York: Institutional Investor (quarterly).

A forum where practitioners and theorists can exchange the latest ideas in portfolio management. Well-researched articles, most of them written by academicians, cover such areas as market behavior, securities management, portfolio strategies, the profession, and much more. Indexed in ABI/I, BPI.

Professional Investor. London: Published for the Society of Investment Analysts by Corporate Finance Publishing Ltd. (monthly).

Contains short articles and news on investment analysis, portfolio management, and related topics, with a British view.

DIRECTORIES OF THE SECURITIES INDUSTRY

For directories of pension funds and their investment managers, refer to the section for "Directories" of pension funds at the end of chapter 19.

The Bond Buyer's Municipal Marketplace. New York: American Banker–Bond Buyer (semiannual).

Arranged geographically, this directory of U.S. municipal bond dealers includes the names of top officials or specialists for each dealer. At end are lists of government officials, associations, regulators, consultants, attorneys, and information/technology services; also a list of discontinued firms.

Commerce Clearing House. *NASD Manual.* Chicago (monthly).

The official manual of the National Association of Securities Dealers, giving bylaws, rules, codes, etc., and a list of member firms.

The CUSIP Directory: Corporate. New York: Standard & Poor's Corporation for the CUSIP Agency (annual, with weekly and quarterly supplements). Also available online and on CD-ROM.

To avoid possible confusion and delays in identifying specific securities, the American Bankers Association's Committee on Uniform Security Identification Procedures (CUSIP) has devised a standard numbering system which is now used by most of the financial community to identify specific securities issuers and issues. This is a directory of CUSIP numbers for over 1,200,000 securities issues. Of the 9 characters, the first 6 digits identify the issuer (which actually arranges the companies alphabetically), the next two numbers and/or letters identify the issue, the last is the "check digit."

If one does not have access to this directory, it may help to know that several reference books described earlier in this chapter include CUSIP numbers; see, for example, the three *Stock & Bonds* annuals covering ASE, NYSE, and NASDAQ companies described in the "Stock Exchange Publications" section of this chapter.

Institute of Chartered Financial Analysts and the Financial Analysts Federation. *Joint Membership Directory.* Charlottesville, VA.

There are separate lists of individuals who are members of each of the local member-societies of the Federation, and a list of members of the ICFA, with a cross-index.

Nelson's Directory of Investment Research. Port Chester, NY: Nelson Publications. 2 volumes (annual).

A useful directory identifying Wall Street research analysts, with volume 1 covering U.S. companies and volume 2, international companies. Volume 1 is arranged in 7 parts, the largest of which is part 2 containing corporate profiles for over 4,500 U.S.-based companies. The data for each usually includes: top officers (often giving age and number of years with company); brief facts such as stock exchange, ticker symbol, fax number, five-year operating summary, number of shareholders, shares outstanding, market value; also investment firms researching the company, ownership summary with names of major shareholders. Part 1 lists over 400 U.S. brokerage and other research firms, giving for each, names of key personnel, including research management and security analysts with industry specialties. Parts 3–7 are indexes: companies by geographic location, by industry groups, analysts listed both alphabetically and by industry specialty; a master index of companies and research sources. Volume 2 provides similar information for over 4,500 corporations and research firms headquartered outside the U.S.

Supplementing this annual is *Nelson's Guide to Institutional Research* (10/yr.), with sections 1 and 2 identifying analysts' research reports for U.S. and foreign companies, section 3 listing research reports by originating firm, and section 4, listing industry reports.

Securities Industry Yearbook. New York: Securities Industry Association.

This directory of SIA member firms gives names of key people, department heads, total equity and subordinated liabilities, net capital requirement, underwriting and syndication data, total employees, number of accounts. A ranked list of firms is at front; brief key industry and market statistics and a list of major exchanges are in back.

Standard & Poor's Security Dealers of North America. New York: Standard & Poor's Corp. (semiannual).

The most complete list of brokers, dealers, underwriters, and distributors of securities in the United States and Canada. It is arranged geographically with an alphabetical index and includes top officers, location of branches, nature of business. At front are addresses of American and foreign stock exchanges.

Who's Who in the Securities Industry. Chicago: Economist Publishing Co. (annual).

Brief biographical information on leaders in the securities industry, including a picture of each person. This is published each year for the annual Securities Industry Association "Convention Issue" of *The Economist* (Chicago) in an early December issue.

Corporate Finance: The IDD Review of Investment Banking includes a list of underwriting firms with details of managed underwriting during the year. This is described in the "New Securities Offerings" section of this chapter.

SECURITIES INDUSTRY ASSOCIATIONS

Association of Investment Management and Research, P.O. Box 3668, Charlottesville, VA 22903.

Investment Company Institute, 1600 M Street, N.W., Washington, DC 20036.

National Association of Securities Dealers, 1735 K Street, N.W., Washington, DC 20006.

Securities Industry Association, 120 Broad Street, New York, NY. 10271.

Security Traders Association, One World Trade Center, Suite 4511, New York, NY 10048.

9

BUSINESS IN AMERICAN SOCIETY

Introductory Business Texts – Business, Society, and the Environment – Business and Government – Business Law – Business Communication – Public Relations – Business History

The first part of this book has been concerned with types of information – bibliographies, indexes, directories, statistical, financial, and other reference sources. Beginning with this chapter the emphasis shifts to the enterprise itself, and here we cover published information on the place of business in American society. It need hardly be mentioned that recent revolutionary social and economic changes are having a profound effect on the way business is conducted. No longer is the business person concerned solely with operating his or her company effectively. Most managers today are earnestly trying to adjust to changing ideas and values and to respond to the public's insistence that business takes a more active role in solving problems of society and environment.

Books may help give the manager a better understanding of these changes and alert him or her to possible implications for future company planning and policy-making. This chapter describes a few recent books, bibliographies or indexes, and journals on social responsibilities and business ethics, as well as on several other important aspects of the external environment of business. We start with the names of several elementary business texts and end with a few suggestions for reading on business history.

INTRODUCTORY BUSINESS TEXTS

The following three texts are written not for the practicing manager but for beginning college students, to provide a simple yet comprehensive overview of the nature of the business enterprise—its organization and management, its traditional functions, its relation to society and the environment, and its regulation. Each is a standard text. Two have been recently revised to cover new developments in matters of social and environmental concern, data processing and information management, statistical techniques, etc. Each uses two-colored type which adds to the book's readability; each contains a chapter on career development and a glossary. Added features usually also include: an outline of objectives at beginning of chapters; real-world examples used throughout; boxed features of added interest; biographical sketches of business leaders with each chapter.

Boone, Louis E., and David L. Kurtz. *Contemporary Business.* 6th ed. Chicago: Dryden Press: 1990. 745, [43] pp.

Mauser, Ferdinand F., and David J. Schwartz. *American Business: An Introduction.* 6th ed. New York: Harcourt Brace Jovanovich, 1986. 729 pp. paper.

Skinner, Steven J., and John M. Ivancevich. *Business for the 21st Century.* Homewood, IL: Irwin, 1992. 864 pp.

The following two books are not textbooks but may still be of interest to persons contemplating business as a career, and wondering what business school courses cover.

Collins, Eliza G. C., and Mary Anne Devanna. *The Portable MBA.* New York: Wiley, 1990. 386 pp.

> A first-rate attempt to give the aspiring manager a beginning familiarity with the essentials of management, and the functions of business, and how they all fit together. Each chapter is written by an MBA faculty person. Part 1 discusses the foundations of management in chapters on management behavior, quantitative analysis, and managerial economics. Part 2 provides a basic understanding of each of 7 important business functions. Short lists for further reading are with chapters.

Germane, Gayton E. *The Executive Course: What Every Manager Needs to Know About the Essentials of Business.* Reading, MA: Addison-Wesley, 1986. 405 pp.

> This book is oriented toward students interested in a business course as taught in the mid-1980s at a business school such as the Stanford Graduate School of Business. Each chapter is written by a member of that faculty and discusses one of 11 course topics such as marketing, finance, accounting. Annotated suggested readings are at end of each chapter.

BUSINESS, SOCIETY, AND THE ENVIRONMENT

Today, as society and business become larger, more complex, and more turbulent, social and economic problems also become more difficult and more urgent. Thus it is important for students and practicing managers to be knowledgeable about the business environment, about company policies and practices as they impact on society, and about social responsibilities of business as seen from the viewpoint of the critic or special interest group. One visible sign of this increased concern is the explosion of writing on every imaginable issue, problem, and possible solution. We cover here only a selection of recent writings on the subject as a whole and on business ethics rather than try to include the many books on any one particular pressing problem area, such as pollution control, minority employment, or consumer protection. However these can easily be located in libraries by using catalogs, bibliographies, and indexes.

For discussions about socioeconomic problems as they relate to specific management functions, refer to recent books in each area. For example, several of the marketing books in Chapter 18 include pertinent chapters on environmental forces that are influencing marketing. For books on the environment of international business see the "International Management" section of Chapter 16. Articles abound, not only in the several journals listed in this section, but in all types of periodicals, whether they are business, technical, or general interest magazines. For easy identification of these many articles, consult the periodicals indexes mentioned in Chapter 2.

Anderson, Jerry W., Jr. *Corporate Social Responsibility: Guidelines for Top Management.* New York: Quorum Books, 1989. 284 pp.

A recent book providing corporate managers and executives with the history and background as well as the present day status of what social responsibility is all about. The first two parts give the background and historical evolution of the concept; the third part examines the legal aspects and interaction process (in 5 chapters), the ethical/moral, and philanthropic interactions and issues; the last part reviews and evaluates the social responsibility audit and the future of social responsibility. Each chapter contains a list of references; many chapters also include real-world scenarios highlighting important issues.

Buchholz, Rogene A. *Business Environment and Public Policy: Implications for Management and Strategy.* 4th ed. Englewood Cliffs, NJ: Prentice-Hall, 1991. 626 pp.

This book is designed to equip students and business managers with the knowledge and skills necessary to handle the public policy dimension of the job effectively. Based on an examination of the previous edition, part 1 is an introduction; part 2 discusses the nature of public policy (history, social context, and business/government relations); part 3 treats public policy issues that affect business operations (antitrust, equal opportunity, safety and health, pollution control, etc.); part 4 focuses on management responses to public policy issues within the context of strategic management. There are occasional quotes from other sources, some of which are separated in dark grey boxes; also diagrams, tables, and other illustrations. Suggested readings are at end of chapters.

Professor Buchholz has also written *Public Policy Issues for Management* (2d ed. Prentice-Hall, 1991) which is a discussion of specific public policy issues facing business; *Principles of Environmental Management: The Greening of Business* (Prentice-Hall, 1993, 433 pp., paper), a text on the physical environment and environmental issues and their significance for management and corporations; and also a book of cases, with title *Management Response to Public Issues: Concepts and Cases in Strategy Formulation* (2d ed., Prentice-Hall, 1989, 388 pp.).

Frederick, William C., James E. Post and Keith Davis. *Business and Society: Corporate Strategy, Public Policy, Ethics.* 7th ed. New York: McGraw-Hill, 1992. 625 pp.

An excellent text both for students and for managers which seeks to relate business to the whole environment in which business operates. Substantially revised in this latest edition, its chapters are arranged within five major parts. The first two discuss in general terms the corporation in society and the corporation in a global society. With this as background, the authors then focus in turn on: the corporation and public policy; responding to corporate stakeholders (covering stockholders, employees, consumers, and the community); social issues in management (women in the workplace, media's influence, accelerating technological and scientific trends, environmental and ecological problems). These authors make their text more interesting by the inclusion of illustrative examples and quotations from other authorities. Ten case studies, a glossary, and a bibliography are at end.

Luthans, Fred, Richard M. Hodgetts and Kenneth R. Thompson. *Social Issues in Business: Strategic and Public Policy Perspectives.* 6th ed. New York: Macmillan, 1990. 646 pp.

This latest edition has been substantially revised to reflect the dramatic changes and social challenges facing all managers today. The heart of the book is now in its third part which examines social issues facing modern business (corporate governance, equal opportunity, employee rights, consumerism issues, ecological issues). The book starts with an overall analysis of the social role in business, and a section on the role of government in business. It ends with two sections—one discussing the challenges facing business (including a chapter on business in the international arena), and the other on managing and controlling the social performance of business. The authors have combined text with "discussion cases and incidents" in each chapters. Real world examples and boxed features appear throughout; a related reading is at the end of each part.

Sethi, S. Prakash, and Cecilia M. Falbe, eds. *Business and Society: Dimensions of Conflict and Cooperation.* Lexington, MA: Lexington Books, 1987. 654 pp. paper.

An anthology intended to give readers exposure to a broad range of issues and to provide the basis for class discussions on changes taking place in the increasingly complex relationship between business and society. Included are usually two-to-five selections on: business-government relations, corporations and stakeholders, sources of public pressure, corporate responses to external pressures, corporate law violations and white-collar crime, corporate political involvement, corporate external communications, corporations in a global economy. The authors are academics and executives. Most selections are taken from other published sources and many include bibliographic references.

Steiner, George A., and John F. Steiner. *Business, Government, and Society: A Managerial Perspective. Text and Cases.* 5th ed. New York: Random House, 1988. 703, [30] pp.

Probably the most widely used text but also of interest to business persons for its broad view of the interrelationships and issues among business, government, and society. Substantially revised in this latest edition, it is now arranged within 6 sections. The first discusses underlying forces in today's interrelationships. Part 2–4 then focus on the business-government relationship, business ideologies and social responsibilities, and ethics in the business system. The last two parts consider major functional issues (pollution, consumerism, minorities), and corporate issues (such as the political process, multinational corporations, and corporate governance). Each chapter begins with a short sketch and ends with a case study. Interesting features (in boxes) are scattered throughout. An appendix and separately paged bibliography are at end of the book.

Sturdivant, Frederick D., and Heidi Vernon-Wortzel. *Business and Society: A Managerial Approach.* 4th ed. Homewood, IL: Irwin, 1990. 361 pp.

Substantially revised because of new and pressing issues managers must confront and successfully deal with, this text "provides tools and builds skills essential to the achievement of corporate social goals" which are so crucial for corporate survival. Sturdivant and his new coauthor devote four of six chapters to the application of socially responsible management in each of the following areas: political and community responsiveness; human investment; consumer welfare; environmental issues. The first two sections set the stage by discussing strategic management of social issues in general, and also the history, ideology, and ethics involved. A case incident is at end of most chapters.

Professor Sturdivant has also written, with James E. Stacey, a book of cases that corresponds to the structure of his text. The title is *The Corporate Social Challenges: Cases and Commentaries* (4th ed., Irwin, 1990, 701 pp., paper).

Business Ethics

Beauchamp, Tom L., and Norman E. Bowie, eds. *Ethical Theory and Business.* 3d ed. Englewood Cliffs, NJ: Prentice-Hall, 1988. 596 pp.

Principally a book of readings, including several case incidents and legal perspectives with each chapter. The first and last chapters are textual discussions of ethical theory and its application to business, and theories of economic justice. The readings chapters cover concepts and theory of: corporate responsibility; the regulation of business; protecting consumers, workers, and the environment; rights and obligations of employers and employees; discrimination and employment practices; advertising and disclosing information; obligations in accounting, finance, and investment. Suggested supplementary readings are at end of chapters.

De George, Richard T. *Business Ethics.* 3d ed. New York: Macmillian, 1990. 486 pp. paper.

In this text De George deals first with the techniques of moral reasoning and argumentation that are needed to analyze moral issues in business. He then raises basic questions about the morality of economic systems. With this as background, he discusses a variety of current and pressing moral issues in business such as workers' rights, whistle blowing, discrimination, trade secrets, corporate disclosure/insider trading, and business ethics as it relates to such topics as advertising and computers. Finally he discusses moral obligations of nations to other nations, of people to other people geographically distant from them, and of one generation to later generations. Suggestions for further reading are at end. This is a good book—comprehensive, clear, and well organized.

Donaldson, Thomas, and Patricia H. Werhane, eds. *Ethical Issues in Business: A Philosophical Approach.* 3d ed. Englewood Cliffs, NJ: Prentice-Hall, 1988. 454 pp. paper.

Another anthology, this one stressing the importance of analyzing business issues from the standpoint of theoretical philosophy by combining theoretical articles about specific issues with articles discussing actual case studies of a decision-making dilemma in business. (Many of the cases are new to this edition). The selections are arranged in five parts: general issues in ethics; morality and corporations; property, profit, and justice; employer-employee relationship; contemporary business issues.

Professor Donaldson has also written a short treatise on the moral theory of international business, with title *The Ethics of International Business* (New York and Oxford, Eng.: Oxford University Press, 1989, 196 pp.), as well as *Case Studies in Business Ethics* (with A. R. Gini as coauthor, 2d ed. published by Prentice-Hall, 1990, 284 pp., paper).

Freeman, R. Edward, and Daniel R. Gilbert. *Corporate Strategy and the Search for Ethics.* Englewood Cliffs, NJ: Prentice-Hall, 1988. 222 pp.

This is a thought-provoking book because it is the first one attempting to demonstrate that questions and issues of corporate strategy are fundamentally ethical issues. The authors argue that we must get much better and more sophisticated in our understanding of ethics. In three parts, they begin by introducing some fundamental ideas to enrich our understanding of corporate strategy. They then address the current literature on corporate strategy and show how attempts to deal with ethics are inadequate. The last part defends their view of ethics and strategy which they call "the personal projects enterprise strategy." Copious notes and a bibliography are at end.

Madsen, Peter, and Jay M. Shafritz, eds. *Essentials of Business Ethics.* New York: Penguin Books, 1990. 407 pp. paper.

A third book of readings is probably not needed yet this collection of essential articles taps social thinkers such as Peter Drucker and Milton Friedman in pinpointing and analyzing everyday problems, dilemmas, and issues that managers must resolve in business. They are arranged in 7 sections running from defining business ethics to multinational ethics.

Reidenbach, R. Eric, and Donald P. Robin. *Ethics and Profits: A Convergence of Corporate America's Economic and Social Responsibility.* Englewood Cliffs, NJ: Prentice-Hall, 1989. 276 pp.

The corporate "ethical crisis," these authors say, is first and foremost a management problem. Thus the core of their book introduces an approach they call a parallel planning system which accommodates concerns of ethics, social responsibility and the demands for corporate profitability. The first four chapter provide background on the ethics crisis, the reasons corporations are losing respect, the concepts, and the importance of the corporation's culture. The rest of the book focuses on their parallel planning system.

Snoeyenbos, Milton, Robert Almeder and James Humber, eds. *Business Ethics: Corporate Values and Society.* Buffalo, NY: Prometheus Books, 1983. 502 pp. paper.

Unlike the Beauchamp anthology above, this collection of essays examines ethical issues arising within the context of business practices. They were chosen for their intelligibility and their potential for encouraging classroom discussion on key issues facing today's business people. Coverage is provided for selections on: ethics and organizations in general; employee obligations; hiring and discharge; employee rights; ethics and the accounting profession; business and the consumer; business and the environment; multinational corporations. Some chapters are reprints of articles; others are original essays. There are a few case incidents, several corporate policy statements, and a short bibliography at end of each section.

Toffler, Barbara L. *Tough Choices: Managers Talk Ethics.* New York: Wiley, 1986. 372 pp.

The two stated purposes of this interesting book are: (1) to present in a public forum the voices of managers talking about their work, the values they bring to that work, the kinds of ethical concerns they have, and their feelings about them; (2) to explore the nature of those ethical problems and how they come about, and to identify the organizational conditions and individual characteristics and actions necessary to allow and assist ethical business behavior. Much of the book consists of the author's thought-provoking interviews with the 33 managers chosen, whose identity has been disguised to guarantee anonymity. It was reprinted in paperback in 1991 with title *Managers Talk Ethics: Making Tough Choices in the Competitive Business World.*

A more recent book based on interviews with 125 CEOs of major U.S. corporations is *Managing With Integrity: Insights from America's CEOs* by Charles E. Watson (New York: Praeger, 1991, 375 pp.). Its practical examples are intended to show that it is possible for the business person to do what is right and still run a profitable company.

Velasquez, Manuel G. *Business Ethics: Concepts and Cases.* 3d ed. Englewood Cliffs, NJ: Prentice-Hall, 1991. 420 pp. paper.

Three of the four parts of this well-written book examine specific moral issues in business: the ethics of markets and prices; environmental and consumer issues; employee issues. The first part provides an introduction to basic ethical theory. Case studies of several actual moral dilemmas faced by businesses are with each chapter. This note is based on inspection of the earlier edition.

Bibliographies and Abstracts

Beck, Patricia Ann. *Business Ethics and Responsibility: An Information Sourcebook.* Phoenix, AZ: Oryx Press, 1988. 204 pp. (Oryx Sourcebook Series in Business and Management).

An annotated bibliography of U.S. books and selected articles published from 1980 to 1986 and arranged by the following topics: business ethics; corporate social responsibility; self-regulation; international business; South Africa; internal corporate affairs (employee rights and discrimination); external corporate affairs (the consumer and the environment); the role of organized religion in business. At end are: a "Core Library Collection," a list of other information sources, a statement of The Sullivan Principles. Note that this does not cover recent books and articles.

Energy Information Abstracts. New York: R. R. Bowker (monthly, with annual cumulation). Online counterpart is *ENERGYLINE.*

This service concentrates on abstracting the many articles and related sources on all types of energy and related topics such as research and development, consumption, and conservation. Each issue is arranged in 21 subject classifications, and there are good indexes.

Environment Abstracts. New York: R. R. Bowker (monthly, with annual bound cumulation). Online counterpart is *ENVIROLINE;* also on CD-ROM.

Similar to the service above, but covering the whole broad area of the environment. The wide range of journal articles, reports, and other sources are arranged within 21 subject classifications such as: air pollution; food and drugs; land use and misuse; population planning and control; solid waste; transportation; water pollution. Subject and author indexes are at end.

Loose-leaf Services on Social Responsibility Topics

A number of loose-leaf legal services and guides are now being published to help the many managers and other specialists who must keep informed on the latest laws, regulations, rulings, and new developments in environmental protection, pollution control, and product safety. Several of these are:

Bureau of National Affairs. *Air & Water Pollution Control; Environment Reporter* (23 volumes), also available online; *International Environment Reporter* (4 volumes); *Job Safety and Health* (biweekly); *Occupational Safety & Health Reporter* (4 volumes), also available full-text online; *Product Safety & Liability Reporter* (4 volumes).

Commerce Clearing House. *Consumer Product Safety Guide* (3 volumes); *Energy Management and Federal Energy Guidelines* (7 volumes); *Food, Drug, Cosmetic Law Reporter* (6 volumes); *Product Liability Reporter* (2 volumes).

Periodicals on Social Responsibilities

Business & Professional Ethics Journal. Gainesville, FL: Center for Applied Philosophy, University of Florida (quarterly).

The publishers say they attempt here to publish articles that focus on issues and professions not covered in related journals, as well as articles exploring the similarities and differences between ethical issues that arise in two or more professions. Recent volumes have included one double issue containing papers from a pertinent conference. Most articles end with bibliographical citations. Indexed in BPI, SSI.

Business and Society Review. Boston: Management Reports, Inc. (quarterly).

An attractively presented and informative journal with short articles covering a wide range of topics on the role of business in a free society. "Company Performance Roundup" in each issue briefly reviews notable achievements or failures of specific companies in areas of public concern. Includes book reviews. Indexed in ABI/I, BPI, PTS/F&S, PAIS.

Journal of Business Ethics. Dordrecht, Holland and Hingham, MA: Kluwer Academic Publishers (monthly).

Focuses on original articles from a wide variety of methodological and disciplinary perspectives concerning business ethical issues, and covering both speculative philosophy and reports of empirical research. Indexed in ABI/I, BPI, PAIS, SSI.

Journal of Environmental Economics and Management. Duluth, MN: Academic Press (bimonthly).

This quarterly contains both theoretical and empirical papers devoted to specific natural resources and environmental issues. The orientation is toward economics, but it also includes interdisciplinary papers in other fields of interest to resource and environmental economists. It is the official journal of the Association of Environmental and Resource Economists. Indexed in ABI/I, SSI, TI.

BUSINESS AND GOVERNMENT

Fritschler, A. Lee, and Bernard H. Ross. *How Washington Works: The Executive's Guide to Government.* Cambridge, MA: Ballinger, 1987. 198 pp. paper.

A useful guide to understanding how the government works, intended for business executives who operate in this complex and changing government environment. Useful data in appendixes includes an explanation of how a bill becomes a law. A good bibliography provides suggestions for further reading.

Petersen, H. Craig. *Business and Government.* 3d ed. New York: Harper & Row, 1989. 543 pp.

Updated to include important changes in public policy, Petersen's text is divided into five parts: beginnings (which focuses on an analysis of the relationship between market structure and industry performance); workable competition and antitrust policy; regulation as an alternative to competition; social regulation (including coverage on product safety, working conditions, pollution); selected topics (government enterprises, patents, wage and price control). Some familiarity with microeconomic theory is presumed.

Schnitzer, Martin C. *Contemporary Government and Business Relations.* 3d ed. Boston: Houghton Mifflin, 1987. 500 pp.

The author's intent here is to fill what he feels is a void in books on government and business by focusing on all areas of government regulation that directly affect business operations. He starts with two sections introducing the whole area of government and business relations and giving a historical background. The rest covers: industrial concentration and antitrust; social regulation of business (including equal opportunity and environmental policy); direct regulation of business; government as a promoter of business; other issues (government stabilization policies, and business and government in a global environment). Recommended readings are at end of chapters.

Shepherd, William G. *Public Policies Toward Business.* 8th ed. Homewood, IL: Irwin, 1991. 452 pp.

The latest revision of this basic university text is intended to instill an ability to analyze the design, effects, and fitness of the three major categories of public policies toward business. These are discussed in parts 2–4 which are on: antitrust policies (with expanded coverage in this edition); deregulation and regulation of utilities; public enterprise and special cases (the latter covers patents, barriers, and antitrust exemptions). Part 1 is an expanded summary of industrial organization called "the setting for policies."

Weidenbaum, Murray L. *Business, Government, and the Public.* 3d ed. Englewood Cliffs, NJ: Prentice-Hall, 1986. 499 pp.

Weidenbaum's book is designed to provide business executives with an understanding of the different ways government policy affects the activities of the modern corporation. This latest revision starts by discussing government regulatory power in both the social and economic areas (the consumer, the automobile, managing the environment, energy, equal opportunity, etc.). It goes on to cover broader governmental powers (industrial policy, foreign trade, the military market, national planning), and then how business responds. Weidenbaum ends by considering the outlook for the American corporation. Nine chapters each contain a case study.

BUSINESS LAW

Anderson, Ronald A., Ivan Fox and David P. Twomey. *Business Law and the Legal Environment.* 14th ed. Comprehensive Volume. Cincinnati, OH: South-Western, 1990. 1,260 pp.

This widely used textbook for a basic course in business law has been extensively revised to include such current and relevant topics as business ethics and the international legal environment. Its 10 major parts cover: the legal and social environment of business; contracts; personal property and bailments; sales; commercial paper; secured transactions, creditors rights, and insurance; agency and employment; business organizations; real property; estates. Case problems are with each chapter; a glossary is at end. A shortened version, containing only the first 7 parts mentioned above, was published with same title (14th ed., Standard Volume; South-Western, 1990, 1,023 pp.). These authors have also written a text that is divided equally between textual material and cases and case problems, with title *Business Law: Principles, Cases, Legal Environment* (11th ed., South-Western, 1992, 1,234 pp.).

Blackburn, John D., Elliot I. Klayman and Martin H. Malin. *Legal Environment of Business.* 3d ed. Homewood, IL: Irwin, 1988. 666 pp.

A well-organized text for business students on the title subject. The authors begin with an introduction to business and law (including a discussion of business ethics). They then study in turn: public law basis of business regulation; private law basis of government regulation (contracts, torts); business and financial markets (security regulation, creditor relations, etc.); business and the marketplace (consumer protection, monopolies, antitrust, international business transactions); business and its employees (labor-management relations, equal employment opportunity). Each chapter consists of about a third case material. Texts of related acts are in appendixes, and also a glossary.

Clark, Robert C. *Corporate Law.* Boston: Little, Brown, 1986. 837 pp.

An introduction which attempts to explore, explain, and illustrate basic principles and connecting themes of corporate law in a clear, concise, and fair way rather than to be a compilation of legal authorities. Included are chapters on: the basic allocation of powers and duties, conflicts of interest, executive compensation, insider trading, the voting system, combinations, mergers, buyouts, tender offers, shareholders, issuance of securities, close corporations, and the meaning of corporate personality.

Corley, Robert N., O. Lee Reed and Peter J. Shedd. *The Legal Environment of Business.* 8th ed. NY: McGraw-Hill, 1990. 903 pp.

When this was originally published in 1966, it was the first text for the first course taught on the title subject. Now in its 8th edition with two different coauthors, it is a well-established text for an environmental course in law, intended to prepare students for decision making in business. Included are sections 4–7 on: conducting business (chapters are on form of organization, liability, international transactions); protecting employees (worker protection, discrimination in employment, right to union activity, unfair labor practices); protecting parties to transactions; protecting society (antitrust and environmental laws). The first three sections cover: an introduction (the law, court systems, litigation, arbitration); constitutional and administrative law in general; contracts and torts. The authors say they have tried to make their writing style clear. Summaries of court cases illustrating the text and summaries of important legislation appear throughout. Text of several statutes and a glossary are at end. In 1986 Professors Corley and Reed published a shortened version of an earlier edition called *Fundamentals of the Legal Environment of Business* (McGraw-Hill, 1986, 643 pp.).

While these books concentrate on public law and the regulation of business,

Professor Corley (with Peter J. Shedd) has also written a text on the *Fundamentals of Business Law* (5th ed., Englewood Cliffs, NJ: Prentice-Hall, 1990, 1,018 pp.) which stresses those aspects of law that are essential to the business decision-making process. Case briefs appear throughout; text of the Uniform Commercial Code (UCC) and a glossary are at end. A slightly longer version, *Principles of Business Law* (14th ed., Prentice-Hall 1984, 1,203 pp.), has four sections that are not in the *Fundamentals* book.

Howell, Rate A., John R. Allison and Robert A. Prentice. *Business Law: Text and Cases.* 4th ed. Chicago: Dryden Press, 1988. 1,426 pp.

Another comprehensive, traditional business law text intended for future business managers, and devoted to such subjects as contracts, agency, sales, commercial paper, property, and business organizations. There are also sections on the legal environment and government regulation of business. The authors use frequent examples to show how legal rules apply to "real world" situations; illustrative court cases are also interspersed. Appendixes contain text of the UCC, the Model Business Corporation Act, several partnership acts, the Constitution, and a glossary.

The two joint authors have also written a related text on *The Legal Environment of Business* (3d ed., Dryden Press, 1990, 784 pp.).

Lane, Marc J. *Legal Handbook for Small Business.* Rev. ed. New York: AMACOM, 1989. 255 pp.

Here is a practical guide intended to alert small business owners to major legal opportunities and pitfalls they may encounter, and to provide a background they must have in order to work efficiently with their attorneys. This edition updates the information on taxes, etc., and includes such new material as protecting corporate officers and directors. There are checklists, figures, and forms with most chapters, and a glossary at end. Mr. Lane, a practicing attorney, has written earlier legal books for non-lawyers such as *Legal Handbook for Nonprofit Organizations* (AMACOM, 1980, 294 pp.).

Lashbrooke, E. C., Jr., and Michael I. Swygert. *The Legal Handbook of Business Transactions: A Guide for Managers and Entrepreneurs.* New York: Quorum Books, 1987. 579 pp.

Every business needs a manual of preventive law for its legal health, say these experienced teachers, and this is what they have tried to write—a practical, yet comprehensive volume covering the principal laws, rules, regulations, and legal principles that every manager or entrepreneur should be familiar with in conducting a business. It is arranged by common situations, and the topics covered include the legal environment, formation and sale of a business, raising capital, buying real estate, negotiating contracts, buying and selling goods, extending credit, collecting accounts, obtaining relief from creditors, managing employees, keeping the workplace safe, record keeping, taxation, business planning. A bibliography is at end.

Metzger, Michael B. et al. *Business Law and the Regulatory Environment: Concepts and Cases.* 7th ed. Homewood, IL: Irwin, 1989. 1,563 pp.

This is the latest edition of what has been a leading text ever since Harold Lusk wrote the first edition in 1935. Now updated once again by a team of five authors, it gives comprehensive coverage both to traditional subjects and to the more nontraditional emerging issues and problems, such as ethical considerations, employment law, computer law, securities regulations, the legal environment. It is arranged in 12 parts, with problem cases at end of most chapters. As in most other business law text, appendixes give text of the UCC, the Constitution, the Revised Model Business Corporation Act, and several other acts. A glossary of legal terms and index of cases is at end.

Yet another recent textbook is *Business Law: Legal Environment, Transactions and Regulation* by George D. Cameron III and Phillip J. Scaletta, Jr. (3d ed., BPI/ Irwin, 1989, 1,338, [283] pp.).

Bibliographies

Goehlert, Robert, and Nels Gunderson. *Government Regulation of Business: An Information Sourcebook.* Phoenix, AZ: Oryx Press, 1987. 425 pp. (Oryx Sourcebook Series in Business and Management).
Part 1 of this useful (but now rather old) bibliography is an annotated core list of books on government regulation of business and industry arranged in four categories (the economics, the politics, regulatory activities, regulatory agencies). The following four parts cover journal articles (not annotated) and dissertations in these same four categories. The last part is an annotated list of basic business reference sources arranged by type of source such as dictionaries and handbooks.

Indexes

Index to Legal Periodicals. New York: H. W. Wilson (monthly, except September, cumulating quarterly and annually). Online counterpart available via *WILSONLINE;* also on CD-ROM as *WILSONDISC.*
Subject and author index to over 500 legal periodicals, yearbooks, etc., in all areas of jurisprudence, including those published in the U.S., Australia, Canada, Great Britain, Ireland, and New Zealand. Tables of those cases and statutes commented upon, and index of book reviews is at end.

Legal Resource Index. Foster City, CA: Information Access Corp. (monthly). Also available online.
This is a monthly cumulating COM (Computer Output Microfilm) production. The microfilm is projected on a screen, somewhat like a TV set, and you operate it yourself to find articles, case notes, book reviews, and other material found in over 800 law journals, pertinent articles from general periodicals, and newspapers.

No effort is made here to cover legal reference sources in any depth. When researching any legal topic one should visit a law library and enlist the assistance of a librarian expert. For instance there are online services, one called *MEAD/LEXIS,* where one can obtain the full text of court decisions, statutes, regulations, and other primary and secondary legal materials. Another, *WESTLAW,* provides online access to legal reporters and other West Publishing Co. legal services.

Dictionaries

Black, Henry C. *Black's Law Dictionary.* 5th ed. St Paul, MN: West Publishing Co., 1990. 1,657 pp.
"Definitions of the terms and phrases of American and English jurisprudence, ancient and modern." This is the standard law dictionary covering all types of law. This latest edition has several coauthors and contributing authors.

Corporate Legal Services

Legal services covering specific aspects of business are described elsewhere in this book: securities regulations in Chapter 8; accounting and tax laws and regulations, Chapters 12 and 16; banking, Chapter 14; insurance and real estate (books only), Chapter 15; antitrust and trade regulation, Chapter 18; and labor laws, Chapter 19.

Prentice-Hall, Inc. *Corporation Guide* and *Corporation* Service. Englewood Cliffs, NJ. 2 loose-leaf services.

The *Corporation Guide* is a handy one-volume service designed to give business executives quick and accurate answers to questions on corporate law from organization to dissolution. *Corporation* Service (6 volumes) contains one volume of "Explanations" covering all phases of corporation law and procedure, and five volumes of state statutes, court decisions, and rulings affecting the operation of business corporations. Two separately published volumes contains *Corporation Forms*.

Periodicals

American Business Law Journal. Abilene, TX: American Business Law Association (Abilene Christian University) (3/yr.).

A professional journal, each issue of which contains five lengthy, scholarly articles, and an occasional book review. The ABLA is an association of teachers of business law and legal environment. The address of the journal changes as ABLA officers change. Indexed in ABI/I, BPI.

Business Lawyer. Chicago: Section of Business Law, American Bar Association (quarterly).

Articles are on a wide range of business, financial, and legal subjects, written by practicing lawyers and of interest to both lawyers (especially those belonging to the section noted above) and to managers. Indexed in ABI/I, PAIS.

Directories

Martindale-Hubbell Law Directory. New Providence, NJ. 22 volumes (annual). Also available online and on CD-ROM.

The 17 numbered volumes consist of a geographic list (vols. 1–15) and an alphabetical index of attorneys, services, and suppliers (vols. 16–17). The geographic volumes are in three parts: bar practice profiles (blue pages) giving vital statistics for attorneys and firms, with ratings; professional biographies (white pages), arranged by law firm and containing biographies for individual attorneys in the firm; directory of services and suppliers (yellow pages). Volume 15 includes profiles of major law schools. The five unnumbered volumes contain the *Martindale-Hubbell Law Digest* (3 vols.) and the *Martindale-Hubbell International Law Directory* (2 vols.).

BUSINESS COMMUNICATION

Handbooks

DiGaetani, John L., ed. *The Handbook of Executive Communication.* Homewood, IL: Dow Jones-Irwin, 1986. 894 pp.

A collection of essays by major communication specialists, with its 64 chapters arranged in 8 parts. Four of these cover writing, reading, speaking, interviewing, and interpersonal skills. The other sections cover such topics as: corporate communication (annual reports, handbooks, manuals, etc.); training and development; telecommunication (electronic meetings, computers, etc.). The editor says this handbook is intended to help managers improve their ability to diagnose communication problems and to solve those problems in order to produce more effective communication in their companies.

Books

Himstreet, William C., and Wayne M. Baty. *Business Communications: Principles and Methods*. 9th ed. Boston: PWS-Kent Publishing Co., 1990. 768 pp.
Significant changes were made in the 8th edition of this well-established introductory textbook. It was divided into 7 major parts to cover: an introduction to communication and organizations; getting ready to write; communication through letters and memorandums; communicating about work and jobs (including a chapter on preparing resumes); listening and speaking for success; communicating through reports; and communicating today and tomorrow (intercultural business communication, and the office of today and tomorrow). An appendix reviews the basics of grammar and mechanics. Sample letters and other illustrations occur frequently; the publisher has made effective use of color to highlight sections and marginal and boxed notes. The 9th edition was not seen for review.

Lewis, Phillip V. *Organizational Communication: The Essence of Effective Management*. 3d ed. New York: Wiley, 1987. 345 pp.
The purpose of this book is to provide managers at all levels with the learning and understanding of the communication process which they need to effectively transmit information within changing organizations. The four parts cover: communication and organizational behavior; the nature of organizational communication; barriers to and cornerstones of organizational communication; managing organizational communication. Appendixes discuss letters and written reports, and employment and the exit interview. Suggested readings are at end of chapters.

Sigband, Norman B., and Arthur H. Bell. *Communication for Management and Business*. 5th ed. Glenview, IL: Scott, Foresman, 1989. 633, [150] pp.
A good, recently revised text that covers the subject in depth. The authors begin with an overview that includes an expanded chapter on the electronic communication revolution. They then consider in turn: writing that works; research and reports (including a chapter on writing proposals, procedures, and business plans); professional speaking and listening; career communication; business correspondence. "Legal Considerations" supplement some chapters. Chapter 7 contains an annotated bibliography of published information sources. Separately paged sections contain cases, readings, a brief guide to usage, and to business letter style and format. Professor Sigband has also written, with David N. Bateman as first author, an introductory text, *Communicating in Business* (3d ed., Scott, Foresman, 1989, 558 pp.).

Guides for Better Writing or Speaking

Hayakawa, S. I., and Alan R. Hayakawa. *Language in Thought and Action*. 5th ed. San Diego, CA: Harcourt Brace Jovanovich, 1990. 287 pp. paper.
Knowing about the role of language in human life and its different uses is basic to an understanding of people and how to communicate with them. In this excellent volume a well-known authority (now with a coauthor) discusses the principles of

semantics and their applications. Hayakawa's imaginative and sometimes amusing examples add much to the interest of his book and may encourage readers to test the principles presented. Includes a bibliography.

Holcombe, Marya W., and Judith K. Stein. *Writing for Decision Makers.* 2d ed. New York: Van Nostrand Reinhold, 1987. 219 pp. paper.

This is a good, short, nontextbook-type book written by two experts to "show you how to plan, organize, and present your thoughts on paper in a way that will produce results." The sub-title reads "memos and reports with a competitive edge." It is full of checklists, guidelines, and pertinent examples of managers' writing. Many of the latter are new to this edition as is a note on writing electronically.

Lesikar, Raymond V. *Basic Business Communication.* 5th ed. Homewood, IL: Irwin, 1991. 666 pp. Sixth edition to be published in 1993.

Regarded as a highly readable and thorough text, this book focuses on writing communication fundamentals, patterns, applications in business. Parts 2–4 cover letter writing. The other three parts deal with other forms of communication: report writing; public speaking, oral reports and other forms of oral communication; specific topics, such as electronic technology, international communication, and business research methods. Adding to the interest of this book is a good use of marginal notes, situation descriptions and challenging problems in boxes, and many examples and problems. Self-help checklists and notes about correct documentation are at end. Two other texts by Lesikar (now coauthored by John D. Pettit, Jr.) are his *Business Communication: Theory and Application* (6th ed., Irwin, 1989, 754 pp.) and *Report Writing for Business* (8th ed., Irwin, 1991, 460 pp.).

Several other useful texts as alternatives to Lesikar are: *Effective Business Communications* by Herta A. Murphy and Herbert W. Hildebrandt (6th ed., New York: McGraw-Hill, 1991, 840 pp.); *Communicating in Business Today* by Ruth G. Newman (with Marie A. Danziger and Mark Cohen as collaborators. Lexington, MA: D. C. Heath, 1987, 626 pp.); and *Communications in Business* by Walter Wells (5th ed., Boston: PWS-Kent Publishing Co., 1988, 632 pp.).

Munter, Mary. *Guide to Managerial Communication.* 3d ed. Englewood Cliffs, NJ: Prentice-Hall, 1992. 174 pp. paper.

"Short, compact, practical, useful and readable" says one reviewer, and he is surely correct. This handy little guide to communication techniques is intended for persons in business, government, and the professions who need to speak or write. The author starts with a chapter on communications strategy. Then she covers writing in three chapters (the process, macro, and micro issues), and speaking, also in three chapters (structure, visual aids, nonverbal delivery skills). Appendixes are on writing formats, correct words, unbiased language, grammar, and punctuation. A bibliography is at end.

Roman, Kenneth, and Joel Raphaelson. *Writing that Works.* New York: Harper & Row, 1981. 105 pp.

Another concise little guide for busy people who must use the written word to communicate, this one focuses on "how to write memos, letters, reports, speeches, resumes, plans and other papers that say what you mean—and get things done." A good list of several "other books that will help you write better" is at end; it includes two frequently cited, brief guides to the craft of writing: *The Elements of Style* by William Strunk and E. B. White (3d ed., New York: Macmillan, 1978, 85 pp., paper); and *The Golden Book on Writing* by David Lambuth and others (New York: Penguin Books, 1976, 81 pp., paper).

Yet another more recently published self-help guide which advocates use of a conversational approach for improving business writing is *Writing Out Loud: A Self-Help Guide to Clear Business Writing* by John L. DiGaetani, Jane B. DiGaetani and Earl N. Harbert (Homewood, IL: Dow Jones-Irwin, 1983, 178 pp.).

Tacey, William S. *Business and Professional Speaking.* 4th ed. Dubuque, IA: Wm. C. Brown Co., 1983. 280 pp. paper.

This book is designed to help people who want to improve their oral communication skills. Not only does Professor Tacey cover preparing and delivering speeches but he also discusses speaking in groups, speaking in meetings, interviewing, listening, voice patterns, and appearance. Examples are used throughout; bibliographies at end of chapters are intended for persons interested in serious study on any chapter topic. Sample speeches for study and analysis are at end of book.

Vik, Gretchen N., Clyde W. Wilkinson and Dorothy C. Wilkinson. *Writing and Speaking in Business.* 10th ed. Homewood, IL: Irwin, 1990. 636 pp.

With a new lead author and a changed title, this is the latest revision of a standard text which is still intended to help students understand communication strategies and to speak and write more effectively and efficiently. It is written from the management point of view. There are five parts: basics of business communication; psychological planning for effectiveness; reporting for management decisions; oral applications of principles; special topics. Checklists and examples are used throughout. Cases are with chapters; a "concise writer's handbook" is at end.

For students who need a basic "guide to suitable style in the typewritten presentation of formal papers both in scientific and in nonscientific fields," consult *A Manual for Writers of Term Papers, Theses, and Dissertations* by Kate L. Turabian (5th ed., revised and expanded by Bonnie B. Honigsblum. Chicago: University of Chicago Press, 1987, 300 pp.).

Periodicals

Journal of Business Communication. Urbana, IL: Association for Business Communication (quarterly).

This is a refereed scholarly journal seeking original research that develops, tests, or advances business, managerial, or organizational communication theory or knowledge. Often includes book reviews. Indexed in ABI/I, BPI.

This association also publishes *The Bulletin* (quarterly) which concentrates on articles of general interest to teachers and practitioners. The March issue contains an ABC membership directory.

Directories

O'Dwyer's Directory of Corporate Communications. New York: J. R. O'Dwyer Co. (annual).

A directory of more than 4,000 companies and 900 associations and federal government departments, providing the following: address, total sales, statement of PR/communications operations (personnel involved, budget, scope of activity). There are geographic and industry indexes.

PUBLIC RELATIONS

Handbooks

Dilenschneider, Robert L., and Dan J. Forrestal. *The Dartnell Public Relations Handbook.* 3d ed., rev. Chicago: Dartnell Corporation, 1987. 875 pp.

The first three parts of this latest edition consist of an overview of public relations and a discussion of external PR. These were written by Dilenschneider with contributions by the staff of Hill and Knowlton. Parts 4 and 5 (by Forrestal) detail the many aspects of internal PR. Part 6 (by David B. Williams) focuses on PR for health care facilities. Appendixes contain case studies, as well as 6 annual lectures (1981–86) on PR, and a bibliography prepared by the Public Relations Society of America.

Lesly's Handbook of Public Relations and Communications. Ed. by Philip Lesly. 4th ed., rev. and updated. Chicago: Probus Publishing, 1991. 874 pp. paper.

Restructured, retitled, and significantly revised to encompass the rapid changes in recent years, this is a comprehensive introduction to public relations and communications in 48 chapters written by the editor plus over 40 PR practitioners. It covers: what public relations is and does (including a chapter on policy, issues, crises, and opportunities); what PR includes (with increased attention paid to the various aspects of public affairs, and chapters also on such topics as investor relations, employee relations, consumer affairs); analysis, research, and planning; the techniques of communication; how an organization utilizes PR (with chapters relating both to profit and nonprofit organizations); the practice of PR. Useful bibliographical sources are in an appendix, including lists of groups, organizations, periodicals, press clipping bureaus, etc.; also a list of PR books, a glossary, and codes of professional standards.

Books

Cutlip, Scott M., Allen H. Center and Glen M. Broom *Effective Public Relations.* 6th ed. Englewood Cliffs, NJ: Prentice-Hall, 1985. 670 pp.

This was a widely used text in the 1980s. Its main focus is on the role of the practitioner, and it is arranged in two parts. Part 1 is devoted to the principles and the process, with four chapters on the process, and others discussing communication, the organizational/social/legal context of public relations, the various publics, the media. Part 2 is on the practice and the profession as it relates to business, associations and labor unions, voluntary agencies/health care/the arts/churches, government, and education. Lists of additional readings are given at end of chapters.

Harris, Thomas L. *The Marketers Guide to Public Relations.* New York: Wiley, 1991. 306 pp.

Harris' book is the first one to cover the emerging discipline of marketing public relations, and it relates how top marketers use this new PR to gain a competitive edge. Arranged in two parts, the first discusses how to understand marketing PR, and the second how to use it for specific purposes. Case examples as they apply to consumer products are used throughout, all based on the author's long-time personal experience and observation. References and a bibliography are at end.

Reilly, Robert T. *Public Relations in Action.* 2d ed. Englewood Cliffs, NJ: Prentice-Hall, 1987. 594 pp.

A beginning undergraduate text that aims to present the profession of public relations in an interesting, comprehensive, and practical form. This edition has increased emphasis on public relations as a management function and also on the skills necessary for entry-level practitioners. Illustrations are used throughout; also explanatory boxed inserts. Suggested readings are with chapters.

Wouters, Joyce. *International Public Relations.* New York: AMACOM, American Management Association, 1991. 308 pp.

As the title above indicates, this introductory book offers an overview of markets abroad and information on challenges and opportunities inherent in a company's moving overseas. It is written for executives and public relations specialists by a public relations professional who has had first-hand experience in establishing a company's products or services in foreign markets. The author includes actual case histories to dramatize the guidelines and techniques that work. The textual portion comprises only the first 175 pages; the rest consists of a resource directory listing pertinent organizations and publications, major communications media (arranged by selected country), and fact sheets on selected nations.

Three alternative introductory texts, well reviewed but not seen for evaluation, are: *Public Relations: The Profession and the Practice* by Otis W. Baskin and Craig E. Aronoff (2d ed., Dubuque, IA: W. C. Brown, 1988, 483 pp.); *The Practice of Public Relations* by Fraser P. Seitel (Columbus, OH: Charles E. Merrill, 1989, 641 pp.); and *Public Relations: Strategies and Tactics* by Dennis L. Wilcox, et al. (3d ed., New York: HarperCollins, 1992). A collection of articles by top practitioners is *Experts in Action: Inside Public Relations* ed. by Bill Cantor (2d ed., New York: Longmans, 1989, 520 pp., paper).

Bibliographies

Passarelli, Anne B. *Public Relations in Business, Government, and Society: A Bibliographic Guide.* Englewood, CO: Libraries Unlimited, 1989. 128 pp.

A selected, annotated bibliography of the public relations literature published in the United States. It is arranged by topic within 7 basic sections, and it includes directories and other reference works as well as books and periodicals.

Periodicals

International Public Relations. London: Published for the International Public Relations Association by Whiting and Birch Ltd. (quarterly).

An international review, with a European and British focus, covering the broad areas of PR and communication. Includes book reviews.

Public Relations Journal. New York: Public Relations Society of America (monthly except semimonthly in June).

Short articles on a wide variety of PR-related subjects; also news of interest to PRSA members. Their "Annual Salary Survey" is in June. Usually one book review is in each issue. A second issue in June is their useful PRSA membership directory called "Register Issue." Indexed in ABI/I, BPI, PTS/F&S, TI; full text on BRS, DATA-STAR, DIALOG, DOW JONES, MEAD/NEXIS.

Public Relations Review. Silver Spring, MD: Communication Research Association (quarterly).

Usually about five well-researched articles in each issue on public relations, applied research, and education. Occasional issues are devoted to a specific theme, e.g. "Ethics in Public Relations" (summer 1989). Includes book reviews. Indexed in ABI/I, BPI, PAIS, TI.

Another journal containing short, practical articles is *Public Relations Quarterly* (Rhinebeck, NY). Indexed in ABI/I, BPI, TI.

Directories

O'Dwyer's Directory of Public Relations Firms. New York: J. R. O'Dwyer Co. (annual).

This describes more than 2,000 PR firms and PR departments of advertising agencies and their branches, with a separate list of PR firms in other countries. For each it usually gives top officers, type of service offered, when founded, number of employees and, in most cases, a list of client companies. At front are several ranked lists of largest U.S. public relations firms and largest PR operations with advertising agencies. There are indexes by geographic location and client company. The publisher now offers also a biographical directory both of public relations and communications executives called *O'Dwyer's Directory of Public Relations Executives.*

Public Relations Journal. "Register Issue." New York (annual; extra issue in June).

An annual directory of individual members of the Public Relations Society of America, with index by geographic location and name of firm.

BUSINESS HISTORY

Beard, Miriam. *A History of Business.* Ann Arbor: University of Michigan Press, 1963. 2 volumes. Out of print.

The first attempt to write a complete history of the businessman. Starting with the heritage of antiquity in Vol. 1, Professor Beard discusses development from the patrician city ruler up through the monopolist of the eighteenth century. In Vol. 2, she continues with the period of the individualist, on up to the organization makers of the twentieth century. This book was originally published in 1938 with title *A History of the Business Man.*

Bruchey, Stuart. *Enterprise: The Dynamic Economy of a Free People.* Cambridge, MA: Harvard University Press, 1990. 645 pp. paper.

A thoughtful study for both students and general readers that retraces the origins of American capitalism from its beginnings at Jamestown up to recent times, describing and analyzing the forces making for change as the U.S. economy developed and matured. Its copious footnotes attest to the author's careful research as well as his long and distinguished career as an economic historian, researcher, and writer.

Chandler, Alfred D., Jr. *Strategy and Structure: Chapters in the History of Industrial Enterprise.* Cambridge, MA: MIT Press, Massachusetts Institute of Technology, 1962. 463 pp. paper.

This highly significant volume is the first scholarly study of the administrative history of American industry. It is based on a survey of almost 100 large industrial companies, with an exhaustive analysis of the four companies that first developed a decentralized, multidivisional structure—du Pont, General Motors, Standard Oil

(New Jersey), and Sears. Extensive bibliographical notes are at end. Professor Chandler has also written, with Richard S. Tedlow, *The Coming of Managerial Capitalism: A Casebook on the History of American Economic Institutions* (Homewood, IL: Irwin, 1985, 877 pp.). This is a compilation of the useful materials used in their HBS course on "The Coming of Managerial Capitalism."

For a study of the evolution of strategy and structure of the 100 largest British industrial enterprises, 1950–1970, in a book inspired by Chandler's classic work, see Derek F. Channon, *The Strategy and Structure of British Enterprise* (Boston, Harvard Business School, 1973, 257 pp. Later distributed by Harvard University Press, but now out of print).

Chandler, Alfred D., Jr. *Scale and Scope: The Dynamics of Industrial Capitalism.* Cambridge, MA: Belknap Press of the Harvard University Press, 1990. 860 pp.

An excellent, truly monumental, work that carries forward the author's prizewinning study of the rise of managerial capitalism in U.S. business enterprises from the 1840s to the 1920s (that book, also highly recommended, was *The Visible Hand: The Managerial Revolution in American Business,* Belknap Press, 1977, 608 pp.). In this more recent study (which was 10 years in the making), Professor Chandler examines the beginning and the growth of managerial capitalism globally by studying the collective histories of the 200 largest manufacturing companies in three important countries (the United States, Great Britain, and Germany) from the 1880s to the 1940s. Three major sections consider the evolving patterns of growth and competitiveness separately for each country, with an introductory section at the beginning setting the stage. Like his earlier book, this one is filled with details about companies, events, changing strategies, challenges, problems, new technologies, etc. The copious bibliographical notes at the end point up the massive research behind the study. An appendix contains separate ranked lists (by industry) of the 200 largest industrial companies in the three countries for three significant points in time (for the U.S. this was 1917, 1930, and 1948; for the other countries it varied somewhat).

Cochran, Thomas C. *200 Years of American Business.* New York: Basic Books, 1977. 288 pp. Out of print.

Professor Cochran is one of our most outstanding business historians. In this wellwritten volume he describes the changing ways in which Americans have managed their businesses from 1776 to the mid-1970s with special emphasis on human relations and organizational innovation. Useful notes and suggested readings are at end. Among Cochran's earlier publications is his *Business in American Life: A History* (New York: McGraw-Hill, 1972, 402 pp.) in which he studies the history of business in relation to its social and physical environment.

Walton, Gary M., and Hugh Rockoff. *History of the American Economy.* 6th ed. New York: Harcourt Brace Jovanovich, 1990. 687 pp.

Professor Walton and his new coauthor now revise this well-established text on American economic history begun back in 1955 by Professor Ross M. Robertson. It retains the chronological sequence of earlier editions and the division of U.S. history into four periods: the colonial era, 1607–1776; the revolutionary, early national, and antebellum eras, 1776–1860; the reunification era, 1860–1920; the modern era, 1920 to the present. More emphasis is now given to the modern era. Selected references are with each chapter.

For persons who want to read a simple, general survey in paperback see *A History of American Business* by Keith L. Bryant, Jr., and Henry C. Dethloff (2d ed., Englewood Cliffs, NJ: Prentice-Hall, 1990, 384 pp., paper). This focuses on individuals and "certain firms which have innovated or pioneered in the creation of administrative structures, technology, or managerial practices," and suggested readings are with chapters for those who want to read further. It should also be noted here that there is an excellent, massive compilation of the views of many well respected economists and business historians on the economic experience and development from the 17th century to the 1970s. That is *Encyclopedia of American Economic History: Studies of the Principal Movements and Ideas* edited by Glenn Porter (New York: Scribner's, 1980, 3 volumes). Finally, for persons interested in tracing the growth of our present-day society from its beginnings, there is a good, nontechnical text on *The Making of Economic Society* by Robert L. Heilbroner (7th ed., rev., Prentice-Hall, 1985, 286 pp.). Although now out of print, it will be found in many libraries.

Bibliographies

Although these bibliographies are still of great value, all but the one by Geahigan are very old and so do not cover histories of companies, industries, and business personalities published since the early 1970s. For the most recent bibliographies one needs to check book reviews in the business history journals noted below, and also consult more general lists of published books, or card catalogs in business libraries.

Geahigan, Priscilla C. *U.S. and Canadian Businesses, 1955–1987: A Bibliography.* Metuchen, NJ: Scarecrow Press, 1988. 589 pp.

This bibliography on the title subject covers not only company historical and biographical studies from 1955–1987 but also works relating to various aspects of a company's operation. It is arranged by two-digit SIC and then alphabetically by company or person. There are indexes by company name, personal name, and author. Canadian companies and people are noted by an asterisk (*) after the name. A useful source despite the fact that it lists both the better company histories and those that are ephemeral without noting which are which. Checking the total number of pages for each citation can help in identifying the longer and thus potentially more useful histories.

Another recently revised bibliography is *United States Corporation Histories: A Bibliography, 1965–1990* by Wahib Nasrallah (New York: Garland Publishing Co, 1991, 511 pp.). This one also includes many of the very short (20 pages or so) historical addresses by company executives which provide no real insight into a company's history. My own *Studies in Enterprise* (Boston: Baker Library, Harvard Business School, 1957, 169 pp.) is now out or print but may be found in business school libraries. It is a listing by subject of selected American and Canadian company histories and biographies of businessmen, but it is useful only for identifying older books.

Larson, Henrietta M. *Guide to Business History* (Harvard Studies in Business History, No. 12). Cambridge, MA: Harvard University Press, 1948. 1,181 pp. Reprinted in Boston by J. S. Canner Co., 1964.

An old but indispensable guide to materials for the study of American business, including annotated lists of business histories, biographies of businessmen, histories of industries, and research and reference sources.

Lovett, Robert W. *American Economic and Business History Information Sources* (Management Information Guide, 23). Detroit, MI: Gale Research Co., 1971. 323 pp.

A selected, annotated bibliography of U.S. and some Canadian works on economic and business history (but only to 1970), as well as on agricultural and labor history and on the history of science and technology. Includes histories of industries, corporate histories, and biographies.

Whitten, David O., ed. *Manufacturing: A Historiographical and Bibliographical Guide.* (Handbook of American Business History, Volume 1). New York: Greenwood Press, 1990. 497 pp.

First of a series of volumes, each will consist of chapters devoted to concise histories of individual industries, supported by bibliographical essays and a bibliography. This first volume covers 23 specific manufacturing industries, each written by an academician or other authority. The introduction is by Professor Mira Wilkins. The bibliographical portion of each chapter is intended to supplement bibliographical materials available in such books as those by Larson and by Lovett above, and so they may be useful for noting the more recent historical material on an industry.

Institute of Chartered Secretaries and Accountants. *Company Histories.* London: 1972. 35 pp.

A complete list of the British company histories in the library of this institute as of 1972. No later list has been published by this institute.

Some British and Irish company and industry histories are also included in the annual "List of Publications on the Economic and Social History of Great Britain and Ireland," appearing in the November issue, each year, of the *Economic History Review.*

Chronology and Encyclopedias

Encyclopedia of American Business History and Biography. New York: Facts on File, 1988– to date. 7 volumes published as of 1991.

This is an on-going series of volumes chronicling America's material civilization as seen through its business leaders and businesses. Each volume focuses on a particular industry, and the profiles are each written by a specialist in the field. The volumes consist of: short company profiles (usually 1-to-3 pages in length), biographies of persons important to the industry (these are usually longer, especially for the most important leaders), and occasional articles on specific aspects of the industry. Most contributions include bibliographical and archival references. The following unnumbered volumes have been published to date: the automobile industry (2 volumes); banking and finance (2 volumes); railroad industry (2 volumes); the iron and steel industry in the 19th century (1 volume).

Robinson, Richard, comp. *United States Business History, 1602–1988: A Chronology.* New York: Greenwood Press, 1990. 643 pp.

Of potential use for reference purposes, this is a chronological description of representative events in the evolution of U.S. business. For each year one can find both "general events" noting how business is interwoven with society, economics, government, etc., and "business events" which identify occurrences in the rise and fall of business enterprises, in managerial practices, in people, etc. A detailed index helps to pinpoint specific people and events. A short bibliography is at end.

Directories

The International Directory of Company Histories. Chicago: St. James Press, 1988–to date. 5 volumes.

This directory consists of two-to-five page historical profiles of 1,250 of the world's largest and most influential companies. It is arranged by industry: vol.1 covers the subjects Advertising to Drugs; vol.2, Electrical & Electronics to Food Services & Retailers; vol.3, Health & Personal Care Products to Materials; vol.4, Mining & Metals to Real Estate; vol.5, Retail to Waste. At end of most profiles is a list of subsidiary companies, and one or more sources for further reading. An index arranged by company and person is in each volume.

Periodicals

Business History. London: F. Cass & Co., Ltd. (quarterly).

Four or five good, scholarly articles in each issue on histories of British industries, companies, and related subjects. Includes book reviews. Indexed in BPI, PAIS.

Business History Review. Boston: Harvard University, Graduate School of Business Administration (quarterly).

An excellent selection of articles on management history, companies, industries, and other topics of interest to business and economic historians. Includes book reviews. Indexed in BPI, PAIS. This journal is slow in publishing.

Economic History Review. Oxford, Eng.: B. Blackwell Ltd. for Economic History Society (quarterly).

Lengthy, professional articles covering all aspects of economic and social history, the history of economic thought, and related disciplines, with special interest for British and European economic historians. Includes book reviews. The November issue each year contains a "List of Publications on Economic and Social History of Great Britain and Ireland." Indexed in SSI.

Journal of Economic History. New York and Cambridge, Eng.: Published by Cambridge University Press for the Economic History Association in co-operation with Rensselaer Polytechnic Institute (quarterly).

Good professional articles on economic history and related aspects of the history of economics. The June issue contains papers presented at the annual meeting of the EHA; also "Summaries of Doctoral Dissertations." Includes book reviews. Indexed in SSI.

Journal of European Economic History. Rome: Banco Di Roma (3/yr.).

Written in English, this journal contains scholarly, well researched articles on European economic history, on individual European countries, and on related topics of interest to European economic history scholars. Includes book reviews. Indexed in PAIS. This journal is slow in publishing.

10

MANAGEMENT

Management Handbooks – Books on Management Principles and Practices – Finding the "Best" Books on Management – Managers – Organization Theory – Project Management – Management Bibliographies and Abstracts – Dictionaries and Encyclopedias – Management Periodicals – Associations – Strategic Management and Planning – Human Factors in Organizations – Organizational Behavior – History of Management Thinking – Managerial Job Descriptions – Functions of Directors – Entrepreneurship/Small Business Management

The managing of any organization in today's fast-paced and changing world is very complex. Computer technology, the development of quantitative techniques, the new social consciousness, the expansion into foreign markets – all these have had a revolutionary impact on management. Business men and women are finding it imperative to keep themselves informed about all new techniques and methods, and this requires not only taking traditional courses and attending seminars but also planning a continuous independent reading program of both books and journals.

This chapter is intended to help the manager by suggesting basic management sources: bibliographies, indexes, abstracts, handbooks, periodicals, and a sampling of useful, general books, most of them quite recent. One will also find here a selection of books and periodicals on strategic planning, on human factors in organizations, on entrepreneurship and small business management. Books on decision making, on the other hand, are described in Chapter 17, because most of them stress quantitative and statistical techniques.

The previous chapter covered material on the social and environmental aspects of business. The remainder of this book will concentrate on management sources, with separate chapters for each of its principal functions as well as a chapter on international management.

MANAGEMENT HANDBOOKS

Except for the British-based *Gower Handbook* below, there have been no recent comprehensive handbooks covering the whole field of management. This may be due primarily to the awesome task such a big undertaking would require. These older handbooks can still be of great value, however, as sources of concise background information in the whole area of business and management even though they do not include discussions of the most recent management policies, practices, and trends. This section contains descriptions of those older management handbooks that are still in print as of 1991.

Fallon, William K., ed. *AMA Management Handbook.* 2d ed. New York: AMACOM, 1983. 1 volume (almost 1,600 pp.).

Originally published in 1970, this excellent, comprehensive one-volume source for concise information on a broad range of management practices and techniques has now been completely revised and updated to incorporate the many changes and innovations of the 1970s (70% new material, says the publisher). It is written as a collaborative effort of over 200 experts, with the material arranged within 14 broad subject areas (finance, human resources management, manufacturing, R & D, etc.). A further outline is at the beginning of each section, and a detailed index is at end of book.

The Gower Handbook of Management. Ed. by Dennis Lock and Nigel Farrow. 2d ed. Aldershot, Hants, Eng., and Brookfield, VT: Gower Publishing Co., 1988. 1,244 pp.

An up-to-date, comprehensive management handbook with a British focus. Sixty-three chapters by over 60 British experts are divided into the 10 basic parts devoted to policy, organization, administration, and to each broad management function. Guides for further reading are at the end of each chapter.

Mali, Paul, ed. *Management Handbook: Operating Guidelines, Techniques and Practices.* New York: Wiley, 1981. 1,522 pp.

Here is another comprehensive one-volume reference source on the managerial state of the art—its concepts, practices, techniques, and guidelines, with 60 authors representing a wide range of expertise. The 67 chapters are arranged within the following 7 sections: development of management; managing the total organization; managing organizational functions; managing the work; managing the human effort; managing resources; managing your self-development. Useful sample management forms and checklists are at the end of each section, and references for further reading at the end of most chapters. A detailed "subject and problem-solving index" is at the end.

Maynard, Harold B., ed. *Handbook of Business Administration.* New York: McGraw-Hill, 1967. 1 volume (various pagings).

Probably the most ambitious attempt to cover the many aspects of management function and practices. Each of the 166 chapters within 17 broad subject areas is written by an expert. Although it does not cover current developments in new management concepts and methods, it is still good for the older "tried-and-true" practices. Bibliographies at the end of most chapters list some older works.

Maynard was a management engineer who edited several other comprehensive and useful handbooks in the early 1970s. One that has just been revised and updated, with William K. Hodson as editor-in-chief, is *Maynard's Industrial Engineering Handbook* (4th ed., McGraw-Hill, 1992, 1 volume, various pagings).

Morrison, Robert S. *Handbook for Manufacturing Entrepreneurs.* 2d ed. Cleveland, OH: Western Reserve Press, 1974. 571 pp.

Morrison has had wide experience as a successful owner/manager of manufacturing firms, and he has written this comprehensive handbook for entrepreneurs, for owners/managers of existing companies, and for students, teachers, and others. He attempts to cover all aspects of owner-managed manufacturing "from the decision to go into business to maintaining the operation after the owner/manager retires." This is a good, practical book, but it is now quite old.

BOOKS ON MANAGEMENT PRINCIPLES AND PRACTICES

Donnelly, James H., James L. Gibson and John M. Ivancevich. *Fundamentals of Management.* 8th ed. Homewood, IL: Irwin, 1991. 840 pp.

This is a standard, undergraduate text. Parts 2–4 of the 7th edition are structured around three fundamental management tasks common to all organizations: managing work and organizations; managing people; and managing products and operations. Part 5 focuses on emerging management issues (entrepreneurship, globalization of business, and management careers). Includes illustrations and special features such as real-world examples, and profiles of managers—to reinforce the textual material. Case incidents and lists of additional references are with chapters; a glossary is at end. The 8th edition was not seen in time to note any content changes. These three professors, with Ivancevich as lead author, have also written a text entitled *Management: Principles and Functions* (4th ed., BPI/Irwin, 1989, 765 pp.) which is structured around the four managerial functions.

Drucker, Peter F. *Management: Tasks, Responsibilities, Practices.* New York: Harper & Row, 1974. 839 pp.

Whatever this well-known management authority writes is always widely read and commented upon, whether it is one of some 25 book titles, one of his numerous articles, or one of his essays appearing from time to time on the editorial page of the *Wall Street Journal.* The latest of his books (as of early 1992) is a collection of previously published articles or essays written over a five-year period on *Managing for the Future: The 1990s and Beyond* (New York: Truman Talley Books/Dutton, 1992, 370 pp.). We have selected two books to describe here, this one being among the best and surely the most comprehensive. Its purpose is to give managers all the information they need in order to prepare for effective performance. It is based on Drucker's many years of experience as a management consultant, and thus it draws to a certain extent on some of his earlier works. He considers first "the tasks" (business performance, performance in the service institution, productive work and achieving worker, social impacts and social responsibilities); in the second section he covers "the manager" (work, job, skills, organization); and lastly he discusses "top management" (tasks, organization, strategies). Because of its length this book may well be treated more as a handbook, to be kept for frequent reference rather than to be read from cover to cover in one sitting. All managers and students will find it a practical, informative, and important book both to read and to consult.

Persons wishing to begin with a selection from Drucker's earlier writings may want to see his *People and Performance: The Best of Peter Drucker on Management* (New York: Harper's College Press, 1977, 366 pp., paper).

Drucker, Peter F. *The Practice of Management.* New York: Harper, 1954. 404 pp.

This management classic was written both to help managers evaluate and improve their performance and to explain to younger persons just what management is and what qualifications one needs to be a good manager. It is still "must" reading for all managers.

DuBrin, Andrew J., R. D. Ireland and J. C. Williams. *Management & Organization.* Cincinnati, OH: South-Western Publishing Co., 1989. 682 pp.

Although there is no edition number in this book, it seems to be a 6th revision of their introductory text. The aim is to help readers develop an appreciation for and understanding of management and its practice, including a knowledge of the concepts and techniques needed to meet today's important challenges. Parts 2–5 focus on the basic functional areas of: planning (and decision-making), organizing (including staffing), leading, controlling. The first section is an introduction and the last two examine managing in special settings (small business and international management), and career management and organizational development. Included are interesting boxed inserts that link chapter material to current events and issues, as well as two-color diagrams and checklists, case incidents, and other learning aids. Bibliographies are with each chapters, and a glossary is at end of book.

Professor DuBrin alone has written what seems to be a shortened version with title *Essentials of Management* (2d ed., South-Western Publishing Co., 1989, 522 pp.). It covers the same basic functional areas, with a chapter added on managing yourself.

Koontz, Harold, and Heinz Weihrich. *Management.* 9th ed. New York: McGraw-Hill, 1988. 687 pp.

This is still one of the better known texts on management theory and practice, emphasizing the essentials of management pertinent to the effective work of practicing managers. This 9th edition is the most comprehensive revision, reflecting the latest findings, techniques, and thinking, but it is still organized around the same functional areas of planning, organizing, staffing, leading, and controlling. An added section in this latest revision covers challenges in the domestic and international environment. Many real-life situations are used throughout the book as well as "perspectives" in boxed inserts to provide additional insights. Two cases and bibliographical references are with each chapter; a glossary is at end of the book. This text has now been published in 16 foreign language editions.

These two authors, with Cyril O. O'Donnell, have also written a concise version of this text to meet the demand for a much shorter book dealing with only the *Essentials of Management* (5th ed., McGraw-Hill, 1990. 538 pp., paper).

McGregor, Douglas. *The Human Side of Enterprise.* New York: McGraw-Hill, 1960. 246 pp. Twenty-fifth anniversary printing was published in 1985, with a foreword by Warren Bennis.

McGregor's current classic has had more influence on managers than any other book of its kind, in the continuing search for better ways of managing, motivating, and developing personnel. In it he presents his Theory Y, a strategy to integrate the individual's goals with those of the organization, and a large portion of the book discusses practical implications of that theory. Also covers the development of management talent.

Newman, William H., E. Kirby Warren and Andrew R. McGill. *The Process of Management: Strategy, Action, Results.* 6th ed. Englewood Cliffs, NJ: Prentice-Hall, 1987. 624 pp.

Substantial revision of an excellent introductory text focusing on those management fundamentals needed both to build a solid foundation for action on today's problems but also for those dealing with future problems. After first introducing the current challenge for managers, the authors examine in turn each of the five basic elements in the process of management that are present in every kind of enterprise: planning, decision making, organizing, leading, and controlling. The last part deals with managing in diverse settings (multinational organizations, small business, service businesses). Case incidents and short annotated bibliographies are with each chapter; a longer managerial decision case is at end of each part.

Odiorne, George S. *The Human Side of Management: Management by Integration and Self-control.* Lexington, MA: Lexington Books, 1987. 236 pp.

Management by objectives is a procedure used in many firms for improving management performance. Professor Odiorne wrote the pioneering work on MBO in 1965, and he followed it with *MBO II* in 1979. This latest book covers MBO and more. It is divided into four parts: the first two cover basic principles of management and successful goal setting to achieve integration and self-control; the third part delves into productivity, training, and management development; the fourth highlights superior-subordinate relationships (mentoring and commitment). Much of the material in this book is taken from *The George Odiorne Letter* (St. Petersburg, FL, MBO, Inc. semimonthly; about $72). It is both readable and practical.

If you prefer a book on MBO by another author, consider *How to Manage by Results* by Dale D. McConkey (4th ed., New York: AMACOM, 1983, 301 pp.). This is the latest revision of a handy paperback that intends to provide operating managers with a timely and comprehensive view of how MBO systems operate.

O'Toole, James. *Vanguard Management: Redesigning the Corporate Future.* Garden City, NY: Doubleday, 1985. 418 pp.

An interesting book based on a three-year study of what Professor O'Toole identifies as 8 vanguard corporations which can serve as models for large American corporations in the future. He begins by talking about how the new management is different from traditional management. With this as background he then reviews how vanguard companies meet the responsibilities to their various stakeholders through observance of four general principles. Then he examines the process by which vanguard leaders change, lead, and sustain their organizations.

Peters, Thomas J., and Robert H. Waterman, Jr. *In Search of Excellence: Lessons from America's Best-Run Companies.* New York: Harper & Row, 1982. 360 pp.

In the 1980s this was a much-read and much-cited report on a search undertaken by two management consultants to find out what makes for corporate excellence and to generalize about what excellent companies seem to be doing that the rest are not. Starting with 62 companies which they soon narrowed to 43, these authors then chose 21 companies to study in depth. From their research emerged 8 basic practices characteristic of successfully managed companies, and each of these is studied in part 3 of this book. There are also two chapters (part 2) providing readers with some background theory. The book is full of practical examples especially from the 14 companies the authors consider to be the best run. Although still worth reading, much has changed since 1982, and both authors have written later books for managers.

Pierce, Jon L., and John W. Newstrom. *The Manager's Bookshelf: A Mosaic of Contemporary Views.* 2d ed. New York: HarperCollins, 1990. 347 pp. paper.

This is a selection of over 30 excerpts or summaries taken from recent popular management books or articles. Its 16 parts usually contain about three selections each, and topics covered include environment trends, organizational culture, strategy and plans, ethics, motivating, entrepreneurship, managerial/leadership styles, women in management. It is intended for managers and students who do not have time to read complete books, to help make them better informed. Best selling authors include Bennis, Drucker, Kanter, Lawler, Leavitt, Odiorne, Peters, Porter, Schein. The summaries, most of which were prepared by academic persons, usually cover the thoughts, philosophies, views, or experiences of these authors. A glossary is at end.

Richard, Max D. *Readings in Management.* 7th ed. Cincinnati: South-Western, 1986. 641 pp. paper.

A good selection of 53 readings arranged in 15 subject chapters. Bibliographies are at end of each chapter for those persons wishing to read further on any topic.

Sloan, Alfred P. *My Years with General Motors.* Ed. by John McDonald, with Catharine Stevens. Garden City, NY: Doubleday, 1964. 472 pp. paper.

This is another management classic—the story of the management of General Motors over the 23 years (1923–1946) when Mr. Sloan served as its chief executive. It is an informative, readable book and provides valuable insight into the kinds of decisions and problems faced by this outstanding administrator. Peter Drucker calls this "the best book on management ever" (see *Fortune*, April 23, 1990, pp.145–153).

Stoner, James A. F., and R. Edward Freeman. *Management.* 5th ed. Englewood Cliffs, NJ: Prentice-Hall, 1991. Approximately 800 pp.

Yet another popular introductory management text organized around the functional approach of planning, organizing, leading, and controlling. The authors say their book is about the job of the manager—how men and women go about managing the people and activities of their organizations so that their goals can be achieved. In this latest thorough revision there is increased emphasis on both the external environment, ethics and social responsibility, and on international management. Adding to the interest are boxed highlights about ethical issues and illustrative case studies; also frequent use of diagrams, tables, and other illustrations. Definitions of key terms appear in the left margin, with an overall glossary at end of book. This annotation is based on examination of the fourth edition.

Strage, Henry M., ed. *Milestones in Management: An Essential Reader.* Oxford, Eng. and Cambridge, MA: Blackwell, 1992. 497 pp. paper.

Just published is another reader (see Pierce/Newstrom above), this one bringing together in one volume what the editor hopes are the best and most influential general management writings from the past 30 years. Strage's 28 selections (from both books and articles) are arranged by the following broad topics: strategy; leadership; globalization; finance; calls to arms; trends. Authors include such well-known names as Drucker and McGregor.

Uris, Auren. *The Executive Deskbook.* 3d ed. New York: Van Nostrand
Reinhold, 1988. 427 pp. paper.

The author says he intends this as a "practical easy-to-find and quick-reading executive tool" for the busy business manager. He offers concise suggestions on handling
problems in 14 areas of management activity such as effective communication,
decision-making, delegation, leadership and motivation, women in management.
He also briefly highlights some key management concepts, and offers a suggested
"management tool kit."

FINDING THE "BEST" BOOKS ON MANAGEMENT

I am often asked for the titles of the so-called "best books" on management,
and so feel it worthwhile to make a few suggestions for finding such lists. Most
management authorities have their own favorite management or organizational behavior titles, and these vary greatly from individual to individual
especially when the experts are recommending some of the more recently
published books. But when it comes to the long-term "classics," the same
names crop up in just about every published bibliography—Barnard, Chandler, Drucker, McGregor and Sloan, to name just a few.

The lists of recommended books which a few companies compile, usually for
their management development programs, may or may not all be considered
classics or "the best," but they *are* important books for "the educated practitioner." Probably the best known of these lists is *The Fifty Books on Business
Management* prepared by the Management Development Institute of General
Electric Company (Croton-on-Hudson, NY: 1978. 11 pp.). This was actually
the second selection of 50 important management books, concentrating on
those published between 1945 and 1978. The original list was *Soundings in the
Literature of Management: Fifty Books the Educated Practitioner Should Know*
by Harry A. Hopf (Ossining, NY: Hopf Institute of Management, 1945, 28
pp.). Although the earlier bibliography has been out of print for many years, a
copy can probably be located in one of the older business school libraries; also it
was reprinted in the original edition of *Sources of Business Information* by
Edwin T. Coman, Jr. (Prentice-Hall, 1949, pp.156–177). Perhaps of more
interest is the later list compiled at GE, although even that one was not widely
distributed outside the firm. If the GE list is no longer available, contact a
library that has a file of the 1978 issues of the *HBS Bulletin* (Harvard Business
School's alumni magazine) where that list was reprinted (without annotations)
in the September/October 1978 issue, pp.22–23.

Deere & Company published a useful, recommended reading list in 1974
called *Staying Ahead: Reading for Self-Improvement,* but that bibliography is
no longer revised or available. It is admittedly difficult to identify these short
lists prepared at a specific company because they are often reproduced only
for internal use. For instance, in 1978, U.S. Home Corporation prepared a
two-page typed list of almost 50 recommended titles, for participants of their
management development program. There must be other similar lists, should
you decide to address an inquiry to several large companies.

One way of identifying the important works of individual persons who have made a significant contribution to the development of management theory and practice is to check the bibliographies contained in books on the "history of management thinking" (see that section in this chapter). These books are especially useful for their discussions of the contributions of each recognized management theorist, and they usually include lists of the major publications of each. See also Howard E. McCurdy's *Public Administration: A Bibliographic Guide to the Literature* (1986), described in Chapter 11, for the names of older books on management and public administration most frequently cited.

Two recently published "readers" described in the previous section may be of value in identifying important management books and articles. These are *The Manager's Bookshelf: A Mosaic of Contemporary Views* (by Jon L. Pierce and John W. Newstrom) for its excerpts or summaries from recent popular management literature, and Henry M. Strage's *Milestones in Management: An Essential Reader,* for its selections from the most influential management writings.

There are also a few books that are compilations of selections from what are called the "classics" of management, but these are usually the choices of just one or two editors and they use the term "classics" loosely to refer generally both to books and articles which the editors feel have had a recognized impact over a period of time. One such collection focuses on organization theory (see book edited by Schafritz/Whitbeck) and two are on organizational behavior (one edited by Matteson/Ivancevich and the other by Natemeyer), described elsewhere in this chapter.

Best Sellers

Business books that sell the most copies in bookstores are not necessarily classics (at least not yet), but they still have a significant impact on current management thinking (or else they serve as a good conversation piece), and so they are "must" reading for the ambitious executive. These books are usually so widely publicized and reviewed that it is easy to identify the one or two titles of the moment if you are a frequent reader of business journals. But what is the "hot" book today will be replaced by a different one tomorrow, and so there is a continual procession of new and interesting books for the manager to read. Some of the books that seem to get the most attention/ promotion today (1991) are accounts of the wrong-doings of business persons rather than those that focus on good business/management practices. Those business books one can purchase as part of a book club (such as the Business Week Book Club) are often "how-to" books intended more for the small business person or entrepreneur.

There ARE noteworthy books being written which, while they may never make the best-seller list, are still highly regarded and well worth reading. How will you know which these are? Sometimes you will hear about them from an acquaintance, but more usually they will come to your attention in the course of regular reading/scanning of current business journals, or by browsing in a library or a large bookstore. One annual list worth checking is "Business Books (year)" in the March 15 issue of *Library Journal* each year. This is a descriptive list of 100 or so of the better business books published during the previous year, and it is currently compiled by Susan S. DiMattia, a respected business information consultant.

MANAGERS

See also the few books on "Leadership" described later in this chapter.

Filley, Alan C. *The Compleat Manager: What Works When.* Middletown, WI: Green Briar Press, 1985. 239 pp. paper. Reprint of 1978 book.

For the practicing manager interested in an easy-to-read treatise on management essentials, here is a good but now rather old book. It briefly covers type of organizations, leadership, decision making, motivating others, managing time, organization structure, selecting good people. There are occasional interesting anecdotes and personal experiences, and a final chapter suggests where to find resources and advice.

Horton, Thomas R. *"What Works for Me:" CEOs Talk about Their Careers and Commitments.* New York: AMACOM, 1986. 436 pp. (paperback edition published in 1989).

An intriguing book in which 16 CEOs talk about their personal approaches to their current jobs, and their earlier assignments leading to those jobs. The interviews run from about 15 to 20 pages in length. At end is a further discussion of the 18 management competencies, and the five qualities of successful CEOs; also a bibliography.

Leavitt, Harold J. *Corporate Pathfinders: Building Vision and Values into Organizations.* Homewood, IL: Dow Jones-Irwin, 1986. 229 pp.

Professor Leavitt divides the managing process into three parts: pathfinding; problem solving; implementing. Of these he focuses here on the visionary, pathfinding part as the one most in need of attention and change by managers and educators today. He talks about the concept (vision, values, determination), how to develop pathfinders, how to become one yourself, how to build pathfinding into the organization, how to maintain it. This is an interesting, thought-provoking book.

Luthans, Fred, Richard M. Hodgetts and Stuart A. Rosenkrantz. *Real Managers.* Cambridge, MA: Ballinger, 1987. 192 pp.

"This is the first book that makes an empirical investigation of what mainstream managers from middle-of-the-road organizations really do in their day-to-day activities and how the successful and effective ones do things differently from their unsuccessful and less effective counterparts." The first four chapters report on a research study of the activities of 457 managers as to what real managers really do, what successful managers really do, and what effective managers really do. The rest of the book discusses, in separate chapters, each of the four types of managers' activities which the authors found in their investigation: traditional management; communication; networking; human resources management. Supplementary readings and references are at end.

Slevin, Dennis P. *The Whole Manager.* New York: AMACOM, 1989. 422 pp.

A self-help manual for practicing managers "to help you better understand managerial effectiveness, personal satisfaction, and personal growth." It is structured like a workbook with frequent checklists, forms, and exercises to help you change your (and others') behavior. Chapters cover such topics as time management, power, leadership motivation, negotiation skills, staffing, health, and life-style. A short reading list is at the end.

Speeches

Executive Speeches. Dayton, OH: Executive Speaker Company (monthly). $60.

For persons who want the text of selected speeches made by executives, here is a monthly source. Each issue contains the text of only about four or five speeches, but it also has the titles of many other speeches in this publisher's Executive Speaker Library which are available to subscribers for a nominal fee. The October 1991 issue is longer than the others, and has the text of 19 commencement addresses. The speeches cover a wide range of business and some nonbusiness topics. A cumulated index is published just once a year and lists the speeches by: topic, speaker, title of the speech, speaker's company or organization, the audience, and a chronological list for the year arranged by issue number.

ORGANIZATION THEORY

Organization theory is the discipline that studies the structure and design of organizations. It is the macro study of organizations whereas organizational behavior (see section later in this chapter) is the micro study emphasizing individuals and groups in organizations.

Handbooks

Nystrom, Paul C., and William H. Starbuck, eds. *Handbook of Organizational Design.* Oxford and New York: Oxford University Press, 1981. 2 volumes.

This comprehensive work will probably be used primarily by researchers, professors, and graduate students since it summarizes and reinterprets research and suggests applications to the design of organizations. Vol. 1, with 22 chapters by 32 professors, analyzes the effects of environments on organizations and discusses the adaptive capabilities of organizations such as planning, forecasting, and innovation. Vol. 2 focuses on processes of change within organizations, including control systems, interdepartmental relations, and job designs—in 23 chapters by 36 professors. Bibliographical references are at the end of each essay.

Books

Barnard, Chester I. *The Functions of the Executive.* Cambridge, MA: Harvard University Press, 1968. 334 pp.

In the introduction to this thirtieth-anniversary edition of Barnard's contemporary classic (1938), Professor Kenneth R. Andrews says that this book "remains today, as it has been since its publication, the most thought-provoking book on organization and management ever written by a practicing executive." Barnard, who was a president of New Jersey Bell Telephone Company, divides his study into two parts: (1) consideration of cooperative systems and the theory and structure of formal organizations; (2) a study of the elements of formal organizations and the functions of executives in cooperative systems. Although well worth the effort, this book is difficult to read and to understand, so readers may benefit greatly by using with it a summary and interpretation by William B. Wolf called *The Basic Barnard: An Introduction to Chester I. Barnard and His Theories of Organization and Management* (Ithaca: New York State School of Industrial and Labor Relations, Cornell University, 1974, 140 pp. paper).

Gibson, James L., John M. Ivancevich and James H. Donnelly, Jr. *Organizations: Behavior, Structure, Processes.* 7th ed. Homewood, IL: Irwin, 1991. 774 pp.

In this newly revised edition the authors have expanded their approach to include worldwide issues, problems, and considerations. They have tried to provide readers with a realistic, relevant and thorough book that illustrates "how organizational behavior theory leads to research and how both theory and research provide the basic foundation for practical applications in business firms, hospitals, educational institutions, and government agencies." The contents are arranged according to the three basic characteristics common to all organizations: behavior, structure, processes. A concluding section focuses on developing organizational effectiveness. Short case problems, bibliographies, and an experiential exercise are at the end of many chapters; a glossary is at end of the book. "Organizations: Close-Ups" are interesting boxed inserts appearing throughout, which report on actual applications of specific concepts or theories. The authors' selection of pertinent readings is called *Organization Close-Ups: A Book of Readings* (6th ed., Business Publications, 1988, 449 pp.).

Jackson, John H., Cyril P. Morgan and G. P. Paolillo. *Organization Theory: A Macro Perspective for Management.* 3d ed. Englewood Cliffs, NJ: Prentice-Hall, 1986. 387 pp.

The macro perspective, these authors say, considers the organization as the unit of analysis. It concerns itself with organizational goals, how the organization is structured, what technologies are used, and how the organization influences and is influenced by its environment. All of these important issues of a sometimes difficult topic are covered in a readable fashion. Interspersed are illustrative examples (boxed) from published sources, tables and diagrams. A related reading is at end of each chapter, as well as suggestions for further reading.

Kast, Fremont E., and James E. Rosenzweig. *Organization and Management: A Systems and Contingency Approach.* 4th ed. New York: McGraw-Hill, 1984. 720 pp.

In this latest edition the authors continue to present their view of the organization as a subsystem of its environmental suprasystem. Their discussion revolves around the following organizational subsystems: environment, social responsibility, and goals; technology and structure; the psychosocial system; the managerial system. There is also a section discussing comparative analysis, including organizational analysis in hospitals, universities, the city. Includes a bibliography at end.

Robbins, Stephen P. *Organization Theory: Structure, Design, and Applications.* 2d ed. Englewood Cliffs, NJ: Prentice-Hall, 1987. 518 pp.

Organization theory is a complex discipline, says Professor Robbins, and so his objective here is to write a book that covers the contemporary material in a rigorous fashion but in a way that will be interesting and relevant to the readers. After his introduction he covers in turn each of the three components in his subtitle. An epilogue looks briefly at organizations in the future. Interesting "OT: Close-Up" boxes are interspersed throughout to illustrate practical applications of OT concepts. Suggested readings are with chapters. Cases are at end of book as well as a glossary, a short, informative appendix on the evolution of OT over time, and another on measures of organization structure. Professor Robbins, with Penny L. Wright as first author, has published a companion volume, *Organization Theory: Readings and Cases* (Prentice-Hall, 1987, 320 pp.).

Robey, Daniel. *Designing Organizations.* 3d ed. Homewood, IL: Irwin, 1991. 586 pp.

The major portion of this text covers 6 aspects of designing the organization structure (part 2), and 6 aspects of designing organization processes (part 3). Part 1 is an introduction and discusses perspectives, a framework and organizational effectiveness; while part 4 takes a look at organizational design in the future. The author has tried to enliven each chapter with "up front," "up close," and "in action" features to bring the real world in to support his theory. Bibliographical notes are with each chapter; 14 cases are at end of book.

Scott, W. Richard. *Organizations: Rational, Natural, and Open Systems.* 3d ed. Englewood Cliffs, NJ: Prentice-Hall, 1992. 414 pp.

The latest revision of a text providing a coherent, integrated introduction to the sociological study of organizations. The emphasis is placed on contemporary theory and research. Its five parts cover: an introduction to organizations; three perspectives on organizations (see subtitle); environments, strategies, and structures; organizations and society. An extensive bibliography is at end.

Shafritz, Jay M., and J. Stevens Ott, eds. *Classics of Organization Theory.* 3d ed. Pacific Grove, CA: Brooks/Cole Pub. Co., 1991. over 400 pp. paper.

Another revision of an anthology that attempts to select from the works of the most significant writers on organization theory those that are most readable for persons without a background in the study of organizations. The 47 chapters are divided into 7 sections as follows: classical organization theory; neoclassical organization theory; the organizational behavior perspective; organization theory as it relates to "modern" structure; to systems, contingency and population ecology; to power and politics; to organizational culture and symbolic management. An introduction contains an overview of organization theory and a useful chronology from 1491 B.C. to 1990 A.D. Bibliographical notes are with many chapters.

Tushman, Michael L., Charles O'Reilly, and David A. Nadler, eds. *The Management of Organizations: Strategies, Tactics, Analyses.* New York: Harper & Row, 1989. 601 pp.

We end this section with a good compilation of readings selected to help managers "better understand how organizations work and how managers deal with organizational and competitive challenges." The editors further state that the book is a synthesis of their various attempts to organize the research in organizational behavior and theory in a way that might be useful to practitioners, with the focus on managerial problem solving. The readings are arranged within 6 sections: managers, strategies, and organizations; formal organization arrangements: structure and systems; informal organization and social processes; understanding and managing individual behavior; organization adaptation and change; executive leadership: does it matter? The authors are respected management thinkers and practitioners.

Two older books still in print as of 1991 and still cited as useful are: *Organization Design* by Jay R. Galbraith (Reading, MA: Addison-Wesley, 1977, 426 pp.), a text on the title subject; and *The Structuring of Organizations: A Synthesis of the Research* by Henry Mintzberg (Englewood Cliffs, NJ: Prentice-Hall, 1979, 512 pp.) which, as the title indicates, is a syntheses of research findings on what organizations really do.

PROJECT MANAGEMENT

According to Kerzner below, "Project management is the planning, organizing, directing, and controlling of company resources for a relatively short-term objective that has been established to complete specific goals and objectives."– p.4. It was difficult to decide just where in this book to include this section since much of the material on project management relates to network planning and management science. These few books are more management oriented and so we decided to include them in this management chapter.

Handbooks

Cleland, David I., and William R. King, eds. *Project Management Handbook.* 2d ed. New York: Van Nostrand Reinhold, 1988. 997 pp.

The purpose of this handbook (a cooperative effort of many individuals) is to serve as a reference quide for the fundamental concepts and techniques of managing projects. While it is meant primarily as a source for practical how-to-do-it information, it also provides a theoretical framework and relates both to public and private organizations of all sizes. Nine interdependent areas are developed: an overview of project and matrix management; the project organization; organizational strategy and project management; life-cycle management; project planning; project implementation; project control; behavioral dimensions and teamwork in project management; the successful application of project management.

Books

Cleland, David I. *Project Management: Strategic Design and Implementation.* Blue Ridge Summit, PA: TAB Books, 1990. 370 pp.

Professor Cleland has written widely on this subject. Here he takes a fresh approach by presenting project management as an integrated part of an effective overall strategy for the long-term management of an organization. Chapters deal with the strategic context of projects (including the role of boards of directors, and stakeholder management), organizational design, project operations (planning, controlling, terminating), interpersonal dynamics (communicating, team development, creativity), and the cultural elements. User checklists and short bibliographies are with each chapter.

Gilbreath, Robert D. *Winning at Project Management: What Works, What Fails and Why.* New York: Wiley, 1986. 329 pp.

This book focuses on failure tendencies and failure avoidance in project management so that you can recognize problem areas and do something about them. Ten separate areas of project performance are examined: people; organizations; perspectives; planning; information; processes; contracting; change; standards; outsiders. A failure/success index is at end.

Graham, Robert J. *Project Management: Combining Technical and Behavioral Approaches for Effective Implementation.* New York: Van Nostrand Reinhold, 1985. 234 pp.

A practical book "about managing people, project management, and change, particularly change in management style for project managers." The author says his overall philosophy "is that project management is mainly people management, and not just planning systems and control techniques." Each chapter examines an aspect of the overall project management process including network planning techniques, people and control interaction, matrix organization. Short bibliographies are with each chapter.

Kerzner, Harold. *Project Management: A Systems Approach to Planning, Scheduling, and Controlling.* 3d ed. New York: Van Nostrand Reinhold, 1989. 987 pp. Fourth edition to be published in 1992.

Here is a more comprehensive study to show how to integrate modern organization theory and practice into project management regardless of size or project complexity, and it covers both the behavioral and quantitative aspects of project planning from beginning to end. Kerzner starts with five chapters providing the basic core of knowledge needed to understand project management. He then treats in turn: support functions (such as time management, conflict resolution); executive involvement and variables for predicting project success; quantitative tools; tradeoff analysis; advanced topics such as software, international project management, future trends. Case studies with chapters are taken from actual situations; a bibliography is at end.

Knutson, Joan, and Ira Bitz. *Project Management: How to Plan and Manage Successful Projects.* New York: AMACOM, American Management Association, 1991. 198 pp.

A short book for the novice on key project management processes and models, written by two experienced practitioners. They start by discussing how to initiate a project and to build a project team. They also cover such topics as: planning and keeping control by using models, managing schedules, costs, resources, dealing with changes, monitoring cost and progress, software support.

Periodicals

Project Management Journal. Drexel Hill, PA: Project Management Institute (quarterly).

Intended as a forum for discussion of project management problems, solutions, applications, and opinions, this quarterly looks for a balance of useful articles both on the theory and practice of project management. Indexed in ABI/I.

MANAGEMENT BIBLIOGRAPHIES AND ABSTRACTS

Bibliographies in the broad area of business are covered in Chapter 2. Following are several general management bibliographies, abstracting services, and booklists. If these do not answer a need, try the bibliographies that are sometimes included in basic management books such as the chapter references in the book by Newman et al. noted in the section above on "Management Principles and Practices."

British Institute of Management. *Management Information: A Comprehensive Catalog of BIM Publications.* London.

This periodic, descriptive list of BIM publications is available on request. Their library publishes a separate *Bulletin* (6/yr.) listing new accessions, new BIM publications, new reading lists. The latter covers over 100 topics and can be purchased both by members and by nonmembers. BIM formerly published a useful short list called *A Basic Library of Management* (1974, 48 pp.), but this is now old and there are no plans for revising.

Conference Board. *Cumulative Index.* New York (annual).

The Conference Board publishes useful periodic reports and other publications covering company policies or practices on various aspects in five broad areas: corporate relations, human resources, management functions, economic and business environment, and consumer research. This is a cumulative subject index to all CB publications. Several examples of *Report* series titles published 1988/90 include: *The Changing Human Resources Function.* 1990 (R-950); *Competitive Intelligence.* 1988 (R-913); *Corporate Directors' Compensation.* 1990 (R-936); *Corporate Experience with Drug Testing.* 1990 (R-941); *Creating Customer Satisfaction.* 1990 (R-944); *Making Total Quality Happen.* 1990 (R-937); *Membership and Organization of Corporate Boards.* 1990 (R-940); *1992: Leading Issues for European Companies.* 1989 (R-921); *Productivity Needs of the United States.* 1989 (R-934); *Survey of Corporate Contributions* (annual, 1990 edition is no. R-942); *Top Executive Compensation* (annual, 1991 edition is no. R-983, and it is described in Chapter 19).

Personnel Management Abstracts. Chelsea, MI (quarterly).

Because this descriptive listing of recent articles for personnel managers includes material on management functions, behavior in organizations, decision making, motivation, planning, etc., it is of value to include in this management section. It consists of an annotated subject listing of articles, with an index by author. A few books are also described at end of each issue.

For an annotated list of 50 recommended management books and for other suggestions on finding the so-called "best" or "most talked-about" books on management, see the section discussing this topic earlier in this chapter.

Two of the bibliographies described in Chapter 11 include some important books on management and administration of interest to business managers as well as to public administrators. These are *The Administrator's Bookshelf* compiled annually by the Medical Group Management Association, and *Public Administration: A Bibliographic Guide to the Literature* by Howard E. McCurdy (1986).

DICTIONARIES AND ENCYCLOPEDIAS

In comparing the dictionaries by French, Johannsen, and Rosenberg, it is important to note that no dictionary with less than 500 pages in as broad an area as management can hope to contain all the terms one might need. Thus it is helpful to have access to more than just one so that you can "shop around" when looking for a particular definition. See also the section for "Business Dictionaries" in Chapter 1.

Banki, Ivan S. *Dictionary of Administration and Management.* Los Angeles, CA: Systems Research Institute, 1986. 1,369 pp.

This dictionary, expanded from an edition published in 1981, is meant to serve as a bridge between the terminology of administration, management, and organization, and those of supportive or applicable sciences, fields, and disciplines. Included is brief information on management-related associations and organizations; also a list of acronyms and abbreviations is at end plus a partially annotated bibliography of resources such as guidebooks, glossaries, bibliographies, abstracts, directories available as of 1986. While the dictionary can be useful for administration, management, supervision, and training terms, it is not an overall business dictionary that covers terms in such functional areas as accounting and finance.

Bittel, Lester R., and Jackson E. Ramsey, eds. *Handbook for Professional Managers.* New York: McGraw-Hill, 1985. 1,000 pp.

This is an excellent (but now rather old) encyclopedic dictionary whose purpose is "to provide managers in all kinds of organizations with (1) clear explanations of fundamental concepts and widely practiced techniques and (2) specific advice about how to apply them successfully." Over 200 major entries (with some 3,000 specific definitions) are well written in simple language by more than 200 expert contributors. These entries, arranged alphabetically, run from "accounting" to "zero-base budgeting," and vary in length from a few pages to about 10 pages. They often contain practical examples; they also usually have cross references to related topics, and lists of additional sources for persons seeking further information about any one subject. At end is a detailed and helpful index.

Another good encyclopedic dictionary, also compiled with help from more than 200 qualified persons, is *The Encyclopedia of Management,* edited by Carl Heyel (3d ed., New York: Van Nostrand Reinhold, 1982, 1,371 pp.).

French, Derek, and Heather Saward. *Dictionary of Management.* 2d ed. Aldershot, Hants, Eng.: Gower Press, 1983. 470 pp.

Contains definitions of nearly 4,000 management and economic terms and techniques chosen because of their use by managers and writers about management. It is meant to be equally useful to American and British readers and so distinguishes varying usage in the two countries. Includes abbreviations and short descriptions of important associations and organizations, but only as of 1983.

Johannsen, Hano, and G. Terry Page. *International Dictionary of Management.* 4th ed. East Brunswick, NJ: Nichols/GP Publishing, 1990. 359 pp. Published also in London by Kogan Page Ltd.

This is a good dictionary covering the whole area of business and management, with its more than 6,000 concisely defined terms, techniques, and concepts of use and interest worldwide. Occasionally it notes U.K. and/or U.S. usage of a term, and often contains cross references. At end is a directory of associations, trade unions, and other organizations referred to in the dictionary; also a list of world currencies and time zones.

Rosenberg, Jerry M. *Dictionary of Business and Management.* 2d ed. New York: Wiley, 1983. 631 pp.

Rosenberg's dictionary contains concise definitions for approximately 10,000 business and management terms in current usage, with some abbreviations, acronyms, associations, etc., and occasional cross-references. Useful supplementary data in an appendix includes units of measurement, interest tables, foreign exchange, relevant quotations, list of graduate business schools, summary of major U.S. business and economic events, 1776–1983. A third edition is announced for publication in 1992, but it will be shorter (384 pp.) and contain fewer definitions (7,500).

MANAGEMENT PERIODICALS

Articles on management topics appear in all varieties of business publications. Even magazines discussing business in general (for instance, *Business Week* and *Fortune*) frequently run articles on important management subjects or touch on them in articles dealing with other topics. Trade journals published for a particular industry or trade also carry management articles. The best commercial indexes and online databases for finding articles on any specific business or management topic are described in Chapter 2.

This is a selection of the most important academic, professional, and trade journals dealing with management subjects in general. A few examples of foreign language management periodicals are also given at the end of this section. Periodicals focusing on organizational behavior, small business management, project management, and strategic management and planning are described elsewhere in this chapter. Business periodicals are listed in Chapter 3; several other international management journals are in Chapter 16; directories of periodicals are in Chapter 7 for persons who need a further list or address/subscription information.

Academy of Management Journal.

Academy of Management Review.

The Executive. Mississippi State, MS: Academy of Management (located at Mississippi State University; quarterlies).

These are three excellent management quarterlies, each with a different focus. The *Journal* has been in existence longest. It publishes scholarly articles and research notes, based on empirical research, in all aspects of management. Many are based on research studies undertaken at various universities, and most are written by academicians. Next in succession is the *Review* where articles concentrate on organizational and management theory. It includes a book review section. The newest quarterly (1987) is *The Executive* which covers full-length articles and "short subjects" on the study and practice of management, with managers and executives as the intended audience. The publisher says this journal aims to form a link in that they look for articles based on sound research and theory but always with practical application and written in a readable style. It also contains book reviews. All three of these periodicals are indexed in ABI/I, BPI; the last is also in full text on DIALOG.

Administrative Science Quarterly. Ithaca, NY: S. C. Johnson Graduate School of Management, Cornell University.

The science of administration in all kinds of organizations is discussed in excellent, authoritative articles that are based both on empirical investigation and on theoretical analysis. Includes book reviews. Indexed in ABI/I, BPI, PAIS, SSI.

Business Horizons. Bloomington, IN: Graduate School of Business, Indiana University (bimonthly).

One of the best academic journals, with useful well written articles on all aspects of management and business planning. Some issues contain a book review section called "Focus on Books." Indexed in ABI/I, BPI, PAIS, PTS/F&S.

Business Quarterly. London, Ontario, Canada: School of Business Administration, University of Western Ontario.

The best Canadian academic journal, with scholarly articles aimed particularly at the Canadian executive. Indexed in ABI/I, BPI, PAIS, PTS/F&S, TI; full text on BRS, DATA-STAR, DIALOG, DOW JONES.

California Management Review. Berkeley: W. A. Haas School of Business, University of California (quarterly).

Another very good academic journal. Articles are on all aspects of enterprises—both public and private—with priority given to those reporting results of original research and analysis. Indexed in ABI/I, BPI, PAIS, TI.

Director. London: Director Publications Ltd. for the Institute of Directors (monthly).

An informative journal, with short articles on a wide range of business and management topics of special interest to British managers. "The European 500" (December issue) includes ranked lists of the top 400 industrial companies, the top 50 banks, and 50 insurance companies. It is based on a study this magazine conducted in cooperation with Kiel University. A few book reviews are in each issue. Indexed in ABI/I, BPI, PAIS.

European Management Journal. Oxford, Eng.: B. Blackwell (quarterly).

A good, relative new (1982) management journal with a European focus. For a descriptive note see listing in Chapter 16.

Harvard Business Review. Boston: Graduate School of Business Administration, Harvard University (bimonthly). Full text online database is called *Harvard Business Review Online.*

One of the most outstanding professional management journals, with practical articles by recognized authorities on all aspects of general management and policy. There are usually about 10 major articles in each issue plus regular feature articles in particular areas such as "Four Corners" (for business insights that cross borders), "In Question" (for perspectives on business issues in progress), "First Person" (for first hand lessons from experienced managers), and an HBS case study. An annual index is in the last issue each year, and a separately published moving "Ten-Year Index" is a subject/author listing of articles published during the ten most recent years. Indexed in ABI/I, BPI, PTS/F&S. Note that *Harvard Business Review Online* is a full text database devoted exclusively to indexing and delivering articles in the *Review*. It can also be accessed full text via BRS, DATA-STAR, DIALOG, MEAD/NEXIS.

International Management. London: Reed Business Publishing Group (monthly).

Billed as "the voice of European business," this business magazine has short, timely articles of practical interest to all managers with operations in Europe. They cover a wide range of management topics, with occasional profiles of companies or individuals. Features include a ranked list of "The Top 500 Industrial Companies" in European Community countries (April issue); usually one book review is in each issue. Indexed in ABI/I, PTS/F&S, TI; full text on BRS, DATA-STAR, DIALOG.

International Studies of Management & Organization. Armonk, NY: M. E. Sharpe, Inc. (quarterly).

Consists of "original articles, generally from a number of countries, written for the journal or drawn from collections of papers prepared for relevant meetings around the world." Each issue, with an academic guest editor, has a theme, and some issues contain papers originally presented at conferences. Several subjects covered in recent issues (as of 1990) are: "Anthropology of Complex Organizations" (Fall 1989); "The Italian Alternative: Flexible Organization and Social Management" (Winter 1990/91); "Organization and Management in China, 1979–1990" (Spring/Summer 1990). Indexed in ABI/I, TI.

Journal of European Business. New York: Faulkner & Gray (bimonthly).

This is a new journal (1989) containing short, practical articles on new trends, policies, and programs of interest to executives operating in Europe. They are usually written by managers, accountants, or other practitioners.

Journal of General Management. Henley-on-Thames, Eng.: Braybrooke Press Ltd. in association with Henley-The Management College (quarterly).

A British academic journal whose aim it is to help keep executives up-to-date with new developments in the theory and practice of general management. Its authoritative articles are of special interest to the European manager. Includes book reviews and a periodic supplement called "Management Updates." Indexed in ABI/I, PAIS.

Journal of Management Studies. Oxford, Eng. and Cambridge, MA: B. Blackwell (bimonthly).

Scholarly articles on organization theory, strategic management, and human resource management, written primarily by British educators and researchers. Includes book reviews in some issues. Indexed in BPI.

The McKinsey Quarterly. New York: McKinsey & Company (quarterly).

This is a good selection of practical articles on management topics that are of interest and/or concern to top management. Occasionally these are reprints of articles, excerpts from books, or interviews, but most are original articles written by McKinsey & Company staff from around the world.

Management International Review. Wiesbaden, Germany: Th. Gabler GmbH (quarterly).

A refereed journal seeking to publish articles based on the theoretical contributions, state-of-the-art surveys, or reports on actual developments in the areas of management, business policy, and transnational corporations. Indexed in ABI/I, BPI, PAIS.

Management Review. Saranac Lake, NY: American Management Association (monthly).

Each issue contains about seven short articles on practical topics of interest to managers. There are also regular features such as "Global Perspective" and "Management in Practice," as well as short book notes. Indexed in ABI/I, BPI, PAIS, TI; also full text on BRS, DATA-STAR, DIALOG, DOW JONES.

Management Today. London: Management Publications Ltd. (monthly).

Begun as the British counterpart to *Fortune,* this popular monthly contains short articles of special interest to British and European managers on managing, companies, industries, and so forth. There are regular columns including a short book review section. "MT 250: Growth & Profit Leagues" (June issue) is an annual list of Britain's largest companies ranked by growth and profits, with other financial data included. Includes a few book reviews. Indexed in ABI/I, BPI, PTS/F&S; also full text on BRS, DATA-STAR, DIALOG, DOW JONES.

SAM Advanced Management Journal. Cincinnati, OH: Society for Advancement of Management (quarterly).

Short, readable articles on current management theory and practice, most written by educators. Each issue has a theme. Includes an occasional book review or "Reading Roundup." Indexed in ABI/I, BPI.

Sloan Management Review. Cambridge, MA: Sloan School of Management, Massachusetts Institute of Technology (quarterly).

One of the best academic journals, designed to provide practicing managers with articles that discuss new techniques, case studies, models, and research trends of practical significance for effective problem solving and decision making. Includes a few book reviews and book notes describing "Recent Management Publications." Indexed in ABI/I, BPI, PAIS, PTS/F&S.

It is a temptation to go on and on in a list such as this. For instance there are respected management journals directed toward one segment of the executive population. Several examples are: *Black Enterprise* (New York: E. G. Graves Publishing Co.; monthly); *High Technology Business* (Boston: Infotechnology Publishing Co.; monthly) for senior managers interested in technological developments; *INC* for new and small business (see listing at end of this chapter); *Journal of Management Consulting;* (Amsterdam: Elsevier Science Publishers B.V.; quarterly); *Working Women* (monthly), one of several journals aimed at women executives.

Several examples of foreign language management periodicals are listed below. Journals focusing on management in specific functional areas are described in the latter part of this book. Remember also to use the directories of periodicals described in Chapter 7 for the names of many other business/management journals.

Foreign Language Management/Business Periodicals

Most countries have their own popular management/business journals, written in the language of the country and concentrating on informative articles and news of interest to managers in that country. It is not possible here to provide a complete list of these, but several examples are given as a starting point.

Canadian Business. Toronto: CB Media Ltd. (monthly).

An English language monthly with business/management articles of interest to Canadian business persons. Ranked lists include: "The Corporate 500" (June issue), with lists also on the "Next 250," "Subsidiaries 100," and "Finance 100"; "The Service 250" arranged by type of service (July); "Canada's 50 Fastest" companies (October). The first annual ranking of top Canadian business schools is in the April 1992 issue. Indexed in ABI/I, BPI, PAIS, TI; also full text on BRS, DATA-STAR, DIALOG, MEAD/NEXIS.

L'Entreprise. Paris (monthly).

This is a well-known French business/management monthly, with articles on a wide-range of topics of potential interest to French managers. Annual features include: "Le Salaire des Chefs" (January); "Spécial Top 100: Le Classement des Cent Fran-çaises Entreprises les Plus Performantes" (May); "Atlas 10,000 Entreprises" (November), including ranked lists of largest companies, arranged by region and city, with a brief introduction to each region. Each issue contains book notes.

Espansione. Milano: Mondadori Business Information (monthly).

Italy's monthly journal for business and management.

L'Expansion. Paris (semimonthly).

Billed as the "premier journal économique français," this well-known French busi-ness journal contains several useful annual issues: "Salaires des Cadres" (May/June issue), giving salaries of executives; a ranked list of top French industrial companies "Les 1000" (a November issue), with this issue also containing ranked lists of other types of companies; "Le Mondial des Entreprises" (also a November issue) includ-ing a ranked list of the 100 largest worldwide companies.

Manager Magazin. Hamburg, Germany and Englewood, NJ. (monthly).

A popular magazine for German-speaking entrepreneurs and managers.

Le Nouvel Economiste. Paris (weekly).

Articles in this French weekly cover the French economy, communication, finance, and individual companies. Two of its special extra issues are: "Le Guide Pratique des Placements" (a March issue) and "Le Nouvel Economiste 5000" (an extra issue in November), which is a ranked list of largest French and European companies, arranged by industry. Includes book reviews.

Revue Française de Gestion. Paris: Fondation Nationale pour l'Enseignement de la Gestion des Entreprises (bimonthly).

A bimonthly patterned somewhat after the *Harvard Business Review* and intended to offer authoritative articles of interest to French managers. One special issue each year is devoted to a particular topic, e.g. the issue for November/December 1989 on management consulting. Includes a few book reviews. A short summary of articles in English is at end.

ASSOCIATIONS

Academy of Management, Mississippi State University, Mississippi State, MS 39762.

American Management Association, 135 West 50th Street, New York, NY 10020.

British Institute of Management, Management House, 64–78 Kingsway, Lon-don WC25 6BL, England.

Society for Advancement of Management, 2331 Victory Parkway, Cincinnati, OH 45206.

STRATEGIC MANAGEMENT AND PLANNING

In the preface to Day's book noted below, he says "the rate of change in the market has clearly outstripped the speed at which a conventionally managed organization can respond." This rapid change is causing organizations of all sorts (both for-profit and those that are not-for-profit) to spend much more time looking into the future, and making plans and decisions that are critical to the organization's survival and prosperity. This process was formerly called "long-range planning." Today, with increasing competition, costs, and complexities both here in the United States and abroad, this management procedure has developed into a broad area now called "strategic management," of which the major part is strategic planning. Fortunately a good body of management literature has also developed on this subject to help give executives the background necessary for learning about the principles and objectives of strategic planning, the strategies and steps to follow, and the various techniques that can be used. There are also many articles being written, in almost every kind of business journal, discussing one or more aspects of strategic planning or relating the experience of an individual company. Following are a few general handbooks, recent books, and periodicals on strategic management and strategic planning. Articles can be located by using one or more of the periodical indexes or online databases described in Chapter 2. See also Chapter 11 for several books focusing on strategic management/planning in non-profit organizations; and in other chapters for strategy relating to specific management functions such as marketing, personnel, operations, or international management. For a few books on the business plan, refer to the section on "The Entrepreneur and New Business Ventures" near the end of this chapter. Finally, see the subsection below on "Competitive Intelligence" for descriptions of a few books covering the tools, techniques, and/or management of a company's efforts to monitor its competitors as part of its strategic planning activities.

Handbooks

Handbook of Business Strategy. 2d ed., ed. by Harold E. Glass. Boston: Warren, Gorham & Lamont, 1991. 1 volume (various pagings). And a supplementary *Yearbook.*

Reflecting the changing needs of managers today, this second edition is significantly different, now with 29 chapters arranged in five parts and written by 45 authoritative contributors from the academic, consulting, and management communities. It is intended to help planning and line managers improve the effectiveness of their strategic planning. The five sections cover: elements of effective strategy; tools for strategic planning; corporate development—mergers and acquisitions; formulating business unit and corporate strategy; strategy implementation. Given the speed of developments in this field, the publisher is wise to issue a *Yearbook* focusing on recent trends and changes.

King, William R., and David I. Cleland, eds. *Strategic Planning and Management Handbook.* New York: Van Nostrand Reinhold, 1987. 644 pp.

Another handbook, this one intended to provide specific guidance and more general insight for real-world managers who will have major responsibility for strategic planning and management in the coming years. Its 37 chapters, each by a leading practitioner, explain and evaluate the various tools and techniques. Among important topics covered are: a strategic view of leadership; strategic management in multinational firms; stakeholder analysis; strategic issues management; implementing strategy; strategic management in small firms and in the public arena; trends in strategic planning. References are at end of each chapter.

Yet another *Handbook of Strategic Planning* has been edited by James R. Gardner, Robert Rachlin and Allen Sweeny (New York: Wiley, 1986, 1 volume, various pagings). This is a "hands-on handbook" in which 33 authors share their practical experiences and present the latest thinking on strategic planning.

Books

Aaker, David A. *Developing Business Strategies.* 3d ed. New York: Wiley, 1992. 394 pp.

We start with a book for managers who need to develop strategies and can benefit from an introduction to the concepts, methods, and strategy alternatives. Its five parts cover: introduction; external analysis; internal analysis; alternative business strategies; implementing and the planning process. Included throughout are useful diagrams, outlines, boxed features, and bibliographical notes.

Andrews, Kenneth R. *The Concept of Corporate Strategy.* 3d ed. Homewood, IL: Irwin, 1987. 132 pp. paper.

This third edition brings up-to-date the concepts of corporate strategy used in teaching business policy at the Harvard Business School. It is addressed to executive readers. Following an introductory chapter on the functions of top managers, Professor Andrews begins with an excellent introductory chapter on the whole idea of corporate strategy. He then deals first with the formulation of corporate strategy in chapters on the company and its environments, its strategists, its responsibilities to society. With this as background he turns to implementation of strategy, with one chapter on achieving commitment to purpose and one covering the period from commitment to results. A final chapter returns to the view of the corporation as an organizational process and considers the problems of strategic management and corporate governance. The substance of this book is essentially the same as the text material in *Business Policy: Text and Cases* by C. Roland Christensen et al. (6th ed., Irwin, 1987, 940 pp.).

Ansoff, H. Igor, and Edward J. McDonnell. *Implanting Strategic Management.* 2d ed. New York: Prentice-Hall, 1990. 520 pp.

A comprehensive treatment of strategic management in turbulent environments, focusing on "designing and implementing a firm's adaptation to changes in its external environment," a response which the authors refer to as the firm's "strategic activity." They arrange their material into 7 parts: evolution of challenges and management systems; planning strategic posture; matching capability to environmental turbulence; managers, systems, structures; real-time strategic response; managing strategic change; overview. Ansoff has had long experience as a manager, teacher, consultant, and writer on corporate strategy. Among his other books is the recent *The New Corporate Strategy* (New York: Wiley, 1988, 258 pp.)

Capon, Noel, John U. Farley and James M. Hulbert. *Corporate Strategic Planning.* New York: Columbia University Press, 1987. 482 pp.

An informative assessment of the state of the art in corporate and strategic planning based on a study of the planning practices in over 100 major U.S. manufacturing corporations. It also tries to identify what are likely to be the interrelationships among a firm's planning system and its environment, strategy, organization structure, and organizational climate. An extensive bibliography is at end. Chapter 11 is a "summary and synthesis" of the study.

Day, George S. *Market Driven Strategy: Processes for Creating Value.* New York: Free Press, 1990. 405 pp.

"The arguments for a new perspective on competitive strategies remain compelling," says this consultant. Here he presents what he hopes is a proven market-driven approach to formulating and implementing competitive strategy at the business-unit level, based on material gathered from many companies. It is arranged in 6 parts: strategic choices in competitive markets; processes for developing market-driven strategies; assessing the competitive position; choosing arenas and advantages; renewing the strategy; issues in implementing market-driven strategies. Bibliographical notes are at end.

Famularo, Joseph J. *Organization Planning Manual.* Rev. ed. New York: AMACOM, 1979. 372 pp. Out of print.

We include this even though it is out of print because it is a practical planning tool for persons interested in seeing: (1) 100 sample organization charts illustrating various types, sizes, and departments of companies as well as varying organizational concepts; (2) over 100 sample position descriptions covering a range of job titles and types of companies; (3) 125 sample policy statements selected from nearly 200 company policy manuals to cover a wide range of specific policies, from accident prevention to union relations and working conditions. The companies are identified only by type of business. In each section samples from hospital administration are included. A glossary is at the end. The data is old but is still of value for background information on a specific topic about which little has been written.

Just announced for publication in 1992 is a new collection of *Organization Charts* (see entry below) which may make part 1 of Famularo no longer so important.

Hatten, Kenneth J. and Mary L. Hatten. *Strategic Management: Analysis and Action.* Englewood Cliffs, NJ: Prentice-Hall, 1987. 1,041 pp.

This is a combined text/casebook on strategy formulation and implementation intended to provide a useful introduction to the concepts and skills needed for the effective management of strategy. The text portion (first 331 pp.) starts with an overview of strategy and strategic management, and then considers, in turn: fundamentals of strategic analysis (including chapters on identifying the strategy and objectives of a business, the strategy evaluation process, competitive analysis); strategic alternatives; strategic administration; multibusiness and corporate strategy; strategy and leadership. A bibliography of suggested readings, arranged by chapter, is at end of the text chapters. Since the use of cases is especially important in developing skills in strategic management, the rest of the book (about 700 pp.) consists of useful cases arranged to correspond with sections in the text. For persons who prefer to have this book without cases, the authors have also written *Effective Strategic Management: Analysis and Action* (Prentice-Hall, 1988, 388 pp.).

Hax, Arnoldo C. and Nicolas S. Majluf. *The Strategy Concept & Process: A Pragmatic Approach.* Englewood Cliffs, NJ: Prentice-Hall, 1991. 430 pp.

To meet the enormous challenges facing managers today, these authors feel that managers must "be able to articulate a vision of the firm with charismatic zeal." They hope their book offers "practicing managers and business students a disciplined process that facilitates the formulation and implementation of strategy to allow this demanding task of identifying and imprinting the vision of the firm to become meaningful reality." The material is arranged within five parts: strategy and process; business strategy; corporate strategy; functional strategy; methodology for the development of a strategic plan (this latter has a step-by-step recommendation). Relevant and real-life applications are used throughout, as are diagrams and checklists. References and a glossary are at end.

McCarthy, Daniel J., Robert J. Minichiello and Joseph R. Curran. *Business Policy and Strategy: Concepts and Readings.* 4th ed. Homewood, IL: Irwin, 1987. 528 pp. paper.

Revision of a basic text, this book emphasizes the conceptual understanding and skill required of executives with policy and/or strategy responsibility. It covers skills required not only in business but also in nonbusiness organizations, and it is addressed to business policy students at all levels, including those in executive development programs. The authors carried out a major consolidation and reorganization with this latest edition, reducing the text portion to 8 concise chapters, and updating and increasing the readings to 24. The authors are on the faculty at Northeastern University.

Mintzberg, Henry, and James B. Quinn. *The Strategy Process: Concepts, Contexts, and Cases.* 2d ed. Englewood Cliffs, NJ: Prentice-Hall, 1991. 1,083 pp.

A new kind of strategy book consisting primarily of readings and cases written, the authors hope, in a style that is sophisticated, eclectic, and lively. It combines theory and practice, and description with prescription. The readings (by the authors as well as by other well-known management thinkers) represent a wide range of issues and perspectives. They have usually been cut in length from the original source to extract the key messages in as concise a manner as possible. Cases are at end of each major part: strategy; organization; context. A bibliography is at end of the book.

Professor Quinn has written an earlier book that is on every list of important books managers should read. It is *Strategies for Change: Logical Incrementalism* (Irwin, 1980, 222 pp., paper). In this, he reports on a study he undertook to document why managers in large companies act and make decisions as they do and what the implications of those actions are for managers and students of strategic planning.

Organization Charts. Ed. by Judith Nixon. Detroit: Gale Research, Inc., 1992. 259 pp.

Just announced for publication in 1992 is this collection of organization charts, culled, the publisher says, from international business journals, annual reports, and direct requests to Fortune 500 companies. It promises to fill a real need for up-to-date charts on the organizational structures in a range of companies and non-profit organizations—both public and private, domestic and foreign, and of different sizes and types. Although it is a reference work rather than a text, it is still logical to include here because it may be helpful in identifying varying company structures, chains of command, lines of communication, etc., of potential use in planning, strategy, and competitive analysis.

Pearce, John A., II, and Richard B. Robinson, Jr. *Strategic Management: Strategy Formulation and Implementation.* 3d ed. Homewood, IL: Irwin, 1988. 987 pp.

Latest edition of an introduction to the critical skills of planning and managing strategic activities, which combines text with cases. The text portion, in three parts, starts with an overview, and then it examines in turn strategy formulation and strategy implementation. Boxed features throughout called "Strategy in Action" give real-world examples of key concepts discussed; also a "Cohesive Case" at end of each chapter applies the chapter material to one company. "Sources for Remote Environmental and Operating Forecasts" are in Chapter 7; bibliographies are with each chapter. Part 4 (over 500 pages) consists of 34 case studies and notes on industries.

Their *Formulation, Implementation, and Control of Competitive Strategy* (4th ed., Irwin, 1991, 390 pp., paper) is a revision of the text portion of the book described above, with an expanded number of real-world examples and a new Cohesive Case. For a recent book of related readings refer to their *Strategic Management Practices: Readings in Strategic Management* (Irwin, 1991, 411 pp.).

Pfeiffer, J. William, ed. *Strategic Planning: Selected Readings.* Revised. San Diego, CA: Pfeiffer & Company, 1991. 407 pp.

Here is a selection of 16 of "the best, most relevant, and most insightful articles" published during the previous decade and organized along the line of the Applied Strategic Planning (ASP) Model which was developed by the publisher. After an overview of the Model, Pfeiffer arranges these selections into four sections: perspective on the need to plan; clarifying the mission; creating a strategy; implementing strategic management. An appendix provides some background on the history of strategic planning.

Porter, Michael E. *Competitive Strategy: Techniques for Analyzing Business, Industry and Competitors.* New York: Free Press, 1980. 396 pp.

This well-written book (a bestseller in the early 1980s) is of special interest to practitioners who need to develop strategy for a particular business and also to scholars who want to understand competition better. It is in three parts. Part 1 presents a series of general analytical techniques for analyzing industries and competitors and translating this analysis into a competitive strategy. Part 2 then shows how these analytical underpinnings can be applied to develop strategy in the following specific types of industry environments: in fragmented industries, in emerging industries, maturing industries, declining industries, and in global industries. Part 3 completes the analytical framework by examining the important types of decisions that confront firms in the context of a single industry—strategic analysis of vertical integration, major capacity expansion, and entry into new businesses. Two items in an appendix are also of potential interest; these are short notes about "Portfolio Techniques as Competitor Analysis Tools" and "How to Conduct an Industry Analysis."

Professor Porter's second book proceeds to the next step by considering how a firm can create and sustain a competitive advantage. It is titled *Competitive Advantage: Creating and Sustaining Superior Performance* (Free Press, 1985, 557 pp.). Arranged in four parts, it covers: principles of competitive advantage; competitive scope within an industry; corporate strategy and competitive advantage; and implications for offensive and defensive strategy. A bibliography is at end. His most recently published research, described in Chapter 16, is *The Competitive Advantage of Nations* (Free Press, 1990, 855 pp.). In this book he investigates why nations gain competitive advantage in particular industries and the implications both for company strategy and for national economies.

Steiner, George A., John B. Miner and Edmund R. Gray. *Management Policy and Strategy: Text, Readings, and Cases.* 3d ed. New York: Macmillan, 1986. 963, [27] pp.

Intended as a capstone course on business policy, the text portion is organized into five parts: the nature and importance of business policy/strategy; key overall forces in policy/strategy formulation and implementation; formulating business policy/strategy; implementing policy/strategy; policy/strategy in varied contexts (entrepreneurship, and not-for-profit organizations). Part 6 consists of 12 significant readings (about 150 pp.); part 7 contains cases (almost 500 pp.). An extensive bibliography is at end.

Professor Steiner has written widely in the field of strategy and planning starting back in 1969 with his comprehensive *Top Management Planning* (795 pp.) which was for many years an indispensable guide that was on most lists of top management books.

Thompson, Arthur A., Jr., and A. J. Strickland III. *Strategy Formulation and Implementation: Tasks of the General Manager.* 4th ed. Homewood, IL: BPI/Irwin, 1989. 366 pp. paper. Fifth edition to be published in 1992.

A major revision with many new features, this is a text for advanced students about the managerial tasks of crafting and implementing strategy. The 10 chapters are arranged within four parts: an overview of managing strategy—tasks, concepts, and process; strategic analysis in single-business companies; strategic analysis in diversified companies; strategic administrative tasks. One or two readings are with each part; "illustrative capsules," set in boxes, are interspersed throughout to highlight experiences of companies. Suggested readings are at end of chapters. The authors use many examples. An explanation of how to prepare a case is in an appendix.

Related books by these authors include: *Readings in Strategic Management* (with William E. Fulmer, 4th ed., BPI/Irwin, 1992, paper); *Strategic Management: Concepts and Cases* (5th ed., BPI/Irwin, 1990, 1,011 pp.).

It is a temptation to make this section longer since strategic management is such an important topic and there have been so many books published recently on the subject. Here are just a few additional titles worth mentioning: *Business Policy and Strategic Management* by Lawrence R. Jauch and William F. Glueck (5th ed., McGraw-Hill, 1988, 940 pp.), combining text with cases; *Introducing Corporate Planning: Guide to Strategic Management* by David E. Hussey (4th ed., Oxford, Eng. and NY: Pergamon Press, 1991, 245 pp., paper), an introductory guide with a British focus; *Making Strategy Happen: Transforming Plans into Reality* by Arnold S. Judson (Oxford, Eng. and Cambridge, MA: B. Blackwell, 1990, 250 pp.), a practical book on how to ensure that a firm's strategic plans actually lead to desired tangible outcomes; *Strategic Management: Formulation and Implementation* by Lloyd L. Byars (3d ed., HarperCollins, 1991, 995, [10] pp.) which combines a text on concepts with cases.

Competitive Intelligence

Fuld, Leonard M. *Monitoring the Competition: Finding Out What's Really Going On Over There.* New York: Wiley, 1988. 204 pp.

A nuts-and-bolts book for the person directly involved in monitoring a company's competitive activities, providing him/her with helpful hints on how to put together a successful monitoring program. Included are discussions on how to gather information from both outside and inside the company, how to organize and store competitive data, how to deliver the information speedily to the company's decision makers. Includes a checklist for competitor monitoring, a survey of corporate intelligence gathering, and a chapter on using your library. Mr. Fuld, who heads his own information gathering firm, has written an earlier book called *Competitor Intelligence: How to Get It; How to Use It* (Wiley, 1985, 479 pp.). This book focuses on the potential tools and techniques covering both traditional sources (published books, databases, etc.) and creative sources and techniques that may reveal vital facts. It is now rather old, but a revision is in progress with tentative publication in late 1994.

For persons who want a similar guide to gathering, analyzing, and using business intelligence, there is a new loose-leaf volume called *Competitive Intelligence Manual and Guide* by Kirk W. M. Tyson (Englewood Cliffs, NJ: Prentice-Hall, 1990, 376 pp.). This is a practical manual in 13 chapters, full of facts, worksheets, checklists, and other aids. One chapter includes a list of published sources useful in gathering information about companies and industries.

Gilad, Benjamin and Tamar Gilad. *The Business Intelligence System: A New Tool for Competitive Advantage.* New York: AMACOM, 1988. 242 pp.

Unlike the Fuld book, this one focuses on showing how to build an organized and ongoing business intelligence system within the organization. Much of it discusses the five functions that constitute the BI system: what information to collect, how to evaluate it, how to store and to analyze it, and how to disseminate it. Included is a short overview of types of BI sources of information, and a longer chapter on the organizational structure for the BI system. A short bibliography is at end. Both authors are experienced consultants.

Oster, Sharon M. *Modern Competitive Analysis.* New York and Oxford: Oxford University Press, 1990. 376 pp.

A book about competitive strategy written by an economist with the result that it focuses on understanding the interplay between the economic conditions faced by an organization and its strategy. Its four sections reflect the ingredients in a dynamic planning process: discussing first the environment faced by an organization; then narrowing in on the organization itself; next the relationship (rivalry) among organizations within an industry; finally dealing with the planning process. It includes many examples from actual companies. Some case suggestions, bibliographical notes, and a glossary are at end.

Rothschild, William E. *How to Gain (and Maintain) the Competitive Advantage in Business.* New York: McGraw-Hill, 1984. 226 pp. Reprinted in 1989.

This is a good, practical guide aimed at "helping executives improve their competitive position by consciously identifying, anticipating, and analyzing current and potential competitors." It is based on the author's many years of experience in all phases of strategic planning. He discusses various techniques and how they can be used to improve strategy and implementation. Includes a chapter on sources (now very old) and resources of competitive intelligence.

Periodicals

Business Strategy Review. Oxford, Eng.: Oxford University Press for the Centre for Business Strategy. (3/yr.).

A relatively new periodical (Spring 1990) containing original nontechnical articles on a wide variety of issues relevant to strategic decisions in modern business. Much of it reflects the research undertaken at the London Business School's Centre for Business Strategy, and most are written by the school's faculty or research staff.

International Review of Strategic Management. Chichester, Eng. and New York: Wiley (annual).

Another new publication, this is an international review that hopes, over time, to provide practicing managers and academics with a critical review of the best developments and practices in strategic management. "Each volume will reflect the state of the art in the topics covered, explore different aspects of a theme relating to strategy, and identify trends and important topics." The first volume (1990) concentrated on the subject of building competitive advantage.

Journal of Business Strategy. Boston: Warren, Gorham & Lamont (bimonthly).

An excellent journal aimed expressly at the practical interests of managers in the area of strategic business planning. Indexed in ABI/I, BPI, PAIS, TI.

Long Range Planning. Oxford, Eng. and Elmsford, NY: Pergamon Press for the Strategic Planning Society and the European Planning Federation (bimonthly).

Articles in this bimonthly cover all aspects of strategy and planning and often have an international flavor. Each issue includes a book review, "Review Briefs," and "A Current Awareness Service for Long Range Planning," which is a selected, annotated list of articles. Indexed in ABI/I, BPI, PAIS, TI.

Planning Review. Oxford, OH: The Planning Forum (bimonthly).

All aspects of corporate and strategic planning are covered by short, practical articles. One book review is in each issue and occasionally abstracts of selected articles. Indexed in ABI/I, BPI, PTS/F&S.

Strategic Management Journal. Chichester, Sussex, Eng. and New York: Wiley (bimonthly).

This international quarterly publishes original material on all aspects of strategic management, both theory and practice. It is meant for both practicing managers and academics. A special issue each summer focuses on one topic, e.g. "Strategic Leaders and Leadership" (Summer 1989). Indexed in ABI/I, BPI, TI.

Services

Commerce Clearing House. *Business Strategies.* Chicago. 4 volumes.

This loose-leaf, continually updated service explains the legal, tax, and accounting ramifications of management decision-making in three "Strategies and Forms" volumes. Volume 3 also has articles on specific aspects of new business planning developments. Volume 4 contains "Ideas & Trends" which reviews new developments, and contains a newsletter called "Business Strategies Bulletin."

Directories

Planning Forum. *Membership Directory.* Oxford, OH (annual). Available to Forum members.

There is an organization index with this directory so one can check the names of the planning executives within specific companies and other organizations. The main list, with addresses, is arranged by individual name.

Associations

The Planning Forum (an international society for planning and strategic management) 5500 College Corner Pike, Oxford, OH 45056.

Strategic Planning Society, 15 Belgrave Square, London SW1X 8PU, England.

HUMAN FACTORS IN ORGANIZATIONS

The study of the interaction of people within organizations spans the field of psychology as well as business. The literature is legion, not only for general books on human behavior but also for those on its several aspects, such as motivation, morale, communication, leadership, group behavior, conflict, and change. The titles of many excellent books on these topics are missing from this very short list, as are the names of important and influential behavioral theorists, such as Chris Argyris, Frederic K. Herzberg, Rensis Likert, Douglas McGregor (listed elsewhere in this chapter), and the teams of Blake/Mouton and Lawrence/Lorsch. The contributions of these and other important theorists are usually discussed in basic books on organizational behavior and, occasionally, in recent texts on personnel/human resources management (Chapter 19). Persons who wish to investigate the writings of any individual can start by reading several of the books on the history of management thinking in the following section of this chapter. The books listed below will also be useful, as will their bibliographies, in identifying specific titles by each theorist. Many general management lists also cite these important works.

The entire area of human relations is an essential part of the literature on personnel administration, and so many of the sources listed in Chapter 19 may also be of interest to persons wanting to read about human factors in organizations. See, for example, the section on "Performance Appraisal" in that chapter.

Handbooks

Frederiksen, Lee W., ed. *Handbook of Organizational Behavior Management.* New York: Wiley, 1982. 604 pp.

OBM is a new approach to understanding, measuring, and managing behavior in organizational settings. This book is a guide to its principles, procedures, and uses, with each chapter written by a different author. Of special interest is its fourth part consisting of seven chapters that review specific applications of OBM such as absenteeism, productivity improvement, performance. This is, generally speaking, a good overall summary of OBM, and its bibliographies with each chapter provide additional reading for persons wanting to pursue any one topic in greater depth.

Lorsch, Jay W., ed. *Handbook of Organizational Behavior.* Englewood Cliffs, NJ: Prentice-Hall, 1987. 430 pp.

In this excellent handbook the editor has brought together more than 30 experts in organizational behavior and management "to provide a concise set of references" that will help managers understand and encourage effective behavior for achieving organizational goals. The first three sections contain essays giving a perspective on the development of the field and its current state. The last three sections, called the core of the book, describe what is known about organizational behavior at various systems levels of organization, in relation to specific applied issues, and in nonbusiness settings. Most of its 27 chapters contain bibliographical references.

ORGANIZATIONAL BEHAVIOR

Davis, Keith, and John W. Newstrom. *Human Behavior at Work: Organizational Behavior.* 8th ed. New York: McGraw-Hill, 1989. 643 pp. Ninth edition will be published in 1992 with authors reversed and title/subtitle reversed.

Latest revision of a beginning text on people at work in all kinds of organizations and how they may be motivated to work together more productively. The section headings are: fundamentals of organizational behavior; motivation and reward systems; leadership and organizational change; organizational environment; social environment. There is also a conclusion and 8 case problems. Useful examples of real organizational situations are used throughout; also diagrams and marginal notes. Bibliographies are at end of chapters; a glossary is at end of book. These professors (in reverse order) have also edited a good book of readings, which can be used with the text, called *Organizational Behavior: Readings and Exercises* (8th ed., McGraw-Hill, 1989, 597 pp., paper).

DuBrin, Andrew J. *Contemporary Applied Management: Behavioral Science Techniques for Managers and Professionals.* 3d ed. Homewood, IL: BPI/Irwin, 1989. 356 pp.

This book provides managers and aspiring managers with a look at the application of a selection of behavioral science and management techniques, methods, and strategies—considering both the strengths and weaknesses of each technique or method. These are arranged in the following five parts: improving individual effectiveness; improving interpersonal relationships; improving the functions of work groups; improving productivity and quality at the organizational level; human research management programs. Bibliographies are at end of chapters. Some previous understanding of human resource management and OB is recommended.

Also of possible interest is a revision of Professor DuBrin's text on *Human Relations: A Job-Oriented Approach* (5th ed., Prentice-Hall, 1992, 558 pp.).

Hackman, J. Richard, ed. *Groups That Work (and Those That Don't): Creating Conditions for Effective Work.* San Francisco: Jossey-Bass, 1990. 512 pp.

The purpose of this study of 27 diverse task-performing teams was two-fold: to find out how work groups function and why some succeed while others fail; to show how leaders and group members can improve work groups' effectiveness. These teams were grouped into 7 categories ranking from top management teams to production teams such as airline cockpit crews. A bibliography is at end.

Hampton, David R., Charles E. Summer and Ross A. Webber. *Organizational Behavior and the Practice of Management.* 5th ed. Glenview, IL: Scott, Foresman, 1987. 876 pp.

Another introductory text, this one recently revised and updated to include new developments in research and theory. It is arranged in three parts: individual, interpersonal, and group behavior (motivation, work and careers, power and influence, communication, etc.); organizational structure and processes (work and organization design, objectives, performance and rewards); managing conflict, adaptation, and change (including leadership, organizational development, evolution, and culture). A few readings, case studies, and selected bibliographies are at end of each chapter.

Hersey, Paul and Kenneth H. Blanchard. *Management of Organizational Behavior: Utilizing Human Resources.* 5th ed. Englewood Cliffs, NJ: Prentice-Hall, 1988. 474 pp. paper.

An extensive revision of a text on behavior within organizations written, the authors hope, as a concise and easy-to-read book that will make the behavioral sciences come alive to operating managers, students, and others who read it. Included are: two chapters discussing motivation; nine tracing the development of modern leadership theory and introducing a "Situational Leadership" concept developed by the authors; seven focusing on applied behavioral science with special attention to One Minute Management and its relationship to Situational Leadership. Bibliographical notes are at end of chapters, and a recommended supplementary reading list is at end of book.

Judson, Arnold S. *Changing Behavior in Organizations: Minimizing Resistance to Change.* Oxford, Eng. and Cambridge, MA: B. Blackwell, 1991. 221 pp.

This short book focuses on how to approach and manage change so that the intended outcomes are actually achieved. Judson starts by discussing how people are affected by change and how they react to it. Then he presents some concepts, principles and guidelines to help managers improve the way they introduce and implement changes in business situations. Bibliographical notes are at end. The initial version of this book was called *A Manager's Guide to Making Changes* (1966).

Luthans, Fred. *Organizational Behavior.* 5th ed. New York: McGraw-Hill, 1989. 637 pp.

Luthans' advanced text aims to provide "a strong conceptual framework for the study, understanding, and application of organizational behavior." This latest edition has been more thoroughly revised than previous editions not only because of the accelerated rate of change facing organizations but also to reflect the global community in which managers now operate. Its first part provides the foundation, with new chapters devoted to organizational culture and the international context of OB. The rest (parts 2–5) are arranged so that one progresses from the micro perspective of individual behavior (personality, perception, attitudes, stress, motivation, and learning), to interpersonal and group behaviors, dynamics, and influence (including chapters on power and on leadership), and finally to the macro end of the spectrum with a study of OB processes and structure. Tables, diagrams, and boxed "application examples" appear throughout; case incidents and readings are at end of chapters.

Matteson, Michael T., and John M. Ivancevich, eds. *Management and Organizational Behavior Classics.* 4th ed. Homewood, IL: Irwin, 1989. 545 pp.

This is a good sampling of 39 classic readings whose objective it is to make readily available outstanding contributions to the management and organizational literature. These readings are arranged in the following sections: foundations for understanding management and organizational behavior; classical management processes; managing individual behavior; managing group behavior; managing organizational behavior. This latter section (16 readings) includes several each on leadership, motivation, decision making, and organizational development. The earlier editions of this book focused just on *Management Classics*. The selections were good and many are not included in this latest expanded edition. Thus readers may want to refer also to the first edition (1977).

Ott, J. Steven, ed. *Classic Readings in Organizational Behavior.* Pacific Grove, CA: Brooks/Cole Publishing Company, 1989. 638 pp. paper.

Another selection, this one contains over 40 of the most widely quoted and/or reprinted writings on OB. They are arranged within 6 chapters to cover: motivation; group and intergroup behavior; leadership; people in organizations: the context; power and influence; and organizational change and development. At front is a useful chronology of the theoretical developments in organizational behavior from 21 B.C. to 1988 A.D.

Yet another good, up-to-date selection of some of the time-tested and often-referenced readings is *Classics of Organizational Behavior* ed. by Walter E. Natemeyer and Jay S. Gilberg (2d ed. Danville, IL: Interstate Printers & Publishers, 1989, 370 pp., paper). Its 32 selections are arranged in 6 sections.

Robbins, Stephen P. *Organizational Behavior: Concepts, Controversies and Applications.* 5th ed. Englewood Cliffs, NJ: Prentice-Hall, 1991. 725 pp.

Here is another introductory OB text from which to choose. This one aims to give students an accurate and up-to-date review of the field while presenting the material in a lively style. As with several other basic texts, it is organized around the three levels of organizational behavior—the individual, the group, and the organization system. Includes "OB Close-Ups," colored boxed features designed to illustrate applications of concepts and elaborate on current issues in OB; also "Point–Counterpoint" debates at end of chapters which present current controversies in OB. Annotated suggestions for further reading are at end of chapters; a glossary is at end of book. Professor Robbins has also revised his *Essentials of Organizational Behavior* (3d ed., Prentice-Hall, 1991).

Rosen, Robert H. (Lisa Berger, collaborator). *The Healthy Company: Eight Strategies to Develop People, Productivity, and Profits.* Los Angeles: J. P. Tarcher, 1991. 315 pp.

This title drew my attention because I am always looking for factors that make for a happy library (organization). It is a practical, readable book on the strategies managers and their companies can use to become healthy, and consequently (one hopes) a more profitable organization. The author has filled his discussion with practical tips and advice, personal questionnaires, observations, research, many company examples, and quotations (in margins) from leaders of healthy companies. The 8 strategies discussed include how to use the power of respect to motivate and inspire commitment, how to manage change, the importance for leaders to know how to follow as well as to lead, and much more. A list of sources consulted is at end.

Steers, Richard M., and Lyman W. Porter, comps. *Motivation and Work Behavior.* 5th ed. New York: McGraw-Hill, 1991. 594 pp.

A selection of excellent readings that "brings together in one volume the major contemporary theories, research, and applications in the area of motivation and work behavior." They are arranged within five parts to cover: initial considerations; theoretical approaches to motivation; central issues in motivation at work; techniques of motivation; motivation theory in perspective. Suggested additional readings are at the end of chapters for persons wishing to study a particular topic in more detail. This book is directed primarily toward advanced undergraduates, graduate students in organizational behavior and industrial psychology, and also general managers.

Professor Steers has also recently revised his *Introduction to Organizational Behavior* (4th ed., HarperCollins, 1991, 675 pp.).

There are other introductory texts that have either been well-reviewed or have been revised several times. Three of these are: *Behavior in Organizations* by H. Joseph Reitz (3d ed., Irwin, 1987, 626 pp.); *Organizational Behavior* by Robert P. Vecchio (Dryden Press, 1988, 576 pp.); *Organizational Behavior* by Don Hellriegal et al. (5th ed., West Publishing Company, 1989, 629 pp.).

Organization Development

The term "organization development" has been defined in varying ways. One short and clear definition is: "Organization Development (OD) is a powerful set of concepts and techniques for improving organizational effectiveness and individual well-being that had its genesis in the behavioral sciences and was tested in the laboratory of real-world organizations" (in French and Bell's *Organization Development: Theory, Practice and Research,* 3d ed., 1989, p.1).

Addison-Wesley Series on Organization Development. Ed. by Edgar H. Schein and Richard Beckhard. Reading, MA: Addison Wesley Publishers. 1969– to date.

This series of concise paperback volumes was begun in 1969 by a number of leading organizational theorists who recognized that the rapidly growing field of organization development was not well understood or well defined and that, since there was no one OD philosophy, it would be of value to let different well-respected authors speak for themselves about specific aspects of this rapidly growing and highly diverse field. The original six books (by Beckhard, Bennis, Blake and Mouton, Lawrence and Lorsch, Schein, and Walton) launched the series; today it has expanded to cover all kinds of organizational areas and technologies. A complete list of the titles in this series (over 20 as of 1990) can be obtained from the publisher. Following are the titles of several of the most recent books to give a feeling for the breadth of subjects covered (arranged alphabetically): *Change by Design* by R. R. Blake, J. S. Mouton and A. A. McCanse (1989); *Designing Organizations for High Performance* by D. P. Hanna (1988); *Managing Conflict: Interpersonal Dialogue and Third Party Roles* by R. E. Walton (2d ed., 1987); *Organization Development: A Normative View* by W. W. Burke (1987); *Organizational Transitions: Managing Complex Change* by R. Beckhard (2d ed., 1987); *Power and Organization Development* by L. E. Greiner and V. E. Schein (1989); *Process Consultation, Volume I: Its Role in Organization Development* by E. H. Schein (2d ed., 1988); *Process Consultation, Volume II: Lessons for Managers and Consultants* by E. H. Schein (1987); *Self-Designing Organizations: Learning How to Create High Performance* by S. A. Mohrman and T. G. Cummings (1990); *Stream Analysis: A Powerful Way to Diagnose and Manage Organizational Change* by J. I. Porras (1987).

French, Wendell L., and Cecil H. Bell, Jr. *Organization Development: Behavioral Science Interventions for Organization Improvement.* 4th ed. Englewood Cliffs, NJ: Prentice-Hall, 1989. 368 pp. paper.

In this book Professors French and Bell tell the story of OD—both its theory and practice, what is going on in the field, what the state-of-the-art is, and what the future of OD might be. It is another revised, updated, and expanded edition to reflect increased interest and usage. Bibliographical "Notes" are at end of each chapter. This note is based on an examination of the previous edition.

Both of these authors, along with Robert A. Zawacki, have edited a good selection of 66 readings called *Organization Development: Theory, Practice and Research* (3d ed., Homewood, IL: BPI/Irwin, 1989, 681 pp. paper). There are "Suggested Additional Readings" at the end of most of its 10 parts, one part of which covers "Application in the Public and Service Sectors."

Another book that describes the underlying concepts, principles, and assumptions of OD (using a systems approach) is *Organization Development and Change* by Thomas G. Cummings and Edgar F. Huse (4th ed., St. Paul, MN: West Publishing Company, 1989, 600 pp.).

Industrial and Organizational Psychology

Kolb, David A., Irwin M. Rubin and Joyce S. Osland, eds. *The Organizational Behavior Reader.* 5th ed. Englewood Cliffs, NJ: Prentice-Hall, 1991. 689 pp. paper.

A selection of readings which attempts "to portray a balanced view of the field of organizational behavior, including basic ideas and concepts, new approaches developed in current research, and emerging perspectives that suggest the future shape of the field." They are arranged within four parts: understanding yourself and other people at work; creating effective work relationships; leadership and management; managing effective organizations. Many of the readings are by such well-known names as Argyris, Bennis, Lawler, Likert, McClelland, McGregor, Schein. The editors have also written a companion text, *Organizational Behavior: An Experiential Approach* (5th ed., Prentice-Hall, 1991, 560 pp.).

Landy, Frank J. *Psychology of Work Behavior.* 4th ed. Pacific Grove, CA: Brooks/Cole Publishing Company, 1989. 715, [58] pp.

A well-reviewed, somewhat rigorous text that emphasizes the individual as the unit of analysis and has a good balance between theory and practice. It is separated into four areas. The first is background/introductory; then chapters 3–9 deal with topics related to personnel psychology (such as job analysis, measures of performance, tests, interviews). Chapters 10–13 discuss the individual's attempts to adjust to the job, people, and organization (in relation to work motivation, job satisfaction, leadership, organizational theory). The last two chapters wind up the text by covering the worker's environment and how it affects effectiveness and well-being. Technical matters are often relegated to chapter appendixes; a bibliography is paged separately at end. The author presumes an introductory course in psychology and some familiarity with basic statistical theory.

Leavitt, Harold J., and Homa Behrami. *Managerial Psychology: Managing Behavior in Organizations.* 5th ed. Chicago: University of Chicago Press, 1988. 353 pp.

This is the latest thorough revision of an excellent and not too difficult book about those concepts of human behavior that are relevant to management problems as seen by a well-known psychologist and his new coauthor, an OB lecturer. They consider, in turn, the individual in the organization, people two at a time (communicating, influencing, commanding, challenging), people in small groups (efficiency and influence in groups), people in large organizations (managing the whole organization), and finally, the relationship between contemporary organizations and their environments. Useful "suggested readings" are included at end.

Leavitt also edited, with Louis R. Pondy and David M. Boje, a good selection of *Readings in Managerial Psychology* (4th ed., University of Chicago Press, 1989, 769 pp., paper).

McCormick, Ernest J., and Daniel R. Ilgen. *Industrial and Organizational Psychology.* 8th ed. Englewood Cliffs, NJ: Prentice-Hall, 1985. 468 pp.

Another widely used text which McCormick (now with a coauthor) has revised for the eighth time to keep abreast of the many changes in methods, techniques, and procedures, and, in this latest edition, to reflect by a change of title the fact that the focus is on the behavior of people at work in all kinds of organizations. They emphasize practical applications, but also cover the "science" of psychology, so the book is excellent for students and managers and is also of special interest to personnel administrators. Twenty-one chapters provide good coverage, especially for a consideration of the various aspects of personnel selection, training and development, as well as the organizational and social context of human work. Bibliographical references are at the end of chapters; appendixes contain statistics and tables.

Organ, Dennis W. *The Applied Psychology of Work Behavior: A Book of Readings.* 4th ed. Homewood, IL: Irwin, 1991. 522 pp.

Professor Organ's latest selection of 37 readings is arranged within 6 sections to cover: organizational behavior: scope and method; the motivational basis of behavior in organizations; organizations and people: patterns of conflict and accommodation; groups and social influence processes in organizations; leadership; organizations: structure, strategy, culture, and environment.

Schultz, Duane P., and Sydney E. Schultz. *Psychology and Industry Today: An Introduction to Industrial and Organizational Psychology.* 5th ed. New York: Macmillan, 1990. 667, 17 pp.

This is the latest revision of an introductory undergraduate text on the principles, practices, problems, and occasional pretenses of industrial/organizational (I/O) psychology. The authors say it aims to be readable and to focus on contemporary on-the-job situations. They arrange it in five parts: the practice of I/O psychology; personnel psychology; organizational psychology; the workplace; consumer psychology. Case incidents are with most chapters; also short, annotated lists of additional readings. A bibliography is at end.

Leadership

People have always been curious about those persons who are considered to be great leaders, and especially about what it is that makes them great. It follows that much has been written on leaders and leadership, not only because of this curiosity but also because effective leadership is vital for success in every kind of organization or endeavor. Despite all of the published studies and analyses, leadership is still a complex subject that is not well understood. We have described here a few recent books—several based on surveys or research conducted by organizational behavior experts, several intended as helpful analyses for practitioners, and one a book of readings. All basic organizational behavior textbooks contain at least one chapter on leadership. Other books can be located by using the *Subject Guide to Books in Print,* and articles can be found by using periodical indexes (Chapter 2). A new *Leadership Quarterly* is described in the "Periodicals" section that follows. In addition the few books on "Managers" described earlier in this chapter may also be of interest.

Bass and Stoghill's Handbook of Leadership: Theory, Research, and Managerial Applications. Ed. by Bernard M. Bass. 3d ed. New York: Free Press, 1990. 1,182 pp.

Listed first is a handbook—a comprehensive analysis and review of the literature on leadership intended more as an essential reference work than as a book to be read from cover to cover. Its 37 chapters are arranged within 8 parts to cover: introduction to concepts and theories of leadership; personal attributes of leaders; power and legitimacy; the transactional exchange; leadership and management; situational moderators; diverse groups; improving leadership, and leadership research. A short glossary and an extensive bibliography are at end. This handbook was originally edited by Ralph M. Stoghill.

Batten, Joe D. *Tough-Minded Leadership.* New York: AMACOM, 1989. 236 pp.

The focus of this practical book "is on the methods, procedures, processes, techniques, and many other overt manifestations of the tough-minded leader." Batten further explains that his concern is "how the leader views, perceives, and responds to life as a whole, in terms of *changed behavior,*" and his book argues for a new style of management he calls "leadership by expectation." Typical chapter titles are: leadership and power; enhancing innovation; build and motivate your team; lead by example; tooling for change. A glossary and a short annotated list of books for new leaders are at end.

Bennis, Warren. *On Becoming a Leader.* Reading, MA: Addison-Wesley, 1989. 226 pp.

Bennis is a respected educator/administrator/writer who has focused much of his research on the study of leadership. In this latest book he focuses on studying the "hows" of leaders by observing and listening to some of the world's most distinguished leaders. In this way he brings to light insights about "how people learn, how they learn to lead, and how organizations help or hinder the process—or, to put it succinctly, how people become leaders." About one third of those leaders he studied are in the field of business; others are from a wide range of activities, but none are politicians. His book is full of concise comments these leaders make about their ideas, beliefs, experiences, etc., which makes for absorbing reading. One of his earlier books, written with Burt Nanus, is *Leaders: The Strategies for Taking Charge* (Harper & Row, 1985, 244 pp.).

Kotter, John P. *A Force for Change: How Leadership Differs From Management.* New York: Free Press, 1990. 180 pp.

Much of Professor Kotter's recent research has centered around the subject of leadership in business, and this is the latest in a series of four books he has written on aspects of this subject. The first one, *The General Managers* (1982), was an in-depth study of 15 successful general managers in 9 companies. Next came *Power and Influence* (1985) in which he argued that many of the complex skills and personal assets general managers possess are also needed by a growing number of middle-level managers and professionals. Then came *The Leadership Factor* (1988) where he tried to demonstrate why most firms do not have sufficient people with those skills needed, and what could or should be done to help them deal with this important problem. It was based on field work, in-depth interviews with executives, and studies of specific corporations. His latest research (title noted above), is based on a survey of 200 senior executives. It focuses on how leadership differs from management, yet why both good leadership and management are essential for business success, especially for complex organizations operating in a changing environment. Research methodology and bibliographical notes are included in each book.

Kouzes, James M., and Barry Z. Posner. *The Leadership Challenge: How to Get Extraordinary Things Done in Organizations.* San Francisco: Jossey-Bass, 1988. 362 pp.

Leadership begins where management ends, say these authors. Their book, written for practitioners, discusses the 5 practices of exemplary leadership which their research revealed and the 10 commitments of leadership they recommend. It is based on a survey of over 500 managers and also selected in-depth interviews. Chapters 3–12 explore these 5 practices and 10 commitments. A final chapter discusses becoming a leader who cares and makes a difference. Practical examples are used throughout the book. Appendixes contain the authors' personal best questionnaire and their leadership practices inventory. Bibliographical notes are at end.

Levinson, Harry. *Executive.* Cambridge, MA: Harvard University Press, 1981. 370 pp.

In 1968 Professor Levinson published a widely acclaimed book on effective business leadership called *The Exceptional Executive* (Harvard University Press, 1968). This newer book was a thorough revision undertaken to meet the challenges of executives in the 1980s who were facing increased complexities in managing companies and also in satisfying changing demands from multiple constituencies. He says this revision was "designed to help senior executives learn more about their role from a psychological point of view and to help them meet the expectations of their organization and the public." In four parts, part 1 defines the problem; part 2 discusses leadership—the tasks of top management, the executive as teacher, etc.; part 3 considers how the executive moves into action, specifying the human needs to be met and dealt with; the last section addresses managing change and some mistakes that executives are likely to make. This book is still "must" reading for thoughtful executives.

Manz, Charles C., and Henry P. Sims, Jr. *SuperLeadership: Leading Others to Lead Themselves.* New York: Prentice-Hall Press, 1989. 245 pp.

As the subtitle indicates, these authors say that the "superleader" is one who leads others to lead themselves. Their book is another one intended for the practitioner, and it focuses "on a new form of leadership in organizations—one designed to facilitate the self-leadership energy within each person." Interesting examples and checklists are used throughout; "profiles in superleadering" are at end of most chapters.

Nash, Michael. *Managing Organizational Performance.* San Francisco: Jossey-Bass, 1983. 361 pp.

Nash, an experienced consultant, feels that successful organizations take an integrated approach to the challenge of performance. Thus the purpose of his book "is to discuss organizational performance in all its various aspects from the strategic to the personal." The arrangement reflects this thesis: part 1 deals with planning, measuring, and controlling performance at the corporate level; part 2 discusses appraising and achieving performance from the divisional to the individual level; and part 3 wraps up the book by bringing together all the links in performance and management. His book is written for the thinking manager or the student as an alternative to standard textbooks. A bibliography of older material is at end.

Rosenbach, William E., and Robert L. Taylor, eds. *Contemporary Issues in Leadership.* 2d ed. Boulder, CO: Westview Press, 1989. 248 pp.

A collection of readings to help provide a broad and integrated understanding of the elusive concept of leadership. The editors arranged their 20 selections into four parts: understanding leadership; people and personalities; style, substance, and circumstance; vision—a focus on the future.

Another short selection of articles by these same editors (with Taylor as first editor) is *Leadership: Challenges for Today's Manager* (New York: Nichols Publishing, 1989, 207 pp.). In five parts, it seeks to stimulate thought and controversy among today's practicing managers.

Sayles, Leonard R. *Leadership: Managing in Real Organizations.* 2d ed. New York: McGraw-Hill, 1989. 310 pp.

Here is a first-rate book designed to help real managers who are struggling to transform the principles of good management into results in "the pressure-filled, fragmented, uncertain world which confronts" them. "The book's focus is middle management and the skills and conceptual understanding required to orchestrate five critical tasks, often simultaneously: monitoring work flows, motivating subordinates, negotiating lateral relationships, working the hierarchy, and introducing change in structure and technology." Chapters cover these and related topics such as asserting authority, gaining power, designing workable and valid controls. Sayles' book is based on firsthand accounts, previous research, published studies by other authors which he cites in footnotes.

Schein, Edgar H. *Organizational Culture and Leadership.* San Francisco: Jossey-Bass, 1991. 358 pp. paper.

Today organizational culture is receiving much more attention in the press, and so it seems useful to include one recent book on the subject here, even though it is not principally on leadership. The book's purpose is, first "to clarify the concept of 'organizational culture' and, second, to show how the problems of organizational leadership and organizational culture are basically intertwined." Divided into three parts, the first discusses what culture is and what it does. Then the focus shifts in part 2 to the origins and evolution of culture; part three deals with problems of cultural evolution and change. The last chapter is on leadership as managed culture change. References are at end.

Abstracting Services

Psychological Abstracts. Arlington, VA: American Psychological Association (monthly, with annual index). Also available online as *PsycINFO,* and on CD-ROM.

Abstracts of worldwide journal articles and also some reports and books in psychology and related disciplines. It is arranged by over 60 topics within 17 major subject areas, including: communication systems; experimental social psychology; applied psychology (management and management training; organizational behavior and job satisfaction; human factors engineering, etc.). Each issue has an index arranged by specific subject, and there is also a separately published and very detailed annual index. The online service contains references to more journal articles than does the print copy.

Sociological Abstracts. San Diego, CA. (5/yr.) Also available online.
Abstracts of international journal articles classified by more than 60 topics within 33 basic categories, including: social psychology; group interactions; complex organizations (management); social change and economic development; policy, planning, forecasting; environmental interactions; studies in poverty. Each issue includes a subject and author index, and there is a separately published annual cumulated index.

Dictionaries

Wolman, Benjamin B., comp. *Dictionary of Behavioral Science.* 2d ed. San Diego, CA: Academic Press, 1989. 370 pp.
Concise definitions of terms covering all areas of psychology and applied psychology and not just the behavioral sciences.

Periodicals

Articles in four of the journals described here are indexed in *Work Related Abstracts* (WRA) as well as in the other general indexes mentioned.

Group & Organization Studies. Newbury Park, CA: Sage Publications (quarterly).
This international journal publishes original research articles and reports that are practical in orientation and directed to group facilitators, trainers, educators, consultants, or managers in organizations. Special attention is given to studies with cross-cultural implications. Typical subjects include leadership, management development, group processes, communication in organizations, consultation, and organization development. Most articles are written by academicians and contain bibliographical references for further study. Indexed in ABI/I.

Human Relations. London and New York: Plenum Publishing Corporation (monthly).
An international "journal of studies toward the integration of the social sciences," with most of the papers written by academicians. This journal is sponsored by the Tavistock Institute of Human Relations, in London. Indexed in ABI/I, SSI, WRA.

Journal of Applied Behavioral Science. Greenwich, CT: Published for the NTL Institute for Applied Behavioral Science by JAI Press (quarterly).
An excellent selection of empirical studies on the theory and practice of planned change. Indexed in ABI/I, SSI, WRA.

Journal of Applied Psychology. Arlington, VA: American Psychological Association (bimonthly).
Short articles reporting on original investigations in many areas of applied psychology of interest to business persons as well as to psychologists and others. Articles tend to be quantitative and are usually written by academicians. Indexed in ABI/I, SSI, WRA.
   The American Psychological Association publishes a number of other journals,

including the *Journal of Personality and Social Psychology,* a monthly that contains original research in all areas of personality and social psychology. Indexed in SSI.

Journal of Organizational Behavior. Chichester, West Sussex, Eng.: Wiley (quarterly).

Called "the international journal of industrial, occupational, and organizational psychology and behavior," this journal aims to report and review the growing research in the organizational behavioral area throughout the world. The authors are usually academicians and each article contains a bibliography. Includes book reviews. Indexed in ABI/I.

Journal of Organizational Behavior Management. Binghamton, NY: Haworth Press (semi-annual).

This journal seeks original research articles that advance the knowledge of applied behavior analysis in work and organizational settings. Authors are usually academic persons. Includes occasional book reviews. Indexed in ABI/I.

The Leadership Quarterly. Greenwich, CT: JAI Press.

This is a new (1990) "international journal of political, social, and behavioral science" which hopes to bring "together diverse scholarship and practice to help better understand and improve the leader's performance and the effectiveness of the individuals, groups, organizations, and societies for which the leader, officer, manager, or administrator is responsible." Usually three or four well-researched articles are in each issue plus about two book reviews.

Organizational Behavior and Human Decision Processes. Duluth, MN: Academic Press (bimonthly).

"A journal of fundamental research and theory in applied psychology," with many of the articles based on the use of quantitative research. Indexed in ABI/I, BPI.

Organizational Dynamics. New York: American Management Association (quarterly).

Billed as "a quarterly review of organizational behavior for professional managers," each issue contains about five informative articles by recognized authorities, most of whom are academicians. Covers a wide range of interesting subjects, with all articles containing a short selected bibliography for persons wanting further information. Indexed in ABI/I, BPI.

Personnel Psychology. Houston, TX (quarterly).

This is a journal of applied research covering personnel psychology and organizational behavior. Excellent articles written primarily by academic authorities, often with bibliographical citations. Includes an especially good book review section on OB and human resources management. Indexed in ABI/I, BPI, WRA.

HISTORY OF MANAGEMENT THINKING

With the exception of only a few recent management classics, cited elsewhere in this chapter (Barnard, Drucker, McGregor, Sloan), no attempt is made in this work to include the important pioneering books on management and organizational behavior. The five historical compilations listed below will be useful for studying the history of management and its writers, especially those in the United States. The bibliographies in each are important for those persons interested in identifying and reading further in the works of any individual pioneer. A few of these early books are still in print, such as Herbert A. Simon's *Administrative Behavior* (3d ed., New York: Free Press, 1976, paper); and Frederick W. Taylor's *Principles of Scientific Management* (New York: Norton, 1967, paper). Other out-of-print books such as Mary Parker Follett's collected papers on *Dynamic Administration* (1941) can be purchased through the "Books on Demand" program at University Microfilms International in Ann Arbor, Michigan. These important classics can usually also be found and borrowed from any large library that has a good business collection.

Duncan, W. Jack. *Great Ideas in Management: Lessons from the Founders and Foundations of Managerial Practice.* San Francisco: Jossey-Bass, 1989. 286 pp.

Professor Duncan says: "The value of heritage in management is that knowing what the early writers had to say is the most efficient way to begin learning how to manage"—cf. p.xv. His book is for present and future managers to increase their knowledge of the past as a way of dealing with the uncertainties of the future. It is in five parts: exploring the seeds of modern management thought; merging the art and science of management; managing purposeful systems; managing the human factor; managing coordination and change. The last chapter presents a summary of the 10 lessons to be learned from classical management literature. A lengthy bibliography is at end.

George, Claude S., Jr. *The History of Management Thought.* 2d ed. Englewood Cliffs, NJ: Prentice-Hall, 1972. 223 pp. paper. Out of print.

A history of management thinking as it evolved from ancient civilizations up through the classical economists of the 19th century; then on to scientific management and early 20th century concepts; the contributions of various minor writers and critics; managerial philosophers such as Follett and Barnard; and concluding with the quantitative school. Includes a good "Selected Bibliography of Management Literature" (pp.189–216), arranged in chronological time periods so that it is convenient to find sources in any era.

The Golden Book of Management. New expanded ed. New York: AMACOM, 1984. 488 pp.

This is "a historical record of the life and work of more than one hundred pioneers." Part 1 is essentially a reprinting of the original *Golden Book* (1956), edited by Lyndall F. Urwick, which consisted usually of three-page descriptions of the accomplishments and publications plus a photograph of 70 of the world's greatest scientific management pioneers, selected by Col. Urwick and the Committee of Scientific Management. Part 2 expands the honor roll by adding 38 more recent "greats" selected by a committee to carry forward the strict criteria of the earlier work. This latter part was edited by William B. Wolf, and it contains similar data for each profile.

Pugh, Derek S., and David J. Hickson. *Writers on Organizations.* 4th ed. Newbury Park, CA: Sage Publications, 1989. 230 pp.

The authors see this as a resource book describing the contributions of prominent writers to the understanding of organizations and their management. The discussions about these 42 authors are arranged by their contribution to: the structure of organizations; the organization in its environment; the management of organizations; decision-making in organizations; people in organizations. In this latest edition many contributions in previous editions had to be dropped to make room for more recent contributions while keeping the book short.

Wren, Daniel A. *The Evolution of Management Thought.* 3d ed. New York: Wiley, 1987. 451 pp.

As the preface states, "this book traces the evolution of management thought from its earliest, informal days to the present by examining the backgrounds, ideas, and influence of the major contributors." In the process it also describes the various stages in this development and the interaction of management thinking with existing economic, social, and political values and institutions. This new edition refines and extends the earlier materials and incorporates recent research findings. It is arranged chronologically to cover: early management; the scientific management era; the social man era; the modern era. A selected bibliography is at end.

MANAGERIAL JOB DESCRIPTIONS

The three sources described here are now old and two are no longer in print. We continue to list them because there seems to be nothing recent that is comparable. They may still be of interest for job descriptions as of the 1970s, and can probably be located for use in a business library. For another outdated source see part 2 of *Organization Planning Manual* by Joseph J. Famularo (1979) described elsewhere in this chapter. See also the appendix in an annual survey on *Executive Compensation* prepared by Ernst & Young and described in Chapter 19. In addition, the executive search firm Heidrick and Struggles published a series of short booklets in the 1970s and early 1980s giving *Profiles of* . . . various top executives, such as a CEO, a chief financial officer, personnel executive, R & D executive, woman officer, black executive, and so forth.

Stessin, Lawrence, and Carl Heyel. *The Encyclopedia of Managerial Job Descriptions.* New York: Business Research Publications, 1981. 2 volumes (loose-leaf). Out of print.

This encyclopedia provides 374 actual functionally organized job descriptions from a wide variety of types and sizes of industries and companies (not identified by name) and running the gamut from directors and CEOs down through supervisory and staff/service functions. The descriptions are arranged within 7 functional sections. For each description one can usually find: nature and scope of the position, reporting relationships, principal and specific accountabilities. This may be a useful source for managers who are reviewing or revising their position analyses and position description programs and want to know how other organizations divided their top job responsibilities in the early 1980s.

Ulery, John D. *Job Descriptions in Manufacturing Industries.* New York: AMACOM, 1981. 161 pp.

Descriptions of 75 typical benchmark jobs for any manufacturing organization arranged within 10 categories, such as administration, controller's group, engineering, materials management. Information given for each includes purpose, duties and responsibilities, organizational relationships.

Wortman, Max S., Jr., and Joann Sperling. *Defining the Manager's Job: A Manual of Position Descriptions.* 2d ed. New York: AMACOM, 1975. 434 pp. Out of print.

Although now quite old, this manual on organization practices is still helpful for preparing and using managerial position descriptions. There are three parts: Part 1 is a survey of 136 organizations that already had position descriptions when this book was published; Part 2 provides information on techniques, methods, and procedures; Part 3, comprising over half of the book, contains descriptions of individual top management and middle management positions. A bibliography of older sources is at end.

FUNCTIONS OF DIRECTORS

Despite a continuing interest in the United States in the changing role of the corporate director, there have been relatively few books published in the past five years to reflect these developments. On the other hand, many articles are being written all the time on various aspects of the role of directors, and so it may be worth a reminder to use the periodical indexes described in Chapter 2, especially *Business Periodicals Index,* and/or the online index, *ABI/INFORM.*

Handbooks

Mattar, Edward P., III, and Michael Ball, eds. *Handbook for Corporate Directors.* New York: McGraw-Hill, 1985. 1 volume (various pagings).

A first-stop source for directors and managers who may need a wide range of information about board composition, organization, rules, procedures, committees, policy-making, functions, relationships, responsibilities, future directors, and more. Over 60 presidents, professors, lawyers, and other experts have contributed these short chapters which the editors have arranged within 15 sections.

Books

Anderson, Charles A., and Robert N. Anthony. *The New Corporate Directors: Insights for Board Members and Executives.* New York: Wiley, 1986. 246 pp.

Two experienced board members offer here their ideas and concepts which they recommend other directors think about in connection with their own responsibilities. These include such functions as nominating, compensation, audit, and finance. The authors address these concepts in the context of real issues by having one or two short cases with most chapters. A chapter at end discusses boards in non-profit organizations.

Braiotta, Louis, Jr., and A. A. Sommer, Jr. *The Essential Guide to Effective Corporate Board Committees.* Englewood Cliffs, NJ: Prentice-Hall, 1987. 178 pp.

A concise guide that seeks to provide guidance to corporate board members on how to make board committees more effective. The second of its three parts contains chapters discussing each of seven types of committees. Part 1 is an introduction on board committees and on the corporate environment; part 3 covers guidelines for preparing committee reports. Appendixes include the text of several related acts, and business conduct guidelines. "Suggested References" are at end of chapters.

Conference Board. *Corporate Directors' Compensation.* New York (annual). This is a short report based on an annual survey of almost 900 U.S. corporations which analyzes directors' compensation and benefits both by industry and by size of company. It is issued in the Conference Board's *Report* series, with the 1991 survey issued as Number 988.

This publisher has also issued other surveys and reports on corporate directors. Their *Report No. 940* was on "Membership and Organization of Corporate Boards" (1990, 40 pp.). Formerly the compensation surveys were issued as their *Corporate Directorship Practices* reports, which were research reports focusing on company policies and practices concerning board committees, such as "The Audit Committee" (1979), "The Nominating Committee and the Director Selection Process" (1981), "The Planning Committee" (1981), "Board Committees in European Companies" (1986). These were usually written either by Jeremy Bacon or James K. Brown. In 1985 the Conference Board's *Executive Bulletin No. 29* discussed "The Legal Vulnerability of Corporate Directors."

The Conference Board in Canada publishes related studies, and several recent ones on *Canadian Directorship Practices* had subtitles: *A Profile 1990* (Report 51-90) and *Compensation of Boards of Directors* (7th ed., 1987, 57 pp., Report 21-87).

Knepper, William E., and Dan A. Bailey. *Liability of Corporate Officers and Directors.* 4th ed., Charlottesville, VA: Michie Company, 1988. 950 pp. And a 1989 Supplement in pocket.
A typical law book covering such topics as duties and liabilities of directors; also chapters on securities laws, disclosure, legal representation, liability insurance. Footnote references to legal citations are on about every page; bibliographic references are at end of chapters.

Lorsch, Jay W., and Elizabeth MacIver. *Pawns or Potentates: The Reality of America's Corporate Boards.* Boston: Harvard Business School Press, 1989. 200 pp.
This is an examination of board governance reality which is based on a questionnaire survey of more than 900 outside directors in 400 companies, and interviews with a much smaller group. The authors start with chapters describing directors and examining power constraints they face. They then move on to studying in turn: the board at work; the balance of power; crisis management; the need to change.

Mace, Myles L. *Directors: Myth and Reality.* [Rev. ed.] Boston: Harvard Business School Press, 1986. 213 pp. paper.
A classic study, published in 1971, is now reprinted in the "Harvard Business School Classics" series with a new preface and an index. It reports on field research Professor Mace conducted in the late 1960s to measure what he felt was the "considerable gap between what directors in fact do and what the business literature said they should do." His book is written for business persons and includes quotes from the many interviews he conducted with executives and with board members of both public and family corporations. The findings are still relevant today.

Waldo, Charles N. *Boards of Directors: Their Changing Roles, Structure, and Information Needs.* Westport, CT: Quorum Books, 1985. 213 pp.
"A key aim of this book is to report on the timeliness, adequacy, and use of financial and other kinds of operating information presently being supplied to the boards of

directors of today's major U.S. corporations." This is covered in chapters 7–11, with chapter 8 describing an in-depth study of director information-providing practices in large manufacturing companies, and chapter 11 consisting of "an information package for directors." The first 6 chapters discuss functions, roles, composition, and legal responsibilities of boards, as well as the changes in use of committees. A bibliography is at end of book.

Two executive search firms publish brief findings of annual surveys on boards of directors. These are: *The Changing Board* (Chicago: Heidrick and Struggles), which consists of tables and brief text based on a survey of directors of Fortune's largest companies; and *Boards of Directors: Annual Study* (New York: Korn/Ferry International). This latter firm also issues separate surveys on U.K. and on Australian boards.

Periodicals

Directors & Boards. New York: Investment Dealers' Digest, Inc. (quarterly).
With a new publisher and new editor, the focus of this quarterly has changed. Each issue is now called "Chairman's Agenda", and it consists of short articles on one topic, such as "Being a Global Leader," or "Governing for Shareholder Value." It calls itself an international journal of leadership and governance directed to the interest of corporate boards and senior management. Indexed in ABI/I, TI.

ENTREPRENEURSHIP/SMALL BUSINESS MANAGEMENT

An increasing number of business persons are expressing interest in learning about entrepreneurship and the management of small firms, and there is also a noticeable trend among some established executives to opt for a second career by striking out on their own. Most business schools now offer courses to meet this demand. There are even several new journals that have come into existence to meet this mounting interest in current sources devoted solely to discussing the problems and interests of new and small business. Thus it is important to know about books, bibliographies, and periodicals that may help entrepreneurs and small business persons. This list does not include the numerous books on "how to make a million"; it is admittedly short, but the bibliographies will suggest further sources of information. Several guides to venture capital companies are listed in Chapter 14.

The Entrepreneur and New Business Ventures

Cohen, William A. *The Entrepreneur and Small Business Problem Solver.* 2d ed. New York: Wiley, 1990. 565 pp. paper.
Subtitled "an encyclopedic reference and guide," this is a one-book source that is intended to answer the most frequently asked questions on starting or expanding your own small business or entrepreneurial project. Its 20 chapters are arranged within 3 parts: financial problem solving (chapters cover such topics as legal aspects, sources of capital and how to get a loan, insurance, leasing or buying equipment, record keeping); marketing problem solving (focusing on how to find and introduce a new product, pricing, advertising, personal selling, how to make money with trade shows, and more); management problem solving (including chapters on recruiting

employees, protecting your idea, how computers can help). Specific examples, forms, checklists are used throughout. Appendixes include directories of related organizations and contacts, a list of SBICs, and a sample business plan.

Mr. Cohen has updated and expanded the second part of this book covering marketing and published it as *The Entrepreneur and Small Business Marketing Problem Solver* (Wiley, 1991, 274 pp., paper).

Dible, Donald M. *Up Your Own Organization! A Handbook for Today's Entrepreneur.* New and Rev. Ed. by Jeannine Marschner. Reston, VA: Reston Publishing Company, 1986. 423 pp. paper. A revision is in progress.

A readable, practical handbook on how to start and finance a new business, in three steps: first, a recognition and objective evaluation of your personal needs and abilities, including the identification of your marketable product and/or service; then a discussion of the preparation of a business plan for the attainment of your goal; and finally, a review of the financial resources necessary to make that plan a reality. This latter section is called "Ali Baba and the Forty Money Sources." Useful data in appendixes includes a recommended reading list, an annotated list of directories and other information sources, lists of venture capital companies and SBICs, several business start-up checklists.

Gladstone, David J. *Venture Capital Handbook.* New and Rev. Englewood Cliffs, NJ: Prentice-Hall, 1988. 350 pp. paper.

Here is a guide that covers the entire process of raising venture capital "from the presentation of the proposal, through the negotiations, the commitment letters, the legal closings, and the due diligence, to the exit by the venture capital company, when the entrepreneur is left to own it all." Mr. Gladstone says it is written from the perspective of how he would react if he were an entrepreneur approaching a venture firm. An appendix contains sample documents and forms, a list of venture capital companies that belong to the NVCA and NASBIC, and a short glossary. Gladstone is a venture capitalist who has reviewed thousands of venture capital proposals in the course of his career.

Hisrich, Robert D., and Michael P. Peters. *Entrepreneurship: Starting, Developing, and Managing a New Enterprise.* 2d ed. Homewood, IL: Irwin, 1992. 641 pp.

The focus in this book is on understanding the entrepreneur and the entrepreneurial process because, these authors say, the entrepreneur is the person who has all the responsibility for the development, growth, and survival of a new business as well as the risks and rewards. They start by talking about the entrepreneurial perspective. With this as background, they examine in turn: starting a new venture and developing the business (including chapters on business, marketing, financial, and organizational plans); financing a new venture; managing the new venture; and lastly, special issues for entrepreneurs (legal, franchising and direct marketing, intrepreneurship, international business). Each chapter begins with the profile of an entrepreneur. Examples are used throughout the book; annotated lists of selected reading are at end of chapters. A glossary is at end of book.

In 1991 Business One/Irwin published essentially the same book as *On Your Own: How to Start, Develop, and Manage a New Business,* with this book targeted for the professional rather than for the student.

McGarty, Terrence P. *Business Plans That Win Venture Capital.* New York: Wiley, 1989. 368 pp.

"The business plan is the cornerstone of any successful business venture" says Ms. McGarty who has had long-time experience advising start-up companies on business planning processes. She directs her book toward the entrepreneur. Part 2 covers each component of the plan: the concept; the market; competition; the development plan; ongoing operations and management; financial portions. Part 1 is an overview and an outline of the business plan; the last part deals with financing the firm after the plan is completed. A sample business plan is at end along with a short list of business management books.

Merrill, Ronald E., and Henry D. Sedgwick. *The New Venture Handbook.* New York: American Management Association, 1987. 356 pp.

Written by entrepreneurs for entrepreneurs, these authors rather ambitiously state in their subtitle that this book has "everything you need to know to start and run your own business." Have they succeeded? The focus is primarily on the start-up process—planning the business and seeing it through its first few years of operation. Chapters cover such topics as building a team, finding your niche, the business plan; chapters 6–11 deal with specific management functions such as marketing. Examples are interspersed along with checklists and exercises. A glossary and a short annotated bibliography of suggested readings are at end.

O'Hara, Patrick D. *The Total Business Plan: How to Write, Rewrite, and Revise.* New York: Wiley, 1990. 288 pp.

Here is another guide to the total business planning process. "It includes market planning, strategizing, research sources, pricing concepts, as well as specific questions entrepreneurs must ask themselves to prepare for presenting the resulting plan to its targeted audience, be it management, a lender, or the investment community." Includes chapters on understanding and evaluating money sources, and on planning and writing the business plan, with outlines for a suggested business and marketing plan.

Timmons, Jeffry A. *New Venture Creation: Entrepreneurship in the 1990s.* 3d ed. Homewood, IL: Irwin, 1990. 677 pp. paper.

An information-packed book "about the actual process of getting a new venture started, growing the venture, successfully harvesting it, and starting again." It uses text, case studies, and hands-on experience to guide students or entrepreneurs through the process, and it is based on the author's considerable research, experience, and teaching in this field. The first three of its six parts discuss the driving forces of entrepreneurship (opportunity recognition, the team, and resource requirements including developing the business plan). The next two parts provide details on financial and "start-up and after" strategies; while the last part aims to help in "crafting a personal entrepreneurial strategy." At end are useful appendixes and an annotated bibliography.

Professor Timmons has more recently coauthored a book (with William D. Bygrave) on *Venture Capital at the Crossroads* (Boston: Harvard Business School Press, 1992, 356 pp.).

Vesper, Karl H. *New Venture Strategies.* Rev. ed. Englewood Cliffs, NJ: Prentice-Hall, 1990. 356 pp. paper.

Vesper concentrates on entrepreneurial strategies—both personal and commercial—which can be used to embark on new business ventures effectively. His frequent use of true-life experiences makes for interesting reading. Topics discussed are: success and failure factors; career departure points; sequences in startup;

sources of and evaluating venture ideas; competitive entry wedges; acquisition finding and dealing. Appendixes discuss corporate venturing and the chemistry of entrepreneurship. A bibliography is at end.

To be published early in 1993 is Vesper's latest book, *New Venture Mechanics*
(Prentice-Hall, 1993, 380 pp., paper). This has some similarities to the book above
but pays more attention to how venture ideas are refined, developed, protected, and
implemented. It also contains numerous examples from real life; an outline and
example of a business plan is at end.

Starting and Managing Small or Growing Businesses

Baumback, Clifford M. *How to Organize and Operate a Small Business.* 8th
ed. Englewood Cliffs, NJ: Prentice-Hall, 1988. 578 pp.

This is the latest edition of one of the better, standard texts covering: making the
decision (the role of small business in the economy, the problems and risks, and the
decision about self-employment); getting started; operating the business (with separate sections devoted to marketing, producing, financing and financial management); regulations; and taxes. A model business plan is used throughout to illustrate
each step. Short "cases in point" are with each chapter, and a few longer cases are at
end. The appendix contains a "Checklist for Organizing and Operating a Small
Business."

Professor Baumback has also published (with Joseph R. Mancuso) a selection of
36 articles by authoritative writers on *Entrepreneurship and Venture Management*
(Prentice-Hall, 1987, 452 pp., paper).

Burstiner, Irving. *The Small Business Handbook: A Comprehensive Guide to
Starting and Running Your Own Business.* Rev. ed. Englewood Cliffs, NJ:
Prentice-Hall, 1989. 356 pp. paper.

Designed as an informative, comprehensive, and nontechnical guide to profitable
small business management for the new or future entrepreneur. Its 26 chapters in 9
parts cover basic functions such as production, marketing, finance, as well as those
discussing the preliminaries of making the decision to start your own business, start-
up issues, managing the organization after it is started, and finally improving the
new business operation. Short bibliographies with each chapter are useful for persons wanting further information.

Edmunds, Stahrl W. *Performance Measures for Growing Businesses.* New
York: Van Nostrand Reinhold, 1982. 247 pp.

"A practical guide to small business management," which provides fairly simple
performance measures that will help small business persons "to improve their feedback control loop, so they know early what corrective actions to take for successful
operations." Included are chapters on performance measures for just about every
aspect of business management in a growing firm (profit, cash control, market
performance, management capacity, taxation, etc.).

Hancock, William A. *The Small Business Legal Advisor.* New York: McGraw-
Hill, 1982. 258 pp.

Written as an informal guide and not as a substitute for legal advice, Hancock
explains how lawyers can assist the small business executive, what laws are relevant
to starting and running a small business, and how one can avoid legal pitfalls.

Handbook of Management for the Growing Business. Ed. by Carl Heyel and
Belden Menkus. New York: Van Nostrand Reinhold, 1986. 586 pp.

This handbook is intended for owners/managers of growing businesses who have reached the stage where informal management must be replaced with more advanced-practice management concepts and techniques. Each of the 10 sections of this "refresher" covers one broad management function (such as marketing, production, human resources), and each of its 38 chapters is written by a specialist in the field. A few recommended sources for further information are at end of chapters.

Kuriloff, Arthur H., and John M. Hemphill, Jr. *Starting and Managing the Small Business.* 2d ed. New York: McGraw-Hill, 1988. 663 pp.

Designed to prepare people who want to start and run their own business with "a rigorous plan" without their having had to take a course in business. The text follows the flow of the business process. The authors start with a section on "what you should bring to your business" (personal factors and sound ideas). They follow this with 5 sections covering: understanding marketing for your small business; discussions of retail, service and manufacturing businesses; achieving proactive financial management; buying a business opportunity (includes chapters on franchising and on key legal matters); some crucial management functions such as business risk, personnel management. At end are several cases and a glossary; also appendixes containing an outline of a business plan, examples of a successful plan (prospectus), examples of basic planning for small business. Work sheets (that can become part of the business plan) and useful annotated bibliographies accompany each chapter.

Lasser (J.K.) Tax Institute. *How to Run a Small Business.* 6th ed. New York: McGraw-Hill, 1989. 334 pp.

A popular guide to small business operations, newly revised and updated and meant both for persons planning a new enterprise and those operating an existing business. It provides a broad background of information, from deciding on a location to operating an efficient plant. It discusses how to deal with such problems as accounting and record systems, computers, extending credit, doing business with the government, insurance, fraud, and theft. Chapters also cover special problems of retailers, wholesalers, mail-order operations, service firms, and franchises.

Longenecker, Justin G., and Carlos W. Moore. *Small Business Management: An Entrepreneurial Emphasis.* 8th ed. Cincinnati: South-Western, 1991. 828, [48] pp.

Another thoroughly rewritten and updated book with a strong emphasis on entrepreneurial opportunities and new venture activities needed for successful small business operations. It is arranged in 7 sections to cover: the nature of small business; exploring entrepreneurial alternatives; launching a new venture (including chapters on the business and marketing plans); small business marketing (with a chapter on distribution channels and international markets); managing small business operations; financial and administrative controls; social and legal environment. Colorful illustrations, diagrams, exhibits appear throughout, along with "Small Business in Action" taken from experiences of real-world entrepreneurs and set off in green boxes. Annotated references and two brief case incidents are with each chapter; at end are further cases and a glossary.

Megginson, Leon C., Charles R. Scott and William L. Megginson. *Successful Small Business Management.* 6th ed. Boston: Irwin, 1991. 851 pp.

These authors designed their text to provide a thorough yet simple and readable introduction for persons wanting to own or manage a small business. This latest revised and updated edition covers new trends and emerging issues of importance to small business such as new computerized technology of potential benefit to small business management. Its 7 sections deal with: the challenge of owning and managing a small business; planning and organizing a business; selecting and leading employees; operating the business; marketing goods and services; financial planning and control; providing present and future security for the business (including business laws, ethics, and taxes). Frequent use of checklists, figures, and forms add to the value of this text. Suggested readings are at end of chapters; cases are at end of each section. Appendixes include checklists for choosing a type of business, handling union organizing, a sample business plan, a management self-evaluation; also at end are short glossaries of business and computer terms.

Pickle, Hal B., and Royce L. Abrahamson. *Small Business Management.* 5th ed. New York: Wiley, 1990. 702, 10 pp.

Yet another well-established, recently revised textbook, these authors say their approach is practice-oriented and the writing style informal. It is written both for students and prospective small business entrepreneurs or operators. The material is in 6 parts to cover: entrepreneurship, small business ownership, and franchising; establishing the firm; managing the small business; management information and merchandise control; marketing the product or service; the government and small business. Expanded coverage is given to the "business plan," with one full chapter plus guidelines and questions with each chapter and in an appendix. Boxed "entrepreneur profiles" and "small business briefs" are scattered throughout. Two case incidents are with each chapter; at end are: a glossary of key words, lists of associations, private sector resources, SBA offices and publications.

Resnik, Paul. *The Small Business Bible: The Make-or-Break Factors for Survival and Success.* New York: Wiley, 1988. 230 pp.

In this book for practitioners, Resnik identifies and examines 10 make-or-break requirements for success in managing your business. Thus it is useful reading for owners/managers as supplementary to a basic small business text. He says it "is as much a 'what-to and why' book as a 'how to' book. The emphasis is on doing a handful of basic, critical things well, rather than doing everything with indiscriminate energy." Interspersed throughout this book are useful checklists. Suggestions for further reading (annotated) are at end.

The only recent book I am familiar with that focuses on management in a medium-sized firm is *To Flourish Among Giants: Creative Management for Mid-Sized Firms* by Robert C. Kuhn (New York: Wiley, 1985, 494 pp.). For several books on the franchising and mail order businesses refer to Chapter 18.

Books on Managing Basic Functions in Small Businesses

It is not possible here to cover the many books written on various functional aspects of small business management; for these you are urged to consult bibliographies, several of which are listed in the next section. What follows are merely a few possible titles which I have noted but not evaluated (unless you find a chapter reference to a description elsewhere in this book). In the case of several older titles, these seem to be the latest books published and are still in print as of 1990.

Finance

Bond, Cecil J. *Credit and Collection for Your Small Business.* Blue Ridge Summit, PA: Liberty House, 1989. 184 pp. paper.

Carey, Omer L., and Dean Olson. *Financial Tools for Small Business.* Reston, VA: Reston Publishing Co., 1983. 269 pp.

Day, Theodore et al. *Taxes, Financial Policy, and Small Business.* Lexington, MA: Lexington Books, 1985. 167 pp.

Horvitz, Paul M., and R. Richardson Pettit, eds. *Small Business Finance.* Greenwich, CT: JAI Press, 1984. 2 volumes. Vol.1 includes an annotated bibliography on small business financing.

Walker, Ernest W., and J. William Petty II. *Financial Management of the Small Firm.* 2d ed. Englewood Cliffs, NJ: Prentice-Hall, 1986. 465 pp. See listing in Chapter 14.

Marketing

Breen, George E., and Albert B. Blankenship. *Do-It-Yourself Marketing Research.* 3d ed. New York: McGraw-Hill, 1989. 261 pp. See listing in Chapter 18.

Davidson, Jeffrey P. *The Marketing Sourcebook for Small Business.* New York: Wiley, 1989. 325 pp.

Davis, Robert T., and F. Gordon Smith. *Marketing in Emerging Companies.* Reading, MA: Addison-Wesley, 1984. 159 pp.

Gordon, John S., and Jack R. Arnold. *Profitable Exporting: A Complete Guide to Marketing Your Products Abroad.* New York: Wiley, 1988. 358 pp. See listing in Chapter 16, with two other guides mentioned in its annotation.

Hayes, Rick S., and Gregory B. Elmore. *Marketing for Your Growing Business.* New York: Ronald Press, 1985. 283 pp.

Holtz, Herman R. *The Secrets of Practical Marketing for Small Business.* Englewood Cliffs, NJ: Prentice-Hall, 1982. 192 pp.

Rice, Craig S. *Marketing Planning Strategies: A Guide for Small or Mid-sized Companies.* Chicago: Dartnell Corporation, 1984. 436 pp.

Smith, Brian R. *Successful Marketing for Small Business.* Brattleboro, VT: Lewis Publishing Co., 1984. 237 pp.

Personnel

Arthur, Diane. *Managing Human Resources in Small and Mid-Sized Companies.* New York: AMACOM, 1987. 278 pp.

Cohn, Theodore, and Roy A. Lindberg. *Practical Personnel Policies for Small Business.* New York: Van Nostrand Reinhold, 1984. 216 pp.

Slimmon, Robert F. *Successful Pension Design for Small- and Medium-Sized Businesses.* 2d ed. Englewood Cliffs, NJ: Prentice-Hall, 1987. 440 pp.

Planning

Brandt, Steven C. *Strategic Planning in Emerging Companies*. Reading, MA: Addison-Wesley, 1981. 187 pp.

Curtis, David A. *Strategic Planning for Smaller Business: Improving Performance & Personal Reward*. Lexington, MA: Lexington Books, 1983. 197 pp.

Lane, Marc J. *Legal Handbook for Small Business*. Rev. ed. New York: AMACOM, 1989. 255 pp. See listing in Chapter 9.

Linneman, Robert E. *Shirt-Sleeve Approach to Long-Range Planning for the Smaller, Growing Corporation*. Englewood Cliffs, NJ: Prentice-Hall, 1980. 290 pp.

Production

Messner, William A. *Profitable Purchasing Management: A Guide for Small Business Owners/Managers*. New York: AMACOM, 1982. 272 pp. See listing in Chapter 20.

Murdick, Robert. *Production-Operations Management for Small Business*. Worthington, OH: Publishing Horizons, 1981. 150 pp. paper.

Bibliographies and Resource Books

Christy, Ron, and Billy M. Jones. *The Complete Information Bank for Entrepreneurs and Small Business Managers*. 2d ed. New York: American Management Association, 1988. 340 pp.

An annotated bibliography in 8 sections. Sections 1–3 contain annotated lists of books: for the entrepreneur (in five categories); for the small business manager (arranged in 13 categories, such as management, finance and accounting, franchising, marketing/advertising/sales); periodicals. Sections 4–8 cover: audio-visual materials; computer systems for small companies; organizations and associations; academic programs; government information and venture capital firms (including a directory of SBICs as well). There are author/title/subject indexes.

London Business School. *Small Business Bibliography*. 2d ed. London: Institute of Small Business Management & Library, London Business School, 1983. 373 pp. And annual updates.

A list (not annotated) of books, pamphlets, articles, theses, and other literature on small business. It is arranged within about 14 subject categories, e.g. entrepreneurship, starting new businesses, financing, taxation, technology and innovation. One section relates specifically to the small firm and its environment in the United Kingdom.

Ryans, Cynthia C. *Small Business: An Information Sourcebook*. Phoenix, AZ: Oryx Press, 1987. 286 pp. (Oryx Sourcebook in Business and Management).

More useful than the bibliography above because of its annotations, this is a well-selected, descriptive list of books published through 1986 on all aspects of starting and operating a small business. It is arranged in 38 categories ranging from accounting to women in business; it seems to cover all important aspects such as planning, finance, production, marketing, data processing, salaries. Adding to its value is a useful general "Core Library Collection" which describes basic reference sources for a small firm's library, such as indexes, dictionaries, directories, handbooks, and periodicals. Pertinent government offices are listed at end along with several indexes to this bibliography and a directory of publishers. Note that this is now rather out of date.

Small Business Sourcebook. Detroit: Gale Research, Inc. 2 volumes (annual). Part 1 of this two-part guide describes sources and services for each of over 200 popular small businesses such as bowling alleys, camera shops, computer stores. For each it may list start-up information, pertinent associations, trade periodicals, reference works, statistical sources, sources of supply, trade shows and conventions, franchises, consultants, educational programs. Part 2 identifies general types of organizations and publications of interest to small business owners, such as government agencies, associations, universities, venture capital firms, incubator centers, some of which are arranged geographically. At end are lists of a few published handbooks, directories, periodicals, indexes, and an index to both volumes. Comprehensive but of use only as a starting point for the uninitiated.

U.S. Small Business Administration. *The Small Business Directory.* Washington, DC: U.S. Government Printing Office, 1990. 5 pp. Formerly the SBA published many booklets, aids, and bibliographies for the small business person. Today their publishing program is almost nonexistent. This is a list of the few booklets, aids, and videotapes still available at a nominal fee in such areas as financial management, management and planning, marketing, personnel management.

Several useful directories of venture capital companies are described in Chapter 14.

Statistics

Financial Research Associates. *Financial Studies of the Small Business.* Winter Park, FL. (annual, loose-leaf). This loose-leaf annual consists of financial and operating ratios for about 50 types of businesses, based on 25,000 financial statements of firms with capitalization under $1,000,000. The ratios are given for four asset size categories. A separate sales volume section contains breakdown of sales and income ratios for four sales size categories; also a section contains ratios based only on the 25% most profitable firms. At end is a five-year trend of figures by category.

NFIB Foundation. *Quarterly Economic Report for Small Business.* Washington, DC. A quarterly report based on survey data obtained from National Federation of Independent Business members, San Mateo, CA. Covers brief discussion with some statistics on credit conditions, prices, compensation, sales, earnings, employment, inventory, capital expenditures, list of the most important problems.

Ranked Lists of Fastest-Growing Companies

Business Month. "The Fastest 100: America's Top Growth Companies." (May 1990). Ranks publicly held companies by sales gains over past four years.

Business Week. "The Best Small Companies." (annual, third or fourth May issue). A ranking of the 100 best small growth companies using three criteria.

FW: Financial World. "The FW Growth 500." (annual, first August issue).
Companies are ranked by EPS growth over five years.

Forbes. "The 200 Best Small Companies in America." (annual, first November issue).
Ranking is by a five-year average of return on equity.

INC. "INC 100." (annual, May issue).
Ranks the 100 fastest growing small public companies by sales growth over five years. Their "INC 500" (December) ranks America's fastest-growing private companies.

Periodicals

Business Age. Milwaukee, WI: Business Trends Communications Corporation (monthly).
Designed to help small business owners and managers (with staffs of from 1 to 100 employees) make better day-to-day business decisions by providing practical articles on all aspects of small business management. Includes short book reviews and other regular columns.

D&B Reports. Murray Hill, NJ: Dun & Bradstreet Credit Services (bimonthly).
Billed as "the Dun & Bradstreet magazine for small business management," each issue usually contains 5 or 6 short, interesting articles plus one or two feature reports on the economy, economic indicators, office technology, Washington, taxes, export/import, sales/marketing. There is also a four-page inserted newsletter called "Dun & Bradstreet Looks at Business" which often includes useful current statistics on business expectations, business starts, business failures, and other brief data of interest to small business. Indexed in BPI.

Entrepreneurship: Theory and Practice. Waco, TX: Hankamer School of Business, Baylor University (quarterly).
Formerly published as the *American Journal of Small Business,* this quarterly continues to publish short, scholarly articles in all areas of entrepreneurship, small business, and family business. Authors are usually academic persons; short bibliographies usually accompany each article. This is an official journal of the United States Association for Small Business and Entrepreneurship. Indexed in ABI/I, BPI, PAIS, TI.

INC. Boston (monthly).
A popular monthly intended for small and growing companies, with practical articles covering a wide range of pertinent topics, interesting stories of successful entrepreneurs, and profiles of companies. Each issue has regular columns; also a table at end of "Initial Public Offerings," and a chart comparing the INC market index with other indexes. Annual features include: "The INC 100" (May), a ranked list of the 100 fastest growing small public companies; "The INC 500" (December), ranking the fastest-growing private companies; "The Most Entrepreneurial Cities in America" (March); "Report on the States" (October) which rates the states on several measures of growth; "The Best-Managed Franchises in America" (October). This monthly is indexed in ABI/I, BPI, TI; available full-text on BRS, DATA-STAR, DIALOG, DOW JONES, MEAD/NEXIS.

Journal of Business Venturing. New York: Elsevier Science Publishing Company (quarterly).

This journal is intended as a forum for articles on "empirical, and rigorously developed theoretical findings that advance our knowledge in four key areas: entrepreneurship, new business development, industry evolution, and technology management." It is published in cooperation with the Snider Entrepreneurial Center, University of Pennsylvania and the Center for Entrepreneurial Studies, New York University. Five or so refereed articles per issue, each usually written by academicians and each containing bibliographical references for further reading. Indexed in ABI/I.

Journal of Small Business Management. Morgantown, WV: Bureau of Business Research, West Virginia University (quarterly).

Each issue contains 7 or 8 short articles by academicians on small business management topics of current professional interest worldwide. It includes also a bibliographic "Resources" section and book reviews. This quarterly is sponsored by the International Council for Small Business and the Small Business Institute Directors' Association, as well as by West Virginia University. Indexed in ABI/I, BPI, PAIS.

A quarterly that focuses on refereed articles, both theoretical and empirical, on effective policies and management of small business throughout the world is *International Small Business Journal* (Wilmslow, Cheshire, Eng.: Woodcock Publications).

Associations

American Federation of Small Business, 407 S. Dearborn Street, Chicago, IL 60605.

International Council for Small Business, c/o Institute of Entrepreneurial Studies, 3674 Lindell Blvd., St. Louis University, St. Louis, MO 63108.

National Federation of Independent Business, 150 West Twentieth Avenue, San Mateo, CA 94403.

National Small Business United, 1155 15th Street, N.W., Washington, DC 20005.

United States Association for Small Business and Entrepreneurship (U.S. affiliate of ICSB), c/o SBDC, 905 University of Wisconsin-Madison, Madison, WI 53706.

11

MANAGEMENT OF PUBLIC AND NONPROFIT ORGANIZATIONS

General Books – Arts Administration – Educational Administration – Health Care Administration – Public Administration – Urban Administration

Organizations of all kinds have been facing new and more complex problems and uncertainties during the past few years due to many of the same factors that make living more complicated today. This has been true particularly for organizations in the nonprofit sector. The health care industry, for instance, has been growing by leaps and bounds. Educational, welfare, arts, government, and urban agencies–all these and many other organizations are trying to cope with almost insurmountable problems that only the most highly qualified managers and policy makers can hope to deal with successfully. Most business schools have responded to this need for better trained managers by introducing courses and programs to give students the skills necessary in these specialized areas. Some schools have even changed their names from "School of Business Administration" to "School of Management" or "College of Business and Administration" to describe more accurately the scope of the programs offered.

The literature has kept pace with this new concern. Many recent texts on organization and management now include a discussion of factors important for the management of both business and nonbusiness organizations. See, for example in Chapter 10, the management and organization books by Donnelly et al., Gibson et al., and Kast; the planning and strategy books by Famularo, McCarthy, and Steiner et al.; and the book by Davis on human behavior. There may be books in each functional area that are pertinent to nonbusiness organizations; see especially the sections covering "Accounting for Governmental and Nonprofit Organizations" in Chapter 12 and "Marketing in Nonprofit Organizations" in Chapter 18.

It is not possible in a book of business information sources to give good coverage to all of this material, but since these new areas of management are so important today, this short chapter is included to call attention to a few pertinent reference sources. These are admittedly spotty and incomplete and are meant merely to identify a handful of books, bibliographies, indexes, abstracts, and periodicals that the reader can use as a basis for pursuing further research in a library that collects material in these and other areas of managing public and nonprofit organizations.

GENERAL BOOKS

Handbooks

Connors, Tracy D., ed. *The Nonprofit Organization Handbook.* New York: McGraw-Hill, 1980. 1 volume (various pagings).

This is the first comprehensive volume devoted exclusively to providing guidelines for improved management in the important area of voluntary-action nonprofit organizations (NPOs). It was prepared under the editorship of an experienced NPO practitioner and educator with the help of 27 experts who wrote its 43 chapters. It covers the following essential areas of management and operations: organization and corporate principles; leadership, management, and control; human resources management; sources of revenue; public relations and communications; fiscal management and administration. This handbook is meant more for reference than for reading from cover-to-cover; suggestions for further reading are with some chapters. This is still useful as background information but it does not reflect changes and new developments in the 1980s.

Oleck, Howard L. *Nonprofit Corporations, Organizations, and Associations.* 5th ed. Englewood Cliffs, NJ: Prentice-Hall, 1988. 1,274 pp.

Written by a lawyer/law professor, this is the revision of a lengthy one-volume reference guide concentrating on the law and operation of nonprofit enterprises of all kinds. A sampling of the many topics covered gives a good idea of its comprehensive scope: nature, types and forms, purpose, bylaws, meetings, committees, directors, trustees, fund raising, lobbying, lawsuits, management techniques, tax exemptions, accounting, trade associations, dissolution, parliamentary law, and more. There is frequent use of forms and also many citations to regulations and cases.

Books

Bryce, Herrington J. *Financial & Strategic Management for Nonprofit Organizations.* 2d ed. Englewood Cliffs, NJ: Prentice-Hall, 1992. 625 pp.

This book aims "to give the reader the perspective and vision to participate successfully in the management of a nonprofit organization either as an employed manager, a trustee, or a corporate volunteer." Its four parts are organized around what the author calls the Four M's—mission, marketing, money, and management. Examples throughout are drawn from a wide scope of nonprofits. Suggested readings are at end of most chapters. The author says his book could be used both as a college level text and as a desk reference.

Drucker, Peter F. *Managing the Nonprofit Organization: Principles and Practices.* New York: HarperCollins, 1990. 235 pp.

Here Mr. Drucker addresses the needs of managers for guidelines and expert advice on how to effectively manage their nonprofit organizations. In his direct and readable style, he talks about the tasks, responsibilities, and practices that must be followed in order to do this. He gives examples and explanations on such topics as mission, goals, leadership, decision making, performance, people development, and he includes interviews with 9 experts that address key issues in the nonprofit sector. As with almost everything Drucker writes, this is a concise, thought-provoking book that will be well read.

Firstenberg, Paul B. *Managing for Profit in the Nonprofit World.* New York: Foundation Center, 1986. 253 pp. paper.

Firstenberg draws on his extensive experience in nonprofit institutions to demonstrate how state-of-the-art management techniques used in successful for-profit enterprises can be applied to nonprofit organizations. Five of his six sections study: the basics; financing growth; planning; professionalism and developing human resources; entrepreneurial management. The last section contains profiles of two nonprofit entrepreneurs. A list of cited works is at end.

Gies, David L., J. Steven Ott and Jay M. Shafritz, eds. *The Nonprofit Organization: Essential Readings.* Pacific Grove, CA: Brooks/Cole Publishing Co., 1990. 402 pp. paper.

This is a collection of what the editors feel are the 31 most important and readable articles or chapters about the nonprofit organization. It consists of three or four articles on each of seven broad topics, including: planning and policy formulation; governance; managing; entrepreneurship; and promotional management.

Hay, Robert D. *Strategic Management in Non-Profit Organizations: An Administrator's Handbook.* New York: Quorum Books, 1990. 398 pp.

Written for administrators, this book aims to provide them with a professional strategic managerial approach to administering the functions of an NPO. A special feature, the author says, is the self-evaluations of various objectives, strategies, and policies related to the functions that each NPO has to perform. The four basic parts are: introduction; determinants of strategy formulation; strategy integration into organizational functions (with chapters focusing on each broad functional area); implementation of strategies. Bibliographical references are with some chapters.

Koteen, Jack. *Strategic Management in Public and Nonprofit Organizations: Thinking and Acting Strategically in Public Concerns.* New York: Praeger, 1989. 227 pp.

Another of the increasing number of recent management books focusing on public and/or nonprofit organizations, this one "directly aims to be operationally useful to busy and harassed executives and their leaders who desperately need to gain practical understanding of strategic insights, processes, and skill." Little or no technical background is presumed. There are 6 major sections: remedies for making a significant difference; new approaches to strategic leadership; establishing a strategic management system; setting the strategic agenda; implementing strategic thrusts by using bite-sized modern program management methods (including chapters on MBO, budgeting by program accountability, team structure); learning from lessons of experience. A bibliography is at end.

McKinney, Jerome B. *Effective Financial Management in Public and Nonprofit Agencies: A Practical and Integrative Approach.* New York: Quorum Books, 1986. 378 pp.

This is an easy-to-read guide for practicing financial managers in public and nonprofit agencies which ties together the fiscal side of financial management systems (budgeting, financing, and controlling) with the management side (planning, programming, and evaluating). The author uses a step-by-step approach, balancing theory with practice, and there are numerous examples. He also discusses such topics as cash, risk, internal control, fiscal health and fraud, waste, and abuse management. At end is a chapter on financial advisory services and a short bibliography.

Powell, Walter W., ed. *The Nonprofit Sector: A Research Handbook.* New Haven, CT: Yale University Press, 1987. 464 pp.

"A collective effort to produce a state-of-the-art review and assessment of scholarly research on the nonprofit sector," sponsored by the Program on Non-Profit Organizations, at Yale University. There are 6 parts: an overview; the nonprofit sector, the state, and private enterprise; organization and management; functions of the non-profit sector; sources of support for nonprofit organizations; comparative perspectives. Bibliographical references are at end of each essay.

Setterberg, Fred, and Kary Schulman. *Beyond Profits: The Complete Guide to Managing the Nonprofit Organization.* New York: Harper & Row, 1985. 271 pp.

The book jacket says: "Written in an engaging, entertaining, and easy-to-understand style, *Beyond Profit* gives you advice you need all taken from real-life experiences, and covers every aspect of the challenge of managing the nonprofit organization: fundraising; carefully defining your focus, goals, and long-range plans; building an effective staff; selecting the perfect board of directors; day-to-day management; budget and finance; publicity; promotion; politicking; and knowing the law." Bibliographic notes are at end.

Wacht, Richard F. *Financial Management in Nonprofit Organizations.* 2d ed. Atlanta: College of Business Administration, Georgia State University, 1991. 545 pp.

One of a growing number of books on one important management function in nonprofit organizations, this text covers the basics of financial management in the nonprofit context, and it discusses both theory and practice. Parts 1 and 2 outline the legal and operational characteristics of nonprofit organizations, and the basic tools of financial management. Parts 3–5 then explain how to apply financial management decision rules in: working capital management, resource-allocation decisions, and long-term financing. Sources for further reading are with each chapter; appendixes and a glossary are at end.

Wolf, Thomas. *Managing the Nonprofit Organization.* New York: Prentice Hall Press, 1990. 310 pp. paper.

Wolf is a leading consultant for the nonprofit field. Here he has expanded an earlier manual on the title subject. In an easy-to-understand manner he covers the whole range of issues: staffing, fund raising, choosing trustees, financing, marketing, computerizing, planning, succeeding. This is a useful short book both for administrators and students.

For a primer to provide volunteer board directors with an overview of basic board mission and action, see *A Working Guide for Directors of Not-for-Profit Organizations* by Charles N. Waldo (New York: Quorum Books, 1986, 132 pp.). Just published and not seen for evaluation is *Strategic Management of Public and Third Sector Organizations: A Handbook for Leaders* by Paul C. Nutt and Robert W. Backoff (San Francisco: Jossey-Bass, 1992, 486 pp.).

A legal guide also not seen is *Starting and Managing a Nonprofit Organization: A Legal Guide* by Bruce R. Hopkins (New York: Wiley, 1989, 264 pp.).

Dictionaries

Ott, J. Steven, and Jay M. Shafritz. *The Facts on File Dictionary of Nonprofit Organization Management.* New York: Facts on File Publications, 1986. 407 pp.

Focuses on terms and phrases found in texts and handbooks on the subject, and includes listings for organizations, laws, court cases, tax implications. A list of books is at end.

Periodicals

Nonprofit Management & Leadership. San Francisco: Jossey-Bass (quarterly).

As evidence of the increasing interest in effective management of nonprofits, here is the first journal (started fall 1990) intended for scholars and thoughtful practitioners. It seeks to publish nontechnical articles focusing on some aspect of nonprofit organization management or leadership such as governance, management of human resources, resource development and financial management, strategy and management of change, and organizational effectiveness. An interview or case study is included in each issue, as well as a book review section. This interesting quarterly is sponsored jointly by the Mandel Center for Nonprofit Organizations at Case Western Reserve University and the Centre for Voluntary Organisation at the London School of Economics and Political Science.

Directories

National Directory of Nonprofit Organizations. Rockville, MD: The Taft Group, 1992. 2 volumes in 3. (annual).

A directory of over 256,000 of the largest nonprofit organizations, with volume 1 (in two parts) covering some 176,000 organizations with reported annual income over $100,000, and volume 2 listing those with incomes of from $25,000 to $99,000. For each organization it usually gives: IRS filing status (denoting the general nature of the organization's activities); employer identification number assigned by the IRS; charitable deduction eligibility; reported annual income; and the activity identifier code. At the end of volume 2 there are indexes by activity and by geographic location (zip code).

ARTS ADMINISTRATION

Caplin, Lee E., ed. *The Business of Art.* 2d ed. Englewood Cliffs, NJ: Prentice-Hall, 1989. 352 pp.

The material presented in the first edition "is a first step toward understanding many aspects of 'survival' among artists in a commerce-oriented society. The artists, dealers, and business professionals who have contributed their thoughts in producing this book hope it will help you discover the types of questions you ought to be asking either yourself or those whom you enlist to help you. . . . Their views on the professional side of art will illuminate and demystify many seemingly technical and complicated details that might seem burdensome to those who just want to make art." Published in cooperation with the National Endowment for the Arts, this collection of practical business tips and techniques is arranged in five parts: planning; protecting; marketing; dealing; finding alternatives. The second edition was not seen for evaluation.

Horwitz, Tem. *Arts Administration: How to Set Up and Run Successful Nonprofit Arts Organizations.* Chicago: Chicago Review Press, 1978. 256 pp. Out of print.

"This book is written for artists and administrators who want to set up arts organizations, reorganize existing ones, or simply think about some of the possibilities open to them," and it focuses especially on small- to medium-sized institutions. More than half of the book deals with the nitty-gritty of arts administration—grant writing, fund-raising, marketing, financial management, etc. There is also a chapter on legal matters explained by an arts attorney. Appendixes include sample by-laws and a bibliography.

Shore, Harvey. *Arts Administration and Management: A Guide for Arts Administrators and Their Staffs.* New York: Quorum Books, 1987. 218 pp.

A short, recently written book for arts administrators, on basic management concepts as they apply to arts organizations. Its major parts are arranged to focus on the five basic functions of managers: planning, organizing, staffing, leadership, control. At end are a glossary and a bibliography.

Turk, Frederick J., and Robert P. Gallo. *Financial Management Strategies for Arts Organizations.* New York: American Council for the Arts, 1984. 186 pp.

A concise book designed to help arts managers and governing boards with the many issues and decisions they need to make by describing generally accepted financial management principles and practices and illustrating them where appropriate. There are short chapters on strategic planning, budgeting, organization, key elements in establishing an effective financial management process (fund accounting, ratio analysis, asset management, etc.). At the time this book was published these authors specialized in services to nonprofit organizations at Peat, Marwick, Mitchell.

Two pertinent arts journals are: *Arts Management* (New York: Radius Group; 5/yr.) and *Journal of Arts Management and Law* (Washington, DC: Heldref Publications; quarterly).

EDUCATIONAL ADMINISTRATION

Unlike the relatively new interest in arts management, the problems of administering educational institutions are so varied and have been with us for so long that whole libraries are devoted exclusively to collecting and making available the overwhelming amount of writings on all aspects and levels of education. In an effort to collect, index, and make available for retrieval the large volume of hard-to-find research reports and documents of potential interest to educators, the U.S. Department of Education in 1960 established its very active Educational Resources Information Center (widely known as ERIC). Besides this national computerized information system, ERIC also maintains a network of clearinghouses, each specializing in a particular aspect of education. The Clearinghouse on Educational Management (ERIC/CEM) is located at the University of Oregon, in Eugene, and its specialized staff can provide information on all aspects of the theory and practice of educational administration. ERIC is also available on CD-ROM.

A Sampling of Recent Books

Here are the names of several relatively recent, useful books found in a quick search of the shelves in an education library, and not seen for evaluation.

Guthrie, James W., and Rodney J. Reed. *Educational Administration and Policy: Effective Leadership for American Education.* 2d ed. Englewood Cliffs, NJ: Prentice-Hall, 1991. 416 pp.

Haller, Emil J., and Kenneth A. Strike. *An Introduction to Educational Administration: Social, Legal and Ethical Perspectives.* New York: Longmans, 1986. 347 pp. Bibliography: pp. 331–342.

Hanson, E. Mark. *Educational Administration and Organizational Behavior.* 3d ed. Boston: Allyn and Bacon, 1991. 406 pp.

Hoy, Wayne K., and Cecil G. Miskel. *Educational Administration: Theory, Research and Practice.* 3d ed. New York: Random House, 1986. 448 pp. Bibliography: pp. 432–470.

Kimbrough, Ralph B., and Michael Y. Nunnery. *Educational Administration: An Introduction.* 3d ed. New York: Macmillan, 1988. 677 pp.

Kotler, Philip, and Karen F. Fox. *Strategic Marketing for Educational Institutions.* Englewood Cliffs, NJ: Prentice-Hall, 1985. 396 pp.

Lewis, James, Jr. *Achieving Excellence in Our Schools . . . by Taking Lessons from America's Best Run Companies.* Westbury, NY: Wilkerson Publishing Co., 1986. 250 pp.

Lunenburg, Fred C., and Allan C. Ornstein. *Educational Administration: Concepts & Practices.* Belmont, CA: Wadsworth Publishing, 1991. 557 pp.

Rebore, Ronald W. *Educational Administration: A Management Approach.* Englewood Cliffs, NJ: Prentice-Hall, 1985. 288 pp. and his *Personnel Administration in Education: A Management Approach.* 2d ed. (Prentice-Hall, 1987, 368 pp.).

Abstracts, Indexes, Periodicals

Since the total volume of publishing on educational topics is so vast and so varied, there is no good single recent bibliographic source covering books on the overall topic of educational administration. As a result, one must search under specific kinds of education, such as school administration or higher education, to find current bibliographies, or recent books with bibliographies, that may be pertinent. For instance, each year the December issue of *American School Board Journal* (Alexandria, VA: National School Boards Association) includes a short list of "The Books You Should Have Read This Year— And Still Can." This reviews and gives capsule summaries for books of value to professional and lay administrators in the management of public schools. The following indexes may help in locating articles and other information.

Current Index to Journals in Education. Phoenix, AZ: Oryx Press (monthly, with semiannual cumulations). Online counterpart is *ERIC*.

This is a descriptive index of articles in approximately 780 major educational and education-related journals. It is based on information submitted by ERIC Clearing-houses and is arranged by the Clearinghouse accession number, with subject and author indexes. There is a section in each issue covering "Educational Management."

Educational Administration Abstracts. Newbury Park, CA: Sage Publications (quarterly).

An excellent source for abstracts of articles, some books, and other sources of information for practicing administrators, educators, and students. Articles are se-lected not only from educational journals but also from basic management, behav-ioral science, and personnel journals. It is arranged within 15 subject headings including: administration and organization; financial administration and manage-ment; policy, planning, and implementation; professional development.

For a simple, good author/subject index to educational periodicals, proceed-ings, yearbooks, and book reviews in the English language see *Education Index* (Bronx, NY: H. W. Wilson Co.; published monthly except July and August, with annual cumulations). Online counterpart can be accessed via *WILSONLINE;* also on CD-ROM as *WILSONDISC.*

The *Educational Administration Quarterly* is a professional journal pub-lished under the auspices of the University Council for Educational Adminis-tration in cooperation with the University of Utah, and published in Newbury Park, CA, by Sage Publications. Book reviews are included.

Associations

Association of School Business Officials International, 11401 N. Shore Drive, Reston, VA 22090.

National Association of College and University Business Officers, One Dupont Circle, Washington, DC 20036.

HEALTH CARE ADMINISTRATION

In the health care field, probably more than in any other nonprofit industry, the growth and expansion in all of its various aspects has been accompanied by a rise in the number of books, journals, and reference tools published to meet the needs of health care administrators for more and better information to help in managing the varied health care organizations and facilities. This short section does not attempt to do justice to this growing literature; it merely provides a sampling of recent books, journals, directories, and bibliographies. A few of these, especially those not annotated, were not seen for evaluation. For other material on this important subject, use the several bibliographies/ abstracts cited; check book reviews in current journals; consult with organiza-tions such as the American Hospital Association Resource Center which regu-larly collects these kinds of information sources. Special attention is called to the core bibliography they compiled in 1989 which is described in the "Bibliog-raphies" section below.

Handbooks

Rowland, Howard S., and Beatrice L. Rowland, eds. *The Hospital Administration Manual.* Gaithersburg, MD: Aspen Publishers, 1991. 1 volume (loose-leaf).

An up-to-date manual for hospital administrators covering administration, organization, planning, financial management, construction and capital formation, information systems, personnel management, quality assurance and risk management, law.

A Sampling of Recent Books

Coddington, Dean C., and Keith D. Moore. *Market-Driven Strategies in Health Care.* San Francisco: Jossey-Bass, 1987. 337 pp.

Two consultants have written this helpful book on the title subject intended for top managers, physicians, trustees, and others interested in health care management. The first of its three parts describes the three major health care market segments (physicians, employers, and consumers). Part 2 covers 10 different strategies for gaining and sustaining competitive advantage, and includes examples and an analysis of strategic implications of each strategy. Part 3 discusses charting the best course. Bibliographical citations are at end.

Herzlinger, Regina E. *Creating New Health Care Ventures: The Role of Management.* Gaithersburg, MD: Aspen Publications, 1992. 508 pp.

Professor Herzlinger aims here to help executives and students in the health care sector (as well as those contemplating being involved) to identify the many "opportunities that currently exist for revolutionizing the health care system and to fully appreciate the painstaking details of management appropriate for their implementations." She has organized her book around the opportunities inherent in the market rather than the needs of those who provide health care. There are five parts, with part 2 describing the three major opportunities for change in health care ventures, and part 3 covering each of the 7 skills of management they require. Part 5 consists of 20 relevant cases. Appendixes provide background information on the structure, financing, and technology of the American health care industry. Suggested readings are with chapters.

Kovner, Anthony R., and Duncan Neuhauser, eds. *Health Services Management: Readings and Commentary.* 4th ed. Ann Arbor, MI: Health Administration Press, 1990. 512 pp.

Pegels, C. Carl, and Kenneth A. Rogers. *Strategic Management of Hospitals and Health Care Facilities.* Gaithersburg, MD: Aspen Publishers, 1988. 296 pp.

"The goal of this book is to assist management to deal with the numerous major and minor changes that are occurring in their respective internal and external environments." It is in 7 parts starting with a description of the strategic planning process and ending with a review of future directions.

Shortell, Stephen M. et al. *Strategic Choices for American Hospitals: Managing Change in Turbulent Times.* San Francisco: Jossey-Bass, 1990. 397 pp.

The results of a three-year study to identify how successful hospitals have managed change. Stephen Shortell, with others, has also written a text on *Health Care Management: A Text in Organization Theory and Behavior* (2d ed., Wiley, 1988, 542 pp.).

Wolper, Lawrence F., and Jesus T. Peña. *Health Care Administration: Principles and Practices.* Gaithersburg, MD: Aspen Publishers, 1987. 548 pp.

Finance

Berman, Howard J., Lewis E. Weeks and Steven F. Kukla. *The Financial Management of Hospitals.* 7th ed. Ann Arbor, MI: Health Administration Press, 1990. 770 pp.

A standard work revised and updated once again to reflect changing laws and practices in the health care financial environment. Its 6 parts cover: introduction; sources of operating revenue; working capital management; resource allocation decisions (corporate planning, budgeting, and control); control and analysis; the future. Suggested readings are with chapters; a glossary and a bibliography are at end.

Cleverley, William O. *Essentials of Health Care Finance.* 3d ed. Gaithersburg, MD: Aspen Publishers, 1992. Over 400 pp.

An easy-to-understand text whose objective it is to improve the understanding and use of financial information by decision makers in the health care industry.

Cleverley, William O. *Handbook of Health Care Accounting and Finance.* 2d ed. Gaithersburg, MD: Aspen Publishers, 1989. 2 volumes.

A comprehensive handbook covering all areas critical to sound financial management, including financial accounting, cost accounting, tax administration, information systems, quantitative methods, insurance.

Suver, James D., and Bruce R. Neumann. *Management Accounting for Healthcare Organizations.* New rev. ed. Chicago: Pluribus Press, 1985. 479 pp.

Human Resources

Haimann, Theo. *Supervisory Management for Healthcare Organizations.* 4th ed. St. Louis, MO: Catholic Health Association of the United States, 1989. 420 pp.

Metzger, Norman, ed. *Handbook of Health Care Human Resources Management.* 2d ed. Gaithersburg, MD: Aspen Publishers, 1990. 560 pp.

Consists of 70 articles written by experts and covering important specific topics in personnel management, employee benefits, and labor relations as they relate to health care organizations. Metzger has also written *The Health Care Supervisor's Handbook* (Aspen Publishers, 1988, 250 pp.) which covers everything from basic communication and motivation to handling employee grievances and dealing with union organizers, for health care managers.

Marketing

There is a budding literature on health care marketing due to the recognition that health care marketers must understand basic marketing concepts and procedures if they want to succeed in their increasingly competitive environment, with lowered funds, increasing demands, and other major problems. This short section cites just three relatively recent books, and an old bibliography. Two journals are included in the "Periodicals" section below. For a good selection of recent material on marketing and advertising in general, see Chapter 18.

Hillestad, Steven G., and Eric N. Berkowitz. *Health Care Marketing Plans: From Strategy to Action.* 2d ed. Gaithersburg, MD: Aspen Publishers, 1991. 255 pp.

A book on how to develop and implement a successful marketing strategy for health care organizations. It follows a step-by-step process.

Kotler, Philip, and Roberta N. Clarke. *Marketing for Health Care Organizations.* Englewood Cliffs, NJ: Prentice-Hall, 1987. 545 pp.

Professor Kotler is a respected marketing specialist, teacher, and author (see his other books cited in Chapter 18). Here he and his coauthor address the marketing problems health care managers are likely to encounter. The book is divided into five major parts: understanding marketing; organizing marketing; analyzing marketing opportunities; planning the marketing mix; supporting the marketing effort.

Leebov, Wendy. *Service Excellence: The Customer Relations Strategy for Health Care.* Chicago: American Hospital Publishing, Inc., 1988. 332 pp. paper.

For an annotated bibliography only of older material published prior to 1984, see *An Annotated and Extended Bibliography of Health Care Marketing* by Philip D. Cooper (Chicago: American Marketing Association, 1984, 186 pp.).

Bibliographies

"Health Care Administration: A Core Collection." In *Hospital & Health Services Administration,* Vol.34, No.4 (Winter 1989), pp.559–576.

This short, useful list is intended to serve as a selection guide for persons wishing to develop a basic resource collection of major authoritative works in health care administration. It was compiled by the staff of the American Hospital Association Resource Center (in Chicago), and it consists of separate lists of 147 books and 87 journals, each arranged in broad subject categories. Those titles considered of first importance are marked with an asterisk. Some but not all of the starred items are also in this shorter selection of mine.

Medical Group Management Association. *The Administrator's Bookshelf.* Denver, CO (annual).

Published every fall for the MGMA annual conference by their Library Resource Center, this is a useful subject list of books on management and on health care that are of potential interest to Association members. Included among the more than 30 subject headings are books relating to basic management functions such as financial management, marketing, personnel management, strategic planning, as well as books on specific health care topics such as geriatrics, home health care/hospices. Includes also reference books and selected periodicals.

Indexes

Health Planning and Administration. Online index available through regular database vendors.

Produced by the National Library of Medicine, this database indexes literature on the nonclinical aspects of the health care industry with records taken from the

Hospital Literature Index, as well as related records from MEDLINE (The NLM's online database covering biomedical literature), and from books and technical reports supplied by the National Health Information Center.

Hospital Literature Index. Chicago: American Hospital Association (quarterly, with annual cumulations).

This subject-author index is "the primary guide to literature on hospital and health facility administration, including multi-institutional systems, health planning, and administrative aspects of health care delivery." See *Health Planning and Administration* above for online counterpart.

Dictionaries

Rhea, Joseph C., J. Steven Ott and Jay M. Shafritz. *The Facts on File Dictionary of Health Care Management.* New York: Facts on File Publications, 1988. 692 pp.

A useful, comprehensive dictionary that covers all areas of health care management, including concepts, theories, laws, organizations, journals, and pertinent basic business terms. At end is a chronology of American health care management, and also an unannotated bibliography.

An alternative dictionary published about the same time is *The McGraw-Hill Essential Dictionary of Health Care: A Practical Reference for Health Managers* by Lee Hyde (McGraw-Hill, 1988, 468 pp.).

Periodicals

Health Care Management Review. Gaithersburg, MD: Aspen Publishers (quarterly).

This quarterly provides an excellent selection of thoughtful articles on management concepts, techniques, and approaches as they relate to health care. Most issues contain descriptions of recent "Books for Health Care Managers." Indexed in ABI/I.

Hospital & Health Services Administration. Chicago: Foundation of the American College of Healthcare Executives (bimonthly).

Another source for scholarly, professional articles on new developments and thinking in the broad field of management that have implications for health service management. Also a good selection of book reviews on management in general and as it relates to hospital and health services administration in most issues. Indexed in ABI/I, TI; full text on BRS, DATA-STAR, DIALOG, DOW JONES, MEAD/NEXIS.

Journal of Health Care Marketing. Chicago: American Marketing Association (quarterly).

This is the official journal of the Academy for Health Services Marketing, affiliated with the AMA. Its purpose is to serve as an outlet for theoretical and empirical research contributions for practitioners and scholars with an interest in health care marketing, and its articles cover all health care areas. In addition to the feature articles, each issue contains short sections containing research in brief, "health care marketing abstracts" from the current literature, one book review, and a "resource guide." This latter usually describes pertinent periodicals, books and other resources. Indexed in ABI/I.

M&M: Medical Marketing and Media. Boca Raton, FL: CPS Communications, Inc. (monthly, except semimonthly in September and October).

A trade journal, with several feature issues: "Healthcare Advertising Review" (March); "Midyear Preview" (extra October issue); "Career and Salary Survey" (November); "Health Care Agency Profiles" (December), which describes over 100 ad agencies having health care interests, and usually giving for each the year founded, number of employees, billings, health care accounts, accounts gained and lost, names of management personnel. Occasional issues contain a stock price table titled "Financial Pulse." Indexed in ABI/I, PTS/F&S; full text on BRS, DATA-STAR, DIALOG, MEAD/NEXIS.

There are other useful professional and trade journals in the medical care area. Several of these are: *Federation of American Health Systems Review* (Little Rock, AR; bimonthly); *Health Industry Today* (Chicago: J. B. Lippincott Co.; monthly. Indexed full text on BRS, DATA-STAR, DIALOG); *Healthcare Financial Management* (Westchester, IL: Healthcare Financial Managment Association; monthly. Indexed in ABI/I, BPI; full text on BRS, DATA-STAR, DIALOG, DOW JONES, MEAD/NEXIS); *Hospitals* (Chicago: American Hospital Publishing; semimonthly—this is billed as "the magazine for health care executives". Indexed in ABI/I, TI; full text on BRS, DATA-STAR, DIALOG, DOW JONES, MEAD/NEXIS); *Modern Healthcare* (Chicago: Crain Communications; weekly—this is called "the business news magazine for healthcare management". Indexed in ABI/I, PTS/F&S); and *Topics in Health Care Financing* (Gaithersburg, MD: Aspen Publishers; quarterly—each issue is devoted to a specific topic. Indexed in ABI/I, BPI).

Directories

Dun's Guide to Healthcare Companies. Parsippany, NJ: Dun & Bradstreet Information Services (annual).

Data on some 15,000 healthcare manufacturers and suppliers, usually including for each a description of the business, officers, sales range, number of employees. Contains geographic and industry indexes as well as medical/diagnostic devices and brand name cross references.

Medical and Health Information Directory. Detroit: Gale Research, Inc. 3 volumes (annual).

Volume 1 describes major medical and health "organizations, agencies and institutions," including hospital management companies, pharmaceutical companies, consultants, associations, government agencies, insurance providers, and more. Volume 2 covers related "libraries, publications, audiovisuals, and database services"; volume 3 covers "health services," including clinics, treatment centers, care programs. Pertinent data is given for each entry. Master name and key word indexes are in each volume.

Medical & Healthcare Marketplace Guide. Philadelphia: MLR Biomedical Information Services (annual).

Most of this guide consists of more than 5,000 company profiles (about four per two-column page) providing names of officers/management, type of business, products/services, brief business history, total sales, medical sales, number of employees, recent financial facts for public companies, phone/fax. Divisions or business units are described following data on the parent company. Includes geographic, executive, products/services, and company indexes. A section for "medical marketplace" contains statistics and brief text on the medical and health care industry, with data for over 200 product/service classifications arranged under five broad categories, such as pharmaceuticals, medical devices. Sources used are listed at end.

PUBLIC ADMINISTRATION

As is the situation in other parts of this chapter, these few texts should not be considered a balanced and representative list of the best of the wide range of books published in the broad area of public administration. They are a sampling of what was found quickly and easily. Persons interested in locating additional material should use the bibliographies noted below, book reviews in journals, references in several recent books (such as those in Cleary noted below), or consult an information specialist in a public administration library.

Handbooks

Handbook of Public Administration. Ed. by James L. Perry. San Francisco: Jossey-Bass, 1989. 660 pp.

A handbook intended as a guide for public administrators at all levels of government and in all types of services to help them fill in the gaps in their knowledge base and to cope with the many challenges facing them. Its 43 original chapters, each written by an academician or other expert, are arranged in 8 parts to cover: public administration in a new era; effective administrative and organizational systems; strengthening relationships with legislatures, elected and appointed officials, and citizens; establishing successful policies and programs; effective budgeting and fiscal administration; managing human resources; improving operations and services; the professional practice of public administration. References are with each chapter. This handbook was sponsored by the American Society for Public Administration.

Handbook of Public Administration. Ed. by Jack Rabin et al. New York and Basel: M. Dekker, 1989. 1,095 pp.

Using a much different approach from the handbook above, this comprehensive work provides perspectives in 13 major subfields of public administration by offering two bibliographical essays in each subfield—one tracing major writers, ideas, theories, and applications chronologically by decade, and the other developing the five greatest ideas or theories associated with each field. Detailed bibliographies or works cited are with each essay, written by expert contributors. Subfields covered include: public budgeting and financial management; decision making; public personnel administration and labor relations; policy sciences; public law and regulation. Useful to students for its opportunity to review the literature of key subjects in public administration. This handbook is no.35 in the "Public Administration and Public Policy Series."

Books

Bozeman, Barry, and Jeffrey D. Straussman. *Public Management Strategies: Guidelines for Managerial Effectiveness.* San Francisco: Jossey-Bass, 1990. 239 pp.

This is a thought-provoking, practical book written primarily for public management practitioners who are either working currently at the strategy level or hope to one day.

Its purpose "is to provide a perspective on public management that emphasizes approaches to monitoring, adapting to, and shaping organizational environments." Chapters identify strategies in finance, marketing, information resources, and interorganizational relationships. The authors also discuss organization design and reorganization as strategic tools, as well as fostering innovation in government. They conclude with a chapter on characteristics of effective strategic public managers.

Straussman has also written a text on *Public Administration* (2d ed., New York: Longmans, 1990, 421 pp.).

Cleary, Robert et al. *Managing Public Progress: Balancing Politics, Administration and Public Needs.* San Francisco: Jossey-Bass, 1989. 281 pp.

"Aims to provide public managers with background information, ideas, techniques, and approaches, and also with a perspective on the forces that affect their official functions." It starts with an introduction detailing the fundamental differences between public administration and private sector management. Then two chapters analyze the political and organizational environment, three examine key personnel issues and human resource skills contributing toward effective public program management, and five chapters focus on tools and strategies for managing public programs. Each chapter is written by a specialist and each contains bibliographical references.

Cohen, Steven. *The Effective Public Manager: Achieving Success in Government.* San Francisco: Jossey-Bass, 1988. 215 pp.

Here is a concise book that "not only describes the problems faced by public managers but also it provides strategies for addressing these problems and personal advice on how to build and maintain a professional reputation and to advance in the bureaucratic hierarchy." It is intended both as a primer on public management and an essay that presents a vision of an effective public manager. A bibliography is at end.

Henry, Nicholas L. *Public Administration and Public Affairs.* 5th ed. Englewood Cliffs, NJ: Prentice-Hall, 1991. 438 pp.

Professor Henry's standard college text is useful especially for its appendixes which contain annotated lists of information sources on public administration and related fields, journals, and organizations; also correct form of address for public officials, and job opportunities. It is revised and updated with much new information about the field, particularly in the area of organizational theory. There are five parts: paradigms of public administration; public organizations; theories, concepts, and people; public management; implementation. This note is based on examination of the 4th edition.

Nigro, Felix A., and Lloyd G. Nigro. *Modern Public Administration.* 7th ed. New York: Harper & Row, 1989. 387 pp.

Combining both theory and practice, this is one of the better textbooks covering administrative organization, management problems, personnel administration, financial administration, administrative responsibility, and international administration. Bibliographies are at end of chapters. These authors have also written a book on *The New Public Personnel Administration.* (3d ed., Itasca, IL: F. E. Peacock, 1986, 478 pp.).

Shafritz, Jay M., and Albert C. Hyde. *Classics of Public Administration.* 2d ed., rev. and expanded. Chicago: Dorsey Press, 1987. 551 pp. paper.

This book brings together what the compilers hope are the 49 most significant, enduring, and readable selections in the field of public administration. They are arranged in chronological order within 6 time periods from 1887 to 1983, and at the beginning of each of these 6 parts is an interesting chronology of landmark events and the evolution of public administration for that time period. Included are selections from the works of several important management pioneers such as Taylor, Follett, Barnard, and McGregor.

Two other books that were not seen for evaluation are: *Public Administration in America* by George T. Gordon (3d ed., New York: St. Martin's Press, 1986, 642 pp.) and *Public Administration: Understanding Management, Politics, and Law in the Public Sector* by David H. Rosenbloom (2d ed., New York: Random House, 1989, 516 pp.).

Bibliographies and Abstracts

Caiden, Gerald E. et al. *American Public Administration: A Bibliographical Guide to the Literature.* (The Public Affairs and Administration Series, 3). New York: Garland Publishing Co., 1983. 201 pp.

A good but now rather old bibliography intended to help students and others locate the best of the reference material, the leading journals and books on American public affairs and administration. There are essentially three parts. The first is an annotated list of abstracts, indexes, and continuing bibliographies; the second is an annotated list of journals which includes a "core list" and those in 12 major subject areas such as American government, education administration, public finance, public personnel administration, urban administration. The last part consists of the names of books (without annotations)—classic texts, core texts, and those in 12 subject areas similar to the headings used in the second part. Professor Caiden is well qualified to compile, with help from his colleagues, this bibliographical effort.

Coleman, James R., and Robert E. Dugan. *Public Administration Desk Book.* Newton, MA: Government Research Publications, 1990. 270 pp. paper.

This is a useful guide describing important reference tools of special interest to public administration researchers and practitioners. It covers directories of people (and their offices and agencies), statistics, dictionaries, handbooks, publishers, periodicals, indexes and abstracts, online and other machine-based services, law and regulatory reporter services, associations, and institutions. The appendix contains "a basic library" of 14 reference sources, and "other guides to public administration information." Title and subject indexes are at end.

International City Managers Association. *ICMA Catalogue: Publications & Services.* Washington, DC (annual).

The ICMA publishes a number of useful practical books and pamphlets in the area of local government management. Several of the most general books described in their 1990/91 catalogue are: *Compensation 90: An Annual Report on Local Government Executive Salaries and Fringe Benefits* (1990); *Managing for Tomorrow: Global Change and Local Futures* (1990); *Managing Local Government: Cases in Decision Making* (1990).

McCurdy, Howard E. *Public Administration: A Bibliographic Guide to the Literature.* New York and Basel: Dekker, 1986. 311 pp.

Part 3 of this four-part guide is a useful list of the 181 most frequently cited books on public administration, with annotations outlining the important contribution of each. These are all older books (most published prior to the 1980s) since it takes a while for a book to gain solid recognition. The list cites some of the most important works in management, organization theory, organizational behavior, as well as those in public administration, bureaucracy, etc. With each entry there is a figure noting how many times the book was cited in the author's original ranking (1972) and in this second ranking (1985). Part 4 lists 1,200 books (not annotated) within 33 specialized subject areas of study, each of which has been cited by experts at least two or three times. The annotated list of 181 titles forms the basis for two essays comprising parts 1 and 2. This is an excellent source for identifying the older classics both in management and in public administration.

A more recently published source is in an article on "The Half-Century's 'Great Books' in Public Administration" by Frank P. Sherwood (in *Public Administration Review*, vol.50 no.2 (March/April 1990), pp.249–264). This identifies the books in public administration that have had significant influence on the academic career of the article's author. It includes a list of 70 books nominated by an informal advisory panel. The overwhelming leader was Herbert A. Simon's *Administrative Behavior* (3d ed., Free Press, 1976). Several other management classics were also on the list of those receiving more than one nomination.

Sage Public Administration Abstracts. Newbury Park, CA: Sage Publications Press (quarterly).

Each issue contains about 250 abstracts of important recent literature—books, articles, pamphlets, speeches, research studies—on public administration. They are arranged in a varying number of subject sections, usually 10 to 15, and including such headings as: administrative structure and organization; administration and politics; public service personnel; taxation, budgeting and finance.

PAIS International in Print may also be of use when looking for articles. See listing in Chapter 2.

Dictionaries

Shafritz, Jay M. *The Facts on File Dictionary of Public Administration.* New York: Facts on File Publications, 1985. 610 pp.

A comprehensive dictionary on "the theory, concepts, practices, laws, institutions, literature, and people of the academic discipline and professional practice of public administration." Includes also terms in related fields. Sources for further information are sometimes given with definitions.

A more recent dictionary, which is arranged in a subject chapter format and not alphabetically by term, is *The Public Administration Dictionary* by Ralph C. Chandler and Jack C. Plano (2d ed., Santa Barbara, CA: ABC-CLIO, 1988, 430 pp.).

Periodicals

International Review of Administrative Sciences. London and Newbury Park, CA: Sage Publications (quarterly). Published also in French and Spanish editions.

Features articles with an international view. Each issue includes book reviews and an annotated list of worldwide books on administrative science in a section called "Bibliography—A Selection." This quarterly is the official organ of the International Institute of Administrative Science, in Brussels. Indexed in PAIS.

Journal of Policy Analysis and Management. New York: Wiley, for the Association for Public Policy Analysis and Management (quarterly).

A successor to *Policy Analysis* and to *Public Policy,* this journal contains a good selection of thoughtful articles on public policy analysis and management. It is intended for persons interested in learning how to formulate better public policy and how to manage public institutions more effectively. Book reviews and a list of books received (by topic) are included in each issue. Indexed in PAIS.

Public Administration Review. Washington, DC: American Society for Public Administration (bimonthly).

An outstanding professional journal, with authoritative articles covering the entire field of public administration. Its book review section consists of group reviews on a specific topic. The March/April 1990 issue contains an interesting article which identifies those books on public administration that have had a significant influence on the academic career of its author; see "The Half-Century's 'Great Books' in Public Administration" by Frank O. Sherwood (pp.249–264). Indexed in ABI/I, BPI, PAIS.

Several other good professional or trade journals are: *Administration & Society* (Newbury Park, CA: Sage Publications Press; quarterly); *The Bureaucrat* (a quarterly journal for public managers, published in Potomac, MD; indexed in ABI/I); *Government Executive* (Washington, DC: Times-Mirror Co., monthly); *Policy Sciences* (an international journal devoted to the improvement of policy making, published quarterly in Amsterdam by Elsevier Scientific Publishing Co.; indexed in PAIS); *Public Budgeting and Finance* (New Brunswick, NJ: Transaction Periodical Consortium, Rutgers State University; a quarterly, indexed in ABI/I and PAIS); *Public Management* (Washington, DC: International City Managers Association; a monthly on local government management; Indexed in BPI and PAIS); *Public Personnel Management* (Alexandria, VA: International Personnel Management Association; quarterly, indexed in ABI/I and PAIS); and *Public Productivity & Management Review* (San Francisco: Jossey-Bass; a quarterly review encompassing all of the various factors influencing the productivity of public and nonprofit organizations and agencies; indexed in ABI/I and PAIS).

URBAN ADMINISTRATION

Abstracts and Periodicals

Sage Urban Studies Abstracts. Newbury Park, CA: Sage Publications Press. (quarterly).

Abstracts of significant books, articles, pamphlets, government publications on all aspects of urban studies. Each issue is arranged under 15 topics such as: housing; transportation and communication; urban development and redevelopment; urban economics; urban planning and land use.

Urban Affairs Abstracts. Washington, DC: National League of Cities (weekly, with semiannual and annual cumulations).

The annual cumulation of this weekly is especially good for its longer selection of abstracts of articles relating to urban information. Subject headings used include: business and industry; community development; environment; finances; health; municipal administration; public administration; transportation.

Three journals on urban policy and planning are: *Journal* of the American Planning Association (Chicago; quarterly); *Journal of Urban Analysis and Public Management* (New York: Gordon and Breach Science Publishers; semi-annual); and *Urban Affairs Quarterly* (Newbury Park, CA: Sage Publications Press; indexed in PAIS).

12

ACCOUNTING/CONTROL AND TAXATION

Accounting Handbooks – Introductory Accounting Books – Advanced Accounting – Cost and Management Accounting – Budgeting and Management Control – Auditing – Financial Statement Analysis – Accounting for Multinational Enterprises – Accounting and Control for Governmental and Nonprofit Organizations – Surveys of Company Accounting Practices – Accounting Services – Management of Accounting Firms – Accounting Indexes and Abstracts – Accounting Dictionaries – Accounting Periodicals – Directories of Accountants – Accounting Associations – TAXATION – Books on Tax Management – Tax Services – Tax Bibliographies and Indexes – Taxation Periodicals

Probably no function of business has such a prolific literature, written over as long a span of history, as does the field of accounting. Its roots go back to the year 2000 B.C. with early records of Babylonian and Egyptian businessmen found preserved on clay tablets and papyrus rolls. There is an interesting and well-documented account of this development in *A History of Accounting Thought* by Michael Chatfield (Rev. ed., Huntington, NY: R.E. Krieger Publishing Co., 1977, 316 pp.).

Today accounting continues to be one of the best documented fields of business. Perhaps this is because accounting practices are always changing to respond to continuously changing needs, pressures, and new interpretations of standards. Thus the books are quickly outdated and must be frequently revised. So it is especially important to watch the date of publication for books in this chapter and, after my book is published, to check in works such as the annual *Books in Print* for a possible later revision of whatever text you want to read.

This chapter contains only a relatively few recent books, important reference works, the best professional journals, and a few trade journals. The broad topic of management information systems is treated separately in Chapter 13; books on mathematical techniques are in Chapter 17.

ACCOUNTING HANDBOOKS

The business person seeking information on accepted practices in accounting as well as knowledge about forms and procedures will often find that handbooks provide the maximum of facts with a minimum of effort. The accounting field is well supplied with useful handbooks, and it is important for these to be kept as up-to-date as possible. Of the handbooks noted below, the one by Davidson/Weil is very good but now too old to cover the latest information. Kay/Searfoss and Carmichael et al. are both excellent, comprehensive, and recent, with the former likely to remain the most up to date because of its useful periodic updates. Ameiss is also recent and is useful as a shorter one-volume sourcebook for quick information.

Listed elsewhere in this chapter are two now rather old cost accounting handbooks by Black and by Davidson, and an auditor's handbook by Cashin.

Ameiss, Albert P., and Nicholas A. Kargas. *Accountants' Desk Handbook.* 3d ed. Englewood Cliffs, NJ: Prentice-Hall, 1988. 724 pp. And *1989 Cumulative Supplement.*

This is a useful one-volume sourcebook for quick information to meet the changing needs of accounting practitioners. This latest edition has been greatly expanded to keep users informed of recent accounting changes including computerized accounting and office management, new FASB standards, inflation accounting, segment reporting, and much more. The three principal sections cover: financial accounting topics; managerial accounting subjects; and standards, procedures and reports. Checklists, charts, and illustrations drawn from business experience appear throughout the handbook.

An alternate ready-reference, instant-answer manual for accounting and tax accounting information is *Accounting Desk Book* by Tom M. Plank and Douglas L. Blensly (9th ed., Prentice-Hall, 1989, 772 pp.).

Carmichael, D.R., Steven B. Lilien and Martin Mellman, eds. *Accountants' Handbook.* 7th ed. New York: Wiley, 1991. 1 volume (various pagings).

The longest-running comprehensive handbook, this has been in existence for some 70 years. The current editors have streamlined and updated it in this latest edition, yet they still aim "to provide in a single reference source an answer to every reasonable question on accounting and financial reporting that may be asked . . ." Its 36 chapters, arranged in 8 major parts, are clearly written by 58 author/specialists, and its usefulness is enhanced both by frequent references to or excerpts from accounting pronouncements and other accounting literature, and also by the use of diagrams, tables, and forms. There are helpful outlines at the beginning of each chapter, and good bibliographies at the end.

Davidson, Sidney, and Roman L. Weil, eds. *Handbook of Modern Accounting.* 3d ed. New York: McGraw-Hill, 1983. 1 volume (various pagings).

Provides comprehensive, authoritative yet concise coverage for both preparers and users of accounting information and incorporates the newest in concepts and techniques (as of 1983) along with time-tested theories and procedures. There are 42 topics written by 50 expert professors or practitioners, and each chapter contains a short bibliography for readers interested in further sources for information. Tables, diagrams, and how-to-do-it forms are scattered throughout. Compound interest, annuity, and bond tables are in an appendix.

Kay, Robert S., and Gerald Searfoss, eds. *Handbook of Accounting and Auditing.* 2d ed. Boston: Warren, Gorham & Lamont, 1989. 1 volume (various pagings). And periodic updates.

An excellent handbook, this is the cooperative work of Touche Ross & Company partners and staff. Now greatly expanded because of many accounting changes, new topics, new pronouncements, etc., its 50 chapters are in 6 parts: financial accounting—general; auditing—general; specific areas of financial accounting and auditing; industries other than financial services (including not-for-profit organizations, and smaller and emerging businesses); financial services industries; the profession and its environment (FASB, etc.). A useful outline is at the beginning of each chapter; major professional pronouncements, a consolidated bibliography, and a good index are at end of the Handbook. Its periodic updates keep this a useful, up-to-date volume.

Lipkin, Lawrence, Irwin K. Feinstein and Lucile Derrick. *Accountant's Handbook of Formulas and Tables.* 3d ed. Englewood Cliffs, NJ: Prentice-Hall, 1988. 627 pp.

Compilation of formulas and tables often used by accountants, including interest, statistical formulas, sampling, inventory, depreciation, cost and production, and ratio analysis.

INTRODUCTORY ACCOUNTING BOOKS

Most standard one-volume texts cover the principles of both of the two basic branches of accounting: financial accounting (concerned with providing financial statements, reports, etc., of interest to bankers, investors, and other outsiders who must make financial assessment of the company); and management accounting (which emphasizes the use of accounting data for internal purposes, to help management in the planning and control functions of the company). Following are just a few of the many books that offer good introductions to the principles of accounting. It is particularly important for books on financial accounting to be either recently published or revised since they must reflect the latest pronouncements of the Financial Accounting Standards Board (FASB).

For persons needing detailed treatment of accounting requirements in individual industries, check under the name of the industry or subject in the *Accountants' Index,* or its online counterpart, noted in the index section of this chapter.

Anthony, Robert N., and James S. Reece. *Accounting Principles.* 6th ed. Homewood, IL: Irwin, 1989. 678 pp. A new edition is in progress, with a possible 1994 publication date.

This upper-level introductory text covers both financial and management accounting in about equal parts. It is a good one for students not planning to take further accounting courses because it focuses on procedural details that the manager or practicing accountant needs to know rather than on the more analytical uses of accounting information. Thus it is shorter than most of the other beginning texts and does not contain questions/problems with chapters. Present value tables appear at the end.

These professor/authors have also revised their *Accounting: Text and Cases* 8th ed., Irwin, 1989, 1,030 pp.) which contains the same material but has cases with each chapter, for use in case-study courses. Professor Anthony's *Essentials of Accounting* (4th ed., Reading MA: Addison-Wesley, 1988) is a short introductory programmed text for the self-study of basic concepts of accounting.

Edwards, James D., Roger H. Hermanson, and R. F. Salmonson. *A Survey of Financial and Managerial Accounting.* 5th ed. Homewood, IL: Irwin, 1989. 848 pp.

A one semester introductory text for students who want a basic understanding of financial and managerial accounting, fairly evenly treated, and in a relatively short text. The major emphasis is on the content of accounting reports and the interpretation and possible uses of this information. International accounting is covered in a supplement to chapter 12. Glossaries are with chapters. These three accounting professors, with Hermanson as lead author, have also written a more comprehensive text on *Accounting Principles* (5th ed., BPI/Irwin, 1992, 1 volume), recently revised to incorporate the important topic of ethics throughout the book.

Fess, Philip E., and Carl S. Warren. *Accounting Principles.* 16th ed. Cincinnati: South-Western Publishing Co., 1990. 1,128, [112] pp.

The latest of many editions, this standard introductory text aims to present the fundamental accounting concepts and principles in a logical, concise, and clear manner. Its 8 parts are typical of most beginning texts, starting with an introduction on the evolution of accounting, and then covering: basic structure of accounting; accounting systems; accounting principles; partnerships and corporations; financial reporting for corporations; managerial accounting principles and systems; planning and control; decision making. Useful features include: real-world examples, boxed features taken from business periodicals, charts/graphs/diagrams, and an ethics discussion case with each chapter; also exercises and problems. Separately paged at end are appendixes including interest tables, a code of ethics, a specimen financial statement, and a glossary.

Granof, Michael H., and Philip W. Bell. *Financial Accounting: Principles and Issues.* 4th ed. Englewood Cliffs, NJ: Prentice-Hall, 1991. 750 pp.

Granof (now with a coauthor) provides a clear understanding of basic financial accounting principles as well as an appreciation of the significant issues currently facing the accounting profession. A distinguishing feature of this graduate-level textbook "is its focus not only on accounting principles that are currently accepted but on alternative possibilities as well." A glossary, and present/future value tables are at end.

Horngren, Charles T., and Gary L. Sundem. *Introduction to Financial Accounting.* 4th ed. Englewood Cliffs, NJ: Prentice-Hall, 1990. 816 pp. And their *Introduction to Management Accounting.* 8th ed. Prentice-Hall, 1990. 826 pp.

A matched pair of introductory texts covering the essentials of financial and management accounting, written by a highly respected accounting professor and his new coauthor. Professor Horngren, with Walter T. Harrison, Jr., has also recently revised a beginning text called *Accounting* (2d ed., Prentice-Hall, 1992, 1,334, [32] pp.), whose aim it is to focus on the most widely used accounting theory and practice with clarity and accuracy so that students will find it easy to study. It covers the usual topics of an introductory text, with useful features such as an emphasis on real-world examples, good use of color for tables and diagrams, and a glossary.

Larson, Kermit D. *Fundamental Accounting Principles.* 12th ed. Homewood, IL: Irwin, 1990. 1,278, 15 pp.

A well-established college text which integrates conceptual principles with their applications to specific business situations. The primary goal is to help students interpret and use accounting information intelligently and effectively. Both financial and managerial accounting topics are covered with an emphasis on the former. In this latest edition new emphasis is placed on ethics. There is effective use of color, with real-world examples, and excerpts from news articles. Exercises, problems, and expanded glossaries are at end of each chapter; appendixes include present and future value tables, explanation of the accounting problem of changing prices, and a sample annual report.

Professor Larson has also written (with Paul B.W. Miller) a beginning text on *Financial Accounting* (5th ed., Irwin, 1992).

Marshall, David H. *A Survey of Accounting: What the Numbers Mean.* Homewood, IL: Irwin, 1990. 508 pp.

Here is a user-oriented text for nonaccountants who want to learn enough about accounting fundamentals to understand financial statements and how financial information is used in the planning, control, and decision making processes. About two-thirds covers financial accounting topics, and one-third managerial accounting.

Meigs, Robert F., and Walter B. Meigs. *Accounting: The Basis for Business Decisions.* 8th ed. New York: McGraw-Hill, 1990. 1,081 pp.

Another popular text designed for a first college-level course. Since the environment of accounting is changing so rapidly, this latest edition has been extensively revised to reflect the shift toward computers, the increasing public interest in income tax policies, and the growing importance of international business activity. It covers both financial and managerial accounting but the emphasis is on financial. Key terms are defined with each chapter.

Nickerson, Clarence B. *Accounting Handbook for Nonaccountants.* 3d ed. Boston: Van Nostrand Reinhold, 1986. 695 pp.

This is an excellent book for the nonfinancial executive who must be well informed about the language of accounting and accounting data. It differs from other books in its approach through the income and funds flow statements rather than through the balance sheet. Nickerson aims to minimize bookkeeping aspects while stressing the importance of transaction analysis and considering in greater depth such critical accounting areas as depreciation, inventory valuation, cost accounting, and budgeting. Present value tables are at end. Still useful, although it does not reflect changes more recent than 1986.

Several other introductory texts include a well-reviewed matched pair of books by Sidney Davidson et al., with titles *Financial Accounting: An Introduction to Concepts, Methods, and Uses* (3d ed., Chicago: Dryden Press, 1988, 896 pp.) and *Managerial Accounting: An Introduction to Concepts, Methods, and Uses* (3d ed., 1988, 1,024 pp.); *Accounting Principles* by Jack L.

Smith et al. (3d ed., New York: McGraw-Hill, 1989, 1,225 pp.); *Fundamentals of Financial Accounting* by Daniel G. Short and Glenn A. Welsch (6th ed., Homewood, IL: Irwin, 1990, 841 pp.; 7th edition to be published in 1993).

ADVANCED ACCOUNTING

Beams, Floyd A. *Advanced Accounting.* 5th ed. Englewood Cliffs, NJ: Prentice-Hall, 1992. 960 pp.

An alternative to the advanced text by Larsen/Mosich noted below under Mosich. This one covers such topics as business combinations, intercompany profit transactions, consolidations, accounting for branch operations, partnerships, dissolutions and liquidations, accounting for state and local governmental units, accounting for nonprofit organizations such as universities, hospitals. Exercises and a list of selected readings are with chapters; a glossary is at end.

Yet another recently revised standard text is *Advanced Accounting* by Charles H. Griffin et al. (6th ed., Irwin, 1991, 1,213 pp.).

Hendriksen, Eldon S., and Michael F. van Breda. *Accounting Theory.* 5th ed. Homewood, IL: Irwin, 1992. 905 pp.

"Designed to provide a frame of reference for junior, senior, and graduate courses in financial accounting and financial accounting theory; seminars on financial accounting standards and issues; seminars on the theory of income and asset valuation." Suggested additional readings are at end of chapters as well as selected CPA examination questions.

Kaplan, Robert S., and Anthony A. Atkinson. *Advanced Management Accounting.* 2d ed. Englewood Cliffs, NJ: Prentice-Hall, 1989. 817 pp.

Major revision of an advanced text that takes a user-decision-oriented approach to the design of management accounting procedures and systems. Included are chapters on such topics as cost-volume-profit analysis, cost analysis for pricing decisions, assigning service department costs, measuring quality, decentralization, and profit centers. Cases are with chapters.

Kieso, Donald E., and Jerry J. Weygandt. *Intermediate Accounting.* 7th ed. New York: Wiley, 1992. 1,459 pp.

In this latest edition of a well written and comprehensive (very long) text, the authors discuss in depth the traditional intermediate financial accounting topics, as well as recent developments in accounting valuation and reporting practices. Special features include a good use of color for ease in understanding, and interviews with prominent persons on relevant accounting topics. Extra instructional aids are included as appendixes with many chapters.

These two authors, with Walter G. Kell, have also written a basic introductory book on *Accounting Principles* (2d ed., Wiley, 1990, 1,230, [46] pp.).

Mosich, A.N. *Intermediate Accounting.* Rev. 6th ed. New York: McGraw-Hill, 1989. 1,364 pp.

This latest edition of a standard text (which originally had Walter B. Meigs as its primary author) still states that its "emphasis throughout is on underlying concepts and on analysis of the problems that arise in the application of the concepts to financial accounting." It is in 6 parts: basic concepts and financial statements; working capital; long-term assets and liabilities; stockholders' equity; more complex accounting topics (accounting for pension plans; leases; income taxes); analytical procedures and statements. Compound interest tables are in an appendix to chapter 5. This is a long book, but frequent use of tables and illustrative examples make it relatively easy to read.

Professor Mosich also co-authored (with E. John Larsen as first author) *Modern Advanced Accounting* (4th ed., McGraw-Hill, 1988, 1,002 pp.). This focuses on relevant new problems of significance to future accountants concerning accounting for partnerships and branches, business combinations, consolidated financial statements (6 chapters), accounting for nonbusiness organizations (including governmental units; 5 chapters), bankruptcy, accounting for multinational enterprises, segment reports, installment sales. Compound interest tables are in an appendix.

Smith, Jay M., and K. Fred Skousen. *Intermediate Accounting: Comprehensive Volume.* 11th ed. Cincinnati: South-Western Publishing Co., 1992. 1,147 pp.

Another well-established text for a second course on accounting principles, with extensive revisions in this latest edition to cover the many changes, to expand the treatment of important topics in financial accounting and reports, and to make the book what these authors hope is "the most teachable and student-oriented text" available. Many new illustrations, real-world examples, and applications have been added. Supplementary materials are with many chapters; appendixes contain a glossary, an illustrative financial statement, and a useful index of references to APB and FASB pronouncements. This 11th edition is also published as a shorter "Standard Volume" (1991, about 900 pp.) which discusses all of the essential topics, and also defines key terms in an appendix.

Welsch, Glenn A., and Charles T. Zlatkovich. *Intermediate Accounting.* 8th ed. Homewood, IL: Irwin, 1989. 1,406 pp.

Here is a widely adopted comprehensive text emphasizing accounting theory and concepts and meant for students who have already had a course in the fundamentals of financial accounting. It covers all the topics normally studied in intermediate accounting, such as inventory, liabilities, operational assets, statement of cash flows, and special reporting problems such as accounting for pension plans, leases, and income taxes. This latest edition has useful exhibits, examples of financial statement disclosures; also a list of official pronouncements on the end papers.

COST AND MANAGEMENT ACCOUNTING

With the growing complexities of business and the resulting emphasis on management systems and quantitative methods, more attention is being paid to writings on that branch of accounting concerned with internal planning, control, and managerial decisions. Several handbooks and books are included in this and the following section on budgeting and management control, but attention is also called to the following chapter, which covers the whole area of management information systems.

Handbooks

Bulloch, James, Donald E. Keller and Louis Vlasho, eds. *Accountants' Cost Handbook: A Guide for Management Accounting.* 3d ed. New York: Wiley, 1983. 1 volume (various pagings).

This is a comprehensive yet concise handbook dealing with the fundamental cost and financial information concepts and principles that apply to the activities of planning, decision making, budgeting, operations control, and reporting. This updated and expanded edition (as of 1983) is based not only on the experience of its expert contributors but also on a review of the literature, occasionally including examples and illustrations of applications quoted from other sources. Suggestions for further reading are with each chapter, but these are now rather out of date.

Shim, Jae K., and Joel G. Siegel. *Management Accountant's Standard Desk Reference.* Englewood Cliffs, NJ: Prentice-Hall, 1990. 616 pp.

Although not as long as most handbooks, this is still a useful working guide to assist practitioners in pinpointing and solving problems in management accounting. The material is arranged within five parts: cost analysis for planning and decision making; planning and performance evaluation; cost accounting; quantitative methods and financial statement analysis; internal evaluation. Useful guidelines, formulas, checklists, charts, sample documents, outlines, and other illustrations appear throughout. An appendix includes a list of software packages and pronouncements of the Cost Accounting Standards Board.

Books

Garrison, Ray H. *Managerial Accounting: Concepts for Planning, Control, and Decision Making.* 6th ed. Homewood, IL: Irwin, 1991. 810 pp.

As the subtitle indicates, this well-received text focuses on the information managers need to plan operations, to conduct activities, and to make decisions. It looks at accounting data through the eyes of those who must use the data in the management of an enterprise. "Real world" examples are used throughout; key terms are defined at end of each chapter.

Another standard text is *Managerial Accounting* by Carl L. Moore et al. (7th ed., South-Western, 1988, 897 pp.).

Horngren, Charles T., and George Foster. *Cost Accounting: A Managerial Emphasis.* 7th ed. Englewood Cliffs, NJ: Prentice-Hall, 1991. 964 pp.

Latest revision of a very good, comprehensive, and widely-used text on cost accounting, with an emphasis on costs for planning and control. It is arranged in 29 chapters within 7 sections to cover all important aspects, including new uses of cost accounting data and insights gained into how changes in technology are affecting the roles of cost accounting information. There is increased use of real-world examples, and colorful visual aids. At the end is a glossary, a short bibliography, and notes on compound interest and interest tables.

Rayburn, Letricia G. *Principles of Cost Accounting, Using a Cost Management Approach.* 4th ed. Homewood, IL: Irwin, 1989. 1,464 pp.

A comprehensive text which the author hopes identifies concepts and principles of cost accounting in a clear, concise, and straightforward manner. The major parts cover: basic cost accounting concepts; product cost allocation and accumulation procedures; cost data for performance evaluation; cost accounting/cost management for decision making; selected topics for further study (including behavioral facts in accounting control); quantitative models for planning and control. Important terms and further readings are listed with each chapter; present value tables and Cost Accounting Standards Board standards are at end of book.

Thomas, William E. *Readings in Cost Accounting, Budgeting and Control.* 7th ed. Cincinnati: South-Western, 1988. 576 pp. paper.

Professor Thomas has arranged this seventh edition of his selection of 45 readings into a sequence he feels is a coherent presentation of the managerial control function. These are: systems for business controls; goals and subgoals; decisions; feedforward; feedback for control; control of decentralized operations; professional responsibilities.

Usry, Milton F., and Lawrence H. Hammer. *Cost Accounting: Planning and Control.* 10th ed. Cincinnati: South-Western, 1991. 903 pp.

The latest revision of this standard text maintains its focus on the twin management functions of planning and control. It is intended to have broad applicability to all phases of business and nonprofit organizations, both large and small. There are five parts, with part 3 dealing with the cost elements of materials and labor from both the planning and control phases. Part 4 covers budgeting and standard costing, and part 5, an analysis of costs and profits. This book was originally the work of Professor Adolph Matz who is now deceased.

BUDGETING AND MANAGEMENT CONTROL

Handbooks

Corporate Controller's Manual. Ed. by Paul J. Wendell. 2d ed. Boston: Warren, Gorham & Lamont, 1989. 1 volume (various pagings). And annual updates.

This comprehensive handbook is intended to help keep the controller up to date on a wide range of important topics. It contains contributions from over 50 experts, and is arranged in 9 sections to cover: the role of the controller; accounting principles; financial reporting; management accounting; treasury functions; human resources; taxes; multinational corporations; special situations (including mergers and acquisitions). Suggested readings are usually with each chapter.

Sweeny, Allen, and Robert Rachlin. *Handbook of Budgeting.* 2d ed. New York: Wiley, 1987. 880 pp.

Brings together in one volume all important aspects of budget preparation, presentation, and utilization for profit and for nonprofit organizations. In its 30 chapters, 29 experts discuss accounting and financial concepts that are basic to the budgeting process, as well as modern budgeting concepts and applications. There are practical working examples of forms, techniques, and reports, and short bibliographies are at the end of some chapters.

Willson, James D., and James P. Colford. *Controllership: The Work of the Managerial Accountant.* 4th ed. New York: Wiley, 1990. 1,218 pp.

The greater role of the controller as a member of management is reflected in this expanded book which is of handbook length and scope. It emphasizes a practical "how to do it" format with its 45 chapters arranged within 6 parts as follows: the broad management aspects of controllership; the planning function of controllership; planning and controlling operations; planning and accounting control of assets, liabilities, and equity interests; accounting reports—principles and applications; some administrative aspects of the controller's department. This book is well written and includes numerous helpful illustrations and examples taken from a wide variety of industries and business situations.

Books

Anthony, Robert N. *The Management Control Function.* Boston: Harvard Business School Press, 1988. 216 pp.

This book focuses on the management control function in organizations and the management control environment. It is also partly a revision of Professor Anthony's *Planning and Control Systems* (HBS, 1965), updating the discussion of the conceptual framework but also going into more detail on certain topics and adding others such as project control. "Notes" and a good, short bibliography are at end.

Anthony, Robert N., John Dearden and Vijay Govindarajan. *Management Control Systems.* 7th ed. Homewood, IL: Irwin, 1992. 1,033 pp.

Normally we have not included case books in this bibliography. However this one has such useful, short preliminary discussions with each of its 17 chapters that we have made an exception here and recommend it for persons preferring brief background summaries. To give an idea of its scope, this major revision is arranged in three parts after an introductory overview. These are: the management control environment (behavior, responsibility centers, profit centers, transfer pricing, investment centers, strategies); the management control process (programming, budget preparation, operations, analysis of operations, incentive compensation); variations in management control (service organizations, financial services organizations, multinational organizations, management control of projects). With each chapter are suggestions for additional readings, and four or more cases.

Belkaoui, Ahmed. *Handbook of Management Control Systems.* New York: Quorum Books, 1986. 355 pp.

"Presents the principal tools and techniques involved in the design and implementation of a management control system in an environment varying in (a) the structure adopted by the organization and (b) the market served by the organization." It is arranged in 9 chapters, three of which focus on control for multinational operations, for nonprofit organizations, and behavioral issues in control. Bibliographies are at end of chapters.

Figgie, Harry E., Jr. *Cutting Costs: An Executive's Guide to Increased Profits.* New York: AMACOM, American Management Association, 1990. 240 pp. paper.

Mr. Figgie is a well-known business executive who has had wide experience in the practical aspects of cost reduction. He intends this book as a primer for heads of small to medium-size companies to show them how reducing costs can increase profitability. Part 1 offers instruction for the first month; part 2 establishes cost reduction priorities; part 3 discusses specific cost reduction techniques in a variety of departmental areas. Includes useful tips, checklists, and calculations techniques. This was also published in 1988 by Probus Publishing Co. with title *The Harry Figgie Guide to Cost Reduction and Profit Improvement.*

Welsch, Glenn A., Ronald W. Hilton and Paul N. Gordon. *Budgeting: Profit Planning and Control.* 5th ed. Englewood Cliffs, NJ: Prentice-Hall, 1988. 661 pp.

As the title indicates, Welsch designed his book as a practical text on profit planning and control within the management process. For this major revision, he has added two coauthors. They say this is the only book covering "all aspects of the budgeting process—from the details of preparing the many schedules that comprise a master budget to the fundamental managerial issues that are affected by the profit planning and control process." Real-world illustrations and cases are used throughout and "suggested references" are at end of chapters.

AUDITING

Handbooks

Cashin's Handbook for Auditors. Ed. by James A. Cashin, Paul D. Neuwirth, and John F. Levy. 2d ed. New York: McGraw-Hill, 1986. 1 volume (various pagings).

An excellent, comprehensive handbook covering all phases of auditing but not updated to cover new techniques and procedures since 1986. Its 50 chapters, written by expert practitioners or academicians, are in 7 parts: principles, standards, and responsibilities; principal types of auditing; planning, evaluation, and administration; audit program objectives and procedures; analytical methods; conclusion, review, and reporting; professional development.

Wallace, Wanda A. *Handbook of Internal Accounting Controls.* 2d ed. Englewood Cliffs, NJ: Prentice-Hall, 1991. 1,068 pp.

More specialized than Cashin, this is a comprehensive handbook that "presents a workable, intuitive approach to designing and/or evaluating both existing and proposed controls. It explains the reasons why particular controls are important, the practical factors that often diminish the effectiveness of well-designed controls, and the effect that can be expected if a particular control is omitted." It is intended for auditors, system designers, and operating managers.

Books

Watch for date of publication in auditing books since it is very important for them to be recent enough to reflect the latest developments and changes in the Statements of Auditing Standards.

Carmichael, D. R., and John J. Willingham. *Auditing Concepts and Methods: A Guide to Current Auditing Theory and Practice.* 5th ed. New York: McGraw-Hill, 1989. 591 pp.

Intended as a practical guide to auditing theory and practice for students who are new to the field. Among other topics the authors explain audit planning and the performance of auditing procedures. There are also chapters on auditing sampling, the effect of computers on the audit, the auditor's report, operational auditing. The authors have also published a good selection of more than 50 readings called *Perspectives in Auditing* (4th ed., McGraw-Hill, 1985, 503 pp., paper). This covers almost all aspects of auditing but reflects trends and accounting changes only as of 1985.

Montgomery's Auditing. By Vincent M. O'Reilly et al. 11th ed. New York: Wiley, 1990. 1,150 pp.

Another revision of Robert H. Montgomery's widely-used, comprehensive text on auditing which has been a standard work ever since it was first published in 1912. It now covers "what auditors do and should do when they perform an audit—and the auditing profession—the institutional framework within which the practice of auditing takes place." The material is arranged within five broad parts: the audit environment; theory and concepts; auditing specific cycles and accounts (such as auditing revenue cycles, investments, income tax); completing the work and reporting the results; auditing specialized industries (banks, educational institutions, health care institutions, high tech companies, brokers/dealers, state and local governments, and more). A shorter revised college text version was published in 1991 (887 pp.) with Philip L. Defliese as lead author.

Robertson, Jack C., and C. T. Zlatkovich. *Auditing.* 6th ed. Homewood, IL: BPI/Irwin, 1990. 765 pp.

Here is a text whose recurring theme is the practical audit method. Students learn by "doing" audits, these authors says, and so they use one recurring audit for much of their book as a "practice case-within-a-textbook." The book is in four parts: introduction to professionalism; general technology of auditing; audit program applications; other attestations and operational auditing.

Sawyer, Lawrence B. *Sawyer's Internal Auditing.* Altamonte Springs, FL: The Institute of Internal Auditors, 1988. 1,291 pp.

This is the third edition, re-titled, revised, and greatly enlarged of Sawyer's IIA-sponsored text, *The Practice of Modern Internal Auditing,* brought up to date (as of 1988) and greatly expanded because of the continuing explosive growth of internal auditing. In successive sections he studies, in depth, internal auditing techniques, scientific methods (including computer auditing), reports, administration of an internal auditing department, and other matters (management, fraud, dealing with people, relations with external auditors and with boards of directors). A final section analyzes each part of the IIA "Standards for the Professional Practice of Internal Auditing." Statistical tables are in appendixes; references and supplementary readings are listed at end of many chapters.

Whittington, O. Ray et al. *Principles of Auditing.* 10th ed. Homewood, IL: Irwin, 1992. 824 pp.

A substantial revision of a standard text which formerly had Walter B. Meigs as its lead author. Its first 10 chapters emphasize the philosophy and environment of the auditing profession (including chapters on standards, ethics, liability, approaches followed in performing audits of financial statements). Chapters 11–17 deal with internal control cycles and obtaining evidence about the various financial statement accounting; chapters 18–19 cover auditors' reporting responsibilities; chapter 20 presents expanded coverage of internal, compliance, and operational accounting. Includes latest pronouncements of the IIA, FASB, etc. Problems are at end of chapters as well as definitions of terms introduced in that chapter.

Three other recently revised textbooks are: *Auditing: An Integrated Approach* by Alvin A. Arens and James K. Loebbecke (5th ed., Prentice-Hall, 1991, 857 pp.); *Auditing: Integrated Concepts and Procedures* by Donald H. Taylor and G. William Glezer (4th ed., Wiley, 1988, 845 pp.); and *Auditing Theory and Practice* by Roger H. Hermanson (5th ed., Irwin, 1989, 776 pp.).

Bibliographies

Formerly the Institute of Internal Auditors published a bibliography covering material published 1969–79. Today they issue only an *Educational Products Catalog* which describes their own publications on auditing and a few books published by commercial publishers. For a description of their bi-monthly *Internal Auditor* refer to the "Accounting Periodicals" section of this chapter.

FINANCIAL STATEMENT ANALYSIS

Bernstein, Leopold A. *Financial Statement Analysis: Theory, Application, and Interpretation.* 4th ed. Homewood, IL: Irwin, 1989. 1,003 pp.

This is probably the best book on financial statement analysis. It aims to give a comprehensive understanding of financial statements and of the tools and methods employed in their analysis. Bernstein says he wrote it for all persons who must make decisions based on financial data (including security analysts, managers, lending officers). Part 2 is devoted to an in-depth analysis of each part of the financial statement; part 3 examines the processes and methodology of financial statement analysis; part 1 is concerned with the relationship between the disciplines of financial analysis and accounting. Practical examples are used throughout. A shortened version of this book has the title *Analysis of Financial Statements* (3d ed., Business One Irwin, 1990, 420 pp.).

An older yet still useful graduate text is *Financial Statement Analysis* by George Foster (2d ed., Prentice-Hall, 1986, 625 pp.).

Donahoe, Alan S. *What Every Manager Should Know About Financial Analysis.* New York: Simon and Schuster, 1989. 223 pp.

Here is a short, easy-to-read book for the busy manager. It is written in simple language from the long experience of a CEO, and so it focuses on the significance and usefulness of financial analysis to top management. Chapters are short, and many examples illustrate key points involved.

Gibson, Charles H. *Financial Statement Analysis: Using Financial Accounting Information.* 4th ed. Boston: PWS-Kent Publishing Co., 1989. 709 pp. (The 5th edition will be published in 1992 by South-Western Publishing Co., Cincinnati, OH).

A novel feature of this book is that one firm is used extensively as an illustration beginning with chapter 5, and also the use of actual statements in illustrations, problems, and cases. The author hopes he has presented a clear, realistic, and balanced treatment of the material. A bibliography is at end.

Merrill Lynch Pierce Fenner & Smith. *How to Read a Financial Report.* 5th ed. New York: 1984. 30 pp.

Here is a helpful little brochure for the individual who knows nothing about financial reports and needs a simple explanation of the various items in a company's balance sheet, income statement, etc., and how these figures can be used to get a general picture of the company's financial health. Merrill Lynch revises or reprints this brochure from time to time and offers it free to interested persons.

A longer paperback explaining 50 key concepts to help users understand the facts is *Keys to Reading an Annual Report* by George T. Friedlob and Ralph E. Welton (New York: Barron's, 1989, 160 pp., paper).

Tracy, John A. *How to Read a Financial Report: Wringing Cash Flow and Other Vital Signs Out of the Numbers.* 3d ed. New York: Wiley, 1989. 164 pp.

This book is meant for the nonaccountant who needs to understand the importance of cash flow and how to read financial statements. It is an informative, short, step-by-step guide using an exhibit throughout to explain the relationships of specific items in the balance sheet, the income statement, and the statement of sources and uses of cash. This makes for a readable, easy-to-follow guide. Accounting terms are explained as they occur.

Another book that uses a fictional company to describe and analyze the parts of the financial statement is *Understanding Financial Statements* by Lyn M. Fraser (3d ed., Prentice-Hall, 1992, 255 pp., paper). An earlier book of possible interest to the British nonspecialist is a practical non-technical guide to *Interpreting Company Reports and Accounting* by Geoffrey Holmes and Alan Sugden (3d ed., Cambridge, Eng.: Woodhead-Faulkner, 1986, 204 pp.).

ACCOUNTING FOR MULTINATIONAL ENTERPRISES

Because of recent rapid developments of the multinational corporation and increased concerns about managing foreign operations, it is important to become familiar with accounting problems as they relate to MNEs. Here are a handbook, four books, and two reference guides to accounting in specific countries. Other books and articles may be found by consulting the *Accountants' Index* or its online counterpart (see "Indexes and Abstracts" section of this chapter).

Handbooks

Choi, Frederick D. S., ed. *Handbook of International Accounting.* New York: Wiley, 1991. 1 volume (various pagings). Annual supplements are planned.
This handbook is intended as a useful reference for those whose interest or responsibilities concern the international dimensions of accounting, reporting, and control. Its 30 chapters are written by both academic and practical contributors, and the editor is an acknowledged expert who has focused most of his teaching and research on this subject. There are 8 basic sections to cover: internationalization of the accounting function; world scene of accounting practices; international financial analysis; international accounting harmonization; technical issues in international accounting; financial reporting and disclosure; analysis, planning, and control issues; international transfer pricing and taxation. A tabular listing of information services is in chapter 10, covering both those providing international, regional, and national coverage, as well as those available in hardcopy and online. Most chapters contain bibliographical references.

Books

AlHashim, Dhia A., and Jeffrey S. Arpan. *International Dimensions of Accounting.* 3d ed. Boston: PWS-Kent Publishing Company, 1992. 252 pp. paper.
Published more recently than the textbook that follows by Arpan/Radebaugh, this short paperback is part of a useful publisher's series that studies the "international dimensions" of specific business functional areas. Written in 7 short chapters by expert professors, it covers such aspects of accounting as financial reporting in MNEs, managerial accounting complexities in international business, auditing. Lists of additional references are with each chapter.

Another short book that is part of a similar publisher's series is *Accounting: An*

International Perspective: A Supplement to Introductory Accounting Textbooks by Gerhard G. Mueller et al. (2d ed., Irwin, 1991, 150 pp. paper).

Arpan, Jeffrey S., and Lee H. Radebaugh. *International Accounting and Multinational Enterprises.* 2d ed. New York: Wiley, 1985. 370 pp.

In this advanced (now rather old) text meant for both accounting students and practicing accountants, the authors have attempted to cover a broad range of issues in order to convey a fundamental understanding of the problems faced by multinational enterprises, as well as appreciation for the ways different countries perceive certain accounting problems and the rationale for how they deal with these problems. A case is provided with most chapters to illustrate the kinds of problems encountered in day-to-day operations; also short bibliographies.

Belkaoui, Ahmed. *Multinational Management Accounting.* New York: Quorum Books, 1991. 292 pp.

"This book explores the major issues that accountants in multinational corporations, and other outside consulting firms, must deal with if they are to understand how the corporation is performing financially, and if they are to effectively advise top management"—book jacket. Professor Belkaoui divides his study into four parts: overview of the international business environment; managing exchange rate risks; organization and controlling; management accounting issues (including international financial analysis, capital budgeting, pricing strategies, the lease-or-buy decision). Bibliographic references are at end of chapters. A companion volume is *Multinational Financial Accounting* (Quorum Books, 1991, 222 pp.).

A related book by the author is *The New Environment in International Accounting: Issues and Practices* (Quorum Books, 1988, 220 pp.) which identifies and examines 7 important new developments in international accounting.

Choi, Frederick D.S., and Gerhard G. Mueller. *International Accounting.* Englewood Cliffs, NJ: Prentice-Hall, 1984. 325 pp. (The second edition will be published in 1992).

Formerly called *An Introduction to Multinational Accounting,* this is an introduction by two respected authorities. The authors cover the financial accounting dimensions with chapters on such topics as foreign currency translation, accounting for inflation, financial reporting and disclosure, analyzing foreign financial statements. There are also chapters on managerial accounting, transfer pricing and international taxation, and one discussing international standards and organizations. Selected references and a case incident are at end of each chapter.

These authors have also edited a useful book of readings on issues and problems called *Essentials of Multinational Accounting: An Anthology* (Ann Arbor, MI: Published for New York University Research Policy Project, the Multinational Firm in the United States and World Economy, by University Microfilms International, 1979, 1 volume, various pagings). There are 85 selections arranged in 7 parts, and a good, annotated bibliography of "Key Book Literature in Multinational Accounting" (10 pp., listing 35 books) is included at the end. A more recent selection of 18 essays to provide an overview of the direction in which international accounting has been moving since 1980 is their *Frontiers of International Accounting: An Anthology* (Ann Arbor, MI: UMI Research Press, 1985, 313 pp., paper).

European Accounting Guide. U.S. Edition. By David Alexander and Simon Archer. New York: Harcourt Brace Jovanovich, 1991. 1,097 pp.

Arranged by country, this provides descriptions of accounting rules and practice in each European country including four in Eastern Europe. For each it covers: background; the form and content of published financial statements; accounting policies and practices in valuation and income measurement—implications for the analyst; expected future developments; specimen financial statements. Authors for each country chapter are usually CPAs in the country.

Orsini, Larry L. et al. *World Accounting.* New York: Matthew Bender, 1990. 3 volumes (loose-leaf).

Intended for financial executives and others involved in international operations, this consists of a country-by-country reference source for current information on accounting and auditing practices, standards, and regulations in 20 countries. Within each country the arrangement is by section for ease in country comparisons. This can be useful as a general reference for the countries it covered, but it is not meant to be definitive.

The American Institute of Certified Public Accountants now publishes a series of booklets on *The Accounting Profession in (name of country).* As of 1990 it covers only 13 countries, but for these, it contains information on the accounting profession, auditing standards, and accounting principles for each.

ACCOUNTING AND CONTROL FOR GOVERNMENTAL AND NONPROFIT ORGANIZATIONS

With more and more nonprofit organizations showing concern about accurate and efficient methods of accounting and financial reporting, a growing literature has aimed specifically to meet their needs. This section describes several books covering the whole area of accounting and control for governmental and nonprofit organizations. For the names of books and articles on accounting dealing with specific types of organizations such as hospitals, educational institutions, and so forth, consult recent issues of *Accountants' Index* or its online counterpart.

Anthony, Robert N., and David W. Young. *Management Control in Nonprofit Organizations.* 4th ed. Homewood, IL: Irwin, 1988. 918 pp.

The thesis of this textbook is that basic control concepts are the same in both profit-oriented and nonprofit organizations but that, because of the special characteristics of nonprofit organizations, the application of these concepts differs in some important respects. The authors focus on both the management control structure and on the steps in the management control process (programming, budgeting, control of operations, reporting on performance, etc.). A few cases are at the end of each of its 17 chapters.

Gross, Malvern J., Jr., William Warshauer, Jr., and Richard F. Larkin. *Financial and Accounting Guide for Not-For-Profit Organizations.* Rev. 4th ed. New York: Wiley, 1991. 686 pp.

This is intended as a practical and professional guide for treasurers and executives of nonprofit (nongovernmental) organizations who need to understand something about the principles of nonprofit accounting, about financial reporting, and about how to communicate their financial activities and financial conditions to members and to the public. Little accounting knowledge is required. This latest edition has been expanded to reflect rapidly changing events in nonprofit accounting and in tax laws. It is arranged in six parts: key financial concepts; financial statement presentation; accounting and reporting guidelines (including chapters on guidelines for specific types of organizations such as health care providers, colleges and universities); controlling the not-for-profit organization; tax and compliance reporting requirements; setting up and keeping the books. Includes a bibliography. Annual supplements are planned to keep the material up to date.

Hay, Leon E., and Earl R. Wilson. *Accounting for Governmental and Nonprofit Entities*. 9th ed. Homewood, IL: Irwin, 1992. 867 pp.

Latest edition of a standard text on accounting for nonbusiness entities, with 14 of its 22 chapters describing the application of generally accepted accounting principles to the activities of state and local governmental units. Separate chapters cover accounting for colleges and universities, health care entities, volunteer health and welfare organizations, the federal government, and other nonprofit organizations. Short lists of references and problems are at end of chapters; a useful glossary and present value tables are at the back of the book. A shorter text, with John H. Engstrom as coauthor, is *Essentials of Accounting for Governmental and Not-for-Profit Organizations* (2d ed., Irwin, 1990, 349 pp., paper).

Henke, Emerson O. *Introduction to Nonprofit Organization Accounting*. 3d ed. Boston: PWS-Kent Publishing Company, 1988. 670 pp. (The 4th edition will be published in 1992 by South-Western Publishing Co., Cincinnati, OH).

Henke has previously written several books on accounting for nonprofit organizations. Here is a revised and greatly expanded version to meet this growing interest in the nonprofit segment of our economy. It is in four parts to cover: nonprofit organization accounting systems; governmental accounting; accounting for other nonprofit organizations (colleges and universities, hospitals, health and welfare agencies and churches); using nonprofit organization accounting data (how to effectively read and interpret financial reports). This text presumes an introductory accounting background. At end are: an appendix containing audits of nonprofit organizations, a glossary, and a bibliography.

Professor Henke's shorter text is *Accounting for Nonprofit Organizations* (5th ed., PWS-Kent Publishing Co., 1989, 408 pp., paper).

SURVEYS OF COMPANY ACCOUNTING PRACTICES

Two guides to accounting rules and practices in foreign countries are described in this chapter's section on "Accounting for Multinational Enterprises."

American Institute of Certified Public Accountants. *Accounting Trends & Techniques*. New York (annual).

This is a useful annual survey of accounting practices, arranged by broad subject (with a more detailed subject index at the end), thus making it possible to compare company accounting practices on many specific topics such as business combinations, contingencies, leases, pensions, and retirement plans. It is based on a study of stockholder's reports for 600 industrial and merchandising corporations, with added excerpts from and comments on unusual accounting treatments found in additional reports.

Institute of Chartered Accountants in England and Wales. *Financial Reporting: A Survey of UK Reporting Practice*. London (annual).

This is somewhat similar to the AICPA guide above, with part 2 providing survey tables and examples based on the financial reports of 300 British industrial and commercial companies. In part 1, contributors address some of the key issues of the day concerning current financial reporting practices, with examples an important part of their review.

The Canadian Institute of Chartered Accountants (Toronto) publishes a biennial survey of annual reports of 300 Canadian public companies called *Financial Reporting in Canada*.

ACCOUNTING SERVICES

The Commerce Clearing House publishes several loose-leaf services, which are important sources for current information on accounting laws, regulations, court decisions, rules, and standards. Loose-leaf services in general are discussed in Chapter 2. Tax services are listed elsewhere in this chapter. Several CCH and FASB accounting services plus an online system are:

Accountancy Law Reporter. (CCH). 2 volumes.

State laws regulating the practice of public accounting. This loose-leaf service is published in cooperation with the American Institute of Certified Public Accountants.

AICPA Professional Standards. Chicago. 2 volumes (loose-leaf).

Volume 1 covers U.S. auditing standards of the American Institute of Certified Public Accountants; volume 2 contains data on accounting and review services, code of professional ethics, bylaws, international accounting standards, international auditing, guidelines, management advisory services, quality control, and tax policy.

Financial Accounting Standards Board. *Accounting Standards: Current Text.* Norwalk, CT. 2 volumes (loose-leaf service).

This service contains an integration of currently effective accounting and reporting standards. Material is drawn from pronouncements and descriptive materials in the AICPA Accounting Research Bulletins, APB Opinions, FASB Statements and Financial Accounting Standards, and FASB Interpretations. Volume 1 covers general standards and volume 2, industry standards.

NAARS (National Automated Accounting Research System).

This is a full text online service produced jointly by the AICPA and Mead Data Central. One part covers a wide range of accounting literature relating to the major official statements, pronouncements, interpretations, and so forth, of important accounting boards, commissions, and associations as well as government regulatory agencies such as the SEC. Included are the publications of the Accounting Principles Board, Financial Accounting Standards Board, Cost Accounting Standards Board, International Accounting Standards Committee, Governmental Accounting Standards Board. The other part consists of full text for financial statements and auditors' reports from annual reports of about 4,200 public companies.

SEC Accounting Rules. (CCH). 1 volume.

Securities and Exchange Commission rules on accounting practices and procedures for financial statements. Includes texts of Accounting Series Releases, Bulletins, and Guides for Registration Statements.

While it is not a legal service, it may be useful to note here the existence of a popularly written guide to current promulgated Generally Accepted Auditing Standards published annually as *Miller Comprehensive GAAS Guide* by Martin A. Miller and Larry P. Bailey (New York: Harcourt Brace Jovanovich).

MANAGEMENT OF ACCOUNTING FIRMS

Kastantin, Joseph T. *Professional Accounting Practice Management.* New York: Quorum Books, 1988. 215 pp.

This book is intended to help the accounting practitioner manage his/her own business practice. The first of five sections discusses basic business considerations such as purpose, goals, insurance, financing. The other four cover in turn: working relationships with staff, partners, bankers, and the IRS; client services; marketing/advertising; "making it work for you" which focuses on administration, financial statements, computers, and other factors. A selected bibliography is at end.

ACCOUNTING INDEXES AND ABSTRACTS

Accountants' Index. New York: American Institute of Certified Public Accountants (biennial through 1970; now quarterly, with last issue an annual cumulation). Available also online as *Accountants.*

An indispensable, comprehensive subject/author index to English-language books, pamphlets, government documents, and major articles from more than 300 periodicals on accounting and related fields of auditing, data processing, financial reporting, financial management, investments and securities, management, and taxation. Includes references for both business and nonbusiness organizations and on accounting in many specific industries. Publication of the print volumes is very slow; use the online counterpart for recent citations.

Accounting Articles. Chicago: Commerce Clearing House (monthly).

A cumulated, annotated loose-leaf service which describes and indexes articles on accounting and management services appearing in accounting, business, economic, management, and other English-language journals. It is arranged topically within 8 major subject sections, and there are two cumulated indexes—by author and by subject.

American Institute of Certified Public Accountants. *Index to Accounting and Auditing Technical Pronouncements.* New York (annual).

As the title indicates, this is a more specialized index, but it is still of great value to accountants and auditors because it is a cumulative index to the current pronouncements of the AICPA, FASB, GASB, SEC, and certain other professional and regulatory bodies. It is arranged alphabetically by subject and gives the section or paragraph number of the accounting or auditing service where each pronouncement may be found.

ACCOUNTING DICTIONARIES

Cooper, W.W., and Yuji Ijiri, eds. *Kohler's Dictionary for Accountants.* 6th ed. Englewood Cliffs, NJ: Prentice-Hall, 1983. 574 pp.

Carrying forward Eric Kohler's tradition for thoroughness, these two editors, with help from 20 other authorities, have extensively revised and updated this excellent, complete dictionary. It describes terms and phrases not only for accounting and auditing but also for such related fields as economics, law, taxation, finance, management science, statistics, computers. Definitions vary from one sentence to several paragraphs and even occasionally to a page or two in length.

Davidson, Sidney, Clyde P. Stickney and Roman L. Weil. *Accounting: The Language of Business.* 7th ed. Sun Lakes, AZ: T. Horton and Daughters, Inc., 1987. 131 pp.

The first 83 pages contain a useful glossary of some 1,400 accounting terms in wide usage. The rest includes a reproduction of GE's annual report, with comments, and a list of official accounting pronouncements (but only as of 1987).

Shim, Jae K., and Joel G. Siegal. *Encyclopedic Dictionary of Accounting and Finance.* Englewood Cliffs, NJ: Prentice-Hall, 1989. 504 pp.

This encyclopedic dictionary covers all major topics in accounting and finance as well as related subjects such as computers and economics. Definitions are usually longer than in a traditional dictionary, and there is frequent use of examples, formulas, tables, and so forth. Both authors are experienced accounting/finance professors.

Siegel, Joel G., and Jae K. Shim. *Dictionary of Accounting Terms.* New York: Barron's, 1987. 472 pp. paper.

Defines approximately 2,500 terms which the authors hope present the working vocabulary of accounting today—covering not only new terms but also updating the traditional language of accounting and its related disciplines. Note that the same authors prepared the dictionary above.

ACCOUNTING PERIODICALS

Articles in all of these journals are indexed in *Accountants' Index,* its online counterpart, and in *Accounting Articles.*

Accounting Horizons. Sarasota, FL: American Accounting Association (quarterly).

A new AAA journal (1987) intended to provide readable, practical articles of interest to accounting practitioners, educators, and students on such topics as accounting policy issues, technical issues, applied research, interpretations of research findings for practical applications.

The AAA continues to publish its excellent quarterly *Accounting Review* which is a professional journal reporting on scholarly research covering all aspects of accounting and intended more for faculty researchers and doctoral students. This latter quarterly includes an excellent book review section, and is indexed in ABI/I, BPI.

CPA Journal. New York: New York State Society of Certified Public Accountants (monthly).

This is probably the best example of a journal issued by a state CPA society, with articles of interest to CPAs (and usually written by CPAs) on accounting, auditing, taxation; also news about new trends, taxes, etc. Indexed in ABI/I, BPI, TI; full text on BRS, DATA-STAR, DIALOG, DOW JONES.

The Financial Manager. Boston: Warren, Gorham & Lamont (bimonthly).

A new (1988) bimonthly for financial and accounting professionals in medium-sized businesses, which focuses on practical articles covering finance, accounting, computers, and taxation.

The Government Accountants Journal. Alexandria, VA: The Association of Government Accountants (quarterly).

Practical articles on government accounting and control. One or two book reviews are in some issues. Indexed in ABI/I.

Internal Auditor. Altamonte Springs, FL: Institute of Internal Auditors (bimonthly).

Contains short articles of interest to auditors and controllers. Includes brief book reviews. Indexed in ABI/I, BPI, TI; full text on BRS, DATA-STAR, DIALOG.

International Journal of Accounting. London: Springer-Verlag London Ltd. or Secaucus, NJ: Springer-Verlag New York (quarterly).

This refereed journal aims "to advance the academic and professional understanding of accounting theory and practice from an international perspective and viewpoint." Articles are well researched and contain bibliographical citations. Includes a few book reviews.

Journal of Accountancy. New York: American Institute of Certified Public Accountants (monthly).

A long-time journal providing articles on new trends and topics of current interest to the practicing CPA, with special emphasis on financial accounting. Contains practitioners' forum, official releases (including new FASB Statements), and a section called "Current Reading." Indexed in ABI/I, BPI, PAIS, TI; full text on BRS, DATA-STAR, DIALOG.

Journal of Accounting, Auditing & Finance. Westport, CT: Greenwood Press (quarterly).

Sponsored by the Vincent C. Ross Institute of Accounting Research at New York University, this journal seeks to publish thoughtful discussions or reports of research on a wide range of subjects of interest and concern to practicing corporate and professional accountants. Indexed in ABI/I, BPI.

Journal of Accounting Research. Chicago: Institute of Professional Accounting, Graduate School of Business, University of Chicago (semiannual).

The *JAR* publishes scholarly articles written primarily by academic persons, with an emphasis on accounting theory. An annual supplement contains the proceedings of the annual Conference on Accounting Research held at the University of Chicago. Indexed in ABI/I, BPI.

Management Accounting. Montvale, NJ: National Association of Accountants (monthly).

Well written, short, and practical articles for corporate decision makers on management accounting and related topics such as auditing, budgeting. They are written by practicing accountants, as well as by managers and educators. Indexed in ABI/I, BPI, PTS/F&S, TI.

National Public Accountant. Alexandria, VA: National Society of Public Accountants (monthly).

Usually this journal has about five short articles in each issue on a wide range of accounting topics of interest to the public accountant, banker, small business person, etc. Includes brief book notes. Indexed in ABI/I, PAIS, TI; full text on BRS, DATA-STAR, DIALOG.

Probably more professional journals are published on accounting than in any other business area. A longer list can be found in the back of CCH's *Accounting Articles*. These include not only official journals of U.S. professional societies but also those of other countries, publications of U.S. state CPA societies, and a few journals published by the larger U.S. accounting firms. A short list is also in *The Accountant's Almanac* (see listing with "Directories" below).

Several useful Canadian and British accounting journals are:

Accountancy. London: Institute of Chartered Accountants in England and Wales (monthly). Indexed in ABI/I. This Institute also publishes a quarterly on *Accounting and Business Research*. Indexed in ABI/I, BPI, PAIS, TI.

The Accountant. Dublin: Lafferty Publications Ltd. (monthly). Short journal focusing on professional development.

CA Magazine. Toronto: Canadian Institute of Chartered Accountants (monthly). Indexed in ABI/I, BPI, TI.

CMA. Hamilton, Ontario, Canada: Society of Management Accountants of Canada (bimonthly). Indexed in ABI/I.

Certified Accountant. London: Chartered Association of Certified Accountants (bimonthly).

Management Accounting. London: Chartered Institute of Management Accountants (monthly). Indexed in ABI/I; full text on DIALOG.

DIRECTORIES OF ACCOUNTANTS

See also a useful descriptive list of 80 leading CPA accounting and auditing firms in *The Corporate Finance Sourcebook* (noted in Chapter 14).

The Accountant's Almanac. New York: Executive Enterprises Publications (annual).

Brings together useful "resources, facts, and statistics for use by accountants in their practice." Most is directory-type information: data on professional organizations, professional development (education, certification, list of periodicals, etc.), list of major accounting firms with addresses of local offices, regulating bodies, *Fortune*'s largest companies with names of their accounting firms; also professional ethics and standards.

Emerson's Directory of Leading U.S. Accounting Firms. Bellevue, WA: Emerson's Professional Services Review (biennial).

A geographic directory of over 3,000 leading U.S. accounting firms that have met the criteria for inclusion based on peer or quality reviews. For each it provides names of key persons, codes referring to approximate size of staff, whether a branch or main office, scope of services. At front is key information about the national offices of the 13 largest firms. A firm index is at end.

Two British associations each publish an annual *List of Members and Firms:* the Institute of Chartered Accountants in England and Wales and the Chartered Association of Certified Accountants. There is also an annual *Directory of Canadian Chartered Accountants* published by the Canadian Institute of Chartered Accountants.

ACCOUNTING ASSOCIATIONS

American Accounting Association, 5717 Bessie Drive, Sarasota, FL 34233.

American Institute of Certified Public Accountants, 1211 Avenue of the Americas, New York, NY 10036.

Association of Government Accountants, 2200 Mt. Vernon Avenue, Alexandria, VA 22301.

Institute of Internal Auditors, 249 Maitland Avenue, Altamonte Springs, FL 32701.

National Association of Accountants, 10 Paragon Drive, Montvale, NJ 07645.

National Society of Public Accountants, 1010 North Fairfax Street, Alexandria, VA 22314.

TAXATION

This section concentrates on tax reference sources of interest to business managers. Most of the books on tax management are now too old to be of interest. The following two seem to be the only relatively recent ones.

BOOKS ON TAX MANAGEMENT

Ruland, William. *Manager's Guide to Corporate Tax.* New York: Wiley, 1984. 370 pp.

In simple language for the manager with no tax or legal training, Ruland attempts to give a basic understanding of corporate tax and how tax issues affect the corporation, as well as an appreciation for tax planning. The first six chapters provide background and summarize basic tax concepts applicable to most businesses. The last six chapters are concerned with tax issues unique to the corporation (dividends, returns of invested capital, form of organization, acquisitions, reorganization, spin-offs and other corporate divisions). It focuses only on topics of general interest and is not intended as a substitute for a tax adviser.

Sommerfeld, Ray M. *Federal Taxes and Management Decisions.* Homewood, IL: Irwin (biennial revision).

Professor Sommerfeld has tried to provide readers with a broad vista of tax planning opportunities and tax traps. He says his goal is "symptom recognition" so that the business person working with an expert tax adviser can recognize and understand important tax consequences of many common business transactions. Most chapters are topical, with the provisions selected for discussion those pertaining primarily to income tax with a lesser emphasis on estate and gift tax.

TAX SERVICES

Federal and state regulations have multiplied so rapidly and have become so complex that it is essential for the businessperson, accountant, banker, and lawyer to have ready access to the very latest in tax laws, regulations, and rulings, to ensure compliance with the law and to minimize the amount of tax paid. Both of the best known loose-leaf service publishers offer complete federal and state tax services, kept right up-to-date with supplementary pages inserted weekly. They also publish several condensed but still useful guides and services. A few U.S. tax services are listed below. Foreign tax services are noted in Chapter 16. Loose-leaf services as a basic source of information are discussed in Chapter 2.

Comprehensive Federal Tax Services

Commerce Clearing House. *Standard Federal Tax Reporter.* Chicago. 19 volumes (annual, with weekly supplements). Available online as *CCH/ ACCESS.*

Prentice-Hall, Inc. *Federal Taxes.* Englewood Cliffs, NJ: 16 volumes (annual, with weekly supplements).

These two services are similar in coverage, and so it is primarily a matter of personal preference as to which one an individual uses. Both give complete information about all federal tax laws, regulations, court decisions, administrative rulings, etc. Each is arranged by topic or Internal Revenue Code section; they have good instructions on how to use the service; they have complete indexes, charts, finding lists, tax planning information, supplementary brochures. They differ somewhat in arrangement of volumes:

Of the 19-volume CCH set, 13 numbered volumes cover income tax, with the 13th devoted to "New Matters, Finding Devices, Editorial Analysis". The other unnumbered volumes cover: *Internal Revenue Code* (2 volumes); *Citator* (2 volumes); *U.S. Tax Cases—Advanced Sheets;* the *Index.* This latter volume contains a complete topical index, tax calendar, tax tables, checklists, tax planning ideas, tax terms, special tables such as annuity and savings bond tables, Bulletin F depreciation rate tables. Two of its many other tax services are: *Federal Excise Tax Reporter* (1 volume), and the multi-volume *U.S. Tax Cases* which publishes the text of all federal court decisions on federal income, excise, estate, and gift taxes.

CCH's online service, *CCH/ACCESS,* provides users with an easy means of finding information and doing tax law research. It consists of the majority of data from their *Standard Federal Tax Reporter* plus also data from other CCH tax services covering federal and state taxes, historical data, and news about recent developments. A CD-ROM product is in progress as of 1991. CCH publishes a number of loose-leaf legal services covering taxes, securities, insurance, labor, etc., in Canada, and also in Australia and New Zealand, and in Mexico.

Prentice Hall's 16-volume tax service consists of: 12 numbered volumes of which all but the last provide detailed data on income taxes arranged by Internal Revenue Code number; volume 12 contains recent developments, new legislation, etc. The other volumes (unnumbered) consist of: an index volume; an American Federal Tax Reports *AFTR 2d, Decisions* current volume; the *Internal Revenue Code* (2 volumes). Separately published from the basic 16-volume set are *Estate & Gift Taxes* (2 volumes); *Excise Taxes* (1 volume); *Federal Regulations* (3 volumes); Federal Tax Citator (4 volumes); *Tax Court Memorandum Decisions.*

Condensed Services and Guides

Although complete tax services are essential, it is often possible to find the tax information needed by using one of the shorter guides or handbooks, which are easier to keep nearby for answering simple tax questions that arise daily. Several of these are:

Commerce Clearing House. *Federal Tax Guide.* 8 volumes.

Prentice-Hall, Inc. *Federal Tax Guide.* 2 volumes.

These are condensed versions of the complete services described above, geared to answer many of the everyday corporate and individual tax questions with clearly written, short explanations. Kept up-to-date for new laws, regulations, and rulings by weekly loose-leaf supplements.

Commerce Clearing House. *U.S. Master Tax Guide.* 1 volume (annual).

Prentice-Hall, Inc. *Federal Tax Handbook.* 1 volume (annual).

Each is a simple, shortcut guide providing basic information on how to prepare income tax returns for individuals, corporations, and small businesses. Each contains paragraph references to its complete services for persons wanting more information. The CCH guide is now also available in an expanded loose-leaf format with updates, as well as on a disk.

State and Local Services

Comprehensive loose-leaf services are published to cover state and local taxes:

Commerce Clearing House. *State Tax Reporter.*

Prentice-Hall, Inc. *State and Local Taxes.*

These are similar services, the choice depending on personal preference. Each publishes a separate volume for each state, providing complete up-to-date coverage on state and local taxes. Each also has an "All States" volume, with charts, tables, and data to show which taxes are imposed by which states.

CCH publishes two other state tax guides: *State Tax Cases Reporter* and *All-State Sales Tax Reporter,* as well as a weekly *State Tax Review* highlighting major laws and other state tax news. Prentice-Hall's related services are: *Sales Taxes; State Income Taxes.*

Commerce Clearing House. *State Tax Guide.* 2 volumes.

Prentice-Hall, Inc. *All States Tax Guide.*

Handy, condensed tax guides that are easy-to-use sources for finding basic state tax laws. They are arranged by type of tax, with state facts given in each section.

TAX BIBLIOGRAPHIES AND INDEXES

Commerce Clearing House. *Federal Tax Articles.* Chicago (monthly).

This loose-leaf service describes federal tax articles (covering income, estate, gift, excise, and employment taxes) that have appeared in tax, legal, accounting, business, and other related journals. It is arranged by Internal Revenue Code section, with indexes by subject and by author.

Index to Federal Tax Articles. Boston: Warren, Gorham & Lamont (quarterly).

A topical index to articles on federal income, estate, and gift taxes that appear in legal, tax, accounting, and a few economic journals. There is an author index, a list of subject headings, and a list of periodicals covered.

Monthly Digest of Tax Articles. Albany, NY: Newkirk Products, Inc.

As the title indicates, each issue digests a selection of current tax articles, many from law journals. Includes a section for cases and rulings.

TAXATION PERIODICALS

Articles in these journals are also indexed in *Accountants' Index* and in its online counterpart.

Journal of Corporate Taxation. Boston: Warren, Gorham & Lamont (quarterly).

Of interest to practicing attorneys and accountants, corporate counsel, and executives, this usually contains three articles plus three to four varying columns on such topics as corporate organizations and reorganizations, closely-held corporations, recent developments.

Journal of Taxation. Boston: Warren, Gorham & Lamont for the Tax Research Group, Ltd. (monthly).

A national professional journal of current tax developments and trends for tax practitioners. Includes summaries of tax decisions, court actions, revenue rulings issued each month, and occasionally an annotated list of "Recent Tax Literature." Indexed in ABI/I, BPI, TI. The Tax Research Group also publishes a monthly *Taxation for Accountants.* Indexed in ABI/I, BPI.

National Tax Journal. Columbus, OH: National Tax Association/Tax Institute of America (quarterly).

Professional journal reporting on research in government finance and taxation. One issue is usually devoted to NTA/TIA symposia proceedings. Indexed in ABI/I, BPI, PAIS.

Tax Executive. Washington, DC: Tax Executives Institute (bimonthly).

Articles are on tax practices and problems and other topics of interest to corporate tax officers. Occasionally includes a few book reviews or notes. Indexed in ABI/I, PAIS.

Taxes. Chicago: Commerce Clearing House (monthly).

"Published to promote sound thought in economic, legal and accounting principles relating to all federal and state taxation." There are signed articles, usually with many legal citations, and also notes by CCH staff members on recent federal and state tax matters and meetings. Indexed in BPI, PAIS.

13

COMPUTERS AND MANAGEMENT INFORMATION SYSTEMS

Management Information Systems – Indexes and Abstracts – Computer Dictionaries – Periodicals – Computer Directories – Associations – Office Management

Business men and women have had ways of getting information and keeping records since ancient times. It has only been with recent rapid developments in computer capabilities that revolutionary changes have occurred in the kinds of data available and in the whole flow of information throughout an organization. Managers and students today are finding it imperative to both understand and know how to use these new systems. For managers the need is to keep abreast of new developments and to be able to talk intelligently with information specialists in a continuing effort to make faster, more accurate decisions and forecasts. Now, with the heavy use of personal computers, it is clear that every employee (and not just the manager) must be familiar with and feel comfortable in using computers in the daily work process. Tomorrow the same is bound to be true also for homemakers and persons in all walks of life.

This chapter then aims to help managers by listing a few current sources on computers and on management information systems (MIS) in general. There is also a short section on office management. Chapter 2 includes a brief discussion on the use of computerized databases as the fastest and most efficient way of conducting literature searches and of retrieving statistical data; chapter 17 covers the important topics of mathematical techniques and decision making. Books on all of these subjects are so quickly outdated that continual use of various bibliographical indexes, abstracting services, and recent journals is particularly important for keeping informed on the latest trends and techniques.

MANAGEMENT INFORMATION SYSTEMS

Handbooks

Handbook of IS Management. Robert E. Umbaugh, ed. 3d ed. Boston: Auerbach Publishers, 1991. 824 pp. To be kept up to date with a Yearbook.

This handbook "is directed to those who have the responsibility for managing and guiding the application of information technology in an organization—both large or small." The chapters, each written by an expert, are arranged within 18 sections. Not only do these sections cover such traditional topics as systems development, security and control, human resources, and database management, but they also cover strategy/planning, management issues, quality improvement, communications networks, technology outlook, and more. Diagrams and checklists are used throughout.

Handbook of Information Resources Management. Ed by Jack Rabin and Edward M. Jackowski. (Public Administration and Public Policy, 31). New York and Basel: M. Dekker, 1988. 567 pp.

"Compiled as an encyclopedic treatment of the major areas in information systems and data administration," this is a basic introduction to the subject, with each chapter written by an expert. It is arranged within four parts: theoretical/technological developments and pedagogic underpinnings; elements in information systems and data administration (including a chapter on information centers); information systems architecture; data adminstration. Usually quite long lists of references are at end of each essay.

Handbook of Systems Management: Development and Support. Ed. by Paul C. Tinnirello. Boston: Auerbach Publishers, 1989. 820 pp. And a supplementary Yearbook.

Up-to-date information is very important in this field, and so it is good to know about a recent handbook with an annual update. This one has over 40 contributors and the chapters are arranged in 15 sections. Sections 1–3 cover the management methodologies area; sections 4–12 discuss the tools and techniques area (such as hardware, software, programming language, testing, and so forth); section 13 deals with career and human resources issues; and sections 14–15 cover understanding business issues.

Books

Bugg, Phillip W. *Microcomputers in the Corporate Environment.* Englewood Cliffs, NJ: Prentice-Hall, 1986. 192 pp.

We start off with a specialized book whose purpose it is "to serve as a guide to those using or planning to use microcomputer technology in corporate settings." It was written especially for those in positions of influencing, supporting, or managing corporate microcomputer resources. First there is an introductory section on the microcomputer revolution. This is followed in turn by sections covering: microcomputer systems (hardware and software); microcomputer applications (word processing, graphs, data communication, and so forth); microcomputer management (including advice on policy and on development and management).

Cash, James I., Jr., F. Warren McFarlan and James L. McKenney. *Corporate Information Systems Management: The Issues Facing Senior Executives.* 3d ed. Homewood, IL: Business One Irwin, 1992. 301 pp. paper.

Designed to help present and future managers better prepare themselves and their organizations to deal with the management of information systems technology

(IT)—computers, telecommunications, and office systems. This latest edition incorporates material on new challenges to competitive advantage posed by the latest technologies, and it pays particular attention to changes in corporate organization, control, response times, and costs. Chapters 1 and 2 begin with an overview and a series of frameworks the authors have found useful for analyzing and structuring problems in this field. With this background, each chapter then deals specifically with issues relating to how the IT activity can be best organized, planned, and controlled. Their book is based heavily on observation of real practice. A useful short descriptive list of general management books and of IT books is at end.

For persons who want this same text with cases added, see their *Corporate Information Systems Management: Text and Cases* (3d ed., Irwin, 1992).

Emery, James C. *Management Information Systems: The Critical Strategic Resource.* New York: Oxford University Press, 1987. 341 pp.

A good introduction, designed to give practicing senior managers the knowledge necessary on management information systems technology without their being technical experts. Focusing on concepts rather than on techniques, the author explains computers and their language, handling routine transactions, decision support systems, the process of developing application software, how to develop an information system, and finally implementing a successful MIS strategy. A few books for further reading are described at end of each chapter; a useful glossary is at end of book.

Fitzgerald, Jerry, and Ardra F. Fitzgerald. *Fundamentals of Systems Analysis.* 3d ed. New York: Wiley, 1987. 769, [130] pp.

A first-rate text for a beginning course in systems analysis and design intended to teach "systems thinking" and to cover all general concepts and problem-solving steps. The heart of the book is in its second part which discusses the 10 steps of systems analysis. The last part covers the tools of systems analysis such as charting, forms design, records retention, report analysis, procedure writing, and so forth. The last chapter covering analysts' research needs contains a useful discussion of basic library reference sources of use to systems analysts (pp.732–768). Selections for further study and short "situation cases" are at the end of each chapter; appendixes and a glossary are separately paged at end.

O'Brien, James A. *Introduction to Information Systems in Business Management.* 6th ed. Homewood, IL: Irwin, 1991. 515, [15] pp.

Another major revision of a standard undergraduate text whose objective it is "to build a basic understanding of the value and uses of information systems for business operations, management decision making, and strategic advantage," while also providing up-to-date coverage reflecting the dynamic changes occurring in this field. It is organized according to the five major areas of the framework for information systems knowledge: foundation concepts; technology; applications; development; management. Useful two-color diagrams and other illustrations appear throughout, with "real-world applications" in boxes. Selected references are with chapters; a glossary is paged separately at end.

A shortened version of this text focuses just on *Computer Concepts and Applications: With an Introduction To Software and BASIC* (3d ed., Irwin, 1989, 470, [124] pp.) Professor O'Brien has also written a modular text for future managers who will use MIS, with title *Management Information Systems: A Managerial End-User Perspective* (Irwin, 1990, 670 pp.).

Thierauf, Robert J. *Executive Information Systems: A Guide for Senior Management and MIS Professionals.* New York: Quorum Books, 1991. 364 pp.

Executive Information Systems (EIS) are designed to provide management with reporting tools for planning, monitoring, and analyzing the company's total operations. This book, both for practitioners and academicians, is structured to follow a logical flow. It starts with an overview of EIS and then focuses in turn on: the hardware and software useful in an EIS environment; the development of EIS; applications (to strategic planning, marketing, manufacturing, finance, personnel). Bibliographies are at end of each of its four parts.

Watson, Hugh J., Archie D. Carroll and Robert I. Mann, eds. *Information Systems for Management: A Book of Readings.* 3d ed. Plano, TX: Business Publications, 1987. 514 pp. paper.

These authors feel that students should know about the four basic aspects of computers and information systems, and so they have arranged their book of more than 30 readings into these four categories: computer hardware and software; computer-based information systems; management of information systems; computer impact on personnel, organizations, and society. The articles were selected for their readability, level of interest, contributions to understanding, and current importance.

Several other books as possible alternatives are: *Information Systems Concepts for Management* by Henry C. Lucas, Jr. (4th ed., McGraw-Hill, 1990, 530 pp.), a textbook for future managers; *Managing the Systems Development Function* by Robert O. Peterson (Van Nostrand Reinhold, 1987, 294 pp.); and *Managing Information Systems: An Integrated Approach* by Eugene J. Wittry (Dearborn, MI: Society of Manufacturing Engineers, 1987, 280 pp.), a well-written book covering both theory and practice. Yet another recent and more specialized book on the effective implementation of advanced information technology in organizations is *Up and Coming: Integrating Information Technology and the Organization* by Richard E. Walton (Boston: Harvard Business School Press, 1989, 231 pp.).

INDEXES AND ABSTRACTS

Computer Database.

Indexes and abstracts online about 360 journals on computers, computer industry, telecommunications, and electronics. A companion database is *Computer ASAP* which provides full text for articles in fewer journals.

Computer Literature Index. Phoenix, AZ: Applied Computer Research (quarterly, with an annual cumulation).

A very useful descriptive subject/author index to computer and data processing literature, with an emphasis on practical material rather than research or academic literature. It includes books, special reports, proceedings, and a selection of the more "durable" articles. The main listing is by subject, and an alphabetic index is at the end.

Computing Reviews. New York: Association for Computing Machinery (monthly). The online counterpart is *COMPUSCIENCE.*

Good, signed reviews of books and articles on computer sciences, classified by specific topics within 11 broad subject fields. Includes computer applications, software, hardware, mathematics of computing. "Books and Proceedings" are covered first, followed by a longer section for "Nonbook Literature." *COMPUSCIENCE,* the online counterpart, includes also the *ACM Guide to Computing Literature* which is an annual index to the world's computing literature.

Data Processing Digest. Los Angeles. (monthly).

A useful monthly digest of the more significant articles (and a few books), arranged by subject and covering all aspects of computer technology and its application to operations and management. It is compiled for the computer professional and the manager who uses computer technology for planning, control, and production.

COMPUTER DICTIONARIES

Covington, Michael, and Douglas Downing. *Dictionary of Computer Terms.* 2d ed. New York: Barron's, 1989. 333 pp. paper.

A useful dictionary covering approximately 1,000 key terms and applications of common commands and functions. Definitions are well-written and the compilers have included in-depth discussions of many terms. At front are lists of selected words by categories to help in finding entries related to a particular topic.

Rosenberg, Jerry M. *Dictionary of Computers, Information Processing, & Telecommunications.* 2d ed. New York: Wiley, 1987. 734 pp. paper.

Probably the most comprehensive of the dictionaries covering the title subjects, this one contains more than 12,000 concise definitions, some of which are quoted from several other sources. Includes symbols, acronyms, abbreviations; there are many cross-references. At end is a list of French and Spanish equivalents for basic terms.

Sippl, Charles J. *Computer Dictionary.* 4th ed. Indianapolis, IN: H.W. Sams & Co., 1985. 562 pp. paper.

Sippl's dictionary is designed to aid in identifying and defining terms and concepts concerned with electronic data processing, information technology, computer science, robotics, and other types of automation. It is now out of date for any recent interpretations of terms.

Spencer, Donald D. *Spencer's Computer Dictionary for Everyone.* 3d ed. New York: Scribner's, 1985. 290 pp.

Expanded in this edition to cover more than 3,000 most frequently used terms, words, acronyms, and abbreviations, this dictionary aims to give simple definitions in easy-to-understand language for the beginner. Includes occasional photographs or drawings. Its author is a computer science consultant who has written widely in the area of computers. This is also out of date for current terms.

PERIODICALS

American Federation of Information Processing Societies. *AFIPS Conference Proceedings.* Reston, VA: AFIPS Press (annual).

These proceedings offer an excellent means of keeping up-to-date on new developments in computer science and technology and their applications. AFIPS is a federation of 5 computer societies; their conference is called the "National Computer Conference."

Computerworld. Framingham, MA: CW Publishing, Inc. (weekly, with some exceptions).

This is "the newsweekly of information systems management," an indispensable weekly newspaper for anyone wanting to keep informed on recent developments and news about computers, systems, and the computing industry, including companies and people. Each issue is usually over 100 pages in length and contains short articles and a few in-depth articles along with all of the current news; also a table showing current prices of specific stocks. Section 2 of a September or October issue (e.g., September 14, 1992) contains "The Premier 100," a ranked list of the most effective IS users, with industry comparisons; "Computerworld's Annual Salary Survey" is in first September issue. Indexed in ABI/I, PTS/F&S, TI; full text on DIALOG, MEAD/NEXIS.

Datamation. Newton, MA: Cahners Publishing Co. (semimonthly).

A trade journal for managers, with short timely articles on data processing and related subjects. A company index is in each issue. Each year there is a ranked list of the top 100 U.S. companies in the data processing industry, called "The Datamation 100," with interesting profiles of each (June 15 issue); an annual "Salary Survey" (December 1). Indexed in ABI/I, BPI, PTS/F&S, TI; full text on BRS, DATA-STAR, DIALOG, DOW JONES, MEAD/NEXIS.

I/S Analyzer. Rockville, MD: United Communications Group (monthly).

Each issue is a short professional report (about 16 pages) on one specific topic of interest to information systems management. Several titles in 1991 issues are: "Fostering Creativity and Innovation"; "High-Performance Computing"; "Information Systems: The Risk and the Return"; "Re-Engineering Existing Systems." Topics covered for the three previous years are listed in each issue. Indexed in ABI/I.

Information & Management. Amsterdam and New York: Elsevier Science Publishers (10/yr.).

This is an "international journal of information systems applications," with articles on a wide range of subjects in the field of applied information systems and aimed at database administrators and managers. Included are case studies, briefings, and articles on techniques. Indexed in ABI/I, ASTI.

Information Strategy: The Executive's Journal. Boston: Auerbach Publishers (quarterly).

As the title indicates, this quarterly aims to publish "articles that will help senior executives decide policy and strategy for business information management." Usually there are five practical articles in each issue plus regular departments covering current news about such topics as executive computing, the legal environment, emerging technologies, competing through information technology; also a short book review section. Indexed in ABI/I, BPI.

InformationWeek. Manhasset, NY: CMP Publications, Inc.

A popular newsmagazine about new developments in IS companies, news about executives, products, etc., of interest to information systems managers and professionals. The annual "IW 500" (mid-September issue) contains ranked lists of the best and the biggest companies (those who use information technology resources most effectively, and those that are the biggest spenders).

Journal of Systems Management. Cleveland: Association for Systems Management (monthly).

This journal publishes short, practical articles of interest to systems and information resource managers. Annotated lists of "Recommended Readings" are in each issue. Indexed in ABI/I, BPI.

MIS Quarterly. Minneapolis: Published jointly by the Society for Information Management and the Management Information Systems Research Center of the University of Minnesota (quarterly).

A professional journal, with state-of-the-art survey articles and refereed articles on both the theory and practice within MIS. Most articles are by academic persons and most include bibliographic references. An annual list of MIS doctoral dissertations is in the June issue. Indexed in ABI/I, BPI.

Another refereed journal is *JMIS: Journal of Management Information Systems* (Armonk, NY: M.E. Sharpe, Inc. (quarterly), also containing well-researched articles by academic persons.

Online. Weston, CT. (bimonthly).

This is a "must" magazine for librarians and other information specialists because it contains feature articles on online information systems, tips for searching, profiles of persons, views of hardware/software, regular columns, and departments, including "The Printout" for news of new databases and other matters. Each issue contains critical book reviews, and recommended reading in journals. Indexed in BPI, PTS/F&S, TI; full text on DATA-STAR, DIALOG, DOW JONES, MEAD/NEXIS.

A companion journal is the bimonthly *Database,* "the magazine of database reference and review," with a format similar to *Online.*

COMPUTER DIRECTORIES

Directories listing computerized databases and other information systems and services can be found in Chapter 2.

The Computer Industry Almanac. New York: Simon & Schuster (annual).

A reference annual on the computer industry that contains much more than just directory information. It covers data on: companies (including a directory and ranked lists from other published sources); products and technologies; people; the international marketplace (including ranked lists of foreign companies); advertising and marketing; education; employment; financial facts; forecasts and sales estimates; history; news items and events; organizations and agencies; publications; research activities; salaries; bits, nibbles and bytes.

Data Sources. New York: Ziff-Davis 2 volumes (semiannual).

This is a comprehensive, periodic directory and buyer's guide. Volume 1 covers hardware and data communications; volume 2, software—data communications and telecommunications. In both volumes, the product data is arranged within subject categories, with a product name and a master index at end. Company profiles are also at end of each volume and usually include for each company the address, telephone/fax, top officers, year established, principal business, sales (when available), whether privately held, number of employees.

Thomas Register's Mid-Year Guide to Data/Information Processing. New York: Thomas Publishing Company (annual).

Published as a supplement to the useful *Thomas Register of American Manufacturers* (described in Chapter 7), this focuses on identifying data/information processing products and services, and software companies. The format is similar, with the basic listing by name of product/service, and a separate description of companies at end.

Each company profile usually includes divisions, names of officials, number of employees, telex and fax numbers, products/systems/services.

ASSOCIATIONS

Association for Computing Machinery, 11 West 42d Street, New York, NY 10036.

Association for Systems Management, 1433 W. Bagley Road, Cleveland, OH 44138.

Computer and Business Equipment Manufacturers Association, 311 First St., N.W., Washington, DC 20001.

Data Processing Management Association, 505 Busse Highway, Park Ridge, IL 60068.

Society for Information Management, 401 N. Michigan Ave., Chicago, IL 60611.

OFFICE MANAGEMENT

Office work in any organization is involved primarily with information processing, so it is useful to include in this chapter several recent texts on the adminstrative management of information.

Handbooks

Minor, Robert S., and Clark W. Fetridge. *The Dartnell Office Administration Handbook.* 6th ed., rev. and enlarged. Chicago: Dartnell Corp., 1984. 974 pp.

A comprehensive handbook on the practices and procedures of office administration, with this latest revision reflecting the changing physical structure of the modern office. Its 36 chapters are divided into the following major sections: administrative management—the basics; office personnel—recruiting and selection; office personnel—administration; guides through the paperwork jungle; office practices and procedures; the office environment; how to improve administrative skills. An appendix includes glossaries of management, communication, and electronic calculator terms. Now too old to be of value for technological changes.

Books

Kallaus, Norman F., and B. Lewis Keeling. *Adminstrative Office Management.* 9th ed. Cincinnati, OH: South-Western, 1987. 784 pp.

This latest edition of a standard text continues to reflect the growing concern for the human resource element in the office as well as the office manager's need to understand rapidly changing office technology. There are four parts: introduction (including a chapter on communication in the office); managing human resources (8 chapters); managing administrative services (7 chapters, including ergonomics in the office, word processing and mailing systems, telecommunications); managing administrative systems (including a new chapter on office automation). An abridged edition of this 9th edition with same title (1988, 496 pp.), concentrates on material in the first two sections with much less on administrative services and systems.

Quible, Zane K. *Administrative Office Management: An Introduction.* 5th ed. Englewood Cliffs, NJ: Prentice-Hall, 1991. 613 pp.

With the increased use of technology in the office, it is important to use a recently revised text which includes a discussion of the subject. This introductory book is more current than the other. Its material in the 4th edition was arranged in five parts to cover: principles of administrative office management; management of the office environment; management of office employees; management of office systems; management of office functions. Mini-cases are with chapters. The 5th edition was not seen for review.

Secretarial Handbooks

Every secretary should have close at hand a good secretarial handbook. The busy executive may also find such a handbook useful for quick references to correct English usage, punctuation, letter writing style, and so forth. We have selected three to cite here, but there are others that may be just as useful.

Doris, Lillian, and Besse May Miller. *Complete Secretary's Handbook.* 6th ed., rev. by Mary A. De Vries. Englewood Cliffs, NJ: Prentice-Hall, 1988. 664 pp.

A standard handbook of essential information for secretaries presented in a concise, easy-to-read manner with frequent quick-reference charts and tables and a good index. It is arranged in four sections to cover: techniques for general secretarial duties (practical data on filing, handling mail and electronic messages, telecommunications, making meeting and travel arrangements, etc.); how to write effective letters and memos; how to write correctly (spelling, punctuation, capitalization); the secretary's handy information guide (including quick reference guide to miscellaneous facts and figures such as abbreviations, forms of address for officials and honorary positions, proof-reading marks, weights/measures/values, interest tables, international time chart); and a glossary of important business terms.

Taintor, Sarah A., and Kate M. Monro. *The Secretary's Handbook.* 10th ed., rev. by Margaret D. Shertzer. New York: Macmillan, 1988. 422 pp.

Published since 1929, this shorter yet still useful handbook is in two parts. Part 1 focuses on grammar, capitalization, punctuation, spelling. The second part covers such topics as goals and attitudes, office machines and other equipment, use of telephone, letter writing, forms of address, filing, preparing reports, making travel arrangements, compiling bibliographies, indexing, taking minutes. The last chapter describes "sources of information for secretaries." Signs and symbols are in an appendix.

Webster's New World Secretarial Handbook. 4th ed. New York: Webster's New World, 1989. 691 pp.

Here is yet another recently revised handbook also containing much information. This one starts with five chapters discussing the secretary today, office equipment and supplies, office correspondence, record keeping, and special functions. Then comes a practical chapter on business English including coverage of business letters and memos, grammar and usage, forms of address, and the spelling of some 33,000 words. The rest of this handbook discusses legal information that might be needed, specialized secretaries (such as legal, medical), travel information (such as foreign currencies, dialing codes, distances), general reference (sources of information, U.S. holidays, signs and symbols, weights and measures).

Periodicals

The Office. Stamford, CN: Office Publications (monthly).

A trade journal covering articles on office management, equipment, and systems. Includes annotated booklists in most issues. Indexed in ABI/I, BPI, PTS/F&S, TI.

Associations

Administrative Management Society, 1101 14th Street NW, Washington, DC 20005.

14

CORPORATE FINANCE AND BANKING

Financial Handbooks – Books on Corporate Finance – Capital Budgeting and Capital Expenditures – Raising Venture Capital and Going Public – Acquisitions and Mergers – Finance Bibliographies – Finance Dictionaries – Finance Periodicals – Corporate Finance Directories – Financial Associations – MONEY, BANKING, AND FINANCIAL INSTITUTIONS – Basic Texts – Financial Markets – Bank Management – Credit Management – Mortgage Banking – Personal Finance – Banking Law and Financial Legal Services – Banking and Financial Tables – Banking Bibliographies – Banking Dictionaries – Financial Manuals and Bank Directories – U.S. Banking and Financial Statistics – Banking Newspapers and Periodicals – Banking and Credit Associations

The broad area of business finance can be divided into three interrelated parts: corporate finance, banking, and investments. This chapter concentrates on two of these: corporate finance; and money, banking and credit. Although a distinction in the literature is sometimes difficult to make, it seems logical to consider investment sources following the chapters on statistics and directories, and so investment management books are described separately in Chapter 8. Books and reference sources in international finance are in Chapter 16; insurance and real estate sources are discussed in Chapter 15; several books on the mathematics of finance are in Chapter 17; those on financial management in nonprofit organizations, in Chapter 11.

As is true in the areas of accounting, control, and MIS, such rapid changes are underway in corporate finance as well as in financial institutions and systems that it is important for published material on these subjects to be updated frequently in order that they not become obsolete. A growing emphasis on analytical techniques, changing financial policies and regulations, the fluctuating state of financial institutions and markets—all of these make it necessary to watch the dates of publication of books and to monitor periodicals, newspapers, and continuously revised services for new trends and developments.

FINANCIAL HANDBOOKS

Below are three relatively recent comprehensive financial handbooks. Several older but much-used handbooks have been deleted from this edition because they do not reflect current developments in the topics they cover. Since these might still be of some background interest for their concise, comprehensive coverage we list them here: *Controller's Handbook* ed. by Sam R. Goodman and James S. Reece (Dow Jones-Irwin, 1978, 1,253 pp.); *Corporate Treasurer's and Controller's Encyclopedia, Revised,* ed. by Sam R. Goodman from Lillian Doris's original book (Prentice-Hall, 1975, 2 volumes); *Encyclopedia of Long-Term Financing and Capital Management* by John F. Childs (Prentice-Hall, 1976, 607 pp.); and *Treasurer's Handbook* ed. by J. Fred Weston and Maurice B. Goudzwaard (Dow Jones-Irwin, 1976, 1,181 pp.). For *The Bankers' Handbook,* ed. by Baughn, Storrs, and Walker, see the "Bank Management" section of this chapter.

Handbook of Corporate Finance. Ed. by Edward I. Altman. New York: Wiley, 1986. 1 volume (various pagings).

Since its first appearance in 1925, the *Financial Handbook* by Julius I. Bogen has been a comprehensive, indispensable guide to corporate finance, money, and banking. Now, thanks to Professor Altman and his panel of distinguished contributors, we have an updated handbook, expanded into two companion volumes of which this is one. It focuses on synthesizing the latest literature and developments (as of 1986) on current corporate finance principles and practices, and it is intended for finance practitioners. Each of its 19 chapters, written by respected experts, covers an important aspect, such as planning and control, forecasting, small business finance, cash management, capital budgeting, mergers and acquisitions, financial decisions for multinational enterprises, bankruptcy and reorganization. A useful chapter on the "Mathematics of Finance" and a list of sources of financial and investment information are in an appendix. Good bibliographical references are at end of chapters; useful tables and diagrams appear throughout; a detailed index is at end. The companion volume, *Handbook of Financial Markets and Institutions* (6th ed., Wiley, 1987), is described in the section covering "Financial Markets."

Handbook of Modern Finance. Dennis E. Logue, ed. 2d ed. Boston: Warren, Gorham & Lamont, 1990. 1 volume (various pagings). And an annual "Update."

Professor Logue's intent in preparing this comprehensive handbook is to produce a one-volume reference book that covers virtually every major issue or question likely to confront business professionals active in business and finance. Its 46 chapters, each by an authority, are organized around 7 major subject areas: the financial system and markets; security analysis, pricing, and portfolio management; short-term financial management; long-term financial management; financial policy (including mergers and acquisitions); personal finance; international dimensions of finance. Charts and tables appear throughout and suggested readings are given in each chapter. The annual "Update"—with cumulative index—reflects emerging trends, new applications, and other changes that affect business operations.

Vancil, Richard F., and Benjamin R. Makela. *The CFO's Handbook.* Homewood, IL: Dow Jones-Irwin, 1986. 642 pp.

This handbook focuses on essays to stimulate the thinking of the chief financial officer concerning policy and administration of corporate financial management. Its 31 chapters are short and readable, with each written by contributors who are either current (or past) CFOs or senior advisors to such executives. Of the 7-part arrangement, two discuss major substantive issues (setting financial policies, in part 2, and international financing, in part 4); two deal with the various aspects of the CFO's role (external, in part 5, and internal, in part 6); the last is aimed at CFOs in diversified firms. The first part considers 5 aspects of corporate and financial strategy.

BOOKS ON CORPORATE FINANCE

Aby, Carroll D., Jr., and Donald E. Vaughn, eds. *Financial Management Classics.* Santa Monica, CA: Goodyear Publishing Co., 1979. 397 pp. paper.

Thirty-three of the older classic readings selected to supplement a basic financial management text. They are concentrated in the following 8 areas: functions of the financial manager; analysis, planning, and control of financial management; working capital management; intermediate and long-term financing; capital budgeting; cost of capital and capital structure decisions; capital markets and stock evaluation; corporate mergers, acquisitions, and reorganizations.

Bowlin, Oswald D., John D. Martin and David F. Scott, Jr. *Guide to Financial Analysis.* 2d ed. New York: McGraw-Hill, 1990. 417 pp. paper.

Here is a concise, no-nonsense book focusing on analytical techniques that business managers need for sound financial decision making. It describes techniques for financial statement analysis, financial forecasting and control, valuation, capital budgeting, evaluating risky investment proposals, estimating rates of return on investment (ROI), working capital, financing, and determining dividend policy. In addition there is a chapter on using financial models. The authors assume some prior knowledge of elementary accounting and algebra. Numerous solved problems are used throughout to illustrate the techniques discussed; other problems are at end of chapters along with lists of "selected references." A few chapter appendixes cover some topics in more depth. Appendixes contain present value and compound interest tables, as well as a glossary.

Brealey, Richard A., and Stewart C. Myers. *Principles of Corporate Finance.* 4th ed. New York: McGraw-Hill, 1991. 924, [66] pp.

Considered one of the best, this is a comprehensive introductory textbook describing the theory and practice of corporate finance, with an effort made to show how to use financial theory in solving practical problems. A course in algebra is a prerequisite and an elementary knowledge of accounting, statistics, and microeconomics is helpful. Parts 1–3 cover investment decisions (value, risk, practical problems in capital budgeting); parts 4–7 focus on financing decisions (including dividend policy, options, debt financing); parts 8–10 consider financial planning, short term financial decisions, and mergers/international finance/pensions. Short lists of suggested readings are at end of chapters; a glossary and present value tables are paged separately at end of the book.

Brigham, Eugene F. *Fundamentals of Financial Management.* 5th ed. Chicago, IL: Dryden, 1989. 855, [31] pp. Sixth edition to be published in 1992.
Professor Brigham's introductory text begins with a discussion of the fundamental concepts in financial management. With this as background he then covers in turn: financial statements and financial forecasting; strategic long-term investment decisions (including capital budgeting, the cost of capital, leverage, dividend policy); working capital management. Each chapter of this well-written book starts with a real-world example. There is a running glossary in the left margin. Mathematical tables at end. A more comprehensive version for MBAs (coauthored by Louis C. Gapenski) is *Financial Management: Theory and Practice* (6th ed., Dryden, 1991, 995, [68] pp.). Brigham has also written, with Gapenski, an intermediate-level text with title *Intermediate Financial Management* (3d ed., Dryden, 1990, 923, [36] pp.).
  Several other books Brigham has coauthored with others are: *Essentials of Managerial Finance* (listed under J. Fred Weston in this chapter); *Introduction to Financial Management,* with B.J. Campsey as first author, which is designed as an introductory text for the general business student and not just the finance major and so is less complex (3d ed., Dryden, 1991, 882, [53] pp.); and *Cases in Financial Management,* also with Gapenski (Dryden, 1990, 304 pp.).

Cohen, Jerome B., Sidney Robbins and Allan Young. *The Financial Manager.* Columbus, OH: Publishing Horizons, 1986. 748 pp.
The authors say their goal in writing this text is to explain the complicated role of the financial manager in clear and explicit terms, and so there is minimal mathematical notation. Parts 1–5 cover the basic topics of a financial management text; part 6 takes up 6 major financial issues and is directed more to the practitioner. These issues are: mergers and acquisitions; repurchasing and other capital structure rearrangements and reorganizations; leasing; financial aspects of multinational operations; corporate tax planning and management; financial aspects of employee pension programs and other forms of extra compensation. Suggested readings are at end of each chapter.

Cooley, Philip L., ed. *Advances in Business Financial Management: A Collection of Readings.* Chicago: Dryden, 1990. 634 pp. paper.
This is a selection of 48 nonmathematical articles published relatively recently and focusing on the ideas of finance and not on methodology. It is intended to add depth to an introductory finance course or just for general reading. They are arranged within 7 parts covering the major topics of financial management.

Finnerty, John D. *Corporate Financial Analysis: A Comprehensive Guide to Real-World Approaches for Financial Managers.* New York: McGraw-Hill, 1986. 566 pp.
As the subtitle says, this book aims to be a comprehensive yet practical survey of the techniques of modern corporate financial analysis with an emphasis on how to apply these techniques to solve the types of problems financial managers regularly encounter. It is arranged in 9 parts, with the first setting the stage, and parts 2 to 8 explaining and interpreting techniques used in analyzing capital investment projects, the dividend decision, working capital, long term financing, and so forth. The last part is a short list of sources of financial information. Practical examples are found throughout.

Hawkins, David F. *Corporate Financial Reporting and Analysis.* 2d ed. Homewood, IL: Dow Jones-Irwin, 1986. 553 pp.

"This book provides the reader with an understanding of the current state of financial reporting practices; the ways in which the corporate financial statements published in annual reports, prospectuses, and proxy statements influence our economic system; the significant consequences of these data for the people who depend on their credibility; and the methods by which competent statement users interpret the data contained in corporate financial reports. It is not a book on accounting methodology." Based on material used for an MBA course that does not presume in-depth understanding of accounting and financial analysis, it is intended for use both in undergraduate and graduate accounting and financial analysis courses at both the introductory and advanced levels. Present value tables are at end.

Helfert, Erich A. *Techniques of Financial Analysis.* 7th ed. Homewood, IL: Irwin, 1991. 502 pp. paper.

Latest edition of a good, concise, practical, and usable overview of the more important tools and techniques of financial analysis without delving into theoretical abstraction. The first five chapters cover: business as a financial system; managing operating funds; assessment of business performance; projections of financial requirements; dynamics of the business system. The last four chapters deal with more specialized topics such as investment analysis, the cost of capital, financing choices, and business evaluation. The book presupposes only some familiarity with fundamental accounting concepts. "Selected References" at end of each chapter suggest other books useful for further reading. Appendixes include a brief overview of inflation concepts, a description of basic financial information sources, and explanations of financial quotations in newspapers.

Higgins, Robert C. *Analysis for Financial Management.* 3d ed. Homewood, IL: Business One Irwin, 1991. 387 pp.

A short book providing nonfinancial executives and business students interested in the practice of financial management with basic standard techniques and recent developments in a practical, intuitive way. It emphasizes the application and interpretation of analytical techniques in decision making, and it assumes no prior background beyond some familiarity with financial statements. Part 1 focuses on an assessment of the financial health of a company. The other three parts then deal in turn with the acquisition and management of new resources as they relate to: planning future financial performance; financing operations; evaluating investment opportunities. International topics are woven into the text. A few suggested readings are described in each chapter; present value tables and a glossary are at end of the book.

Ross, Stephen A., and Randolph W. Westerfield. *Corporate Finance.* 2d ed. Homewood, IL: Irwin, 1990. 833, [55] pp.

This is intended as an MBA text of moderate difficulty emphasizing modern fundamentals of theory and finance, and making the theory come to life with contemporary examples. Throughout the book, the concept of valuation and the role of financial markets are used as themes to demonstrate the corporate decision-making process. The usual topics are covered in 7 parts, including one devoted to a complete discussion of risk. The last part discusses two special topics: mergers and acquisitions, and international corporate finance. Math tables and a glossary are paged separately at end. Basic algebra is the only prerequisite. These professors, with Bradford D. Jordan, have written a shorter text on the *Fundamentals of Corporate Finance* (Irwin, 1991, 758 pp.).

Schall, Lawrence D., and Charles W. Haley. *Introduction to Financial Management.* 5th ed. New York: McGraw-Hill, 1988. 856 pp.

Another effort to give students a thorough introduction to financial management, with all the essential topics covered in 6 parts and 25 chapters. A little background in accounting, mathematics, and economics is assumed. At the end are interest tables, suggested readings, and a glossary. A short "Sources of Financial Information" includes explanations on how to read stock and bond price quotations.

Serraino, William J., Surenda S. Singhvi and Robert M. Soldofsky. *Frontiers of Financial Management: Selected Readings.* 4th ed. Cincinnati: South-Western Publishing Co., 1984. 454 pp. paper.

The 36 articles in this revised collection were selected for their "managerial viewpoint; a concern for real and relevant problems that financial and other top-level managers must confront; and a judicious introduction of new approaches to subjects including models, simulations, and alternative formulations of the goals." This is a good selection with many of the articles written by well-known experts. It is arranged within 11 categories similar to the section headings in most introductory financial management texts.

Another collection of 21 readings (in 7 parts) designed for an advanced level financial course is *Issues and Readings in Managerial Finance* ed. by Ramon E. Johnson (3d ed., Chicago: Dryden, 1987, 448 pp.).

Shapiro, Alan C. *Modern Corporate Finance.* New York: Macmillan, 1990. 1,045, [46] pp.

Professor Shapiro is not new to this field since he has written a well-received text on *Multinational Financial Management* (described elsewhere). This is another well-written graduate-level text intended "to make accessible to students and practitioners alike the practical implications for corporate financial management of the exciting new theoretical breakthroughs in financial economics." It "emphasizes two related issues: how companies create value and how corporate finance can facilitate the process of value creation," with the focus on how the financial manager can add value to the firm. The usual topics are well-covered in its 7 parts. He tries to integrate domestic and international financial management throughout, and he also makes extensive and good use of examples. References are at end of chapters.

Spiro, Herbert T. *Finance for the Nonfinancial Manager.* 3d ed. New York: Wiley, 1988. 282 pp. paper.

This book originated in a series of university extension courses and is geared to meet the needs of mature and motivated managers who wish to increase their understanding of financial management. It is not a how-to book but rather an exploration of relevant financial concepts coupled with selected demonstrations of their application to the solution of problems facing financial management in all types of organizations. Reorganized and updated, it covers such important topics as capital budgeting, cash flow, leasing, credit management, capital structure, and much more. Present and future value tables plus a glossary are at the end.

Van Horne, James C., and John M. Wachowicz, Jr. *Fundamentals of Financial Management.* 8th ed. Englewood Cliffs, NJ: Prentice-Hall, 1992. 816 pp.

The purpose of this excellent, introductory text "is not only to provide an understanding of how funds are raised and allocated within a company, but to inspire an interest in what goes on in corporate finance." This latest edition, now with a coauthor, has been substantially rewritten to reflect ever-changing conditions, and it requires a minimum of math. The 8 parts are: introduction; valuation; tools of financial analysis and planning; working capital management; investment in capital assets; the cost of capital, capital structure, and dividend policy; intermediate and long-term financing; special areas of financial management (including mergers and international financial management). Useful appendixes are with several chapters on such topics as inflation and financial analysis, accounting treatment of leases, option pricing. Problems and short bibliographies are at the end of chapters; present value tables are at end of book.

Professor Van Horne has also revised his standard text on *Financial Management and Policy* (8th ed., Prentice-Hall, 1989, 852 pp.). A longer book, this one aims to develop an understanding of financial theory and the application of analytical techniques to problems involving financial decisions, as well as to expose readers to the institutional material necessary for an understanding of the environment in which financial decisions are made.

Walker, Ernest W., and J. William Petty II. *Financial Management of the Small Firm.* 2d ed. Englewood Cliffs, NJ: Prentice-Hall, 1986. 465 pp.

Most of the books on financial management are aimed at large companies; this one relates the same financial theories and techniques to the small firm. It is meant for the serious student who has a sound basis in financial accounting and an understanding of statistics and microeconomics. There are five parts: introduction and forms of organization; planning; investment decision making; valuation; sources of financing (including a chapter on going public). References accompany each section; present value tables are at the end.

The titles of two other books on small business finance are given in the small business management section of Chapter 10.

Weston, J. Fred, and Eugene F. Brigham. *Essentials of Managerial Finance.* 9th ed. Chicago: Dryden, 1990. 931, [31] pp.

A well-established undergraduate text focusing on the role of the financial manager in maximizing the value of the firm. This latest revision is in 7 parts. The first two deal with introductory material and essential concepts. The others examine: financial analysis, planning, and control; working capital management; capital budgeting; the cost of capital, leverage, and dividend policy; strategic long-term financial decisions. Increased coverage in this edition includes ethical issues, with international finance and small business finance discussed in relevant chapters. A few mathematical tables are at end; a separate insert card contains present value tables. A running glossary appears in the margin.

These two authors, with other coauthors, have written related texts. For instance, Weston, with Thomas E. Copeland, has written a more comprehensive graduate-level text on *Managerial Finance* (9th ed., Dryden, 1992, 1,182, [32] pp.), and a more difficult theory text called *Financial Theory and Corporate Policy* (3d ed., Reading, MA: Addison-Wesley, 1988, 946 pp.). Several books Brigham has coauthored are cited under his name in this section.

A few other books worth considering are: *Foundations of Financial Management* by Stanley B. Block and Geoffrey A. Hirt (6th ed., Irwin, 1992, 700 pp.) which attempts to present the concepts of finance in an interesting manner; *Principles of Managerial Finance* by Lawrence J. Gitman (6th ed.,

HarperCollins, 1991, 886, [97] pp.), latest edition of an introductory, under-graduate text that aims to make the factual material as easy as possible; *Corporate Financial Analysis* by Diana R. Harrington and Brent D. Wilson (3d ed., Dow Jones-Irwin, 1989, 316 pp.), a short book whose objective it is to discuss financial analysis as it relates to decision making; *Basic Financial Management* by John D. Martin et al. (5th ed., Prentice-Hall, 1991), an introductory overview with a managerial orientation; and *Essentials of Managerial Finance* by John J. Pringle and Robert S. Harris (2d ed., Scott, Foresman, 1987, 811, [98] pp.), a text for beginning students which places emphasis on developing a sound conceptual framework.

For a selection of books on international financial management, refer to Chapter 16.

CAPITAL BUDGETING AND CAPITAL EXPENDITURES

Handbooks

Kaufman, Mike, ed. *The Capital Budgeting Handbook.* Homewood, IL: Dow Jones-Irwin, 1986. 776 pp.

This is the first attempt to integrate the many facets of capital budgeting into a handbook which covers both traditional material and current viewpoints. It is written by over 30 business practitioners/consultants/academicians for the practical use of business persons. The chapters are grouped into five major sections: strategic planning of capital expenditures; preparing the capital budget; initiating a capital project; financing capital expenditures; implementing a capital project.

Books

Bierman, Harold, Jr., and Seymour Smidt. *The Capital Budgeting Decision: Economic Analysis and Financing of Investment Projects.* 7th ed. New York: Macmillan, 1988. 557 pp.

These authors advocate the present value method in their well-established introductory study on how to evaluate investment proposals. The book moves from the simple to the complex. Part 1 covers capital budgeting with certainty; part 2 deals with specific aspects of capital budgeting such as replacement decisions, leasing, timing; part 3 then discusses capital budgeting with uncertainty. Part 4 contains cases. Present value and other tables are in an appendix.

Professor Bierman has also written a book on *Implementing Capital Budgeting Techniques* (Rev. ed., Cambridge: Ballinger, 1988, 108 pp.). This reviews the state of the art today by surveying 257 financial officers of the largest Fortune industrial companies, requesting them to identify problems of implementation. Bibliographical notes are at end of the book.

Clark, John J., Thomas J. Hindelang and Robert E. Pritchard. *Capital Budgeting: Planning and Control of Capital Expenditures.* 3d ed. Englewood Cliffs, NJ: Prentice-Hall, 1989. 620 pp.

In this edition the authors have expanded certain topics and introduced new material to keep the subject matter current. It is arranged in 8 parts: introduction to capital budgeting and discounted cash flow; evaluation of projects under conditions of unchanging risk; underlying assumptions of DCF evaluation techniques; risk analysis and capital budgeting; capital asset pricing applied to capital budgeting; mathematical programming and multiperiod analysis; strategic management; special applications (capital budgeting for the multinational company, and lease analysis). References are at end of chapters; case studies are with some chapters. Compound interest and annuity tables are in an appendix. This book is intended for persons with a working knowledge of algebra and basic statistics.

Grant, Eugene L., W. Grant Ireson and Richard S. Leavenworth. *Principles of Engineering Economy.* 8th ed. New York: Wiley, 1990. 591 pp.

A long-term, well-recognized text that "explains the principles and techniques needed for making decisions about the acquisition and retirement of capital goods by industry and government." Part 2 of its four parts covers the procedures and methods for evaluating alternatives (including equivalent uniform annual cash flow, present worth, internal rate of return); part 3 focuses on techniques for handling special situations (such as economy studies for retirement and replacement, capital budgeting, sensitivity analysis, mathematics of probability). Part 1 starts the book off by discussing basic concepts, principles and financial mathematics; part 4 ends by covering special applications. Appendixes include compound interest tables and a bibliography.

Another standard text is *Engineering Economy,* by G.J. Thuesen and W.J. Fabrycky (7th ed., Englewood Cliffs, NJ: Prentice-Hall, 1989. 717 pp.).

Marino, Bernard D. *Handbook of Capital Expenditure Management.* Englewood Cliffs, NJ: Prentice-Hall, 1986. 258 pp.

Intended for financial managers, a large part of this book is devoted to the mechanics of the capital expenditure management process, with the capital budgeting procedure detailed in 5 chapters, and several other chapters on techniques for evaluating capital expenditures, on cash flow aspects, and on funding alternatives. The last chapter examines the management of capital expenditures both from the organizational and the human perspectives. Forms, diagrams, and tables appear throughout; present value tables are at end.

Smith, Gerald W. *Engineering Economy: Analysis of Capital Expenditures.* 4th ed. Ames, IA: Iowa State University Press, 1987. 584 pp.

Another recognized text on the engineering economy, this one dealing "with the concepts, principles, techniques, and reasoning applicable to the planning of long-term facilities." Section headings include: time and money; methods of comparing alternatives; income tax considerations; multi-outcome considerations—risk and uncertainty; capital budgeting considerations. Useful charts, diagrams, tables appear throughout. A good, short bibliography is at the end, along with interest tables, random digits, and other useful data.

Expenditures for New Plants and Equipment

Data Resources, Inc. *Annual DRI/McGraw-Hill Spring Survey of Business Plans for New Plants and Equipment.* Lexington, MA (annual).

Key findings based on a periodic survey of capital expenditures in over 300 companies. Statistics (by broad industry) usually give actual spending plans for one year, projected plans for the coming year, and for a three-year trend into the future. Tables cover: plans for capital spending; expansion versus modernization; building, motor vehicles, and other machinery and equipment; capacity expansion and utilization rates; sales expectations; real sales expectations; inflation expectations. DRI publishes this annual release of about 22 pages in cooperation with McGraw-Hill. They also publish a *Capital Spending Memo* (6/yr).

U.S. Bureau of the Census. *Census of Manufactures.* Washington, DC.

Statistics on capital expenditures are included in this census and also in the *Annual Survey of Manufactures* taken in the years between each five-year census. These give new capital expenditures for each 4-digit SIC industry.

U.S. Bureau of the Census. *Plant and Equipment Expenditures and Plans.* Washington, DC (quarterly).

Formerly published in the *Survey of Current Business,* this is now a separate 7-page quarterly giving actual and planned expenditures for plant and equipment for basic manufacturing and nonmanufacturing industries. The figures are in both current and constant dollars.

Periodicals

The Engineering Economist. Norcross, GA: Joint Publication of the American Society for Engineering Education and the Institute of Industrial Engineers (quarterly).

Articles devoted to current thinking on problems of capital investment. It includes critical book reviews. Indexed in ABI/I, BPI, TI.

RAISING VENTURE CAPITAL AND GOING PUBLIC

Besides these several handbooks and books, note the useful guidebooks prepared by accounting firms mentioned at the end of this section. Note also the first directory below which is of interest not only for its descriptive list of venture capital companies but also for its inclusion of short chapters (which vary each year) on pertinent topics of interest to entrepreneurs. For books of a more general nature on starting and expanding new or small businesses, see the last section of Chapter 10. Sources for lists of "New Securities Offerings" are described in Chapter 8; several "Corporate Finance Directories" are described near the end of this chapter.

Handbooks

Gladstone, David J. *Venture Capital Handbook.* New and rev. Englewood Cliffs, NJ: Prentice-Hall, 1988. 350 pp. paper.

Here is a guide that covers the entire process of raising venture capital "from the presentation of the proposal, through the negotiations, the commitment letters, the legal closings, and the due diligence, to the exit by the venture capital company, when the entrepreneur is left to own it all." Gladstone says it is written from the perspective of how he would react if he were an entrepreneur approaching a venture firm. An appendix contains sample documents and forms, a list of venture capital companies that belong to the NVCA and NASBIC, and a short glossary. Gladstone is a venture capitalist who has reviewed thousands of venture capital proposals in the course of his career.

Handbook for Raising Capital: Financing Alternatives for Emerging and Growing Businesses. Ed. by Lawrence Chimerine, Robert F. Cushman, and Howard D. Ross. Homewood, IL: Dow Jones-Irwin, 1987. 666 pp.

Written to meet the needs of small and midsized businesses, this handbook explains in nontechnical language the advantages and disadvantages of each alternative and the strategies to be employed by companies seeking financing. Each chapter is written by a qualified financial or legal authority. The subjects covered include such topics as borrowing from banks, venture capital financing, going public, mergers & acquisitions, leveraged buyouts, long-term borrowing, and much more.

Books

Arkebauer, James B. (Ron Schultz, collaborator). *Cashing Out: The Entrepreneur's Guide to Going Public.* New York: HarperBusiness, 1991. 320 pp.
This is a step-by-step guide written by a consultant who has specialized in advising and assisting companies in the process of going public. It is arranged in five parts to cover: an overview of the process; assembling the IPO team; before the offering; the public offering process; completing the public offering.

Bartlett, Joseph W. *Venture Capital: Law, Business Strategies, and Investment Planning.* New York: Wiley, 1988. 514 pp.
The objective of Bartlett's book "is to provide a resource which can be used at several different levels, which can be read not only by attorneys and accountants but by venture capitalists, entrepreneurs, financial and other business consultants, and anyone interested in becoming involved with venture capital." The emphasis is on early stage financing. The bibliography at end will refer readers to other more specialized material. Bartlett is a lawyer and so the footnotes usually contain citations to cases, statutes, and regulations.

Field, Drew. *Take Your Company Public: The Entrepreneur's Guide to Alternative Capital Sources.* New York: New York Institute of Finance, 1991. 259 pp.
This book focuses on an alternative path for raising public capital which the author calls a "direct public offering" (DPO). It is written by a pioneer in applying direct-marketing technology to selling securities. Mr. Field starts by discussing the traditional path, an initial public offering (IPO), and its advantages; then he presents a step-by-step guide to the DPO process. An annotated bibliography and a glossary comprise about 75 pages at the end.

Henderson, James W. *Obtaining Venture Financing: Principles and Practices.* Lexington, MA: Lexington Books, 1988. 366 pp.
Developed as an introductory course in venture financing, this will also be of use to owners of entrepreneurial ventures. The broad areas covered are: planning and analysis (including a chapter on the business plan); accounting and finance concepts (chapters on tools of financial management, evaluating cash flow, credit analysis, forms of business organizations); special topics (transferring business ownership and the changing financial environment). Short bibliographies are at end of chapters.

Silver, A. David. *Up Front Financing: The Entrepreneur's Guide.* Rev. ed. New York: Wiley, 1988. 238 pp.
This helpful guide for entrepreneurs seeking financing is written by an experienced venture capital investment banker. Silver focuses on over 20 approaches to low-cost financing, from deal money and franchise money to facilities management contracts and state funding programs, with the advantages and disadvantages for each.

Three Ernst & Young accounting partners have written a book providing entrepreneurs and professional advisers with 15 innovative financing strategies, to help when financing new product development, expanding into new markets, or just keeping pace. This is *The Ernst & Young Guide to Raising Capital* by Daniel R. Garner et al. (New York: Wiley, 1991, 355 pp. paper).

Sutton, David P., and M. William Benedetto. *Initial Public Offerings.* Chicago: Probus Publishing Company, 1990. 354 pp. paper.

Yet another guide for entrepreneurs, this one says it contains "all you need to know about taking a company public." The authors follow the whole process from the decision and preparation for going public through such considerations as selecting the underwriter, disclosure guidelines, the prospectus, the offering, and finally stock trading and ongoing responsibilities. Almost half of the book consists of appendixes containing a sample prospectus, questionnaires, forms for SEC filings, and so forth.

Trends in Venture Capital. Needham, MA: Venture Economics (annual).

A five-part annual review of the venture capital industry, including recent developments such as new fund formation, acquisitions, and initial public offerings of venture-backed companies. Includes analyses of 10 major industries, with directories of companies in each that are funded by venture capital. Includes some statistics and a few graphs.

Deloitte Haskins & Sells has prepared two useful guidebooks to assist entrepreneurs through the difficult steps of raising the capital they need. One is *Raising Venture Capital: An Entrepreneur's Guidebook* (London: 1983, 122 pp., paper). The other, *Raising Venture Capital in Europe: An Entrepreneur's Guidebook* (1984, 116 pp. paper), is published in cooperation with the European Venture Capital Association.

Several accounting firms have published useful little guides to going public. These are: *Deciding to Go Public: Understanding the Process and Alternatives* (Cleveland, OH: Ernst & Whinney, 1984, 139 pp.); *Strategies for Going Public: An Entrepreneur's Guide* by Leslie Wat (New York: Deloitte Haskins & Sells, 1983, 112 pp.); *Taking Your Company Public* (New York: Price Waterhouse, 1988, 71 pp.). For a comprehensive handbook on the underwriting process with a legal focus, see the annual *Going Public Handbook: Going Public, the Integrated Disclosure System and Exempt Financing* by Harold S. Bloomenthal and his law firm, Holme Roberts & Owen (New York: Clark Boardman, 1991, 1 volume, various pagings). It is intended "for the practitioner who is not a specialist in the field, but who represents companies wishing to go public or which have recently gone public."

Directories of Venture Capital Companies

Pratt's Guide to Venture Capital Sources. Needham, MA: Venture Economics (annual).

More than half of this useful guide consists of a directory of over 800 American and Canadian venture capital companies. Information given for each includes project preferences (minimum investment range, preferred investment range, type of financing, miminum operating data), geographic, and industry preferences. The first part contains short chapters discussing venture capital topics, most of which are written by venture capitalists. These vary from year to year but usually cover: sources of business development financing; how to raise venture capital; when and how to go public.

Venture Economics also publishes a monthly loose-leaf *Venture Capital Journal* which contains news of the month, a special report, news about specific venture companies, news of venture-backed IPOs in registration, statistics of Venture Capital 100 companies (stock price and P/E ratios).

In 1991 Venture Economics published the fifth edition of a companion directory, *The Venture Capital Report Guide to Venture Capital in Europe*, which describes more than 500 European firms. It is arranged by country and provides information similar to that in the directory above. There are also short articles at the beginning on the European venture capital scene written by leading experts, and a list of VC associations.

National Association of Small Business Investment Companies. *NASBIC Membership Directory*. Washington, DC annual.

Arranged alphabetically by state, this directory lists over 200 SBICs and SSBICs. For each, one can find data similar to other directories, such as preferred levels of loans or investments, investment policy, industry, and geographic preferences. Small Business Investment Companies (SBICs) and Specialized Small Business Investment Companies (SSBICs) are financial institutions created to make equity capital and long-term credit available to small, independent businesses. SBICs are licensed by the U.S. Small Business Administration, but they are privately organized and managed.

Silver, A. David. *Who's Who in Venture Capital*. 3d ed. New York: Wiley, 1987. 468 pp.

The directory portion of this book describes U.K. and Canadian venture capital funds, giving for each the average size of investment, investment criteria, names of portfolio companies, and brief facts about leading venture capitalists (education, prior positions, directorships). To use this latter data, the reader must know the fund for which each individual works since there is no index. The first 100 pages contain several essays on topics of interest to entrepreneurs and venture capitalists.

Venture Capital in Europe: EVCA Yearbook. London: Peat Marwick McLintock for the European Venture Capital Association.

The last half of this annual is a directory of EVCA member-firms, arranged by country in Europe, with brief data on each usually including type of firm, senior executives, type of financing, minimum and preferred investments, industry and geographic preferences, contact person. The first half contains summary information and facts on venture capital in each European country. At end is EVCA's code of conduct.

The Venture Capital Report Guide to Venture Capital in Europe. By Lucius Cary. 5th ed. Henley on Thames, Oxon, U.K.: 1991. 960 pp. Revised every two years.

This edition has expanded its coverage into Europe (previous editions were limited to U.K. firms), but it still focuses mostly on U.K. venture capital companies. For each firm it gives the usual facts found in most such directories plus brief information on the decision-making process, key management, a table providing profile of investments, and examples of investments. At front is a chapter on the business plan and on the personal experiences of four entrepreneurs. Includes a list of members of the British Venture Capital Association.

That association, the BVCA, also publishes an annual *Directory* (London) which gives basic information about each member firm.

Two other directories are: *Membership Directory,* listing some 200 member-firms of the National Venture Capital Association (Washington, DC), but giving only the address of each firm; and *Directory of Members* of the Western Association of Venture Capitalists (Menlo Park, CA) which gives basic data on each firm similar to what is found in the directories above.

ACQUISITIONS AND MERGERS

Few books have been published recently on mergers and acquisitions. Most seem to be focused on just one or more aspects, such as corporate takeovers. Below are several of the more recent handbooks, books, periodicals, and reference works. One can find many articles on all aspects of the subject, and these can be located by using several business periodical indexes or online databases mentioned in Chapter 2. Directories of M&A intermediaries are described in the section covering "Corporate Finance Directories." For persons inexperienced in the practice of securities law or practitioners needing a refresher course, a loose-leaf legal guide called *Going Public and the Public Corporation* by Harold S. Bloomenthal (New York: Clark Boardman Co., 1986– to date) may be helpful.

Handbooks

BenDaniel, David J. and Arthur H. Rosenbloom. *The Handbook of International Mergers and Acquisitions.* Englewood Cliffs, NJ: Prentice-Hall, 1990. 375 pp.

More specialized and shorter than the two handbooks below, this one focuses on providing a "road map" setting forth the general issues in most international M&A transactions, with contributions from a team of hands-on practitioners. It covers strategic planning, law, accounting, tax, financing, personnel issues, valuation, pricing, and negotiation. A bibliography arranged by broad topic is at end. The editors hope to update this with pocket supplements.

Levine, Sumner N., ed. *The Acquisitions Manual.* New York: New York Institute of Finance, 1989. 599 pp.

Intended as a practical guide to negotiating and evaluating business acquisitions, this manual contains chapters by the editor and other authorities on such aspects of the acquisition process as the steps in identifying acquisition candidates, the advertising campaign, valuation/financing/accounting, and the acquisition contract. What makes this guide useful as a continuing resource are its chapters on information sources and on understanding and analyzing financial statements, as well as its informative chapter appendixes on such topics as online databases, key business ratios, directories of financing sources. One can also find here examples and explanations of sample agreements, checklists, and other documents needed in the acquisition process. Short lists of references are with some chapters.

The Mergers and Acquisitions Handbook. Milton L. Rock, editor-in-chief. New York: McGraw-Hill, 1987. 518 pp.

This is a compendium of state-of-the-art knowledge and practice on mergers, acquisitions, and divestitures, with each chapter written by a qualified professional. It is intended for the practicing professional as a practical guide to all stages and facets of the M&A process. The 46 chapters are organized into 9 parts: planning and strategic issues; cases of growth and diversification; organizing to merge and acquire; pricing, negotiating and deal structuring; finishing touches; after the merger; LBOs, divestitures and other modes; regulation, communication, and defenses; M&A experiences in three industries.

There is an earlier, more comprehensive merger handbook which is now out of print but may still be available in libraries. It is *Handbook of Mergers, Acquisitions and Buyouts* edited by Steven J. Lee and Robert D. Colman (Englewood Cliffs, NJ: Prentice-Hall, 1981, 747 pp.). It is not a step-by-step guide but rather a book that concentrates (in 39 chapters and 14 topical areas) on essential information needed by nonprofessional practitioners to better understand this important subject.

Books

Bing, Gordon. *Corporate Acquisitions.* Houston: Gulf Publishing Co., 1980. 248 pp.

Now somewhat out of date, this book is for individuals who wish to learn how either to acquire one substantial business or to establish a continuous program of multiple takeovers that would last indefinitely. It is written primarily for serious buyers and presents a systematic approach—describing what must be accomplished and how to do it step by step, beginning with acquisition objectives and the buyer's capabilities, and ending with a discussion of the negotiation and the transition following close of the deal. The appendix contains an outline of a transaction summary and management report, outline of a contractual agreement, and a preclosing acquisition checklist.

Clark, John J. *Business Merger and Acquisition Strategies.* Englewood Cliffs, NJ: Prentice-Hall, 1985. 223, [4] pp.

"Intended as a practical guide for managers who contemplate combination as the road to corporate growth or who seek to fend off unwanted suitors." The theme centers on the need of a well-conceived acquisition strategy as a component of strategic planning, and each chapter focuses on one strategy such as financial analysis, or negotiating the terms. Brief case histories, problems, and exhibits are used throughout. Short bibliographies are at end of each chapter.

Cooke, Terence E. *Mergers and Acquisitions.* Oxford and New York: B. Blackwell, 1986. 284 pp.

This book, with a British focus, covers the major areas affecting mergers and acquisitions from an economic, accounting, and finance basis. It is in five parts: trends, causes, and performance; controls in the U.K. and in some other major industrial countries; a framework for assessment of acquisitions; other areas of special importance (including accounting and taxation); success at acquisitions and defense. The appendix includes a merger and acquisitions information checklist on acquiring a company, prepared by Price Waterhouse accounting firm. A bibliography is at end.

A follow-up book by Cooke is *International Mergers and Acquisitions* (B. Blackwell, 1988, 516 pp.). This was written in association with Arthur Young International, and part 2 highlights key issues in each of 16 industrial countries.

Freier, Jerold. *Successful Corporate Acquisitions: A Complete Guide for Acquiring Companies for Growth and Profit.* Englewood Cliffs, NJ: Prentice-Hall, 1990. 401 pp.

As the subtitle indicates, Freier aims here to offer a complete guide to the techniques and strategies today's small-to-medium companies need in order to develop and implement an acquisitions program which will work successfully for financial growth and profit. It is written in easy-to-understand language for owner-executives. Throughout he uses practical examples, checklists, charts, and tables.

Ravenscraft, David J., and F. M. Scherer. *Mergers, Sell-Offs, and Economic Efficiency.* Washington, DC: Brookings Institution, 1987. 290 pp. paper.

This is a research study on "the consequences of mergers and takeovers for the subsequent performance of the company and the production of the manufacturing sector more generally." The methodology includes use of stock market events, case studies, and also the Federal Trade Commission's Line of Business data. This latter covered some 6,000 mergers and takeovers in 471 manufacturing corporations for the years 1950–1976.

Reed, Stanley F., and Lane & Edson, P. C. *The Art of M & A: A Merger, Acquisition, Buyout Guide.* Homewood, IL: Dow Jones-Irwin, 1989. 960 pp.

An entrepreneur and members of a law firm have cooperated here to write this nuts and bolts book which looks "at the process of accomplishing an acquisition: how does it happen; who does what; what are the necessary parts and players; and how do they fit together?" Using a question and answer format, it starts with questions relating to deciding what to buy and finding the company. It then continues through each step up to closing the deal, discussing special issues relating to public company acquisition and to transactions with international aspects. A table of cases cited is at the end.

Scharf, Charles, Edward E. Shea and George C. Beck. *Acquisitions, Mergers, Sales, Buyouts and Takeovers: A Handbook With Forms.* 4th ed. Englewood Cliffs, NJ: Prentice-Hall, 1991. 526 pp.

A practical guide to all phases of buying and selling businesses, including legal, tax, securities and accounting aspects, and foreign company acquisitions and ventures. The authors use a practical "how-to-do-it" method and includes numerous forms, practical examples, sample calculations, model agreements, and checklists.

For a nontechnical guide to what managers must know about M&As, refer to *The Ernst & Young Management Guide to Mergers and Acquisitions* edited by Stephen L. Key (New York: Wiley, 1989, 330 pp.). Each chapter, by a recognized expert, addresses a component of a successful acquisitions program.

Dictionaries

The Dealmaker's Dictionary of Merger and Acquisition Terminology. Ed. by Donnan Mandell. San Diego, CA: Buyout Publications, 1984. 203 pp. paper.

A useful paperback dictionary providing concise definitions for the new terms and buzzwords associated with merger and takeover activity—such as "golden parachutes" and "greenmail"—that are usually not found in a regular dictionary. Also covered are commonly used accounting and legal terms relating to mergers and acquisitions.

Periodicals

Acquisitions Monthly. Tunbridge Wells, Kent, Eng.: Tudor House Publications (U.S. office is in Washington, DC).

Each issue of this rather expensive monthly ($360 as of 1991) contains about five articles focusing on topics of interest especially to British and European participants. Some are on takeover activity in a specific country, and include ranked lists. Each issue also usually has one M&A profile, current news and comments, and a monthly list of acquisitions arranged by SIC industry. About one third of the issue consists of a roster of mergers and acquisitions (see section below for description). The "Annual (year)" issue contains a list of companies acquired during the year, giving buyer and price; also the same data arranged by 4-digit SIC, a list of management buyouts, and an index of articles published during the year.

Mergers & Acquisitions. Philadelphia: MLR Publishing Company (bimonthly).

Billed as "the journal of corporate venture," each issue usually contains four or five articles on the state of the art in merger/acquisition/divestiture methodology, with a round-table feature and continuing news reports on sell-offs, joint ventures, takeover defenses, Washington update, the world scene, the M&A database. What makes this journal especially useful is its continuing roster of U.S. mergers/acquisitions/divestitures, foreign investments in the U.S., and U.S. investments abroad (for description see section below). Its annual *Almanac & Index* is published as issue no. 6 (May/June) each year and contains a statistical profile of merger/acquisition/divestiture activity, lists of largest transactions, divestitures, largest foreign acquisitions of U.S. interests, and more; also a "Roster Cross-Index" of mergers reported in issues of M&A each year, and an index of major articles for the year. This journal is indexed in ABI/I, PTS/F&S, TI.

A European companion bimonthly is *M & A Europe* (Geneva: IMC Business Communications SA). This reports on the latest merger and acquisitions strategies, techniques, and trends. It is somewhat similar to the American bimonthly above, but there is no roster section. The "Almanac" issue (January/February) contains an "Annual M & A Review" which includes a ranked list of the "Top International Deals in Europe," and rankings of top deals in various industries. This publisher has recently announced a separate *M & A Europe Handbook* (1991) which is a reference guide containing a directory of key professionals and intermediaries, databases, sources of information, summaries of regulations, checklists, and more.

Lists of Mergers and Acquisitions

Acquisitions Monthly. Tunbridge Wells, Kent, Eng.: Tudor House Publications (U.S. office is in Washington, DC).

About one third of each issue contains details about specific recent mergers and acquisitions including: new and completed bids for U.K. public companies; completed acquisitions for U.K. private companies; U.K. divestments; U.K. acquisitions of North American companies; other U.S. acquisitions; U.K. acquisitions of foreign companies; other foreign acquisitions; management buyouts. At end is a monthly list of the most recent acquisitions arranged by SIC number. The "Annual (year)" issue lists companies acquired during the year, management buyouts, and the list of companies arranged by SIC industry. Published separately by this monthly is their *International Directory of Mergers & Acquisitions Intermediaries* (annual?)

which is arranged by country. The publisher also has an acquisitions database called *AMDATA*.

Merger & Acquisition Sourcebook. Santa Barbara, CA: Quality Services Company (annual).

The first two chapters in the 1991 volume list top mergers and acquisitions for the previous year, arranged by SIC industry. The first contains, for each, details of the terms, purchase price, effective date, total sales, and net income; the second gives only partial data for private or foreign companies and for subsidiaries. Chapters 3–8 contain: featured transactions taken from the publisher's *Acquisition/Divestiture Weekly Report* (an expensive weekly offering a statistical summary of each week's transactions); financial data on potential takeover targets; buybacks; terminations; foreign transactions; M&A data, with an industry focus, and including a ranked list of the 50 largest acquisitions of public companies. An alphabetical index of companies is in the last chapter.

The Merger Yearbook: Domestic. New York: Securities Data Company.

Consists primarily of a list of U.S. corporate acquisitions, mergers, divestitures, and leveraged buyouts, arranged by SIC industries. For each it usually gives names of the target company and buyer, value (price if known), type of deal, effective date, and a brief statement about the event. At front is a summary for the year in charts and tables (including ranked lists of the top 10 financial, target, and acquiror advisors); at end are company and investor indexes. A companion volume is *The International Merger Yearbook* which covers acquisitions and mergers involving foreign targets.

Securities Data Company produces two databases: *Mergers and Corporate Transactions Database* and *International Merger and Corporate Transactions Database*, both with descriptive information on mergers.

Mergers & Acquisitions. Philadelphia: MLR Publishing Company (bimonthly).

About half of each issue consists of a roster of U.S. mergers/acquisitions/divestitures, arranged by two-digit SIC, with data for each completed deal giving details of the terms, the principals involved, effective date, and some financial figures (usually total revenues and net income). There are also shorter lists of foreign acquisitions in the U.S. and U.S. acquisitions abroad with similar details given. A "Roster Cross-Index" of mergers, etc., reported in recent past issues of M&A is published separately in the *Almanac & Index* issue each year (see separate listing under "statistics" below). There is an online *M&A Data Base* which corresponds in part to this roster but contains more information.

Three annual lists of top "deals of the year" appear in: *Business Week* (a mid-April issue), containing a list of the top 100; *Fortune* (first February issue), which has a shorter list; and *Institutional Investor* (March issue), listing 20 of the largest deals. A list of announced or completed M&As for the previous year is in *The Corporate Finance Sourcebook* which is described in the "Corporate Finance Directory" section of this chapter. Two databases are: the *M & A Data Base,* mentioned above as corresponding to the rosters in *Mergers and Acquisitions* magazine; and a DIALOG database, *M & A Filings,* which abstracts merger and acquisitions documents released by the SEC.

Statistics

Mergers & Acquisitions. *Almanac & Index.* Philadelphia: MLR Publishing Company (annual).

This is issued annually as No. 6 (May/June) of the journal. The almanac portion contains brief but useful data on mergers and acquisitions such as ranked lists of 100 largest transactions, largest divestitures, largest foreign acquisitions of U.S. interests, top cancellations, merger activity by industry area. The "Roster Cross-Index" indexes all merger activity reported in *M&A* during previous year; there is also an index of major articles in *M&A*.

Mergerstat Review. Schaumburg, IL: Merrill Lynch Brokerage & Valuation (annual, and quarterly supplement).

A statistical review and summary of the merger and divestiture industry with many charts, tables, and brief text. Includes merger data by industry, data on such topics as tender offers, foreign buyers/sellers, divestitures; also lists of largest transactions, ranked list of top transactions completed or pending during previous year by price paid, largest acquisitions, roster of transactions for previous year giving price paid, method of payment, etc.

Some overall industry data can be found in several of the annual lists of mergers in previous section.

Directories

For directories of types of financing sources see "Corporate Finance Directories" section of this chapter.

Directory of M&A Intermediaries. New York, SDC Publishing (annual).

This directory profiles over 500 investment banks, business brokers, law firms, and other merger and acquisitions intermediaries, arranged geographically by state. A few foreign intermediaries are described in a separate section. For each it usually gives names of officers, services offered, recent M&A activity, financings arranged, fee considerations, transaction size, and geographic coverage. There are five indexes: by company, M&A professionals, industry preference, international activity, type of firm.

A companion annual is *Directory of Buyout Financing Sources,* profiling over 500 U.S. firms that provide debt and equity for buyouts. Separate sections cover: U.S. senior lenders; U.S. mezzanine lenders, providers, and equity investors; a very few foreign firms. There are four indexes similar to those mentioned above, but no index by the types of companies it covers, which are venture capital firms, merchant banks, private LBO (leveraged buyout) investment firms, and more.

Directory of Merger and Acquisition Firms and Professionals. New York and Boston: Walker and Company. (annual; first edition published in 1990).

The company profiles section provides details on more than 900 firms, including when established, key personnel, services offered, industry specialization, number of deals completed recently, fee arrangement, list of typical deals and transactions. There is also a biographical profiles section with details on over 2,700 individuals often with professional and educational history, publications, or articles. Includes an index to industry expertise, and a list of largest M&A firms in the U.S. and Canada.

International Directory of Mergers and Acquisitions Intermediaries. Ed. by Rita Shackleton. Tunbridge Wells, Kent, Eng.: Tudor House Publications, Ltd. (annual?).

Arranged by geographic location, this contains profiles of foreign intermediaries. Basic information for each is similar to the directory noted above, including contacts, types of transactions undertaken, transaction history. This directory is a publication of the British journal *Acquisitions Monthly*.

FINANCE BIBLIOGRAPHIES

Brealey, Richard, and Helen Edwards. *A Bibliography of Finance.* Cambridge, MA: MIT Press, 1991. 822 pp.

This comprehensive bibliography (not annotated) covers English-language books and articles of lasting importance that were written by financial economists and professors, with the articles appearing in approximately 120 periodicals, primarily financial journals. The entries are divided into 40 main subject areas and further into over 350 subdivisions. The 40 main headings cover not only corporate finance topics such as financial planning, working capital, mergers, capital expenditures, but also many investment subjects such as valuation of common stock, options, hedging instruments, cash dividends, and more. The time range runs from 1730 through 1989. An author index is at end. The compilers are a professor and a librarian at the London Business School.

FINANCE DICTIONARIES

American Bankers Association. *Banking Terminology.* 3d ed. Washington, DC: The Association, 1989. 409 pp. paper.

This is an ABA-sponsored dictionary which not only defines new banking terminology but also updates the existing language of bankers. Some 20 bankers were collaborators. Appendixes include bank performance ratios, a glossary of economic indicators, lists of Federal Reserve banks, and other bank-related organizations.

Downes, John, and Jordan E. Goodman. *Dictionary of Finance and Investment Terms.* 3d ed. New York: Barron's, 1991. 537 pp. paper.

This is the finance/investment dictionary I usually turn to first because its definitions are well-written, easy to understand, and they sometimes include useful examples. This latest edition defines more than 3,000 terms including the new terminology as well as updated definitions for the "traditional language." There are ample cross-references; abbreviations and acronyms are at the end. This useful dictionary also appears as part 4 of the authors' *Barron's Finance and Investment Handbook* (3d ed., Barron's, 1990, pp.163–565).

For persons who need a longer dictionary (some 5,000 entries) that includes newer terminology and some buzz words, *The Wall Street Dictionary* by R.J. Shook and Robert L. Shook (New York Institute of Finance, 1990, 470 pp. paper) can be considered. However its definitions are generally too short to be of as much value as most of the other finance dictionaries in this section.

Encyclopedia of Banking and Finance. Originally edited by Glenn G. Munn; then by F.L. Garcia; 9th ed., rev. and expanded by Charles J. Woelfel. Rolling Meadows, IL: Bankers Publishing Co., 1991. 1,097 pp.

This latest edition of an excellent one-volume encyclopedia covering the whole area of banking and finance has been updated and expanded once again to cover the tremendous changes and technological developments in banking and financial systems that have occurred in the past 10 years. Its almost 4,200 entries vary in length from one paragraph to several pages in double-columns. The definitions are well written, often with discussions of the historical background, uses, illustrative examples, statistical data, and citations to applicable laws and regulations. Glossaries are included with some entries, and bibliographies are with many entries for persons who wish to read about any topic in more depth. Besides defining a wide range of financial terms, this encyclopedia also gives information on financial organizations and on the major U.S. (and some foreign) stock and commodity exchanges.

Fitch, Thomas P. *Dictionary of Banking Terms.* New York: Barron's, 1990. 698 pp. paper.

Here is a newly compiled dictionary which promises to be one of the best with its clear, concise definitions of more than 3,000 key terms relating to banking, finance, investment, and money management.

Moffat, Donald W., ed. *Concise Desk Book of Business Finance.* 2d ed. Englewood Cliffs, NJ: Prentice-Hall, 1984. 382 pp.

A good, concise dictionary for financial terms, concepts, theories, and formulas which is easy to use and includes useful cross-references.

The Money Encyclopedia. Ed. by Harvey Rachlin. New York: Harper & Row, 1984. 669 pp.

This is a good encyclopedic dictionary which explains every facet of the money system—from personal finance to corporate operations, from individual money-related matters such as insurance and wills to the worldwide economic system. The entries vary in length from one paragraph to five or more pages, and each is signed by one of over 130 expert contributors representing authoritative finance firms and organizations. Included are entries on financial organizations and exchanges, as well as helpful discussions on such topics as how to purchase a new automobile, how to calculate interest rates, how to read the financial pages. This dictionary would be enhanced, I feel, if there had been more cross-references.

The New Palgrave Dictionary of Money & Finance. Ed. by Peter Newman, et al. London: Macmillan Press Ltd.; New York: Stockton Press, 1992. 3 volumes.

Just published is this new encyclopedic dictionary covering more than 1,000 essays in the field of money and banking, written by some 800 expert contributors, most of them from North America or Britain. Many are over two double-column pages in length, with suggestions for further reading included. While most of these essays are original to this book, a few pertinent ones are taken (with revisions) from a companion work, *The New Palgrave: A Dictionary of Economics* (1987), which is described in Chapter 3. This potentially useful dictionary is expensive ($595) but can probably be found in large libraries with a good finance collection.

Richards, Robert W. *The Dow Jones-Irwin Dictionary of Financial Planning.* Homewood, IL: Dow Jones-Irwin, 1986. 377 pp.

Intended for use both by professional and lay persons, this dictionary focuses on terminology (some 3,000 entries) in the wide-ranging area of financial planning. Included are selected terms from the fields of accounting, business law, estate planning, insurance, investments, real estate, retirement planning, and taxation. A subject index by broad topic is at end.

Rosenberg, Jerry M. *Dictionary of Banking and Financial Services.* 2d ed. New York: Wiley, 1985. 708 pp.

Professor Rosenberg used his *Dictionary of Business and Management* as a point of departure for the first edition of this more specialized dictionary. With this new edition he has expanded the coverage to about 15,000 terms, many of which are taken from a broad base of related fields. His concise definitions, some reprinted from other dictionaries, make for a certain unevenness, with occasional definitions just too short to be very helpful. However, it does cover more terms, and so is more comprehensive than most other dictionaries. A number appears at the end of those citations quoted from another copyrighted source; a list of these cited dictionaries is at the end of the book. A third edition is announced for publication in 1992, but the title will be changed to *The Dictionary of Banking,* and it will be much shorter (384 pp.).

Seglin, Jeffrey L. *Bank Administration Manual: A Comprehensive Reference Guide.* 3d ed., revised. Rolling Meadow, IL: Bank Administration Institute, 1988. 427 pp.

This manual has elements of both a dictionary and an encyclopedia, and it is designed as an easy-to-use comprehensive reference on banking. Entries are arranged alphabetically—some definitions are brief and others cover the topic in depth, including one or more suggestions for further information.

FINANCE PERIODICALS

Banking periodicals are listed elsewhere in this chapter; investment magazines are in Chapter 8; insurance and real estate magazines in Chapter 15; international financial periodicals are in Chapter 16.

The Continental Bank Journal of Applied Corporate Finance. New York: Stern Stewart Management Services, for the Continental Bank (quarterly).

A relatively new (1988) quarterly, with each issue consisting of about 8 to 10 well-researched articles focusing on a particular broad topic. Subjects in several recent issues (as of 1991) include: corporate restructuring; financing the middle market; global finance; workouts and bankruptcy. Most of the authors are respected academicians or finance experts. A roundtable discussion appears in many issues.

Corporate Finance. New York: CF-VH Associates (monthly).

Usually four short, practical articles of interest to the "financing strategist" are in each issue, often about people, financial problems, or companies; also regular sections on such topics as financing strategies, internal company finance, and "The Month in Finance" (lists of new issues and leading underwriters of new issues). At end of issue is a special report with a different topic covered in each issue, e.g. cash management, mergers & acquisitions, pensions, and there is usually a directory of firms included on each topic. Special annual features include: "The (year) International Corporate Finance Register" (January), describing the 250 largest manufacturing firms outside the U.S.; "Corporate Finance Register" (June), with brief facts about the 250 largest U.S. nonfinancial corporations, including biographical data on each firm's CEO and CFO, and names of the treasury staff.

A monthly with same title is published in London by Euromoney Publications; it is described in Chapter 16.

Financial Executive. Morristown, NJ: Financial Executives Institute (monthly).

Each issue usually contains authoritative yet readable articles on business and financial management topics of interest to FEI members, plus continuing features. Indexed in ABI/I, BPI, TI.

Financial Management. Tampa, FL: Financial Management Association, University of South Florida (quarterly).

Instructive, scholarly articles on financial management, written primarily by academicians. Indexed in ABI/I, BPI, TI.

Financial Planning. Atlanta, GA: Financial Services Information Company for the International Association for Financial Planning (monthly).

Billed as "the magazine for financial service professionals," this monthly contains articles and news on trends, events, and people of interest to IAFP members. Regular departments cover such topics as regulation, industries in motion, planning, investments, resources (occasionally including a book review). Annual features include: a two-part "Annual Broker-Dealer Survey" (June and July) which contains ranked lists (by three size-categories) of financial planning and insurance firms giving vital statistics and statistics by each source of revenues; and "A Comparative Survey of Variable Life and Annuity Contracts" (September). Indexed in PAIS.

Institutional Investor. New York: Institutional Investor (monthly).

A practical journal of interest to money managers and available in both a domestic and an international edition. Its articles are on such topics as money management, corporate finance, pensions, mergers and acquisitions, investor relations, and profiles of specific money managers. Almost every issue contains an annual feature article. For a more complete list of these see entry for this journal in Chapter 8. Several relating to corporate finance and banking are: "Deals of the Year" (January issue), ranking noteworthy financings of the past year; "The (year) M & A Sweepstakes" (March), ranking top M&A advisers for U.S.-based companies; "The World's Largest Banks" (July); "The Best Annual Reports" (September). Specific directories in issues include: "The (year) M&A Directory" (November), listing leading M&A specialists; "The (year) Real Estate Directory" (December), giving corporate executives in charge of real estate. This journal is indexed in ABI/I, BPI, PAIS, TI; also in full text on BRS, DATA-STAR, DIALOG, MEAD/NEXIS.

An "International Edition" contains some of the same material but concentrates more on articles of interest to international money managers.

Journal of Business Finance & Accounting. Oxford, Eng.: B. Blackwell (quarterly).

An international quarterly for authoritative refereed articles on a wide spectrum of interrelated financial matters, including accounting as it relates to finance. Most of the articles are by academic persons. Indexed in ABI/I.

Journal of Cash Management. Baltimore: The Treasury Management Association (bimonthly).

This journal contains short articles on treasury management techniques and methodology on timely topics of interest to treasury professionals. Occasional features in recent issues (1991) include: "Compensation Survey" (January/February); "Commercial Banking in (year)" (July/August); "Directory of Major Cash Management Banks" (July/August). Indexed in ABI/I.

Journal of Finance. New York: American Finance Association (5/yr.).

A widely respected professional journal covering theoretical and technical articles on all phases of finance. Most articles are by academic persons, and many contain mathematical formulas. The quarterly issues include a good book review section. The third issue (in July each year) contains "Papers and Proceedings" of the annual AFA meeting. Indexed in ABI/I, BPI, PAIS.

The Eastern Finance Association and the Midwest Finance Association jointly publish a quarterly called *The Financial Review,* (Statesboro, GA: School of Business, Georgia Southern College). The Southern Finance Association and the Southwestern Finance Association jointly sponsor the *Journal of Financial Research* (Tempe, AZ: College of Business, Arizona State University, quarterly). Both are indexed in ABI/I, BPI.

Journal of Financial and Quantitative Analysis. Seattle: University of Washington, Graduate School of Business Administration in conjunction with the Western Finance Association (quarterly).

An academic journal for theoretical articles on the title subject, and so most articles are mathematically oriented. The fifth issue each year (November) contains "Proceedings" of the WFA annual meeting. Indexed in ABI/I BPI.

CORPORATE FINANCE DIRECTORIES

Most of the corporate finance directories concentrate on just one type of finance and so will be described with books on that subject. For instance, directories of banks, venture capital companies, and merger and acquisition firms appear elsewhere in this chapter; directories of insurance and real estate companies are in Chapter 15, and investment management companies and securities dealers in Chapter 8. (Check the index for exact pages).

The Corporate Finance Bluebook. Wilmette, IL: National Register Publishing Co. (annual).

This directory is useful for its listing of the top financial officers in more than 5,200 American nonfinancial companies. For each company, it provides the names, titles, and telephone numbers of the officers in charge of about 11 finance functions such as cash management, employee benefits, international finance, investor relations, leasing, management information services, pension administration, planning and development. Also listed are the outside firms providing about 10 different financial services for the company, the names of U.S. wholly-owned subsidiaries of parent companies. Other brief data are: year founded, number of employees, a few financial figures, stock exchange/ticker symbol/CUSIP no. for public companies. Seven indexes are at front: complete list of firms and subsidiaries; private companies; index by SIC; index by geographic location; outside service firms client index (listed by type of service, e.g. auditors, business brokers, and including clients of each firm); index by name of officers; and officer index by each financial function.

The Corporate Finance Sourcebook. Wilmette, IL: National Register Publishing Co. (annual). Available also on disk.

Arranged in 18 sections, this is an impressive directory of all types of firms that are sources for corporate financing, with important details given for each firm. The sections cover: U.S. venture capital lenders, major private lenders, commercial finance and factors, leasing companies, commerical banks, U.S.-based foreign banks, investment banks, foreign investment banks in the U.S., business intermediaries (business brokers), leading pension managers, U.S. banks offering master trust services, leading corporate cash managers, business insurance brokers, corporate real estate services, security analysts (arranged by industry specialty), CPA accounting and audit firms, international venture capital companies, and leading merchant banking firms. The last section lists all corporate securities public offerings during the past three years, giving pertinent data such as issuing date, offering price. At end is a list of mergers and acquisitions for the previous year with pertinent data about each.

Sunday Telegraph Business Finance Directory. London: Graham & Trotman in association with the *Sunday Telegraph* (annual).
This is a useful "guide to sources of corporate finance in Britain." It describes, in turn, companies in 12 different types of institutions offering finance for business: recognized banks and licensed deposit takers; venture capital companies; business expansion scheme fund managers; stockbrokers; licensed dealers and investment managers; public sector institutions; finance houses; factoring companies; leasing companies; insurance companies; investment trusts; accountants. Three indexes help in identifying the companies.
A somewhat similar directory covering Canada is *The Guide to the Canadian Financial Services Industry* (Toronto: Flagship Publishers Corporation; annual).

FINANCIAL ASSOCIATIONS

American Finance Association, School of Business, New York University, 100 Trinity Place, New York, NY 10006.

Financial Executives Institute, PO Box 1938, 10 Madison Ave., Morristown, NJ 07960.

Financial Management Association, Graduate School of Business, University of South Florida, 4202 Fowler Ave., Tampa, FL 33620.

Institute of Certified Financial Planners, Two Denver Highlands, 10065 E. Harvard Ave., Denver, CO 80231.

International Association for Financial Planning, Two Concourse Pkwy., Suite 800, Atlanta, GA 30328.

MONEY, BANKING, AND FINANCIAL INSTITUTIONS

BASIC TEXTS

Horvitz, Paul M., and Richard A. Ward. *Monetary Policy and the Financial System.* 6th ed. Englewood Cliffs, NJ: Prentice-Hall, 1987. 532 pp.
Latest revision of a basic textbook, with emphasis placed on monetary policy. The material is divided into 6 parts: operations of the financial system; financing the economy (chapters cover financing business, the consumer, housing, government, international); banking regulation and development; central banking; monetary theory; monetary policy. Suggested readings are listed at the end of chapters; a glossary is at end of the book.

Hultman, Charles W. *The Environment of International Banking.* Englewood Cliffs, NJ: Prentice-Hall, 1990. 288 pp. paper.

Intended to supplement a standard money/banking textbook, the purpose of this concise volume "is to provide a basis for an understanding of international commercial banking and the framework within which it occurs, particularly in terms of the U.S. interest in such activity in recent years." The chapters are arranged within three parts: basic nature of international banking; foreign commercial banking in the U.S.; U.S. commercial banks in overseas activities. A bibliography is at end.

Kamerschen, David R. *Money & Banking.* 9th ed. Cincinnati: South-Western Publishing Co., 1988. 663 pp.

Another well-established introductory text both on monetary theory and policy and on commercial banking, with the core of the book dealing with the former.

Kaufman, George G. *The U.S. Financial System: Money, Markets, and Institutions.* 4th ed. Englewood Cliffs, NJ: Prentice-Hall, 1989. 732 pp. Fifth edition to be published in 1992.

In this introductory text, Professor Kaufman places emphasis on important current issues in financial institutions and monetary policy with a balance given to theory and practice. The first five parts develop the microanalysis of the U.S. financial system, discussing the development and operation of financial markets and financial institutions, as well as international finance. The last two parts study the macrostructure of the economy by discussing the Federal Reserve System and other topics in monetary theory and policy. This latest edition has been thoroughly revised and updated to incorporate the many recent changes in the financial system. An introductory course in economics is a prerequisite; mathematics is used sparingly; references to additional readings are at end of chapters.

Kidwell, David S., and Richard L. Peterson. *Financial Institutions, Markets, and Money.* 3d ed. Chicago: Dryden Press, 1987. 710 pp.

The authors present here a revision of their text with a balanced view emphasizing both financial institutions, markets and financial instruments, and also banks and monetary policy. The material is divided into 7 major parts: the financial system; central banking; commercial banking; nonbank financial institutions; financial markets; monetary policy; the international financial system. Useful features include boxed items containing interesting background or current events material, "profiles in finance" at beginning of each major part, good use of two colors in diagrams, tables, and so forth. Lists of annotated, selected references are at end of chapters. A glossary is at end of the book. This text assumes the reader has had an introductory economics course.

Mayer, Thomas, James S. Duesenberry and Robert Z. Aliber. *Money, Banking, and the Economy.* 4th ed. New York: Norton, 1990. 425 pp.

Revised a fourth time to incorporate the many new developments such as the savings and loan bailout, this is a standard, introductory text that is organized into five parts to cover: the financial structure; the supply of money; money, national income, and price level; monetary policy; the international monetary system. Suggestions for further reading are with chapters.

Mishkin, Frederic S. *The Economics of Money, Banking, and Financial Markets.* 3d ed. New York: HarperCollins, 1992. 739, [67] pp.

Professor Mishkin says he has tried to convey the excitement of recent developments and important concepts in the field in an understandable and interesting way. In this major revision he has developed a comprehensive economic framework for analyzing financial markets and institutions. He has also tried to show the increasing importance of international trade and financial markets to our economy by integrating international topics throughout the book. It is still arranged in 7 parts to cover the subjects mentioned in the title. The publisher uses color effectively, especially in graphs, charts, and other illustrations. Interspersed throughout are special interest and "global perspective" boxes (in color) as well as useful "following the financial news" inserts to help students interpret financial data found in newspapers. At end are mathematical appendixes and a glossary.

Ritter, Lawrence S., and William L. Silber. *Principles of Money, Banking, and Financial Markets.* 7th ed. New York: Basic Books, 1991. 644 pp.

Another leading introductory text, this one of use either for a course on money and banking or on financial institutions and markets. This latest edition still hopes to maintain its conversational style while focusing attention throughout on the increasing role of computers and communication technology in the financial sector. It is arranged within 6 parts to cover: the basics; intermediaries and banks; the art of central banking; monetary theory; financial markets and interest rates; international finance. There are useful suggestions for further reading at end of most chapters; a glossary is at end of book.

Several alternative texts are: *Money, Banking, and Economic Analysis* by Thomas D. Simpson (3d ed., Englewood Cliffs, NJ: Prentice-Hall, 1987, 562 pp.) which tries to strike a balance between an analytical and a descriptive/historical emphasis; *Money, Banking and Financial Markets* by Robert D. Auerbach (3d ed., New York: Macmillan, 1988, 832 pp.) who covers the subjects well in 9 parts, and with good use of two-color boxed explanations, tables, and diagrams; *Money and the Economy* by John T. Klein (6th ed., New York: Harcourt Brace Jovanovich, 1986, 560 pp.), a readable but rigorous account of the relationship of money to aggregate economic activity; *Money, Banking, and the U.S. Economy* by Harry D. Hutchinson (7th ed., Englewood Cliffs, NJ: Prentice-Hall, 1992, 552 pp.), a standard undergraduate text whose objective it has been to present this introduction in as clear and understandable a way as possible.

FINANCIAL MARKETS

For books on investing in the stock, bond, and money markets see Chapter 8. Books on international finance, banking, and the international capital market are in Chapter 16; statistics on the U.S. capital market are included in the "U.S. Banking and Financial Statistics" of this chapter; international financial statistics are in Chapter 5.

Handbooks

Handbook of Financial Markets and Institutions. 6th ed. by Edward I. Altman. New York: Wiley, 1987. 1 volume (various pagings).

This companion volume to the *Handbook of Corporate Finance* (see description in section for "Financial Handbooks") focuses on financial markets, institutions, and investments, synthesizing the latest literature and developments. Like the other volume, it also is intended for financial practitioners, and each of its 27 chapters is written by a respected expert. New chapters have been added on such topics as investment banking, the microcomputer and investments, the bond rating process, asset pricing models, and small business financing. Also like its companion volume, the appendix has a chapter on "Mathematics of Finance" and a list of sources of financial and investment information. Good bibliographical references are at end of chapters; useful tables and diagrams appear throughout; and a detailed index is at end.

Books

Dougall, Herbert E., and Jack E. Gaumnitz. *Capital Markets and Institutions.* 5th ed. Englewood Cliffs, NJ: Prentice-Hall, 1986. 294 pp. paper.

Revised once again to reflect the many changes and developments, this new edition still aims "to present a general and uncomplicated discussion of the institutions operating in the capital market," to assess the demand and supply of funds in these markets, and to analyze the interplay of these forces. It contains chapters on the major sources of capital market funds (banks, thrift institutions, insurance companies, pension and retirement plans, investment companies, real estate trusts) as well as chapters on the uses of funds (federal securities, state and local government bonds, corporate securities, mortgage market). A bibliography is at the end. This paperback belongs to the useful "Foundations of Finance" series, edited by Ezra Solomon, that provides short, authoritative essays on current thinking about individual financial topics.

Fabozzi, Frank J., and Franco Modigliani. *Capital Markets: Institutions and Instruments.* Englewood Cliffs, NJ: Prentice-Hall, 1992. 726 pp.

A new textbook which describes the wide range of instruments for financing, investing, and controlling risk that are available in today's financial markets. The authors arrange the material within 6 parts: financial institutions; asset pricing and derivative markets; the equity market; interest rate determination; the debt market; foreign exchange and global financial markets.

Fraser, Donald R., and Peter S. Rose, eds. *Readings on Financial Institutions and Markets.* 4th ed. Homewood, IL: Irwin, 1990. 431 pp. paper.

For persons who want a book of readings, this is an updated selection covering major developments in the operation and regulation of financial markets and institutions. They are arranged in 7 parts, three of which cover: instruments of the money and capital markets; international finance; financial innovation. These two professors have written other books including an eight-part text (with Rose as lead author) titled *Financial Institutions: Understanding and Managing Financial Services* (3d ed., Plano, TX: Business Publications, 1988, 762 pp.).

Henning, Charles N., William Pigott and Robert H. Scott. *Financial Markets and the Economy.* 5th ed. Englewood Cliffs, NJ: Prentice-Hall, 1988. 638 pp.

Paul Nadler says this text "explains money and banking in simple terms, it gives a good picture of the other financial institutions, and it shows the workings of the money and capital markets in terms the student can not only understand but can also examine with interest."—cf. Foreword. The aim of this latest edition is to cover the financial part of macroeconomics, while "the heart of the book is still the determination of interest rates through the generation of saving, the flow of saving through financial institutions and markets, and the demand for borrowing." Each of its 17 chapters ends with a short bibliography that contains useful annotations including mention of the significance of the reading.

BANK MANAGEMENT

Handbooks

Aspinwall, Richard C., and Robert A. Eisenbeis, eds. *Handbook for Banking Strategy.* New York: Wiley, 1985. 800 pp.

The emphasis in this compilation of 24 papers by 26 contributors is on changes in financial institutions and markets and their implications for the development of effective strategies. Thus half of the book consists of 12 chapters (part 4) which examine implications for effective management, addressing not only analytical approaches and resource issues, but also critical uncertainties. The first two parts consist of two papers each on the role of financial intermediaries in general and on major forces for change. Part 3 has 8 papers on specific manifestations of banking change in the markets served by banking institutions—in terms of customers, services, suppliers, and regulation.

Baughn, William H., Thomas I. Storrs and Charles E. Walker, eds. *The Bankers' Handbook.* 3d ed. Homewood, IL: Dow Jones-Irwin, 1988. 1,347 pp.

Over 100 contributors, many of whom are practicing bankers, have written chapters in this handbook on commercial banking and major changes affecting this important industry. Included are sections on organization, control, credit services, investment instruments and markets, retail and wholesale banking, marketing bank services, bank regulations. This is a comprehensive and useful background reference. Earlier Mr. Baughn also edited, with Donald R. Mandich, *The International Banking Handbook* (Dow Jones-Irwin, 1983, 858 pp.) which is described in the "International Finance and World Trade" section of Chapter 16.

Books

Channon, Derek F. *Global Banking Strategy.* New York and Chichester, Eng.: Wiley, 1988. 389 pp.

A respected British management professor examines here the trends and changing patterns in multinational banking which must be addressed to avoid problems in the near future. His chapters cover: the evolution of multinational banking; multinational banks and the foreign exchange market; industrial development; the debt bomb; the changing nature of corporate banking; retail banking; the delivery system revolution. It ends with two chapters, one discussing the strategic impact of regulation and deregulation, and the other, implications for economic management.

Compton, Eric N. *Principles of Banking.* 4th ed. Washington, DC: American Bankers Association, 1991. 461 pp.

Revised once again to cover rapid changes in the industry, this is an overview of commercial banking that the nonbanker can understand. It includes chapters covering history, fundamentals of bank accounting, deposits, payments, credit, bank services, and regulations/controls. A glossary is at end. Short lists of sources for further information are with most chapters.

Garcia, F.L. *How to Analyze a Bank Statement.* 7th ed. Boston: Bankers Publishing Co., 1985. 223 pp.

A well-researched and detailed guide to the financial statements of banks and bank holding companies, including reporting requirements, forms and content of statements, and techniques of analysis.

Hempel, George H., and Donald G. Simonson. *Bank Financial Management: Strategies and Techniques for a Changing Industry.* New York: Wiley, 1991. 514 pp.

"The purpose of this book is to present the financial concepts, strategies, and techniques that will help bank managers to be successful" in a changing financial environment. Part 1 of its 7 parts discusses this changing nature of bank financial management. The other parts cover: measuring and evaluating bank performance; basic financial instruments and techniques; bank asset management; bank liability management; new financial strategies; integrative bank financial management decisions. Appendixes explain specific approaches/calculations.

Hempel coauthored (with Howard D. Crosse) a now quite old but still well-recognized book on *Management Policies for Commercial Banks* (3d ed., Prentice-Hall, 1980, 356 pp.).

McMahon, Robert J. *Bank Marketing Handbook: How to Compete in the Financial Services Industry.* Rolling Meadows, IL: Bank Administration Institute, 1989. 360 pp.

Bank marketing is of increasing importance in bank management, and so we include here a book intended to help improve the bank marketing management process. It starts with an introductory section and then studies in turn: bank marketing strategy (customer behavior, bank products and services, pricing); bank marketing action (selling, advertising, public relations); bank marketing management. A final chapter talks about the future. Diagrams and checklists appear throughout; "sources for additional reading" are at end.

Nadler, Paul S. *Commercial Banking in the Economy.* 4th ed. New York: Random House, 1986. 199 pp. paper.

A readable, informative paperback that examines the role of the banking industry as a link between credit control and economic activity and provides an understanding of what banking is as a business. Special emphasis is placed on recent changes.

Reed, Edward W., and Edward K. Gill. *Commercial Banking.* 4th ed. Englewood Cliffs, NJ: Prentice-Hall, 1989. 472 pp.

This book aims to provide both professionals and students with a description and analysis of the operations of commercial banks from a managerial view. It covers such topics as structure, organization and management, deposits, cash and liquidity management, investments, trust services, and international banking. There are also 7 chapters on lending since it is the major business of commercial banks, and 2 chapters on profitability and bank capital. Selected bibliographies are at end of chapters.

For persons who want a research-oriented book that examines the tremendous structural changes in American banking since the second World War and the impact of these changes on bank performance in serving the public, see *The Changing Structure of American Banking* by Peter S. Rose (New York: Columbia University Press, 1987, 419 pp.).

CREDIT MANAGEMENT

Cole, Robert H. *Consumer and Commercial Credit Management.* 8th ed. Homewood, IL: Irwin, 1988. 468 pp. Ninth edition just published in 1992.

What credit is, what it does, and what it can and cannot do—for persons involved in the management of credit and collection activities. In the 8th edition of this standard work, two parts are devoted to the basics of understanding consumer credit and the management/analysis of consumer credit, and two parts to business credit and management/analysis of commercial credit. Revised chapters in this latter section discuss the credit services of Dun & Bradstreet, Inc., other credit reporting agencies, and the analysis and interpretation of financial statements. There is also one chapter each on international trade credit and on control of credit operations. Lists of suggested readings are provided in each chapter, and a glossary is at end of the book.

For "a helpful reference glossary of commercial and legal words and phrases most commonly used in the business office," see *The Dictionary of Business and Credit Terms* by Ben Berman (New York: National Association of Credit Management, 1983, 208 pp.).

MORTGAGE BANKING

Mortgage Banking: A Handbook of Strategies, Trends and Opportunities. Ed. by Jess Lederman. Chicago: Probus Publishing Company, 1989. 573 pp.

Intended as an in-depth, timely source for mortgage banking participants at all levels, this handbook contains the practical information and advice of 36 experts. Its 30 chapters are arranged in 6 sections: review of the mortgage banking industry; programs for mortgage origination; opportunities in the secondary market; shaping mortgage banking operations for success; developments in mortgage servicing; issues in mortgage banking.

PERSONAL FINANCE

It usually is best to consult recent books on personal finance if you want to factor in to your financial planning a consideration of such problems as inflation, new tax laws, and other current conditions. The books below are relatively recent; three are textbook-type books and the other two are practical guides for interested persons.

Hallman, G. Victor, and Jerry S. Rosenbloom. *Personal Financial Planning.* 4th ed. New York: McGraw-Hill, 1987. 475 pp.

These authors say they consider personal financial planning as the process of determining an individual's or a family's total financial objectives, considering alternative plans or methods for meeting those objectives, selecting the plans and methods that are best suited for the person's circumstances, implementing, and periodically reviewing those plans. Their book addresses these needs in five sections: coordinated financial planning; using insurance effectively; accumulating capital and income tax planning; planning for retirement; estate and tax planning. A checklist and review forms are at end.

Klott, Gary L. *The New York Times Complete Guide to Personal Investing.* New York: Times Books, 1987. 612 pp.

Although limited to the subject of investments, this is still a useful guide because of its practical, non-textbook approach to one aspect of personal finance. It covers a wide range of investment choices, with tips on how best to select them, and tax consequences as of 1987. Klott covers not only stocks and bonds and short term investments but also collectibles, precious metals, commodities, tax shelters, real estate investments, savings plans, international investments, and business investments.

Quinn, Jane B. *Making the Most of Your Money.* New York: Simon & Schuster, 1991. 934 pp.

The subtitle of this handbook is "Smart Ways to Create Wealth and Plan Your Finances in the 90s." Miss Quinn, who is a personal finance columnist with *Newsweek* and several other journals, provides here an easy-to-read and simple-to-understand guide to an eight-step system for personal financial planning. The 8 steps, in 32 chapters, are: building your base (including coverage on keeping records, banking, writing a will); finding the money; your safety net (insurance, etc.); your own home; paying for college; understanding investing (including chapters on how to pick a mutual fund, working with a stockbroker, how to use bonds, and so forth); retirement planning; making it work. Appendixes contain useful planners, tables, and other supplementary aids. The author sums it all up wisely by saying that "the broad principles of personal finance will stay the same; save money, borrow intelligently, invest for growth."

Another well-known personal finance columnist has recent written a shorter practical guide called *Sylvia Porter's Your Finances in the 1990s* (New York: Prentice Hall Press, 1990, 346 pp.).

Stillman, Richard J. *Guide to Personal Finance: A Lifetime Program of Money Management.* Englewood Cliffs, NJ: Prentice-Hall, 1988. 504 pp.

Professor Stillman, whose specialty is the field of money management, has once again revised his well-organized undergraduate text which aims to provide fundamental personal finance concepts so that students and others can develop "a lifetime program of money management." He examines 24 components of his personal finance model which he groups into 6 interrelated parts: achieving financial health; spending money wisely (for food, clothing, personal health, cars, appliances, taxes); housing and other real estate; insurance; investing in stocks, bonds, investment companies; retirement and estate planning (including wills and trusts). Useful data in an appendix includes a list of periodicals and services, a glossary, a bibliography, and material on the computer's role.

Wolf, Harold A. *Personal Financial Planning.* 8th ed. Boston: Allyn and Bacon, 1989. 696 pp.

As with other texts on this subject, the goal of this one is to provide the reader with an understanding of the principles of personal finance and to help him/her develop better skills in making the correct financial decisions. This latest edition contains significant revisions and changes in response to increased complexities and rapid changes. It is divided into five parts: introduction; managing your income and your assets (consumer credit, automobiles and major appliances, taxes, housing, etc.); planning and managing your insurance program; managing your investments; retirement and estate planning. Useful tables and charts are found throughout. Suggested readings and case incidents are with chapters; a glossary is at end of book.

BANKING LAW AND FINANCIAL LEGAL SERVICES

Commerce Clearing House. *Bankruptcy Law Reporter.* Chicago. 3 volumes (biweekly).

This loose-leaf service spans the whole field of bankruptcy and debt relief law embodied in the federal Bankruptcy Act and related federal statutes. Gives explanations, text of laws, interpretative reports of congressional committees, general orders, specimen forms.

Commerce Clearing House. *Federal Banking Law Reporter.* Chicago. 6 volumes (loose-leaf).

Comprehensive, continuing coverage of federal banking laws, regulations, rulings, court decisions, explanations, forms. Includes data on the Federal Reserve System, National Banking Acts, financial institutions, deregulation and monetary control, and related federal banking loan rules.

Prentice-Hall, Inc. *Control of Banking.* Englewood Cliffs, NJ. 2 volumes, with biweekly supplements (loose-leaf).

Reports on federal controls governing the operation and financial practices of financial institutions, including rules, regulations, interpretations, opinions of federal agencies, and latest court decisions.

Schroeder, Milton R. *Bank Officer's Handbook of Commerical Banking Law.* 6th ed. Boston: Warren, Gorham & Lamont, 1989. 1 volume (various pagings). Kept up to date with supplements.

Good for its nontechnical coverage of information on the ordinary legal problems that arise in the regular course of the banking business.

BANKING AND FINANCIAL TABLES

Financial Publishing Company. *Financial Compound Interest and Annuity Tables.* 6th ed. Boston: 1980. 2,113 pp. Out of print.

Provides the six standard compound interest and annuity tables for the greatest number of periods, and it has the easiest-to-use format. Examples of applications of these tables to practical problems are an aid to the novice. The six standard tables are: amount of 1; amount of 1 per period; sinking fund, or periodic payment which will amount to 1; present worth of 1; present worth of 1 per period; partial payment, or periodic payment worth of 1 today.

There are other shorter volumes that give compound interest tables for a lesser number of rates. See, for example, *Handbook of Interest and Annuity Tables* by Jack C. Estes (New York: McGraw-Hill, 1976, 466 pp.).

Financial Publishing Company. *Monthly Payment Direct Reduction Loan Amortization Schedules.* 13th ed. Boston: 1980. 2,075 pp. And supplementary revised edition, 1987 (300 pp.).

A comprehensive set of amortization schedules "showing the division each month of the payment between interest and principal on a $1,000 loan." In the back is a "points discount table" and a "monthly payment per $1,000" table carried out to 6 places after the decimal.

Financial Publishing Company has other specialized books of tables, e.g. continuous compounding growth tables, simple interest tables, mortgage payment and values tables, expanded bond values, U.S. Treasury Bills tables.

Johnson, Irvin E. *Instant Mortgage-Equity: Extended Tables of Overall Rates.* Lexington, MA: Lexington Books, 1980. 454 pp.

This book, written by an appraiser for appraisers and for other nonmathematicians, was published in conjunction with the National Association of Independent Fee Appraisers. The major part contains OAR tables (Precomputed Mortgage-Equity Overall Rates) for the valuation of income property. This latest volume extends the tables of Overall Rates to provide for mortgage interest rates from 12½ to 30%. Compound interest and annuity tables are also included. There is some discussion of new procedures at the beginning, but a more detailed explanation of mortgage-equity theory, techniques, and procedures, with problems and solutions, is in Johnson's earlier *The Instant Mortgage-Equity Technique* (Lexington Books, 1972, 374 pp.).

Mason, James J., ed. *American Institute of Real Estate Appraisers Financial Tables.* Chicago: The Institute, 1981. 473 pp.

Since this book is intended for use with the Institute's courses, each of its 9 sets of financial factors is prefaced by its formulation, brief explanation, and examples of use. Special features are: the continuous compounding and discounting factors; annuities changing in constant amount and constant ratio; sinking fund factors for annual payments with daily interest; part-paid-off for monthly, direct reduction loans; and straight-line J-Factors for income adjustment in mortgage/equity analysis.

Thorndike, David. *Thorndike Encyclopedia of Banking and Financial Tables.* 3d rev. ed. Boston: Warren, Gorham & Lamont, 1987. 1 volume (various pagings). And a supplementary *Yearbook.*

Consists of 6 types of tables: loan payment and amortization; compound interest and annuity; interest; savings and withdrawal; installment loan, leasing, and rebates; investment (discount price, mortgage, and bond price and yield). The *Yearbook* updates are usually in two parts: the first has updated banking and financial tables; the second contains "banking and financial information," including interest rates and investment yields tables, foreign exchange rates, international weights and measures, and more. A glossary of banking and financial terminology is at end of the *Yearbook.*

See also *Barron's Real Estate Handbook* by Jack C. Harris and Jack P. Friedman described in Chapter 15 for a desk reference book that contains mortgage payment and other financial tables of interest in real estate financing.

BANKING BIBLIOGRAPHIES

American Bankers Association. *Banking Literature Index.* Washington, DC: The Association (monthly, with annual cumulations).

Of interest to bank librarians and bank researchers is this monthly list, by subject, of the significant articles on banking and bank management selected by the ABA library reference/research staff from an examination of almost 200 periodicals. Journals covered include not only the major banking journals but also related periodicals in finance, law, and management.

American Bankers Association. Stonier Graduate School of Banking. *Cumulative Catalog of Theses.* Washington, DC: 1977?– to date. 3 volumes published as of 1991.

The first volume describes Stonier School banking theses completed from 1937–1961; the second, 1962–75; the third, 1976–88.

Deuss, Jean. *Banking in the U.S.: An Annotated Bibliography.* Metuchen, NJ: Scarecrow Press, 1990. 164 pp.

A well-selected, descriptive bibliography of recent (as of 1989) basic English-language books on the history, organization, regulation, and management of U.S. banks and banking with an emphasis on the banking industry. It is arranged in 12 sections by subjects such as commercial banking, savings institutions, investment banking. There are also sections covering basic statistics, reference works, periodicals, and newspapers. Appendixes include a chronology of banking, lists of agencies, and associations. The selections are based on the author's long experience as a leading bank librarian. We hope she will consider a periodic revision to keep it up to date.

The Fed in Print: Business & Banking Topics. Philadelphia: Federal Reserve Bank of Philadelphia (semiannual).

This is a subject index to publications of the Federal Reserve Research Departments (including the periodic business or economic reviews of the 12 Federal Reserve district banks), and also to the analytical articles in the *Federal Reserve Bulletin.*

FINIS: Financial Industry Information Service. Online database.

A specialized database abstracting articles on the marketing of financial services that appear in more than 200 core business journals, banking magazines, financial industry newsletters, district Federal Reserve bulletins, house organs of a few financial institutions, several daily newspapers. This database is produced by the Bank Marketing Association.

BANKING DICTIONARIES

A selection of the better dictionaries on banking and finance is described in the "Finance Dictionaries" section of this chapter.

FINANCIAL MANUALS AND BANK DIRECTORIES

Moody's Bank & Finance Manual. New York: Moody's Investors Service. 4 volumes (annual, with semiweekly supplements).

Volume 1 of this basic financial manual covers U.S. banks and trust companies, savings and loan associations, and federal credit agencies. Volume 2 covers insurance, investment and finance companies, real estate companies, real estate investment trusts. Volumes 3–4 describe unit investment trusts. Information for each company that has standard coverage usually includes a brief financial history, officers and directors, comparative income statements, balance sheets, information on capital stock, record of dividend payments, recent stock price range. Blue pages in each volume contain some general banking and finance statistics and also lists of largest banks, mutual savings banks, S&Ls, bank holding companies, insurance, and investment companies. Companies having complete coverage usually have more information including a copy of the company president's annual letter to shareholders.

The three principal directories of banks and one rating service are:

Bankers' Almanac and Year Book. East Grinstead, West Sussex, Eng.: T. Skinner Directories. 2 volumes.

Volume 1 is a directory of British and international banks, giving officers, correspondents, balance sheet statistics. General information at end includes list of British banking associations; U.K. amalgamations, absorption, liquidations; Bank of England statistics; currencies of the world. Volume 2 contains country, town, and geographic indexes. Published separately is an annual *Bankers' Almanac World Ranking* which ranks the top 3,000 international banks by total assets, with an added section by country and also an alphabetical index.

Polk's Bank Directory. North American Edition. Nashville, TN: R.L. Polk (semiannual and bimonthly supplements).

Geographic list of North American banks, giving telephone/cable/fax, officers and directors, correspondents, out-of-town branches, assets, and liabilities. Supplementary information includes maps for each state, state banking officials, legal holidays, list of bank holding companies, transit numbers, list of bank related associations, ranked list of largest banks. A companion volume is the "International Edition," which is arranged geographically.

Quarterly Bank and Savings & Loan Rating Service. Frederick, MD: LACE Financial Corporation.

For persons interested in checking bank ratings, this is a continuously revised list (arranged geographically) of 13,000 commercial banks, 500 savings banks, 2,900 S&Ls, and 100 bank holding companies. For each it gives total assets, net income, liquidity, asset quality, capital earnings % of assets, and LACE rating. The ratings are given quarterly for the past year. Ranked lists of the 100 largest banks and bank holding companies are at front.

Sheshunoff Information Services, in Austin, TX, publishes an alternate source for bank ratings called *The Bank Holding Company Quarterly: Ratings & Analysis.* It is somewhat similar in that it gives other financial figures for the U.S. bank holding companies (BHCs) and subsidiary banks it covers, and has ranked lists of BHCs at front in 16 categories, such as assets. At end is a short list of foreign BHCs.

Thomson Bank Directory. Skokie, IL: Thomson Financial Publishing (semiannual).

Volumes 1–2 contain a geographical listing of U.S. banks (head office and branches) with data for each including when established, key officers, principal correspondents, phone/telex/fax/cable, rank in state and in nation, some financial data (for most banks); volume 3 is a comparable directory of international banks arranged by country. Brief demographic and financial facts are at beginning of each state section, including ranked lists of the 5 largest banks in the state. At front of volume 1 is a "reference and banking information" section which includes facts about the Federal Reserve banks and other regulatory agencies, some banking statistics, lists of banking associations, state banking officials, ranked lists of 500 largest U.S. commercial banks and 200 largest bank holding companies, the ABA routing numbers for individual banks by Federal Reserve district. The international volume has lists of: the 100 largest world banks, banking and trade associations, foreign exchange rates. For many years this directory was published by Rand McNally as *Rand McNally International Bankers Directory.*

A companion directory is *Thomson Savings Directory,* a semiannual directory of U.S. savings banks, arranged in a similar manner and giving about the same information.

Several specialized directories are:

National Council of Savings Institutions. *Directory.* Washington, DC (annual).

A geographic list, this one containing, for each bank, key executives, type of charter, insuring agency, total assets, and deposits.

Trusts & Estates. *"Directory of Trust Institutions."* Annual, in 13th issue, published December 15.

This geographical directory of over 4,000 bank and trust companies in the U.S. and Canada gives names of principal trust and estate planning officers and occasionally the value of the bank's trust assets. There are lists of state banking associations, state banking authorities, and other organizations at the front; also a glossary of fiduciary terms.

The U.S. Savings and Loan Directory. Chicago: Rand McNally and Company. 2 volumes (annual).

Arranged geographically, this usually includes, for each S&L: when the firm was established, insuring agency, type of charter and ownership, number of employees, top officers, financial data, branches. A map plus demographic and financial industry statistics are at beginning of each state section. At front of volume 1 are names of officers and federal, state, and industry organizations and agencies, a ranked list of the 500 largest savings institutions, routing numbers of banks. This directory is endorsed by the United States League of Savings Institutions.

An alternate is the *Directory of American Savings and Loan Associations* (Baltimore, MD: T.K. Sanderson Organization; annual) which gives only officers, branches, total assets for each S&L.

Who Owns What in World Banking. London: Financial Times Business Information, Ltd. (annual).

Here is a corporate relationship directory of major world banks and consortia, giving domestic and international subsidiaries and affiliated interests, and percentage figures for holdings when available. A companion volume, *Who is Where in World Banking* (annual), is a guide to the overseas representation of the major world banks, classified by financial center.

Several other directories of foreign banks are: *Merrill Lynch Euromoney Directory* (London: Euromoney Publications Ltd.; annual) which lists over 4,000 banks, brokers, and other organizations in the international money and capital markets, arranged by country; *Bankers Handbook for Asia* (Hong Kong: Asian Finance Publications, Ltd.; annual), a guide to banks and finance companies in Asia, plus those in countries in the Iran/Arab region; *The MEED Middle East Financial Directory* (London: Middle East Economic Digest; annual) which is a directory, by country, of the principal banks and other financial institutions.

For ranked lists of largest American banks see *Moody's Bank & Financial Manual;* also notes about the following newspapers or periodicals listed elsewhere in this chapter: *American Banker* and its annual compilations of ranked lists called "Ranking the Banks: Top Numbers"; *Savings Institutions.* Ranked lists are also often found in directories such as *Rand McNally* (described above). For foreign bank rankings see: *Bankers' Almanac* above; the periodical *The Banker* (which ranks largest U.S., Asian, Arabian, and European banks); and *Euromoney* (described in Chapter 16) for lists of the world's largest banks, and 100 top banks in Asia, Latin America, and the Arab world.

U.S. BANKING AND FINANCIAL STATISTICS

International financial statistics are listed in Chapter 5; statistics on government finance in Chapter 4.

American Bankers Association. *Statistical Information on the Financial Services Industry.* 5th ed. Washington, DC: 1989. 1 volume (various pagings).

Statistical tables and a few charts covering financial institutions, including sources and uses of funds, capital, earnings, structure, payment systems, international banking; also consumer attitude and trends, economic and demographic trends influencing the financial services industry. This is revised every two or three years; statistics are usually three or more years old and so this is better for background rather than for current data.

American Financial Services Association. *Finance Facts Yearbook.* Washington, DC.

Brief text, with statistics and charts, on consumers—their income, spending, finance and credit management, as well as the consumer installment credit industry. Includes a bibliography. Former name of this association was National Consumer Finance Association.

Bank Marketing Association. *Analysis of (year) Bank Marketing Expenditures.* Washington, DC (annual).

Data in the volume covering 1990 is based on a questionnaire survey received from more than 850 commerical banks. It includes marketing expenditures by expenditure type, budget by market size and type, budgeting for bank services, and use and compensation of ad agencies. Each year it also covers a varying specialized area of bank expenditures such as the use of direct mail as is found in the issue covering 1990.

Board of Governors of the Federal Reserve System. *Banking and Monetary Statistics* (1914–1941). Washington, DC: 1943. 979 pp. And *Banking and Monetary Statistics, 1941–1970.* Washington, DC: 1976. 1,168 pp. Updated by an *Annual Statistical Digest.*

Contains a wealth of historical banking and financial statistics, much of it going back to the year 1914. Included are data on Federal Reserve banks and other member banks, bank debits, bank income, bank suspensions, bank holding companies; also statistics on nonbank financial institutions, currency, money rates and security markets, U.S. government finance, gold, international finance, consumer credit.

Another historical volume the Board published in 1959 is *All Bank Statistics, 1896–1955,* which gives state-by-state statistics on assets, liabilities, and number, for all commercial banks, for national banks, state commercial banks, unincorporated banks, and mutual savings banks.

Board of Governors of the Federal Reserve System. *Federal Reserve Bulletin.* Washington, DC (monthly).

The "Financial and Business Statistics" section in each issue of this Bulletin is the best single source for current U.S. banking and monetary statistics. It includes Federal Reserve bank statistics, financial statistics for commercial banks, money and capital market rates, government securities, mortgage markets, consumer installment credit, flow of funds, etc.; also international financial statistics, interest and exchange rates, and selected economic measures such as the Federal Reserve Board's index of industrial production. Several of these tables are continuations of statistics in the historical *Banking and Monetary Statistics* listed above. More detailed historical flow of funds figures are in the Board's annual *Flow of Funds Accounts: Financial Assets and Liabilities Year-End* covering a 24-year run of flow data, and quarterly statistics in their *Flow of Funds Accounts, Seasonally Adjusted and Unadjusted* issued as Statistical Releases. There are other FRB statistical releases published on specific financial subjects. The articles in the *Federal Reserve Bulletin* are indexed in ABI/I, BPI, PAIS; also in full text in MEAD/NEXIS.

Dun & Bradstreet, Inc. *The Business Failure Record.* New York (annual).
These failure statistics are quoted by location (each state and 50 largest U.S. cities), by industry, age of business, liability size, cause of failure. For current statistics see D & B's *Monthly Business Failures;* also center grey pages of occasional issues of *D&B Reports* (bimonthly).

The *Annual Report of the Director* of the U.S. Administrative Office of the United States Courts includes bankruptcy statistics as Tables F, 1–2, 8. These give U.S. District Court bankruptcy petitions commenced, terminated, or pending during the calendar year, by state; business and nonbusiness cases commenced according to chapters of the Bankruptcy Act, by circuit and district; and adversary proceedings figures. Overall totals are in the *Statistical Abstract of the United States.*

Mortgage Bankers Association of America. *Financial Statements and Operating Ratios for the Mortgage Banking Industry.* Washington, DC (annual).
Operating ratios and balance sheet statistics, based on the experience of almost 200 mortgage banking companies. Statistics are by size of mortgage loans serviced and by percentage of income property loans serviced to total loans serviced. The MBA also publishes an annual *Loans Closed and Servicing Volume for the Mortgage Banking Industry.* Their monthly *Mortgage Banker* includes a short "vital statistics" section covering current figures on housing and lending activity, interest rates, etc.

Savings & Home Financing Source Book. Washington, DC: Office of Thrift Supervision of the Treasury Department (annual).
Consists of national thrift and financial data (including FSLIC-insured thrift institution balance sheet data); thrift and financial statistics for FHL bank districts and states; mortgage debt and mortgage loan data.

There are other sources for U.S. banking statistics. See, for example, the annual *Statistics on Banking* of the Federal Deposit Insurance Corporation which publishes financial statistics on FDIC-insured commercial banks, trust companies, and savings banks; also the Bank Administration Institute's annual *U.S. Bank Performance Profile,* with composite balance sheet, income statement and performance ratios for each state.

Periodic business and economic reviews of the 12 Federal Reserve District banks and letters from specific U.S. banks are good sources for current data on financial as well as regional economic conditions.

Persons needing to identify the many other statistical sources may want to consult *A Guide to Statistical Sources in Money, Banking, and Finance* by M. Balachandran (Phoenix, AZ: Oryx Press, 1988, 119 pp.). This is a selected, annotated bibliography primarily to serial reference sources for statistics, arranged geographically to cover, first, U.S. state, regional, and national sources, and then those for foreign countries, and general international sources. Databases are described at the end.

BANKING NEWSPAPERS AND PERIODICALS

ABA Banking Journal. New York: Published for American Bankers Association by Simmons-Boardman Publishing Corp. (monthly).

The official publication of the ABA (formerly called *Banking*), this journal is a good source of information on banking trends, new and improved banking techniques, news and special reports of interest to bankers. Several annual directory features include: "Bankers' Guide to Services" (January issue); "Bankers' Guide to Washington" (April); "Bank Operations Buyers Guide" (May). Indexed in ABI/I, BPI, PAIS, TI; full text on BRS, DATA-STAR, DIALOG, DOW JONES, MEAD/NEXIS.

American Banker. New York: American Banker-Bond Buyer (5/wk).

This important daily financial newspaper covers news about bank developments and trends, pending legislation, national and international monetary affairs, executive changes, and so forth. Each issue contains a statistical table called "Daily Financials" which gives money market statistics such as bankers acceptances, certificates of deposit, and also Treasury bill futures, bond futures. The Tuesday issue each week contains financial services firms' stock price quotations in a table called "Weekly Market Summary". Various issues throughout the year include excellent ranked lists of largest banks or other financial institutions. See, for example, "American Banker 300" ranking top commercial banks by deposit/assets (a late March issue and again in mid-September); "The Top 500 Banks in the World" which also covers banks ranking from 500 to 1000 (late July); "Foreign Banks in the U.S." (early March); top bank holding companies (late April); "Top 100 Mortgage Servicing Firms (mid-May); "Top 300 Thrift Companies" (late May); top bank performers (early June); "Top 100 Trust Banks" (late June); "Top 300 Mortgage Banking Companies" (third week in October); "Top Finance Companies" (late October). These approximate issue dates are taken from 1989 issues and they sometimes vary from year to year. Two online versions of this financial newspaper are *American Banker Full Text* and *American Banker News Service*. Selected articles are also indexed in PTS/F&S, TI; full text on DATA-STAR, DIALOG, DOW JONES, MEAD/NEXIS.

American Banker publishes two separate annual compilations. The first, *American Banker Yearbook* is designed as a reference tool for financial services executives. It is arranged in 6 parts to cover: articles on key financial trends and developments; dates and events of the previous year; statistics (primarily the useful ranked lists of banks and other financial institutions); a digest of the best *AB* surveys and special reports; directories of banks, associations, etc.; a topical index of articles in *American Banker* during the previous year. The other annual is the more specialized *Ranking the Banks: Top Numbers* which contains many more of the ranked lists than are cited above. The 1991 volume is more than 150 pages in length. It contains almost 100 ranked lists for commercial banks, bank holding companies, world banking, thrifts, and mortgages, including also the 100 highest paid bank executives. Because of its usefulness, the publisher also issues a *Top Numbers Update,* containing ranking tables appearing in *American Banker* during the first half of the next year, as well as including corrections, revisions, and several special tables.

Bank Management. Rolling Meadows, IL: Bank Administration Institute (monthly).

Formerly called *The Magazine of Bank Administration,* this monthly still contains practical articles both on management and finance and on operations and technology of interest to BAI members. Indexed in ABI/I, BPI, TI.

Bank Marketing. Chicago: Bank Marketing Association (monthly).

Short articles on advertising, marketing, and public relations, of interest to bank managers. Indexed in ABI/I, BPI, PTS/F&S, TI.

The Bankers Magazine. Boston: Warren, Gorham & Lamont (bimonthly).

Often an issue contains 4 to 10 practical and informative articles focusing on a particular topic covering any of a wide range in the banking and money management field. There are also regular departments discussing the international scene, bank regulation, human resources, and so forth. This magazine is written by bankers for bankers and has been in existence since 1846. Indexed in ABI/I, BPI, PTS/F&S, TI.

Bankers Monthly. New York: Hanover Publishers, Inc.

A national trade magazine containing short, practical articles on all aspects of bank management. Regular departments in each issue include marketing strategy, technology update, disks and videos, and "Banker's Bookshelf." Each issue also usually contains a page of statistics on "Jumbo CD Rates." Indexed in ABI/I, BPI, PAIS, TI.

Business Credit. Columbia, MD: National Association of Credit Management (monthly, except for combined July/August issue).

Published for many years as *Credit and Financial Management,* this monthly still contains short articles, regular columns, and news of interest to credit managers. Includes also a few book reviews. Indexed in ABI/I, BPI, TI.

Journal of Commercial Bank Lending. Philadelphia, PA: Robert Morris Associates (monthly).

Practical articles of interest to bank loan and credit officers. The September issue includes an annual "Analysis of Finance Company Ratios." Indexed in ABI/I, BPI, PAIS.

Journal of Money, Credit and Banking. Columbus, OH: Ohio State University Press (quarterly).

A continuing source for research studies on monetary policy, banking, and credit, written primarily by professors and economists, and often with a quantitative emphasis. Includes book reviews. Indexed in ABI/I, BPI.

Money. New York: Time, Inc. (monthly).

This is a widely read journal for the layman, with popularly written articles on personal and family finance, and on such topics of current interest and concern as money management, investments, taxes, insurance, careers. "The Money Rankings" is an annual ranked list of some 900 top mutual fund performers arranged by type of fund (February issue). "Fund Watch" (in each issue) contains brief current data on top performers. Indexed in ABI/I, BPI, TI; also full text on DATA-STAR, DIALOG, DOW JONES, MEAD/NEXIS.

Mortgage Banking. Washington, DC: Mortgage Bankers Association of America (monthly).

Provides articles and news on real estate finance of interest to MBA members. Each issue includes "Vital Statistics," containing tables for interest rates, housing activity, lender activity (long-term mortgage loans closed), secondary market yields. Includes also one or two book reviews. An annual feature is "The MBA Cost Study: Measuring Performance" (January issue). Indexed in ABI/I, BPI, TI; also full text on BRS, DATA-STAR, DIALOG.

Savings Institutions. Chicago: United States League of Savings Institutions (monthly).

About 7 feature articles are in each issue; also regular feature columns for real estate finance, money market, appraisal reports, and so forth. Ranked list of top savings institutions is in a varying issue, e.g. July/August 1989. Former title was *Savings and Loan News.* Indexed in ABI/I, BPI, TI.

A smaller association, the National Council of Savings Institutions, also publishes a monthly called *Bottomline,* with short articles and news of interest to NCSI members.

Trusts & Estates. Atlanta, GA: Communications Channels, Inc. (monthly, with 13th issue in December).

In existence since 1904, this journal aims at keeping estate planners and administrators informed through articles and news. The 13th issue, published December 15, is a "Directory of Trust Institutions." Indexed in ABI/I, BPI.

United States Banker. Greenwich, CT: Kalo Communications Inc. (monthly).

Another long-published journal, this one servicing the financial services industry, and including articles on specific banks, on people, strategies, and trends. Each issue has a table giving financial statistics for the largest U.S. banks called "U.S. Banker Index." About every other issue contains a short section for news of interest to the Northeast banker. Special annual features include: "U.S. Banker M & A Advisor Rankings" (March); "Annual Compensation Survey" for CEOs (June); "U.S. Banker 100" (July), ranked by performance; "Ranking the Second 100 Banks" (September); "Ranking the Top Thrifts" (October); "Ranking the 300 Banks" (November). Indexed in ABI/I, BPI, PAIS, TI; full text on BRS, DATA-STAR, DIALOG, DOW JONES, MEAD/NEXIS.

The World of Banking. Washington, DC: World of Banking Publishing Co. (bimonthly).

Billed as "the international magazine of bank management," each issue of this bimonthly is devoted to short articles on a particular banking or financial services trend or development of interest to bankers around the world. Indexed in ABI/I, PAIS.

Some of the largest banks publish bank letters or bulletins, which are useful sources for current regional financial and economic information. A few examples of foreign bank letters are included in Chapter 5. The monthly *Federal Reserve Bulletin* usually contains one to three reports or surveys on recent financial trends such as domestic financial developments, U.S. international transactions, survey of finance companies, financial developments of small banks. Each issue also contains Federal Reserve Board announcements, statements, and publications, statements to Congress, legal developments, as well as statistics which are described in the "U.S. Banking and Financial Statistics" section of this chapter. Articles in the *FRB* are indexed in ABI/I, BPI, PAIS; also full text on MEAD/NEXIS.

Several good foreign periodicals are:

The Banker. London: Financial Times Business Information, Ltd. (monthly).
Excellent articles and news on banking and monetary policy of worldwide interest.
Annual ranked lists of banks in 1991 include: "Top 100 Japanese Banks" and top
security houses (January issue); "U.S. Top 300" (June); "Top 1,000 World Banks"
(July); "Top 100 Latin American Banks" (August); "Europe's Top 500" (September); "Top 200 Asian Banks" (October); "Top 100 Arab Banks" (November); "Top
100 African Banks" (December). Special directories in issues include: "Foreign
Banks in New York" (March); "Foreign Banks in London" (November). Indexed in
ABI/I, BPI, PAIS, TI; also full text on DIALOG.

Banking World. London: The Chartered Institute of Bankers (monthly).
A monthly resulting from the merger of two established magazines—*Bankers' Magazine* and the *Journal of the Institute of Bankers*. It provides short practical articles on
banking in the U.K. and overseas for practicing bankers, as well as educational
articles and other news of interest to Institute members. One page of economic/
financial charts is in each issue. Includes book notes. Indexed in ABI/I, PAIS.

Canadian Banker. Toronto: Canadian Bankers' Association (bimonthly).
Articles on Canadian and international bank management and monetary policy.
Aims to be a forum for discussion rather than a medium for association news.
Contains a few book reviews. Indexed in ABI/I, BPI, PAIS.

Journal of Banking & Finance. Amsterdam: North-Holland (quarterly).
Aims "to provide an outlet for the increasing flow of scholarly research concerning
financial institutions and the money and capital markets within which they function." Emphasis is on applied and policy oriented research; it is international in
scope. Includes book reviews. Indexed in ABI/I, BPI, TI.

Savings Banks International. Geneva, Switzerland: International Savings
Banks Institute (quarterly).
Articles in this journal are on savings banking and finance; many are either on a
specific bank or on savings bank practices in a particular country. Usually one issue
a year contains some varying ISBI statistics.

BANKING AND CREDIT ASSOCIATIONS

American Bankers Association, 1120 Connecticut Avenue, N.W., Washington, DC 20036. (The American Institute of Banking is a division of ABA).

American Financial Services Association, 1101 14th Street, N.W., Washington, DC 20005. They publish a bimonthly called *Credit*.

Association of Bank Holding Companies, 730 15th Street, N.W., Washington, DC 20005.

Bank Administration Institute, 60 Gould Center, 2550 Golf Rd., Rolling Meadows, IL 60008.

Credit Research Foundation, 8815 Center Park Drive, Columbia, MD 21045.

Independent Bankers Association of America, One Thomas Circle, N.W., Suite 950, Washington, DC 20005.

International Credit Association, 243 N. Lindbergh Blvd., St. Louis, MO 63141. They publish the bimonthly *Credit World.*

Mortgage Bankers Association of America, 1125 15th Street, N.W., Washington, DC 20005.

National Association of Credit Management, 8815 Center Park Drive, Columbia, MD 21045.

National Council of Savings Institutions, 1101 Fifteenth Street, N.W., Washington, DC 20005.

Robert Morris Associates, the National Association of Bank Loan and Credit Officers, 1650 Market Street, Suite 2300, Philadelphia, PA 19103.

United States League of Savings Institutions, 1709 New York Avenue, Suite 801, Washington, DC 20006.

15

INSURANCE AND REAL ESTATE

INSURANCE – Risk and Insurance – Life/Health Insurance – Property/Liability Insurance – Insurance Bibliographies and Indexes – Insurance Dictionaries – Insurance Law and Legal Services – Information About Insurance Companies – Insurance Statistics – Insurance Periodicals – Insurance Directories – Insurance Associations – REAL ESTATE – Real Estate Principles and Practices – Real Estate Management and Appraisal – Real Estate Finance and Investing – Real Estate Law – Housing and Real Estate Bibliographies and Indexes – Real Estate Dictionaries – Real Estate Operating Statistics – Housing and Real Estate Statistics – Real Estate Periodicals – Real Estate Directories – Real Estate Associations

INSURANCE

Insurance companies have developed into big business today due to the fact that risk and misfortune are daily possibilities, and most individuals and businesses are prudent enough to want to plan ahead either to avoid a loss entirely or to reduce it significantly by sharing the burden with someone else. However, most people know very little about the industry itself. The first half of this chapter attempts to help correct this situation by suggesting a selection of recent books and reference sources on risk and insurance in general and also on several major insurance lines. For books and reference sources on employee benefits and pension plans see the "Pension and Employee Benefit Planning" section of Chapter 19.

RISK AND INSURANCE

Athearn, James L., S. Travis Pritchett and Joan Schmitt. *Risk and Insurance.*
6th ed. St. Paul, MN: West Publishing Company, 1989. 745 pp.

A standard introductory text on how to manage risk and make the best use of insurance, this covers all principal types of insurance and other risk handling techniques. Short "consumer applications" features are at end of chapters. A glossary and specimen insurance policies are at the end; also a mortality table and a list of state insurance commissioners.

Bickelhaupt, David L. *General Insurance.* 11th ed. Homewood, IL: Irwin, 1983. 989 pp.

This is the latest edition of a popular textbook. It aims to provide fundamental and applied concepts of insurance and risk in five parts: insurance, risk, risk management, and insurance; life and health insurance; property and liability insurance; the structure and operations of the insurance business; the future of insurance. Appendixes include compound interest and present value tables, life insurance premium calculations, special and allied fire lines.

Greene, Mark R., and James S. Trieschmann. *Risk and Insurance.* 7th ed. Cincinnati, OH: South-Western Publishing Company, 1988. 785 pp.

Designed as a first course in insurance to cover basic ideas, problems, and principles found in all types of modern insurance and other methods of handling risk. The first 3 of its 8 parts are general in nature and include discussions of the insurance institution and the legal environment. The next two parts cover personal risk management, with part 4 focusing on life/health and income, and part 5 on property/liability. The last three parts are on: business risk management; government and insurance; international insurance. "Boxed Features" throughout highlight current applications; useful appendixes include insurance ratings, interest tables, a glossary, a bibliography.

Vaughan, Emmett J. *Fundamentals of Risk and Insurance.* 5th ed. New York: Wiley, 1989. 781 pp.

This is designed as a college-level survey of risk and insurance that is consumer oriented. The main emphasis is on the insurance product and its use within the risk management framework. There are three sections, with the first examining the concepts/nature/principles of risk and insurance, and the others dealing with life/health and property/liability. Bibliographies are at end of chapters; sample insurance policies and a glossary are in an appendix.

Williams, C. Arthur, Jr., and Richard M. Heins. *Risk Management and Insurance.* 6th ed. New York: McGraw-Hill, 1989. 836 pp.

Presents a balanced introduction to the two title subjects. Major consideration is given to business and related family risk management, with 29 of its 34 chapters devoted to the risk management function, risk identification and measurement, the major tools, insurance contracts (by line), implementing an insurance decision, and international risk management. Two further chapters cover unique aspects of family risk management, and one deals with government regulation of insurance. Suggestions for additional reading and definitions of key concepts are with chapters; explanations of mathematical calculations are in an appendix. Professor Williams was solely responsible for this edition.

An older but still useful book addressing risk management from the analytical framework of financial management is *Corporate Risk Management: A Financial Exposition* by Neil A. Doherty (McGraw-Hill, 1985, 483 pp.).

LIFE/HEALTH INSURANCE

A few reference sources on unemployment insurance are included in Chapter 19 under "Pension and Employee Benefit Planning."

Black, Kenneth, Jr., and Harold D. Skipper, Jr. *Life Insurance.* 11th ed. Englewood Cliffs, NJ: Prentice-Hall, 1987. 608 pp.

For many years this has been the best-known integrated life and health insurance textbook, first written by the much respected S. S. Huebner and more recently with Professor Black as coauthor. Now Black and a new coauthor have substantially revised the text to alter its emphasis from a factual account to one that combines current information with use in the life and health insurance marketplace. The 9 parts cover: an introduction; types of life insurance products; aspects of life insurance evaluation; uses in personal financial planning; uses, types, and evaluation of health insurance; the mathematics of life and health insurance; selection and classification; employee benefit plans; organization, management, and regulation of companies.

Mehr, Robert I., and Sandra G. Gustavson. *Life Insurance: Theory and Practice.* 4th ed. Plano, TX: Business Publications, 1987. 675 pp.

Another comprehensive, well-established text integrating theory and practice of life and health insurance. This latest edition updates the material and gives expanded emphasis to the link between financial planning and insurance, and to new life and health insurance products.

Services

Prentice-Hall, Inc. *Life Insurance Planning.* Englewood Cliffs, NJ. 1 volume (loose-leaf with monthly supplements).

Focuses on up-to-date information on both personal and corporate life insurance planning and is of special use for insurance salespersons. Includes sections on: financial problems and insurance solutions; retirement planning; pension and profit sharing plans; business insurance; and more. Real-world examples are used throughout. Included with this service is a separate semimonthly volume for new *Life Insurance Ideas.*

PROPERTY/LIABILITY INSURANCE

The following books are the only two relatively recent texts I could find on property and liability insurance. There are other earlier books and a very old (1965) comprehensive handbook that was included in the first edition of my book. For other up-to-date information one can find pertinent chapters in the general books covering all lines of insurance, and there are also articles in current periodicals that can be located by using the periodic indexes described elsewhere in this chapter.

Huebner, S. S., Kenneth Black, Jr., and Robert S. Cline. *Property and Liability Insurance.* 3d ed. Englewood Cliffs, NJ: Prentice-Hall, 1982. 630 pp.

This latest revision by the latter two authors continues to strive for as comprehensive coverage as possible, with the emphasis on perils and insurance coverages. Four of its eight parts deal with the various historical divisions of property and liability exposures (fire, marine, consequential loss insurance, and other direct damage insurance). The other parts focus on insurance of liability exposures, multiple line coverages, and the functional aspects of insurance. Although the book is meant to give basic principles and concepts both for students and for new agents or brokers, it does presume an introductory course in insurance.

Smith, Barry D., James S. Trieschmann and Eric A. Wiening. *Property and Liability Insurance Principles.* Malvern, PA: Insurance Institute of America, 1987. 280 pp.

A readable text which begins with a discussion of uncertainty and the role of insurance, and then examines: insurance policies, property and liability insurance contract provisions, the insurance business (including financial performance and regulations, marketing, underwriting, claims, and other functions), and finally risk management.

Published about the same time by the same publisher is a well-reviewed textbook on one type of insurance, *Inland Marine Insurance* by Roderick McNamara et al. (Insurance Institute of America, 1987, 2 volumes, paper).

Services

The Fire, Casualty & Surety Bulletins. Cincinnati, OH: National Underwriter Co. 5 volumes (loose-leaf service, with monthly supplements).

A comprehensive loose-leaf service providing good background information and explanations on all types of property/liability insurance. The volumes cover: management; sales; fire/marine; casualty/surety; companies and coverage; and personal lines.

INSURANCE BIBLIOGRAPHIES AND INDEXES

Insurance Periodicals Index. New York: NILS Publishing Co. in association with the Insurance & Employee Benefits Division, Special Libraries Association. 2 volumes (annual). Available also online.

A detailed subject index to articles in over 35 insurance periodicals, compiled by a group of insurance librarians. There is an index by author.

Insurance Information Institute. *Books in Insurance: Property, Liability, Marine, Surety.* 11th ed. New York: 1983. 25 pp.

This is a useful selected and annotated list of books and periodicals on property/liability insurance, arranged by subject and revised every five years or so.

Weiner, Alan R. *The Insurance Industry: An Information Sourcebook.* (Oryx Sourcebook Series in Business and Management). Phoenix, AZ: Oryx Press, 1988. 278 pp.

A useful, annotated guide to the wide variety of material on the insurance industry. It begins by describing general insurance and risk management reference sources. This is followed by subject sections on: lines of insurance; insurance operations; the legal environment; consumer guides; miscellaneous; insurance careers; a "core library collection" (bibliographies, dictionaries, periodicals, statistics, etc., essential in building a library). The rest of this bibliography lists related organizations, educational institutions, libraries, databases, and supervisory authorities. This should be revised to be of continued use.

INSURANCE DICTIONARIES

Davids, Lewis E. *Dictionary of Insurance.* 7th rev. ed. Savage, MD: Littlefield Adams, 1990. 504 pp. paper.

A dictionary of terms in insurance and related fields compiled for laypersons, students, and insurance people. This latest edition includes a directory of insurance organizations and state commissioners of insurance.

Ingrisano, John R., and Corinne M. Ingrisano. *The Insurance Dictionary: The A to Z of Life and Health.* 3d ed. Chicago: Dearborn Financial Publishing, 1990. 342 pp. paper.

A recent and more specialized dictionary, this covers over 3,500 terms and phrases, not only basic life and health terms, but also a wide range of related subjects, organizations, and agencies.

Rubin, Harvey W. *Dictionary of Insurance Terms.* 2d ed. New York: Barron's, 1991. 465 pp. paper.

Defines more than 3,000 key terms used in life, health, property, casualty, and other types of insurance, often with illustrative examples. This dictionary is useful for both insurance practitioners and consumers.

INSURANCE LAW AND LEGAL SERVICES

Commerce Clearing House. *Insurance Law Reporter.* Chicago. 2 volumes (loose-leaf).

This service reports on new decisions in major insurance areas handed down by federal and higher state courts. One volume contains "Fire and Casualty Insurance Law Reporter" and the other, "Life, Health and Accident Insurance Reporter." Prior bound volumes of cases for each are available. CCH publishes a separate service for new decisions involving motor vehicle insurance statutes called *Automobile Law Reporter.*

There are two complete, multivolume treatises covering all types of insurance law and including the substance of the law, with practical illustrations and also appellate court cases. These are: George J. Couch's *Couch Cyclopedia of Insurance Law* (2d ed. revised, by Ronald A. Anderson, Rochester, NY: Lawyers Cooperative Publishing Co., 1987– to date, 26 volumes) and *Insurance Law and Practice* by John A. Appleton and Jean Appleman (St. Paul, MN: West Publishing Co., 1943– to date, 26 volumes in 59, as of 1990). Annual pocket supplements at the back of each volume in both services keep them up-to-date.

INFORMATION ABOUT INSURANCE COMPANIES

For ranked lists of largest insurance companies see *Moody's* below; also both editions of *Best's Review* and several other magazines described in the "Insurance Periodicals" section of this chapter.

Argus F.C., and S. Chart. Cincinnati, OH: National Underwriter Co. (annual).

Financial statement figures in tabular format for companies writing property and liability lines. For some 1,500 companies there are financial and operating statistics covering the last two years. Includes also group totals, classification of business by lines written, list of corporate relationships, rankings of companies by net premiums written. A companion volume is *Argus Health Chart* (annual) containing financial statistics on health insurers and also data on Blue Cross and Blue Shield plans.

Assecuranz Compass. *Yearbook for International Insurance Matters.* Brussels.
A worldwide financial manual covering more than 13,000 insurance, reinsurance, and related organizations. For each it usually includes activities, officers and directors, phone/fax/telex, year established, financial statistics. Indexes are by geographic location and type of activity.

Best's Aggregates & Averages: Property-Casualty Edition. Oldwick, NJ: A. M. Best Co. (annual).
Statistics are by company for stock, mutual, reciprocal, and "Lloyds" organizations and contain balance sheet and operating data and statistics by line underwriting experience, all in tabular form; also various aggregate and average figures. A companion annual is *Best's Aggregates & Averages: Life-Health Edition.*

Best's Flitcraft Compend. Oldwick, NJ: A. M. Best Co. (annual).
Gives information on company operations, policy analysis, policy premiums, cash values, and current dividend illustrations for most U.S. insurance companies. At end is data on annuities and settlement options, cash value tables, mortality tables, compound interest and discount tables, mortgage amortization tables, text of the Federal Social Security Act, analysis of Medicare.

Best's Insurance Reports: International Edition. Oldwick, NJ: A. M. Best Co. (semiannual).
This is a companion financial manual to the two described below, covering foreign insurance companies that offer insurance policies. It is arranged by company and includes a geographic index.

Best's Insurance Reports: Life-Health. Oldwick, NJ: A. M. Best Co. (annual).
The best-known financial manual for U.S. and Canadian life/health companies, usually giving for each: a brief corporate history; management and operation; assets and liabilities; investment data; operating comment; Best's rating; statistics on company development; insurance in force; new business issued; accident and health written. At front is a list of state officials; at end a list of name changes, retired companies, and reinsurance.

Best's Insurance Reports: Property-Casualty. Oldwick, NJ: A. M. Best Co. (annual).
A companion financial manual to the one above, for U.S. property/casualty insurers and branches of foreign insurance companies operating in the U.S. At end are: a directory of other insurers, underwriting organizations, name changes and retired companies, the list of companies arranged by state, a list of the 200 largest American property/casualty companies.

Best's Key Rating Guide: Property-Casualty. Oldwick, NJ: A. M. Best Co. (annual).
Provides ratings and financial size categories along with selected financial data showing the financial condition and operating results of about 1,700 prominent property/casualty insurance companies. At end are: list of retired companies, table showing states in which companies are licensed to operate, data on underwriting

organizations, list of 200 largest American p/c companies. List of state officials in charge of insurance at front.

Best's Trend Report: Life-Health Insurance Companies. Oldwick, NJ: A.M. Best Co. (annual).

This trend report contains a five-year tabulation of Best's Ratings, and the results of the selected Best's Profitability, Leverage, and Liquidity Tests for more than 1,300 U.S. legal reserve life/health insurance companies. There is also a companion annual with title *Best's Trend Report: Property-Casualty Insurance Companies.*

Canadian Insurance. "Annual Review of Statistics." June issue each year.

Useful statistics on the Canadian insurance industry, including a five-year trend of underwriting experience for specific companies, ranked list and growth in the property/casualty market, ranked lists of leaders by provinces.

The journal *Canadian Underwriter* also publishes a useful "Annual Statistical Issue" (extra issue in June each year) which contains Canadian underwriter experience by company, insurance by type of nationality in Canada, a directory of life insurance companies in Canada, and much more.

Life Financial Reports: Financial and Operating Results of Life Insurers. Cincinnati, OH: National Underwriter Co. (annual).

Provides concise (one-page) financial information on over 1,000 life insurers plus detailed corporate and operating statistics on more than half of these companies. Useful especially for libraries that cannot afford *Best's* yet need basic financial facts about leading companies. A companion volume is their *Life Rates & Data* (annual), which gives premium rates, cash values, dividends costs, and policy conditions for the life plans of insurers.

Moody's Bank & Financial Manual. New York: Moody's Investors Service. 4 volumes (annual).

Volume 2 of this basic financial manual includes U.S. insurance companies. The information for each company usually covers brief financial history, officers and directors, income and balance sheet statistics, underwriting and investment results, recent stock price range. Center blue pages include ranked lists of largest insurance companies.

World Insurance. Chicago and London: St. James Press. (annual).

Brief information on insurance companies arranged alphabetically by country. For each it gives activities, classes of insurance written, officers, directors, subsidiaries, recent developments, three-year summary financial statistics. At beginning of each country listing are: basic economic and risk statistics, list of chamber of commerce and insurance organizations, insurance regulatory body for the country.

INSURANCE STATISTICS

American Council of Life Insurance. *Life Insurance Fact Book.* Washington, DC (biennual, with a condensed "Update" in intervening years).

Statistics, charts, and brief interpretative text on the U.S. life insurance business. Includes life insurance ownership, annuity benefit payments, assets, pension and retirement programs, life expectancy, and much more. At end are: mortality tables, list of state insurance officials, names of organizations, a glossary. This Council also publishes periodic general, investment, legislative, etc., bulletins for its members.

The Canadian Life & Health Insurance Association in Toronto publishes a similar but shorter annual fact book called *Canadian Life Insurance Facts.*

Association of British Insurers. *Insurance Statistics.* London (annual).

For persons needing U.K. insurance statistics, this booklet contains brief text with statistical tables, usually for a five-year period, covering: life insurance; general insurance; investments. Sources for the statistics are listed at end. It is published by the ABI in collaboration with Linked Life Assurance Group.

Health Insurance Association of America. *Source Book of Health Insurance Data.* Washington; DC (biennial; with *Update* in alternate year).

A useful statistical report on the U.S. private health insurance business. Includes tables on major forms of health insurance (such as hospital, major medical, disability, and dental insurance); also data on claims and premiums, government health care programs, medical care costs, disability and health care utilization, and more. Contains a short glossary and list of historic dates. The alternate year *Update* reproduces and updates those tables for which data is most frequently requested.

Insurance Information Institute. *The Fact Book: Property/Casualty Insurance Facts.* New York (annual).

Brief text with basic statistics and facts on the property and casualty insurance business, including dollar and cents data and losses by categories; also list of organizations and state insurance commissioners as well as a glossary.

Life Insurance Marketing and Research Association. *Monthly Survey of Life Insurance Sales in the United States.* Farmington, CT.

This is an example of one of several brief statistical reports of this association. They also publish a similar monthly survey for insurance sales in Canada.

Metropolitan Life Insurance Co. *Statistical Bulletin.* Baltimore (quarterly).

Text and brief statistics on accidents, mortality, health problems, birth trends, death rates, and other topics of interest to the life insurance industry.

U.S. National Center for Health Statistics. *Vital Statistics of the United States.* Washington; DC: U.S. Government Printing Office. 3 volumes (annual).

Slow in publishing, this is the definitive publication for U.S. vital statistics, containing extensive data and analysis on births (vol. 1), mortality (vol. 2 in 2 parts), marriages and divorces (vol. 3). "Life Tables" are in section 6 of vol. 2. Current and provisional statistics appear in their *Monthly Vital Statistics Report* (which contains an annual supplement). Statistics for other countries are included in the UN's *Demographic Yearbook.*

INSURANCE PERIODICALS

All of the periodicals in this list are indexed in *Insurance Periodicals Index,* which is described in the "Insurance Bibliographies and Indexes" section of this chapter. Journals on employee benefits and pension planning are described in the last section of Chapter 19.

American Society of CLU and ChFC. *Journal.* Bryn Mawr, PA (bimonthly).

Publishes scholarly articles "to advance the philosophy and practice of professionalism in the fields of insurance and financial services." Each issue includes regular departments on such topics as information management, financial planning, tax planning. There are also book reviews. CLU stands for Chartered Life Underwriters, and ChFC stands for Chartered Financial Consultants. Indexed in BPI.

Best's Review: Life/Health Insurance Edition. Oldwick, NJ: A.M. Best Co. (monthly).

Short, practical articles of special interest to life/health insurance executives and agents, with recent news about companies and industry developments. Includes frequent annual statistical tables, some of them ranking companies, e.g. leading life companies in three categories (July); the 500 leading life companies in total premium income (July); leading companies by assets (October); 20-year dividend comparisons (July); 10-year dividend comparisons (August). Indexed in ABI/I, BPI, TI; full text on BRS, DATA-STAR, DIALOG, DOW JONES, MEAD/NEXIS.

Best's Review: Property/Casualty Insurance Edition. Oldwick, NJ: A.M. Best Co. (monthly).

Similar journal to the one preceding but meant for property/casualty executives and agents. Special annual statistical tables includes ranked list of 250 leading property/casualty companies and groups (July). Indexed in ABI/I, BPI, TI; full text on BRS, DATA-STAR, DIALOG, DOW JONES, MEAD/NEXIS.

Business Insurance. Chicago: Crain Communications, Inc. (weekly).

A national news magazine for corporate risk, employee benefits, and financial executives. Each issue contains a "BI Industrial Stock Report." The "Annual Agent/Broker Profile Issue" (mid-June) has a ranked list of 100 largest U.S. brokers with profiles of each. The basic articles are also indexed in ABI/I, BPI; full text on DATA-STAR, DIALOG, MEAD/NEXIS.

Journal of Risk and Insurance. Orlando, FL: American Risk and Insurance Association (quarterly).

Contains authoritative, original research on all aspects of risk, insurance, and risk management topics, with the articles written primarily by academic persons. Cites recent court decisions; includes book reviews and a section called "From the Library Shelf" consisting of abstracts of current articles arranged by topic. Indexed in ABI/I, BPI, PAIS, TI; full text on BRS, DATA-STAR, DIALOG, MEAD/NEXIS.

Life Association News. Washington, DC: National Association of Life Underwriters (monthly).

Articles on selling methods and news of interest to NALU members. Includes book reviews. Indexed in ABI/I.

National Underwriter: Life & Health/Financial Services Edition. Cincinnati, OH: National Underwriter Company (weekly).

A weekly newspaper for life/health/financial services agents, brokers, and executives providing news about companies, agency activity, business trends, legislation, associations, and so forth. An annual "Life & Health Statistics Review" (second June issue) contains ranked lists of the top 300 life insurance companies by various categories and also a ranked list of the top 300 or so health insurers. Indexed in ABI/I, BPI, TI; also full text on BRS, DATA-STAR, DIALOG, DOW JONES, MEAD/NEXIS.

A similar weekly for the property/casualty/risk field is *National Underwriter: Property & Casualty/Risk & Benefits Management*. One of several annual issues is "Property & Casualty Premium Rankings" (third May issue) which ranks 700 stock companies. Indexed in the same sources as its companion weekly.

Risk Management. New York: Risk and Insurance Management Society (monthly).

Articles cover new developments, regulations, and news of interest to professional risk managers and related financial executives. Indexed in ABI/I, BPI, TI; full text on BRS, DATA-STAR, DIALOG.

Rough Notes. Indianapolis, IN (monthly).

A journal for insurance agents and brokers covering selling techniques, agency management, office management. Indexed in ABI/I.

Society of Chartered Property and Casualty Underwriters. *CPCU Journal.* Malvern, PA (quarterly).

In-depth studies on current problems and issues, analysis of legislation, management, marketing, etc. Indexed in ABI/I.

International Insurance Monitor (Bronxville, NY: Chase Communications Group, Ltd. monthly) is a journal containing insurance news that is worldwide in scope (Indexed in ABI/I). Two Canadian trade journals are: *Canadian Insurance* (Toronto: Stone & Cox Ltd., 13/yr. Indexed in ABI/I); *Canadian Underwriter* (Don Mills, Ont.: Wadham Publications, Ltd. 13/yr.). Each has very useful annual statistical issues described in the company information section of this chapter.

INSURANCE DIRECTORIES

Agent's & Buyer's Guide: The Markets Handbook. Cincinnati, OH: National Underwriter Co. (annual).

Arranged by subject line of property/casualty insurance covered, this is a list of underwriting firms that are specialists in excess and surplus lines, running all the way from abortion clinics to yachts. An alphabetical list of companies is at end.

A companion volume for life/health is *Who Writes What in Life and Health Insurance* (Cincinnati: National Underwriter Co., annual).

Insurance Almanac. Englewood, NJ: Underwriter Printing and Publishing Co. (annual).

A company directory (U.S.) for the 6 principal lines of insurance (including Lloyds companies) giving, for each, officers, type of insurance written, territory covered. Includes also a directory of related services (inspection, investigation, audit, appraisal, reporting), agents and brokers, actuaries and consultants, adjusters, organizations, state officials, management, and insurance groups.

The Insurance Directory and Year Book. Brentwood, Middlesex, Eng.: Buckley Press Ltd.

Provides brief information about insurance companies in the U.K., including when established, names of directors, regional officers; also underwriting and other statistics; data on associations, clubs; and official bodies.

Society of Actuaries. *Year Book.* Schaumburg, IL.

Directory of officers and members; also other Society data such as constitution, by-laws, committees.

Who's Who in Insurance. Englewood, NJ: Underwriter Printing and Publishing Co. (annual).

Brief biographical sketches of U.S. insurance leaders. The same publisher also compiles a *Who's Who in Risk Management* (annual).

INSURANCE ASSOCIATIONS

American Council of Life Insurance, 1001 Pennsylvania Avenue, N.W., Washington, DC 20004-2599.

American Insurance Association, 1130 Connecticut Avenue, N.W., Washington, DC 20036.

American Society of CLU and ChFC, 270 Bryn Mawr Avenue, Bryn Mawr, PA 19010.

Health Insurance Association of America, 1025 Connecticut Avenue, Suite 1200, Washington, DC 20036.

Independent Insurance Agents of America, 127 Peyton, Alexandria, VA 22314.

Insurance Information Institute, 110 Williams Street, New York, NY 10038.

Life Insurance Marketing and Research Association, P.O. Box 208, Hartford, CT 06141.

National Association of Life Underwriters, 1922 F Street, N.W., Washington, DC 20006.

Risk and Insurance Management Society, 205 East 42d Street, New York, NY 10017.

REAL ESTATE

The second half of this chapter is concerned with listing selected recent books on real estate as a business—principles and practices, management and appraisal, finance, and investing, and the basic reference sources including statistics on housing. There has been no attempt to cover the many books being written on the important problems of urban development and urban renewal, although several abstracting services and periodicals on urban affairs are described in Chapter 11.

REAL ESTATE PRINCIPLES AND PRACTICES

Handbooks and Desk Books

Harris, Jack C., and Jack P. Friedman. *Barron's Real Estate Handbook.* 2d ed. New York: Barron's, 1988. 700 pp.

More a desk reference than a handbook, almost half is a dictionary (also published separately). The rest consists of a series of 8 important financial tables (monthly mortgage payments, loan progress tables, mortgage value tables, premiums for assumable loans, etc.), and short sections on real estate opportunities, government regulations, real estate careers, and buyers' and sellers' guides. Measurement tables and a bibliography (arranged by subject) are at end.

Seldin, Maury, and James H. Boykin, eds. *The Real Estate Handbook.* 2d ed. Homewood, IL: Dow Jones-Irwin, 1990. 1,055 pp.

Many of the 75 authors of the 58 chapters in this handbook are well-known real estate practitioners or academicians. They provide a comprehensive, authoritative reference work which the editor has arranged within five major parts: real estate transactions; real estate marketing; real estate analyses; real estate financing (discussing traditional financial and new financing sources in almost 300 pp.); real estate investment (dealing with 9 different types). There is a good index at end. These editors have also edited a book, by a variety of authors, on the various methods of *Real Estate Analysis* (American Society of Real Estate Counselors and Dow Jones-Irwin, 1990, 1 volume).

Books

Dasso, Jerome, and Alfred A. Ring. *Real Estate: Principles and Practices.* 11th ed. Englewood Cliffs, NJ: Prentice-Hall, 1989. 524 pp.

First written by Ring, then by Ring with Dasso, and now with Dasso as lead author, this is a long-time comprehensive, introductory text that has always been on every list of basic recommended real estate books. This most recent revision starts with two introductory chapters on real estate as a business and as a commodity. It then proceeds by dividing the material into the following major parts, each of which takes up important components of the decision-making cycle: defining property rights; acquiring ownership rights (including a chapter on brokerage operations and practices); finance; markets; value analysis, and investment. An appendix contains time value of money tables; there is also a glossary.

Ficek, Edmund F., Thomas P. Henderson and Ross H. Johnson. *Real Estate Principles and Practices.* 4th ed. Columbus, OH: Merrill Publishing Company, 1987. 604 pp.

This latest revision of an undergraduate text continues the authors' effort "to present real estate principles and practices primarily from a practical, business point of view while providing the appropriate legal, economic, mathematical, social, and ethical background." Lists of suggested supplementary readings are with chapters. Appendixes include a glossary, present value and amortization tables, lists of associations and state commissioners, code of ethics.

Industrial Real Estate. 4th ed. Washington, DC: Society of Industrial and Office Realtors of the National Association of Realtors, 1984. 721 pp.

The fourth edition still "serves both as a textbook on industrial real estate brokerage and as a ready reference for real estate practitioners." Its 18 chapters are arranged in four parts: the economics of industrial real estate (site selection, space, real estate as an investment, income tax considerations); major functions of the industrial real estate broker; supplementary activities (for example, real estate lending, leasing, valuation); industrial real estate development (industrial parks, aids to industrial development, etc.). A Canadian supplement provides a short overview of real estate in Canada. References are at end of each chapter. This is now out of date.

Karvel, George R., and Maurice A. Unger. *Real Estate: Principles and Practices.* 9th ed. Cincinnati, OH: South-Western, 1991. 720 pp.

Latest edition of a traditional text, for practitioners as well as for students, which continues to provide a study both of theory and practice, with its effects on the local and national economy. Based on an examination of the 8th edition which had Professor Unger as lead author, this is in 7 parts: overview; property rights; real estate brokerage; property ownership; real estate financing and investment; property valuation and management; planning for the future. Appendixes included compound interest tables and a glossary.

Professor Unger has also recently revised his *How to Invest in Real Estate* (2d ed., McGraw-Hill, 1991, 162 pp.), a short book designed for the individual who is relatively unlearned in real estate. He coauthored (with Ronald W. Melicher) *Real Estate Finance* (3d ed., South-Western, 1989, 423 pp.).

McMahan, John. *Property Development.* 2d ed. New York: McGraw-Hill, 1989. 488 pp.

"This book is about the fundamentals of the real estate development process. After the historical and economic stage has been set, the book pursues each of the fundamentals in a step-by-step fashion in much the same manner that a well-organized developer would approach a new project. The emphasis throughout is on the important role played by each of the fundamentals and how they mesh into a smoothly functioning process." A bibliography is at end. McMahan is an experienced real estate investment adviser and educator.

Saft, Stuart M. *Real Estate Development: Strategies for Changing Markets.* New York: Wiley, 1990. 1 volume (various pagings).

An overview that attempts "to walk the reader through the steps involved in developing a parcel of land. It reviews general concepts, the entities in which title to the property can be held, the tax considerations, the manner of contracting for and purchasing the land, the uses of land, zoning and environmental concerns, acquisition and development, permanent financing, construction, and leasing concerns for developers who want to retain the property and lease it to users." An extensive appendix contains sample forms.

Wurtzebach, Charles H., and Mike E. Miles. *Modern Real Estate.* 4th ed. New York: Wiley, 1991. 805, [15] pp.

This is a well-written, introductory text that is presented from a decision-making view. It is arranged in 9 major parts to cover: the analytical framework; the legal environment; valuation and the appraisal process; brokerage and management; real estate finance; taxation; investment analysis; real estate development; public policy and prospects for the future. Real-life examples and bibliographical citations are found throughout; compound interest tables and a glossary are at end.

REAL ESTATE MANAGEMENT AND APPRAISAL

Appraisal Institute. *The Appraisal of Real Estate.* 10th ed. Chicago: 1992. 768 pp.

Latest edition of an AI-sponsored textbook on the fundamentals of real estate appraisal and on current appraisal techniques. Appendixes include financial tables, a review of mathematics in appraising, and a list of selected readings and information sources.

Downs, James C., Jr. *Principles of Real Estate Management.* 12th ed. Chicago: Institute of Real Estate Management, 1980. 386 pp.

A standard beginner's text (now very old) on real estate management, with this latest edition arranged in four parts: dimensions of real estate and its management; techniques; scope (chapters on rental housing, condominiums and cooperatives, office buildings, shopping centers); entrepreneurial role of real estate management. A glossary and a few sample forms are in an appendix.

Institute of Real Estate Management. *Managing the Shopping Center.* Chicago: 1983. 435 pp.

Written by a team of shopping center specialists, this officially sponsored book guides the new manager through the processes and procedures of effective management in all types of shopping centers. Beginning with the manager's original assignment to a center and the creation of a management plan, the text then focuses on the "how-tos" of day-to-day concerns such as property maintenance, record keeping, advertising. A glossary and short bibliography are at end. Although I am not covering books on each type of real estate, I feel this is a good example of a text on one important part of the industry, but it is now rather out of date.

Lindeman, Bruce. *Real Estate Brokerage Management.* 2d ed. Englewood Cliffs, NJ: Prentice-Hall, 1988. 276 pp.

Anyone considering owning or operating a real estate brokerage business will want to use a book such as this one. It is oriented toward the practical application and organization form of the business, and is arranged within four parts: real estate brokerage and its business environment; management and personnel; marketing management; the professional brokerage. Short case experiences are with most chapters; all chapters contain suggestions for further reading.

Silverman, Robert A., ed. *Corporate Real Estate Handbook.* New York: McGraw-Hill, 1987. 202 pp.

This is not a typical handbook, but rather a book of 14 essays written by persons active in corporate real estate. The first part contains 8 essays intended to help senior real estate executives understand and evaluate strategy; the second part consists of 6 essays offering junior practitioners a survey of how best to perform the 6 most common operations activities.

REAL ESTATE FINANCE AND INVESTING

The important reference sources on mortgage banking and financing (including savings and loan statistics, mortgage lending, real estate appraisal and financial tables, amortization tables) are described in the "Money and Banking" section of Chapter 14.

Handbooks

Miles, Martin J. *Real Estate Investor's Complete Handbook.* Englewood Cliffs, NJ: Prentice-Hall, 1982. 572 pp.

Miles says his book provides the real estate professional with quick answers to almost any question on real estate investments. Its 162 sections are in 21 chapters arranged in alphabetical format from "annuities" to "taxes." Numerous formulas, examples with solutions, tables, forms, checklists, and other illustrations are used throughout. The last 100 pages consist of tables for: annuities; monthly payments; depreciation; day numbers.

Books

Brueggeman, William B., Jeffrey D. Fisher and Leo D. Stone. *Real Estate Finance.* 8th ed. Homewood, IL.: Irwin, 1989. 836 pp. Ninth edition to be published early in 1993 by first two authors.

A well-established text originally written by Henry E. Hoagland. It is now substantially revised to cover the many changes in financing real estate, and it gives increased attention to decision making. The authors begin by studying legal instruments and other considerations in real estate finance. This is followed by sections on: financing residential properties; financing and investing in income-producing properties; financing real estate development; institutional sources of funds and the secondary mortgage market; real estate investment performance. Compound interest tables are at end.

Greer, Gaylon E., and Michael D. Farrell. *Investment Analysis for Real Estate Decisions.* 2d ed. Chicago: Longman Financial Services Publishing, 1988. 530 pp.

Each part of this readable textbook covers a subject fundamental to informed investment decision making. These are: basic issues; market research; forecasting cash flows; income tax considerations; measuring investment performance; the risk element; the investment analysis process illustrated; real estate as a security. Examples and tables are used throughout. Recommended readings are with chapters; case problems are at end of each part. Financial tables, symbols, and a glossary are at end.

Greer has also written *The New Dow Jones-Irwin Guide to Real Estate Investing* (Homewood; IL: Dow Jones-Irwin, 1989, 330 pp.).

Hines, Mary Alice. *Guide to International Real Estate Investment.* New York: Quorum Books, 1988. 348 pp.

Professor Hines has written widely in the field of real estate. Here she examines 6 principal types of property investment on a worldwide basis, as well as such topics as real estate values, differences in international law, financing, taxation—all as they relate to international real estate investment.

Three other recent books by Hines are: *Global Corporate Real Estate Management: A Handbook for Multinational Business and Organizations* (Quorum Books, 1990, 262 pp.); *Marketing Real Estate Internationally* (Quorum Books, 1988, 239 pp.); *Shopping Center Development and Investment* (2d ed., Wiley, 1988, 418 pp.).

Jaffe, Austin J., and C. F. Sirmans. *Fundamentals of Real Estate Investment.* 2d ed. Englewood Cliffs, NJ: Prentice-Hall, 1989, 414 pp.

An introduction to the real estate investment process using as a basis an equity valuation model. The five parts cover: basic concepts; the investment environment; financial analysis (this is the core of the book, and it covers operating, financing, and reverse decisions); investment criteria (including a chapter on discounted cash flow models); a conclusion. Includes numerous examples and illustrations, and one case study. Bibliographies are at end of chapters; real estate tables are at end of book. This text presumes its users have had introductory courses in economics and financial management. Some basic algebra is used.

Sirota, David. *Essentials of Real Estate Finance.* 6th ed. Chicago: Real Estate Education Company, 1991. Approximately 320 pp. paper.

This is a popular text revised and updated once again to cover subjects that are essential in real estate finance. Appendixes explain the mathematics of real estate finance and major laws affecting the savings industry. A glossary is at the end.

Professor Sirota has also revised his *Essentials of Real Estate Investment* (3d ed., Real Estate Education Company, 1988, 254 pp., paper) which is an easy-to-read text covering all of the basic concepts of the title subject.

Wiedemer, John P. *Real Estate Finance.* 6th ed. Englewood Cliffs, NJ: Prentice-Hall, 1990. 328 pp.

The author's primary emphasis in this basic book on the methods and elements of real estate finance is on residential financing since this comprises two-thirds of all mortgage lending. Among the topics covered are a discussion of money and interest rates, mortgage money, mortgage documents, federal government underwriting programs, property analysis, commercial loans, settlement procedures. Terminology is explained in a glossary at end.

Professor Wiedemer has also revised his text on *Real Estate Investment* (4th ed., Prentice-Hall, 1989, 321 pp.).

Two alternative texts on finance are: *Real Estate Finance* by C. F. Sirmans (2d ed., New York: McGraw-Hill, 1989, 550 pp.); *Real Estate Finance* by Ronald W. Melicher and Maurice A. Unger (3d ed., Cincinnati: South-Western, 1989, 423 pp.). Two further books on real estate investment worth citing are: a recent text on *Real Estate Investment: Strategy, Analysis, Decisions* by Stephen A. Phyrr et al. (2d ed., New York: Wiley, 1989, 962 pp.), not seen for evaluation but well reviewed; and *How to Invest in Real Estate* by Maurice A. Unger (2d ed., New York: McGraw-Hill, 1991).

REAL ESTATE LAW

Kratovil, Robert, and Raymond J. Werner. *Real Estate Law.* 9th ed. Englewood Cliffs, NJ: Prentice-Hall, 1988. 639 pp. Tenth edition to be published in 1992 with authors reversed.

The standard work on real estate law revised to cover new developments and rapid changes that have occurred in recent years. It is comprehensive but made easy to use by a numbered paragraph format within its 48 chapters and also by frequent comments and examples.

Real Estate Law Digest. Rev. ed. Boston: Warren, Gorham & Lamont. 2 volumes (annual, with cumulative supplements).

A classified digest of selected federal and state court decisions on all phases of real estate law. It summarizes facts, issues, rulings and refers to the law report where the case is reported in full. Includes an index and table of cases.

HOUSING AND REAL ESTATE BIBLIOGRAPHIES AND INDEXES

American Institute of Real Estate Appraisers. *Bibliography of Appraisal Literature (1981–1986).* Chicago, 1987. 71 pp. and an annual *Update.*

A subject listing of periodical literature on real estate appraisal, kept up to date with an annual *Update.* Prior to this 1987 edition, the Institute published two earlier lists with the title *Real Estate Appraisal Bibliography;* the first was published in 1973 and the second in 1981 to cover the literature published from 1973 to 1980. The AIREA has now merged into the Appraisal Institute.

Harris, Laura A. *The Real Estate Industry: An Information Sourcebook.* (Oryx Sourcebook Series in Business and Management). Phoenix, AZ: Oryz Press, 1987. 170 pp.

An annotated bibliography of English-language real estate sources published 1980–1986 and arranged in four parts. The first is a "Core Library Collection" which describes basic general works and reference sources (such as bibliographies, dictionaries, directories, handbooks, periodicals). Next is a "general literature" section describing books in each of 25 subject categories such as appraisal, finance, property management. The last two parts describe real estate periodicals and other sources of information (associations, government agencies, maps, etc.).

Society of Industrial Realtors. *Industrial Real Estate: An Annotated Bibliography.* Washington, DC: 1982. 34 pp.

A selected, annotated list of books, reports, and articles, arranged by 14 subjects such as appraisal, brokerage, industrial parks, investment. It covers primarily the literature published during the 12 years prior to 1982, and it includes a selected list of periodicals.

REAL ESTATE DICTIONARIES

Please note the fact that many of the real estate books included in this chapter contain useful glossaries.

American Institute of Real Estate Appraisers. *The Dictionary of Real Estate Appraisal.* 2d ed. Chicago: 1989. 366 pp.

This expanded edition is the latest of several dictionaries on real estate appraisal sponsored by the AIREA. Its definitions are short yet clear and include terms in fields related to real estate. There is ample use of cross-references; and the source is cited if a definition is taken from another dictionary or handbook. At end is a bibliography of books, periodicals, and reference sources.

Blankenship, Frank J. *Prentice-Hall Real Estate Investors Encyclopedia.* Englewood Cliffs, NJ: Prentice-Hall, 1989. 539 pp. paper.

An encyclopedic dictionary of terms you will encounter in real estate investing. Each concise definition is followed by advice to investors and "an expanded explanation of the use of the term in everyday investing situations." Includes illustrative examples, checklists, timely topics.

Friedman, Jack P., Jack C. Harris and J. Bruce Lindeman. *Dictionary of Real Estate Terms.* 2d ed. New York: Barron's, 1987. 329 pp. paper.

A useful dictionary of over 1,200 real estate terms using concise and practical definitions. Often examples are given on the use for a specific term, and occasionally there are helpful illustrations. Includes diagrams, cross-references, organizations, plus a few mortgage and measurement tables at end.

This same dictionary appears in *Barron's Real Estate Handbook* by Harris and Friedman (2d ed., Barron's, 1988, 700 pp.) along with 8 important financial tables, several short chapters on such topics as real estate careers, measurement tables, and a bibliography.

Reilly, John W. *The Language of Real Estate.* 3d ed. Chicago: Real Estate Education Co., 1989. 467 pp. paper.

This is a good comprehensive dictionary of almost 2,400 real estate terms which gives, for each term, a basic definition (usually longer than in the other dictionaries), several applications, and useful cross-references. An appendix contains list of abbreviations, a sample form, the realtors code of ethics.

Among the several other dictionaries is *Real Estate Dictionary* comp. by Michael C. Thomsett (Jefferson, NC and London: McFarland & Company, 1988, 220 pp.) which defines some 1,000 terms and phrases.

REAL ESTATE OPERATING STATISTICS

Building Owners & Managers Association International. *BOMA Experience Exchange Report.* Washington, DC (annual).

Gives operating income and expense data for office buildings in the U.S. and Canada, with data in dollars per square foot, per year, for total building rentable area, and for total office rentable area. All of this statistical analysis is given both for private sector properties and for government office buildings in more than 90 U.S. cities and about 25 Canadian cities. There are also general tables by location/size, age/size, age/height.

Institute of Real Estate Management. *Income/Expense Analysis: Conventional Apartments.* Chicago (annual).

Apartment building income/expense data for elevator buildings, unfurnished; low rise buildings (for two unit size categories); garden type buildings; furnished buildings. For each, statistics include median income and operating costs, by selected metropolitan areas, by regions, by age groups.

Three companion annuals are: *Income/Expense Analysis: Office Buildings, Downtown and Suburban* (with metropolitan area, regional and national reports by building size, age group, rental range, building type); *Expense Analysis: Condominiums, Cooperatives & Planned Unit Developments* (expense data by metropolitan area, region, age groups, and price range); *Income/Expense Analysis: Federally-Assisted Apartments.* These four combined annuals report on the operational experiences of more than 10,000 buildings and developments in the U.S. and Canada.

Urban Land Institute. *Dollars & Cents of Shopping Centers: A Study of Receipts & Expenses in Shopping Center Operations.* Washington, DC (triennial).

Detailed operating statistics for four categories of U.S. shopping centers (super regional, regional, community, neighborhood) by geographic area and by age group; also for Canadian shopping centers. The statistics in the 1990 edition are based on data from more than 700 centers.

An alternative source for operating expenses by region and size is *ICSC Shopping Center Operating Cost Analysis Report* (New York: International Council of Shopping Centers; annual?).

HOUSING AND REAL ESTATE STATISTICS

The first two governmental series listed below are the best sources for U.S. housing statistics. Statistics on the building and construction industry are covered in Chapter 6.

U.S. Bureau of the Census. *1980 Census of Housing.* (HC) and *1980 Census of Population and Housing* (PHC). Washington, DC: U.S. Government Printing Office.

These censuses are taken every 10 years in the year ending with zero. The *Census of Housing* for 1970 was in 7 volumes, each with many parts. The volumes for 1980 are listed below:

HC80-1A: *General Housing Characteristics* (one per state)—gives statistics on housing items for counties, SMSAs, urbanized areas, cities, and other geographical areas.

HC80-1B: *Detailed Housing Characteristics* (one per state)—includes tenure, vacancy status, number of persons per room, type of structure, condition and plumbing facilities, financial characteristics—by geographic location.

HC80-2: *Metropolitan Housing Characteristics.*

HC80-3: *Subject Reports*—covering such topics as mobile homes, condominium housing, and mover households.

HC80-4: *Components of Inventory Change.*

HC80-5: *Residential Finance.*

Volumes in the 1980 *Census of Population and Housing* include:

PHC80-1: *Block Statistics* (one for each state and one per SMSA)—housing and some population data for individual city blocks.

PHC80-2: *Census Tracts* (one for each state and one per SMSA). Gives socioeconomic data by census tract.

PHC80-3: *Summary Characteristics for Governmental Units and Standard Metropolitan Statistical Areas* (one per state).

PHC80-4: *Congressional Districts of the 98th Congress.*

For sample survey statistics published in non-census years, see *American Housing Survey: Housing Characteristics for Selected Metropolitan Areas* (*Current Housing Reports* series no. H-170). This is published jointly by the Bureau of the Census and the Dept. of Housing and Urban Development, and it contains housing characteristic statistics for 44 selected metropolitan areas. However it is published in a four-year sequence and so only 11 metropolitan areas are covered in any one year, with 1988 data the latest published as of 1991. Among other statistics from sample survey data is *American Housing Survey for the United States in (year)* (*Current Housing Reports* series no. H-150). There are further reports published in the *Current Housing Reports* series devoted to such specific topics as housing vacancies and home ownership.

National Association of Real Estate Investment Trusts. *REIT Facts: A Statistical Profile of the REIT Industry in (year).* Washington; DC (annual).

A statistical review of recent industry trends including an industry profile, an industry balance sheet, financial data, a list of qualified REITs, and more. The NAREIT also publishes an annual *Fact Book* which is an overview of the industry's history, organization, laws and regulations affecting REITs, and includes a glossary. Their *Directory of Members* is described elsewhere.

Society of Industrial and Office Realtors. *Comparative Statistics of Industrial and Office Real Estate Markets.* Chicago (annual).

This contains a one-page market review and forecast for each of more than 100 U.S. metropolitan areas and a very few Canadian, English, and Mexican cities. The section covering industrial real estate markets includes statistics on: sales prices of industrial buildings by size (square feet), lease prices, site prices, construction costs, vacancy indicators, composition of absorption, outlook, and brief demographic data (including median household income, cost of living, and rank). The office real estate markets section has some of this same data for metropolitan areas plus such figures as rental rates, utility rates, parking ratios. At front is a general overview of real estate conditions. This annual is published in cooperation with Landauer Associates, Inc.

U.S. Bureau of the Census. *Census of Government, Vol. 2: Taxable Property Values and Assessment-Sales Price Ratios.* Washington, DC: U.S. Government Printing Office.

This census is taken every 5 years in the years ending with 2 and 7. Volume 2 tabulates the amounts of assessed values (gross and net) for local general property taxation by those counties and cities having a population of 50,000 or more.

Urban Land Institute. *ULI Market Profiles.* Washington, DC (annual).

Another source for market profiles of metropolitan areas, this one reports or updates profiles on 57 real estate and development markets in the U.S. and Canada each year. For each area there is a discussion and brief statistics covering: development climate, residential market, retail market, office market, hotel market, industrial market.

REAL ESTATE PERIODICALS

Appraisal Journal. Chicago: Appraisal Institute (quarterly).

Authoritative articles on real estate appraisal and real estate financing. Includes book reviews. Indexed in ABI/I, BPI, PAIS, TI. Now published separately by this Institute is *The Appraiser* (monthly) which covers news about regulatory, legislative, and other issues of interest to appraisers; and *The Quarterly Byte,* a newsletter for current computer information relevant to the appraisal business.

The Society of Real Estate Appraisers in Chicago publishes a quarterly called *Real Estate Appraiser & Analyst.* Indexed in ABI/I, TI. This Society has now merged into the Appraisal Institute.

Journal of Housing. Washington, DC: National Association of Housing and Redevelopment Officials (bimonthly).

Billed as "the magazine of housing and community development issues," this journal contains primarily news about new developments, government programs, legislation, court decisions, and NAHRO members. Includes annotated lists of books, reports, and periodicals. The May/June issue includes a "Buyer's Guide." Indexed in ABI/I, PAIS, SSI.

Journal of Property Management. Chicago: Institute of Real Estate Management (bimonthly).

Articles cover management practices, procedures, and related topics on property management, including specific types of property. Each issue contains a "computer section"; also regular departments for legal, tax, and other news of interest to members, and one or two book reviews. Indexed in ABI/I, BPI, PAIS, PTS/F&S.

Journal of Real Estate Research. American Real Estate Society (quarterly).

A relatively new journal (1986) emphasizing scholarly real estate research that produces results which are of interest to the decision-maker. The address of this Society changes about every year; in 1991 it was: University of North Dakota; Grand Forks; ND 58202.

Journal of Real Estate Taxation. Boston: Warren, Gorham & Lamont (quarterly).

Usually three articles in each issue on the title subject; also regular departments relating to partnerships, condominiums and cooperatives, taxation. Indexed in ABI/I.

Monitor. Clearwater, FL: Maclean Hunter Media, Inc. (10/yr.).

This trade journal covering articles and news on the development, management, and design of shopping centers and retail chains is billed as "The Shopping Center Industry Magazine." Prior to 1988 its title was *National Mall Monitor*. Special annual issues include: "Top 50" (January), a ranked list of leading companies in three categories: management, development, acquisition; "Annual Top 50 Survey of Open Centers" (March); including ranked list for the same categories; "Leading Builders & Contractors" (July), a ranked list.

National Real Estate Investor. Atlanta, GA: Communication Channels; Inc. (monthly).

An important magazine for news about real estate developments, finance, investment, and management. Each issue includes articles discussing real estate developments in about five different cities or areas. Useful ranked lists in annual survey issues include: the Top 100 Developers (January); the Top 100 Office Developers (March); the Top 50 Industrial Developers (April); the Top 50 Retail Developers (May); the Top 75 Property Managers (June); the Top 50 Real Estate Investors (September). Each of these lists gives descriptive data about each firm such as types of projects, major development projects for the previous year, total square feet under construction. Its annual "Directory Issue" (a mid-year issue) is described under "Directories" below. Indexed in ABI/I, PAIS, TI; full text on BRS, DATA-STAR, DIALOG, MEAD/NEXIS.

Real Estate Finance. Boston: Federal Research Press (quarterly).

This is a quarterly review of commercial finance techniques, with articles on today's financing strategies as well as case studies of actual financing deals. Authors are leading real estate professionals. Indexed in ABI/I.

Real Estate Law Journal. Boston: Warren, Gorham & Lamont (quarterly).

Research articles on the legal and tax aspects of real estate; also news about legislation, case digests. Includes a subject "survey of articles," a "digest of selected articles," and occasional book reviews. Indexed in ABI/I, PAIS.

Real Estate Review. Boston: Warren, Gorham & Lamont (quarterly).

This quarterly is sponsored by the Real Estate Institute, New York University. It contains informative and readable articles by real estate, legal, and accounting experts, on all aspects of real estate and related subjects. Indexed in ABI/I, BPI, PAIS, TI.

Real Estate Today. Chicago: National Association of Realtors (10/yr.).

Covers short articles on real estate management, sales, and commercial investment. Indexed in BPI, TI.

Shopping Center World. Atlanta, GA: Communication Channels, Inc. (monthly).

Short articles on such topics as shopping center trends, financing, leasing, operations; also geographic reviews for a region or state, and occasional product spotlights. Ranked lists and other special features include: "The Top 100 Owners of Shopping Centers" (January issue); "The Top 100 Managers of Shopping Centers" (March); "Annual Ranking of Strip Center Owners" (August); "Annual Ranking of Leading Retail Contractors" (September); "Product & Service Directory" (extra issue in September); "Buyers' Guide to Products & Services" (October); "Annual

Leasing Guide & Chain Store Expansion Plans Survey" (December). Most of the ranked lists also contain an alphabetical list of firms giving names of top officers.

REAL ESTATE DIRECTORIES

Moody's Bank and Financial Manual includes financial information on U.S. real estate companies and real estate investment trusts. See listing in the "Insurance" section of this chapter. Directories of major U.S. homebuilders and several ranked lists of builders, designers, and contractors are included in the "Construction Industry" section of Chapter 6.

Employee Relocation Council. *E-R-C Directory.* Washington, DC (annual).
   Geographical lists of real estate appraisers, brokers, and relocation service companies.

National Association of Real Estate Investment Trusts. *Directory of Members.* Washington, DC (annual).
   This is more than a directory since it gives, not only address and names of officers and trustees for each member firm, but also the types of investment, number of shareholders, assets, liabilities and equity statistics, stock price range, and occasionally public offerings and private placements of debt and equity. Lesser information is given for associate companies (auditors, lawyers, etc.) in a separate list at end.

National Real Estate Investor. "Directory Issue." (annual, a mid-year issue).
   Especially handy because of its lists (arranged geographically) of a wide variety of real estate-related firms: appraisers, architects, asset managers, associations, builders/ contractors, business/office parks, computer services, corporate real estate managers, developers, economic & industrial development authorities, environmental consultants, equity investors & investment companies, executive search firms, financial services, hospitality services, hotel franchises, institutional & pension fund advisers, limited partnerships, professional services, property managers, real estate brokers & agents, real estate consultants & counselors, title insurance companies, national marketplace. Also included in this issue is an annual "Compensation Report."

National Roster of Realtors. Cedar Rapids, IA: Stamats Communications Inc. 2 volumes (annual).
   A directory, arranged geographically, of individuals who are members of the National Association of Realtors. Information on associations is at front of volume 1.

The Real Estate Directory of Major Investors, Developers and Brokers. Wilmette, IL: Reed Publishing (USA) Inc. (annual).
   This directory is in five sections to cover: real estate investors, brokers and developers, service firms, international real estate firms, companies engaged in real estate finance. For each company it usually gives: names of key personnel, average purchase price/investment range per property preference, size of portfolio, investment structure, geographic preference, number of transactions completed in last 12 months. There are 6 indexes: by property preference, by investment range, by type of firm, by geographic location, by geographic preference, by name of personnel.

Shopping Center Directory. Chicago: National Research Bureau. 4 unnumbered volumes (annual).
   A comprehensive directory of U.S. shopping centers, arranged in four volumes covering: the East, Midwest, South, and West, with each volume arranged by state

and then by city. Data for each shopping center usually includes statistics on the center, owner, leasing agent, original developer, center management, architect/engineer, names of tenants. Each volume contains an index of the centers, as well as indexes of new centers, centers expanding, centers with space available, centers by gross leasable area, owners and leasing agents.

Site Selection and Industrial Development. Norcross, GA: Conway Data, Inc. (bimonthly).

In two parts to cover the former *Site Selection Handbook* and *Industrial Development* magazine. Each issue focuses on a different site selection "issue", including a different useful geographic directory. These are: "Geo-Corporate Issue" (February) containing a geographic directory of companies with names of executives in charge of planning new facilities; "Geo-Economic Issue" (April), listing over 4,600 development organizations worldwide; "Geo-Technology Issue" (June), with a list of university engineering and scientific programs; "Geo-Life Issue" (August), giving quality of life factors in specific U.S. and Canadian cities (temperature, cost of living, unemployment, crime, etc.); "Geo-Political Issue" (October), with key votes, by state, of U.S. Congressmen, and names of city mayors; "Geo-Sites Issue" (December), with a geographic directory of business parks around the world. The "Industrial Development" section of each issue contains articles and news of interest to industrial developers and real estate managers.

U.S. Real Estate Register. Wilmington, MA (annual).

Section 2 (yellow pages) is an alphabetical list of companies involved in real estate and industrial development professions. Section 3 lists these companies by more than 100 specific subject categories such as: architects/engineers; developers; industrial parks; joint ventures; mortgage bankers. Section 1 is a list of real estate managers.

REAL ESTATE ASSOCIATIONS

Appraisal Institute, 875 N. Michigan Avenue, Suite 2400, Chicago, IL 60611.

NACORE International (National Association of Corporate Real Estate Executives), 440 Columbia Drive, Suite 100, West Palm Beach, FL 33409.

National Association of Real Estate Brokers, P.O. Box 56483, Washington, DC 20041.

National Association of Real Estate Investment Trusts, 1129 20th Street, N.W., Washington, DC 20036.

National Association of Realtors, 430 North Michigan Avenue, Chicago, IL 60611. (This is a federation of state and local real estate boards. Two institutes affiliated with this association are: American Institute of Real Estate Appraisers and Institute of Real Estate Management).

National Center for Housing Management, 1275 K Street, N.W., Washington, DC 20005.

Property Management Association of America, 8811 Colesville Road, Silver Spring, MD 20910.

Society of Industrial and Office Realtors, 777 14th Street, N.W., Washington, DC 20005. (Affiliated with National Association of Realtors).

16

INTERNATIONAL MANAGEMENT

International Economics – International Finance and World Trade – International Management – International Financial Management – Political and Financial Risk Assessment – International Marketing – International Business Bibliographies – Dictionaries – Tax and Trade Guides for Specific Countries – Reference Data for Exporters – International Management Periodicals – Directories – Associations

The rapid development of international business in the period following World War II brought with it many new and important challenges for management. Added to the usual problems of managing a domestic company, the international or multinational corporation/enterprise (MNC or MNE) must concern itself with many complex questions in connection with political, economic, and social differences between nations. The literature has lagged behind this growth in international business for several reasons: the wide range of complicated factors that must be considered, rapidly changing events, and diversity of opinion, to name a few. Although the time lag in book publishing has lessened significantly, the reasons for it point up the particular importance of periodicals in this field. Current articles offer the most up-to-date information on global political, economic, and governmental activity, on continuing management efforts to adjust to changing environments, and they also have the advantage of being able to present various opinions on how to solve specific business problems. Not only are business and economic periodicals of value, but it is assumed the person with international interests also reads current U.S. and foreign affairs journals and one or more U.S. and foreign newspapers.

This chapter describes a selection of recent books, periodicals, and a few reference sources on the topics listed above. The following reference materials are covered elsewhere in this book: directories of foreign companies in Chapter 7; foreign statistical sources and foreign economic trends in Chapter

5; financial manuals for foreign companies in Chapter 8; books on accounting for multinational enterprises in Chapter 12.

INTERNATIONAL ECONOMICS

Fieleke, Norman S. *The International Economy Under Stress.* Cambridge, MA: Ballinger, 1988. 253 pp.

The author says this short book "is an analytical survey of the major disruptions and challenges facing the international economy, primarily during the period 1970–87. The discussion will be intelligible to the sophisticated layperson and the advanced undergraduate and may constitute a useful reference for the expert." It is copyrighted by the Federal Reserve Bank of Boston which supported the author's work on this survey. Bibliographical notes and suggestions for further reading are at end of chapters.

Lindert, Peter H. *International Economics.* 9th ed. Homewood, IL: Irwin, 1991. 682 pp.

Professor Lindert has now completely taken over revision of Professor Charles P. Kindleberger's classic text. It is still arranged in the following five parts: parts 1 and 2 deal with the microeconomic aspects of international economics (covering international trade theory and trade policy); a macroeconomic and financial focus comprise parts 3 and 4, which deals with understanding foreign exchange, and income and foreign exchange; part 5, factor movements, examines the special problems raised by the partial international mobility of human and other assets. Supplementary explanations and formulae are in appendixes; suggested readings are with chapters and a bibliography is at the end.

An alternative undergraduate text is *The International Economy* by Peter B. Kenen (Englewood Cliffs, NJ: Prentice-Hall, 1989. 482 pp.).

Terpstra, Vern, and Kenneth David. *The Cultural Environment of International Business.* 3d ed. Cincinnati: South-Western, 1991. 252 pp. paper.

An interesting book which tries to help the reader to better understand the complexities of the environment that are critical to success in international business. It studies 8 major components of the cultural environment, noting international differences in each component and discussing implications for international business. These 8 components are: culture; language; education; religion; values; technology; social organization; political environment. An epilogue provides an overview of the "environment and issues." A bibliography is at end.

Vernon, Raymond, and Louis T. Wells, Jr. *Economic Environment of International Business.* 5th ed. Englewood Cliffs, NJ: Prentice-Hall, 1991. 226 pp. paper.

Although these authors have borrowed frequently from concepts of economic theory, they state that this book is different both in purpose and content from a standard textbook on international economics and that it "is intended to introduce the reader to a manager's perspective in the fields of international payments, international trade, and international investment." Thus they have attempted "to present the institutions, forces, and problems that are involved when business managers try to operate in many economies at once, and to sort out the threats and promises that develop when they try to link their operations across national boundaries." First they examine the firm from within, then the firm and the nation, and finally the international environment. A few suggested readings are at end of chapters. This useful paperback has also been published as a bound textbook with title *Manager in the International Economy* (6th ed., Prentice-Hall, 1991, 470 pp.) which the authors have expanded for teaching purposes to include a fourth section containing 12 cases. Professors Vernon and Wells are respected teachers, researchers, and writers on international business.

INTERNATIONAL FINANCE AND WORLD TRADE

See also a subsequent section on international financial management.

Handbooks

Baughn, William H., and Donald R. Mandich, eds. *The International Banking Handbook.* Homewood, IL: Dow Jones-Irwin, 1983. 853 pp. Out of print.

A good but now rather old overview of this complex and important industry, with its 51 chapters organized around the following major issues and functions involved in international banking: the international financial system; international credits; international banking services; foreign exchange; special institutions and programs; approaches to world financial markets; managing international banking activities; legal and regulatory framework for international banking; the future of international banking. Most of its authors are top banking executives.

George, Abraham M., and Ian H. Giddy, eds. *International Finance Handbook.* New York: Wiley, 1983. 2 volumes.

For the first time we have, in these two massive volumes, a vast compendium of practitioner-oriented information on the major tasks and tools of international financing, banking, and investment, intended for the intelligent nonspecialist. There are 56 contributors—both practitioners and scholars and all recognized authorities. The Handbook is divided into 8 parts with each part self-contained and treated as a guide to that particular subfield. These are: introduction; the foreign exchange markets; the Eurocurrency markets; national banking, money, and bond markets (chapters cover each important country); the international bond market; international equity markets (chapters for each of 10 country or regional markets); special financing techniques and sources; the management of international finance. Bibliographies are with each chapter. At end of volume 2 is an appendix covering the mathematics of international finance, and a glossary. There is also a list of periodicals containing articles, surveys, statistics, or other data on the financial and business conditions in various countries.

Books

Aliber, Robert Z. *The International Money Game.* 5th ed., rev. New York: Basic Books, 1987. 372 pp.

Widely recommended as a good and highly readable introduction to the international monetary system—its history, its strengths and weaknesses, its likely future evolution. The first of two parts examines the structure of national monies, with the focus on tensions between economic pressures toward integration of national monetary policies and political pressures toward decentralization. The last half, "Living with the System," studies some of the direct and indirect consequences of segmenting the world into 100 currency areas, with each chapter focusing on a particular issue.

Bank for International Settlement. *Annual Report.* Basel, Switzerland.

Of potential interest to persons needing a good, annual survey of financial markets and international monetary developments during the previous year. This report usually examines the following topics: general economic development; international trade and payments; developments in domestic and international financial markets; monetary developments and policy; the international monetary system. It also contains an annual update on activities of the Bank.

Caves, Richard E., Jeffrey A. Frankel and Ronald W. Jones. *World Trade and Payments: An Introduction.* 5th ed. Glenview, IL: Scott, Foresman, 1990. 784 pp.

The latest edition of this introductory text still combines descriptive material with world trade theory and balance of payments, and it is still geared for undergraduates who have already taken a standard course in the principles of economics. It starts by explaining the simplest model of trade between nations, and with each subsequent part it builds upon this model in studying: the patterns of trade and the distribution of income; commercial policy; balance of payments, income, and money; international financial markets and their macroeconomic implications. The last two parts are entirely new sections written by the second author who is new to this edition. Suggestions for further reading are with each chapter; mathematical supplements are at end of book.

Cominx, Raymond G.F. *Foreign Exchange Today.* Rev. ed. Cambridge, Eng.: Woodhead-Faulkner, 1980. 171 pp.

With the advent of floating exchange rates and frequent and continuing currency crises, there has been a growing need for executives and other commercial users to have better grounding in foreign exchange practices and movements. This little book is still one of the better ones written as an easy-to-understand overview of foreign exchange as of 1980. The first 6 chapters deal with the origin and recent history of the foreign exchange markets, the structure and main factors influencing exchange rates. The last 6 chapters concentrate on the practical aspects of foreign exchange techniques (including simple explanations of spot and forward exchange rates), on accounting procedures and forecasting. An excellent glossary and a short bibliography are at end.

The Eurocurrency Market Handbook. 2d ed. By Eugene Sarver. New York: New York Institute of Finance, 1990. 621 pp.

Here is a detailed overview of the full scope of the Eurocurrency market. Its 9 sections break the material down into: Eurocurrency market size and profit; historical development; Eurocurrency bank centers (with information on each); the principal nondollar Eurocurrency markets; interbank Eurocurrency trading; Eurocurrency market instruments; syndicated Eurocurrency bank credits; Eurocurrency market supervision; the Eurobond market. Useful appendixes include a glossary, a chronology, directories of Euromarket institutions and of databases, and much more. A bibliography is at end.

Riehl, Heinz, and Rita M. Rodriguez. *Foreign Exchange and Money Markets: Managing Foreign and Domestic Currency Operations.* 2d ed. New York: McGraw-Hill, 1983. 453 pp.

Provides a good, practical, integrated discussion of foreign exchange markets and money markets for persons who have had no previous acquaintance with these subjects. Part 1 provides a basic understanding of the functioning of the two markets; part 2 applies this generalized knowledge to specific problems involved in the treasury department (operations in the trading room, funds management in both markets, management of exposure to exchange risk); part 3 discusses issues involved in controlling treasury operations. A glossary and a bibliography of sources of data arranged by country are at end.

For a practical, up-to-date guide, see *The Foreign Exchange and Money Markets Guide* by Julian Walmsley (Wiley, 1992, 513 pp.). It starts with background information on the markets, and then explains and covers: money market calculations; foreign exchange calculations; derivatives (financial futures, interest rates and currency swaps, options); risk issues. Appendixes and a short list of further readings are at end.

Root, Franklin R. *International Trade and Investment.* 6th ed. Cincinnati: South-Western Publishing Co., 1990. 696 pp.

This book offers the reader an integrated treatment of theory, policy, and enterprise in international trade and investment. Professor Root has integrated these three topics for each of the principal international economic flows which form the four basic sections of his book: international trade; international payments; international development; international investment/multinational enterprise. Lists of selected readings are at end of most chapters.

Roussakis, Emmanuel N., ed. *International Banking: Principles and Practices.* New York: Praeger, 1983. 528 pp.

An informative synthesis of the thinking of 23 experts on international banking, the objective of which "is to provide important insights into, and a frame of reference for understanding, the various aspects of international banking, with special emphasis on international lending policies, procedures, and considerations." Includes also chapters on risk and credit analysis. Suggested references are with most contributions; a glossary is at end.

Weisweiller, Rudi. *How the Foreign Exchange Market Works.* New York: New York Institute of Finance, 1990. 212 pp. paper.

Here is an up-to-date simple explanation of the foreign exchange market written by a London-based financial authority. The author starts with why and how the market works and, from there, explains the five common choices or problems for firms, the background of Bretton Woods, Eurodollars and Eurobonds, gold, the capital movement, the new instruments, financial futures, and more. A bibliography and a glossary are at end.

Another guide to foreign exchange dealings is *Basic Handbook of Foreign Exchange: A Guide to Foreign Exchange Dealing* by Claude Tygier (2d ed., London: Euromoney Publications, 1988, 252 pp., paper).

INTERNATIONAL MANAGEMENT

Handbook

Walter, Ingo, and Tracy Murray, eds. *Handbook of International Business.* 2d ed. New York: Wiley, 1988. 1 volume (various pagings).

First published in 1982, this excellent, comprehensive, yet clear and concise reference work on international business is now revised and greatly expanded into two companion volumes. The first volume, with title above, presents an overview of the global environment of the business firm, assessing a wide spectrum of considerations ranging from the factors driving international trade and competition to public policies dealing with international markets. Each chapter, written usually by a qualified academician, contains a guide for further reading.

The second volume, *Handbook of International Management* (1988, various pagings), deals with managerial issues confronting firms doing business internationally, including marketing management, corporate and financial planning, country and political risk, and much more. Its authors are also primarily academic persons, and it also includes bibliographies and an index. These handbooks are intended as a practical source for executives, managers, accountants, and others involved in international business.

Books

Austin, James E. *Managing in Developing Countries: Strategic Analysis and Operating Techniques.* New York: Free Press, 1990. 465 pp.
Professor Austin's book is intended to help both current and future managers involved or interested in doing business in or with developing countries. It has evolved out of his research, teaching, and work in developing countries. The first of its two parts presents as background the components of what he labels the Environmental Analysis Framework. The larger second part focuses on how to deal with strategic and operating problems in each of the core functional areas of management. Extensive bibliographical notes are at end. Professor Austin has also prepared (with Tomas Kohn) a book of 30 case studies, with title *Strategic Management in Developing Countries* (Free Press, 1990, 691 pp.).

Baker, James C., John K. Ryans, Jr., and Donald G. Howard. *International Business Classics.* Lexington, MA: Lexington Books, 1988. 576 pp. paper.
This book brings together a good selection of what the authors have chosen as the 34 best articles written on international business. It is arranged in the following sections: multinational; cultural aspects of global business; business-government interactions of global operations; management and control of resources; exploring global markets; financial management; strategic planning. Such well known names as Root, Terpstra, and Vernon are among the authors.

Ball, Donald A., and Wendell H. McCulloch, Jr. *International Business: Introduction and Essentials.* 4th ed. Homewood, IL: BPI/Irwin, 1990. 774 pp.
A readable, practical, yet comprehensive introduction to international business. The first two of its four parts describe the nature of international business, and examine the international environment (organizations and the monetary system). With this as background, the authors next study the uncontrollable forces affecting international business with which its management must cope (financial, economic, physical, social, political, legal, labor, competition) and, finally, how management deals with these environmental forces (with chapters covering important functions of management). Interspersed throughout are boxed quotes from readings called "worldview"; also interesting anecdotes, examples, tables, diagrams, and marginal definitions. Supplementary reading lists and a mini-case are with chapters; a glossary and a list of "Sources of Economic and Financial Information" are at end of the book.

Bartlett, Christopher A., and Sumantra Ghoshal. *Managing Across Borders: The Transnational Solution.* Boston: Harvard Business School Press, 1989. 274 pp.

Bartlett and Ghoshal have based their book on a five-year worldwide research project that involved interviews with over 200 managers in 9 of the world's leading companies. Its "objective was to gain a rich undertanding of the organizational and administrative tasks facing managers in companies with worldwide operations in a time of major environmental change." They start by discussing the transnational challenge. With that as background they then focus first on characteristics of the transnational, and then on building and managing them. Copious notes and a bibliography at end point up the wide range of literature consulted for this study.

Business International Corporation. *Organizing for International Competitiveness: How Successful Corporations Structure Their Worldwide Operations.* New York: 1988. 119 pp.

This is an example of the various research reports BIC publishes that are based on studies of actual companies. Most are too short (about 100 pages) to treat a topic in great depth and most are overpriced for the individual or nonsubscribing company (prices usually range from $295 to $595). This one reports on how 11 successful companies organize their businesses for international competitiveness, and what organizational trends are most promising for the future. It includes data on how companies organize for specific functions, and it has some organizational diagrams.

Try locating a library near you that subscribes to BIC publications and services if you want to consult one or two of these expensive reports. Examples of several published in 1990 are: *Corporate Culture for Competitive Edge: A User's Guide; Managing for Global Excellence: Building the Total Quality Company; Marketing Strategies for Global Growth and Competitiveness; Successful Financial Strategies for the New Europe.*

Daniels, John D., and Lee H. Radebaugh. *International Business: Environments and Operations.* 6th ed. Reading, MA: Addison-Wesley, 1992. 805, [45] pp.

This text is meant for a first course in international business in an upper-level college course. As the subtitle indicates, it is written both from an environmental and an operational perspective, and it emphasizes the managerial viewpoint. The material is arranged in 7 parts: background; comparative environmental frameworks; theories and institutions—trade and investment; world financial environment; the dynamics of international business-governmental relationships; corporate policy and strategy; functional management, operations, and concerns. Useful features include: real-world examples; outline of major points in left margin; a short case at beginning and end of each chapter; bibliographical notes with chapters; a glossary at end of book.

Just published but not seen for comparison is a shorter book these authors wrote in the "Kent International Dimensions of Business Series" (see entry below) called *International Dimensions of Contemporary Business* (Boston: PWS-Kent Publishing Co., 1992, 214 pp.).

Doz, Yves. *Strategic Management in Multinational Companies.* New York: Pergamon, 1986. 243 pp. paper.

Based on extensive research of selected multinational companies in 6 industries, Professor Doz analyzes "the types of strategic choices and organizational capabilities that underly the success (or explain the failures) of MNCs in trading off needs for responsiveness and needs for integration. Success in managing such trade-offs [he says] is the key to MNC survival and success in the 1980s." This book is intended for practicing managers, policy makers, and students and so aims to be readable in style, avoiding abstractions and complex language.

Ferguson, Henry. *Tomorrow's Global Executive.* Homewood, IL: Dow Jones-Irwin, 1988. 265 pp.

Intended for the in-service executive or senior manager facing a new world of global competition, this book focuses on planning a market related global strategy and acquiring the attitudes and skills needed to execute it. Starting with the development of global strategies, Ferguson discusses in successive chapters the global executive as planner, motivator, operator, timer, communicator, researcher, networker, negotiator. Includes occasional useful checklists the author has used in seminars, and examples from his experience overseas especially in India. Lists of references and research organizations are at end.

Grub, Phillip D., Fariborz Ghadar and Dara Khambata, eds. *The Multinational Enterprise in Transition: Selected Readings and Essays.* 3d ed. Princeton, NJ: Darwin Press, 1986. 534 pp.

Forty-one leading observers of the multinational enterprise have contributed to this book whose objective it is to provide business executives and students "with a better understanding of the changing context in which business is conducted on a global basis." Its 31 chapters are arranged within 10 sections to focus on each management function and to explore governmental and political risk factors. This is the third revision of a basic selection of readings to supplement key texts in the field.

Harris, Philip R., and Robert T. Moran. *Managing Cultural Differences.* 3d ed. Houston: Gulf Publishing Company, 1991. 638 pp.

This book describes and studies high performance strategies and key insights that today's global managers need in order to understand, cooperate with, motivate, and lead people from diverse cultural backgrounds. It is organized into three major units: cultural impacts on global management; cultural impacts on international business; cultural specifics and business/service abroad (chapters covering each broad geographic area). The fourth unit consists of four appendixes containing instruments for data-gathering and analysis, surveys, and questionnaires. Incidents, case studies, self-assessment tools, figures, and tables appear throughout the book. A comprehensive bibliography is at end.

The Kent International Dimensions of Business Series. Boston: PWS-Kent Publishing Company.

This publisher's paperback series has been developed to offer supplemental material in business school courses on the international dimensions in specific functional areas of business, with each book written by a respected author in his/her field. There have been 10 books published as of mid-1992, and each title begins: *International Dimensions of. . . .* They cover: *Accounting* (3d ed., by D.D. AlHashim and J.S. Arpan, 1992, 252 pp.); *Business Policy and Strategy* (2d ed., by J. Garland, R.N. Farmer and Marilyn Taylor, 1990, 235 pp.); *Contemporary Business* (by John D. Daniels and Lee H. Radebaugh, 1992, 214 pp.); *Financial Management* (2d ed., by W.R. Folks, Jr., and R. Aggarwal, 1988, 239 pp.); *Human Resource Management* (by P.J. Dowling and R.S. Schuler, 1990, 256 pp.); *Information Systems and Technology* (by P. Candace Deans and Michael J. Kane, 1992, 196 pp.); *The Legal Environment of Business* (2d ed., by M. Litka, 1991, 246 pp.); *Management* (2d ed., by A. Phatak, 1992, 235 pp.); *Marketing* (2d ed., by V. Terpstra, 1988, 185 pp.); and *Organizational Behavior* (2d ed., by N. J. Adler, 1991, 313 pp.).

Kolde, Endel-Jakob. *Environment of International Business.* 2d ed. Boston: Kent Publishing Co., 1985. 528 pp.

Professor Kolde offers here a text devoted exclusively to an analysis of environmental factors in international business. He has structured the book "according to the primary sources of problems confronting international business: trade and payments systems, issues and ideas of North-South dialogue, the contrasts and accommodations between the communist East and the capitalist West, the multinationalization of business enterprises, the sociocultural heterogeneities impacting on international business, international integration and the rise of supranational economic systems, and the assimilation of international expertise into administrative professions." Suggested readings are at end of each of its 8 parts.

Leontiades, James C. *Multinational Corporate Strategy.* Lexington, MA: Lexington Books, 1985. 228 pp.

This book aims "to apply the latest methods and techniques [as of 1985] of corporate strategy to the special situation of multinational firms, and the emphasis is on the relationship of the firm to its external environment. It is organized around two levels of strategic analysis (in parts 2 and 3): strategy at the regional global level (with chapters on international portfolio strategy, as well as on competitive, marketing, and logistics strategy); strategy at the national level (including appraisal of new national environments, entry strategy, new product introduction, and political assessment). Part 4 examines methods of coordinating strategy across national borders. Bibliographical "notes" are at end. The stimulus for this book stems from Professor Leontiades' teaching at the Manchester Business School in England, but it will also be of value to business persons involved in international markets.

Porter, Michael E. *The Competitive Advantage of Nations.* New York: Free Press, 1990. 855 pp.

Professor Porter has concentrated much of his research on competitive strategy. Two earlier bestselling books are described in Chapter 10's section on strategic planning. In this his latest research study he investigates why nations gain competitive advantage in particular industries and the implications for company strategy and for national economies. His research was carried on over a four-year period and involved over 30 researchers, many of whom were based in one of the 10 important nations he studied. The book is in four parts: foundations (which presents his theory and an overview of the project); industries (in which he applies his theory to explain the histories of four representative industries); nations (where he applies the theory to the 10 nations studied); and finally, implications of the theory for company strategy and for government policy. Appendixes contain supplementary tables on national trade patterns. Notes and a bibliography are at the end.

An earlier book edited by Professor Porter is *Competition in Global Industries* (Boston, MA: Harvard Business School Press, 1986, 581 pp.). These are papers presented at a Colloquium held at Harvard in April 1984, and "its central focus is on the problems of international competition in industries and on the ways a firm can configure and coordinate its international activities in order to gain a competitive advantage over domestic and foreign rivals."

Robock, Stefan H., and Kenneth Simmonds. *International Business and Multinational Enterprises.* 4th ed. Homewood, IL: Irwin, 1989. 826 pp.

This excellent introductory, graduate-level text is the result of the authors' long experience in teaching international business courses and their aim to write a book for relatively advanced students that both challenges intellectually and that focuses on the development of management skills in handling the problems of multinational business. Its 6 principal sections follow a logical progression: the nature and scope of international business; the framework for international transactions; global business strategy; the nation-state and international business; multinational operations management; emerging issues. Part 7 contains cases and problems. Although there is no bibliography, the extensive footnotes will be a helpful aid to more extensive research. There are also a few quotations from other sources set off in boxes.

Ronen, Simcha. *Comparative and Multinational Management.* New York: Wiley, 1986. 636 pp.

The purpose of this text is "to heighten the awareness of managers and students of organizations to the complexity of operating in other cultures and in unfamiliar nations." To accomplish this Professor Ronen has divided his material into three parts. The first discusses background considerations, and the second, the various attitudinal and behavioral differences. The last section on managing the MNC includes chapters discussing environmental considerations, design and process, subsidiary-host country relations, and staffing the MNC foreign subsidiary. A bibliography is at end of book.

Vernon, Raymond. *Storm Over the Multinationals: The Real Issues.* Cambridge, MA: Harvard University Press, 1977. 260 pp.

This book is intended as the capstone volume for the 12-year Multinational Enterprise Project at the Harvard Business School. Professor Vernon attempts "to filter out the polemic and the propaganda" and to summarize and interpret the state of knowledge on the international spread of large enterprises. He draws heavily on the substantive research conducted both by him and his colleagues, and his book includes useful bibliographical notes at end.

The aim of the large-scale Multinational Enterprise Project was to identify the problems of U.S.-based multinational enterprises in the fields of finance, organization, production, marketing, and business-government relations, and also to explore the effects on international trade, capital movements, technology transfer, and nation states. Several of the more important books to come out of this project are: Professor Vernon's thought-provoking treatise, *Sovereignty at Bay: The Multinational Spread of U.S. Enterprises* (New York: Basic Books, 1971, 326 pp.); *Managing the Multinational Enterprise: Organization of the Firm and Ownership of the Subsidiaries* by John M. Stopford and Louis T. Wells, Jr. (New York: Basic Books, 1972, 223 pp.); *Money in the International Enterprise: A Study of Financial Policy* by Sidney M. Robbins and Robert B. Stobaugh (Basic Books, 1973, 231 pp.); *The European Multinationals* by Lawrence G. Franko (New York: Harper & Row, 1976, 276 pp.). In addition there were three volumes providing tabulations of the substantial body of statistical data collected. Two are compiled by James W. Vaupel and Joan P. Curhan: *The Making of Multinational Enterprise: A Sourcebook of Tables Based on a Study of 187 Major U.S. Manufacturing Corporations* (1969) and *The World's Multinational Enterprises: A Sourcebook of Tables Based on a Study of the Largest U.S. and non-U.S. Manufacturing Corporations* (1973), both now distributed by the Harvard University Press. The third statistical volume continues the data in the first volume through 1975, and it is *Tracing the Multinationals: A Sourcebook on U.S.-Based Enterprises,* by Joan P. Curhan, William H. Davidson and Rafan Suri (Cambridge, MA: Ballinger, 1977, 430 pp.). In the course of its 11 years, this Multinational Enterprise Project produced 21 books, 11 doctoral dissertations, and some 168 articles.

Vernon-Wortzel, Heidi V., and Lawrence H. Wortzel, eds. *Global Strategic Management: The Essentials.* 2d ed. New York: Wiley, 1991. 545 pp. paper.
This is a good selection of readings which the editors have put together as "the 'essentials'—the ideas, concepts, techniques, and knowledge that provide the best possible base for strategic management in a global environment." The 38 selections are arranged in 8 parts to cover, first, strategic planning, competitive analysis, and the political environment. This is followed by sections devoted to each of five basic management functional areas.

Wilkins, Mira. *The Emergence of Multinational Enterprise: American Business Abroad from the Colonial Era to 1914.* Cambridge, MA: Harvard University Press, 1970. 310 pp. And a later volume: *The Maturing of Multinational Enterprise: American Business Abroad from 1914 to 1970* (Harvard Studies in Business History, 27). Harvard University Press, 1974. 590 pp.
An excellent two-volume comprehensive study of the history of American multinational enterprise from colonial times to 1970, carefully researched from published literature, archival records, and interviews with many businessmen. The author confines her study "to foreign investments by U.S. businessmen and business organizations which involved managerial responsibility, the possibility of a voice in management, and direct business purpose." Each book is an independent work, and each includes a lengthy bibliography and bibliographical notes.
More recently Professor Wilkins has completed an excellent, in-depth study of *The History of Foreign Investment in the United States to 1914* (Harvard University Press, 1989, 1,055 pp.). It is arranged in two parts with the first covering the years 1607–1874 and the second, 1875–1914. Because of the sheer quantity of the material, it is divided by industry. Copious bibliographical notes and a bibliography at end (over 350 pp.) attest to the research involved in this study.

INTERNATIONAL FINANCIAL MANAGEMENT

See also "Accounting for Multinational Enterprises" section in Chapter 12.

Handbooks

Aliber, Robert Z., ed. *The Handbook of International Financial Management.* Homewood, IL: Dow Jones-Irwin, 1989. 859 pp.
This handbook documents developments in national financial markets and discusses opportunities and challenges for corporate financial managers in the new international financial environment. The 27 chapters, written by a core of contributing authors, are arranged in four parts: financial markets and institutions—the players; regulatory practices—the rules; the management decisions (including such topics as currency risk management, evaluation of exchange-rate forecasts, capital investment and management in global business, financial innovation); the environment. Appendixes contain a few statistical tables from such sources as the IMF, and profiles of major international lending agencies.

Sweeny, Allen, and Robert Rachlin, eds. *Handbook of International Financial Management.* New York: McGraw-Hill, 1984. 1 volume (various pagings).

An earlier handbook with the same title as the one above, this one was written for practitioners by 21 practicing professionals, and it focuses on the specific skills, concepts, and techniques that must be employed by those in charge of financial management in global enterprises. Among its 19 chapters are those covering capital budget analysis, foreign acquisitions and mergers, licensing, auditing, performance evaluation, lease financing.

Books

Donaldson, J. A. *Corporate Currency Risk.* London: Financial Times Business Information Ltd., 1980. 121 pp. paper.
Donaldson offers a practical guide on foreign exchange exposure management written for corporations that need to use the foreign exchange market.

Eiteman, David K., and Arthur I. Stonehill. *Multinational Business Finance.* 5th ed. Reading, MA: Addison-Wesley, 1989. 679 pp. Sixth edition to be published in 1992.
An excellent and thorough book revised and updated as the field of international business finance has evolved. It identifies major trends and themes that continue to differentiate international financial management from its domestic counterpart, and it points up the importance of global integration of money and capital markets. The major sections cover: the international financial environment; foreign exchange risk management; capital markets and financing instruments; direct foreign investment decisions (including a chapter on political risk management); management of ongoing operations. The text presupposes a basic finance course and some knowledge of international economics. Bibliographies are at end of chapters; a glossary is at end of book.

Lessard, Donald R., ed. *International Financial Management: Theory and Application.* 2d ed. New York: Wiley, 1985. 594 pp.
Here are 34 readings selected in an effort to offer the best available treatments on both the positive and normative levels of those subjects most relevant to international financial management. Lessard arranges these within four parts: the first two deal primarily with the positive theory, the last two with the normative theory. These latter parts focus on the tactical aspects and on investment and long-term finance. Most of the selections (by over 30 authors) are new to this edition and were chosen because they "lie on the frontier of international financial management."

Rodriguez, Rita M., and E. Eugene Carter. *International Financial Management.* 3d ed. Englewood Cliffs, NJ: Prentice-Hall, 1984. 638 pp.
In this latest edition of an upper-level text, the authors have reduced their emphasis on balance of payments and international capital markets, and expanded their discussion of treasury management in the multinational firm. Part 1 still focuses on the international financial environment; part 2 discusses major problems encountered by firms in financing large international operations; while part 3 covers issues associated with capital budgeting and foreign investment. There is a mix of theory, practice and institutional description in this text. A few exercises or cases are with some chapters; short bibliographies are with each chapter; a glossary and present value tables are at end of book.

Shapiro, Alan C. *Multinational Financial Management.* 4th ed. Boston: Allyn and Bacon, 1992. 729pp.

Another advanced text covering all the traditional areas of corporate finance, this one is well-written "from the perspective of a multinational corporation, concentrating on those decision elements that are rarely, if ever, encountered by purely domestic firms." These "elements" include multiple currencies, differing tax systems, multiple money markets, exchange control, political risks, and more. The book is arranged in 6 sections. Bibliographies accompany chapters; a few chapters have appendixes containing more technical material; one or more cases are at end of each part; a glossary is at end. This book presumes knowledge of basic corporate finance, economics, and algebra.

Professor Shapiro has written a shorter version called *Foundations of Multinational Financial Management* (Allyn and Bacon, 1991, 600 pp.) providing students and practitioners with a readable text on the essentials. He has also recently revised his *International Corporate Finance* (2d ed., Cambridge, MA: Ballinger, 1988, 211 pp.). This is intended as a short, readable survey and synthesis for corporate executives and professional investors to give them a conceptual framework within which they can develop financial policies appropriate for a multinational firm.

Venedikian, Harry M., and Gerald A. Warfield. *Export-Import Financing.* 3d ed. New York: Wiley, 1992. 469 pp.

Another revision and update of Gerhard Schneider's standard book (1974) covering all aspects of foreign trade financing, and including the latest changes in market conditions and regulations. It is arranged in the same three parts: first, discussing facilities, institutions and services involved and how they interact; then how transactions are executed, including the role of foreign exchange and techniques for hedging; and lastly, the tools, techniques, and vehicles for financing international trade, from letters of credit to bankers' acceptances. The final chapter covers "recent innovations." Supplementary data in appendixes include the text of the Export Trading Company Act of 1982.

POLITICAL AND FINANCIAL RISK ASSESSMENT

In today's turbulent world there is an emerging function within international companies and banks whose purpose it is to study, monitor, and predict the political and financial risk involved in investing in or operating in specific countries. Interest in this new corporate concern is beginning to be reflected in the number of books, studies, services, and articles being written on the topic. Following are a few relatively recent books, two expensive country risk services, and two semiannual country risk rankings published in periodicals.

Global Risk Assessments: Issues, Concepts & Applications. Ed by Jerry Rogers. Riverside, CA: Global Risk Assessments, Inc.

This is a book series of original articles "intended to advance understanding of the international business environment assessment and management field" and also to serve as a forum for cross-talk among professionals. Begun in 1983, articles can be either theoretical or issues oriented, and a new volume is published about every two years. Book 3 (1988) contains 14 articles, many of which report on actual developments, processes, and reflections of professionals working with political risk issues on a day-to-day basis.

Kobrin, Stephen J. *Managing Political Risk Assessment: Strategic Response to Environmental Change.* Berkeley: University of California Press, 1982. 224 pp.

Kobrin feels that political risk assessment is an emerging managerial function. As this title indicates, his book "focuses on the management of political risk assessment. It explores, both theoretically and analytically, such topics as the relationship between a business firm and its environment, the development of organizational structures to facilitate effective assessment and their institutionalization, communication between staff groups and line managers, and the use of assessments in planning and decision making. It deals with the fundamental issues of organizational response, strategically and structurally, to environmental change." His approach is interdisciplinary, applied, and exploratory, and he uses as a basis for his study a questionnaire survey of U.S.-based international firms and selected follow-up interviews. References to published literature appear throughout the book, and a useful bibliography is at end. "Political Risk Assessment Methods" in use as of 1982 are discussed briefly in an appendix.

Krayenbuehl, Thomas E. *Country Risk: Assessment and Monitoring.* Lexington, MA: Lexington Books, 1985. 180 pp.

Written by a Swiss bank official, the aim of his book is to offer guidance to international lending officers or investors on how better to assess and monitor country risk, and how to understand the complexities and endless number of factors involved in cross-border lending and investing. It begins with an overview and then considers, first, "assessment of country risk" (with one of its chapters describing several country risk ratings services), and then "monitoring of country risk." A final part discusses the outlook for financing and lending. A bibliography is at end.

Raddock, David M. *Assessing Corporate Political Risk: A Guide for International Businessmen.* Totawa, NJ: Rowman & Littlefield, 1986. 212 pp.

Raddock actually wrote only the first of four parts in this guide, which discusses questions he feels the international business person needs to know in assessing political stability and economic integrity. The other three parts are written by contributors and consist of: five country studies; approaches to devising methodologies and models (the bootstrapping approach, and the Frost and Sullivan method); suggestions for financial structuring against risk and political risk insurance.

A more specialized book that focuses primarily on a political risk service called "Business Environment Risk Information" (BERI), developed by its author, is *Country Risk Assessment: Theory and Worldwide Practice* by Professor F. T. Haner with John S. Ewing as collaborator (New York: Praeger, 1985, 329 pp.).

Country Risk Services

These are two expensive services intended for large international companies who may need outside help in monitoring the international political and financial environment. Persons interested in investigating these services in more detail should contact the publishers for more details and current information on prices. Others may find the short rankings that follow these services to be adequate for a broad assessment of the creditworthiness of countries.

Economist Intelligence Unit. *Country Risk Service.* New York: Business International (quarterly). Also available online.

An expensive service intended primarily for banks and large corporations that are lending, trading or investing in developing and indebted countries and so need to assess these countries' creditworthiness. This service covers 73 countries (including 7 in Eastern Europe), with each country report updated quarterly. The reports provide a brief assessment of recent political and economic developments, prospects for the coming two years, and external financing requirements (each is usually about 15 to 18 pages in length including 5 pages of statistical tables). One can subscribe on a country-by-country basis with the minimum order being 7 countries ($3,510 as of 1991, and each subsequent report costing $312). The publisher also offers a quarterly *Risk Ratings Review* ($4,400 alone, or provided at no change with a minimum order). The EIU is a division of Business International.

Political Risk Services. *World Country Report Service.* Syracuse, NY. 7 volumes, loose-leaf.

This is another expensive service ($5,750 in 1990) consisting of 85 country reports of about 50 pages per report, each giving key political, economic, and forecast data of interest to companies operating abroad. They are updated on a rotating basis, with subscribers also receiving a monthly "Political Risk Letter" and other consultation benefits. The publisher also offers a *Political Risk Yearbook* to academic libraries ($1,000), consisting of the 7 volumes with no updates. Companies needing outside help in monitoring the international political environment should contact PRS for further information.

Each year two directors of PRS (William D. Coplin and Michael K. O'Leary) write a short article covering a "World Political Risk Forecast" for the *Planning Review* which includes a "Political Risk & Economic Forecast Chart" for some 85 countries (e.g. issue for January/February 1991).

Country Financial Risk Rankings

Euromoney. "Country Risk" ratings (annual in September issue).
Rankings are based on public sector syndicated loans.

Institutional Investor. International Edition. "Country Credit Ratings" (semi-annual in March and October issues).
I.I.'s rankings are based on surveys from leading international bankers concerning their estimates of the creditworthiness of each country.

Planning Review. "World Political Risk Forecast." (annual, e.g. January/February 1991 issue).
This includes a "Political Risk & Economic Forecast Chart" which forecasts key risk factors for some 85 countries.

INTERNATIONAL MARKETING

Albaum Gerald et al. *International Marketing and Export Management.* Reading, MA: Addison-Wesley, 1989. 407 pp.
A book that studies export management, with exporting viewed as involving marketing processes and activities. Consequently it contains chapters on the various elements of the marketing mix as well as export-based entry modes and channels. It is not a manual of the procedural aspects of exporting but rather a text oriented toward understanding the management of export operations and decision making,

and it is directed toward practices of small and medium-sized firms. Several case studies are with each chapter; also short bibliographies.

Cateora, Philip R. *International Marketing.* 7th ed. Homewood, IL: Irwin, 1990. 870 pp.

This latest edition of a comprehensive and much-used text reflects businesses' changing orientation from international marketing to a more encompassing global marketing view. It still focuses on the planning and strategic problems confronting companies that market across cultural boundaries, while also considering the effects of increased competition. It is in five parts: an overview; the cultural environment of global marketing; global marketing management (covers such topics as planning, researching, developing advertising and promotion, personal selling and personnel management, pricing, distribution system, logistics); corporate context of marketing (financing, coordinating, and control); cases. Interesting boxed notes taken from other sources are scattered throughout the text. A bibliography is at end. A shorter version of an earlier edition, written for the executive, is *Strategic International Marketing* (Dow Jones-Irwin, 1985, 428 pp.).

Cundiff, Edward W., and Marye T. Hilger. *Marketing in the International Environment.* 2d ed. Englewood Cliffs, NJ: Prentice-Hall, 1988. 608 pp.

Another textbook in which the authors say they "have emphasized examples, concepts, coordinating, and relationships that are essential to planning, executing, and controlling marketing strategy from a multinational or international point of view." The five-part arrangement covers: an introduction and background; the environment for international marketing; management tools; building international strategy (pricing, promotion, product, and distribution strategy); strategic planning and control. Appendixes contain: an outline for an international marketing plan; a compendium of secondary sources of information; a glossary; a "diary" of an export shipment. At end of each chapter is usually a concise reading and two case applications.

Gordon, John S., and Jack R. Arnold. *Profitable Exporting: A Complete Guide to Marketing Your Products Abroad.* New York: Wiley, 1988. 358 pp.

Here is a step-by-step guide on how to enter and succeed in the export marketplace for managers and owners of small- to medium-sized companies who have had no special background in the export business. It begins by helping you to identify your export potential and to establish yourself in the marketplace; then it discusses each aspect such as transportation, insurance, finance, legal requirements, exporting to specific countries. Appendixes contain lists of agencies, organizations, embassies of interest to U.S. exporters; also a glossary and short list of reference books.

An alternate guide is *The Marketer's Guide to Selling Products Abroad* by Robert E. Weber (New York: Quorum Books, 1989, 258 pp.) which is arranged in three parts: deciding to export; handling documentation; marketing abroad (this latter includes chapters on product servicing, advertising, patents, trademarks, political risks, foreign trade fairs, traveling the territory). It also has useful appendixes. Some persons may want to see a shorter but still handy step-by-step guide published by the federal government in cooperation with Federal Express Corp. The title is *A Basic Guide to Exporting* (1992 edition, Washington, DC: U.S. Department of Commerce, 1992, 1 volume, various pagings; paper). This guide is full of helpful information for the small business person interested in getting into exporting, and it includes appendixes containing an export glossary, lists of federal, state, and local sources for assistance, and a short selected bibliography of reference sources.

Haar, Jerry, and Marta Ortiz-Buonafina. *Import Marketing: A Management Guide to Profitable Operations.* Lexington, MA: Lexington Books, 1989. 230 pp.

While the preceding book is intended to help U.S. exporters, this one is a guide for U.S. importers and foreign exporters who want to understand the U.S. market and the fundamentals of importing. It begins with an overview of the international monetary environment, and then offers a step-by-step guide to import-marketing strategy and the import function. A bibliography is at end.

Jain, Subhash C., and Lewis R. Tucker, Jr. *International Marketing: Managerial Perspectives.* 2d ed. Boston: Kent Publishing Company, 1986. 466 pp. paper.

A selection of 27 readings on international marketing strategy that blend theory and application, 5 of which are new to this edition. They are arranged in 8 sections including: the nature and environment of international marketing; analysis of foreign market opportunities; selections on strategies as they relate to the product, pricing, distribution, promotion; planning and implementing marketing programs. Selected references are at end.

Among Professor Jain's other books is a textbook on *International Marketing Management* (3d ed., Boston: PWS-Kent Publishing Co., 1990, 758 pp.), and a book on *Export Strategy* (New York: Quorum Books, 1989, 253 pp.), which outlines for marketing and strategic planning executives a step-by-step procedure for formulating a successful export strategy.

Kaynak, Erdener. *The Management of International Advertising: A Handbook and Guide for Professionals.* New York: Quorum Books, 1989. 284 pp.

Here is a guide to the theory and practice of international advertising which the author says could serve either as a handbook, a reference work, or a textbook. The material is arranged in 7 chapters beginning with a conceptual framework on marketing and advertising planning in global markets. The other chapters cover: the development of multinational advertising strategy; comparative advertising systems; cross-cultural and cross-national advertising practices in unlikely environments; internationalization of advertising agencies; advertising and development; legal restraints. Diagrams and other tables appear throughout. References are at end of chapters and in a bibliography at end of the book.

Keegan, Warren J. *Global Marketing Management.* 4th ed. Englewood Cliffs, NJ: Prentice-Hall, 1989. 783 pp.

Another often-cited text which attempts to introduce students and practitioners to a systematic treatment of marketing on a global scale. Professor Keegan starts with a conceptual overview of the world market environment. From this he focuses in turn on: analyzing the global marketing environment; formulating multinational marketing strategies (decisions on product, pricing, channel, promotion); the overall process of planning, organizing, and controlling a multinational marketing program. Usually one case study and a bibliography are with each chapter.

Root, Franklin R. *Entry Strategies for International Markets.* Lexington, MA: Lexington Books, 1987. 269 pp.

Addressed primarily to all company managers actively interested in pursuing international market opportunities, here is a book that "focuses on three fundamental questions: (1) How should managers decide which international markets to enter, if any? (2) How should managers decide their mode of international market entry? (3) How should managers decide their international marketing plans—their product, channel, price, and promotion strategies?" Professor Root uses an entry-planning model which identifies key decisions and their relationships, and this model serves to structure the entire book. Useful checklists, tables, and boxed excerpts from other sources are used throughout; supplementary readings are listed at end of chapters. This is a revised and updated version of a book published in 1982 as *Foreign Market Entry Strategies.*

Terpstra, Vern, and Ravi Sarathy. *International Marketing.* 5th ed. Chicago: Dryden Press, 1991. 714 pp.

Professor Terpstra's text (now with a co-author) covers the whole range of international marketing involvement from small exporters to multinationals, focusing on the problems and decisions facing managers in this regard. The latest edition has been extensively revised to cover the contemporary environment, and these increased problems/challenges, emphasizing the importance of linking international marketing with the overall strategy of the firm. The material is still arranged within three parts: international environment; international marketing management (this is the major part of the book, and it follows the format used in general marketing texts); coordinating international marketing. Several short cases and lists of further readings are with most chapters. A folded world map is inserted.

Thorelli, Hans, and S. Tamer Cavusgil, eds. *International Marketing Strategy.* 3d ed. New York: Pergamon, 1990. 640 pp. paper.

Most of the 50 readings (arranged within 7 parts) are new to this latest edition, but they still aim to be a selection of the best material available. The editors have focused on selections with managerial applications which they hope will be of equal use to executives and students. Some are case studies of actual successes or failures in international marketing, and some discuss industries or companies located outside of North America. Lists of further readings are with each part. A short list of general books is at the end along with a glossary and several useful indexes.

INTERNATIONAL BUSINESS BIBLIOGRAPHIES

Most of the bibliographies on this subject are either too old to include here, or they are all-inclusive computer-produced lists with no descriptive annotations and only what I call a "blind" subject index which makes them a nuisance to use effectively and easily. However, attention is called to the suggested readings in many texts, especially those in the more recently published books. See also bibliographies of foreign economic and business statistics sources listed in Chapter 6. The index following lists only the publications of one publisher.

Business International. *Publications Index.* New York (annual).

This index is available to subscribers and covers information in BI periodicals, research reports, and reference services as well as in the basic publications of the Economist Intelligence Unit (now a division of BI). It is arranged by country, after first indexing citations that are worldwide in scope. A descriptive list of BI/EIU publications is at front.

BI research reports and other publications are usually short studies of practical interest to firms actively concerned with foreign management and markets. Many persons will find them too expensive to purchase, but possibly they can be located in a large business library that subscribes. Several examples of recent research reports are cited in the "International Management" section of this chapter. BI periodicals and their two important reference services are described elsewhere in this chapter. For other BI and EIU publications listed in this book, check in my index at end.

DICTIONARIES

Herbst, Robert, and Alan G. Readett. *Dictionary of Commercial, Financial, and Legal Terms.* 4th ed. Thun, Switzerland: Translegal, Ltd., 1989. 3 volumes.

A multilingual dictionary covering a wide range of commercial/financial/legal terms in three languages. They were revised over a period of years, with: vol.1 (English/German/French), the 4th edition; vol.2 (German/English/French), the 4th ed., revised and enlarged; and vol.3 (French/English/German), the 2d ed., revised and enlarged. It does not give definitions but only the names of each term in the other languages, and so it is designed more for exporter/importers, bankers, accountants, lawyers, and others who want to translate a specific term or phrase.

Hoogvelt, Ankie (Anthony G. Puxty, collaborator). *Multinational Enterprise: An Encyclopedic Dictionary of Concepts and Terms.* New York: Nichols Publishing Co., 1987. 261 pp. Published originally in the U.K.

First attempt at a dictionary of terms and concepts covering all the dimensions of the multinational enterprise. Useful definitions are usually longer than just one paragraph, and there are numerous cross-references. A selected bibliography and list of references are at end.

Presner, Lewis A. *The International Business Dictionary and Reference.* New York: Wiley, 1991. 486 pp.

This is an excellent, comprehensive dictionary of over 1,500 terms aiming to give an "accurate cross-disciplinary interpretation of the vocabulary of international business." Its explanations are well-written and often include useful examples. Cross-references are plentiful. Extensive appendixes provide: lists of international information sources and organizations; geographic reference guides of key terms specific to one region; topical reference guides for foreign language key terms; and international law key terms. A bibliography at end lists sources used.

Walmsley, Julian. *A Dictionary of International Finance.* 2d ed. New York: Wiley, 1985. 222 pp.

Simple yet useful definitions of English-language terms, organizations, and acronyms on international finance, trade, banking, and related topics such as the futures and options markets. There are frequent cross-references and usually a bibliographical citation following each entry for persons interested in pursuing a definition in more depth. Mr. Walmsley is a British foreign exchange expert.

TAX AND TRADE GUIDES FOR SPECIFIC COUNTRIES

Bureau of National Affairs. *International Trade Reporter: Export Shipping Manual.* Washington, DC. 3 volumes (loose-leaf).

A compendium of useful shipping facts concerning nearly 200 countries. Included are such facts as: ports and shipping routes, government and business information offices, principal imports and exports, time differential, holidays, tariff system, import and exchange controls, documents needed, shipping/labeling/packing details, postal rates, warehousing, travel requirements, and more. Export reference data at back of volume 3 contains communications rates, weights and measures, free trade zones, embassies and consulates, data on export controls.

Business International Corporation. *Investing, Licensing & Trading Conditions Abroad.* New York (loose-leaf service, with monthly supplements). This is a regularly updated but expensive service ($1,595 per year as of 1991) to help busy executives decide about investing in, licensing in, or exporting to the world's major countries. For each of about 50 countries, these analyses usually give current information on the state's role in industry, organizing for foreign investments, rules of competition, price controls, licensing, remittability of funds, corporate and personal taxes, incentives, capital sources, labor, foreign trade.

Commerce Clearing House. *Doing Business in Europe.* Chicago. 2 volumes (loose-leaf).

For each European country this service contains legal information on foreign investment, forms of business, investment and finance, tax system, business incentives, employment law, property (including patents and trademark law), competitive rules, arbitration procedures, environmental rules, court systems. There is also brief introductory data on the political structure of the country, the economy and economic development, sources of the country's law. This volume can be purchased separately or as part of the CCH *Common Market Reporter* described in the following section.

Coopers & Lybrand. *International Tax Summaries: A Guide for Planning and Decisions.* New York: Wiley (annual).

Revised and updated annually, this is an overview of the tax systems of 105 countries in which Coopers & Lybrand has accounting offices. Each country chapter runs from 10 to 15 pages and covers income tax laws on individuals, corporations, and nonresidents; each has a short specimen tax computation. The whole volume is over 1,000 pages in length.

Diamond, Walter H. *Foreign Tax and Trade Briefs.* New York: Matthew Bender & Co. 2 volumes (loose-leaf).

Basic data on taxation and trading laws and information for the principal countries of the world where American capital is frequently invested.

Europa World Year Book. London: Europa Publications. 2 volumes (annual). Distributed in the U.S. by Gale Research, Inc.

An important international encyclopedia, with vol.1 covering information on international organizations, plus countries from Afghanistan to Jordan; and vol.2 devoted to all other countries (Kenya to Zimbabwe). The kinds of data provided for each country usually include: recent history, economic affairs, basic economic statistics, constitution, government, political parties, diplomatic representation, judicial system, religion; also lists of leading newspapers, periodicals, publishers, radio & TV, banks, insurance companies, trade and industrial organizations, trade fairs, railroads, shipping firms, tour organizations.

Europa also publishes 6 regional yearbooks: *Africa South of the Sahara; The Far East and Australasia; The Middle East and North Africa; South America, Central America, and the Caribbean; The USA and Canada; Western Europe.*

These give much the same sort of directory information as well as concise data about the geography, the government, basic economic statistics, and a "Who's Who" section for information on prominent people in the countries covered by each yearbook.

Prentice-Hall, Inc. *U.S. Taxation of International Operations.* Englewood Cliffs, NJ. 1 volume (loose-leaf, semimonthly).

Analyses written by leading international tax practitioners to give practical ideas and techniques for tax-savings programs both for U.S. corporations and for American citizens operating and/or investing abroad. The principal sections are: tax ideas; planning; operations.

Price Waterhouse. *Information Guide* Series. New York: The Company.

Most of the guides in this series are on "Doing Business in" over 60 countries where Price Waterhouse has offices; most are over 100 pages in length and are revised frequently. Each usually covers data on the investment climate, doing business (exchange controls, regulatory agencies, business entities, labor relations, etc.), audit and accounting, taxation practices. A few guides are on more general topics such as "Corporate Taxes" in over 80 countries (biennial); "Individual Taxes: A Worldwide Summary" (annual); "Foreign Exchange Information: A Worldwide Summary" (annual); "U.S. Citizens Abroad" (annual).

U.S. International Trade Administration, Dept. of Commerce. *Overseas Business Reports.* Washington, DC: U.S. Government Printing Office.

A series of reports for about 100 countries. Most of the recent ones have the title "Marketing in (name of country)." These usually contain brief information on industry trends, foreign trade outlook, transportation and utilities, distribution and sales channels, advertising and research, credit, trade regulations, investment, shipping documents, taxation, labor and employment, guidance for business travelers, sources of economic and commercial information, market profile.

REFERENCE DATA FOR EXPORTERS

Bureau of National Affairs. *International Trade Reporter.* Washington, DC. 5 volumes (a weekly service). Full text of current developments is also available online.

The "Weekly Reports" (2 volumes) cover the latest international trade developments and changing regulations. Supplementary to this is a 2 volume "Reference File" which contains an analysis of all import laws, plus fully-indexed texts of import statutes, regulations, Executive Orders, forms, and lists; and also a "Decisions Binder" including digests and full text of judicial and administrative decisions in major fields of import law. Their *Export Shipping Manual* is described in the previous section.

Business International Corporation. *Financing Foreign Operations.* New York. 2 volumes (loose-leaf, with semimonthly supplements).

Part 3 covers domestic financing for each of about 38 countries that lend funds, and it includes information on currency considerations, foreign exchange regulations, the monetary system, sources of capital, short-term financing techniques, medium- and long-term financing, equity financing, capital incentives, cash management, short-term investment instruments, trade financing, and insurance. Part 1 discusses general techniques for international financing; Part 2 deals with cross-border sources of financing. A two-page bimonthly update called "Financial News Bulletin" gives brief current data for some countries. At end of volume 2 is an "Interest Rate & Foreign Exchange Rate Updater."

Commerce Clearing House. *Common Market Reporter.* Chicago. 4 volumes (loose-leaf).

Three volumes of this service provide information on the pertinent laws, regulations, rulings, and court decisions needed to guide firms doing business in Common Market countries. The fourth volume (volumes are not numbered), *Doing Business in Europe,* is described in the previous section.

Euromoney International Finance Yearbook. London: Euromoney Publications.

A reference source on international finance, combining some statistical data with authoritative comment and reference material on all important sectors and disciplines. In part 1 senior bankers in 13 principal centers analyze their current state of business; part 2 consists of "sector reviews" for 9 sectors such as debt management, equity funding, mergers and acquisitions; part 3, "Economic and Financial Data," contains 4-year statistical tables, including foreign exchange rates, interest rates, financial futures' rates.

Exporters' Encyclopaedia. Parsippany, NJ: Dun & Bradstreet Information Services (annual, with semimonthly supplements).

A comprehensive world marketing reference guide in 6 sections. Section 2, "Export Markets," comprises the major part of this guide, giving the following important market information for specific countries: country profile (including such items as population, language, currency, banks, weights & measures, metric requirements for import, electric current); communications data (including postal information); key contacts (such as consulates, embassies, chambers of commerce); trade regulations; documentation for shipping; marketing data (regulations and agreements); transportation (data on foreign trade zones, air cargo service, shipping information, ports, sailings); business travel (passport regulations, hotels, holidays, travel hints). Other shorter sections in this guide contain: general export information; communications (including postal regulations and rates); government agencies and organizations that are information sources; transportation data (important facts about U.S. ports and trade zones). Semimonthly *Updates* contain changes. There is also a separate volume, *Export Documentation Handbook* (1986) consisting of "footnotes" on documentation required, issued to facilitate the work of exporters and forwarders.

Reference Book for World Traders. Queens Village, NY: Croner Publications, Inc. 3 volumes (loose-leaf, with monthly supplements).

This service is designed as a handy guide to information about foreign countries for persons in international trade and market research. Data for each country (in vols.2–3) includes facts about the climate, exchange rates, holidays, hotels, office hours, passports, religion, ports, and so forth; also lists of consulates and other information sources in the U.S., chambers of commerce, customs brokers and freight forwarders, associations, market research organizations, statistics sources, trade directories, periodicals that are trade oriented, and sometimes a short bibliography. Vol.1 contains export basics, organizations/publications, postal information, foreign exchange rates, shipping lines and airlines directories, U.S. ports, trade fairs (by industry), conversion tables, glossary of terms, and other useful data.

The Times Atlas of the World. 8th ed. New York: Times Books, 1990. 1 volume.

This atlas is especially good for its coverage of foreign countries.

U.S. Custom House Guide. Philadelphia: North American Publishing Co. (annual).

A basic reference volume in three parts. Part 1A, the "Ports Section," gives data for the principal U.S. ports (including names of customs and port authority officials, description of the port, directories of custom house brokers, foreign freight forwarders, foreign trade zones, steamship lines and agents, truckmen, warehouses, and so forth). At end of part 1 are lists of: embassies and legations, airlines, common carriers, U.S. foreign-trade zones. Part 2 contains the complete *Harmonized Tariff Schedule of the United States* annotated, a classified schedule of imported commodities giving current rates of duty for each, with an alphabetical index to the import commodities; part 3 has U.S. Customs regulations, with appendix and index. Received with this volume is a monthly *Global Trade* which contains short articles and news on high-volume shipping and related services of interest to importers, exporters, brokers, and forwarders.

U.S. International Trade Commission. *Harmonized Tariff Schedule of the United States Annotated.* Washington, DC: U.S. Government Printing Office (issued irregularly, with supplementary sheets).

A classified list of import commodities, giving rates of duty for each. An alphabetical index is at end.

The ITC has also published: (1) *The Tariff Schedules of the United States Converted into the Format of the Brussels Tariff Nomenclature* (U.S. Government Printing Office, 1975, 9 volumes), useful for comparative purposes because the BTN is the standardized product classification system used by most trading nations of the world; (2) *History of the Tariff Schedules of the United States Annotated* (U.S. Government Printing Office, 1981), a loose-leaf volume containing "the staged rates, amendments and modifications, and statistical notes" to the TSUSA.

U.S. Office of Export Administration. *Export Administration Regulations.* Washington, DC: U.S. Government Printing Office (annual, with irregular updates).

A loose-leaf service containing official export control regulations, with instructions, interpretations, and explanatory material. Current changes are announced in their *Export Administration Bulletin.*

J.P. Morgan & Company publishes a separate annual *World Holiday and Time Guide.*

INTERNATIONAL MANAGEMENT PERIODICALS

Asian Wall Street Journal. Hong Kong: Dow Jones Publishing Co. (daily). Also available online.

Format and coverage is similar to the American edition of the *Wall Street Journal,* for Asian business and financial news. Includes stock market prices, commodity futures, international debt issues, and other financial statistics. Indexed in PTS/F&S; full text on Dow-Jones. There is also an *Asian Wall Street Journal Weekly,* published in New York and containing weekly news.

Business America. Washington, DC: International Trade Administration, U.S. Department of Commerce (biweekly). Order from U.S. Government Printing Office.

Billed as "the magazine of international trade," this biweekly covers current news of interest to world traders on the U.S. economy and on international business. Each issue contains useful features such as "International Trade Exhibitions," listing Commerce Dept.-sponsored trade promotion events; a "Calendar for World Traders" listing meeting and seminars. Special issues include: an annual "World Trade Outlook" (mid-April) giving current economic trends and prospects for U.S. business around the world; lists of "World Commercial Holidays in (year)" and "World Trade Fair Schedule" for the next year (last December issue). Descriptions of "New Books and Reports" are in some issues. A quarterly compendium of statistical information called "Current International Trade Positions of the United States" are in an issue for March, June, September, December. Indexed in ABI/I, BPI, TI; also full text on BRS, DATA-STAR, DIALOG, DOW JONES, MEAD/NEXIS.

Business International. New York: Business International Corporation (weekly).

BI is an 8-page weekly report for managers of worldwide operations, providing current news and developments in marketing, finance, licensing, exporting, taxation, planning, government, and all other functional areas; also news about companies, checklists, and occasional statistical tables. Indexed in PTS/F&S.

BIC publishes similar periodic news reports for managers in particular geographic regions: *Business Asia; Business China* (bimonthly); *Business Eastern Europe; Business Europe; Business Latin America.* They also publish a weekly, *Business International Money Report,* an 8-page news sheet for the international financial executive providing news about changes in worldwide financial regulations, hedging and financing instruments, companies; also statistical tables such as monthly lists of exchange rates and interest rates for countries.

Columbia Journal of World Business. New York: Columbia Business School, Columbia University (quarterly).

This professional journal offers a good selection of serious articles on current events, issues, and trends of interest to anyone with responsibilities and interests in global business. Includes occasional book reviews. Indexed in ABI/I, BPI, PAIS, TI.

Corporate Finance (London). London: Euromoney Publications; U.S. subscriptions handled in New York by Reed Business Publishing (USA). (monthly).

A monthly intended for corporate financial executives and covering international financial techniques and markets. Each issue contains short feature articles plus special sections providing news about "deals & dealmakers," profiles of an industrial sector or a country. Occasionally there are supplements to specific issues, e.g. "Mergers, Acquisitions, Divestments" (December 1991 supplement). The October issue each year focuses on "Technology in Treasury Management."

Euromoney. London: Euromoney Publications, Ltd. (monthly). Also available online.

An informative magazine covering the world's capital and money markets, with good short articles and news about European money markets. Supplements with most issues focus on a specific country or financial topic. "Key Figures" in each issue include tables for interest rates, Salomon Brothers international bond market performance indices, the favored currencies, trade-weighted exchange rates from Smithsonian, secondary bond market turnover, futures and options, swap database. Special annual features, based on an examination of 1990 issues, include: "The Global Leaders in Mergers and Acquisitions" (February); "Annual Financing Report" (supplement to March issue) which contains ranked lists of top lead managers for Eurobonds, syndicated loans, commercial paper, international equities, by types of issue or currency; with similar ranked lists in "The Euromoney Global Financing Guide" (September); "Foreign Banks in London" (April); "Annual Foreign Exchange Review" (May); "The Euromoney 500," a ranked list of the world's largest banks (June); "The World's Top Money Managers" (July); "Latin America 100" banks (September); "The World's 100 Best Banks," and "The Asian 100" banks (December). Also of interest is "Euromoney Country Risk Ratings" (September) which ranks countries by loan risk. All in all this monthly has many useful features and issue supplements. Indexed in ABI/I, PTS/F&S, TI; full text on BRS, DATA-STAR, DIALOG, DOW JONES, MEAD/NEXIS.

Euromoney Publications issues three other more specialized monthly reviews: *Corporate Finance* (London), described above; *International Financial Law Review* which analyzes and monitors changes in the law as it applies to international financial transactions; *Trade Finance,* for news and trends in export, import, and project finance.

European Management Journal. Oxford: B. Blackwell (quarterly).

This quarterly aims to publish authoritative articles on any topic relating to management policies, strategies, and trends which focus on the European perspective. The authors are usually academics, with a few who are practitioners; their writing style tends to be such that managers using English as a second language will have no problems. It is sponsored jointly by the European School of Management and the Scottish Business School at the University of Glasgow. Includes reviews of "Books for Managers."

Finance & Development. Washington, DC: International Monetary Fund and the World Bank (quarterly).

Published in Arabic, French, Chinese, German, Portuguese, and Spanish editions as well as in English, this quarterly contains short articles on international finance and development. Each issue has a page of charts on the "World Economy in Transition." Includes book reviews. Indexed in ABI/I, BPI, PAIS; full text on DIALOG.

Financial Times. London (daily). Also available online, and on CD-ROM as of 1992.

An important British newspaper that provides worldwide coverage for business, financial, and economic news, including news of companies and some general news. Its useful financial tables for current stock prices and other figures are noted more fully in Chapter 8 in the section for United Kingdom investment sources. A separately published *Monthly Index to the Financial Times* (which cumulates annually) began in 1981. In addition there are several databases for information from this newspaper: *Financial Times Company Information Database* for abstracts of company and business news items; *Financial Times Currency and Share Index Database,* a time series for statistics on stocks, indexes, and so forth; and *Financial Times Fulltext* for complete text of all articles.

Global Finance. New York: Global Finance Joint Venture (monthly).

Usually four or five short, practical articles in each issue of interest to money managers and other global finance persons. Regular departments include those on corporate financing, international finance, technology, country weightings (for global equity portfolios); also "Global Trends" charts. The January 1989 issue contains tabular data on "The World's Principal Exchanges."

International Currency Review. London: World Reports (UK) Ltd. (bi-monthly).

Useful as a review of selected global currency-related economic and financial developments, with most of each issue containing "currency and country economic reviews" for each of the principal currencies. Indexed in PAIS.

The International Economy. Washington, DC: The International Economy Publications (bimonthly).

A new periodical (1987) on international economic policy intended for officials and banking executives who influence international economic policy making. It contains timely articles on a wide range of fiscal, political, and economic issues. Regular features include "Country Risk-Watch" and "Emerging Markets Scoreboard." Some issues contain book reviews.

International Financing Review. London: IFR Publishing Ltd. (weekly).

Current news and other important developments in international finance, international capital markets, etc. Much of each issue contains news about credit marketing in specific countries and specific bond markets. Statistics in each issue usually include figures on international bond issues, commercial paper & syndicated facilities, Eurobond rating. "The League Tables" (first January issue) have statistics for Eurobonds as does the "Half-Year League Tables" (first July). Another journal of this publisher, with articles on a wide range of topics, is *The Journal of International Securities Markets* (quarterly).

International Management. London: Reed Business Publishing Group (monthly).

Billed as "Europe's business magazine," this has short, timely articles of practical interest to all managers with operations in Europe. They cover a wide range of management topics, and include occasional profiles of companies or individuals. Features include a ranked list of "The Top 500 Industrial Companies" in European Community countries (April issue). Usually one book review is in each issue. Indexed in ABI/I, PTS/F&S, TI; full text on BRS, DATA-STAR, DIALOG.

International Monetary Fund. *IMF Survey*. Washington, DC (23/yr.).

This is a newsletter, with each issue usually containing brief information on IMF activities, news of economic and financial trends, and national economies. Includes varying statistical tables and a few charts. There are editions published in French and Spanish as well as in English. The IMF also publishes *Staff Papers* (4/yr) which contains lengthy staff research papers on international monetary policies and problems. Two useful IMF statistical publications are described in Chapter 5.

International Studies of Management & Organization. Armonk, NY: M.E. Sharpe, Inc. (quarterly).

For descriptive note see listing in Chapter 10.

JIBS: Journal of International Business Studies. Columbia, SC: Published jointly by the Academy of International Business and the University of South Carolina, College of Business Administration (quarterly).

A refereed journal that publishes primarily the results of significant basic or applied research in international or comparative business. Its authors are largely academicians, and its principal audience usually consists of scholars, researchers, and teachers. Most articles include footnotes or bibliographies. Each issue contains book reviews and also abstracts of doctoral dissertations. Indexed in ABI/I, BPI, PTS/F&S, PAIS, TI; full text on BRS, DATA-STAR, DIALOG.

Journal of International Economics. Amsterdam: Elsevier Publishers B.V. (quarterly).

This is "the principal outlet for analytical work in the pure theory of international trade and balance-of-payments analysis and also for institutional, empirical, and econometric work of high quality and general professional interest." Includes book reviews. Indexed in ABI/I, TI.

Journal of World Trade. Geneva: Werner Publishing Co. (6/yr).

Well-documented research papers of wide interest on international trade, monetary policies, antitrust policy, environmental problems, etc., from a legal, economic, public policy view. Includes occasional book reviews. Indexed in ABI/I, PAIS, TI.

Law and Policy in International Business. Washington, DC: Georgetown University Law Center (quarterly).

Scholarly articles on a broad range of topics, with a legal focus. Usually includes book notes and a book review. Indexed in ABI/I, PAIS.

Northwestern University School of Law publishes the *Northwestern Journal of International Law & Business* (3/yr.) which contains scholarly articles on the analysis of private international law.

Management International Review. Wiesbaden, Germany: Th. Gabler GmbH (quarterly).

This "journal of international business" is a refereed quarterly which aims to advance and disseminate international applied research in the fields of management and business policy, international business, and transnational corporations. Most of its articles are written by academic persons and include bibliographical references. Indexed in ABI/I, BPI.

Multinational Business. London: Economist Publications Ltd. (quarterly).

Usually there are three short articles in each issue on international management and the strategic aspects of decision-making for multinational executives, as well as regular columns, quarterly news of interest to the international business person, and occasional charts. A regular feature (grey pages) gives a summary of recent major "Acquisitions and Mergers." There are also notes about multinational management strategies, a literature review, legal roundup, quarterly currency focus. Indexed in ABI/I, PAIS.

World Financial Markets. New York: Morgan Guaranty Trust Company of New York (monthly).

An excellent financial newsletter (each issue about 20 pages in length), with an appendix giving up-to-date statistics, by country, for international bond issues and bank credits, central bank discount rates, money and money market rates, Treasury bill rates, commercial bank deposit rates, domestic government and corporate bond yields, commercial bank lending rates to prime borrowers; also tables for exchange rates, Eurocurrency deposit rates.

DIRECTORIES

Most directories of interest to the international business person are described elsewhere in this book. Chapter 7 includes directories of U.S. international and foreign companies as well as those listing foreign subsidiaries of U.S. companies. Several directories containing lists of foreign trade associations, universities, and other learned societies, and foreign periodicals are also covered in Chapter 7. Financial manuals covering foreign companies are described in Chapter 8; directories of foreign banks in Chapter 14; directories of foreign market research firms in Chapter 18. *Europa World Year Book,* an international encyclopedia described elsewhere in this chapter, includes for each country the names of chambers of commerce, trade associations, as well as banks, railways, shipping companies, and airlines. It also describes the most important international organizations.

American Export Register. New York: Thomas International Publishing Co. 2 volumes (annual).

Volume 1 and part of volume 2 list exporting companies by product line, giving for each only the address and telephone number. An alphabetical list of these companies in volume 2 also gives major products exported, market areas served, person in charge of export sales, cable address, telex, TWX, and fax numbers. The last half of volume 2 contains lists of: embassies, consulates, international chambers of commerce, world trade center clubs, local associations and government services relating to trade, banks, custom house brokers in the U.S., freight forwarders, air cargo carriers, ports, steamship lines. Conversion tables are at front of volume 1.

Directory of Leading U.S. Export Management Companies. 3d ed. Fairfield, CT: Bergano Book Co. and Johnston International Publishing Co., 1991. 154 pp. paper.

Export management companies serve as the export department of a manufacturer, handling all foreign marketing details from identifying customers and promoting sales to shipping and even extending credit. This is a directory of the leading firms in the U.S., arranged by state. For each it usually gives the address, phone/fax/telex/ cable, year established, contact person, products and/or services provided. A supplementary directory of export consultants is at end. Includes alphabetical and product indexes.

Directory of United States Importers. New York: Journal of Commerce (annual).

This directory covers the U.S., Canada, and Puerto Rico. It lists, by state, over 25,000 importers, usually giving for each, when firm was established, type of business handled, number of employees, officers (often including purchasing agent, traffic manager, and import manager), bank reference, port of entry, custom house broker, telex, fax, and cable address. An alphabetical index is at front. Includes customs information, and lists of foreign trade zones, associations, banks, consulates, embassies, world ports; also names of companies by a Harmonized Commodity Description and Coding System.

Marconi's International Register. Larchmont, NY: Telegraphic Cable & Radio Registrations (annual).

Of possible use for persons who need the postal address, cable address, telex, answer back code, fax number, or telephone numbers of the principal firms of the world that have international contacts. This alphabetical list also briefly states the nature of each business. In the back are: an international trade index, listing companies by industry and then by country; a list of attorneys by specialty and country; a cable address index. Telex, fax, and telephone numbers can also be found in other directories.

Trade Shows Worldwide. Detroit: Gale Research, Inc. (annual).

This is an international directory of trade shows, their sponsors and organizers, convention facilities, service providers. The section covering trade shows provides details on sponsorship, attendance, space rental price, number of exhibits, audience, dates and locations for as far in advance as is known. At end are some information sources, rankings of space and hotel rooms needed, a master index, and geographic and subject indexes.

A list of "International Trade Fairs" appears annually in *Business America,* either in a late December or early January issue. Each issue of this same periodical has some data on upcoming overseas trade shows and U.S. promotions abroad in a section called "Worldwide Business Opportunities". *Croner's Reference Book for World Traders* also has a short list of trade fairs in its first volume.

World Chamber of Commerce Directory. Loveland, CO (annual).

Most of each issue is a list of U.S. and Canadian chambers, arranged by state (or province) and then by city. The section for foreign chambers is short and is arranged by country. Supplementary lists include: geographic list of U.S. economic development organizations; U.S. convention and visitors bureaus; foreign embassies in the U.S.; U.S. embassies; dean of diplomatic corps.

Addresses of Chambers of Commerce can also be found in several other directories in this section as well as in the previous section covering "Reference Data for Exporters." See annotations for each item or consult the index.

Yearbook of International Organizations, Vol.1: Organization Descriptions and Index. Munich & New York: Published for the Union of International Associations by K. G. Saur. Also available on CD-ROM.

An excellent, comprehensive directory of over 27,000 international organizations of all types, usually giving for each: year founded, aim, structure, top officer, consultative status, activities, events, publications, countries in which there are members. It is arranged in 13 sections with a detailed index at front containing organization names (in all working languages), subject keywords, initials. There are two other volumes, one a geographical volume, the other a subject volume.

ASSOCIATIONS

American Association of Exporters and Importers, 11 West 42d Street, New York, NY 10036.

Publishes a biennial membership directory.

American Society of International Executives, c/o A.M. Swartz, 18 Sentry Parkway, Suite 1, Blue Bell, PA 19422.

Bankers Association for Foreign Trade, 1600 M Street, N.W., 7th floor, Washington, DC 20036.

International Trade Council, 3144 Circle Hill Road, PO Box 2478, Alexandria, VA 22305.

National Foreign Trade Council, 100 E. 42d Street, New York, NY 10001.

United States Council for International Business, 1212 Avenue of the Americas, New York, NY 10036.

World Council of Management (CIOS), c/o Malaysian Institute of Management, 227 Jalan Ampang, Kuala Lumpur 16-003, Malaysia.

17

MANAGEMENT SCIENCE AND
STATISTICAL METHODS

Mathematics for Management – Mathematical Tables – Statistics for Business and Economics – Decision Making and Decision Theory – Abstracting Services and Bibliographies – Statistical Dictionaries – Mathematical and Statistical Periodicals – Directories of Statisticians – Mathematical and Statistical Associations – Quantitative Methods and Operations Research – Operations Research Abstracts and Indexes – MS/OR Periodicals – MS/OR Associations

The importance of quantitative techniques and statistical analysis in making managerial decisions is already well known. Use of this scientific approach in solving business problems developed rapidly following World War II. As computer capabilities increased, new and more sophisticated mathematical and statistical techniques were devised, and the application of these techniques brought revolutionary changes in all areas of business where decisions are made. In today's fast-paced business world probably the most important factor in effective corporate performance is the quality of decisions made. Thus, the administrator who is unfamiliar with the concepts, techniques, and language of mathematics and statistics is at a decided disadvantage. This chapter lists a selection of books and reference sources that executives may find useful in learning how to solve problems and to make decisions. First are the names of several basic mathematics books that may be useful before reading books on the subjects that follow—statistics for business and economics, decision making and decision theory and, finally, operations research (often called "management science"). Many of these books include problems with each chapter as a teaching aid. For books on systems analysis and management information systems see Chapter 13. Books on quantitative methods as used in specific functional areas of business are described with books on that function, e.g. finance (Chapter 14), marketing (Chapter 18), production/operations (Chapter 20).

MATHEMATICS FOR MANAGEMENT

Bowen, Earl K., Gordon D. Prichett and John C. Saber. *Mathematics: With Applications in Management and Economics.* 6th ed. Homewood, IL: Irwin, 1987. 993 pp.

An introductory text intended to explain the value of math as a tool in solving actual problems. The authors begin by discussing linear equations and functions, and then go on to focus in turn on linear programming, vectors/matrices/summation, the mathematics of finance, elementary probability and statistics and, finally, both differential and integral calculus. Each chapter contains explanations, examples, and answered exercises. One year of secondary school algebra is a prerequisite, with appendixes helping students to review the fundamentals of sets, algebra, and graphing.

Childress, Robert L. et al. *Mathematics for Managerial Decisions.* 2d ed. Englewood Cliffs, NJ: Prentice-Hall, 1989. 662 pp.

Provides "an introduction to the important quantitative tools of sets, matrices, linear programming, calculus, and probability in a manner that permits the non-mathematically inclined students to . . . grasp the basic mathematical concepts." Includes examples that apply to business administration, and suggested readings; logarithms and mathematical tables are in an appendix.

Cissell, Robert, et al. *Mathematics of Finance.* 8th ed. Boston: Houghton Mifflin, 1990. 611, [109] pp.

The most recent revision of a standard introduction to the mathematics used in finance, for students of economics, business, and accounting; also suitable for all students since it emphasizes transactions that are important to individuals and families. Based on an examination of the 7th edition, the authors begin by discussing simple interest and then proceed to bank discount, compound interest, annuities, amortization and sinking funds, bonds, capital budgeting and depreciation, life annuities, and life insurance. They end with a chapter on stocks. Practical problems are used throughout to illustrate the applications of formulas and tables. There is a good selection of mathematical tables in the separately paged section at end. Requires a college or good high-school algebra course.

Muksian, Robert. *Financial Mathematics Handbook.* Englewood Cliffs, NJ: Prentice-Hall, 1984. 486 pp.

A handbook of mathematical formulas written for persons "who must use mathematical concepts in their work but are not, necessarily, mathematically oriented. The basic approach is to 'do the algebra for you'"; and each formula is followed by an example of its use, with numerical solution. There are six chapters on mathematics of finance, five on financial decision making, three on federal taxes and depreciation, two on marketing, and one on statistics. About 200 pages at end contains tables of compound interest for $1.

Shao, Stephen P., and Stephen P. Shao, Jr. *Mathematics for Management and Finance.* 5th ed. Cincinnati: South-Western Publishing Co., 1986. 813 pp. Sixth edition to be published in 1992.

Designed as a first text in mathematics for students in business administration, this edition is brought up to date to cover basic aspects and applications of calculators and computers. Part 1 is a review of basic and modern math; part 2 discusses mathematics in business management; parts 3–4 cover mathematics in investment (basic topics and applications). Drills and exercises are included throughout; over 150 pages of math tables are at end. Only a high-school algebra course is needed to understand this book.

MATHEMATICAL TABLES

These are just two of the many reference volumes devoted exclusively to providing mathematical and statistical tables and mathematical formulas. A few useful tables and formulas are also found in the appendixes of most textbooks listed in this chapter. For several compilations of banking, amortization, and other financial tables see Chapter 14.

Beyer, William H., ed. *CRC Standard Mathematical Tables.* 29th ed. Boca Raton, FL: CRC Press, 1991. 725 pp.

A frequently revised compilation covering a wide range of formulas and tables, including algebra of sets, determinants and matrices, logarithm tables, calculus, probability and statistics, binomial distribution, and financial tables. CRC stands for Chemical Rubber Company.

Burington, Richard S. *Handbook of Mathematical Tables and Formulas.* 5th ed. New York: McGraw-Hill, 1973. 500 pp.

This handbook is designed as an aid in any field where mathematical reasoning, processes, and computations are required. Formulas, definitions, and theorems from elementary mathematics are in Part 1; Part 2 contains tables of logarithms, square root, interest, etc. Includes a bibliography and glossary of symbols.

STATISTICS FOR BUSINESS AND ECONOMICS

Since this author is far from an expert on the contents of books in this chapter, much reliance has been placed on book prefaces in describing contents and especially in stating the degree of mathematical expertise necessary for understanding each. Also after checking numerous book reviews (especially those in the *Journal* of the American Statistical Association) it seems likely that the perfect statistics book does not exist. However the books described below all seem to be considered among the best.

For persons who may be confused by some terms used, all of these books explain the various statistical technqiues. Professor Hamburg in his *Basic Statistics,* for example, gives a short, simple explanation of the difference between descriptive statistics and statistical inference, and he also explains such terms as "Bayesian decision theory" (pp. 4–5). All textbooks on business statistics include problems, exercises, and statistical tables. Those by Freund et al., Hamburg, and Levin also contain good bibliographies which, although very short, do list several recommended books on each of about five statistical topics such as probability and statistical decision theory. For books on statistical quality control see Chapter 20.

Handbooks

Bruning, James L., and B. L. Kintz. *Computational Handbook of Statistics.* 3d ed. Glenview, IL: Scott, Foresman, 1987. 372 pp. paper.

For persons who want a step-by-step analysis of computational procedures to use in applying statistical tests to experimental findings, here is a practical handbook that requires almost no previous mathematical knowledge. "Each test or analysis is illustrated by a clearly worked example, and all computational steps and procedures are expressed verbally rather than in mathematical symbols." Most examples deal with experimental findings in the field of behavioral and social science. This note is based on examination of the previous edition.

Books

Berenson, Mark L., and David M. Levine. *Basic Business Statistics: Concepts and Applications.* 4th ed. Englewood Cliffs, NJ: Prentice-Hall, 1989. 904 pp.

A standard beginning text that attempts to make the study of basic statistics meaningful, rewarding, and comprehensible, now revised once again to incorporate recently developed methods. The authors examine the usual topics found in beginning texts including also data collection and presentation, and using the computer for descriptive statistical analysis. A review of arithmetic and algebra plus other math tables are in appendixes.

Freund, John E., Frank J. Williams and Benjamin M. Perles. *Elementary Business Statistics: The Modern Approach.* 5th ed. Englewood Cliffs, NJ: Prentice-Hall, 1988. 738 pp. Sixth edition to be published in 1993.

Latest revision of a good, basic text on the techniques, theories, and tools of statistics in decision making, whose aim it is to describe the modern approach to decision making in the face of uncertainty. Only an elementary mathematical background is required. Included are chapters on index numbers, probability, decision analysis, sampling; also 7 chapters on the various techniques used in decision making (inferences about means, standard deviations, and proportions; analysis of variance; linear regression; correlation, etc.). This book has an attractive format, with good use of diagrams; formulas are set off in boxes for ease in identifying; each chapter indexes key terms. Computer printouts and simulations are used throughout. Statistical tables and a useful bibliography are at end.

Hamburg, Morris. *Basic Statistics: A Modern Approach.* 3d ed. New York: Harcourt Brace Jovanovich, 1985. 548 pp.

This text for a first course in statistics is a shortened, more informal, and intuitive version of Professor Hamburg's *Statistical Analysis for Decision Making* (4th ed., Harcourt Brace Jovanovich, 1987, 701, [130] pp.). It covers descriptive statistics, probability, statistical inference, and statistical decision theory. The book is written for students of business and public administration and assumes only a modest mathematical background. Includes mathematical tables, symbols, short cut formulas, and a bibliography.

Hildebrand, David K., and Lyman Ott. *Statistical Thinking for Managers.* 3d ed. Boston: Duxbury Press, 1991. 1,014 pp.

The authors feel that statistics texts must reflect the wide availability of computers and so their introduction to statistical thinking shifts away from computation and focuses more on judgment, selection, and interpretation. They cover the usual subjects, including three chapters on statistical inference and good coverage on regression analysis. A chapter at end is on data management and report preparation. Some calculus is included but students who lack a calculus course can skip these sections. A short bibliography is at end. This note is based on an examination of the second edition.

Levin, Richard I., and David S. Rubin. *Statistics for Management.* 5th ed. Englewood Cliffs, NJ: Prentice-Hall, 1991. 862, [2] pp.

Professor Levin hopes his beginning text is written so that students will enjoy learning about statistics rather than have anxiety about it. He covers all the usual topics and techniques and discusses how and when to apply them to decision-making situations. Many intuitive explanations are used rather than complicated statistical proofs, and only a course in high-school algebra is assumed. The book is visually attractive, with many learning aids such as illustrations, explanations, marginal notes, exercises; short glossaries are at end of chapters. The bibliography on pp. 856–858, while short, lists several recommended books in each broad area of statistics.

Schlaifer, Robert. *Probability and Statistics for Business Decisions: An Introduction to Managerial Economics Under Uncertainty.* New York: McGraw-Hill, 1959. 732 pp.

This is a classic nonmathematical introduction to probability and statistics that is Bayesian and decision oriented. "The analysis which it recommends is based on the modern theory of utility and what has come to be known as the 'personal' definition of probability; the author believes, in other words, that when the consequences of various possible courses of action depend on some unpredictable event, the *practical* way of choosing the 'best' act is to assign values to consequences and probabilities to events and then to select the act with the highest expected value." Professor Schlaifer, who pioneered the development of decision making for the business manager, has also written an *Introduction to Statistics for Business Decisions* (Melbourne, FL: R. E. Krieger Publishing Co., 1982, 392 pp.; reprint of 1961 edition) which covers both classical and Bayesian statistics.

Wonnacott, Thomas H., and Ronald J. Wonnacott. *Introductory Statistics for Business and Economics.* 4th ed. New York: Wiley, 1990. 815 pp.

Another well-received introductory text where only high school algebra is a prerequisite. It is in five parts: basic probability and statistics; inference for means and proportions; regression (relating two or more variables); topics in classical and Bayesian inference; special topics for business and economics (decision trees, index numbers, etc.). The authors say their objective is to make statistics lively, practical, and clear for nonmathematical students. Examples are used to introduce new material. At end are statistical tables, a bibliography, and a glossary of common symbols.

Three other undergraduate texts requiring only a high-school algebra course are: *Statistical Techniques in Business and Economics* by Robert D. Mason and Douglas A. Lind (7th ed., Homewood, IL: Irwin, 1990, 910 pp.); *Statistics for Business and Economics: Methods and Applications* by Edwin Mansfield, (4th ed., New York: Norton, 1991, 689, [A1–117] pp.); and *Statistics for Modern Business Decisions* by Lawrence L. Lapin (5th ed., San Diego: Harcourt Brace Jovanovich, 1990, 1,021 pp.).

DECISION MAKING AND DECISION THEORY

For books on quantitative methods used in decision making see later section in this chapter on "Quantitative Methods and Operations Research."

Ackoff, Russell L. *The Art of Problem Solving: Accompanied by Ackoff's Fables.* New York: Wiley, 1978. 214 pp.

For all persons "who either make their living at, or derive fun from solving problems—or both," here is a book on creative problem solving that benefits from the long experience of its author, a respected authority on management science and operations research. In part 1 on "The Art," Ackoff uses clever short fables to illustrate his points, and these should not be ignored. Part 2 on "Applications" provides a more realistic view of what is involved in creative problem solving by describing some specific problems. Suggested readings (now very old) are at end. Although written with a light touch this book does require close attention, but it is well worth the effort.

Braverman, Jerome D. *Management Decision Making: A Formal/Intuitive Approach.* New York: AMACOM, 1980. 241 pp.

It is Braverman's contention that managers can solve most complex decision problems by simplification of various techniques and approaching the application in a logical, consistent manner. Thus he has attempted in this book "to explain and illustrate these procedures in a way that will require of the reader no background other than the ability to follow directions, to reason logically, and to perform some simple arithmetic." The procedures he describes include: the payoff table, decision criteria, decision trees, measuring uncertainty, the formal intuitive method, and additional tools for intuitive decision makers.

Fabrycky, W.J., and G.J. Thuesen. *Economic Decision Analysis.* 2d ed. Englewood Cliffs, NJ: Prentice-Hall, 1980. 431 pp.

For students taking business or managerial economic courses, this text "presents methods and techniques of analysis for optimizing the economic outcome of managerial decisions." It is arranged in four parts: introduction; evaluating economic alternatives; estimates, risk, and uncertainty; economic decision models. Knowledge of calculus would be helpful in studying this book but only a college algebra course is necessary. Appendixes contain explanations of several theories, interest tables, and a bibliography.

Harrison, E. Frank. *The Managerial Decision-Making Process.* 3d ed. Boston: Houghton Mifflin, 1987. 542 pp.

This book studies decision making from the perspective of "an integrated and interdisciplinary decision-making process in which rational decision makers pursue choices that will provide acceptable outcomes within discernible boundaries." In so doing Harrison bridges a gap by fusing the behavioral sciences and the quantitative disciplines. His interdisciplinary approach is shown in chapter titles which include decision making as it relates to the environment, to values, psychology, sociology, social psychology, and politics; also techniques and implementation of the decision. A glossary and an extensive bibliography of books and articles are at end.

Nutt, Paul C. *Making Tough Decisions: Tactics for Improving Managerial Decision Making.* San Francisco: Jossey-Bass, 1989. 609 pp.

Much of Professor Nutt's research and extensive writing has revolved around strategic decision making. This book, intended both for managers and students, aims "to offer a critical review of decision making and suggest remedies that are responsive to these criticisms." It is organized into five parts: the nature of tough decisions; what inhibits and misleads decision makers; decision-making processes; key steps in decision making; techniques that support the decision process. At end are three appendixes, a glossary and a bibliography.

Another recent book on the subject which involves in-depth interviews and the authors' research is *Tough Choices: The Decision-Making Styles of America's Top 50 CEOs* by Warren J. Pelton, Sonja Sackmann and Robert Boguslaw (Dow Jones-Irwin, 1990, 163 pp.).

Raiffa, Howard. *Decision Analysis: Introductory Lectures on Choices Under Uncertainty*. Reading, MA: Addison-Wesley, 1968. 309 pp.

Professor Raiffa's informal style and studied effort to keep the mathematical demands to a minimum make this an excellent book for independent reading by anyone who has to make important decisions. His approach is that of Bayesians who, in their analysis, take explicit account of the risk inherent in any possible course of action (expressed as "subjective probabilities") and the decision maker's attitude toward taking risk (expressed as "utilities"). This book starts with a simple noncontroversial problem and proceeds by introducing complicated features into this decision problem one at a time. It is now quite old but is still included in most lists of the better books on decision theory.

Schlaifer, Robert. *Analysis of Decisions Under Uncertainty*. New York: McGraw-Hill, 1969. 729 pp. Reprinted in 1978 by R. E. Krieger Publishing Co., Melbourne, FL.

An excellent nonstatistical introduction to logical analysis of the problems of decision under uncertainty, intended for the business decision maker, not the mathematician. Primarily concerned with large-scale problems and emphasizes the use of digital computers to solve many problems. It is in three parts: basic principles; basic methods for arriving at preferences and probabilities; special problems involving acquisition and use of information obtained by sampling or experimentation. Includes mathematical tables. Professor Schlaifer's two earlier books are listed in the previous section of this chapter.

Two other books are: *The Logic of Intuitive Decision Making: A Research-Based Approach for Top Management* by Weston H. Agor (New York: Quorum Books, 1986, 182 pp.) which, as the title indicates, talks about how to use intuition to help make key decisions both at work and in one's personal life; and *Top Decisions: Strategic Decision-Making in Organizations* by David J. Hickson et al. (San Francisco: Jossey-Bass, 1986, 290 pp.), which is based on Bradford studies of strategic decision-making, carried out in the U.K.

ABSTRACTING SERVICES AND BIBLIOGRAPHIES

Balachandran, Sarojini. *Decision Making: An Information Sourcebook*. (Oryx Sourcebook Series in Business and Management) Phoenix, AZ: Oryx Press, 1987. 128 pp.

A selective, annotated bibliography of English language books, reports, dissertations, and journal articles published prior to early 1986. It is arranged in four sections: methodology of managerial decision making; applications; decision aids; quantitative techniques. At end is a "Core Library Collection" containing a basic collection of reference materials such as bibliographies, dictionaries, indexes, periodicals as well as a short list of general books and several devoted to mathematical tables.

Statistical Theory and Method Abstracts. Voorburg, Netherlands: International Statistical Institute (quarterly).

Abstracts, in English, of articles in worldwide journals, reports, proceedings, arranged within these 16 main sections: mathematical methods; probability theory; probability distributions; sampling distributions; estimation; hypothesis testing; association and dependence; regression analysis; analysis of variance; sampling; design of experiments; theory of stochastic processes; statistical inference for stochastic processes; operations research; special topics-applications; general features.

The American Statistical Association and the Institute of Mathematical Statistics jointly sponsor an annual *Current Index to Statistics: Applications, Methods and Theory,* which lists articles on statistics arranged by author, subject, and keyword.

STATISTICAL DICTIONARIES

Encyclopedia of Statistical Sciences. Samuel Kotz and Norman L. Johnson, editors-in-chief. New York: Wiley, 1982–1988. 9 volumes.

This major work aims "to provide information about an extensive selection of topics concerned with statistical theory and the applications of statistical methods in various more or less scientific fields of activity." There are over 4,000 entries and over 750 eminent contributors. Although it is intended for readers who do not have detailed information about the topics but wish to learn more, it still assumes some mathematical competence. Already in 1989 there is a supplement to update this encyclopedia and incorporate the newest information (1989, 762 pp.).

Marriott, F.H.C. *A Dictionary of Statistical Terms.* 5th ed. Harlow, Essex, Eng.: Longman Scientific & Technical; and New York: Wiley, 1990. 223 pp.

Revision of a useful, authoritative dictionary defining statistical terms in current usage, which was originally compiled by two British statistical experts, Maurice G. Kendall and William R. Buckland. It has been brought up to date with about 400 new entries, and it is still published under the auspices of the International Statistical Institute.

MATHEMATICAL AND STATISTICAL PERIODICALS

American Statistical Association. *Journal* (formerly called *JASA*). Alexandria, VA (quarterly).

Excellent, authoritative articles by professors and statisticians, with most articles giving bibliographic citations. Each issue is in three parts: "Applications and Case Studies"; "Theory and Methods"; "General"—with greatest attention given the second part. Includes good, critical book reviews in the "General" section.

American Statistician. Alexandria, VA: American Statistical Association (quarterly).

Short, practical articles on statistics of special interest to statistical educators.

Annals of Probability and **Annals of Statistics.** Hayward, CA: Institute of Mathematical Statistics (bimonthly).

Each of these bimonthlies publishes original contributions, one on the theory/application of probability and the other on the theory of statistics.

Decision Sciences. Atlanta, GA: Decision Sciences Institute, College of Business Administration, Georgia State University (quarterly).

Research papers by academic persons covering concepts, theory, and techniques of decision sciences; applications and implementation; education; notes and communications. Indexed in ABI/I, BPI, TI.

International Statistical Review. Voorburg, Netherlands: International Statistical Institute (3/yr).

Usually there are about 6 research papers or critical surveys in each issue on a wide range of statistical subjects and the most relevant aspects of probability; also brief reports on recent activities in the statistical world.

Journal of Business & Economic Statistics. Alexandria, VA: American Statistical Association (quarterly).

A journal whose aim it is to publish articles of high quality and significance on applied problems in business and economic statistics. These "include measurement problems such as those encountered in the measurement of employment, unemployment, income, output, anticipations and other significant economic variables, construction of price and output indexes, and related topics."

Royal Statistical Society. *Journal.* Series A,B,C. London (3/yr.).

This Journal is published in three series. "Series A (Statistics in Society)" contains papers of general statistical interest that are substantive rather than technical and tend to focus on economic, industrial, social, medical or governmental issues; it includes book reviews. "Series B (Methodological)" covers methodological and theoretical research of interest to statisticians. Series C is published separately as *Applied Statistics*. It promotes papers motivated by real practical problems, with the papers giving a simple presentation of new or recent methodology, using practical examples. This latter includes book reviews and statistical software reviews.

Society for Industrial and Applied Mathematics. *SIAM Review.* Philadelphia, PA (quarterly).

Devoted primarily to expository and survey papers on topics of interest to applied mathematicians. Includes book reviews; also sections on problems and solutions. This society publishes 8 other journals including *SIAM Journal of Applied Mathematics* (6/yr). Both are indexed in ASTI.

DIRECTORIES OF STATISTICIANS

Directory of Statisticians. Alexandria, VA: American Statistical Association (quinquennial?).

A directory of the combined memberships of the ASA, the Biometric Society, and the Statistical Society of Canada. Sometimes out of date since latest edition published as of 1989 is for 1985.

MATHEMATICAL AND STATISTICAL ASSOCIATIONS

American Statistical Association, 1429 Duke Street, Alexandria, VA 22314.

Decision Sciences Institute, University Plaza, Atlanta, GA 30303.

International Statistical Institute, 428 Prinses Beatrixlaan, NL-2270 AZ, Voorburg, Netherlands.

Royal Statistical Society, 25 Enford Street, London W1H 2BH, England.

Society for Industrial and Applied Mathematics, 3600 University City Science Center, Philadelphia, PA 19104.

QUANTITATIVE METHODS AND OPERATIONS RESEARCH

The terms "management science" and "operations research" are often used interchangeably in the literature that studies the application of quantitative methods to solving management problems. Here is a selection of several general books on this subject.

Bierman, Harold, Jr., Charles P. Bonini and Warren H. Hausman. *Quantitative Analysis for Business Decisions.* 8th ed. Homewood, IL: Irwin, 1991. 742 pp.

A well-established introductory text about managerial decision making. It presents a general approach for managers to use when faced with decision problems, as well as specific quantitative tools for particular types of problems, and it is meant for readers who do not have an extensive mathematical background. The four parts cover: models and decision making; decision analysis; mathematical programming; deterministic and probabilistic models (including chapters on such topics as inventory control, queuing theory, simulation, PERT, Markov processes). Problems and short bibliographies are with chapters; mathematical tables are in an appendix.

Budnick, Frank S., Dennis McLeavey and Richard Mojena. *Principles of Operations Research in Management.* 2d ed. Homewood, IL: Irwin, 1988. 988 pp.

The authors say the "primary objective in this book is to demonstrate the contribution OR/MS can make in support of decision making. To accomplish this we present a comprehensive and (we hope) lucid survey of OR/MS techniques, illustrating their applicability in decision-making settings." Because this book is intended for users, there is a strong emphasis on realistic scenarios through examples, exercises, and cases. An attempt is made to relegate mathematical proofs and other quantitative materials to appendixes or advanced sections that can be omitted. The only prerequisite is an understanding of basic algebra and basic statistics.

Hillier, Frederick S., and Gerald J. Lieberman. *Introduction to Operations Research.* 5th ed. New York: McGraw-Hill, 1990. 954 pp.

Now in its fifth revision, this is considered a standard text for an upper-level college course or a first-year graduate school course, with the bulk of the book devoted to the mathematical methods of OR. Based on an examination of the previous edition, this starts with an introduction on OR and an overview of the modeling approach. The authors then cover "the topic of linear programming, a prominent area of OR concerned largely with how to allocate limited resources among the various activities of an organization. Part 3 deals with the broad topic of mathematical programming, including integer and nonlinear programming. Part 4 considers a number of probabilistic models that take into account the uncertainty associated with future events in order to analyze certain important problems." (pp. 11–12). The mathematics required has been kept, for the most part, at a relatively elementary level. Problems and a few references are at end of chapters; appendixes contain tables and review several methods or equations.

Levin, Richard I. et al. *Quantitative Approaches to Management.* 7th ed. New York: McGraw-Hill, 1989. 848 pp.

Latest edition of a good, standard introductory text whose aim it has been to make it possible for persons with a modest background in math to understand the MS/OR field and gain an understanding of how it is applied to our lives. It covers all the important MS/OR techniques: probability concepts, forecasting, decision theory, inventory models, linear programming, special-purpose algorithms, integer programming, heuristics, simulation, queuing theory, network scheduling, Markov analysis. The thrust is toward applications, with many problems included. Glossaries are with each chapter; mathematical tables and a bibliography are at end.

Several other relatively recently revised texts requiring only beginning algebra are: *Quantitative Concepts for Management: Decision Making Without Algorithms* by Gary D. Eppen, F. J. Gould and Charles Schmidt (3d ed., Prentice-Hall, 1988, 752 pp.) which emphasizes concepts of successful modeling in decision making; *Quantitative Methods for Business Decisions, With Cases* by Lawrence L. Lapin (4th ed, Harcourt Brace Jovanovich, 1988, 847 pp.), a complete treatment of basic management science methodology; and *Operations Research: An Introduction* by Hamdy A. Taha (4th ed., Macmillan, 1987, 876 pp.).

OPERATIONS RESEARCH ABSTRACTS AND INDEXES

International Abstracts in Operations Research. Amsterdam: Published for International Federation of Operational Research Societies by Elsevier Science Publishers (6/yr.).

Abstracts (in English) for articles in worldwide journals, arranged by specific topic within four orientation areas: process oriented; application oriented; technique oriented; and professionally oriented. Subject and author indexes are in each issue.

OR/MS Annual Comprehensive Index. Baltimore: The Institute of Management Sciences and the Operations Research Society of America. Also available online.

This has expanded to an annual index of articles in some 150 OR/MS and related journals. It was formerly published irregularly as *The OR/MS Index* and covered only a small selection of journals.

MS/OR PERIODICALS

Interfaces. Providence, RI: Published jointly by The Institute of Management Sciences and the Operations Research Society of America (bimonthly).

Since the purpose of this journal is to improve communication between managers and MS/OR professionals, most articles are on the use or application of MS/OR in commerce, industry, government, or education, and they are usually nonmathematical in approach. Includes book reviews. Indexed in ABI/I, BPI, TI.

Management Science. Providence, RI: The Institute of Management Sciences (monthly).

Significant articles reporting both on new methodological developments in management science and on the problems of developing and converting management theory to practice. Many articles require familiarity with undergraduate mathematics. Indexed in ABI/I, BPI.

For a journal on *Marketing Science* sponsored jointly by the Institute of Management Sciences and the Operations Research Society of America, see Chapter 18.

Omega. The International Journal of Management Science. Marsh Barton, Exeter, Devon, Eng., and Elmsford, NY: Maxwell Pergamon Macmillan (bimonthly).

Reports on developments in management science, including research results and applications. Indexed in TI.

Operations Research. Baltimore, MD: Operations Research Society of America (bimonthly).

Covers refereed articles on a broad range of MS/OR topics of interest to the practitioner and researcher in three substantive categories: OR methods, data-based operational science, the practice of OR. Included are observations of operating systems, case histories of applications, the history, policy, practice, future, and arenas of application of OR. Indexed in ABI/I, BPI.

OR: The Journal of the Operational Research Society. Oxford, Eng., and Elmsford, NY: Published for the Operational Research Society by Macmillan Press, Ltd. (monthly).

Addressed to OR practitioners, researchers, teachers, and students, this monthly covers papers on the theory, practice, history, or methodology of OR, and it includes case studies. Indexed in ABI/I, BPI.

Several other foreign periodicals are: *Cahiers du Centre d'Études de Recherche Opérationelle* (Bruxelles; quarterly); *European Journal of Operational Research* (Amsterdam: Elsevier Science Publishers and sponsored by the Association of European Operational Research Societies, 6/yr.); *INFOR*. a Canadian journal published jointly for the Canadian Operational Research Society and the Canadian Information Processing Society (Downsview, Ontario, Can.: University of Toronto Press, quarterly); and *Zeitschrift Für Operations Research* (Heidelberg, Ger.: Physica Verlag; Secaucus, NJ: Springer Verlag New York, Inc., 6/yr.).

MS/OR ASSOCIATIONS

The Institute of Management Sciences, 290 Westminster Street, Providence, RI 02903.

International Federation of Operational Research Societies, c/o Helle Welling, IMSOR, Building 321, DK-2800 Lyngby, Denmark.

Operational Research Society, Neville House, Waterloo Street, Birmingham B2 5TX, England.

Operations Research Society of America, Mt. Royal and Guilford Avenues, Baltimore, MD 21202.

18

MARKETING

Marketing Handbooks – Marketing Books – Marketing in Non-profit Organizations – Consumer Behavior – Marketing Channels – Business Marketing – International Marketing – Marketing Research – Pricing – Product Development – Public Policy and Marketing – Sales Management – Selling and Salesmanship – Marketing Bibliographies and Abstracting Services – Marketing Dictionaries – Marketing Guides – Marketing Reports on Industries and Locations – Consumer Expenditure Studies – Marketing Periodicals – Marketing and Market Research Directories – Marketing Associations – Sales Promotion – Advertising Handbooks and Books – Advertising Statistics – Advertising Dictionaries – Advertising Periodicals – Advertising Directories – Advertising Associations – Direct Marketing – Retailing – Franchising – Retailing Statistics – Retailing Periodicals – Directories of Retail Stores – Retailing Associations – Service Industries

The same new forces that have brought about social and economic changes in other areas of business are also evident in business activities concerned with the marketing of goods and services to consumers and industry. A more systematic, analytic approach to solving complex marketing problems (aided by rapidly developing data processing techniques); increased importance given to knowledge about what the consumer wants and how s/he behaves; an awakened concern for the environment; and rapid growth in the services sector—these topics are all receiving much more attention in the current literature on marketing and advertising.

This chapter describes a selection of recent books, periodicals, and reference guides on major marketing subjects. Advertising and retailing materials are described at the end in order to list their reference sources separately rather than to interfile them with the statistics, periodicals, and directories pertaining to the whole area of marketing. There is also a new section on service industries. Related topics described in other chapters are: physical distribution, or logistics (including purchasing and transportation), in Chapter 20; public relations and social responsibilities, in Chapter 9; and international marketing, in Chapter 16.

MARKETING HANDBOOKS

Both of these handbooks are useful as comprehensive yet concise sources of basic marketing information, but neither one reflects recent developments. Several more specialized handbooks are listed in the sections for marketing research, sales management, sales promotion, and advertising.

Britt, Steuart H., and Norman F. Guess, eds. *The Dartnell Marketing Manager's Handbook.* 2d ed. Chicago: Dartnell Corp. 1983. 1,293 pp.

Most of its 76 chapters are written by a team consisting of a marketing professor and a marketing executive, with a total of 132 experts collaborating on this comprehensive reference volume. Covers all important topics: 5 chapters on organization and staffing; 6 chapters on establishing objectives; 12 on marketing research; 12 on developing the marketing plan; 11 on putting the marketing plan into action for consumer products and services; 4 on planning for industrial products; 12 on promoting products and services; 6 on international marketing; and 2 on appraising and controlling the marketing program. Useful suggestions for reading are at end of each chapter for persons wanting to read further on any topic.

Buell, Victor P., ed. *Handbook of Modern Marketing.* 2d ed. New York: McGraw-Hill, 1986. 1 volume (various pagings).

Another comprehensive single source for a concise, practical, and balanced treatment of all aspects of marketing and marketing management, in 107 chapters, each written by one of more than 100 authorities. There are 19 broad sections: the modern concept of marketing; identification and classification of markets; planning the product line; efficient distribution of products and services; pricing products and services; marketing research and marketing information systems; marketing planning; marketing organization; controlling marketing operations; marketing management; the marketing mix; selling and sales management; market communications; customer services; financing marketing operations; packaging; legal aspects; specialty marketing; international marketing. Selective bibliographies are at end of most chapters.

MARKETING BOOKS

Boone, Louis E., and David L. Kurtz. *Contemporary Marketing.* 7th ed. Fort Worth, TX: Dryden Press, 1991. pp. 683, [51] pp.

A good introductory undergraduate text with a strong marketing planning/strategy orientation. The usual marketing topics are well covered. This latest edition places more emphasis on the marketing of services and on the integration of materials on global marketing. It is well-written, and uses attractive colored illustrations, diagrams, and tables throughout. Two "theme" boxes are also interspersed, one containing examples of "the competitive edge" and the other covering a "focus on ethics." Video cases and computer applications are with each chapter. An appendix discusses careers in marketing; a glossary is at end.

Cravens, David W. *Strategic Marketing.* 3d ed. Homewood, IL: Irwin, 1991. 833 pp.

This revised text "is designed around a strategic marketing planning approach with a clear emphasis on how to do strategic analysis and planning." The chapters are arranged within five parts: business and marketing strategies; marketing situation analysis; designing marketing strategy; marketing program development; implementing and managing marketing strategy. Professor Cravens incorporates material on the global dimensions throughout his book. He also provides many how-to guides to assist the reader in applying the analysis and planning approaches developed in the text. There are also diagrams and tables throughout, bibliographical notes with chapters, a few cases with each part, and "comprehensive cases" at the end.

Enis, Ben M., and Keith K. Cox. *Marketing Classics: A Selection of Influential Articles.* 7th ed. Boston: Allyn and Bacon, 1991. 578 pp. paper.

Latest revision of a much-used selection of more than 35 widely quoted articles, chosen because of their enduring significance to marketing thought. They are arranged in five parts: marketing philosophy; buyer behavior; marketing strategy; the marketing program; implementing and extending marketing. Among many important articles this book includes Professor Theodore Levitt's classic "Marketing Myopia" which is probably the most frequently quoted marketing article written. There are other published collections of great writings in the field of marketing.

Jain, Subhash C. *Marketing Planning & Strategy.* 3d ed. Cincinnati: South-Western Publishing Company, 1990. 916 pp.

Here is a comprehensive text revised and updated to provide students with a clear understanding of market strategy and its importance for making policy decisions in competitive situations. After an introductory section, the author covers the material as follows: strategic analysis (including chapters on understanding competition, the customer, and on scanning the environment); strategic capabilities and direction (discussing strengths/weaknesses and objectives/goals); strategic formulation; strategy implementation and control; and finally, a section focusing on the four components of marketing strategy (product, pricing, distribution, promotion). Bibliographic notes are with chapters; 22 pertinent cases are at end.

Kotler, Philip. *Marketing Management: Analysis, Planning, Implementation, and Control.* 7th ed. Englewood Cliffs, NJ: Prentice-Hall, 1991. 756 pp.

Professor Kotler's excellent graduate-level text focuses on the major decisions facing marketing executives and top management and offers an analytical approach. This substantial revision strengthens the discussion of strategic marketing while also reflecting new problems facing companies and new concepts and technologies needed to deal with these problems. There are 6 parts, starting with background on the societal, managerial and strategic underpinnings of marketing. This is followed in turn by sections on: analyzing marketing opportunities; researching and selecting target markets; designing marketing strategies (includes a chapter on strategies for the global marketplace); planning marketing programs (describing each element of the marketing mix); organizing, implementing and controlling marketing effort. Frequent use of diagrams and itemized lists, set off in different color, add to the interest of this book.

Four other books by Kotler are worth mentioning: a book of 39 practical readings he edited with Keith Cox called *Marketing Management and Strategy: A Reader* (4th. ed., Prentice-Hall, 1989, 406 pp.); *Strategic Marketing for Non-Profit Organizations* (4th ed., Prentice-Hall, 1991, 644 pp.) which is described elsewhere in this chapter; two beginning texts, with Gary Armstrong as coauthor: *Marketing: An Introduction* (2d ed., Prentice-Hall, 1990, 592 pp.) and *Principles of Marketing* (5th ed., Prentice-Hall, 1991, 711 pp.). These latter two books are almost alike except that the first gives only the basics and so is shorter. Both have appendixes containing a short glossary, and discussions about marketing arithmetic and marketing careers.

Luck, David J., O. C. Ferrell and George H. Lucas, Jr. *Marketing Strategy and Plans: Marketing Management.* 3d ed. Englewood Cliffs, NJ: Prentice-Hall, 1989. 514 pp.

These professors have written a different sort of text for an upper level undergraduate or graduate course which presents and examines managerial principles for selecting marketing strategies and for determining plans. Using a strategic decision model, parts A to C examine: the situation analysis (the environment, for example); market strategy; marketing progress (the marketing mix and so forth). These are the building blocks of strategy decisions, say the authors. They then utilize the model in studying decisions concerning strategy in the corporation as a whole (part D), and finally implementation of plans in the actual market environment (part E). Cases are at end of each part.

McCarthy, E. Jerome, and William D. Perreault, Jr. *Basic Marketing: A Managerial Approach.* 10th ed. Homewood, IL: Irwin, 1990. 734 p.

This is a substantial revision of a widely used, beginning marketing text which strives for clear and interesting communication by way of new examples, new teaching aids such as graphs, figures, and colored illustrations. The emphasis is still on marketing strategy. Half of its 22 chapters are concerned with developing a marketing mix out of the four Ps (product, place, promotion, price). Other important areas covered include target markets, the environment, customers, marketing plans and programs, control, strategy for international markets. Appendixes with three chapters discuss economic fundamentals, marketing arithmetic, and career planning. Short case incidents and a glossary are at end; computer-aided problems are in a separate booklet. A shortened version of this text is *Essentials of Marketing* (5th ed., Irwin, 1991, 526 pp.). A Canadian edition of the *Essentials* text focuses on the Canadian market (2d ed., Irwin, 1988). Stanley J. Shapiro is joint author.

Professor McCarthy (with John F. Grashof and Andrew A. Brogowicz) have revised a good selection of *Readings and Cases in Basic Marketing* (5th ed., Irwin, 1987, 365 pp. paper).

Paley, Norton. *The Manager's Guide to Competitive Marketing Strategies.* New York: American Management Association, 1989. 390 pp.

A step-by-step guide to the title subject, with frequent forms, tables, and short case incidents. Paley's first two parts describe five key strategies, and the framework for competitive analysis (both external and internal). Part 3 discusses marketing research and the marketing plan; part 4 is devoted to specific strategies and tactics with an emphasis on product, pricing, distribution, and promotion strategies. Checklists for developing competitive strategies are at end.

Sheth, Jagdish N., and Dennis E. Garrett. *Marketing Management: A Comprehensive Reader.* Cincinnati: South-Western, 1986. 1,026 pp. paper.

The authors say their purpose in selecting these 54 readings was "to expose students of marketing to the latest viewpoints regarding the paramount questions which marketing practitioners must address. Therefore . . . [they] have selected articles . . . that are generally much more rigorous and provocative than those usually found in most marketing management readings books." The four-part arrangement covers: marketing strategy, planning, and control; marketing and the environment; managing the marketing mix; broadening the marketing concept. These two authors have also published a readings book on *Marketing Theory: Classic and Contemporary Readings* (South-Western, 1986, 872 pp., paper).

Stanton, William J., and Charles Futrell. *Fundamentals of Marketing.* 8th ed. New York: McGraw-Hill, 1987. 666 pp.

Once again Professor Stanton (now with a co-author) has revised his standard introductory text to incorporate recent developments and new concepts and also to reflect the major social and economic forces presenting challenges for business and especially for marketing. The central theme remains the same—"that marketing is a total system of business action rather than a fragmented assortment of functions and institutions." Major sections are on: modern marketing and its environment; target markets; the product; the price; distribution; promotion; marketing in special fields (services, nonbusiness organizations, international); implementing and evaluating the marketing effort. Effective use of color and illustrations have been added in this edition. A few cases are at end of each section; an appendix contains a glossary, and short reviews of marketing arithmetic and careers in marketing.

Stevens, Robert E., David L. Loudon and William E. Warren. *Marketing Planning Guide.* New York: Haworth Press, 1991. 289 pp. paper.

For persons who may want a practical guide just on marketing planning, here is a book for the practitioner or student that emphasizes techniques and tools. It is arranged into 6 parts: introduction; situation analysis; objectives; strategy/strategy variables, and financial impact; controlling the marketing plan; planning analysis. Worksheets and a few bibliographical references are at end of chapters; a sample marketing plan is at end of book.

Several other recent books include: *Strategic Market Management* by David A. Aaker (3d ed., New York: Wiley, 1992, 394 pp., paper), a concise strategy text; *Marketing Management: A Strategic Approach* by Harper W. Boyd and Orville C. Walker (Homewood, IL: Irwin, 1990, 899, [18] pp.), a graduate strategy text; *The Practice of Marketing Management: Analysis, Planning, and Implementation* by William A. Cohen (New York: Macmillan, 1988, 695 pp.); *Managing the Marketing Functions: The Challenge of Customer-Centered Enterprise* by Stewart A. Washburn (New York: McGraw-Hill, 1988, 370 pp.), a practical book on how to manage in 6 broad opportunity areas; *Marketing* by William G. Zikmund and Michael D'Amico (3d ed., New York: Wiley, 1989, 694 pp.), an introductory text.

MARKETING IN NONPROFIT ORGANIZATIONS

Professor's Kotler's book is about the only recent full-length treatment on this topic. Many current articles on specific aspects of marketing in nonprofit organization can be identified by using the several indexes described in Chapter 2. For the names of a few books on managing nonprofit organizations in general, see Chapter 11.

Advances in Nonprofit Marketing: A Research Annual. Ed. by Russell W. Belk. Greenwich, CT: JAI Press.

A periodic collection of about 8 research papers exploring a wide range of issues in the area of nonprofit marketing. Useful bibliographical references are with each paper. Authors are usually academicians. Three volumes have been published as of 1991.

Kotler, Philip, and Alan R. Andreasen. *Strategic Marketing for Nonprofit Organizations.* 4th ed. Englewood Cliffs, NJ: Prentice-Hall, 1991. 644 pp.

Professor Kotler is well known as the author of one of the better textbooks on marketing. Here he uses his considerable expertise to provide (now with a coauthor) a useful book on the marketing concepts and problems of nonprofit organizations. It is arranged within 5 basic parts to cover: developing a customer orientation; strategic planning and organization; developing and organizing resources; designing the marketing mix; controlling marketing strategies. Throughout one can find checklists, hints, narratives of experiences, and sample materials drawn from nonprofit sources. Bibliographical notes are at end of most chapters.

Earlier Professor Kotler edited (with O. C. Ferrell and Charles W. Lamb) *Strategic Marketing for Nonprofit Organizations: Cases and Readings* (3d ed., Prentice-Hall, 1987, 386 pp. paper). He also wrote (with Roberta N. Clarke) an excellent text focusing specifically on *Marketing for Health Care Organizations* (Prentice-Hall, 1987, 545 pp.).

Lovelock, Christopher H., and Charles B. Weinberg. *Public and Nonprofit Marketing.* 2d ed. Redwood City, CA: The Scientific Press, 1989. 520 pp.

This book is the result of over 15 years' collaboration by these two professors in teaching and conducting research on marketing as it relates to public and nonprofit management. It is designed for use by managers, trustees, and students who need a framework for looking at marketing issues, and to help public and nonprofit organizations develop strategies to achieve their objectives. They start with an overview, and then study in turn: exploring and pursuing marketing opportunities (including a chapter on competitive strategy); understanding customers; planning and pricing the product; making contact with the customer; organization and implementation; resource attraction. Bibliographies are with chapters; a glossary is at end.

CONSUMER BEHAVIOR

Berkman, Harold W., and Christopher Gilson. *Consumer Behavior: Concepts and Strategies.* 3d ed. Boston: Kent Publishing Company, 1986. 650 pp.

An academician and a marketing executive have combined forces to offer what they hope is a readable text intended to help students apply an insider's knowledge of consumer behavior to real-world marketing strategies. After an introductory overview, they treat in turn: environmental influences, individual influences, decision making. Includes illustrations, tables, charts, and boxed features. Suggested readings are at end of chapter; models of consumer behavior are in an appendix.

Engel, James F., Roger D. Blackwell and Paul W. Miniard. *Consumer Behavior.* 6th ed. Chicago: Dryden Press, 1990. 789, [37] pp.

A comprehensive text on the concept of consumer behavior, with many practical implications and examples for its various processes and facets. After an introduction and overview the basic sections cover: environmental influences; individual differences; psychological processes; consumer decision processes and behavior; consumer analysis and marketing strategy; an epilogue on consumerism and social responsibility. This edition has been extensively revised. Illustrations and diagrams appear throughout; also "consumer in focus" boxed features show how consumer research is applied and used. Includes bibliographical footnotes; a glossary is at end.

Hawkins, Del I., Roger J. Best and the late Kenneth A. Coney. *Consumer Behavior: Implications for Marketing Strategy.* 5th ed. Homewood, IL: BPI/Irwin, 1992. 674 pp.

Meant as a useful yet enjoyable beginning text to give future managers and marketing people a managerial understanding of consumer behavior and its utilization in developing market strategy. Substantially revised in this latest edition, the material is arranged in five sections: introduction; external influences; internal influences (including motivation, lifestyle, attitudes); consumer decision process; organizational buying behavior. Charts, diagrams, and other illustrations are used throughout, also helpful boxed explanatory matter. Cases are at end of each section; bibliographical references are with each chapter. A consumer behavior audit is in an appendix.

Kassarjian, Harold J., and Thomas S. Robertson. *Perspectives in Consumer Behavior.* 4th ed. Englewood Cliffs, NJ: Prentice-Hall, 1991. 616 pp. paper.

A wide selection of readings with this latest edition focusing both on leading-edge articles and classics, and on empirical as well as theoretical articles. The 31 selections are arranged in 6 sections: information search and acquisition; learning and decision processes; affect, motivation, and personality; attitudes, beliefs and values; social processes; class and culture. Most sections contain a review paper that surveys the topic and presents the existing literature.

Schiffman, Leon G., and Leslie L. Kanuk. *Consumer Behavior.* 4th ed. Englewood Cliffs, NJ: Prentice-Hall, 1991. 680 pp.

The authors hope this is a complete and readable text that maintains a balance of basic behavioral concepts, research findings, and applied marketing examples. The material is divided into five parts: introduction; the consumer as an individual (needs, motivation, perception, attitudes, etc.); consumers in their social and cultural settings (e.g. the family, social class, influence of culture, cross-cultural consumer behavior); the consumer's decision-making process; applications to marketing of service organizations, nonprofit markets, and ethics and public policy considerations. Illustrations, colored tables, and diagrams are used throughout. Bibliographic endnotes are with chapters; a glossary is at end of book.

Settle, Robert B., and Pamela L. Alreck. *Why They Buy: American Consumers Inside and Out.* New York: Wiley, 1986. 351 pp.

This is an attempt to help marketing professionals and technicians understand their consumer publics, written in practical language rather than the technical language of behavioral scientists. The authors start with a look at consumer needs, motives and personalities, and then they look at people's perception, their learning about options, and their attitudes. After this they consider in turn, social roles, family, social class, culture, life stages, family cycles, lifestyles, demographics, and finally what buyers are doing when they make a choice in the marketplace.

Two alternative texts are: *Consumer Behavior in Marketing Strategy* by John A. Howard (Englewood Cliffs, NJ: Prentice-Hall, 1989, 375 pp.) which focuses on providing the conceptual and technical tools needed; and *Consumer Behavior and Marketing Strategy* by J. Paul Peter and Jerry C. Olson (2d ed., Homewood, IL: Irwin, 1990, 608 pp.), written as a more integrative, strategic marketing approach.

Periodicals

Journal of Consumer Research. Provo, UT: Graduate School of Management, Brigham Young University (quarterly).

Since this journal is sponsored by nearly a dozen scholarly associations, the articles sought usually have an interdisciplinary content or interest. They discuss empirical research on consumer behavior and each usually includes useful bibliographical footnotes. Most of the authors are academic persons. Included as sponsoring associations (among others) are: the American Marketing Association; the American Association for Public Opinion Research; the Association for Consumer Research. Indexed in ABI/I, BPI, TI; full text on BRS, DATA-STAR, DIALOG, DOW JONES, MEAD/NEXIS.

MARKETING CHANNELS

Rosenbloom, Bert. *Marketing Channels: A Management View.* 4th ed. Chicago: Dryden Press, 1991. 707 pp.

The objective of Rosenbloom's book is "to provide a management focus to the marketing channels literature within a comprehensive and integrated managerial framework." He arranges the material into five parts: marketing channel systems; developing the marketing channel; managing the marketing channel; appraising the marketing channel; additional perspectives (direct selling and international channel perspective). A sixth part of over 100 pages contains cases. An attempt is made to present the material clearly and concisely; it includes many examples and vignettes.

Stern, Louis W., and Adel I. El-Ansary. *Marketing Channels,* 4th ed. Englewood Cliffs, NJ: Prentice-Hall, 1992. 621 pp.

This thorough book studies marketing channels from both strategic and managerial frames of reference, and so the "core" is in the third of four parts which covers "channel management—planning, coordinating, organizing and controlling." The first two parts lay the groundwork by discussing the emergence and components of marketing channels, while the last part deals with channel management in other contexts (in the international arena and in service industries). There are frequent charts, exhibits, and bibliographical footnotes. Technical and professional appendixes are with some chapters.

These authors (with James R. Brown) have rewritten this text for an undergraduate course and published it as *Management in Marketing Channels* (Prentice-Hall, 1989, 514 pp.)

BUSINESS MARKETING

Business marketing (formerly called "industrial marketing") is defined in Haas's book as "the marketing of goods and services to organizational customers and prospects as opposed to marketing to individuals and households."

Today there is a growing interest in this subject as evidenced by the increase in the number of books written during the past five years. See also the two business marketing periodicals described in the "Marketing Periodicals" section.

Bingham, Frank G., Jr., and Barney T. Raffield III. *Business to Business Marketing Management.* Homewood, IL: Irwin, 1990. 744 pp.

A new textbook focusing on the special elements and requirements of business markets. It is arranged in 6 parts to give strong emphasis to the unique elements of the buyer-seller connection. These parts are: introduction; how buyers buy; identifying the customer; making and moving the goods; promoting and selling the goods; trends in business to business marketing. Coverage includes transportation management, marketing of services, ethical considerations, international marketing. Boxed "business-to-business marketing in action" features are scattered throughout; also tables, diagrams, and other useful illustrations. Annotated suggested readings and short cases are with each chapter; two longer cases are at end.

Haas, Robert W. *Business Marketing Management: An Organizational Approach.* 5th ed. Boston: PWS-Kent Publishing Co., 1992. 900 pp.

The title of this latest revision has been changed from *Industrial Marketing Management* in order to better reflect the more contemporary nature of the subject. The primary emphasis is on marketing management and decision making as it relates specifically to business marketing. The first major section is an expanded one on understanding the business marketing environment, and it includes a chapter on the global nature of business marketing. Parts 2–5 then cover: organizational customers and market behavior; the business marketing process (segmentation, planning, strategy, and intelligence gathering); the business marketing mix; business marketing performance. Part 6 consists of cases (covering about 200 pp.). Frequent useful examples, charts, and tables are found throughout; suggested additional readings are at end of chapters; a glossary is at end of the book.

Hutt, Michael D., and Thomas W. Speh. *Business Marketing Management: A Strategic View of Industrial and Organizational Markets.* 4th ed. Fort Worth, TX: Dryden Press, 1992. 749 pp.

Another of several good, recent texts on business marketing, this one presents a managerial approach. It is well written, with relevant material drawn from such areas as the behavioral sciences, logistics, strategic management. The five parts focus on: the environment; the organizational buying process; assessing market opportunities; formulating business marketing strategy (chapters included on managing the product line, product development, global markets, innovation, services, marketing channels, pricing, communication); evaluating strategy and performance. Illustrations, tables, charts appear throughout; also vignettes called "Inside Business Marketing," "Ethical Business Marketing," and "The Global Marketplace" which are quotes from other interesting sources. A sixth part contains cases.

Patti, Charles H., Steven W. Hartley and Susan L. Kennedy. *Business-to-Business Advertising: A Marketing Management Approach.* Lincolnwood, IL: NTC Business Books, 1991. 286 pp.

"A key objective of this book is to help improve the productivity of business-to-business advertising through better management of the advertising function." It is structured into three parts that move through the decision-making processes of advertising: pre-campaign ideas; campaign decisions; post-campaign evaluation. A selection of about three readings are with each chapters, along with a list of further recommended readings. Appendixes include a list of organizations as sources of advertising information. This book is published in association with the Business/ Professional Advertising Association.

Powers, Thomas L. *Modern Business Marketing: A Strategic Approach to Business and Industrial Markets.* St. Paul, MN: West Publishing Company, 1991. 642 pp.

Professor Powers says he wrote his text because of the need to study the many recent changes in business marketing, especially those relating to the growing complexities of marketing high technology industrial products and services. His book is a balance between strategy and implementation, and it is divided into five parts of which the fifth consists of 12 in-depth cases. Parts 1–4 cover: introduction; developing business marketing strategies; strategic elements of the business marketing program (with chapters on such topics as channel organization, physical distribution, sales force management, advertising and sales promotion, pricing); international and future issues. Short boxed vignettes throughout contain quotes from published sources. Bibliographical notes and a case incident are with each chapter; a glossary is at end.

Sherlock, Paul. *Rethinking Business to Business Marketing.* New York: Free Press, 1991. 188 pp.

This is a short, practical book on company-to-company marketing and selling. It is intended as an "easy to read 'complete blueprint' of how to think about, plan, and implement the marketing and sales of your product." The second of its three parts discusses various aspects of designing and implementing the marketing plan, including chapters on selling, distribution, use of literature, advertising, trade shows, and much more. Tom Peters says in the foreword that this book "is at once widely challenging, deadly serious, and absurdly fun."

Just revised again but not seen for evaluation is *Industrial Marketing Strategy* by Frederick E. Webster (3d ed., Wiley, 1991, 365 pp.). This is a concise text focusing on the strategic problems facing the business/industrial marketer.

INTERNATIONAL MARKETING

The several books on international marketing and advertising, and on profitable importing and exporting, selected for inclusion in this book, are described in the "International Marketing" section of Chapter 16 which focuses on international management. In addition, basic marketing texts now usually include a chapter on global or international marketing. Sources on foreign statistics and economic trends are described in Chapter 5.

MARKETING RESEARCH

Most of the better marketing research texts include a chapter that describes and discusses secondary data useful in undertaking a market research project. We have noted those that are in the books below because they can serve as excellent guides to marketing research sources and statistics, both for the librarian and for the beginning market researcher. For descriptions of several marketing research journals see the "Marketing Periodicals" section of this chapter.

Handbooks

Worcester, Robert M., and John Downham, eds. *Consumer Market Research Handbook.* 3d ed. New York: McGraw-Hill, 1988. 864 pp. paper.

Substantially revised and updated, this latest edition consists of 26 chapters, each written by a practitioner. It is arranged in two parts, with one devoted to discussions of techniques and the other to the use of consumer market research. The authors draw primarily from the U.K. research scene, but the editors say the thinking incorporates ideas and experiences from many countries. A bibliography at end of book is arranged by chapter. This latest edition is sponsored by the European Society for Opinion and Marketing Research (ESOMAR).

Books

Aaker, David A., and George S. Day. *Marketing Research.* 4th ed. New York: Wiley, 1990. 739, [41] pp.

This textbook has a strong decision-making orientation; its latest revision incorporates recent dramatic developments caused by computer and related technologies. There are five parts: the marketing research process; data collection (9 chapters discussing exploratory and secondary research, descriptive research, causal research, sampling); data analysis; special topics in data analysis (such as factor analysis, regression analysis); applications (new product analysis forecasting and advertising research). Two chapters in part 2 discuss secondary sources of marketing data and the major syndicated marketing surveys. Examples are drawn both from the private and public sectors. A few cases accompany chapters; a glossary is at end of book.

Boyd, Harper W., Jr., Ralph Westfall and Stanley F. Stasch. *Marketing Research: Text and Cases.* 7th ed. Homewood, IL: Irwin, 1989. 816 pp.

A standard text arranged in the following four parts: introduction; basic concepts; the marketing research process (including data collection, sampling, data analysis); selected applications of marketing research (chapters on product, advertising, market and sales analysis research). The chapters on data analysis and techniques are presented in what the authors hope is a nontechnical language that undergraduates can understand. Chapter 6 on "Secondary Data" describes principal census data, a few general guides, commercial marketing information, databases, and other miscellaneous marketing or statistical data. Usually two case incidents are with each chapter.

Breen, George E., and Albert B. Blankenship. *Do-It-Yourself Marketing Research.* 3d ed. New York: McGraw-Hill, 1989. 261 pp.

As the title indicates, this is a "do-it-yourself" guide for the business person in a small or medium-sized firm, intending to show how to do marketing research simply and inexpensively. It does not assume knowledge of statistics. The authors follow a logical sequence beginning first with a simple explanation of what marketing research is and how to evaluate a problem and plan a study. They then describe kinds of research, the various methods for collecting pertinent information, and finally how to write a report or choose an outside research firm if that seems indicated. There are many diagrams, forms, and other illustrations. Chapter 4 briefly outlines "how to find existing marketing information."

Churchill, Gilbert A., Jr. *Marketing Research: Methodological Foundations.* 5th ed. Chicago: Dryden, 1991. 1,070 pp.

Churchill studies the market research process as a series of steps in this comprehensive text. His arrangement follows the six stages in the process: formulate the problem; determine the research design; design the data collection methods and forms; design the sample and collect the data; analyze and interpret the data; prepare the research report. His chapter on "Data Collection: Secondary Data" in the third section contains an appendix describing basic published sources of marketing information. In-text examples and boxed "Research Realities" appear throughout. Cases are at end of each part; a glossary and a few mathematical tables are at end of book. Professor Churchill has also written *Basic Marketing Research* (Dryden, 1988, 765 pp.) which is an introductory, undergraduate text.

Green, Paul E., Donald S. Tull and Gerald Albaum. *Research for Marketing Decisions.* 5th ed. Englewood Cliffs, NJ: Prentice-Hall, 1988. 784 pp.

This latest edition broadens the methodological scope of the book but still emphasizes the place of modern analytical tools, such as multivariate analysis, in the design and conduct of marketing research. It is a simpler and more streamlined version than were the first few editions, and it is also more pragmatic and user-oriented. The text presumes some background in statistics. Several short cases are at end of each of its five parts; a few statistical tables are in an appendix.

Hague, Paul N. *The Industrial Market Research Handbook.* New York: F. Watts, 1988 (1985 in the U.K.). 344 pp.

Most marketing research books are oriented toward consumer goods and markets; this one concentrates on business-to-business sales. Its five parts cover: information that can be made available by market research (market size, structure, etc.); the uses of market research; organizing the project; methods; processing and presenting the data. At end is a short introduction to the important statistical methods. The author is a British consultant and manager, and so there is a British focus to the book.

Lehmann, Donald R. *Market Research and Analysis.* 3d ed. Homewood, IL: Irwin, 1989. 879 pp.

Professor Lehmann approaches market research by attempting to explain the methods most commonly used: what they are, how they work, and what their weaknesses are. His target reader is the user rather than the producer of market research, and he stresses "practicality over purity." The four-part arrangement covers: basic concepts (including a chapter on sources of information); collecting information and preparing for analysis (with a chapter describing the major market research suppliers that is more detailed than is found in most texts); analytical methods; applications (such as sales forecasting, product research, industrial marketing research). Tables, charts, and graphs are found throughout; bibliographies are at end of each chapter. Most of the mathematics has been relegated to appendixes. A good, short list of the other market research texts is on pages 16–17.

Luck, David J., and Ronald S. Rubin. *Marketing Research.* 7th ed. Englewood Cliffs, NJ: Prentice-Hall, 1987. 683 pp.

Revised once again to reflect the many changes and new developments up to 1987, this popular undergraduate-level text now integrates microcomputers with the study of marketing research. It also emphasizes practical issues from the user's perspective. Its five parts cover: fundamentals; planning the research project (including a chapter describing basic "secondary data"); performing the data collection; processing and analyzing data; and finally presentation and follow-through (including managing research and ethical issues). Several case incidents are with each chapter; statistical tables and codes of ethics are in appendixes.

Zikmund, William G. *Exploring Marketing Research*. 4th ed. Chicago: Dryden Press, 1991. 834 pp.

One final alternative for an introductory text, this one aims to present a comprehensive and practical perspective, pointing up the energy and creativity of marketing research rather than focusing entirely on advanced statistical techniques. It is organized into 7 parts to follow the logic of the marketing process. Chapter 6, in part 2, on secondary data and database search and retrieval systems, has a useful appendix describing "Selected Secondary Sources." Several case incidents are with each chapter; part 7 consists of four cases with computerized databases. Real examples, exhibits, and boxed features appear throughout; a glossary and statistical tables are at end.

Bibliographies

Dickinson, John R. *The Bibliography of Marketing Research Methods*. 3d ed. Lexington, MA: Lexington Books, 1990. 1,025 pp.

This is a comprehensive but not annotated bibliography devoted to research on how to do research in marketing—perhaps too overwhelming for most persons, with over 14,000 entries classified under some 214 headings plus many more subheadings. These are all organized into three broad categories: the marketing-research function; data-collection methods; data-analysis techniques. There are author and subject indexes.

PRICING

Most of the information on pricing can be found in older books, in chapters of general books on marketing, or in journal articles. Following are four relatively recent books.

Monroe, Kent B. *Pricing: Making Profitable Decisions*. 2d ed. New York: McGraw-Hill, 1990. 502 pp.

The objective of this book is to provide a systematic presentation of the factors to consider when setting prices and to show how pricing alternatives can be developed and analyzed. Professor Monroe reviews the effect of price on demand and the effect of costs on pricing decisions. He discusses pricing strategies in general and the problems of administrating the pricing function. He also considers special topics (such as competitive bidding, pricing for export markets). At the end he reviews the material and makes recommendations. Suggested readings are at end of chapters; a glossary is at end of the book.

Montgomery, Stephen L. *Profitable Pricing Strategies*. New York: McGraw-Hill, 1988. 174 pp.

This is a short book "designed to help managers learn and make profitable use of the critical skills of planning and managing pricing activities." Montgomery begins with what he calls "the basics" and then turns to such specifics as setting prices, pricing under uncertainty, price forecasting, international pricing, the economics of price functions, and price planning. He ends with a chapter on implementing pricing strategy. References and a glossary are at end.

Morris, Michael H., and Gene Morris. *Market-Oriented Pricing: Strategies for Management.* New York: Quorum Books, 1990. 200 pp.

Another short, readable book, this one attempting to provide direction on how market-based pricing can be achieved. It starts by examining pricing programs, and then different aspects of customer evaluation (including the psychology of pricing). Among other topics, the authors explore cost-based pricing, competitive analysis, product line pricing, legal and ethical aspects, and lastly, how computers can serve pricing managers. Suggested readings are at end.

Nagle, Thomas T. *The Strategy and Tactics of Pricing: A Guide to Profitable Decision Making.* Englewood Cliffs, NJ: Prentice-Hall, 1987. 351 pp.

Nagle's book was written not only as a text but also as a guide for the manager or staff assistant charged with making or recommending price decisions. His first 8 chapters give a good "overview of the strategy and tactics of pricing and a basic structure that can be applied immediately to improve pricing decisions. The last five chapters develop certain issues in greater depth to make the basic structure more useful." Examples are used throughout; bibliographical notes are at end of chapters.

PRODUCT DEVELOPMENT

Several of these books below are now rather old, but they are still in print as of 1991.

Bobrow, Edwin E., and Dennis W. Shafer. *Pioneering New Products: A Market Survival Guide.* Homewood, IL: Dow Jones-Irwin, 1987. 234 pp.

This is a short, practical "'how to' book that will serve as a guide for the systematic approach to developing and marketing new products that pioneer new business ground and survive in the marketplace." Includes useful diagrams, lists, charts, and occasional bibliographical footnotes.

Crawford, C. Merle. *New Products Management.* 3d ed. Homewood IL: Irwin, 1991. 564 pp.

Latest revision of a recommended text that provides a management approach to new product development. Crawford has arranged his text according to the following topics: overview and preparation; the ideation stage; concept evaluation; commercialization; structure/environment. Applications and short cases are with chapters; a "product innovation process chart" is in Chapter 2. Appendixes include an "ideation stimulator checklist," a glossary, and a bibliography.

Hisrich, Robert D., and Michael P. Peters. *Marketing Decisions for New and Mature Products.* 2d ed. New York: Macmillan, 1991. 516 pp.

This book presents "a hands-on approach to methods and applications than can minimize the risk of new product development and provide managers with the techniques and understanding to plan, manage, and control products and services over their life cycle." Annotated selected readings are at end of each chapter.

Kuczmarski, Thomas D. *Managing New Products: The Power of Innovation.* 2d ed. Englewood Cliffs, NJ: Prentice-Hall, 1992. 304 pp.

Kuczmarski says his book is a practical guide for management and new product managers on how to improve the success rate of internally developed new products and services. It is based on his experience in working directly with over 200 companies on ways to improve innovation and new products management. He starts with a chapter on the 10 key success factors. This is followed by chapters on: conducting a diagnostic audit; developing of a new product strategy; managing the process; structuring and leading the organization; rewarding and motivating champions; innovation for the future; creating newness for nonprofit organizations.

Pessemier, Edgar A. *Product Management: Strategy and Organization,* 2d ed. New York: Wiley, 1982. 668 pp. Reprinted in 1986.

Probably the most cited book in its field, this is a comprehensive text written for graduate students by a business professor who has concentrated much of his research on product policy and management. Pessemier examines in depth the essential components of product management, including practical methods of analysis, strategy formulation, and implementation, as well as the organization and control of the innovation/product function. Bibliographical references are at end of chapters; a glossary is at end of book.

Servi, Italo S. *New Product Development and Marketing: A Practical Guide.* New York: Praeger, 1990. 180 pp.

Written by a practitioner for practitioners, this is a short up-to-date guide to the why, what, how, who of the new product development process. It ends with "three outstanding examples of new product development." A selected bibliography is at end.

Souder, William E. *Managing New Product Innovations.* Lexington, MA: Lexington Books, 1987. 251 pp.

Based on a 10-year project to gather life-cycle data from 289 new product development innovations, the author feels he has written a unique book showing the best ways to manage new product innovations based on what he found in the real world. His chapters cover costs, organizing, managing, climate for success, picking winners, and much more. A final chapter distills Dr. Souder's findings into 10 principles for managing new product innovations.

Urban, Glen L., John R. Hauser and Nikhilesh Dholakia. *Essentials of New Products Management.* Englewood Cliffs, NJ: Prentice-Hall, 1987. 340 pp.

These authors have attempted to cover the major concerns in each phase of the new product development process and to emphasize particularly managerial issues, concepts, and methods. It is therefore organized around the chronological decision steps in new product development: innovation strategy, opportunity identification, designing new products, testing and improving products, and managing the life cycle. Throughout the book are real-world examples and useful diagrams; recommended readings are at end of chapters. There is little or no mathematical exposition, but a fundamental course in management and some familiarity with market research is useful.

Wheelwright, Steven C., and Kim B. Clark. *Revolutionizing Product Development: Quantum Leaps in Speed, Efficiency, and Quality.* New York: Free Press, 1992. 364 pp.

The result of a six-year in-depth research project in which the authors studied how designers, engineers, marketers, manufacturers, and senior executives of some companies combine their skills to build competitive advantage around product and process development. The first part focuses on the front end of the development process; chapters 6–10 cover the management of individual development projects; the final chapters shift to the concepts for effective organization and management of product and process development. Bibliographical notes are at end.

Just published is a revision of George Gruenwald's *New Product Development* (2d ed., NTC Business Books, 1992, 454 pp.). This is a guide to developing products and services and is based on the author's long-time practical experience.

Periodicals

Journal of Product Innovation Management. New York: Elsevier Science Publishing Company (quarterly).

This is an international quarterly sponsored by the Product Development and Management Association. Its purpose is to publish informative and thought-provoking articles on the research, experiences, and insights of academics, consultants, and practicing managers in the broad area of product innovation management. Articles are well researched, usually with a bibliography of sources consulted. Each issue has an "Abstracts" section describing pertinent articles selected from other journals. Occasionally it contains one book review. Indexed in ABI/I.

PUBLIC POLICY AND MARKETING

The books on antitrust and trade regulation that were in my previous edition are now too old to be listed again, and no recent books seem to have been written that are targeted for the business person. However one can find excellent and comprehensive treatises meant more for the legal profession in almost any law library. This section still cites the useful, comprehensive CCH legal service on trade regulation and antitrust, one periodical on this subject, two (now rather old) books on marketing law for the business person, and an annual covering research on public policy and marketing. Refer to Chapter 9 for names of books and reference sources in the general area of business, society, and the environment, on public policies toward business, and on business law. Several books on consumer behavior are listed elsewhere in this chapter. For better coverage of books on consumer protection, product safety, etc., check in library card catalogs or in a bibliography such as the annual *Subject Guide to Books in Print*.

Commerce Clearing House. *Trade Regulation Reporter.* Chicago. 7 volumes (loose-leaf, with weekly supplements).

A comprehensive service covering important federal and state laws, court decisions, Federal Trade Commission decisions, rules, controls, guides, FTC complaints and orders, advisory opinions, etc., relating to trade regulation, antitrust, and pricing. Vol. 7 contains current trade cases, which give recent court decisions and consent decrees. Vol. 7 also contains a cumulative index and a current topical index, while vol. 1 has a basic topical index, a table of cases, and finding lists. There is a separate set of bound volumes for past *Trade Cases*.

Persons who do not need such detailed coverage may want to investigate a similar two-volume service of the Bureau of National Affairs called *Antitrust & Trade Regulation Report*. It covers activities of the FTC and the Antitrust Division of the Department of Justice concerning antitrust and trade regulation; also legislative court decisions and special analyses of major developments. There are weekly updates, and it is also available online in full text.

Posch, Robert J. *What Every Manager Needs to Know about Marketing and the Law.* New York: McGraw-Hill, 1984. 328 pp. paper.

Written for all management professionals, this book tells you "both how to get things done within the framework of government regulations and how to keep government regulations from impinging on your management discretion." Posch (an attorney with an MBA degree) begins by discussing the need for your firm to develop a profit preservation center and then he focuses in turn on the law as it affects product decisions, channel policy, pricing policy, credit disclosure laws, promotion policy. Section 7 is a "guide to dunning compliance." The book is written simply, with good use of checklists for review and overview.

A short book, slightly older but also useful for its concise information written in nonlegal language, is *Marketing Law* by Joe L. Welch (Tulsa, OK: Petroleum Publishing Co., 1980, 158 pp.).

Stern, Louis W., and Thomas L. Eovaldi. *Legal Aspects of Marketing Strategy: Antitrust and Consumer Protection Issues.* Englewood Cliffs, NJ: Prentice-Hall, 1984. 550 pp.

This was written both for marketing executives and students as "a readily useable resource for obtaining a relatively detailed working knowledge of risks and opportunities which inhere in our legal system's regulation of marketing activities," and yet to know when to obtain further advice from legal counsel. The emphasis is on legal issues which arise from two major areas of public policy concern (antitrust law and consumer protection law), and the presentation is organized around the four elements of the "marketing mix" (pricing, product, channels of distribution, and promotion). Usually two legal cases are discussed at the end of each chapter.

Periodicals

Antitrust Bulletin. New York: Federal Legal Publications (quarterly).

Lengthy research articles on both American and foreign antitrust and trade regulation, written primarily by practicing attorneys and a few economists who have both a conceptual and a practical interest in the field. Includes book reviews. Indexed in ABI/I, PAIS.

Journal of Public Policy & Marketing. Chicago: American Marketing Association (semiannual).

Formerly published annually by the Division of Research, University of Michigan, this is intended to serve the growing interest group addressing the legal and regulatory impacts on marketing activities as well as to show how marketing techniques can be used by public policy makers. Each issue is usually over 200 pages; articles are well-researched and usually include bibliographies. Indexed in ABI/I.

SALES MANAGEMENT

It is important for sales management books to be kept right up-to-date to reflect the many recent changes in the external environment that may call for a changed emphasis in sales programs. Watch for more recent books, and also monitor articles in journals. For a description of the monthly *Sales & Marketing Management* see the sections for "Marketing Periodicals" and "Marketing Statistics." A *Sales Compensation Handbook* edited by John K. Moynahan

(1991) is described in the "Wage and Salary Administration" section of Chapter 19.

Handbooks

The Dartnell Sales Manager's Handbook. 14th ed. John P. Steinbrink, ed. Chicago: Dartnell Corporation, 1989. 1,272 pp.

Since its first appearance in 1934 this handbook has been an essential and practical one-volume reference work for concise information about sales policies and practices of American companies. The 14th edition has been updated to meet present-day policies and practices. Now in 46 chapters, it is arranged in the following sections: sales and marketing today; managing the sales function; sales planning and control; sales policies; marketing channels; managing the sales force. The "Ready-Reference Section," at end, contains a bibliography, glossary, legal data and contract forms, directories of business directories, of sales training aids and sales/marketing executives, data on promotion law, and on how to advertise consumer credit.

Books

Calvin, Robert J. *Managing Sales for Business Growth.* New York: AMACOM, American Management Association, 1991. 325 pp.

Unlike the texts described below, this is an action-oriented book for smaller or growing companies to help them maximize sales through effective sales management. Chapters cover important aspects of managing sales personnel (hiring, training, compensating, motivating, and evaluating); also management topics such as organizing, forecasting, planning, communications. The last two chapters focus on the use of computers, and on exporting.

Futrell, Charles. *Sales Management.* 3d ed. Chicago: Dryden, 1991. 609 pp.

This is a basic, readable introductory text to all major elements of sales management, written by a salesperson turned professor. It is arranged in 7 parts: introduction; sales planning; staffing the sales force; training the sales force; directing the sales force; sales force analysis and evaluation; social responsibilities of sales managers. Case incidents, and a profile of a successful sales manager are with chapters.

Stanton, William J., and Richard H. Buskirk. *Management of the Sales Force.* 7th ed. Homewood, IL: Irwin, 1987. 704 pp.

An established text on the management of an outside sales force and its activities, completely revised and brought up-to-date to reflect current changing conditions as of 1987. Its five major sections cover: introduction: sales-force staffing and operations (selecting, training, compensating, supervising, motivating); sales planning (forecasting, budgeting, territories, sales quotas); evaluation of sales performance; a forward look (ethical and social responsibilities and also careers in sales management). Two or three cases are with each chapter.

An introductory text on the same subject is *Sales Force Management: Planning, Implementation and Control* by Gilbert A. Churchill, Jr., Neil M. Ford and Orville C. Walker, Jr. (3d ed. Homewood, IL: Irwin, 1990, 845 pp., with 4th edition to be published in 1992.). This is arranged in three parts similar to those in the subtitle.

Still, Richard R., Edward W. Cundiff and Norman A.P. Govoni. *Sales Management: Decisions, Strategies and Cases.* 5th ed. Englewood Cliffs, NJ: Prentice-Hall, 1988. 638 pp.

Latest revision of another standard book, with part 1 focusing on the interrelationships of personal selling and marketing strategy; part 2, the problems of organizing the sales effort; part 3, an in-depth analysis of sales-force management; and part 4, techniques of controlling the sales effort. Cases appear at the end of each part.

Several other introductory undergraduate texts are: *Sales Management: Concepts and Cases* by Douglas J. Dalrymple (3d ed., New York: Wiley, 1988, 681 pp.); *Sales Management: Analysis and Decision Making* by Thomas N. Ingram and Raymond W. LaForge (Chicago: Dryden Press, 1989, 752 pp.); and *Sales Management: Text and Cases* by Thomas R. Wotruba and Edwin K. Simpson (2d ed., Boston: PWS-Kent Publishing Co., 1992, about 600 pp.).

Services

Dartnell Corporation. *Sales Force Compensation.* Chicago (biennial). About $165 plus mailing.

Most of the 1990 volume contains the results of a mail survey of some 250 companies in 20 industries, and it was conducted jointly by Dartnell Corporation and the Personnel Corporation of America. It focuses on sales productivity, sales management, and sales compensation, and spans 15 levels of sales executives, managers, and representatives. In addition, there is information on incentive plan design practices, telemarketing, benefits, training, and expense practices. There are 7 parts, with the second part giving statistics on current levels of pay, and the third on pay and performance. Some tables are given by company size, by type of product/service, type of buyer, industry. Position descriptions are in an appendix. The previous volume was in a loose-leaf format and contained some different tables.

SELLING AND SALESMANSHIP

Books on sales promotion are described elsewhere in this chapter.

Kurtz, David L., and H. Robert Dodge. *Professional Selling.* 6th ed. Homewood, IL: Irwin, 1991. 444 pp.

Latest edition of an introductory text on professional selling and steps in the sales process. It is in 6 parts to cover: professionalism in selling; foundations; pre-call preparation; making the sales presentation; securing sales today and tommorow (closing, demonstrations, sales resistence, and objections); additional dimensions (selling to organizational buyers, retail selling, selling real estate and insurance, managing the sales force). Diagrams and illustrations are found throughout as well as boxed features such as "Professional Selling in Action." A sales career profile is at beginning of each chapter, with case incidents at end of the chapter. At end of book is a directory of software and a glossary. These authors have written a shorter version called *Fundamentals of Professional Selling* (Homewood, IL: Irwin, 1989, 280 pp.).

A recently revised edition of another introductory text is *Professional Selling* by B. Robert Anderson (4th ed., Prentice-Hall, 1991, 455 pp.).

Pederson, Carlton A., Milburn D. Wright and Barton A. Weitz. *Selling: Principles and Methods.* 9th ed. Homewood, IL: Irwin, 1988. 644 pp.

A good traditional text on selling arranged in five parts: the field of selling; knowledge and skill required for successful selling; the sales process; special applications of sales principles; improving the sales representative's personal effectiveness. Suggested readings and a few case problems are with each chapter.

Russell, Frederic A., Frank H. Beach, Richard H. Buskirk and Bruce D. Buskirk. *Selling: Principles and Practices.* 12th ed. New York: McGraw-Hill, 1988. 602 pp. 13th edition will be published in 1992.

This 12th edition of a popular book on sales concepts and techniques is written by the last two authors, and it is intended to be as useful to students as it is to the self-taught entrepreneur. It still provides comprehensive coverage on each important selling topic, with chapters also on retail selling, industrial selling, ethics, legal aspects, sales management, and telemarketing. At the beginning of each chapter is a short "profile" interview with one of a wide variety of persons engaged in selling.

MARKETING BIBLIOGRAPHIES AND ABSTRACTING SERVICES

Other abstracts or indexes may be useful in looking for current marketing information especially articles on the marketing of specific products. For example, PROMT (see listing in chapter 6) abstracts articles on new products and technologies, market size, market share, market trends, plans, and strategies. *Predicasts F & S Index* (see chapter 2) often cites articles giving sales, consumption, or market share data for specific products and/or industries under the sub-heading "Market Information."

American Marketing Association. *Bibliography Series.* Chicago. (irregular).

Until 1980 this was a numbered series, each on a different topic, with most describing articles and a few other nonbook sources. The *Bibliography Series* is still being published at irregular intervals, but it is no longer a numbered series. Several of the more recent titles are: *An Annotated and Extended Bibliography of Health Care Marketing* ed. by P.D. Cooper et al. (1984, 186 pp.); *Services Marketing: An Annotated Bibliography* ed. by R.P. Fisk and P.S. Tansuhaj (1985, 256 pp.); *An Annotated and Extended Bibliography of Higher Education Marketing* ed. by K.K. Constantine (1986, 71 pp.); and *Marketing 2000: Future Perspectives on Marketing: An Annotated Bibliography* ed. by Allen E. Smith et al. (1989, 293 pp.).

Goldstucker, Jac L., ed. *Marketing Information: A Professional Reference Guide.* 2d ed. Comp. by Otto R. Echemendia. Atlanta: College of Business Administration, Georgia State University, 1987. 436 pp. A third edition is scheduled for publication in 1993.

This is a useful marketing directory/bibliography, in two parts. Part 2 is a good, annotated list of marketing books, handbooks, bibliographies, directories, periodicals, etc. These are broken down into 22 subject fields such as advertising, channels of distribution, franchising, industrial marketing, international marketing, pricing, product management, retailing, sales promotion. Part 1 provides a descriptive directory of associations, marketing research, services and consulting organizations, largest 300 advertising agencies, special libraries and information center collections, research centers, continuing education, and U.S. government agencies and organizations. Title and publisher indexes are at end.

Herold, Jean. *Marketing and Sales Management: An Information Sourcebook,* (Oryx Series in Business and Management, No.12). Phoenix, AZ: Oryx Press, 1988. 167 pp.

An annotated bibliography arranged by marketing topic and covering primarily reference sources (bibliographies, abstracts, databases, directories, periodicals, plus a few guidebooks/handbooks). It describes English language material published through 1986 with a few items published in 1987. Like most of the other Oryx Series bibliographies this has a "core library collection" listing those sources considered of most value, but also like others in the Series, it is now quite out of date.

Journal of Marketing. "Marketing Literature Review" section. Chicago: American Marketing Association (quarterly).

A continuing bibliography of marketing-related articles selected from the online database ABI/INFORM, and arranged in more than 20 subjects within the broad areas of: the marketing environment; marketing functions; special marketing applications; marketing research; other topics. Each issue of this journal also contains good critical book reviews.

PTS Marketing and Advertising Reference Service database (MARS).

This database abstracts articles on marketing and advertising of consumer products and services industries, covering not only specific products such as foods, consumer electronic products, but also producer organizations, the activities of advertising and public relations organizations, information on advertising campaigns, marketing strategies, market size and market share, advertising industry trends, and issues. Over 140 key publications are covered including basic advertising journals, consumer-oriented trade journals, newsletters, business methods journals, and advertising columns of major newspapers. As of 1991 more and more full-text articles are available on this database.

Three other sources may also be of interest: a descriptive listing of the top 150 marketing books and articles called *Marketing Megaworks* by Larry M. Robinson and Roy D. Adler (NY: Praeger, 1987, 211 pp.). Since this selection was based on the number of times each was cited from, 1972–76, it tends to be the older books and articles that have influenced marketing thought the most. Five of the top 20 ranked books are still available in more recent editions. The second suggestion may be of most interest to persons in the U.K. for it is a semiannual British abstracting service called *Market Research Abstracts* (London: Market Research Society). It covers articles on marketing and advertising, and is arranged by broad topic. Lastly, for a directory of business and marketing source material arranged by name of each foreign country, see *European Directory of Marketing Information Sources* (and its international companion directory) described in the "Bibliographies and Indexes" section of Chapter 5.

MARKETING DICTIONARIES

Bennett, Peter D., ed. *Dictionary of Marketing Terms.* Chicago: American Marketing Association, 1988. 220 pp.

Greatly expanded from several previous AMA glossaries, this is a good dictionary of marketing terms prepared by a group of academicians, each of whom covered the subset of the marketing discipline/profession in which s/he is an expert. Their initials are found with each definition they prepared. A list of references is at the end.

A somewhat similar dictionary with a British flavor is *Dictionary of Marketing & Advertising* by Michael J. Baker (2d ed., New York: Nichols Publishing, 1990, 271 pp.). It is also a collaborative effort of the staff of Strathclyde University's Department of Marketing; occasionally its definitions are longer than those in the Bennett dictionary.

Graham, Irvin. *Encyclopedia of Advertising.* 2d ed. New York: Fairchild Publications, 1969. 494 pp.

An encyclopedic dictionary of "more than 1,100 entries relating to advertising, marketing, publishing, law, research, public relations, publicity and the graphic arts." Still useful for older, well established terms but does not reflect new words, concepts, and usages of the 1970s and 1980s.

Imber, Jane and Betsy-Ann Toffler. *Dictionary of Advertising and Direct Mail Terms.* NY: Barron's, 1987. 514 pp. paper.

This is the most recently compiled advertising dictionary, defining some 3,000 key terms on "all facets of advertising today, including broadcast, print, direct-mail, and direct-response advertising, along with trade, corporate, and classified advertising." Definitions are clear, and there are many useful cross-references. Includes entries for related organizations and associations.

Ostrow, Rona and Sweetman R. Smith. *The Dictionary of Retailing.* New York: Fairchild Publications, 1985. 256 pp.

Defines and explains the many retailing words and phrases in practical and nontechnical terms. Definitions are short but good and include cross references and a few capsule biographies of historical figures.

Shapiro, Irving J. *Dictionary of Marketing Terms.* 4th ed. Totowa, NJ: Littlefield, Adams & Co., 1981. 276 pp. paper.

Concise definitions for over 5,000 terms of interest to managers.

MARKETING GUIDES

The market researcher has a wide variety of statistical sources at his/her disposal when undertaking any research project. Chapters 4 through 6 in this book describe the more important U.S. and foreign statistical volumes and also statistics on individual manufacturing and on agricultural and mining industries. Statistics on retail and wholesale business, as well as advertising expenditures, can be found elsewhere in this chapter. Don't overlook the useful descriptions of market research sources and statistics that are often found in books on marketing research (see note with "Marketing Research" section).

Note about MSA and Other Regional Categories—Some years ago the federal government established geographic standards in order to make for consistency in collecting marketing statistical data for U.S. metropolitan areas. The most widely used designation was for SMSAs (Standard Metropolitan Statistical Areas), and one could find not only detailed census figures by SMSA but also statistics in such commercial sources as those noted below. In 1983 the government replaced the SMSA and SCSA (Standard Consolidated Statistical Area) designations with three new categories in an attempt to improve marketing data. Of these, the most used category now is MSA (Metropolitan Statistical Area) which is defined as one or more counties around a large urban area with at least 50,000 population, adjacent areas of which have close economic and social ties to the principal county. The second category, PMSA (Primary Metropolitan Statistical Area), is an area that has more than one million population including a large urbanized county with over 100,000 population, and closely connected counties nearby. Both of these categories are defined in terms of counties except for the New England states which are defined in terms of cities and towns. The third and largest category is that for CMSAs (Consolidated Metropolitan Statistical Areas), rather like the former SCSAs, and comprising at least two PMSAs. Most of the U.S. marketing sources below use these new designations; the census begins to reflect this change in federal government statistics with the 1987 economic censuses. For better definitions of these three categories, and for a list of MSAs, check in either the Editor & Publisher *Market Guide* or in *Sales & Marketing Management* "Survey of Buying Power," first part.

Below are several periodic guides that provide recent statistical estimates for such important marketing barometers as population, households, income, buying power, and retail sales.

United States and Canada

Editor & Publisher. *Market Guide.* New York (annual).

Contains market data for U.S. and Canadian daily newspaper cities covering facts and figures about: location, transportation, population, households, banks, autos, gas and electric meters, principal industries, climate, tap water, retailing, retail outlets, newspapers. Also gives the following marketing statistics: E&P estimates by county, newspaper city, and MSA (Metropolitan Statistical Area) for population, disposable income, income per capita and per household, households, crop and livestock value, total retail sales, number of retail stores, sales estimates for 9 retail store groups (lumber/hardware, general merchandise, food, auto, gasoline, apparel, furniture, eat/drink, drugs). Rankings of most of these marketing data, by MSA, leading counties and cities, are at front of volume. This annual guide has been published since 1924.

Financial Post. *Canadian Markets.* Toronto: Maclean Hunter Ltd. (annual).

A useful source for demographic data arranged by Canadian province, city, and town. For each it usually gives: population (by age and sex), marital status, mother tongue, housing, private households, families, level of schooling, labor force, occupations by major groups, income, vital statistics, new vehicle registration, average household expenditures, building permits, homes built, manufacturing industries, taxation statistics, newspapers. For CMAs (Census Metropolitan Areas) it also gives data on lifestyles and on radio and TV stations. At front are the following tables: buying power indices (population, personal disposable income, retail sales) for provinces, Canadian census divisions, metropolitan areas, cities, and towns; forecasts of population, households, income, retail sales by province and metropolitan area; retail sales for 6 types of stores; rankings of income and retail sales.

Handbook of Canadian Consumer Markets. Ottawa, Ontario, Can.: Conference Board of Canada (biennial).

A good collection of over 235 statistical tables (with some graphs) drawn from a wide variety of sources and providing data arranged in the following 6 subject areas:

population, employment, income, expenditures, production and retail trade, prices. These statistics are also available as a marketing database which is updated on a regular basis.

The Lifestyle Market Analyst. Wilmette, IL: Standard Rate & Data Service (annual).

This is a new (1989) and potentially useful "reference guide for consumer market analysis" arranged in three sections. Section 1 has "market profiles" for each ADI market, giving demographic statistics (age, marital status, income levels, education, children at home, race, etc.) and also data on lifestyles (what portion of the market's households have persons who participate in each of 56 activities/interests, such as photography, gardening, specific sports, reading, stock/bond investments). Section 2 is arranged by each of these 56 lifestyle interests, with the ADI ranking given for each. Section 3, "consumer segment profiles," analyzes each of the demographic characteristics cited in section 1, and coordinates them with what lifestyle interests the segment prefers. A fourth section lists consumer magazines and direct mail lists (no addresses provided) targeted to each lifestyle profile.

Rand McNally Commercial Atlas & Marketing Guide. Chicago: Rand Mc-Nally & Co. (annual).

A popular atlas, covering maps for each state in the U.S. The marketing data at the front includes: population, income, and sales data for counties, basic trading areas, and MSAs (from the "Survey of Buying Power") as well as number of households, per capita income, effective buying index, retail sales and sales for general merchandise, apparel, food, and drug stores, and for passenger cars; population (past, present, and future) for MSAs and for counties; population for Ranally metro areas. There are also maps for trading areas, MSAs, zip codes; useful data such as postal regulations and rates, railroad and highway distances, lists of airlines, railroads, colleges and universities, ranked lists of *Fortune* largest companies, and much more. Some of that data taken from another source may not be as up-to-date as you can find by checking the original source.

Rand McNally also publishes a separate annual *Road Atlas* covering the U.S., Canada, and Mexico. It includes city and metropolitan area maps, and national parks.

Sales & Marketing Management. New York (monthly, with extra issues in June, August, October).

This journal publishes three useful annual statistical issues. These are:

(1) "Survey of Buying Power" issue (annual, extra August issue).

Marketing and economic researchers usually turn to this important issue first when they seek current estimates showing U.S. regional variations in population, income, retail sales, and buying power. It is in three sections, the most useful of which is section C which gives the following current statistics for each Metropolitan Statistical Area (MSA), county, and many cities: population, population by age group categories, number of households, retail sales for 6 store groups (food, eating and drinking, general merchandise, furniture/furnishings/appliances, automotive, drug), and effective buying income (EBI) by % households. Section A has survey highlights. Section B contains regional and state summaries and metro rankings for most of the same data as is in Section C. This special issue has been published every year since the 1930s. For many years it appeared as the May 10 issue; then it was changed successively to a June, then a July, and most recently (1989) to the extra

August issue. Market Statistics, New York, which generates the data for this survey, maintains an up-to-date data bank for these demographic and sales statistics. Formerly this special issue contained comparable statistics for Canadian provinces, counties, and cities. These Canadian statistics must now be requested separately each year by subscribers using the title *Survey of Buying Power: Canadian Data*.

(2) "Survey of Media Markets" (annual, extra October issue).

The third part of this Survey has tables for "Media Market Projections" consisting of % change over five years for population, EBI, and total retail sales for each metro area. The first section has highlights; the second, "Media Market Profiles," contains, for each Arbitron ADI market, population by age group and total blacks and Hispanics, number of households, EBI, total retail sales, and a buying power index. Section 4, "Merchandise Line Sales," contains ranked lists of metro areas for each of 10 retail merchandise lines.

(3) "Sales Manager's Budget Planner" (annual, extra June issue).

Section 2 contains "Metro Market Profiles" for 94 major U.S. metro markets and for 6 in Canada. Data given includes vital statistics, meal & lodging costs, names of hotels/motels, meeting sites and restaurants (with rates or prices), airport-to-city transportation, daily auto rental rates. Section 3 has useful tables and graphs on compensation and expenses including training, incentives, sales support (such as equipment costs), and transportation costs.

Sourcebook of Zip Code Demographics. Fairfax, VA: CACI (annual).

For each U.S. zip code this gives census statistics and proprietary marketing estimates for: population, number of households, housing profile, age distribution, median age, race, education, employment profiles, % distribution of households by income, purchasing potential. This latter measures potential demand for 13 types of products/services such as apparel, footwear, groceries, video rental, dining out, auto aftermarket, furniture, investments, savings, loans. At end are tables for "Business Statistics" which give (for each zip code area) number of firms, estimated employment, and top five SIC codes ranked by employment. The "1990 Census Edition" will be published in 2 volumes, with vol. 1 published in 1991 and containing part of this data, and vol. 2 to be published in 1992.

Standard Rate & Data Service. Wilmette, IL.

In three of the SRDS monthly publications (those for newspapers, spot radio, spot television), marketing statistics are included near the front of each issue. These give state, county, city, metropolitan area estimates for population, households, household income (% distribution by income size), household expenditures for 7 retail groups (food, drug, general merchandise, apparel, home furnishings, automotive, service stations), number of passenger cars, black and Spanish population. Metropolitan area rankings for these same marketing statistics are at front, as are rankings of Areas of Dominant Influence (ADI) and Designated Market Areas (DMA).

Europe and International

Consumer Europe. London: Euromonitor Publications, Ltd. (biennial). Distributed in U.S. by Gale Research, Inc., Detroit.

A statistical guide to over 500 major consumer products bought by consumers in 17 European countries. Data quoted is usually sales or consumption, market value, % change, per capital volume and value, market share among countries. Statistics for each product usually cover a 6-year period. It is arranged within 17 major sections, with a list of sources and associations at end of each section. A few projections are at end.

European Marketing Data and Statistics. London: Euromonitor Publications, Ltd. (annual). Distributed in the U.S. by Gale Research, Inc.

For each European country, statistics cover: economic indicators, foreign trade, environmental data, advertising patterns, consumer prices and costs, consumer market sizes, consumer expenditure patterns, retailing, households and household facilities, health and living standards, literacy, communications, travel and tourism. Sources of data are noted at bottom of page; basic information sources are at front.

A companion volume providing data on many of the same categories is *International Marketing Data and Statistics.* This covers 153 non-European countries. This publisher also has a little pocketbook guide to *The A–Z of UK Marketing Data* (4th ed., 1990) that gives brief figures on around 400 consumer products, occasionally including market share in the U.K.

MARKETING REPORTS ON INDUSTRIES AND LOCATIONS

The publishers of some trade journals issue statistical surveys or outlooks for their industry that are often included as annual issues of their journal. References to several can be found in Chapter 6. Newspaper publishers in some large cities publish periodic consumer analyses that give buying habits and brand preferences of families in their market area. Two examples are the Milwaukee Journal's annual *Consumer Analysis,* and the Omaha World Herald's *Consumer Preference Study.* A few newspaper publishers also issue market or media studies that contain statistics for the market area.

In addition, many commercial research firms or publishers compile and publish market research reports or services providing current trends and an outlook for specific industries or products. Topics run the gamut from "abrasives" to "zirconium." The vast majority of these are too expensive to be found in a public or university library; corporate libraries probably have those that are written on subjects in which they have a special interest. Although the reports themselves may not be easily located, it is helpful to have access to the directories described below for use in identifying these reports, especially the first for its coverage of reports published in the United States.

Directories of Market Research Reports

Findex. Bethesda, MD: Cambridge Information Group Directories (annual, with mid-year supplement). Available also online.

This directory describes over 12,000 marketing research reports, studies, and surveys from some 500 domestic and foreign publishers. It is arranged by 12 broad industry classifications, with a more detailed subject index and publisher's index at end. For each report, it usually gives title, date, paging, price (many unfortunately cost more than $1,000), and a brief description of contents. Since some of the reports in the annual volume are somewhat out of date, it is important to note that the listing within each subject category is chronological, with the most recent reports described first. A separate list of a few company reports prepared by investment research firms is included, but most are short, expensive, and not right up-to-date. Subscribers to *Findex* receive a quarterly *Information Catalog* that, along with the mid-year supplement, will be useful for their descriptions of the most recent market research reports.

Marketsearch: International Directory of Published Market Research. London: Arlington Management Publications, Ltd. in association with the British Overseas Trade Board (annual, with semiannual supplement). U.S. orders can be addressed to: MacFarlane & Co., Atlanta, GA 30318.

More then 19,000 published market research studies are identified in this directory which covers over 150 countries. The directory section itself (part 2) is arranged according to the British Standard Industrial Classification scheme. For each report, it usually gives title, countries covered, brief statement of products/services offered, number of pages, date, source, and price. An alphabetical product index is at front; a source index (publishers) and a list of reports by name of publisher are at end.

Bibliographies of Market Share Information

Market Share Reporter. Detroit: Gale Research, Inc. (annual).

Begun in 1991, this is an annual compilation of published market share data on companies, products, and services as taken from periodicals and brokerage reports for several previous years. It is organized into chapters by two-digit SIC categories, and then by four-digit numbers. For each it usually gives: remarks on characteristics, a list of products or producers and their % market share, source of the data. Occasionally an entry includes a pie chart illustrating the data. There are five indexes: by source; place names; products/services/issues; companies; brands. Four categories of market share data are covered: corporate market share; institutional shares (countries, states, etc.); brand market share; product/commodity/service/facility shares; other shares. Thus it identifies more than just market share for products, but also such data as product rankings by country or state, some ranked lists of companies, etc. Much of its inclusion of data from brokerage reports is based on use of the database *Investext.*

CONSUMER EXPENDITURE STUDIES

The principal U.S. government source for current personal consumption expenditure by type of expenditure is the "National Income and Product Accounts" issue of the U.S. Department of Commerce, *Survey of Current Business* (annual, July issue). This is described in Chapter 4. Current quarterly expenditure statistics for major products are in each monthly issue of the *Survey.* For other current sources of statistics on consumer expenditure see: *European Marketing Data and Statistics; International Marketing Data and Statistics; Yearbook of Labour Statistics;* also the "Annual Consumer Expenditures Study" in *Supermarket Business* (September issue).

The Bureau of Labor Statistics has been gathering information on the spending patterns and living costs of American consumers for a long time. Beginning in 1983 this sample "Consumer Expenditure Survey" became an ongoing project, with data collected in two ways, by an Interview survey and by a Diary survey. The Interview survey was designed to obtain data on the types of expenditures respondents can easily recall, including relatively large expenditures, such as those for property, automobiles, and major appliances, and those occurring on a regular basis such as rent, insurance premiums, and utilities. The Diary survey collects data on frequently purchased smaller items, such as food and beverages, tobacco, housekeeping supplies, nonprescription drugs, personal care products and services. Formerly these survey results were published separately as *BLS Bulletin* numbers (e.g. Bulletins 2245 and 2246 for data covering 1982–83). More recently the interview/diary data has been integrated. The latest annual integrated data (as of 1991) is in the Bureau of Labor Statistics' *Bulletin 2354* titled "Consumer Survey, 1987" (published June 1990, 153 pp.). Here are statistical tables giving figures on consumer expenditures for specific products arranged by consumer units such as income size, family size, age, race, geographic region (for selected MSAs), occupation of reference person, and more. Much of this CES data is also available on tapes and on diskettes.

For a recent commercially published reference book that is based on data from the CES see:

Ambry, Margaret K. *Consumer Power: How Americans Spend Their Money.* Ithaca, NY: New Strategist Publications, 1991. 461 pp. Also in paperback. A compilation of statistics tracking the spending of some 25,000 U.S. households. The tables are organized by product and services in the following categories: food and alcoholic beverages; housing (shelter and utilities); housing (operations and utilities); apparel and apparel services; transportation; health care; entertainment; personal care/reading/education/tobacco products; financial products and services; cash contributions; gifts, other items. For each, it has tables on spending for specific items (e.g. food products) by age, income, and type of household, with aggregate expenditures for 1988 and projections for 1995 and 2000. The last chapter contains summary tables giving average spending, share of spending tables, indexed expenditure tables, and aggregate expenditure tables. A glossary is at end along with a brief description of the BLS "Consumer Expenditure Survey" from which this data was taken. If this is to be a useful marketing tool, it must be updated periodically.

British statistics are in *Family Expenditure Survey,* published annually by the Great Britain Department of Employment; also in *United Kingdom National Accounts,* an annual publication of their Central Statistical Office. National account statistics for U.N. and OECD countries include consumer expenditure statistics, and these publications are described in Chapter 5.

MARKETING PERIODICALS

Articles in some of these periodicals are also indexed in the database *MARS* as well as in the indexes noted with each journal below. *MARS* is the *PTS Marketing and Advertising Reference Service* described in the "Marketing Bibliographies and Abstracting Services" section of this chapter. Several more specialized marketing periodicals are described with books on each topic in previous sections of this chapter. These are: *Journal of Consumer Research; Journal of Product Innovation Management; Antitrust Bulletin;* and *Journal of Public Policy & Marketing.* Advertising, retailing, and direct marketing periodicals are listed in sections on those subjects later in this chapter.

Academy of Marketing Science. *Journal.* Greenwich, CT: JAI Press (quarterly).

Publishes articles on marketing science that are written by Fellows of the Academy. Book reviews are in some issues. Indexed in PAIS.

American Marketing Association. *Marketing News.* Chicago (biweekly).

A widely-read biweekly newspaper noted for its short, timely articles, news about the AMA, its members, and the marketing industry. Frequent columns are contributed by well-known practitioners or academic persons. Occasionally an issue focuses on a particular topic such as marketing research, business-to-business marketing, creativity and innovation in marketing. "The Honomichl 50" (last May or first June issues) is a ranked list of the 50 top market research organizations which also contains profiles of each. It was taken from Jack Honomichl's annual report. This newspaper is indexed in ABI/I, BPI, TI; full text on BRS, DATA-STAR, DIALOG, MEAD/NEXIS.

Business Marketing. Chicago: Crain Communications, Inc. (monthly).

This is the new title of *Industrial Marketing,* a long-established trade journal on advertising and selling to business, industry, and the professions. It includes regular departments on trade shows, marketing law, communication effectiveness, and more. Features include: "Ad Volume Review & Forecast" (semiannual, in March and September); the " 'Top 100' Business-to-Business Marketers in America" (October), a ranked list, with profiles of each company; "Ad Spending Forecasts by Industry" (November). Each issue has book reviews and a short list of market reports. Indexed in ABI/I, BPI, PTS/F&S, TI; full text on DATA-STAR, DIALOG.

Industrial Distribution. Newton, MA: Cahners Publishing Co. (monthly).

Covers articles and industry news of interest to industrial distributors and also marketing/operations ideas. The July issue each year contains an "Annual Survey of Distributor Operations," and the November issue has a "Salary Survey." Indexed in ABI/I, BPI, TI; full text on BRS, DATA-STAR, DIALOG, DOW JONES, MEAD/NEXIS.

Industrial Marketing Management. New York: Elsevier Science Publishing Co. (quarterly).

Articles in this international journal are within the broadly defined area of its title and include marketing research, sales management, product and marketing planning, buyer behavior, forecasting, and so forth. They are aimed at both business people and scholars. Indexed in ABI/I, BPI.

Journal of Consumer Marketing. Santa Barbara, CA: Grayson Associates (quarterly).

One of three Grayson Associates quarterlies addressed to a particular market segment, this one focuses on easy-to-read articles of interest to consumer market practitioners seeking new ideas and applications in making managerial decisions and to marketing teachers who want examples of how the theories taught in class work in the "real world." Occasional issues include a few book reviews.

The two companion quarterlies are *Journal of Business & Industrial Marketing* and *Journal of Services Marketing.* All three journals are indexed in ABI/I.

Journal of Macromarketing. Boulder: Business Research Division, University of Colorado (semi-annual).

Research papers on the effect of social programs on marketing practice, with most articles by academicians. The Spring 1990 issue contains an annotated "Macromarketing Bibliography" by George Fisk. Includes book reviews. Indexed in ABI/I.

Journal of Marketing. Chicago: American Marketing Association (quarterly).

This is the leading marketing journal, both for academic persons and for marketing executives. Articles are on concepts, theory, trends, new ideas, and techniques in a wide range of marketing management topics. Each issue contains the following useful regular features: a "Marketing Literature Review" section (see bibliographies section for description); a good critical book review section; brief information on current legal cases, arranged by topic. Indexed in ABI/I, BPI, TI; full text on BRS, DATA-STAR, DIALOG, MEAD/NEXIS. A cumulative index has been published covering volumes 1–52 (1936–1987).

Journal of Marketing Research. Chicago: American Marketing Association (quarterly).

Another good but more specialized journal of the AMA, this one for professional articles on concepts and quantitative methods used in solving marketing research problems. Each issue has a section called "Research Notes and Communications" and a book review section. Indexed in BPI, TI; full text on BRS, DATA-STAR, DIALOG, MEAD/NEXIS.

Market Research Society. *Journal,* London (quarterly).

Professional articles on market research with a British or multicountry flavor. Includes book reviews. Indexed in PAIS.

Marketing Research: A Magazine of Management & Applications. Chicago: American Marketing Association (quarterly).

Unlike the AMA's *Journal of Marketing Research* above, the aim of this new magazine (1989) is to provide practical, concise articles and information for practicing market researchers. Each issue usually contains about 6 feature articles plus regular departments on such topics as new technologies, legislative issues, statistical tips, demographic and social change, software reviews. There are also book reviews.

Marketing Science. Providence, RI: The Institute of Management Sciences and Operations Research Society of America (quarterly).

A refereed journal that aims to publish a wide variety of high quality quantitatively oriented papers in the areas of marketing models, measurement, theory, and applications.

Sales & Marketing Management. New York: Bill Communications Inc. (monthly except for the three months in which they publish special issues).

This widely known trade journal began publication in 1918 as *Sales Management.* It is best known for its excellent special issues which are described in the "Marketing Guides" section of this chapter. Indexed in ABI/I, BPI, PTS/F&S, TI; full text on BRS, DATA-STAR, DIALOG, DOW JONES, MEAD/NEXIS.

Several British and Canadian marketing periodicals are: *European Journal of Marketing* (Bradford, Yorkshire, England: MCB Publications Ltd; usually about 8 issues per year); *Marketing* (London: Haymarket Magazines Ltd., weekly); *Marketing* (Toronto: Maclean Hunter Ltd.; a Canadian trade weekly); *Marketing and Research Today* (London: Published for the European Society for Opinion and Marketing Research by Elsevier Science Publishers B.V., quarterly).

MARKETING AND MARKET RESEARCH DIRECTORIES

American Marketing Association. *International Directory & Marketing Services Guide.* Chicago (biennial).

Of most use for its roster of AMA members which contains an index by affiliation for each member. At the front is a listing of firms that provide marketing services, e.g. advertising and market research firms, consultants. For each, one can find names of top officers and location of branches.

American Marketing Association. New York Chapter. *Greenbook: International Directory of Marketing Research Companies and Services.* New York (annual).

This is the most useful marketing research directory. It is arranged alphabetically, and there are indexes: by specialization, by topic of computer programs offered, by geographic location, by name of principal officer. For each firm it gives address, phone/fax, location of branch offices, top officers, brief description of scope of activity.

Bradford's Directory of Marketing Research Agencies and Management Consultants in the United States and the World. Fairfax, VA: (triennial).

This is no longer as useful as the directory above because it does not describe the scope of activity of each firm it lists, and it is primarily U.S. companies with a very few from other countries. It is arranged by state (not city) and gives only address and top officer. The index by type of service is not helpful; there are two other indexes: alphabetical, and by name of top officer. Includes also list of associations and several rather old SMSA rankings.

European Society for Opinion and Marketing Research (ESOMAR). *Directory.* Amsterdam: The Society (annual).

The first part is a list of European market research societies and organizations, arranged by country, and including officers and activities or services offered. The second part (blue pages) is a directory of individuals who are members, also arranged by country. At end is a list of marketing or market research associations in each country.

The Market Research Society publishes an *International Directory of Market Research Organisations* (London; biennial). Arranged by about 70 countries, the data for each firm includes company description, product group expertise, research turnover, data services, international affiliation, number of staff, contact person, name of subsidiary or parent company.

MARKETING ASSOCIATIONS

American Marketing Association, 250 South Wacker Drive, Suite 220, Chicago, IL 60606.

Product Development and Management Association, Graduate School of Business, Indiana University, P.O. Box 647, Indianapolis, IN 46223.

SALES PROMOTION

Handbooks

Riso, Ovid, ed. *The Dartnell Sales Promotion Handbook.* 7th ed. Chicago: Dartnell Corporation, 1979. 1,206 pp.

A comprehensive desk-reference book intended to give sales promotion practitioners all the information they may need to evaluate the probable success of a promotion and to develop the plan once a decision to adopt it has been made. There are 44 chapters arranged within four parts: 5 chapters are on responsibilities and organization; 22 chapters on techniques and tools, such as catalogs, sales letters, sales manuals, mailing lists, displays, contests; 10 chapters on channels of distribution; 7 chapters on special related topics, such as controlling expenditures, measuring results, computers, sales promotion. A very practical compilation, with many illustrations, charts, examples; lists of business directories, business and professional publications, media, and so forth, are at end. However please note that this is very out of date.

Ulanoff, Stanley M., ed. *Handbook of Sales Promotion.* New York: McGraw-Hill, 1985. 607 pp.

Not as comprehensive as the handbook above but more up-to-date, this one has 30 chapters written by 35 contributors. It is divided into 8 parts: the nature of sales promotion; manufacturers' sales promotions to consumers; retailers' sales promotions; manufacturers' sales promotions to retailers, distributors, and sales forces; special personal sales promotions; the management of sales promotion; the creation and distribution of sales promotion items and services; sales promotion and the law. An appendix includes lists of organizations and periodicals, and a glossary.

Books

Blattberg, Robert C., and Scott A. Neslin. *Sales Promotion: Concepts, Methods, and Strategies.* Englewood Cliffs, NJ: Prentice-Hall, 1990. 513 pp.

A new effort by two professors, the aim of their text is to serve as a "guide to sales promotion literature as well as to assist the reader in understanding the research and practical issues associated with the design and execution of sales promotions." They have arranged the material into four parts: conceptual underpinnings; methods for analyzing sales promotions (coupons, trade deals, retail promotions); substantive findings and issues; sales promotion planning. A bibliography is at end.

Engel, James F., Martin R. Warshaw and Thomas C. Kinnear. *Promotional Strategy: Managing the Marketing Communication Process.* 7th ed. Homewood, IL: Irwin, 1991. 753 pp.

Based on a grounding in consumer behavior, these authors provide a complete view of promotional strategy from a managerial point of view, emphasizing an understanding of the factors molding and shaping effective strategic thinking. They study each component part of the overall promotion mix (advertising, sales promotion, personal selling, direct marketing, public relations, and other communications tools). Examples of real-world applications appear throughout, many as boxed "promotion in action" features, and there are other illustrations as well. Bibliographical notes are at end of chapters.

Govoni, Norman, Robert Eng and Morton Galper. *Promotional Management.* Englewood Cliffs, NJ: Prentice-Hall, 1986. 578 pp.

This text aims to foster an understanding of the role of promotion in overall marketing strategy and to identify key elements of promotional management. Those key elements are discussed in parts 3 to 5 of its 6 parts: advertising and advertising management; personal selling and sales management; sales promotion and public relations. Parts 1–2 provide the foundations and the setting; part 6 zeros in on the total promotional program—its evaluation and control, and its legal and social aspects.

These authors have more recently published a book of 28 readings entitled *Promotional Management: Issues and Perspectives* (Prentice-Hall, 1988, 305 pp., paper). It is arranged in parts that correspond to their text, and it blends classic articles with those that are more recent.

ADVERTISING HANDBOOKS AND BOOKS

Handbooks

Stansfield, Richard H. *The Dartnell Advertising Manager's Handbook.* 3d ed. Chicago: Dartnell Corporation, 1982. 1,088 pp.

An extensive compilation which covers important topics such as advertising department organization, campaign planning, agency selection, copywriting, media, research, sales literature, the budget. It is oriented toward industrial advertising but can also be applied to consumer advertising. There are many case histories, frequent illustrations, and a glossary at end. Although this is called a second edition, there are in fact few changes from the 1969 edition, and so most of the data, examples, illustrations unfortunately do not reflect the many changes and developments of the 1970s.

Books

Two more specialized books described elsewhere are: *Business to Business Advertising* by Charles H. Patti et al., listed in the "Business Marketing" section of this chapter; *The Management of International Advertising* by Erdener Kaynak, listed in the "International Marketing" section of Chapter 16.

Aaker, David A., and John G. Myers. *Advertising Management.* 3d ed. Englewood Cliffs, NJ: Prentice-Hall, 1987. 564 pp.

This text draws from and integrates contributions from the behavioral and management sciences. "The focus is on decision making, specifically those decisions involved with setting advertising budgets and objectives, creating advertising campaigns, developing media strategies, and measuring advertising results." The authors explain their approach to the management of advertising as "sophisticated, thoughtful, and state-of-the-art while being practical and relevant to planning, decision making and control." It is arranged in 6 parts; one case is with each part except for the last.

Albion, Mark S., and Paul W. Farris. *The Advertising Controversy: Evidence on the Economic Effects of Advertising.* Boston: Auburn House Publishing Co., 1981. 226 pp.

Albion and Farris wrote this book to review, summarize, and evaluate the extensive research literature on the issues and evidence regarding advertising's economic impact. They bring together different viewpoints on this hotly debated topic and present their own opinions in a final chapter. A list of the books and many articles they consulted is at the end.

For a classic and comprehensive study see *The Economic Effects of Advertising* by Neil H. Borden (Salem, NH: Ayer Company Publications, 1976, 988 pp.; this is a reprinting of the original book published in Chicago by Irwin in 1942).

Bogart, Leo. *Strategy in Advertising: Matching Media and Messages to Markets and Motivation.* 2d ed. Lincolnwood, IL: NTC Business Books, 1990. 406 pp.

An excellent book on good advertising strategy written for the practicing professional. It considers "how much money to spend, where, and in what kind of message units, with what frequency, directed at what targets." Bogart speaks from practical experience. He writes well, and the book is full of interesting facts and data. Useful bibliographical notes are with each chapter.

Bovée, Courtland L., and William F. Arens. *Contemporary Advertising.* 4th ed. Homewood, IL: Irwin, 1992. 718, [57] pp.

A comprehensive, beginning undergraduate text which aims to present advertising as it is actually practiced. It is arranged in five parts, covering first advertising perspectives, and then in turn: developing marketing and advertising strategies; creating advertisements and commercials; advertising media; special types of advertising (local, international, corporate, noncommercial advertising, and public relations). All sorts of advertisements, diagrams, charts are found throughout, as are boxed features called "Ad Labs" and "Checklists." Appendixes contain both a marketing and an advertising plan outline, discussion of career planning (including sources of information), and a glossary.

Dunn, S. Watson et al. *Advertising: Its Role in Modern Marketing.* 7th ed. Chicago: Dryden Press, 1990. 605 pp.

This standard text combines theory and practice and focuses on general principles and on decision making rather than on techniques. It has been extensively revised again to reflect rapid changes in the advertising industry. Its four parts are organized around the following problems of modern advertising and promotion: the environmental structure (marketing communication, social, economic and ethical issues, influence of government and industry regulation); organizational structure; advertising campaign planning (13 chapters on such topics as selling objectives, message tactics, media tactics, measuring effectiveness); special-purpose advertising (retail, business-to-business, institutional, international). Illustrations are used extensively, many of them in color; also "ad insights" are interesting boxed features. Those key terms in bold-face are defined in a glossary at end. Bibliographies are at end of chapters.

Fletcher, Alan D., and Thomas A. Bowers. *Fundamentals of Advertising Research.* 4th ed. Belmont, CA: Wadsworth Publishing Co., 1991. 364 pp.

Advertising research is discussed in most introductory advertising texts. Here is a book for persons wanting a more in-depth discussion, especially about research techniques and major advertising research suppliers. It is arranged in four parts: the nature of research; conducting advertising research; syndicated research sources; the outlook. Published sources for secondary data are discussed in Chapter 4. Tables of random numbers and addresses of research companies and information sources are in appendixes at end.

Gardner, Herbert S., Jr. *The Advertising Agency Business: The Complete Manual for Management and Operation.* Lincolnwood, IL: NTC Business Books, 1988. 229 pp.

"This book is intended as a working tool to help agency management run their business right." The author, who has had a long career in agency administration and finance, covers the subject in 6 parts: the fundamentals; financial operation; ownership; organization and operations; new business (the lifeblood of an agency); some general observations.

McGann, Anthony F., and J. Thomas Russell. *Advertising Media: A Managerial Approach.* 2d ed. Homewood, IL: Irwin, 1988. 452 pp.

A well-written, thorough introduction for future media planners and salespersons to the important managerial decisions involved in planning, buying, and evaluating advertising media. It is divided roughly into three parts to cover: basic marketing principles as they relate to the advertising media function; characteristics of each media; management of the media function. A glossary is at end.

Ogilvy, David. *Ogilvy on Advertising.* New York: Vintage Books, 1985. 224 pp.

An excellent book for practical advice from a veteran advertising man, addressed to persons who are seeking ways to improve techniques and to succeed in the advertising profession. It is full of interesting and throught-provoking comments and is easy to read. Illustrated with many advertisements.

Russell, J. Thomas, and Ronald Lane. *Kleppner's Advertising Procedure.* 11th ed. Englewood Cliffs, NJ: Prentice-Hall, 1990. 718 pp.

Professor Otto Kleppner's long-time standard textbook is now written by two other professors who have tried to carry on his tradition while making the many changes necessary to continue the book as an up-to-date overview of the history, purpose, and role of advertising in our multifaceted economy. They take students through a progression from the general to the specific, with the first three major parts covering: the background of advertising, the planning and research functions, and advertising as a business. The final three parts deal successively with the techniques and execution of advertising (chapters discuss each medium), the creation and production of advertising, and lastly the other environments of advertising (retail, international, legal, economic, and social aspects). The book is full of colored illustrations, diagrams, tables. Reading suggestions are with chapters; a glossary and short lists of periodicals and associations are at end.

Salz, Nancy L. *How to Get the Best Advertising From Your Agency.* Homewood, IL: Dow Jones-Irwin, 1988. 204 pp.

This is a practical guide for those persons who deal with agency people on a daily basis on how to work more productively with ad agencies and how to get better advertising. It first explains the things an agency does and how, and then it explains the client's role in instructing, assisting, interpreting, encouraging, and evaluating the agency's work. The author speaks from long personal experience in the advertising business.

Sandage, C.H., Vernon Fryberger and Kim Rotzoll. *Advertising: Theory and Practice.* 12th ed. New York and London: Longmans, 1989. 483 pp.

Now in its 12th edition, this popular introduction is still intended to give students a broad perspective and penetrating understanding of advertising. The authors have organized the material in 6 sections around the following questions: what is attempted; by whom; to reach which markets; using what strategic strategies and techniques; through which media, at what cost; with what effect? It is full of illustrations, and there are references at end of each chapter.

Sissors, Jack Z., and Lincoln Bumba. *Advertising Media Planning.* 3d ed. Lincolnwood, IL: NTC Business Books, 1989. 461 pp.

The emphasis in this introduction is on planning for consumer media, and the authors' goal is to explain media planning concepts and techniques as practiced by the leading media departments in American advertising agencies. Included as chapter 13 is a sample annotated media plan. Selected readings are listed with each chapter; a glossary is at end.

ADVERTISING STATISTICS

Advertising Age. Chicago: Crain Communications, Inc. (weekly).

This important advertising weekly publishes several annual issues or features of special interest:

(1) "100 Leading National Advertisers" (last September issue).

For each company these marketing profiles provide useful facts about their marketing operations such as sales and earnings, leading product lines and brands, how they rank nationally, share of market for important brands, advertising expenditures by media; also names of marketing personnel and agency account executives, both for parent companies and for their principal divisions or brands. This issue also has three tables: a ranked list of the "Top 100 Leading Advertisers"; "Ad Spending by 100 Leaders"; and "National Ad Spending by Category" (ad spending by media for about 30 industries or products). There are also ranked lists of the top 25 companies in each medium.

(2) "100 Leading Media Companies" (last June issue).

This includes a ranked list of the 100 leading media companies by revenue; shorter lists of media companies by specific type of media; also lists of properties of leading media arranged by type of media.

(3) "Agency Report" (last March issue; mid-April in 1992).

For a description of this issue see the "Advertising Directories" section of this chapter.

(4) "Research Business Review" (first June issue).

Ranks the "Top 50 U.S. Research Organizations," both marketing and advertising, by research revenues, with profiles of each.

(5) "The Top 200 Brands" (quarterly, usually in mid-February, May, August, November issues).

Ranked lists of brands by ad spending.

(6) "The Advertising Fact Book" (first January issue).

Beginning in 1992, the publisher has collected and updated the more important ranked lists for easy access in one special issue. These are: the 100 leading national advertisers; the 100 leading media companies; the world's top 50 advertising organizations; top 200 U.S. agency brands; total U.S. ad spending by category and media; total national ad spending by media; the top 100 magazines.

Advertising Statistics Yearbook. Henley-on-Thames, Oxon, Eng.: Advertising Association.

The first of this four-part statistical compilation is the largest, and it consists of media statistics by type of media for over 10 years. The other parts cover: advertiser statistics (including advertising expenditures by product sector, advertising/sales ratios, ranked lists of the top advertisers and top brands); advertising agency statistics (ranked list of U.K. agencies and those elsewhere in the world, plus a list of those in each European country); miscellaneous statistics. Some of the media statistics are from MEAL data (Media Expenditure Analysis Ltd.).

LNA/Arbitron Multi-Media Service. New York: Leading National Advertisers, Inc. 3 volumes (quarterly).

This is an expensive service published in three parts: (1) *Company/Brands $,* which gives year-to-date advertising expenditures in 9 media by company and then by principal brands; (2) *Class/Brand $,* in which the 9 media expenditure statistics are given by PIB (Publishers Information Bureau) product classifications for each brand, company, and classification, with quarterly and year-to-date data; (3) *Ad $ Summary,* an index by brands, showing the 9 media expenditures, media used, parent company, and PIB classification for each brand. This latter also contains ranked totals and a ranked list of the 1,000 leading advertisers by nine-media spending: it is the only part of the service that can be purchased separately.

   PIB publishes an even more expensive monthly service called *PIB/LNA Magazine Service* (3 volumes). This analyzes magazine advertising, with month-by-month advertising expenditures and linage by industry, by brand, by name of magazine. Volume 1 covers "Magazine Totals and Class Totals;" volume 2, "Brand Detail;" volume 3, "Indexes" (parent name index, brand index, product index). For further information contact the publisher in New York City.

World Advertising Expenditures. Mamaroneck, NY: Starch INRA Hooper in cooperation with the International Advertising Association (annual).

Five-year estimates of expenditures in various media categories for 58 countries, as well as per capita advertising expenditures and expenditures as a % of GNP. Data at end include inflation rates, by country, for 1984–88, and list of sources of expenditure data by country.

For advertising expenditure statistics in the U.K. and other countries, by media, see notes with *Campaign* and with *International Journal of Advertising* (U.K.) in "Periodicals" section of this chapter. In addition NTC Publications Ltd. (in U.K.) publishes for the Advertising Association and the European Advertising Tripartite a separate but very expensive quarterly called *European Advertising & Media Forecast* which gives statistics and forecasts for U.K. expenditures by media and product group. For Japan, the *Dentsu Japan Marketing/Advertising Yearbook* (Tokyo: Dentsu, Inc.) contains useful expenditure statistics for major media in Japan over several years, as well as a directory of Japanese ad agencies, market research and PR terms, and various media—all written in English.

ADVERTISING DICTIONARIES

Graham's *Encyclopedia of Advertising* for older terms and the *Dictionary of Advertising and Direct Mail Terms* by Imber and Toffler are described in the "Marketing Dictionaries" section of this chapter.

ADVERTISING PERIODICALS

Articles in most of the periodicals described here are indexed in the database *MARS* as well as in the indexing sources noted with each journal. *MARS* is the *PTS Marketing and Advertising Reference Service* described in the "Marketing Bibliographies and Abstracting Services" section of this chapter.

Advertising Age. Chicago: Crain Communications, Inc. (weekly).

Since the 1930s *Advertising Age* has been an important weekly newspaper, with current news of interest to advertising and marketing people. A special report in some issues features a product group (e.g., automotive or computer marketing), a type of media, or other topics of potential interest to subscribers. Several of its most useful special issues or features are described in the "Advertising Statistics" section of this chapter. Beginning in 1992 each issue contains a company index for companies with "significant mentions" in the issue. Indexed in ABI/I, PTS/F&S, TI; also full text on DATA-STAR, DIALOG, MEAD/NEXIS.

Advertising Age's Euromarketing. London: Crain Communications, Inc. (weekly).

A weekly newsletter (usually 6 pages per issue) for news items and features on marketing, advertising, and the media in Europe. It is quite expensive ($350) but persons interested in European marketing will find it useful for its news of companies, people, brands, and for its occasional ranked lists of top brands in European advertising agencies, and so forth. Each week there is a short ranked list of top spenders in one product category.

Adweek. New York: BPI Communications

Adweek is actually 6 different weeklies, each of which is devoted to publishing national and local marketing and advertising news and information of interest to advertising professionals in that region (New England, the East, Southeast, Midwest, Southwest, and West). Each is published locally. They also publish *Brandweek* (formerly *Adweek's Marketing Week*) which is of national interest. Indexed in BPI; also full text on MEAD/NEXIS. *Adweek* publishes an annual *Adweek Agency Directory* which is described in the next section of this chapter. In addition *Adweek/ New England* publishes a useful short guide to facts and figures on New England media called *Adweek's Guide to New England Markets & Media.*

Campaign. London: Haymarket Publishing Ltd. (weekly).

An important British news weekly for advertising and related topics. An annual list of "The Top 100 Advertisers" (supplement to last April) gives advertising expenditures for top U.K. advertisers by media, with name of ad agency. These statistics are taken from MEAL (Media Expenditure Analysis Ltd.) data. An extra issue in February ranks the "Top 300 Agencies" in the U.K., with profiles for many. Each issue contains tables for "Sharewatch," "Accountwatch," and "Accounts on the Move." Indexed in PTS/F&S.

International Journal of Advertising. London: Published for the Advertising Association by Cassell Educational Ltd. (quarterly).

This is an international, professional review covering all aspects of marketing communications from the academic, practitioner, and public policy perspectives. About 8 original articles are in each issue: the authors are usually academicians, both

American and foreign. The first two issues each year usually have short articles on "International Advertising Expenditure Trends." Prior to 1989 this expenditure data was given in more detail. Indexed in ABI/I, PAIS, TI.

Journal of Advertising. Athens, GA: Published by the American Academy of Advertising at the University of Georgia (quarterly).

Short but well-researched articles often written by academicians and usually including a bibliography. Covers a wide range of topics with the aim to publish articles that contribute to the development of advertising theory and its relationship to advertising practices and processes. Issues through 1989 included book reviews. A five-year index is in the last 1986 issue. Indexed in ABI/I, BPI, PAIS, TI; also full text on BRS, DATA-STAR, DIALOG, MEAD/NEXIS.

Journal of Advertising Research. New York: Advertising Research Foundation (bimonthly).

Covers original research on advertising and marketing, with short papers, many of which are written by academic persons. Center gray pages contain "Research Currents," comments and opinions expressed at ARF conferences and workshops or from the research community. Indexed in ABI/I, BPI, TI.

MediaWeek. New York: A/S/M Communications, Inc.

A trade journal for media personnel. In 1991 it absorbed *Marketing & Media Decisions* which included a number of useful brand reports, a directory of brands, and some media costs data. I was not able to verify whether these features are being continued in this new weekly. Indexed in ABI/I, BPI, TI; full text on BRS, DATA-STAR, DIALOG, DOW JONES, MEAD/NEXIS.

ADVERTISING DIRECTORIES

Largest Advertisers

Information about the largest U.S. advertisers is in *Standard Directory of Advertisers*. It includes name of advertising agency, advertising appropriations, media used, etc. A similar directory for Canadian companies is *National List of Advertisers*. Both of these directories are described in Chapter 7. See also the annual "100 Leading National Advertisers" issue of *Advertising Age* mentioned in the "Advertising Statistics" section of this chapter.

Media Directories

The basic directories of newspapers and periodicals are described in Chapter 7.

Advertisers Annual. East Grinstead, West Sussex, Eng.: Reed Information Services. 3 volumes.

A specialized British directory now expanded to 3 volumes. The first, "Advertising," contains lists of advertising agencies, sales promotion, and public relations firms, giving such pertinent data for each as names of executives, when established, number of employees, clients, and sometimes total billing. It also contains a directory of leading national advertisers, and an agency client index. Volume 2, "Media," is in two parts, one giving data on U.K. media (British newspapers, magazines, TV, radio and outdoor advertising), and the other covering media in non-U.K. countries and including advertising agencies for those countries. Volume 3 is a classified list of

"Services" and supplies, such as direct marketing firms, graphic designers, poster printers.

Broadcasting & Cable Market Place. New Providence, NJ: R.R. Bowker (annual).

Formerly the *Broadcasting Yearbook,* this annual contains a wealth of directory and some market data in 11 sections, with some of it taken from other Bowker publications. Includes data on U.S. and Canadian radio, TV stations, cable, satellites, programming services, services and suppliers, associations/events/education/awards, books/periodicals/videos, laws and regulations, government agencies. Market statistics include figures on the radio market, an Arbitron ADI market atlas (containing a map for each TV market with number of TV households by county), TV markets ranked by size, network delivery by market, cable penetration by market.

Standard Rate & Data Service. Wilmette, IL.

This service offers separate directories giving advertising rates, specifications, and circulation for publications, broadcast stations, and so forth, in the following advertising media: *Business Publication Rates and Data* (monthly in three parts); *Card Deck Rates and Data* (semiannual); *Community Publication Rates and Data* (a semiannual which profiles weekly newspapers and shopping guides); *Consumer Magazine and Agri-Media Rates and Data* (monthly); *Direct Mail List Rates and Data* (bimonthly); *Newspaper Rates and Data* (monthly); *Spot Radio Rates and Data* (monthly); *Spot Radio Small Markets Edition* (semiannual); *Spot Television Rates and Data* (monthly). Among other specialized SRDS publications are: *Hispanic Media and Markets* (quarterly); *Newspaper Circulation Analysis* (annual); *Print Media Production Data* (quarterly); *Special Issues* (5/yr.). The three services for newspapers, spot radio, spot television include marketing statistics for states, counties, cities, and metropolitan areas (see "Marketing Guides" section of this chapter for description).

Similar volumes covering all media in Great Britain and Canada are published by Maclean Hunter Ltd. These are titled *British Rates and Data* (monthly) and *Canadian Advertising Rates and Data* (monthly). In addition, publishers in 6 European countries each have similar directories written in the language of each country. Those countries covered are Austria, France, Italy, Mexico, Switzerland, and Germany.

Television & Cable Factbook. Washington, DC: Warren Publishing. 2 unnumbered volumes in 3 (annual).

One of these three large annual volumes covers "TV Stations," a directory of U.S. television stations, arranged geographically and including for each, a map, a few technical facts, personnel, TV households for the area served. Separate lists cover such special topics as public/educational TV stations, and lesser information is given for TV stations in Canada and other foreign countries. It also contains lists of supplementary organizations and services, some of which also appear in the "Services" volume. The "Cable" volume contains a descriptive directory of cable systems arranged by state/city. The "Services" volume contains many useful descriptive lists of related service organizations both for TV and for cable, such as consultants, attorneys, publications, market and audience research organizations, associations, labor unions, brokerage and financing firms, public relations and promotion, TV set makers, manufacturers and suppliers of equipment, a buyers guide, FAA department, cable penetration (state by state), ranked list of largest U.S. cable systems.

Advertising Agencies

Advertising Age. "Agency Report." (annual, in a March or April issue).

Contains useful profiles of the "World's Top 50 Advertising Organizations," with facts for each usually including income and volume, billings by major office, names of officers, number of employees, and some data on subsidiaries. Other lists include a ranking of over 500 "U.S. Agency 'Brands'," by gross income; top 25 "U.S.-Based Consolidated Agencies," by worldwide, U.S. and non-U.S. gross income; top "Foreign Agencies by Gross Income," arranged by over 70 countries; "Top 10 Agencies by U.S. Media Billings" in 14 media categories.

Adweek Agency Directory. New York: BPI Communications (annual).

Formerly published separately for each of the 6 geographic regions and received with subscriptions to *Adweek,* this is still arranged by region and then by state, but it is now all in one volume (cost is $225). The data for each of its more than 3,800 U.S. advertising agencies, PR firms, and media buying services usually includes: key personnel, fields served, billings by medium, major accounts, number of employees at that location, year founded, subsidiaries/divisions/affiliations, fax number. At end are three indexes: by company, by fields serviced/services offered, by subsidiaries/divisions under parent company. At front are: ranked lists of the largest ad agencies (for each region and worldwide), top 15 holding companies, and a list of advertising associations, clubs, and networks. *Adweek* also publishes an annual *Adweek Client/Brand Directory,* with information on some 6,000 brand-name products.

Standard Directory of Advertising Agencies. Wilmette, IL: National Register Publisher Co. (3/yr.).

For each U.S. agency, this directory gives specialization, officers, account executives, approximate annual billings, % by media, names of accounts. A ranked list of the largest agencies is at front, as well as a list of name changes and a special market index. At end are lists of media service organizations, sales promotion agencies, public relations firms, and an alphabetical list of personal names.

A new companion volume, *Standard Directory of International Advertisers & Agencies,* includes a directory of foreign advertising agencies with a geographic index, and a ranked list of the top 50 worldwide agencies. Complete description in Chapter 7.

The American Association of Advertising Agencies publishes an annual *AAA Roster and Organization* which gives names and addresses of member firms and association committees. There is a list of Canadian advertising agencies in *National List of Advertisers,* which is described in Chapter 7, and a descriptive list of British ad agencies in *Advertisers' Annual,* volume 1, noted above.

ADVERTISING ASSOCIATIONS

American Advertising Federation, 1400 K Street, N.W., Suite 1000, Washington, DC 20005.

American Association of Advertising Agencies, 666 Third Avenue, 13th Floor, New York, NY 10017.

Association of National Advertisers, 155 East 44th Street, New York, NY 10017.

International Advertising Association, 342 Madison Avenue, New York, NY 10017.

DIRECT MARKETING

Julian Simon (see book below) recommends the checking and reading of more than just one book on the mail-order business since they do not always cover exactly the same topics. Also he feels it is of value to "keep them around and reread them from time to time. You can appreciate the wisdom in these books only after you have gotten into the business."—cf. p. 519.

Handbooks

Hodgson, Richard S. *The Dartnell Direct Mail and Mail Order Handbook.* 3d ed. Chicago: Dartnell Corp., 1980. 1,538 pp.

A comprehensive but now rather old one-volume compendium of 49 chapters covering methods, techniques, and important problems of direct mail and mail order. Includes practical illustrations and examples throughout. An appendix has reference data, such as a direct mail bibliography, a glossary, a list of business directories, postal rates and regulations, guidelines of the direct mail association, but this is also out of date.

Nash, Edward L., ed. *The Direct Marketing Handbook.* 2d ed. New York: McGraw-Hill, 1992. 827 pp.

This is a completely revised handbook that provides a foundation on direct marketing theory and its practical applications, with more emphasis on the former in this edition. Its 52 chapters by over 50 professionals are arranged within the following 8 sections: strategy and planning; databases and mailing lists; alternative media; creative tactics; production methods; fulfillment planning; financial and tactical planning; applications (with chapters discussing such specific areas as subscription marketing, financial services marketing, catalog marketing, customer loyalty programs).

Books

Cohen, William A. *Building a Mail Order Business: A Complete Manual for Success.* 3d ed. New York: Wiley, 1991. 584 pp.

Written from Cohen's personal experience as a practitioner and seminar leader, this is a comprehensive and practical book that takes you from the beginning of how to get your mail-order business started, through all aspects, topics, and techniques he feels are needed for success in mail order. In this revision most chapters have been revised and much material added, including an enlarged appendix, continuing guidelines for ethical practices, a sample mail order marketing/business plan, lists of associations, advertising agencies, sources of mailing lists. Frequent use of examples, short subtopics, illustrations of all sorts, add to the interest of this "nuts and bolts" book.

Ljungren, Roy G. *The Business-to-Business Direct Marketing Handbook.* New York: AMACOM, 1989. 456 pp.

At the title indicates, this book focuses solely on business-to-business direct marketing rather than on consumer direct marketing, and it draws on the long-term practical experience of its author. There are three parts: direct marketing mix (sales support, market segmentation, business lists, marketing data base); managing the direct marketing effort; direct marketing strategies (including profiles of successful strategies). Supplementary data such as postal service rules, tables of sample sizes for responses, are in appendixes.

Nash, Edward L. *Direct Marketing: Strategy, Planning, Execution.* 2d ed. New York: McGraw-Hill, 1986. 445 pp.

The author's intention in writing this book is still to take the reader step by step along the road to eventual success in any direct marketing endeavor, and he tries to make this as interesting and fast-moving as he feels the subject is. He starts with background chapters on strategic planning, the marketing plan, and the proposition. From this he focuses on mailing lists, the various media, research, testing, and other topics dealing with the science and art of advertising. He ends with chapters on direct marketing economics and hopes for the future.

Roman, Ernan. *Integrated Direct Marketing: Techniques and Strategies for Success.* New York: McGraw-Hill, 1988. 239 pp.

Mr. Roman defines integrated direct marketing as "the art and science of managing diverse media as a cohesive whole"—cf. p.5. His book aims to offer a framework for implementing IDM and to note its potential as a force in realizing greater profits and more job satisfaction. He starts by discussing this new marketing philosophy and then he studies each of the decision making areas that can make or break the synergistic effect of IDM. These include: media selection and implementation, strategic planning, ongoing project management, creative excellence, development of database resources. Interspersed are case histories he calls "Cases in Point" and also "Words from the Wise" which are short cautions or advice. A "management checklist" is at end, as well as a bibliography and an appendix containing guidelines on selection and maintenance of systems and applications software.

Simon, Julian L. *How to Start and Operate a Mail-Order Business.* 4th ed. New York: McGraw-Hill, 1987. 597 pp.

Designed both for newcomers and for experienced mail-order operators, this book runs through the important steps on how to proceed and what to do in starting and operating a mail-order business. Among other things Simon discusses finding a product, tactical decisions in advertising, mail-order media, catalogs, filling orders, mailing, use of computer programs, and general management. Useful data (such as copyright information and descriptions of types of successful mail-order businesses) is in an appendix. There is also a helpful partially annotated bibliography.

Stone, Bob. *Successful Direct Marketing Methods.* 4th ed. Lincolnwood, IL: NTC Business Books, 1988. 575 pp.

Another book intended for both students and seasoned professionals, this one is written by a well-known advertising agent who has specialized in direct marketing. Stone has arranged his text in four parts which cover: the world of direct marketing; choosing media for your message; creating and producing direct marketing; managing your direct marketing business (mathematics and research techniques). Reflecting recent trends and developments are the addition of new chapters on business-to-business marketing, data base marketing, and fund raising for worthy causes. There are useful checklists, tables, illustrations throughout; a glossary and an appendix on careers in direct marketing are at end.

Statistics

Direct Marketing Association. *Statistical Fact Book.* New York (annual).

Much expanded, this is now over 200 pages in length and full of statistics and many charts or graphs arranged in the following sections: direct response advertising, media (including data on the catalog and telephone as well as direct mail) lists/

databases, markets, basic management information (including postal information).
For each it usually gives data on consumer attitudes, buying habits, costs, trends,
projections. Many of these facts are taken from other sources.

Directories

Direct Mail List Rates and Data. Wilmette, IL: Standard Rate & Data Service
(bimonthly).

This directory lists over 55,000 mailing lists arranged by some 200 market classifications. It is in three sections to cover: business lists, consumer lists, farm lists. For
each list it usually gives source, rental rates, commissions. There are also separate
sections for co-op lists, list brokers, list compilers. Other media services of SRDS
are listed in the "Advertising Directories" section of this chapter.

One can obtain mailing list catalogs from most mailing list brokers at a nominal
fee. Several examples are American Business Lists, Inc., *List of 14 Million Businesses* (Omaha); Ed Burnett Consultants, Inc., *The Burnett Guide to Sales Leads
Prospects Lists* (Englewood, NJ); Edith Roman Associates, Inc., *Edith Roman
Direct Mail Encyclopedia* (New York).

The Direct Marketing Market Place. Boca Raton, FL: Hilary House Publishers (annual).

Of possible interest to direct marketers, this directory lists: direct marketers of
products and services (catalog and retail sales, financial, credit card, and investment
services, fund raising, etc.); service firms and suppliers to direct marketing companies (printers, list brokers and managers, computer services, telephone marketing,
etc.); creative and consulting services (agencies, artists, copywriters, etc.); also lists
of organizations, associations, meetings, courses, awards, etc. For each it includes
description of the firm's product or service, names of key executives, sometimes
number of employees, gross sales or billings, advertising budget and expenditures
spent in direct marketing media, countries in which business is conducted. Indexes
of companies and individuals are at end.

The Directory of Mail Order Catalogs. 4th ed. Lakeville, CT: Grey House
Publishing 1989. 406 pp. paper.

Contains brief descriptions of over 7,000 active U.S. companies that sell directly to
the consumer. It is arranged by product specialty, and usually gives for each mail
order house: the address, phone, those credit cards accepted, officers, frequency of
publication, catalog price and length, mailing list size, sales volume. Product and
company indexes are at end.

An alternative source is *Mail Order Business Directory* (Coral Springs, FL: B.
Klein Publications; biennial).

The United States Mail Order Industry. A Maxwell Sroge Report. Homewood, IL: Business One Irwin, 1991. 227 pp. paper.

Maxwell Sroge is a leading source for information on the U.S. mail order industry,
and he has published several previous guides. Section II of this latest report contains
two-page profiles of 25 consumer mail order companies and 25 business-to-business
mail order companies. Brief data for each includes nature of business, officers,
history, financial statistics, types of advertising/promotion, list information, comments. Section I (in 8 chapters) covers short discussions, facts, charts and other
information on the industry, demographic trends, major factors affecting growth,

statistics, performance, mergers & acquisitions, international mail order, and new marketing technologies.

Periodicals

Direct Marketing. Garden City, NY: Hoke Communications Inc. (monthly).

A monthly trade journal containing articles and news on the art/science of selling to consumer and business markets using direct response advertising. A "Direct Marketing Directory" is in each issue. Annual features include: a ranked list of "Mail Order's Top 250+" (July); "List Industry Overview" (August); "Mail Order Overview" (September); "International Mail Order Guide" (November), this latter being an overview of the mail order market in 12 countries. The October 1987 issue contained an annotated list of "Direct Marketing Books for Business and Non-Profit Use" (pp.165–180) arranged by broad topic. Indexed in ABI/I, BPI, PTS/F&S, TI; full text on BRS, DATA-STAR, DIALOG, DOW JONES, MEAD/NEXIS.

Journal of Direct Marketing. New York: Wiley, for the Direct Marketing Educational Foundation (quarterly).

This is a new quarterly (1987) whose purpose it is to publish significant articles on direct marketing that either present new ideas or methods, or help advance the current level of education and practice. About five well-researched articles are in each issue, most of them written by academic persons. Each issue also contains a short "abstracts" section for selected articles of interest appearing in other journals. The *Journal* is edited by the Medill School of Journalism at Northwestern University in cooperation with the DMEF.

Associations

Direct Marketing Association, 11 West 42d Street, New York, NY 10036.

RETAILING

Berman, Barry, and Joel R. Evans. *Retail Management: A Strategic Approach.* 4th ed. New York: Macmillan, 1989. 679 pp.

A beginning text with a strategy and decision-making orientation, covering all important topics and including many interesting real-world examples, illustrations, diagrams, and tables. Case incidents are with each chapter; appendixes include a glossary, a discussion of careers in retailing, and a list of selected firms seeking college graduates for retail-related positions.

Davidson, William R., Daniel J. Sweeney and Ronald W. Stampfl. *Retailing Management.* 6th ed. New York: Wiley, 1988. 876 pp.

Another revision of a standard text which incorporates changes that have occurred and increasing concerns about strategic planning and productivity in connection with retail management. Its 18 chapters are arranged in 6 parts: understanding the external environment; retailing management and strategy; creating internal environments; merchandise management; operations and human resources management; review and prospect. Case incidents are at end along with departmental merchandising and operating results tables and retailing career information. There is also a bibliography.

Mason, J. Barry, and Morris L. Mayer. *Modern Retailing: Theory and Practice.* 5th ed. Homewood, IL: BPI/Irwin, 1990. 826 pp.

Here is a comprehensive text meant for middle- and upper-level management and focusing on decision-making tasks these persons face. Part 6 (deciding how to compete: the marketing plan) provides the "nuts and bolts" in 8 chapters covering strategies in pricing, inventory, advertising, communication, layout, etc. The other major parts cover: the retail structure; retailing strategy; monitoring the environment affecting strategy development; understanding markets in which to compete; deciding how to compete—the financial and human resources plan; measuring success and identifying opportunities. Real-world examples appear throughout; short cases are with chapters as are definitions of key concepts and bibliographical notes. Career material is in an appendix. These two authors, with Hazel F. Ezell, have also written an undergraduate text called *Retailing* (4th ed., Irwin, 1991, 701 pp.).

Samli, A. Coskun. *Retail Marketing Strategy: Planning, Implementation, and Control.* New York: Quorum Books, 1989. 353 pp.

This graduate-level text goes beyond the usual how-to-do-it undergraduate book to study retail marketing strategy in the three key phases noted in the subtitle above. After an overview, Samli first explores the externalities of retail marketing strategy development (four chapters), followed by three chapters that bring external factors closer to the individual store. He then covers alternate strategies, store image, and retailing mix components important for implementing strategy (promotion, merchandise mix, pricing). In closing he studies how to determine the effectiveness of the strategy implemented (covering store loyalty, information systems, and control). This book is based on the author's many years of teaching, research, and consulting.

Three other recently revised introductory texts are: *Basic Retailing* by Irving Burstiner (2d ed., Irwin, 1991, 770 pp.); *Retail Marketing: For Employees, Managers, and Entrepreneurs* by Warren G. Meyer et al. (McGraw-Hill, 1988, 580 pp.); and *Retailing* by Gerald Pintel and Jay Diamond (5th ed., Prentice-Hall, 1991, 653 pp.).

FRANCHISING

Boe, Kathryn L., William Ginalski and DeBanks M. Henward III. *The Franchise Option: Expanding Your Business Through Franchising.* 2d ed. Washington, DC: International Franchise Association, 1987. 153 pp. paper.

This little book describes what franchising is, how it works, what it takes to be successful, and how to undertake the development of a franchise system. It is a practical guide meant for potential franchisers, and takes a step-by-step approach. It capitalizes on the longtime experience of the two coauthors, with the lead author bringing it up to date to include recent industry developments, growth, and changes in laws. The text of the FTC's Franchise Rule, a bibliography, and a glossary are at end.

Brown, Harold. *Franchising: Realities and Remedies.* Rev. ed. New York: Law Journal Seminars-Press, 1989. 1 loose-leaf volume (various pagings). With periodic updates.

A comprehensive treatise focusing on the legal aspects of franchises and meant for attorneys, legislators, administrators as well as for franchisees. There is a companion "Forms Volume."

Statistics

Franchising in the Economy. Washington, DC: International Franchise Association Educational Foundation in conjunction with Horwath International (annual).

Statistics in the U.S. section of this annual survey report include: sales, establishments, and employment for about 20 types of franchised businesses, usually for a three-year period; also number of establishments by state, and investments for one year. Beginning in 1991, this is called "International Edition," and contains also a section on franchising in the U.K., and several pages also for Australia. This was formerly published by the International Trade Administration of the U.S. Department of Commerce.

Bibliographies

Heckman, Lucy. *Franchising in Business: A Guide to Information Sources.* New York: Garland Publishing, 1989. 224 pp.

A selected, annotated bibliography of books, articles, pamphlets, and other publications published from 1956 through mid-1988 on the title subject. These are divided into 8 sections according to broad types of sources such as introductory guides, directories, bibliographies, financing, legal, franchising in the U.S., and international sources. An appendix describes organizations, abstracts/indexes, and online databases. This is the first in a publisher's series of "Research and Information Guides in Business, Industry, and Economic Institutions."

Directories

Foster, Dennis L. *The Rating Guide to Franchises.* New York: Facts on File Publications, 1988. 298 pp.

The profiles in this directory of more than 300 U.S. and Canadian franchises are longer than those in most directories. They are arranged by broad industry categories (e.g., business services, food services), and for each the data given usually includes initial investment, franchisor's service, contract highlights, fees and royalties, how long in operation, number of outlets, initial fee, any disputes or litigation, advertising, length of training program, rating in 6 criteria including experience, financial strength, satisfied franchisees.

Mr. Foster has also prepared *The Encyclopedia of Franchises and Franchising* (Facts on File, 1989, 465 pp.). This is an alphabetical listing of franchises giving brief facts, and interspersed are also franchising terms, and other data. At end is a ranked list of franchisors by size of outlet, and also by type of franchise.

Franchise Annual. Lewiston, NY: Franchise News.

Covers over 4,500 franchisors with separate lists for those in the U.S., Canada, and overseas. It is arranged by type of franchise and, for each firm, it usually gives: description of operation, when established, number of units, franchise fee total investment needed, whether financing is available, contact person. Miscellaneous data at front includes sample contract clauses, FTC rules, and summary of state regulations.

Friedlander, Mark P., Jr., and Gene Gurney. *Handbook of Successful Franchising.* 3d ed. Blue Ridge Summit, PA: Liberty Hall Press, 1990. 520 pp.

Arranged by type of franchise, this contains brief profiles of franchise companies, usually giving for each a description of operations, when established, number of franchises, financial assistance available, training provided, managerial assistance available. The data was taken from two U.S. Department of Commerce publications with updating by the compilers. Appendixes list sources of franchising information, and also government and nongovernmental assistance programs. At front is a franchise overview, advice about important things to know, and a sample franchise agreement.

International Franchise Association. *Franchise Opportunities Handbook.* Washington, DC (annual?).

This continues what the IFA formerly published as *Directory of Members,* and it assumes the title of a defunct directory formerly published by the U.S. International Trade Administration. It is a descriptive listing both of full members and of associate members, and it is arranged by industry-type of franchise. Data for each franchise usually includes: type of business, number of outlets, cash investment required, qualifications, contact person. Miscellaneous data at front on franchising includes the IFA code of ethics, organizations as sources of information. A descriptive list of IFA publications at end includes their bimonthly magazine with title *Franchising World* (which is indexed in BPI).

The Source Book of Franchise Opportunities. By Robert E. Bond and Christopher Bond. Homewood, IL: Dow Jones-Irwin (annual?).

Here is yet another recent directory arranged by type of business. This one lists more than 3,700 franchise opportunities but gives details on only 1,000. That data includes: history (when established, number of units, geographic distribution, number of employees), finances (investment needed, fees, agreements), franchise training/support assistance provided. Supplementary lists with each category give names and addresses of the other franchises. An annotated bibliography of franchising sources is at front.

Associations

American Franchise Association, 2730 Wilshire Blvd., Suite 400, Santa Monica, CA 90403.

International Franchise Association, 1350 New York Avenue, Suite 900, Washington, DC 20005.

RETAILING STATISTICS

Statistics published every fifth year by the Bureau of the Census provide valuable data on some 100 kinds of retail and 150 service businesses. These volumes of the *Census of Retail Trade,* the *Census of Service Industries* and *Enterprise Statistics* are described in Chapter 4. The Bureau's annual *County Business Patterns* is also described there. Current but very general statistics are in the Bureau's *Monthly Retail Trade: Sales and Inventories* and earlier data in *Retail Trade: Annual Sales, Year-end Inventories, Purchases, Gross Margin, and Accounts Receivable, by Kind of Retail Store.* Annual estimates of sales for from 6 to 9 basic retail store categories, by geographic area, are found in publications listed in the "Marketing Guides" section of this chapter. Operating ratio figures for many types of retail businesses are described in Chapter 6.

It is impossible to cover here the statistical sources for each type of retail business, but we have listed below a few trade journals (that have annual statistical issues) and annual operating studies for three important categories of retail business. To find data on other specific store and service groups, consult trade journals (several directories of periodicals arranged by subject are described in Chapter 7), publications of trade associations, indexes such as *Predicasts F & S Index United States* and *Statistical Reference Index*.

Retail Chains

Chain Store Age Executive. New York: Lebhar-Friedman (monthly).

Now combined with *Shopping Center Age,* this is a news magazine for retail chain and shopping center executives. Special issues include: "Annual Survey of Retail Credit Trends" (January, section 2); "Physical Supports Census" (July); "State of the Industry" (August, section 2), which gives recent developments in each major segment, and includes a ranked list of top U.S. retail chains called "The Exec 100"; "Annual Survey of Retail Information Systems Expenses and Trends" (September, section 2); "Survey of Executive Compensation in the Retail Industry" (November, section 2). Usually about four issues each year contain a table giving current sales (revenues) and earnings of leading stores in some 14 types of retail categories. Indexed in ABI/I, PTS/F&S, TI; full text on BRS, DATA-STAR, DIALOG, DOW JONES, MEAD/NEXIS.

Retailing—Worldwide

Retail Trade International. London: Euromonitor Publications Ltd. 2 volumes in 3 (annual).

Statistical data on the structure of the retailing business in major countries, with vol. 1 (in 2 parts) covering 18 European countries, and vol. 2, the other areas of the world. For each country one can usually find useful data on social and economic background, consumer expenditures, trends in retail sales, number of retail establishments, major retailers, food distribution, nonfood distribution, forecasts.

Department, Specialty, and Discount Stores

Discount Merchandiser. New York: Macfadden Holdings, Inc. (monthly).

Two annual features in this useful trade journal are: (1) "The True Look" of the discount industry (June issue), containing useful statistics and charts including trends in sales, size, and square footage by state, sales shares by major department, ranked list of the top 50 to 60 companies; also data on wholesale clubs, catalog showrooms, and sales of about 38 retail outlet types. (2) "DM's Annual Presidents' Roundtable on the State of the Industry" (December). A "Scoreboard" table in most issues gives financial statistics for leading companies. Indexed in ABI/I, PTS/ F&S, PAIS, TI; also full text on DIALOG.

Discount Store News. New York: Lebhar-Friedman (biweekly).

This newspaper for the discount department store industry has the following annual issues of possible interest: (1) "Annual Discount Industry Report" 2 parts (in the July issues). Part 1, "Chain Analysis," includes a ranked list of DSN's Top 150 Chains, and other tables with brief text on top specialty discount chains; part 2 is a "Merchandising and Productivity Analysis." (2) "Annual Brand Survey" 2 parts (in the October issues). Part 1 is a store manager survey on the best brands in 15 categories; part 2 is their "Consumer Survey." (3) a report on national and regional economic trends is in the May issue. Indexed in TI; full text on BRS, DATA-STAR, DIALOG, DOW JONES, MEAD/NEXIS.

Fairchild's Retail Stores Financial Directory. New York: Book Division, Fairchild Fashion Group (annual).

Financial manual for general merchandising chains, discount chains, mail order firms, drugstores, food stores, shoe stores, etc. Includes names of officers and directors; subsidiaries (if any); number of stores; sales and earnings; income account, assets, and liabilities. Ranked lists of leading stores/chains are at front, by type of store.

International Mass Retail Association. *Operating Results of Mass Retail Stores.* New York: Cornell University for the IMRA (annual).

Financial and operating performance indicators for the self-service discount department store industry. Expense statistics are given by sales size categories. Section 2 is their "Mass Retailers' Merchandising Report," which the Association formerly published separately. This has a few tables giving stock turns, markup, markdown, gross margin, sales per square foot—all by specific department in discount stores.

National Retail Federation. Financial Executives Division. *Department and Specialty Store Merchandising and Operating Results;* and *Financial and Operating Results of Department & Specialty Stores in (year).* New York (annuals).

Two useful annual sources for operating statistics by sales volume categories for department and specialty stores. The first (MOR) gives merchandising and inventory data (markdown, gross margin, stock turns, etc.), sales and expenses—all by specific store departments. The second (FOR) has sales, personnel, merchandising and earnings data, as well as expenses by natural division and expense centers.

Drugstores

Drug Store News. New York: Lebhar-Friedman (biweekly).

A trade journal for managers of drug chains. Its "Annual Report: State of the Industry" is in two parts, with part 1 (last April issue) covering merchandise categories, and part 2 (first May issue) focusing on drug chain profiles, with a ranked list of leading drug chains. A reprinting of the annual *Nielsen Annual Report: A Review of Retail Drug Trends* (first December issue) consists of charts and brief text summarizing retail drug sales, health and beauty aids (H&BAs), space allocation, and more. (Nielsen did not publish this separately in 1991.) This biweekly is indexed in PTS/ F&S, TI; full text on BRS, DATA-STAR, DIALOG, MEAD/NEXIS.

Drug Topics. Oradell, NJ: Medical Economics Co. (semimonthly, except monthly in December).

This is called "the newsmagazine for today's pharmacies." Special features include: a two-part report on a survey of pharmacist salaries (second March and first April issues); "Annual Rx Review" (second March); "The OTC/HBA Battleground" from Nielsen data (second April); "Independent Superstars of (year)" (second October); "Annual Business Outlook" (December). Many issues contain a "Business Barometer," one page of current statistics. Indexed in ABI/I, BPI, PTS/F&S, TI; also full text on BRS, DATA-STAR, DIALOG, DOW JONES, MEAD/NEXIS.

Lilly Digest. Indianapolis: Eli Lilly and Co. (annual).

Operating data for more than 1,800 independent community pharmacists. The operating ratios include 30 categories of averages both according to annual sales volume and daily prescription activity.

Food Stores

Convenience Store News. New York: BMT Publications (17/yr.).

A news journal for the convenience store business that includes an annual two-part *Industry Report* containing statistics, charts, and brief text (last May and last June issues). A ranked list of the "Top 50" convenience store chains is in a mid-July issue. These two features are also published as a separate booklet. An "Annual Buyers' Guide" is published separately in December.

Food Marketing Institute. *The Food Marketing Industry Speaks: Detailed Tabulations.* Washington, DC (annual).

This is a companion publication to their annual *Food Marketing Industry Speaks*, which has brief text, and charts on the state of the food marketing industry. The "Detailed Tabulations" volume contains the actual detailed statistics gathered by the annual survey of FMI members. Other FMI publications include an annual *Facts About Store Development Trends,* and a monthly abstract of articles (see note below).

Food Marketing Institute. *Supermarket Financial Performance Study.* Washington, DC (annual).

Key operating costs and financial performance statistics for supermarket chains in each of three sales size categories, including specific expenses by responsibility center as % of net sales. This annual takes the place of Cornell University's *Operating Results of Food Chains* and the FMI's *Headquarters and Distribution Center Cost Review.* Two other FMI annuals are: *Operating Results of Independent Supermarkets* and *Annual Financial Review.*

Progressive Grocer. Stamford, CT (monthly).

This top grocery/supermarketing trade journal contains several useful annual features: (1) "Annual Report of the Grocery Industry" (part 2 of April issue). It gives data on competition, buyer/seller relations, operations (statistics on sales volume and regions), costs and prices, consumers, the outlook; also supermarket number and sales by market area. (2) "Supermarket Sales Manual" (July and August issues). This two-part manual examines the product performance of many products in terms of supermarket sales, % categories sales and % change over previous year. The July issue covers about 280 lines in over 30 grocery and perishable food categories; the August issue, about 146 lines in over 20 merchandise and health and beauty aids categories. (3) *Nielsen Review of Retail Grocery Store Trends* (October and November). These are a reprint of this Review which Nielsen Marketing Research publishes separately. (However they say no separate review was published in 1991). The first part gives statistics, charts, and brief text on overall trends, sales, data on coupons, advertising, scanning update, and store characteristics; the second covers space allocation and HBA products. (4) "Outlook" (December or January) is usually an article on prospects for the coming year. Articles in this journal are indexed in BPI, PTS/F&S, TI; full text in BRS, DATA-STAR, DIALOG, DOW JONES, MEAD/NEXIS.

Published separately is *Progressive Grocer's Market Scope.* This is an annual containing statistics for specific market areas, based on the marketing categories used by four syndicated services or market area categories. It is in four sections, and the data given in each includes demographic facts, supermarket sales as % of total food sales, identification of buying offices of individual supermarkets in each area, giving number of supermarkets and market share. The market categories are from: Nielsen Scantrack; ADI (Arbitron's Areas of Dominant Influence); MSAs; and IRI InfoScan (Information Resources, Inc.).

SN Distribution Study of Grocery Store Sales. New York: Fairchild Publications (annual).

Supermarket News publishes this statistical study separately. It is in five parts: (1) a statistical profile of the top 50 market areas ranked by supermarket sales; (2) information on the grocery store business in many other market areas; (3) profiles of leading food chains, with a ranked list of leading U.S. and Canadian chains; (4) grocery store statistical profile giving store numbers and sales; (5) a calendar of industry events and a directory of associations.

Supermarket Business. New York: Fieldmark Media, Inc. (monthly).

The most useful statistical issue in this monthly is their "Annual Consumer Expenditures Study" (September) which contains two-year comparable figures on the amount spent in grocery stores and supermarkets for more than 700 categories of food, non-food, and health and beauty aids (HBAs). Also included for each product is % of total store, and dollar and % margins. The "Annual Product Preference Study" issue (March) gives expected changes in demand patterns for some 350 product categories, with the tables showing use of specific products by age group, with % growth. Indexed in ABI/I, PTS/F&S, TI; full text on BRS, DATA-STAR, DIALOG, DOW JONES, MEAD/NEXIS.

Supermarket News. New York: Fairchild Publications (weekly).

This is a useful weekly trade newspaper. Its annual statistical *SN Distribution Study of Grocery Store Sales* is described above. Indexed in PTS/F&S, TI; full-text on BRS, DATA-STAR, DIALOG, DOW JONES, MEAD/NEXIS.

The Food Marketing Institute publishes a monthly (with annual cumulation) *Reference Point: Food Industry Abstracts,* which consists of abstracts of the most comprehensive and timely articles on food retailing and related topics.

Restaurants and Hotels

Hotel & Motel Management. Cleveland: Edgell Communications, Inc. (21/yr.).

A "newspaper for the lodging industry," it contains scattered ranked lists such as "All-Suite Lodging Chains" (e.g. February 26, 1990); "H&MM's Top Lodging Interior-Design Firms" (April 3, 1989); "Top 50 Economy/Limited-Service Lodging Chains" (mid- or late April); "Franchise Report" (August 19, 1991). Indexed in BPI, PTS/F&S, TI; full text on DATA-STAR, DIALOG.

Hotels. Des Plaines, IL: Cahners Publishing Co. (monthly).

This trade journal covers the hotel industry worldwide. Several annual features and ranked lists are: "Industry Forecast" (January issue); "Top Design Firm Ranking" (June); "Top 300 Hotel Giants Ranking" (July); "The Great Hotel Restaurants of the World" (August); "Buyer's Guide" (December). Indexed in TI. This journal was formerly called *Hotels & Restaurants International.*

Lodging Hospitality. Cleveland: Penton Publishing Co. (monthly).

This is known as "the management magazine of development, operation, and marketing" for hotels, motels, and resorts. "Lodging's 400 Top Performers" (August issue) ranks leading hotels by categories (center city, resort, suburban, highway, and airport), and also 50 lodging chains, and top management companies. The "Almanac" issue (December) includes a directory of manufacturers, products and services, a trade name index, and a short "lodging industry census." Indexed in TI; full text on BRS, DATA-STAR, DIALOG, DOW JONES.

National Restaurant Association. *Restaurant Industry Operations Report for the United States.* Washington, DC: NRA in cooperation with Laventhal & Horworth.

Performance measures and income and expense account data for restaurants, both those with full-menu tableservice and with limited-measure tableservice.

Nation's Restaurant News. New York: Lebhar-Friedman (weekly).

The first August issue of this newsweekly for the foodservice industry features a useful "NRN's Top 100". This ranks the top 100 restaurant chains by U.S. systemwide foodservice sales. Separate ranked lists are for foodservice revenues, sales and revenue growth, sales per unit, total number of U.S. units, growth in franchise units. It also contains segment profiles for such segments as sandwich chains, pizza chains, hotel chains, with shorter ranked lists in each category. "Stock Market Tables" are in each issue. Indexed in TI; also full text on BRS, DATA-STAR, DIALOG, DOW JONES, MEAD/NEXIS.

Pannell Kerr Forster. *Trends in the Hotel Industry.* Houston (annual).

This is a statistical review incorporating operating and financial data on hotels and motels. It is based on an annual survey of some 1,000 establishments and covers: hotels and motels; transient hotels; resort hotels; motels both with and without restaurants. A similar annual covering private clubs is *Clubs in Town & Country*.

Restaurant Business. New York (18/yr.).

The second September issue each year features a useful "Annual Restaurant Growth Index" which spotlights trends and sales within each of 8 major segments plus statistical profiles for each metro area and ADI (giving sales and number of units for eating places, fast food stores, and restaurants, and % market share for the latter two), and summary ranked tables for each category in the profile. The second July issue has a ranked list of the "Top 50 Growth Chains," with recent trends for each; the second March issue features an annual "Franchising Report," with segment reports covering 111 major markets and a ranked list of the top 50 franchise systems. Other features are: "The Top 100 Chains" (second November issue) with profiles of each; "The Presidents' Forecast" (December). Each issue contains a one-page "Business Barometer." Indexed in BPI, TI; full text on BRS, DATA-STAR, DIALOG, DOW JONES, MEAD/NEXIS.

Restaurant Hospitality. Cleveland (monthly).

Called the "magazine of high-volume restaurant management," this monthly has an annual ranked list called "RH 500" independent restaurants (June issue) which gives number of employees, dining seats, average dinner check, as well as total sales by which each is ranked. Indexed in ABI/I, TI: also full text on BRS, DATA-STAR, DIALOG, DOW JONES.

Restaurants & Institutions. Des Plaines, IL: Cahners Publishing Co. (bi-weekly).

This trade journal serves the total foodservice industry. A two-part "400: Ranking" (the two July issues) contains, in its first part called "Financial Report," a ranked list of restaurants and other foodservice companies giving sales, number of units, average unit sales volume; part 2, "Menu Concepts," includes ranked lists of companies both by type of menu specialty, and various categories such as hotels, hospitals. Other features include: "Industry Forecast" (first January issue); "R&I's Top 100 Independents" (first March) which ranks top restaurants and includes number of seats, dinner check, people served, as well as sales; "R&I's Jobs (salary) Survey" (mid-December). Indexed in TI; full text on BRS, DATA-STAR, DIALOG, DOW JONES.

For persons seeking current articles indexed in more detail than can be found in general business periodicals indexes, see *Lodging and Restaurant Index* (West Lafayette, IN: Published quarterly, with annual cumulations, by the Restaurant, Hotel, and Institutional Management Institute at Purdue University in cooperation with the Consumer and Family Sciences Library at Purdue). It is a subject listing of the most important articles in over 40 trade and research journals in the hospitality industry.

RETAILING PERIODICALS

Journal of Retailing. New York: New York University (quarterly).

An academic journal containing well-researched papers on subjects of interest to retailers, written primarily by academic persons. Includes book reviews in most issues. Indexed in ABI/I, BPI, PAIS, TI; full text on BRS, DATA-STAR, DIALOG, DOW JONES.

Stores. New York: National Retail Federation (monthly).

Directed toward retail executives, this monthly contains short articles of practical interest; also news about the industry and news from the National Retail Federation. Includes annual ranked lists of "The Top 100 Department Stores" (July), and the "Top 100 Specialty Chains" (August). Section 2 of the February 1991 issue consists of the first "Ernst & Young's Survey of Distribution/Transportation/Warehousing Trends in Retail." It contains text and statistics on operations and inventory management for four segments of the retail industry. This monthly is indexed in BPI, TI.

DIRECTORIES OF RETAIL STORES

Fairchild's Financial Manual of Retail Stores is described in the "Retailing Statistics" section of this chapter. For U.S. directories of department and specialty stores, food stores, and the many other types of retail stores consult either the *Directories in Print* or the *Guide to American Directories,* both described in Chapter 7.

RETAILING ASSOCIATIONS

There are trade associations for almost every type of retail business. A good list is in the annual *Encyclopedia of Associations,* which is described in Chapter 7. (Check under key word in its index). Here are the names of only a few of the best known or more general retailing associations.

Food Marketing Institute, 1750 K Street, N.W., Suite 700, Washington, DC 20006.

International Center for Companies of the Food Trade and Industry, 3800 Moor Place, Alexandria, VA 22305 (food chains).

International Mass Retail Association, 1901 Pennsylvania Avenue, NW, 10th floor, Washington, DC 20006.

National Retail Federation, 100 West 31st Street, New York, NY 10001 (department and specialty stores).

SERVICE INDUSTRIES

Rapid growth in the services sector as well as increased competition and other recent changes have spurred a rising need to study service management and service marketing as it differs from goods marketing. This has resulted in the publication of recent books focusing on service management and marketing, the inclusion of courses in business school curriculums, periodic conferences or institutes, increased number of articles treating the various aspects of this subject, and even a journal devoted specifically to publishing articles on service marketing. This section describes several books or readings volumes, and the new journal. No attempt is made to cover books on marketing of specific types of services such as health care firms, legal services, or professional services. Chapter 11 does contain a few sources on the management of several types of public or nonprofit organizations including health care. The previous section in this chapter describes several periodicals and statistical sources on the hotel and restaurant industries.

Books

Albrecht, Karl. *At America's Service: How Corporations Can Revolutionize the Way They Treat Their Customers.* Homewood, IL: Dow Jones-Irwin, 1988. 241 pp.

We start with a practical how-to book on how any service organization can become a high quality service performer if its leaders are really determined to do so, and it is based on the author's personal observations and experience. He starts by explaining what service management is, and what are its common blunders and pitfalls. With this as background, he then covers the tools and techniques of service management including how to launch and implement a service quality program in its five phases.

Bateson, John E.G. *Managing Services Marketing: Text and Readings.* Chicago: Dryden Press, 1989. 591 pp.

An advanced MBA text on management problems of services marketing managers, with readings accompanying each chapter. It is divided into three parts: basic building blocks needed; the service marketing mix (product, pricing, communications, profit); marketing implementation. Bibliographical references are at end of many chapters and readings.

Grönross, Christian. *Service Management and Marketing: Managing the Moments of Truth in Service Competition.* Lexington, MA: Lexington Books, 1990. 298 pp.

This book offers a theoretical framework and practical advice on how to pursue a market-oriented service strategy and manage service competition. It is intended for managers in both service and manufacturing firms who are facing service competition as well as for students of service management. Professor Grönross, a Scandinavian pioneer in this field, further states: "it is more a how-to-think book than a what-to-do book, although it also includes practical advice about how to cope with special situations." A bibliography is at end.

Heskett, James L., W. Earl Sasser, Jr., and Christopher W. L. Hart. *Service Breakthroughs: Changing the Rules of the Game.* New York: Free Press, 1990. 306 pp.

These authors say the major objective of their book is to identify elements common to methods that successful service firms adopt for activating strategies, to examine the implications, and to suggest ways to avoid mistakes. They address developing such elements as service quality and productivity, management demand and supply, building blocks such as networks, information technologies, and people. Their study is based on five years of research in 14 service industries. Bibliographical notes are at end.

Professor Heskett has focused much of his recent research on the service industry. See also his earlier *Managing the Service Economy* (Boston: Harvard Business School Press, 1986, 211 pp.) which presents the results of an intensive analysis to determine which management strategies have given leading service companies their competitive advantage.

Johnson, Eugene M., Eberhard E. Scheuing and Kathleen A. Gaida. *Profitable Service Marketing.* Homewood, IL: Dow Jones-Irwin, 1986. 303 pp.

The purpose of this book "is to help service managers learn how their businesses can grow and prosper through the application of modern marketing concepts and practices. It analyzes the nature of services, the service environment, the service marketing management cycle, and the service marketing mix." Two of the authors are marketing professors and the third is a marketing manager.

Lovelock, Christopher H. *Services Marketing.* 2d ed. Englewood Cliffs, NJ: Prentice-Hall, 1991. 526 pp.

This revises and updates the author's textbook which combines text with readings and cases. It is arranged in four parts to cover: understanding services; strategic issues; tools for service marketers; challenges for senior management. A selected bibliography is at end.

Lovelock also recently revised his book of readings and cases, with title *Managing Services: Marketing, Operations, and Human Resources* (2d ed., Prentice-Hall, 1992, 472 pp.).

Zeithaml, Valarie A. et al. *Delivering Quality Service: Balancing Customer Perceptions and Expectations.* New York: Free Press, 1990. 226 pp.

Based on a seven-year research effort, this well-written book documents the role that leadership plays in delivering excellent service. The authors address three questions: what is service quality? what causes service-quality problems? what can organizations do to solve these problems and improve their service? They use a "gaps model" that features four gaps which need to be closed to offer excellent service, and these are discussed in four of the nine chapters. Their research methods are described in appendixes; "notes and references" are at end.

Persons wishing to consult the literature on service marketing published prior to 1985 may want to use *Services Marketing: An Annotated Bibliography* by Raymond P. Fisk and Patriya S. Tansuhaj (Chicago: American Marketing Association, 1985, 256 pp., "Bibliography Series"). It describes books, conference proceedings, dissertations, and journal articles published from 1964 to 1985.

Periodicals

Journal of Services Marketing. Santa Barbara, CA: Grayson Associates (quarterly).

This is a relatively new (1987) academic journal written to provide practitioners of marketing with new ideas on a wide range of services marketing topics that will be applicable to their daily work. Its easy-to-read articles are well researched, with each containing managerial implications and bibliographical citations. A few book reviews as well as a list of upcoming marketing events are in each issue.

Statistics and Directories

It is impossible to cover here the statistical or directory sources published on every type of service business. Attention is called to the *Census of Service Industries* compiled every fifth year by the Bureau of the Census. It provides useful (but sometimes rather out of date) statistics for about 150 kinds of service businesses. To find other statistics and current information on the many service types, use such sources as *Predicasts F & S Index United States* (and its foreign counterparts), the *Statistical Reference Index,* and perhaps also the *MARS* database. For a comprehensive directory of leading service firms, see *Dun's Directory of Service Companies* (annual), which is described in Chapter 7. To identify the many more specific directories, consult either the *Directories in Print* or *Guide to American Directories,* also in Chapter 7.

19

HUMAN RESOURCES/PERSONNEL MANAGEMENT (INCLUDING INDUSTRIAL RELATIONS)

HUMAN RESOURCES/PERSONNEL MANAGEMENT – Handbooks – Books on Human Resources/Personnel Management – Interviewing – Job Analysis – Performance Appraisal – Supervision – Training and Development – Wage and Salary Administration – Executive Job Hunting – Personnel Bibliographies and Abstracts – Personnel Dictionaries – Personnel Services – Human Resources/Personnel Periodicals – Personnel Management Associations – INDUSTRIAL RELATIONS – Labor Economics and Labor Relations – Arbitration and Collective Bargaining – Industrial Relations Bibliographies and Abstracts – Industrial Relations Dictionaries – Labor Services – Labor Statistics – Industrial Relations Periodicals – Labor Directories – Industrial Relations Associations – Pension and Employee Benefits Planning

The well-known behavioral theorist Rensis Likert said in his *Human Organization* (New York: McGraw-Hill, 1967, p.1): "Every aspect of a firm's activities is determined by the competence, motivation and general effectiveness of its human organization. Of all the tasks of management, managing the human component is the central and most important task, because all else depends on how well it is done." Today this activity is often called "human resources management" rather than just personnel administration, to note the more comprehensive approach of considering the personnel function in relation to overall company planning and strategy as well as its close ties with human relations.

Since human resources management does draw upon many of the theories and techniques used in the behavioral sciences, the dividing line in listing books is often hazy. Thus readers will also want to check the books and periodicals on management in general (Chapter 10) for information on HRM, especially the section on "Human Factors in Organizations."

HUMAN RESOURCES/PERSONNEL MANAGEMENT

HANDBOOKS

Famularo, Joseph J., ed. *Handbook of Human Resources Administration.* 2d ed. New York: McGraw-Hill, 1986. 1 volume (various pagings).

Practical, comprehensive handbook for the beginner covering all aspects of human resources in the workplace and brought up to date to cover the latest developments, legislation, and attitudinal changes, but only as of 1986. Its 80 chapters, each written by a qualified HR practitioner, are arranged in 18 parts to include: organization and operation; development of human resources; recruitment/selection/placement; training and development; wage and salary administration; employee benefits; employee appraisal and assessment; employee services/safety/health; government controls; labor relations; international HRM; acquisitions and mergers; special problems; communicating; records/reports/statistics; human resources research. Short lists of selected readings are at end of chapters.

Levesque, Joseph D. *The Human Resource Problem-Solver's Handbook.* New York: McGraw-Hill, 1992. 1 volume (various pagings).

A desktop guide to handling and solving some of the more difficult people problems in the workplace, with considerable emphasis given to legal aspects of each problem area. It is intended to give full background, explanations, factors to consider, and approaches. In three parts, the author covers, first, problems involving discriminatory actions; then solving problems related to employment rights; and finally, solving problems involving difficult employees and workplace control mechanisms. References at end are arranged by chapter.

SHRM-BNA Series on Human Resource Management. Washington, DC: Society for Human Resource Management and the Bureau of National Affairs Books, 1988–90. 6 volumes, paper.

The books in this series provide practical as well as theoretical advice and insights on the topics they cover, and each is written by an experienced team of professionals and academics. They are: vol. 1, *Human Resource Management: Evolving Roles and Responsibilities* ed. by Lee Dyer (1988, 288 pp.); vol.2, *Human Resource Planning, Employment and Placement* ed. by Wayne Cascio (1989, 295 pp.); vol.3, *Compensation and Benefits* ed. by Luis R. Gomez-Mejia (1989, 306 pp.); vol.4, *Employee and Labor Relations* ed. by John Fossum (1990, 310 pp.); vol.5, *Developing Human Resources* ed. by Kenneth N. Wexley (1991, 273 pp.); vol.6, *Managing Human Resources in the Information Age* ed. by Randall S. Schuler (1991, 243 pp.).

BOOKS ON HUMAN RESOURCES/PERSONNEL MANAGEMENT

Burack, Elmer H., and Nicholas J. Mathys. *Human Resource Planning: A Pragmatic Approach to Manpower Staffing and Development.* 2d ed. Lake Forest, IL: Brace-Park Press, 1987. 421 pp.

We start with a specialized book providing a pragmatic framework for the planning of manpower and careers in organizations. It is based on the authors' experience with the human resource planning and development in many organizations, and the book is organized so the reader will understand both the "how" and the "why" of human resource planning system design and implementation. A bibliography is at end.

Caruth, Donald L., Robert M. Noe III, and R. Wayne Mondy. *Staffing the Contemporary Organization: A Guide to Planning, Recruiting, and Selecting for Human Resource Professionals.* New York: Praeger, 1990. 311 pp. paper.

This is intended as a working reference for practitioners and others seeking practical guidance on staffing procedures, policies, techniques, and problems. It integrates a number of human resource topics not usually treated together in one volume: human resource planning, legal aspects of staffing, recruiting, selecting, performance appraisal, career development, and so forth. Bibliographical notes are with chapters and a list of recommended books is at end.

Cascio, Wayne F. *Applied Psychology in Personnel Management.* 4th ed. Englewood Cliffs, NJ: Prentice-Hall, 1990. 736 pp.

An interdisciplinary-oriented personnel psychology text designed to be forward-looking and progressive while integrating psychological theory with tools and methods. Major sections in the 3d edition (the one seen for evaluation) covered: contemporary issues; strategy and outcomes in personnel decisions; fundamental concepts in applied measurement; developing a foundation for personnel decisions; attracting, selecting, and placing personnel; developing and rewarding personnel; ethical issues. A lengthy bibliography is at end. This book presumes familiarity with personnel management and some background in fundamental statistics.

Professor Cascio has written a number of other books, including a well-received text on *Managing Human Resources: Productivity, Quality of Worklife, Profits* (2d ed., McGraw-Hill, 1989, 736 pp.) which, as the subtitle indicates, ties productivity, quality of worklife, and profits to HRM activities; and *Costing Human Resources* (3d ed., PWS-Kent Pub. Co., 1991, 300 pp.).

DeCenzo, David A., and Stephen P. Robbins. *Personnel/Human Resource Management.* 3d ed. Englewood Cliffs, NJ: Prentice-Hall, 1988. 637 pp.

Here is a readable text for a one-semester course that has a balanced coverage of the HRM field and uses interesting examples. Its 6 parts cover: important environmental influences; acquisition of human resources; development of human resources; motivation; maintenance (including compensation, benefits, safety, labor relations, collective bargaining); research and the future. Interesting boxed features and other illustrations are used throughout. Lists of additional readings are with chapters; a glossary is at end of book.

Foulkes, Fred K., ed. *Strategic Human Resources Management: A Guide for Effective Practice.* Englewood Cliffs, NJ: Prentice-Hall, 1986. 451 pp.

A selection of what the editor hopes are the best readings available (as of 1986) written by over 40 leading human resources practitioners, academicians, consultants concerning the practical aspects of managing people in the late eighties. It starts with a few interviews with human resource leaders. Then the readings are arranged in sections to cover: human resources in relation to top management goals and

strategies; the human resources function; topics of continuing and strategic importance to both human resources and line managers; new directions for the future.

**Heneman, Herbert G., III, Donald P. Schwab, John A. Fossum and Lee D.
Dyer.** *Personnel/Human Resource Management.* 4th ed. Homewood, IL:
Irwin, 1989. 740 pp.

Latest edition of a well-written text by four respected professors who approach the
subject from a management view and who structure the book around a P/HR model.
They have arranged the material in 9 basic parts: P/HR management and its environment; individuals and jobs; employee performance; HR planning; external staffing;
internal staffing and development; compensation; labor relations; work environment. Many examples of actual organization practice are given. A case is with most
parts.

Ivancevich, John M. *Human Resource Management: Foundations of Personnel.* 5th ed. Homewood, IL: Irwin, 1992. 796, [60] pp.

Another readable beginning text on P/HRM, with this latest edition switching title
and subtitle. Based on an examination of the 4th edition, it focuses both on people
who work directly in this field, and those who, as employees, are influenced by it.
The 6 major parts were: an introduction; analysis, planning and staffing; performance evaluation and compensation; training and development for better performance; labor relations and safety and health; work scheduling, quality of life, and
evaluation of P/HRM. Interesting boxed features highlighted real situations and
individual P/HRM managers. Definitions of key terms were with chapters, and a
glossary was at end of book. Appendixes include sources of information.

Milkovich, George T., and John W. Boudreau. *Human Resource Management.* 6th ed. Homewood, IL: Irwin, 1991. 740 pp.

This standard text approaches the study and practice of human resource management from one basic premise—"decisions about human resources make a difference." Thus, the authors take a diagnostic, decision-making approach to the subject. They cover both theory and practical techniques, with cases at the end of each
part to provide readers with an opportunity to develop their own skill. The 6 parts
cover: assessing conditions (both external and internal); planning and setting objectives; external staffing; employee development; human resource activities as they
relate to compensation; and human resource activities as they relate to employee/
labor relations. Bibliographical notes are with chapters.

Odiorne, George S. *Strategic Management of Human Resources.* San Francisco: Jossey-Bass, 1984. 356 pp.

Professor Odiorne has written widely on the management of human resources and
on management by objectives. In this book he goes beyond the usual techniques of
personnel and employee relations, by applying the tools of strategic planning to
personnel management. The middle two parts focus on managing high-performing
employees and managing poor performers. The last part describes practical applications of the human portfolio in strategic planning, while part 1 starts with a primer
on research and on applications of the economic theory of human capital. A bibliography is at end.

Sherman, Arthur W., and George W. Bohlander. *Managing Human Resources.* 9th ed. Cincinnati, OH: South-Western, 1992. 726 pp.

Started some years ago by Professor Herbert J. Chruden, with this edition his coauthors are taking over its preparation. The book has always attempted to blend behavioral science principles with traditional personnel and labor relations philosophies. The 8th edition (the latest seen for examination) was arranged in 7 parts to cover: human resources management in perspective; meeting human resources requirements; developing effectiveness in human resources; creating a productive work environment; fostering employee-management relationships; implementing compensation and security; other dimensions of HRM (auditing and international HRM). Suggested readings were at end of chapters; 12 cases were at end of the book.

Tracey, William R. *Critical Skills: The Guide to Top Performance for Human Resources Managers.* New York: AMACOM (American Management Association), 1988. 356 pp.

A practical guide to the 15 skills (primarily communication skills) which the author feels are crucial to HR management in all types of enterprises. These skills, discussed in 15 short chapters, are: listening; speaking; writing; problem sensing; inquiring; problem solving; decision making; hiring; motivating; delegating; appraising; coaching; counseling; negotiating; team building. Useful lists of further readings are included with each chapter.

Werther, William B., Jr., and Keith Davis. *Human Resources and Personnel Management.* 3d ed. New York: McGraw-Hill, 1989. 628 pp.

This is a popular college text, the purpose of which is to explain, in a readable manner, the personnel department's role in dealing with human resources. It introduces the challenges of modern personnel management and presents key concepts, issues, and practices, but the emphasis is on the practical applications of this knowledge so that readers will gain a useful understanding of the subject—cf. p.xxiv. This major revision is organized into 6 basic parts to cover the usual topics of an HR text. Interesting real-life examples are used throughout, set off in blue type. Bibliographical notes are with chapters; a glossary is at end.

INTERVIEWING

When searching for books on this topic it is wise to look at several before deciding which one or ones will best suit your need. Two of the books described below are written for interviewers, and three are guides for interviewees. No single book stands out for its excellent treatment of every aspect of the subject.

Drake, John D. *The Effective Interviewer: A Guide for Managers.* New York: AMACOM, 1989. 387 pp.

Drake's "how to" book for managers focuses primarily on the employment interview, and much is based on his personal experience. He starts with chapters on finding the best candidate for the job and on college recruiting interviews. He then goes on to discuss such topics as knowing what to ask about in the interview, evaluating data (including a chapter describing Drake's "Hypothesis Method"), selling the job to the candidate, performance appraisal, the exit and termination interviews. Appendixes include a list of tested questions to ask, and a short list of suggested readings.

Faux, Marian. *The Executive Interview.* New York: St. Martin's Press, 1985. 177 pp.

A practical little book that offers advice on how to get through an executive job interview and how to create the "chemistry" needed to get the job you want. Chapters are short, with chapter titles including: how to get an executive interview; homework—the key to smooth interviewing; psyching out the interviewer; blockbuster questions; self-confidence and anxiety.

Fear, Richard A., and Robert J. Chiron. *The Evaluation Interview.* 4th ed. New York: McGraw-Hill, 1990. 246 pp.

Here is another practical book, this one primarily on the evaluation interview as a selection device, and it guides the reader, step-by-step, through the complete procedure for handling job applicants. It is now also concerned with the use of time-tested interview techniques in retaining, developing, and motivating individuals, with part 5 covering applications of techniques in the campus interview, in "visioning," in teambuilding, and in feedback. Useful supplementary material is in appendixes.

Goodale, James G., *The Fine Art of Interviewing,* Englewood Cliffs, NJ: Prentice-Hall, 1982. 201 pp.

This is a short, clearly written book providing the fundamentals on how to plan and conduct 6 kinds of interviews, with one chapter devoted to each: selection, performance appraisal, counseling, career planning, disciplinary, and exit. Practical examples are used throughout; bibliographical notes are at end.

Medley, H. Anthony. *Sweaty Palms Revised: The Neglected Art of Being Interviewed.* Rev. ed. Berkeley, CA: Ten Speed Press, 1991. 194 pp.

Here is a short, down-to-earth book written from the view of the interviewee, to give helpful hints about how to conduct oneself in an employment interview. Included are chapters on types of interviews, how to prepare, how to control the contents of the interview, how to handle stress/fear, how to dress. There are also short chapters on honesty, when to discuss salary, discrimination, and so forth. A list of commonly asked questions is at end; also evaluation factors used by interviewers, and a bibliography.

For persons interested in a question and answer book intended to help prepare persons for their job interview, there is a book titled *The Complete Q and A Job Interview Book* by Jeffrey G. Allen (New York: Wiley, 1988, 213 pp.).

JOB ANALYSIS

Ghorpade defines job analysis as "a managerial activity . . . directed at gathering, analyzing, and synthesizing information about jobs, information that serves as the foundation for organizational planning and design, human resource management, and other management functions" (p.2 of book described below). We list here just two recent publications—a handbook and a book.

Handbooks

Gael, Sidney, ed. *The Job Analysis Handbook for Business, Industry, and Government.* New York: Wiley, 1988. 2 volumes.

An excellent, comprehensive handbook covering job analysis topics and issues, with each of its 83 chapters written by a recognized authority. It is presented in such a way that it will be of interest to practitioners in the government, labor unions, universities, the military, as well as in business and industry. Among its 10 sections, two cover uses for job analysis results in organization administration and in HRM, one is on planning, four are devoted to industrial engineering, human factors engineering, worker-oriented and work-oriented approaches. The last section focuses on applications in a variety of jobs or processes. References are with each chapter.

Books

Ghorpade, Jai. *Job Analysis: A Handbook for the Human Resource Director.* Englewood Cliffs, NJ: Prentice-Hall, 1988. 348 pp.

This is a good, practical guide to job analysis intended for human resource professionals. It is organized into 6 chapters: introduction; job information—nature and measurement; methods and systems; job description; worker specification; uses of job information. Diagrams, tables, forms appear throughout; appendixes (over 100 pages) provide questionnaires, checklists, and other ready-made job analysis instruments. A bibliography is at end.

PERFORMANCE APPRAISAL

Henderson, Richard I. *Practical Guide to Performance Appraisal.* Reston, VA: Reston Publishing Co., 1984. 404 pp.

A guide for supervisors and managers that "describes the whys and hows of performance appraisal and what management and performance specialists can do to make the process successful." Henderson covers such areas as standards and goals, designating performance measurement procedures and instruments, uses of appraisal data and information, the interview process, training opportunities. A useful, annotated bibliography of books and selected articles (the latter arranged in four major categories) provides a good means of identifying other material written on this subject. This book was simultaneously published under the title: *Performance Appraisal,* 2d edition.

Mohrman, Allen M., Susan M. Resnick-West, and Edward E. Lawler, III. *Designing Performance Appraisal: Aligning Appraisals and Organizational Realities.* San Francisco: Jossey-Bass, 1989. 227 pp.

According to the preface, this "is a balanced discussion of the technical aspects of appraisal, the contextual realities affecting appraisal, and the process of design." Its aim "is to help the reader design processes so that the result will be appraisal systems that can be used and that work." The first part discusses developing effective appraisal systems, and the last part, key issues in designing performance appraisal systems. A bibliography is at end.

Patten, Thomas H., Jr. *A Manager's Guide to Performance Appraisal.* New York: Free Press, 1982. 188 pp.

In 45 short chapters, Patten examines 45 practical guides which he says "are nononsense rules of thumb for managers who must 'give' performance reviews to subordinates as part of their work." He makes it clear throughout of his strong conviction that a Management by Objectives-based performance appraisal system is far superior to any other method. A list of recommended books (published prior to

1982) is at end for more in-depth treatments of specific facets. This is an easy-to-read guide for the busy executive.

Rausch, Erwin. *Win-Win Performance Management/Appraisal: A Problem Solving Approach.* New York: Wiley, 1985. 311 pp.

The author hopes this book is both "a practical source of ideas for solving problems related to performance management, and a valuable reference on management concepts and techniques which maintain and strengthen a viable performance management process." It is arranged in four parts covering: an overview of performance management; considerations in setting up or revising a performance management system; working effectively within an existing system; essential skills required. Appendixes include sample forms and procedures.

Swan, William S. (Phillip Margulies, collaborator). *How To Do a Superior Performance Appraisal.* New York: Wiley, 1991. 223 pp.

Here is a recent, practical, step-by-step guide to the "Swan Approach" to performance appraisal which the author feels reduces defensiveness and conflict while increasing quality and productivity. Part 1 is a background survey; part 2 discusses in 6 chapters his recommended approach. Swan's last section addresses the aspect dreaded by employees and managers which is the face-to-face discussion of the appraisal. Mr. Swan is a consultant who has specialized in performance appraisal.

Timpe, A. Dale, ed. *Performance: The Art & Science of Business Management.* New York: Facts on File Publications, 1988. 378 pp.

A compendium of practical knowledge, research, and theory relating to performance and how to improve it. Its 51 essays are arranged in 7 parts to cover: performance—an organizational and cultural correlation; factors of behavior and attitude; management—a critical performance link; task definition—undefined and unclear expectations; performance appraisal—a diagnosis; improving appraisal effectiveness; appraisal feedback techniques. References are with most essays; a bibliography is at end.

A book on *Managing Organizational Performance* by Michael Nash is described in Chapter 10.

SUPERVISION

Bittel, Lester R., and John W. Newstrom. *What Every Supervisor Should Know: The Complete Guide to Supervisory Management.* 6th ed. New York: McGraw-Hill, 1990. 614 pp.

Extensive revision and updating of an elementary text intended to cover all important aspects of supervision and to offer practical advice about how to handle real-life, on-the-job situations in a readable manner. The first 7 sections deal with: supervisory management introduction; planning and control; organizing, staffing, and training; activating the work force; managing problem performance; improving department productivity; legal concerns. The last three sections contain: a personal development portfolio; career planning; appendixes. Applications and case incidents are with chapters.

George, Claude S., Jr. *Supervision in Action: The Art of Managing Others.* 4th ed. Reston, VA: Reston Publishing Co., 1985. 424 pp.

Written in a direct, easy-to-read, and easy-to-understand manner, this is a good book both for practicing and for potential supervisors. It deals with such areas as:

using time wisely, communications, motivating employees, handling discipline and grievance, making decisions, leading meetings, organization, performance evaluation, measuring work, and much more. A glossary is at end.

Haimann, Theo, and Raymond L. Hilgert. *Supervision: Concepts and Practices of Management.* 4th ed. Cincinnati: South-Western Publishing Co., 1987. 472 pp. paper. Fifth edition to be published in 1992, with authors reversed.

The objective of this introductory text is to help students and new supervisors analyze the many issues and problems confronting supervisors, and to offer advice for their solutions. It focuses on the managerial process by examining traditional managerial functions (planning, organizing, staffing, directing, controlling) as each relates to a supervisor's job. Short case problems are with each part.

Rue, Leslie W., and Lloyd L. Byars. *Supervision: Key Link to Productivity.* 3d ed. Homewood, IL: Irwin, 1990. 494 pp. paper. Fourth edition to be published in 1992.

A popular undergraduate text focusing on essential issues of supervision and emphasizing the supervisor's role in improving productivity in modern organizations. The material is arranged in the following five sections: basic skills required to supervise; supervising the individual; supervising the group; the supervisor's environment (discusses safety, ethics, politics); the supervisor and productivity. The authors stress real-world applications by using numerous examples. Checklists, tables, diagrams are set off in color; additional readings are listed with some chapters.

Steinmetz, Lawrence L., and H. Ralph Todd, Jr. *Supervision: First-Line Management.* 5th ed. Homewood, IL: Irwin, 1992. 560 pp.

Just revised again but not as yet seen, this text is designed for use in colleges or other organization courses (e.g. hospitals). It offers students and managers practical alternatives for approaching supervision effectively. Based on an inspection of the 1983 edition, the sections cover: introduction; supervisory skills (decision making, motivation); the supervisor's role in leadership; training and control; communicating and working with people; supervision, discipline, and the law; the supervisor and social responsibility. A glossary is at end.

Stone, Florence M., ed. *The AMA Handbook of Supervisory Management.* New York: AMACOM, 1989. 550 pp.

This book brings together a large selection of short, practical articles that appeared originally in *Supervisory Management* magazine. They were chosen to help guide managers toward becoming more effective and efficient in overseeing the work of others. These contributions from more than 130 experts are divided into 14 parts, each representing a skill area such as communication, delegation, or discipline.

Periodicals

Supervisory Management. New York: American Management Association (monthly).

This is now a 12-page monthly news bulletin, published as a forum for authoritative views in the form of one-to-two page practical articles and news briefs. Indexed in ABI/I, BPI; full text on DIALOG.

Supervision. Burlington, IA: National Research Bureau (monthly).

Another monthly, this one focusing more on the industrial relations aspects of supervision, with short, practical articles of interest to "front line" supervisors. Indexed in ABI/I, BPI; full text on DIALOG.

TRAINING AND DEVELOPMENT

General books on human resources/personnel management usually include a chapter on training and development. For a good selection of the many recent articles use *Work Related Abstracts* described in the "Personnel Bibliographies and Abstracts" section of this chapter.

Handbooks

Craig, Robert L., ed. *Training and Development Handbook: A Guide to Human Resource Development.* 3d ed. New York: McGraw-Hill, 1987. 878 pp.
Completely revised and updated to incorporate the latest advances in human resource development (HRD), this is a comprehensive source of basic information on employee training and development published under the sponsorship of the American Society for Training and Development. Its 49 chapters, each by a specialist, are arranged in five main sections. Coverage ranges from how to determine what training is needed and how to administer employee training activities, to how to measure training results. Useful bibliographies are with most chapters for persons seeking further information on each topic.

Nadler, Leonard, and Zeace Nadler, eds. *The Handbook of Human Resource Development.* 2d ed. New York: Wiley, 1990. 1 volume (various pagings).
An updated overview and guide to HRD which focuses on models, concepts, and practices. There are 31 contributed chapters arranged in the following five sections: the field of human resource development; program areas of HRD; international areas of HRD; human resource areas related to HRD; the future of HRD.

Books

Bolt, James F. *Executive Development: A Strategy for Corporate Competitiveness.* New York: Harper & Row, 1989. 212 pp.
The author's goal "is to show CEOs and other executives how executive development can be used to achieve strategic objectives," and in so doing he describes how leading corporations have gone about educating and developing their senior executives. He starts by talking about the changing nature of executive development, and then he goes on to discuss: managing organizational change (using GE and Xerox as examples); global competition (case studies at Motorola and Emhart); deregulation at two telecommunications firms; a major corporate transformation at Weyerhauser; and lastly the new leaders, as at General Foods. These company cases reflect Bolt's experience as a consultant in executive development at a number of companies.

Caruth, Donald L., Robert M. Noe III, and R. Wayne Mondy. *Staffing the Contemporary Organization: A Guide to Planning, Recruiting, and Selecting for Human Resource Professionals.* New York: Quorum Books, 1988. 309 pp.

Intended as an on-the-job resource book for human resource professionals in all types of organizations, this is a systems book covering the entire range of staffing (human resource planning, legal aspects, recruiting, selecting, interviewing, performance appraisal, career development, and so forth). References are with chapters; a bibliography is at end.

London, Manuel. *Managing the Training Enterprise: High-Quality, Cost-Effective Employee Training in Organizations.* San Francisco: Jossey-Bass, 1989. 341 pp.

Mr. London says his purpose here is to examine how organizations educate employees and to consider policies and programs for improving the educational process. Part 1 reviews developing training strategies; part 2 considers important administrative functions; part 3 concentrates on ways to enhance training effectiveness. A bibliography is at end. This book is one of several this author has written in the area of employee development and career decisions. It is based on his years of research, teaching, and practical experience.

McCall, Morgan W., Jr., Michael M. Lombardo and Ann M. Morrison. *The Lessons of Experience: How Successful Executives Develop on the Job.* Lexington, MA: Lexington Books, 1988. 210 pp.

Here is a different approach to developing executive talent—a practical book based on the actual experiences of managers and executives concerning the "lessons" learned from experience that have changed or developed them as managers. It is intended to help people take charge of their own development and to help organizations do a better job of development by making more efficient use of the developmental experiences they have to offer their high-potential managers (cf. p.13). Useful checklists and tables are found throughout; notes and a bibliography are at end of book.

Nadler, Leonard, and Zeace Nadler. *Developing Human Resources.* 3d ed. San Francisco: Jossey-Bass, 1989. 248 pp.

This is a well-written book on human resource development—what it is, what HRD people do, how they do it, and how it relates to the needs of organizations and individuals. The authors use a three-part HRD model: definition and scope; areas of activity; roles of HRD practitioners. The first three parts of the book discuss each of these aspects; the last part covers relationships and trends. Practical examples are used throughout; an extensive bibliography is at end.

Not seen but well-reviewed is *Principles of Human Resource Development* by Jerry W. Gilley and Steven A. Eggland (Reading, MA: Addison-Wesley, 1989, 386 pp.) which covers what HRD is and how it is practiced.

Yearbooks

Training and Development Yearbook. Richard B. Frantzreb, editor. Englewood Cliffs, NJ: Prentice-Hall, 1991.

This yearbook documents the most significant writings on training and development year-by-year, selecting the best from an abstracting newsletter called *Training and Development Alert.* The 1991 volume arranges the articles in the following categories: training administration; program design, development, and implementation; training technology; trainers and trainees; training techniques; training programs. The last section is a "trainer's almanac" containing directories of organizations, conferences, software, courses for trainees, reference books, journals. Subject and name indexes are at the end.

Directories of Training and Development Programs

Bricker's International Directory: University Development Programs. Princeton, NJ: Peterson's Guides (annual).

A descriptive guide, revised annually, for those English-language university executive development programs that meet specified standards of excellence. It covers both general management programs and those in functional areas for programs offered in the U.S., Canada, Europe, Great Britain and Ireland, Australia and Southeast Asia. The details provided include profile of participants, subject matter, methods of instruction, tuition, duration, facilities, faculty, special features. For descriptions of short-term programs (two-to-four days in length), see their annual *Bricker's Short-Term Executive Programs.*

A newly published (1991) descriptive guide to European management programs is *European Master's Degrees in Management* (Bussum, The Netherlands: International Management Education Consultancy; annual?).

Training and Development Organizations Directory. 5th ed. Detroit: Gale Research, Inc. 1991. 677 pp. Available also online.

This directory describes over 2,300 U.S. and Canadian firms, institutes, and other agencies offering training, professional, and personal development programs for business, industry, government, and individuals. Includes geographic, subject, and personal name indexes. Revised about every three years.

Periodicals

Training and Development Journal. Alexandria, VA: American Society for Training and Development (monthly).

Short articles on all aspects of training and development and news of interest to ASTD members. Includes book reviews and regular columns for new products, training tools, and position openings. Indexed in ABI/I, BPI, TI; full text on BRS, DATA-STAR, DIALOG, DOW JONES.

Training: The Magazine of Human Resources Development. Minneapolis: Lakewood Publications (monthly).

This monthly is written for training professionals and managers responsible for developing their organizations' human resources. It features short, practical, readable articles plus regular departments providing news of seminars, new products, employment opportunities, review of one book and one film. Special issues include an annual "Industry Report" (October) which surveys employer-sponsored training in the U.S.; an annual "Trainers' Salaries" survey (November). Published separately as an August supplement is a "Marketplace Directory," a geographic list of training meeting facilities, giving facts about each. Indexed in ABI/I, BPI, TI; full text on BRS, DATA-STAR, DIALOG.

Associations

American Society for Training and Development, Box 1443, 1630 Duke Street, Alexandria, VA 22313.

WAGE AND SALARY ADMINISTRATION

Handbooks

Moynahan, John K. ed. *The Sales Compensation Handbook.* New York: AMACOM, American Management Association, 1991. 303 pp.

More specialized than the handbook following, this one is written as a practical guide for the sales or human resources manager, in developing solutions to sales compensation problems in today's competitive world. Its 21 chapters move from the more general to the specific. The first three chapters provide background on understanding the sales/marketing/organizational context. It then covers: the analytical processes; the fundamentals in building and strengthening the system (salary design/ administration, incentives, etc.); special selling roles, internal equity. The last two chapters conclude by helping one determine if the plan is working and whether changes are needed. Numerous practical examples appear throughout; a glossary is at end. This book combines the extensive experience of 14 authorities from TPF&C, a Towers Perrin Company consulting firm.

Rock, Milton L., and Lance A. Berger, eds. *The Compensation Handbook: A State-of-the-Art Guide to Compensation Strategy and Design.* 3d ed. New York: McGraw-Hill, 1991. 628 pp.

Intended to "describe the entire process a practitioner should follow in order to put together a totally effective compensation program according to the best contemporary standards." Its focus is on performance-based approaches to compensation. Each of its 43 chapters is written by a leading expert, and they are arranged within the following 7 parts: introduction; wage and salary administration; contingent compensation; executive compensation; computers and compensation; performance and compensation; corporate culture and compensation.

Books

Balkin, David B., and Luis R. Gomez-Mejia, eds. *New Perspectives on Compensation.* Englewood Cliffs, NJ: Prentice-Hall, 1987. 363 pp. paper.

For use as a supplement to a text, this brings together the recent thoughts and opinions of 42 leading compensation authors, researchers, consultants, practitioners. Twenty-seven of its 33 papers were written especially for this volume, and they are all arranged in 11 chapters. The purpose of the compilation is to look at those areas usually covered in compensation textbooks, but from several perspectives rather than just one, to reflect the complexities of the field.

Fay, Charles H., and Richard W. Beatty, eds. *The Compensation Sourcebook.* Amherst, MA: Human Resources Development Press, 1988. 510 pp.

Most of this sourcebook consists of readings intended as "a handy reference work of tools and techniques, alternative methodologies, new developments and strategic considerations available to the compensation field." Many of its 65 articles and other selections are from the American Compensation Association. They are arranged within 12 sections, including compensation planning, group incentives, benefits, executive compensation, international compensation. At the end are "resource materials" such as checklists, outlines of factors in compensation administration that can be used as transparency masters for overheads in an oral presentation.

Mr. Fay has also coauthored (with Marc J. Wallace, Jr.) a book on *Compensation Theory and Practice* (2d ed., Boston: PWS-Kent Pub., 1988, 423 pp., paper) which analyzes compensation developments and presents the link between theory and practice.

Foulkes, Fred K., ed. *Executive Compensation: A Strategic Guide for the 1990s.* Boston: Harvard Business School Press, 1991. 550 pp.

Here is a practical guide intended for those persons responsible for the key decisions about executive compensation "who want to think about the design, implementation, and communication of executive compensation plans that will be strategic, cost-effective, and responsible to the short- and long-term needs of the business." Its chapters, each written by a leading authority, are divided into three parts. The first sets the stage by covering the past and present of executive compensation; the second defines and develops the strategic approach; the third describes the application of the strategic approach in a variety of settings and situations. Bibliographical notes are with most essays; a glossary is at end of the book.

Henderson, Richard I. *Compensation Management: Rewarding Performance.* 5th ed. Englewood Cliffs, NJ: Prentice-Hall, 1989. 578 pp.

This is a well-written book on basic compensation (not just on executive compensation), which analyzes and describes the foundation of the reward system for almost all organizations. It "explains how to build the foundation for a compensation program. It then further explains how to develop the superstructure and, finally, how to enclose the framework and provide an acceptable and workable compensation system that stimulates employee effort and values contribution." A glossary is at end.

Lawler, Edward E., III. *Strategic Pay: Aligning Organizational Strategies and Pay Systems.* San Francisco: Jossey-Bass, 1990. 308 pp.

Drawing on his long experience as a researcher, consultant, and teacher in the areas of compensation and organizational effectiveness, Lawler focuses here on identifying for managers the choices that need to be made in order to develop a strategically designed pay system that will improve organizational effectiveness. He begins by discussing the competitive challenge faced by business today, and the objectives and principles of pay systems. With this as background he then covers in turn: different ways of paying for performance; how to determine an individual's base pay; administering pay systems; and applying pay strategies (including a discussion of two cases that show the development of a strategic pay approach for organizations). A bibliography is at end.

Milkovich, George T., and Jerry M. Newman. *Compensation.* 3d ed. Homewood, IL: BPI/Irwin, 1990. 627 pp.

Latest revision of a basic text that focuses on the design and management of compensation systems, with the authors structuring it around a "pay model." The first three of its six sections examine: internal consistency: determining the structure (including consideration of both job analysis and job evaluation); external competitiveness: determining the pay level; employee contributions: determining individual pay. The last three parts cover: employee benefits; government's role and compliance; managing the system (including budgets, compensating specific groups, the union role). Tables, diagrams, and bibliographical notes are used throughout; a glossary is at end.

Sibson, Robert E. *Compensation.* 5th ed. New York: AMACOM, 1990. 400 pp.

The fifth edition of a good, practical book written for managers of personnel, those who work in the field of personnel management, and compensation professionals. It examines all aspects of compensating employees in the context of the current business environment, and it is updated and expanded to cover the different ideas, approaches, and practices made necessary by changes in business and the work force, by an increase in technology, and a greater diversity of jobs. This text reflects the many years experience of its author, a business consultant/compensation specialist.

Surveys of Executive Compensation

Executive Compensation. New York: Ernst & Young (biennial; annual, 1982–). $350.

The 18th survey (1990) is a summary of a study of the salary and bonus compensation levels of more than 1,000 CEOs, about 8,500 top executives from about 1,200 companies spanning 24 industries and 5 geographic areas. These surveys are conducted by James A. Giardina and Thomas S. Tilghman of Ernst & Young. For 28 executive positions, the tables give average base salary, average bonus, and total compensation for bonus companies, as well as total compensation in all companies—by sales volume size and by broad industry. Appendixes include executive job descriptions.

INC. *Executive Compensation Study.* Boston: INC Publishing Company (annual).

This is an annual statistical study of executive compensation, benefits, and perquisites, with tables broken down by revenue ranges and by geographic region. The 1990 volume is based on a survey of 860 companies. Topics covered include: compensation and personal profiles for the CEO, COO, CPO, chief marketing, manufacturing, sales, and human resources officers. There are also sections covering: executive compensation policies; executive bonus and incentive practices; benefits; company financial data; economic expectations. There was no study published in 1991, and so this publication's future is cloudy.

Sibson & Company. *Annual Report: Executive Compensation.* Chicago and New York.

Another report on an annual survey, this one covering more than 600 leading companies and giving useful summary statistics with brief text on executive trends and practices. Included are statistics on executive salaries, annual and long-term incentives, executive benefits, perquisites, and employment contracts.

Survey of Executive Salaries & Fringe Benefits: United Kingdom. London: Inbucon Management Consultants (annual).

Here is an annual survey for salaries of British executives. The 1987 volume is based on over 600 returned questionnaires covering over 7,000 executives. It compares salary size level by job, ranks, size of company, geographical region, industry group. There are also separate sections for directors' salaries, fringe benefits, data processing staff, personnel specialists.

Top Executive Compensation. New York: Conference Board (annual).

An annual survey of the five highest paid executives in over 600 companies issued within the *Conference Board Reports* series (the 1991 edition was Report No. 983, and contains the 1990 survey). Graphs and statistics are given for 13 individual manufacturing industries and 7 broad manufacturing industries. It also contains an analysis of the prevalence of various elements in the executive compensation package, such as bonus and stock option plans. For their annual survey of *Corporate Directors' Compensation,* see listing in Chapter 10.

Wyatt Data Services Company. *ECS [Executive Compensation Service] Reports.* Fort Lee, NJ. 2 volumes (annual).

These reports partially take the place of the American Management Association's expensive *Executive Compensation Service.* They are based on Wyatt's continuing survey of executive compensation in 7,500 contributing organizations. The report on "Top Management" focuses on salary, bonus, and total compensation data for over 50 top management positions, with figures covering more than 40 industries and up to 9 sales or asset levels. Other more specialized "domestic reports" cover: boards of directors; middle management; sales and marketing management; supervisory management; professional and scientific personnel; technical and skilled trades personnel; office personnel. Their "International Reports" series consists of an annual Canadian Report, a report on "Top Remuneration for Europe and USA," separate annual reports for each of 17 European countries, and several more specialized reports. Like the former AMA reports, these are quite expensive, with each report (as of 1989) varying in price from $390 to $640 plus $5 shipping/handling. For further information contact Wyatt Data Services Company, 2 Executive Drive, Ft. Lee, NJ 07024.

Among several other annual surveys are: The American Compensation Association's *Report on the (year) Salary Budget Survey* (Scottsdale, AZ) which supplies information from data on more than 2,800 U.S. firms and almost 180 Canadian firms; *AMS Management Salaries Report* (Washington DC: Administrative Management Society) which is based on an annual salary survey of some 16 middle-level managerial and 4 supervisory positions in over 850 companies and over 40 metropolitan areas in the U.S. and Canada; and *Executive Compensation Study* (New York: Towers, Perrin, Forster & Crosby), primarily a graphic presentation of an annual study among 325 of the nation's largest companies and focusing on two positions—the CEO and CFO.

Six annual surveys published in periodicals or newspapers contain salary statistics for specific top executives. See: (1) *Business Week,* "Executive Compensation Scoreboard" (first May issue) which gives compensation and pay-performance analysis for the top two executives in over 300 public companies, by industry; (2) *Forbes,* "Corporate America's Most Powerful People: The Pay" (last May issue) which is arranged alphabetically and provides for each CEO—his/her age, compensation components, years with company, place of birth, degrees, professional background, stock owned, company sales and profits; (3) *Forbes,* "The Best 200 Small Company's Chief Executives" (mid-November), arranged alphabetically by company and gives salary facts for each, including some of the same data as the issue noted above; (4) *Fortune,* "The Great CEO Pay Sweepstakes" (mid-June issue), ranking 200 CEOs by compensation received; (5) *Wall Street Journal,* "The Boss's Pay" (a mid-April issue, e.g. April 17, 1991, section R1–12), includes a table, arranged in 8 industry categories, and then by company, giving salary/bonus, long-term compensation, total direct compensation for CEOs, based on a survey of over 350 proxies; (6) *Chief Executive,* "CEO Compensation Survey" (September) with its list by industry. In addition, *Sales and Marketing Management* (November) contains a "salary sampler" which is a ranked list of compensation for a sampling of top sales and marketing executives.

To identify other annual salary surveys appearing in specific trade journals, check in the index under "Salary surveys in periodicals."

Periodicals

Compensation & Benefits Management. Greenvale, NY: Panel Publishers (quarterly).

This was started in 1984 as a practical forum for executives, managers, and professionals responsible for the total compensation package. Its short articles offer practical information and ideas about all aspects of compensation and benefits planning, implementation, and management. Indexed in ABI/I, TI; full text on BRS, DATA-STAR, DIALOG, DOW JONES, MEAD/NEXIS.

Compensation and Benefits Review. New York: American Management Association (bimonthly).

Useful not only for its several feature articles on compensation, pensions, etc., but especially as a source for keeping up-to-date on what is being published elsewhere on this subject. It includes condensations of noteworthy articles and also annotated lists of articles and a few books. Indexed in ABI/I, BPI.

EXECUTIVE JOB HUNTING

With the increasingly uncertain job market we felt it of possible interest to include several books here on executive job hunting. If you cannot easily locate these books, there are other good ones which you may find in a library nearby. When undertaking a job search it is often wise to look at a number of guides before deciding which one or two will best serve your particular need.

Boll, Carl R. *Executive Jobs Unlimited.* Updated ed. New York: Macmillan, 1980. 197 pp.

One of the best books for obtaining practical advice when undertaking an executive job search. Boll starts by admitting that job hunting is hard work, and he goes from there to discussing the resumé, the broadcast letter, interviews, advertising, and other more specialized topics such as changing from government to industry, executive search firms. He wraps it up with brief advice for when you are back on the payroll. This is based on the author's longtime experience and is full of real-life experiences.

Bolles, Richard N. *What Color is Your Parachute? A Practical Manual for Job-Hunters & Career Changers.* Berkeley, CA: Ten Speed Press (annual).

With this catchy title and good promotion, Bolles's book is the guide for all job hunters that is cited most often. It is not my favorite for executive job changes, but its lengthy appendix includes a useful annotated list of books arranged by over 20 subject categories. There is also a "quick job-hunting map" and a resources guide for locating professional help. The text portion is based on a distillation of the experiences of many persons seeking jobs. Three of its seven chapters focus on Bolles's three basic steps to effective job-hunting and career change: knowing what you want to do; deciding where you want to do it; identifying the person who has the power.

Bostwick, Burdette E. *Resumé Writing: A Comprehensive How-To-Do-It Guide.* 4th ed. New York: Wiley, 1990. 335 pp. paper.

We are including here just one of several possible books on resumé writing—this one is considered one of the best. It stresses resumés at the management level although it is intended for all job seekers, and it takes the reader step by step through the writing process. There are examples and explanations throughout with supplementary examples in an appendix. There is also a chapter for sales and broadcast letters, and several relating to job searching techniques and suggestions.

Burton, Mary L., and Richard A. Wedemeyer. *In Transition.* New York: HarperBusiness, 1991. 248 pp.

Based on the authors' Harvard Business School Club of New York's Career Seminars, here is a practical guide for managers needing advice on career transition. They start by presenting the five basic concepts underlining the process. Part 2 then focuses on "getting to know you—the product," taking the reader through the self-exploration and self-awareness process. Part 3 is on developing a self-marketing campaign. The book is full of comments and quotes from participants. A checklist and several other lists are at end, along with a list of suggested readings.

Holton, Ed. *The MBA's Guide to Career Planning.* Princeton, NJ: Peterson's Guides, 1989. 363 pp. paper.

This is a practical guide written especially to help MBAs with career planning and the job-hunting process. It hopes to "teach you the concepts, theories, and techniques and show you how to make them work in your own personal way," and it is based on the author's experience both as an MBA and as a business school program and placement director. A useful "Career Resources" bibliography at end covers books, directories, and associations, in specific career areas of interest such as careers in accounting, human resources management, marketing; also general information, career planning, and placement.

A readable paperback intended as another career guide for MBAs is *How to Turn Your MBA into a CEO* by Robert W. Lear (New York: Macmillan, 1987, 222 pp.). It focuses on three topics: career strategy; interviewing; evaluating jobs. Case histories are at end along with an appendix on using your business library.

Lucht, John. *Rites of Passage at $100,000+.* New York: Viceroy Press, 1988. 745 pp.

The subtitle of this book states that it is an "insider's guide to absolutely everything about executive job-changing." Has the author succeeded? Lucht is an experienced recruiter. He discusses four main routes to a different job: personal contact; networking; executive recruiting (6 chapters); and direct mail (3 chapters). He also covers resumés, answering ads, interviews, negotiating your employment contract, outplacement, self-employment, and even increasing contacts. It is a concise, chatty book, full of "do's" and "don'ts." Appendixes contain a list of company directories useful in job searching, and a list of leading executive recruiters.

Directories of Recruiters

Baird, Robert B. *The Executive Grapevine: The Corporate Directory of Executive Recruitment Consultants.* London: Executive Grapevine (annual).

Profiles of management consulting firms in the U.K., Ireland, and Europe that offer executive search and selection services. Data provided for each firm usually includes: address, a few officers, statement of purpose, functions/industries/salary range covered, fees, location, other services. Indexes are by geographic location, function, industry covered, salary range, location of placement.

Directory of Executive Recruiters. Fitzwilliam, NH: Kennedy Publications (annual).

For each of more than 2,100 firms, this specifies the functions, industries, minimum salary handled, and key contact persons both for retainer recruiting firms and for contingency recruiters (in separate sections). Indexes are by function, industry, geographic location, and individual name. At the front are over 100 pages containing tips for candidates and for clients, and also a glossary. At end is a short annotated list of what the publisher feels are the best books on job searching. The publisher also issues *The Directory of Outplacement Firms* (6th ed., 1990).

Sibbald, John. *The Career Makers: America's Top 100 Executive Recruiters.* New York: Harper Business, 1990. 384 pp.

Unlike the other two directories, most of part 2 consists of two-page profiles of persons who are top executive recruiters. For each it usually gives education, employment history, special interests, representative and significant placements, what each person looks for in a candidate, minimum salary level handled, and geographic scope. In addition there is a list of the top two percenters. An index is arranged by specialization. This selection is based on survey responses from CEOs of Fortune's largest companies and retainer executive search firms. Part 1 has four chapters on "Working with the Top Executive Recruiters."

PERSONNEL BIBLIOGRAPHIES AND ABSTRACTS

Several of the bibliographies listed in the "Industrial Relations" section of this chapter are also useful for locating current literature on personnel administration and human relations.

Personnel Management Abstracts. Chelsea, MI (quarterly).

The major part of each issue is a useful annotated subject listing of recent periodical articles dealing with the management of people and organizational behavior; there is an author index. At the end are several pages providing abstracts of a few new books.

U.S. Office of Personnel Management. Library. *Personnel Literature.* Washington, DC: U.S. Government Printing Office (monthly, with annual index).

A continuing list of new books, pamphlets, articles added to the OPM library, arranged by over 50 subject headings and including subject descriptors with each entry. The annual index is by author and subject.

Work Related Abstracts. Warren, MI: Harmonie Park Press (monthly looseleaf service).

A good comprehensive, annotated index of articles and some books covering labor, personnel, and organizational behavior, in loose-leaf format. It is arranged in 20 broad sections for such subjects as: behavior at work; personnel management; compensation and fringe benefits; education and training; labor-management relations; negotiation process and dispute settlement. A detailed subject index is at front of each volume, and there is a separate annual "Subject Heading List."

PERSONNEL DICTIONARIES

Shafritz, Jay M. *The Facts on File Dictionary of Personnel Management and Labor Relations.* 2d ed., rev. and expanded. New York: Facts on File, 1985. 534 pp.

A comprehensive and useful dictionary that covers not only the words, terms, abbreviations, phrases, and processes of personnel management and labor relations but also laws, court cases, notable persons, journals, organizations, unions, and tests. Often a definition includes name of a book or article discussing the topic in more depth. There are occasional diagrams or tables which add to the value of this work.

PERSONNEL SERVICES

Bureau of National Affairs. *BNA Policy and Practice Series.* Washington, DC. 17 volumes. And weekly or biweekly supplements. Also available online.

This is a comprehensive loose-leaf reference guide providing up-to-date information on personnel policies, practices, and procedures, and it is of value to anyone involved in employer-employee relations. There are five sections: *Personnel Management* (3 volumes), which is a practical guide to everyday nonlegal problems of employer-employee relations, covering all important subjects, such as induction and orientation, training and employee education, absenteeism and turnover, community relations (a useful feature is its inclusion of annotated lists of books and articles with each discussion); *Labor Relations* (3 volumes), consisting of federal and state labor laws, explanations of National Labor Relations Board and court rulings; *Fair Employment Practices* (4 volumes), covering federal and state laws dealing with equal employment opportunity; *Wages and Hours* (3 volumes), for federal wage-hour laws and regulations; *Compensation* (3 volumes), covering all aspects of compensation policies and plans and also including occasional lists of books and articles with some sections. A final volume contains a weekly *Bulletin to Management* and bi-weekly *Fair Employment Practices Summary of Latest Developments*.

Bureau of National Affairs. *PPF Surveys.* Washington, DC (usually two numbers per year).

These Personnel Policies Forum Surveys pamphlets report on company policies and practices of BNA Personnel Policy Forum members, who represent all types of enterprises. There were 147 surveys published as of mid-1990, with latest numbers covering such topics as: No.145, "Employee Award Programs" (September 1987); No.146, "Recruiting and Selection Procedures" (May 1988); No.147, "Wage and Salary Administration" (June 1990).

Commerce Clearing House. *Human Resources Management.* Chicago. 5 loose-leaf volumes and a biweekly newsletter.

A five-unit set for human resources professionals that can be purchased separately. The five titles are: *Equal Employment Opportunity; Compensation* (2 volumes); *Employment Relations; Personnel Practice/Communications; OSHA Compliance.* The biweekly newsletter is called *Ideas and Trends*. Another CCH service is *Payroll Management Guide*.

Prentice-Hall, Inc. *Personnel Management.* Englewood Cliffs, NJ: 3 volumes. And periodic updates.

These three volumes can be purchased separately. The one on "Communications" covers methods, ideas, forms, etc., used in communicating company rules and policies (both written and oral) to employees; the "Compensation" volume provides the latest developments and trends in compensation practices; "Policies and Practices" has concise, practical information on a wide range of personnel techniques used by employers, including employee selection, training, promotion, discipline.

Among other personnel services, Prentice-Hall also offers the following looseleaf services with periodic supplements: *Executive Compensation* (3 volumes), which offers guidance on various compensation packages for top executives; *Personnel Management Guide* (1 volume), a guide to employee management options; *Public Personnel Administration; Policies and Practices for Personnel* (1 volume).

HUMAN RESOURCES/PERSONNEL PERIODICALS

All of these periodicals are indexed in *Work Related Abstracts,* which is described elsewhere in this chapter. More specialized periodicals covering compensation, supervisory management, and training and development are described in previous sections of this chapter. Later in the chapter are periodicals on industrial relations and employee benefits.

HR Magazine. Alexandria, VA: Society for Human Resource Management (monthly).

Formerly called the *Personnel Administrator,* each issue of this monthly usually contains about 10 short articles, of which four usually focus on a specific theme and the rest are on any of a wide range of HRM topics such as compensation and benefits, employee and labor relations, communications, or recruitment; also one book review and several pages of book notes. Indexed in ABI/I, BPI, PAIS, TI.

Human Resource Management. Ann Arbor: Wiley, for the School of Business Administration, University of Michigan (quarterly).

This journal aims to publish short, easy-to-read articles and research reports relevant to the effective use of human resources. There are usually 5 to 7 articles in each issue on specific topics of interest to managers, executives, and administrators. Includes book reviews and book notes. Indexed in ABI/I, BPI, PAIS.

Human Resource Planning. New York: Human Resource Planning Society (quarterly).

Seeks articles that "disseminate and encourage the development of leading edge theory, research, and practice in strategic HRM." About five or six articles per issue; bibliographical citations with each. Indexed in ABI/I, BPI, TI.

Personnel. New York: American Management Association (monthly).

Billed as "the human resources management magazine of the American Management Association," this contains short, practical articles on a wide range of HR topics. Includes also a continuing section on new HR development, and occasionally annotated booklists. Indexed in ABI/I, BPI; full text on BRS, DATA-STAR, DIALOG, DOW JONES.

Personnel Journal. Costa Mesa, CA (monthly).

This trade journal calls itself "the management magazine for human resources executives." Its short, interesting, and practical articles may cover any of the many P/HR topics, such as employee communications, compensation and benefits, recruitment, training and development, HR information systems, legal issues. Indexed in ABI/I, PAIS, TI.

Personnel Management. London: Personnel Publications Ltd. (monthly).
Published on behalf of the Institute of Personnel Management, this monthly is useful for its articles with a British view. Includes book reviews. Indexed in ABI/I, BPI, TI.

Personnel Psychology. Houston, TX (quarterly).
Publishes empirical research dealing "with all aspects of personnel psychology, including employee selection, training and development, job analysis, productivity improvement programs, work attitudes, labor-management relations, and compensation and reward systems." It contains excellent articles written primarily by academic authorities, often with bibliographical citations. Included is a good book review section on organizational behavior and human resources management. Indexed in ABI/I, BPI.

Public Personnel Management. Alexandria, VA: International Personnel Management Association (quarterly).
Articles are on personnel and labor relations topics of special interest to personnel managers in the public sector. Indexed in ABI/I, BPI.

PERSONNEL MANAGEMENT ASSOCIATIONS

Institute of Personnel Management, IPM House, Camp Road, London SW 19 4 UW, England.

International Personnel Management Association, 1617 Duke Street, Alexandria, VA 22314.

Society for Human Resource Management, 606 N. Washington Street, Alexandria, VA 22314.

Tavistock Institute of Human Relations, Tavistock Centre, 120 Belsize Lane, London NW3 5BA, England.

INDUSTRIAL RELATIONS

LABOR ECONOMICS AND LABOR RELATIONS

Books

Fossum, John A. *Labor Relations: Development, Structure, Process.* 4th ed. Homewood, IL: Irwin, 1989. 495 pp. Fifth edition to be published in 1992.
As the subtitle indicates, this well-written book focuses on three aspects of labor relations, with three chapters addressing development issues, one examining union structure, nine chapters (the greatest emphasis) on process aspects (including union organizing, wage and nonwage bargaining, contract negotiations, impasse resolution, grievance arbitration). The last three chapters cut across all three areas in discussing: public sector labor relations; employee relations in nonunion organizations; challenges to collective bargaining. Fossum covers important recent changes in labor relations, and overall he presents a balanced perspective on the subject. He has been heavily influenced by the classic *A Behavioral Theory of Labor Negotiations* by Richard E. Walton and Robert B. McKersie (Reprint of 1965 edition with a

new introduction is published as 2d edition, Ithaca, NY: ILR Press, 1991, 437 pp., paper). Useful examples, cases, and exhibits make for a readable text.

Kerr, Clark, and Paul D. Staudohar, eds. *Industrial Relations in a New Age.* San Francisco: Jossey-Bass, 1986. 419 pp.

This is a compilation of 90 short readings which seek to make a contribution to thinking and deciding about the problems of industrial relations, with its central theme the organization of work in industrial society. It goes beyond subjects traditionally included in books on industrial relations to cover such topics as the meaning of work, the changing work force, job satisfaction, the quality of work life, and worker participation in management. Most selections have been shortened to cover only key issues and passages, and each was originally written by a recognized name such as John Dunlop and D. Quinn Mills. Short lists of additional reading are with each chapter.

A useful book of *Readings in Labor Economics and Labor Relations* was edited by Richard L. Rowan (5th ed., Irwin, 1985, 403 pp., paper).

Mills, Daniel Quinn. *Labor-Management Relations.* 4th ed. New York: McGraw-Hill, 1989. 670 pp.

Professor Mills has included material from related disciplines (personnel, human behavior in organizations, labor economics) in this latest revision of his book about the interaction of employers and workers. Throughout the text there runs the central theme of the power inherent in the relation of employer to employee and the various limitations imposed, whether by law, union power, or management self-discipline, on the way in which power is exercised. Each of its 9 major parts (sections A to I) describe aspects of this relationship, including one on labor-management relations in the public sector. At end is a section containing arbitration exercises. A list of selected readings is with each chapter.

Reynolds, Lloyd G., Stanley H. Masters and Coletta H. Moser. *Labor Economics and Labor Relations.* 10th ed. Englewood Cliffs, NJ: Prentice-Hall, 1991. 610 pp.

With the 9th edition of this good, standard textbook covering both title subjects, Professor Reynolds added two coauthors. Now they have revised the book once again to include the latest research findings and new trends. The first half begins with a simple model of the labor market, followed by discussions of supply and demand, wage determination, and an examination of several important policy issues (including discrimination in employment, changes in average wage rates, unemployment). The second half focuses on the unionized sector of the economy, including five chapters on aspects of collective bargaining, and two on how unions affect the operation of the economy. Suggested readings are with chapters; a glossary of concepts is at the end. These authors have also edited a book of *Readings in Labor Economics and Labor Relations* (5th ed., Prentice-Hall, 1991, 469 pp., paper) which follows the general organization of the text.

Sloane, Arthur A., and Fred Witney. *Labor Relations.* 7th ed. Englewood Cliffs, NJ: Prentice-Hall, 1991. 513pp.

A text on union-management relations, with part 3, on collective bargaining, the longest of its three parts. That third part examines the negotiation, administration, and major contents of the labor agreement, and it includes 12 arbitration cases drawn from the authors' experience. This latest revision covers new material on such topics as plant closings, health care benefits, recent developments in labor law, as well as enlarged treatment of minorities and women in unions, quality of work life programs, employee stock ownership plans, union political activity.

ARBITRATION AND COLLECTIVE BARGAINING

It has been predicted that negotiating skills in all kinds of disputes (not just those relating to labor) will become increasingly important for future success in management. Thus perhaps it is not surprising that there have been several recently revised or new books on this subject. Raiffa's book below may be of interest for all managers who must negotiate almost daily in the process of making management decisions.

Begin, James P., and Edwin F. Beal. *The Practice of Collective Bargaining.* 8th ed. Homewood, IL: Irwin, 1989. 638 pp.

One of the better texts, this one is updated once again to cover current developments in the organization, activities, and issues of collective bargaining in the United States. Special chapters are devoted to public sector bargaining and to unions in other countries. A chronology of collective bargaining events, 1786–1984, is in Chapter 2. Short cases are at end of book.

Chamberlain, Neil W., and James W. Kuhn. *Collective Bargaining.* 3d ed. New York: McGraw-Hill, 1986. 493 pp.

This text considers the history, nature, problems, and potential of collective bargaining, but it is brought up to date to reflect research and change only as of 1986. There are 6 parts, including the following: form and content; power and politics; law and regulation; the economic reach.

Coulson, Robert. *Business Arbitration—What You Need to Know.* 3d ed. New York: American Arbitration Association, 1986. 178 pp.

Here is an uncomplicated little guide to business arbitration meant to "help you to understand how arbitration can be used by you to better manage your own business controversies." At end is a code of ethics for arbitrators, significant court decisions, arbitration statutes, and text of several arbitration acts. Bibliographies are with each chapter. This book does not reflect changes since 1986.

Fisher, Roger, William Ury and Bruce Patton. *Getting to YES: Negotiating Agreement Without Giving In.* 2d ed. New York: Penguin Books, 1991. 200 pp. paper.

We all negotiate something just about every day, and these authors feel this is often not done very well. So they have developed a method they call "principled negotiation" by which issues (whatever the disagreement) are decided by merit rather than through a haggling process. Their useful concise guide lays out the four principles of this method and then answers questions most commonly asked about it. The book is full of common sense and good advice, and much is based on the authors' wide experience. It reads easily and has interesting examples.

For persons wanting more detail about effective handling of "people issues" in negotiations, Mr. Fisher has written (with Scott Brown) *Getting Together: Building Relationships as We Negotiate* (Penguin Books, 1988). Mr. Ury has tackled perhaps a more difficult problem in his *Getting Past No: Negotiating with Difficult People* (New York: Bantam Books, 1991, 161 pp.).

Gottlieb, Marvin, and William J. Healy. *Making Deals: The Business of Negotiating.* New York: New York Institute of Finance, 1990. 194 pp.

According to the publisher's note, *Making Deals* argues that the best negotiations provide opportunities for all parties to achieve their objectives and to come away satisfied. This is a practical book that analyzes current trends, shows how to develop strategies and tactics for many different deal-making situations. It is full of scenarios and real-life examples.

Kochan, Thomas A. *Collective Bargaining and Industrial Relations: From Theory to Policy and Practice.* 2d ed. Homewood, IL: Irwin, 1988. 496 pp.

Substantially changed in this second edition, Kochan's goal is to use recent research to introduce students to the changing material of collective bargaining and industrial relations. He introduces a three-tier model which "focuses more directly on how the strategic choices of management, labor, and government decision makers influence the process and results of bargaining." Chapters describe and analyze the environment, structure, and process of the collective bargaining system. A chapter at end covers collective bargaining in the public sector.

Raiffa, Howard. *The Art and Science of Negotiation.* Cambridge, MA: The Belknap Press of Harvard University Press, 1982. 373 pp. paper.

Like the Fisher et al. book, this one is not about labor negotiations specifically but rather about all types of negotiating. Thus it is addressed to all persons who must negotiate—be they diplomats, military officers, lawyers, politicians, or business people. Raiffa attempts to explain in "relatively" nonmathematical language some of the science (theory) of negotiation or intervening—to show that a systematic and conscious analysis can help in the negotiation process and that a blend of the art with analytical, problem-solving skills can make for better dispute settlement. First he studies negotiations involving two parties and one issue, then two parties with many issues, and finally many parties with many issues. Interesting case examples are used throughout. A bibliography is at end.

Taylor, Benjamin T., and Fred Witney. *Labor Relations Law.* 5th ed. Englewood Cliffs, NJ: Prentice-Hall, 1987. 862 pp.

A text for persons with little legal background on "the major trends in the law of collective bargaining, the reasons for these trends, and their consequences on the overall function of collective bargaining." Includes text of important labor acts in an appendix; also a bibliography and index of labor cases, but only as of 1987.

INDUSTRIAL RELATIONS BIBLIOGRAPHIES AND ABSTRACTS

Human Resources Abstracts. Newbury Park, CA: Sage Publications (quarterly).

For the professional interested in current and changing ideas covering human, social, and manpower problems and solutions, this is a continuing abstract of recent literature arranged in 17 subject sections of which several are: labor markets and participation; education, training, and career development; hiring and personnel practices; work life and work environment; organizations and management; labor and industrial relations; earnings and benefits; employment and unemployment; human resources and society.

Industrial Relations Law Journal. Berkeley: School of Law, University of California (quarterly).

Each issue has an abstracts section consisting of short summaries of recent labor law articles.

International Labour Office. *International Labour Documentation.* Geneva, Switzerland (monthly).

A descriptive subject listing, in English, based on current acquisitions in the ILO library, and covering the fields of labor relations, labor law, employment, working conditions, vocational training, labor-related aspects of economics, social development, rural development, technological change, etc. There are also editions published in French and Spanish. This monthly is difficult to use for searching because it has no cumulation, but there is now a machine-readable version called *LABORDOC* which eliminates that problem for persons having access to a computer terminal.

A companion database to *LABORDOC* is the ILO's *LABORINFO* which contains records of material used in the preparation of their *Social and Labour Bulletin.*

Massachusetts Institute of Technology. Industrial Relations Library. *Library Accessions Bulletin.* Cambridge, MA (bimonthly).

This is a good, descriptive list of selected books, pamphlets, and articles added to the MIT Industrial Relations Library. Each issue is arranged by some 50 subjects and includes publications on organizational behavior and human resource management as well as on industrial relations and labor.

New York State School of Industrial and Labor Relations, Cornell University. Martin P. Catherwood Library. *Library Acquisitions List.* Ithaca, NY (monthly).

The Catherwood Library probably has the largest industrial relations collection in the U.S. This is a monthly list of new books and pamphlets added to their collection. It is arranged by the Library of Congress classification system, a subject scheme.

Princeton University. Industrial Relations Section. *Selected References.* Princeton, NJ (5/yr.?).

Instead of an accessions list, Princeton's Industrial Relations Section offers a series of four-page annotated bibliographies, each on a topic of current interest. The March issue each year describes "Noteworthy Books in Industrial and Labor Economics." Other titles in 1991 included: "Self-Directed and Self-Managed Work Teams," "Suggestion Systems."

Work Related Abstracts. Warren, MI: Harmonie Park Press (monthly loose-leaf service).

A good, comprehensive, annotated index of articles and some books covering labor, personnel, and organizational behavior, in loose-leaf format. It is arranged in 20 broad sections for such subjects as: labor force and labor market; labor-management relations; labor unions and employee organizations; negotiation process and dispute settlement. A detailed subject index is at front of each volume, and there is a separate annual "Subject Heading List."

The U.S. Bureau of Labor Statistics publishes a quarterly *BLS Update,* which is a descriptive listing of their recent publications. They have also recently updated the periodic description of their *Major Programs: Bureau of Labor*

Statistics which includes the names of publications covering their research programs in employment and unemployment, prices and living conditions, compensation and working conditions, productivity and technology, and employment projections.

INDUSTRIAL RELATIONS DICTIONARIES

See also the *The Facts on File Dictionary of Personnel Management and Labor Relations* by Jay M. Shafritz (2d ed., rev. and expanded. New York: Facts on File, 1985, 534 pp.) listed elsewhere in this chapter.

Roberts, Harold S. *Roberts' Dictionary of Industrial Relations.* 3d ed. Washington, DC: Bureau of National Affairs, 1986. 811 pp.

This excellent encyclopedic dictionary of industrial relations terms was completely revised, updated, and expanded in 1986 by the Industrial Relations Center at the University of Hawaii in Manoa. Included are short summaries of important cases and major labor laws, notes about international unions. Source references with most entries are useful for persons seeking further information, but only for sources published prior to 1986.

LABOR SERVICES

Bureau of National Affairs. *Daily Labor Report.* Washington, DC (5/wk.). Available also online in full text.

Important for those executives and industrial relations specialists who must have immediate notification, analysis, and interpretations of major U.S. labor developments. It covers news of congressional activity, important NLRB decisions, full text of important federal and state court rulings, arbitration awards, significant bargaining negotiations, equal employment opportunity developments, news of management and union strategy. It also includes basic statistics and economic data of use in bargaining.

BNA ONLINE produces over 80 online versions of many BNA publications and services. Some are in full text, but not all are in the labor field. For a complete annual listing of BNA online services, consult one of the directories of online services described in Chapter 2, such as *Information Industry Directory.*

Bureau of National Affairs. *Labor Relations Reporter.* Washington, DC 14 volumes (loose-leaf, with semiweekly supplements). Available also online, much in full text.

This comprehensive labor service gives full text coverage on current labor relations and developments, state laws, fair employment practices, wages and hours, labor arbitration. The volumes are broken down as follows: *Master Index* (1 volume); *Labor Relations Expediter* (2 volumes), contains annotated discussions of the origin, development, and current status of all important labor relations topics, analyses of leading cases and rulings, text of federal labor laws and regulations, etc.; *Analysis— News and Background Information* (1 volume); *Labor-Management Relations* (1 volume), weekly coverage on all published decisions of the National Labor Relations Board, federal and state court decisions relating to labor-management issues; *State Laws* (2 volumes); *Fair Employment Practice Manual and Cases* (3 volumes), provides text of federal and state laws, orders, and regulations, etc.; *Wages and Hours* (3 volumes), full text of wage-hour and equal pay regulations, laws, etc.;

Labor Arbitration (1 volume), weekly reports of labor dispute settlements, full text of awards, settlements, biographical directories of arbitrators.

Backing up this service are their several bound "Reference Library" series for past labor laws, decisions, etc., in the following sets: *Labor Relations Reference Manuals* containing digest of NLRB decisions and text of court decisions on labor relations; *Wage and Hour Cases,* covering both federal and state laws; *Labor Arbitration Reports; Fair Employment Practice Cases.* Cumulative digests and indexes provide easy access to these bound volumes. Their *Labor Relations Yearbook* is a one-volume summary of the year's major labor events, including conferences, studies, background, and economic data.

Several more specialized BNA labor services are: *Affirmative Action Compliance Manual for Federal Contractors* (2 volumes); *BNA Policy and Practice Series* (described elsewhere in this chapter); *BNA's Employee Relations Weekly* (2 volumes), also online in full text; *Collective Bargaining Negotiations & Contracts* (2 volumes, biweekly); *Construction Labor Report* (weekly); *EEOC Compliance Manual* (2 volumes); *Employment Guide* (biweekly); *Government Employee Relations Report* (4 volumes, weekly); *Labor Relations Week* (2 volumes), also online in full text; *Union Labor Report* (2 volumes, weekly).

Commerce Clearing House. *Labor Law Reporter.* Chicago. 16 volumes (looseleaf, with weekly or biweekly supplements).

A comprehensive, continuing guide to federal and state labor relations and wage-hour rules. It includes: laws, administrative interpretations, rulings, statutes, regulations, rules and forms; NLRB and court decisions; union contracts, arbitration procedures. The volume coverage is as follows: *Federal Labor Relations* (6 volumes) contains federal labor relations and union control rules, statutes, regulations, etc.; *Federal Wages-Hours* (2 volumes) covers federal controls, statutes, regulations, etc.; *State Laws* (3 volumes) gives a state-by-state breakdown of labor relations for employees in both industry and government; *Union Contract-Arbitration* (1 volume) explains arbitration principles; *Employment Practices Guide* (4 volumes) covers federal and state laws on discrimination, etc.

Backing up this service are the following bound volumes for historical data: *Labor Cases,* which gives full-text federal and state court decisions; *NLRB Decisions,* which digests all Board decisions; *Labor Arbitration Awards; Employment Practices Decisions* rendered both by federal and state courts.

Commerce Clearing House. *Labor Law Course.* Chicago (annual).

A one-volume reference or self-study course on the essentials of labor law, with an emphasis on broad federal statutes. It covers labor unions, labor relations, unfair labor practices, contract clauses, arbitration, wage-hour controls.

Two other CCH legal services are: *EEOC Compliance Manual* and *Employment Safety and Health Guide* (4 volumes). Three annual summary guidebooks reflecting current laws, decisions, rulings, etc., are: *Guidebook to Fair Employment Practices; Guidebook to Federal Wage-Hour Laws; Guidebook to Labor Relations.*

Prentice-Hall, Inc. *Labor Relations Guide.* Englewood Cliffs, NJ: 3 volumes (loose-leaf, with weekly supplements).

Volumes 1–2 contain explanations of labor laws, full texts of federal labor laws and regulations, pertinent data both parties should know about bargaining, and a cost-of-living index. The third volume covers "Occupational Safety and Health."

A closely related service is *Industrial Relations Guide* (1 volume, with biweekly supplements), a guide for solving industrial relations problems, with emphasis on arbitration awards and union contract clauses, and including many actual examples.

Four other Prentice-Hall services are: *Equal Employment Opportunity Compliance Manual* (2 volumes, monthly); *Payroll Guide* (2 volumes, weekly); *Personnel Management* (described elsewhere in this chapter); and *Termination of Employment: Employer and Employee Rights* (1 volume, monthly).

Check elsewhere in this chapter for: a textbook on *Labor Relations Law* by B. T. Taylor and F. Witney; a monthly *Labor Law Journal;* a quarterly *Industrial Relations Law Journal.*

LABOR STATISTICS

The Bureau of Labor Statistics publishes a variety of useful statistical publications, some quite general and indispensable, as in the case of the two listed below, and others covering specialized labor subjects such as consumer prices (see "Commodity and Consumer Prices" section in Chapter 6), indexes of labor productivity and wages in specific industries. For a good monthly indexing service (cumulating annually and also available online) that describes the major labor statistics published by the federal government, see *American Statistics Index* (described in Chapter 4). See also continuing BLS bibliographies mentioned in section for "Industrial Relations Bibliographies and Abstracts" above. Much of the BLS statistics is also available online and on CD-ROM.

U.S. Bureau of Labor Statistics. *Handbook of Labor Statistics.* Washington, DC: U.S. Government Printing Office (biennial; formerly annual).

A valuable, one-volume compendium of major BLS statistics, with each table giving statistics for as many years as they were compiled. These statistics cover: population, labor force, employment status; special labor force data; nonagricultural payroll employment, hours and earnings; occupational employment statistics; employment and wages; productivity; compensation; prices and living conditions; work stoppage, occupational injuries and illness; foreign labor statistics; employee benefits. "Technical Notes" at beginning of each section describe major statistical programs and identify the tables derived from each. This handbook is issued in the BLS *Bulletin* series, with the 1989 volume issued as *Bulletin* No. 2340. A new edition is due in 1992.

U.S. Bureau of Labor Statistics. *Monthly Labor Review.* Washington, DC: U.S. Government Printing Office.

This is an indispensable monthly publication for current labor statistics covering employment, unemployment, hours, earnings, consumer and producer price indexes, collective bargaining, productivity, work stoppages.

Several more specialized current statistical monthlies of the BLS are: *CPI Detailed Report* (consumer prices indexes and rates of change for U.S. and 27 metro areas); *Current Wage Developments; Employment and Earnings; Producer Price Indexes.*

Labor statistics are found in other U.S. government publications. The various economic census volumes give number of employees and size of payroll by industry and by location. (These are described in Chapter 4). The decennial *Census of Population* in its "Subject Reports," Series PC80-2 for 1980, published special statistical reports on occupations by industry, journey to work, earnings by occupation and education, among other subjects.

Foreign Labor Statistics

International Labour Office. *Yearbook of Labour Statistics.* Geneva, Switzerland.

Statistics are for some 180 countries or territories, usually for the past 10 years, and they cover: population, employment, unemployment, hours of work, wages, labor costs, consumer prices, occupational injuries, strikes and lockouts. "References and Sources" (at end) list, by country, the principal sources of national labor statistics. The ILO quarterly *Bulletin of Labour Statistics* contains current figures on employment, unemployment, hours of work, wages, consumer prices. A "Retrospective Edition on Population Censuses, 1945–1989" was published in 1990.

Organization for Economic Cooperation and Development. *Labour Force Statistics.* Paris (annual). Data also available on magnetic tape and on diskettes.

OECD country-by-country statistics on population, the labor force, employment and wage earners by broad industry, unemployment rates, for the past 20 years. National sources for statistics are at front. A current *Quarterly Labour Force Statistics* contains country statistics and charts for employment and unemployment for most recent five years.

Great Britain. Department of Employment. *British Labour Statistics Yearbook* London: H. M. Stationery Office.

Statistics include wages and hours, earnings, retail prices, employment, unemployment, family expenditures, trade unions, industrial disputes, industrial accidents, labor costs. For past figures see their *British Labour Statistics: Historical Abstract, 1886–1968* (1971). Current figures are in their monthly *Employment Gazette.*

Many other countries publish national labor statistics. For a list of these consult the "References and Sources" section in the ILO's *Yearbook of Labour Statistics,* mentioned above. The Bank of Japan, for instance, publishes detailed wholesale price index tables in their *Price Indexes Annual.*

INDUSTRIAL RELATIONS PERIODICALS

Most of these industrial relations periodicals are indexed in *Work Related Abstracts* described elsewhere in this chapter.

Arbitration Journal. New York: American Arbitration Association (quarterly).

Scholarly articles on labor arbitration, with a "Review of Court Decisions" in each issue; also usually one book review and recent additions to the AAA library. Indexed in ABI/I, BPI.

British Journal of Industrial Relations. London School of Economics (3/yr.).

"A journal of research and analysis covering every aspect of industrial relations in Britain and overseas." Includes book reviews and a "Chronicle" of recent statistics, government policies, and activities. Indexed in ABI/I, PAIS.

Great Britain. Department of Employment. *Employment Gazette.* London: H. M. Stationery Office (monthly).

Most useful for its continuing monthly British labor and employment statistics, including retail prices, and industrial disputes. The articles on labor research also often contain statistics. Indexed in PAIS.

Industrial & Labor Relations Review. Ithaca: New York State School of Industrial and Labor Relations, Cornell University (quarterly).

An outstanding academic journal, with research papers on a wide range of labor topics relating both to the public and private sector. Useful features in each issue include a good book review section, and notes about "research in progress," arranged by subject. Indexed in ABI/I, BPI, PAIS, SSI.

Industrial Relations. Berkeley: Institute of Industrial Relations, University of California (3/yr.).

Billed as "a journal of economy and society," this contains articles, symposia, and research notes on all aspects of the employment relationship, with special attention to pertinent developments in the fields of labor economics, sociology, psychology, political science, law. Indexed in ABI/I, BPI, PAIS, TI.

Industrial Relations Journal. Oxford, Eng.: B. Blackwell (quarterly).

Well-researched articles on industrial relations with a British and European focus. Abstracts in both English and French at beginning of each issue. Includes book reviews. Indexed in ABI/I.

Industrial Relations Law Journal. Berkeley: School of Law, University of California (quarterly).

Usually two or three lengthy articles are in each issue intended to present current developments in the labor and employment law field for scholars, practitioners, and students. Contains also a descriptive list of recent publications and abstracts of current labor-related articles. Indexed in ABI/I.

International Labour Review. Geneva, Switzerland: International Labour Office (bimonthly).

A good source for current information about labor conditions in specific countries outside the United States. Authoritative articles also cover social and economic problems as they relate to labor. Includes book reviews and book notes. Indexed in ABI/I, BPI, PAIS, SSI.

Labor Law Journal. Chicago: Commerce Clearing House (monthly).

This monthly provides "a continuing survey of important legislative, administrative and judicial developments and signed articles on subjects pertaining to legal problems in the labor field." Proceedings of the annual meeting of the Industrial Relations Research Association are in the August issue each year. Indexed in BPI, PAIS.

U.S. Bureau of Labor Statistics. *Monthly Labor Review.* Washington, DC: U.S. Government Printing Office.

An indispensable monthly for current U.S. labor information. Each issue contains four or five studies by BLS researchers, many with statistical tables. Useful features include: research summaries; major labor agreements expiring during the following month; recent developments in industrial relations; significant decisions in labor cases; technical notes. There are excellent current labor statistics in each issue; also book reviews, and a subject listing of selected books and articles received by the BLS. Indexed in ABI/I, BPI, PAIS, SSI.

LABOR DIRECTORIES

Directory of U.S. Labor Organizations. Washington, D.C.: Bureau of National Affairs (biennial). Also available online.

A directory of national unions, professional, and state employee associations, giving for each the top officers, total membership, names of publications. At front is a directory of AFL-CIO headquarters and central bodies; appendixes have statistical tables on union membership and earnings.

For Canada, see *Directory of Labour Organizations in Canada* (Ottawa, Ontario, Can.: Bureau of Labor Information, Supply and Services Canada; annual).

Descriptive lists of labor unions, labor associations, and federations are also included in the directories of U.S. associations that are described in Chapter 7.

INDUSTRIAL RELATIONS ASSOCIATIONS

American Arbitration Association, 140 West 51st Street, New York, NY 10020.

Industrial Relations Counselors, P.O. Box 1530, New York, NY 10101.

Industrial Relations Research Association, 7226 Social Science Building, University of Wisconsin, Madison, WI 53706.

International Industrial Relations Association, c/o ILO, CH-1211, Geneva 22, Switzerland.

International Labour Office, 4 route des Mouillons, CH-1211, Geneva 22, Switzerland (U.S. branch office is at: 1750 New York Ave., N.W., Washington, DC 20006).

Labor Research Association, 80 East 11th Street, New York, NY 10003.

PENSION AND EMPLOYEE BENEFITS PLANNING

Handbooks

Employee Benefits Handbook, 3d ed. Ed. by Jeffrey D. Mamorsky. Boston: Warren, Gorham & Lamont, 1992. 1 volume (various pagings).

Because of rapid changes, this comprehensive, practical guide has been revised once again to incorporate the latest concepts, techniques, and thinking in all aspects of employee benefits. Each of its 58 chapters is written by one or more expert contributors representing a diversity of disciplines. The sections focus on: benefit objectives and administration; replacement income in the event of retirement; legal requirements; replacement income in the event of disability, unemployment, and death; financial protection against extraordinary or catastrophic costs; specialized plans (stock ownership plans, flexible/cafeteria plans, tax-deferred annuities, and others). Each chapter is preceded by an outline; tables, charts, and illustrative examples are used throughout.

Rosenbloom, Jerry S., ed. *The Handbook of Employee Benefits: Design, Funding and Administration.* 2d ed. Homewood, IL: Dow Jones-Irwin, 1988. 1,170 pp.

So much is taking place in the employee benefits field that it is helpful to have another relatively recent handbook. This is a comprehensive guide to the objectives, design, costing, funding, implementation, and administration of employee benefits plans. It is intended as a handy reference book both for students and for the professional. There are 55 chapters in 10 major sections, each covering a major component of the employee benefit planning process and each written by an expert. Practical examples, charts, and graphs are used throughout.

Books

Allen, Everett T., Jr. et al. *Pension Planning: Pensions, Profit-Sharing and Other Deferred Compensation Plans.* 7th ed. Homewood, IL: Irwin, 1992. 500 pp.

Completely restructured to reflect dynamic developments in the pension field, this latest edition of a comprehensive text is now arranged in 6 parts to cover: environmental influences of private pension plans; tax and legal requirements; defined contribution plans; design considerations for defined benefit plans; operational and administrative aspects; miscellaneous considerations. The coauthors are Joseph J. Melone, Jerry S. Rosenbloom, and Jack L. Van Derhei.

Employee Benefit Research Institute. *Fundamentals of Employee Benefit Programs.* 4th ed. Washington, DC: 1990. 355 pp. paper.

Here is a readable primer which has as its goal the education of interested persons about the extent and importance of employee benefits and the many changes being made by employers and by lawmakers. The first part (34 chapters) describe the many private-sector benefit programs (such as profit sharing plans, ESOPs, IRAs, health insurance). Part 2 (10 chapters) discusses the various public-sector benefit programs. Each chapter ends with a bibliography.

McGill, Dan M., and Donald S. Grubbs, Jr. *Fundamentals of Private Pensions.* 6th ed. Homewood, IL: Irwin, 1989. 785 pp.

Revised once again to reflect regulations, rulings, interpretations, and other developments, this comprehensive text is arranged in five parts: introduction; plan design; valuation of pension plan liabilities; financial management of a pension plan (including chapters on management policy and operations, and on pension accounting); other qualified asset accumulations plans (profit sharing, stock bonus and ownership plans, thrift and deferred arrangements, individual retirement plans, federal tax treatment of qualified plans, etc.). A few statistical tables, and lists of case citations, statutes, rules, and regulations are at end.

Rosenbloom, Jerry S., and G. Victor Hallman. *Employee Benefit Planning.* 3d ed. Englewood Cliffs, NJ: Prentice-Hall, 1991. 500 pp.

Employee benefits are a rapidly growing, more complex, and increasingly important form of employee compensation. Therefore it is important for managers and their consultants to become knowledgeable about the various types and how they fit into a cohesive and well-organized company plan. This book's purpose is to help make this possible by discussing benefits as they relate to: risk management; death; medical expenses; profit sharing and savings plans; stock bonus and employee stock ownership plans; other retirement plans; flexible benefits/cafeteria plans; unemployment. There are also chapters on funding as well as on designing and evaluating the employee benefit plan.

Three further texts not seen for evaluation are: *Employee Benefits* by Burton T. Beam, Jr., and John J. McFadden (2d ed., Homewood, IL: Irwin, 1988, 539 pp.); *Employee Benefit Programs: A Total Compensation Perspective* by Robert M. McCaffery (Boston: PWS-Kent Publishing Co., 1988, 250 pp.); and *Social Insurance and Economic Security* by George E. Rejda (4th ed., Englewood Cliffs, NJ: Prentice-Hall, 1991, 452 pp.).

Bibliographies

Gunderson, Nels L. *Pension Funds: An Annotated Bibliography.* Metuchen, NJ: Scarecrow Press, 1990. 136 pp.

A short bibliography of selected U.S. books, articles, directories, dissertations arranged in 29 subject categories, from "accounting standards and practices" to "terminations." Only the book citations are annotated, and most of these were published no later than 1987.

International Foundation of Employee Benefit Plans. *Employee Benefits Resource Guide.* 2d ed. Brookfield, WI: 1990. 29 pp.

A short bibliography containing book abstracts, descriptions of journals, services, and databases on employee benefits, as well as a directory of several industry-related government agencies. The Foundation also produces *EBIS* (Employee Benefits InfoSource), an online database which abstracts worldwide literature on employee benefits plans, with a focus on that published in the U.S. and Canada.

Services

Bureau of National Affairs. *Pension Reporter.* Washington, DC 3 volumes (weekly). Also available online in full text.

A weekly report providing information on the latest developments in legislation, regulations, court decisions relating to pensions and employee trust funds. One volume contains a "Reference File" for important materials, forms, and text.

Commerce Clearing House. *Pension Plan Guide.* Chicago: 7 volumes (looseleaf, with weekly supplements).

This is the most comprehensive of the services, covering major aspects of pensions, profit sharing and other employee benefits, and blending planning and operating guidance with full information on the tax and legal rules in point. There are five numbered volumes and also a separate volume covering "Plans and Clauses."

CCH also publishes: *Compliance Guide for Plan Administrators* (3 volumes); *Employee Benefits Management* (5 volumes); *Individual Retirement Plans Guide; Pensions and Deferred Compensation;* and *Unemployment Insurance Reports with Social Security.* There is also an annual paperback *Guidebook to Pension Planning,* which briefly spans the whole scope of pension plans.

Prentice-Hall, Inc. *Pension and Profit Sharing.* Englewood Cliffs, NJ. 4 volumes (loose-leaf, with weekly supplements).

Up-to-date information on pension and profit sharing planning, law and legal considerations, taxation, requirements for qualifying, etc.

Two other services are: *Pension and Profit Sharing Forms* and *Plan Administrator's Compliance Manual* (2 volumes) which is a semimonthly report on latest developments, regulations, requirements for all types of benefit plans.

Statistics

Employee Benefits. Washington, DC: U.S. Chamber of Commerce (annual).
Statistics, graphs, and brief text based on an annual survey. Figures include employee benefits by type of benefit and by industry; employee benefits as % of payroll for same categories as well as by region and by size of company; also related topics such as benefits costs, payroll deduction.

U.S. Social Security Administration. *Social Security Bulletin.* Washington, DC: U.S. Government Printing Office (monthly).
Each issue contains current operating statistics for income maintenance programs, social security trust funds, OASDI (Old-Age, Survivors, and Disability Insurance) cash benefits, public assistance, black lung benefits, unemployment insurance (often with statistics given from 1940 to date); also quarterly tables for some statistics including medicare benefits. Usually one or two articles, with statistics, are in each issue, and occasional issues contain a few abstracts of current articles of interest. Includes a separate "Annual Statistical Supplement." Indexed in ABI/I, BPI, PAIS.

Periodicals

Employee Benefits Journal. Brookfield, WI: International Foundation of Employee Benefit Plans (quarterly).
Short, informative articles on all aspects of employee benefits, with some issues focusing on a particular area such as health care issues. Abstracts of "Current Literature" in each issue are selected from *EBIS—Employee Benefits InfoSource,* the Association's database which covers worldwide literature on employee benefits. Indexed in ABI/I, BPI, TI.

The *Benefits Quarterly* is published at the same address by the International Society of Certified Employee Benefit Specialists. It is a refereed quarterly for professional papers representing original research and is geared for the employee benefits practitioner. Each issue has a "legal-legislative regulatory update," as well as abstracts from the literature, both books and articles, which are also selected from the database *EBIS*. Indexed in ABI/I.

Journal of Pension Planning & Compliance. New York: Panel Publishers (quarterly).
A professional journal concerned primarily with the financial, tax, and legal aspects of pension planning and compliance, and often written by accountants, lawyers, or academic persons. Indexed in ABI/I, PAIS.

Pension World. Atlanta, GA: Communication Channels, Inc. (monthly).
Articles focus on pension planning, employee benefits, investment strategy, and portfolio management as applied to pension funds; also news of interest to plan sponsors and investment managers. Annual surveys or directories include: "Software Product Directory" (March); "State Retirement System Investment Survey" (August); directory of "Real Estate Portfolio Managers" (September); "Master and

Directed Trust Services" (December). Indexed in ABI/I, BPI, PAIS; full text on BRS, DATA-STAR, DIALOG.

Pensions & Investments. Chicago: Crain Communications (biweekly).

"The newspaper of corporate and institutional investing." Extracts from a quarterly statistical table called PIPER (Pensions and Investments' Performance Evaluation Report) appears in four issues each year (second February, first May, second August and November). These give comparative performance data on over 400 equity funds, some 150 fixed income funds, and 163 balanced/TAA funds managed by investment counseling firms. Among other special annual issues and/or directories are: "Investment Bank Ranking" (first January issue); profiles of "The 1,000 Largest Pension Funds" (second January issue, described in the following section listing "Directories"); "Directory of Investment Advisers" (second May); "Directory of International and Global Managers" (second June); "Foreign Business Survey" (second July); "Real Estate Investment Management Survey" (first September); "Directory of Investment Management Consultants" (first November). Indexed in ABI/I, BPI; full text on DATA-STAR, DIALOG.

Two other periodicals devoted to benefits are: *Benefits & Compensation International* (London: Pension Publications Ltd.; monthly); *Employee Benefit Plan Review* (Chicago: C. D. Spencer & Associates; biweekly). Both are indexed in ABI/I, and the latter is also in BPI and TI. The domestic edition of *Institutional Investor* includes articles on pension funds and funding. It is described in the "Finance Periodicals" section of Chapter 14.

Directories

Institutional Investor. "The (year) Pensions Directory." New York (annual, in January issue).

A directory of the 500 largest corporate employee-benefit funds, major state, county, and city employees funds; also the money managers that manage these assets. The February issue contains "The (year) Pension Olympics" which is a ranked listing of all money managers that gained or lost pension accounts from the nation's 500 largest ERISA funds during the previous year. The ranking is by net gains or losses, and there is an index by company.

The Money Market Directory of Pension Funds and Their Investment Managers. Charlottesville, VA: Money Market Directories (annual). ("Update Supplement" published each July).

The first section is a geographical directory of more than 22,000 tax-exempt employee benefit funds, including corporate, union, local and state government funds, endowment and foundation funds. For each fund it usually gives, when applicable, facts on the retirement plan, pension plan, profit sharing plan, stock ownership plan, and/or endowment fund; also financial officers, benefits administrator, custodian of fund. Following this is: a ranking of funds by asset; a geographic list of investment managers (advisers, banks, insurance companies), with indexes and a ranking by tax-exempt funds under management; list of clients of investment managers and banks; directory of global custodians; real estate services; international investment firms; investment banking services; consultants and clients; information services and industry associations; institutional research firms; research analysts by industry groups; traders by specialty.

For persons interested in one U.S. geographical area only, the publisher also now offers four separate *Regional Directories* listing corporate pension fund sponsors with tax-exempt pension assets between $1 million and $5 million.

Pensions & Investments. "The 1,000 Largest Funds" (annual, second January issue).

Contains profiles of the nation's 200 largest pension funds, usually giving for each: total assets, defined benefits contribution mix and defined contribution asset mix; also names of equity managers and key personnel involved. This issue also ranks the 1,000 top pension funds/sponsors by asset size range, and the top 200 in various categories.

W G & L Pension and Benefits Fact Book. Boston: Warren, Gorham & Lamont (annual).

This brings together basic information and data on employee benefits, with an emphasis on tables, numbers, and statistics. It includes coverage of benefits legislation, social security, unemployment insurance, taxation of benefits, federal and state tax rates, withholding tables, actuarial tables, deferred compensation survey findings, fringe benefits survey findings, health care and cost containment efforts, Dow Jones and other averages, lists of associations, periodicals, government agencies. An almanac of information at end contains lists of holidays, telephone area codes, time zones, foreign currencies, weights and measures, and more; also a glossary.

Wyatt Company. *Top 50: A Survey of Retirement, Thrift and Profit Sharing Plans Covering Salaried Employees of 50 Large U.S. Industrial Companies as of January 1, (each year).* New York (annual).

A survey giving basic provisions of the qualified pension plans for U.S. salaried employees of 50 large companies, identifying these companies by name. There are also tables illustrative of company benefits in relation to number of years of service, as well as provisions of thrift/savings plans and profit sharing plans.

Associations

International Foundation of Employee Benefit Plans, 18700 W. Bluemound Road, PO Box 69, Brookfield, WI 53008.

20

PRODUCTION AND OPERATIONS MANAGEMENT

Handbooks – General Books – Production and Inventory Control – Industrial Engineering – Manufacturing Processes – Industrial Robotics and Automated Manufacturing – Motion and Time Study – Quality Control – POM Bibliographies – POM Periodicals – POM Associations – Industrial Research – Materials Management (Including Purchasing) – BUSINESS LOGISTICS – General Texts – Physical Distribution Bibliographies – Logistics Dictionaries – Logistics Periodicals – Logistics Directories – Logistics Associations – Traffic and Transportation – Traffic and Transportation Bibliographies – Traffic and Transportation Dictionaries – Transportation Financial Manuals – Traffic and Transportation Periodicals – Traffic and Transportation Directories – Traffic and Transportation Associations

Profound changes have been occurring in the production and operations functions, and this has been reflected in the contents of books and articles on POM. First one noted changes in the 1970s due to increased use of computers, management information systems, and technological advances; now journal articles are full of management concerns about such problems as quality control, costs, industrial research, foreign competition. Today the POM function is receiving much more of management's attention and will, it is likely, continue to play an increasingly important role in the operation of an enterprise. This chapter describes a selection of the latest books and reference sources on the whole POM field and also on some of its major components including the broad areas of materials management and business logistics. There is some overlapping of coverage within this chapter because of variations in both terminology and subjects treated in the recent literature.

Basic statistical methods and quantitative books are described in Chapter 17; management information systems in Chapter 13. Sources for production statistics of individual commodities and products are listed in Chapters 4 through 6.

HANDBOOKS

Several more specialized handbooks covering the automated factory, industrial engineering, manufacturing processes, production and inventory control, purchasing, quality control, and warehousing are listed elsewhere in this chapter.

International Handbook of Production and Operations Management. Ed. by Ray Wild. London: Cassell Educational Ltd., 1989. 653 pp.

Essays solicited especially for this volume and intended to identify, describe, and examine the principal issues and topics relating to effective POM. Its 35 selections, most written by academic experts in both the U.S. and Europe, are arranged in 8 parts: policies and objectives; facilities and capacities; technologies; research, design, and development; planning and control; quality and service; human resources; maintenance and renewal. References to further sources are with each essay.

Manufacturing High Technology Handbook. Ed. by Donatis Tijunelis and Keith E. McKee. New York: Marcel Dekker, 1987. 773 pp.

The editors intended this handbook "to assist the innovation process for manufacturing tools and techniques by providing a quick resource of current manufacturing technologies—an introduction, overview, and reference source covering as much as possible the range of technologies." The emphasis is on state-of-the-art information that can be easily read by managers, manufacturing practitioners, or specialists. The chapters, each by one or more expert contributors are arranged in 8 parts: the field of manufacturing technology; computer-integrated manufacturing; flexible manufacturing systems; numerical control; robotics; material selection and processing; quality, quality assurance, and automated inspection; advanced manufacturing systems design and management tools. Bibliographical references are at end of most chapters.

Production Handbook. Comp. by John A. White. 4th ed. New York: Wiley, 1987. 1 volume (various pagings).

A much needed, fully-revised and contemporary handbook on production management and design, expanded to meet dramatic changes occurring in production management during the five years prior to 1987. Its 63 chapters, each by a recognized author, are organized within 8 sections. The first is an introduction, and the others focus successively on: manpower, methods, machines, material, money, space, and system. There are useful diagrams, charts, and tables throughout. References are at end of many chapters, and a detailed index is at end of book.

GENERAL BOOKS

Adam, Everett E., Jr., and Ronald J. Ebert. *Production and Operations Management: Concepts, Models, and Behavior.* 4th ed. Englewood Cliffs, NJ: Prentice-Hall, 1989. 620 pp. Fifth edition to be published in 1992.

This book aims to introduce the basics of production/operations management in a readable, comprehensive, integrative way and to reflect recent changes in management practices and research. The focus is on management and so the material is organized around the planning, organizing, and controlling theme, with a balance between quantitative aspects and important behavioral applications. Supplements with some chapters discuss techniques and methodology at a more rigorous quantitative level. Useful examples are found throughout, set off in colored boxes; glossaries and literature references are with each chapter.

Amrine, Harold T., John A. Ritchey and Colin L. Moodie. *Manufacturing Organization and Management.* 5th ed. Englewood Cliffs, NJ: Prentice-Hall, 1987. 548 pp.

A nontechnical introduction to the principles, practices, and functions of manufacturing management designed to help both practitioners and students. After an introductory section, this book covers: manufacturing systems design (organization and planning, design of manufacturing processes, industrial equipment, methods engineering, work measurement, materials handling, physical facilities); manufacturing control (including inventory control, purchasing, production planning and control, quality control, maintenance engineering); manufacturing relationships (relation to various functions such as personnel, labor relations, research, financial, and marketing management).

Buffa, Elwood S., and Rakesh K. Sarin. *Modern Production/Operations Management.* 8th ed. New York: Wiley, 1987. 548 pp.

This latest revision of Professor Buffa's popular introductory text focuses on a simpler but more quantitative step-by-step development. "It begins with relatively simple, well-defined subject matter in operations planning and control, such as forecasting and inventory planning and control. Modular information is cumulated toward more complex materials that deal with system design . . ." (including new technologies such as CAD/CAM and robotics); finally, two chapters cover strategic implications of operations. Present value, queuing, and random digit tables are in an appendix. References are at end of chapters.

Chase, Richard B., and Nicholas J. Aquilano. *Production and Operations Management: A Life Cycle Approach.* 6th ed. Homewood, IL: Irwin, 1992. 1,062 pp.

The life cycle approach adopted in this book follows the progress of the productive systems within 6 parts: the nature and context of operations management; product design and process selection; design of facilities and jobs (including just-in-time production systems, forecasting, capacity planning and location, linear programming, facility layout, job design and measurement); startup of the system; the system in steady state (discussing such topics as inventory systems, job shop scheduling and control, materials management, and purchasing); improving the system. Charts, diagrams, tables are used throughout; mathematical tables are in appendixes, and selected bibliographies are with chapters.

The authors have also written (with Professor Aquilano as lead author) *Fundamentals of Operations Management* (Irwin, 1991, 732 pp.).

Hall, Robert W. *Attaining Manufacturing Excellence.* Homewood, IL: Dow Jones-Irwin, 1987. 290 pp.

Mr. Hall wrote this book to inform middle and upper level managers of manufacturing companies about the momentous changes underway in the management of manufacturing. Included are discussions on such topics as total quality, just-in-time manufacturing, attaining total people involvement, synchronizing the company. This is a readable book that gives the basics without going into exhaustive detail.

Hayes, Robert H., Steven C. Wheelwright and Kim B. Clark. *Dynamic Manufacturing: Creating the Learning Organization.* New York: Free Press, 1988. 429 pp.

Writing for general managers, these respected academicians continue to address their concerns about the decline in American industry's competitiveness and the importance of *Restoring Our Competitive Edge: Competing Through Manufacturing* (written by the first two authors; Wiley, 1984). In this more recent work they focus on the "infrastructure" of a manufacturing company—the management policies, systems, and practices that must be at the core of a world-class organization. They identify such key activities as capital budgeting, performance measures, the manufacturing process, and human resource management—discussing how each interacts to foster growth and competitive advantage. This is an important book for concerned executives.

Kaplan, Robert S., ed. *Measures for Manufacturing Excellence.* Boston: Harvard Business School Press, 1990. 408 pp.

Twelve papers by 24 business school professors presented at a colloquium held in January 1989 and presenting a summary of performance measurement in manufacturing organizations in the late 1980s. They are grouped into four categories: measures of organizational improvement; measures to facilitate organizational learning; measures for product design improvements; measures for product management and evaluation.

Krajewski, Lee J., and Larry P. Ritzman. *Operations Management: Strategy and Analysis.* 2d ed. Reading, MA: Addison-Wesley, 1990. 871, [21] pp.

This is a comprehensive, well written, introductory text addressing both the strategic importance of operations management and its analytic tools, with the strategic/managerial issues woven into the fabric of each chapter. The meat of the book is in its third part on operating decisions where the authors cover each aspect such as forecasting, materials management, scheduling, material requirements planning. Part 1 starts by discussing positioning decisions (product planning and quality management). Then part 2 focuses on design decisions (work measurement, layout, etc.). Part 4 ends by studying operations as a competitive weapon. Little math is required for the body of the book, with a quantitative supplement included at end. Tables, diagrams, and other illustrations are used throughout; also boxed material containing real-world applications. Selected references are with chapters; a glossary is at end of the book.

McClain, John O., L. Joseph Thomas and Joseph B. Mazzola. *Operations Management: Production of Goods and Services.* 3d ed. Englewood Cliffs, NJ: Prentice-Hall, 1992. 740 pp.

An upper-level undergraduate or graduate text intended "to give future managers an understanding of the variety and importance of the management decisions faced in the operations area in different organizations and to help them learn how to approach operations management problems." Chapters cover operating problems such as forecasting, inventory control, work-force scheduling, and production planning. The book also analyzes design issues such as equipment selection, facility location, and capacity analysis. Included within all this is consideration of project management, total quality management, just-in-time production systems, logistics, and technological innovation. A final chapter focuses on strategic issues. Problems and references are with chapters. The operations research techniques of queuing, simulation, and linear programming are treated in technical appendixes; also mathematical tables such as random numbers and present value.

Moody, Patricia E., ed. *Strategic Manufacturing: Dynamic New Directions for the 1990s.* Homewood, IL: Dow Jones-Irwin, 1990. 390 pp.

Here is a collection of 19 essays on the latest manufacturing techniques and trends, with recommendations on how to effectively implement these strategies. Arranged within 6 parts, 2 of the essays are on the historical perspective; 3 on the strategic manufacturing planning process; 4 on new strategies; 3 on tactics (including one on Just-In-Time for white collar work); 3 on management focus; 2 on dynamics of change.

Tompkins, James A. *Winning Manufacturing: The How-to Book of Successful Manufacturing.* Norcross, GA: Institute of Industrial Engineers, 1989. 223 pp. paper.

As the subtitle indicates, Tompkins offers here a how-to book for manufacturing managers, focusing on the things that need to be done for a manufacturing enterprise to succeed. It covers everything, from product development, to inventories, to marketing, and it is full of useful charts, lists, and practical advice. Short bibliographies are with chapters, and useful supplementary outlines are in appendixes.

Two further texts are *Production/Operations Management: Concepts and Situations* by Roger W. Schmenner (4th ed., New York: Macmillan, 1990, 797 pp.) and *Operations Management: Decision Making in the Operations Function* by Roger C. Schroeder (3d ed., New York: McGraw-Hill, 1989, 794 pp.), an introductory POM text with operations treated as a major functional area of business. For a book that "explains how firms have dealt with the problems of time-compressing different segments of the value-delivery chain," see *Time-Based Competition: The Next Battleground in American Manufacturing* ed. by Joseph D. Blackburn (Homewood, IL: Business One Irwin, 1991, 314 pp.).

PRODUCTION AND INVENTORY CONTROL

Handbooks

Greene, James H., ed. *Production and Inventory Control Handbook.* 2d ed. New York: McGraw-Hill, 1987. 1 volume (various pagings).

Substantially revised and expanded to reflect the many changes and broadened scope of production and inventory control since 1970, this comprehensive desktop reference book is still sponsored by the American Production and Inventory Control Society. Most of its 87 contributing experts are members. There are 31 chapters arranged within 9 sections to cover: production and inventory management; strategic business planning; information requirements; tactical planning and control; manufacturing information systems; warehouse and distribution operations; just-in-time concepts and applications; managing the function; techniques and models. Diagrams and other illustrations are used throughout; bibliographies are with most chapters.

Books

Lipman, Burton E. *How to Control and Reduce Inventory.* Rev. ed. East Brunswick, NJ: Bell Publishing, 1988. 218 pp.

A practitioner offers 6 basic steps to successful inventory control and reduction which he derived from the learning experiences of a number of operating divisions and companies. Supplementary material is written by Joseph A. Bennardo. Includes a short glossary and a bibliography that has not been revised since the previous edition.

Plossl, George W. *Production and Inventory Control: Principles and Techniques.* 2d ed. Englewood Cliffs, NJ: Prentice-Hall, 1985. 443 pp.

Still used and often referred to is this volume which focuses on the fundamentals of production and inventory control, the mechanics and the tools of the trade, but updated only to reflect changes as of 1985. Included is coverage on such aspects as materials control systems (including MRP and MPS), branch warehouse control, E.O.Q. theory and application, and aggregate inventory management. Mathematical and data-processing subjects are treated lightly, with a few quantitative techniques discussed in an appendix. Problems, case studies, and a bibliography are at end.

A related volume by this author is *Production and Inventory Control: Applications* (Atlanta: G. Plossl Educational Services, 1983, 301 pp.). A short and more general book written recently is Plossl's *Managing in the World of Manufacturing: How Companies Can Improve Operations to Compete Globally* (Prentice-Hall, 1991, 189 pp.).

Tersine, Richard J. *Principles of Inventory and Materials Management.* 3d ed. New York and Amsterdam: North Holland, 1988. 553 pp.

As this title indicates, the primary emphasis is on inventory systems and their impact on materials management. Alternative systems covered are: independent demand systems, discrete demand systems, dependent demand systems (material requirements planning), distribution inventory systems, and single order quantity systems. There are also chapters on inventory system changes and limitations, just-in-time and in-process inventory, inventory valuation and measurement, and simulation. Throughout the book there are numerous examples of solved problems to extend the reader's understanding. A bibliography at end lists books on inventory control, purchasing, logistics, and related topics.

Vollmann, Thomas E., William L. Berry and D. Clay Wybark. *Manufacturing Planning and Control Systems.* 2d ed. Homewood, IL: Dow Jones-Irwin, 1988. 904 pp. (Third edition to be published in 1992.)

Incorporating recent changes and developments, this is an examination of the MPC system and key challenges facing manufacturing companies today. The first half is devoted to the basics (such as material requirements planning, capacity planning, shop-floor control, purchasing, scheduling, production planning), and the balance of the book (beginning with chapter 12) to advanced concepts supporting the basics. Diagrams and tables are used throughout; references, questions, and problems are with chapters.

INDUSTRIAL ENGINEERING

Maynard's Industrial Engineering Handbook. William K. Hodson, editor in chief. 4th ed. New York: McGraw-Hill, 1992. 1 volume (various pagings).

Just announced for publication in 1992 is a long-awaited revision of the *Industrial Engineering Handbook* which Harold B. Maynard originally edited in 1971. It promises to be another excellent, comprehensive, and up-to-date source (see also the handbook following) on the techniques, procedures, and applications of industrial engineering. The third edition was arranged within 13 sections with each of its over 80 chapters written by an expert contributor.

Salvendy, Gavriel, ed. *Handbook of Industrial Engineering.* 2d ed. New York: Wiley, 1992. 1 volume (various pagings).

Especially valuable because it is so comprehensive (2,780 pages), and it covers the latest in techniques, methods, procedures, and practices of industrial engineering. This essential one-volume handbook is the work of more than 100 expert authors, and it is meant for managers at all levels of both manufacturing and service companies as well as for industrial engineers. A good feeling for its scope can be seen by listing the topics covered in the 14 sections of the first edition (with 107 chapters): industrial engineering function; organization and job design; methods engineering; performance measurement and control of operation; evaluation, appraisal, and management of human resources; ergonomics/human factors; manufacturing engineering; quality assurance; engineering economy; facilities design; planning and control; computers and information processing systems; quantitative methodologies for industrial engineers; optimization in industrial engineering. Useful tables, graphs, diagrams, itemized lists, formulas appear throughout. Bibliographies with each chapter will help the person who wants to read further on any topic.

The monthly *Industrial Engineering* is described in the "POM Periodicals" section of this chapter. *Engineering Index Monthly* abstracts technical articles on engineering and applied science and is described in Chapter 2.

MANUFACTURING PROCESSES

Amstead, B.H., Phillip F. Ostwald and Myron L. Begeman. *Manufacturing Processes.* 8th ed. New York: Wiley, 1987. 721 pp.

A comprehensive reference work meant primarily for engineering and technology students, technicians, and practitioners. It gives the fundamentals of basic manufacturing processes such as welding, metal cutting, drilling and boring machines, as well as many new technologies such as computer applications, robots, computer-aided manufacturing. Each process or kind of machinery is briefly described. Included are useful diagrams and pictures, and, where applicable, such data as measurement, tolerance, advantages/limitations. A complete index of materials, processes, and equipment is at end; also a bibliography arranged by chapter.

Another useful reference work that provides essentially the same sort of information is *Materials and Processes in Manufacturing* by E. Paul De Garmo, J. Temple Black and Ronald A. Kohser (7th ed., New York: Macmillan, 1988, 1,172 pp.). These authors arrange their descriptions within 7 parts: materials; measurement and quality assurance; casting processes; forming processes; material removal processes; joining processes; processes and techniques related to manufacturing.

Brady, George B., and Henry R. Clauser. *Materials Handbook: An Encyclopedia for Managers, Technical Professionals, Purchasing and Production Managers, Technicians, Supervisors and Foremen.* 13th rev. ed. New York: McGraw-Hill, 1991. 1,056 pp.

An encyclopedic dictionary describing properties and uses for many materials, including metals, minerals, woods, chemicals, plastics, textiles.

Tver, David F., and Roger W. Bolz. *Encyclopedic Dictionary of Industrial Technology: Materials, Processes and Equipment.* New York and London: Chapman and Hall, 1984. 353 pp.

This dictionary "covers a wide range of subjects from industrial materials, minerals, metals, plastics and synthetic fibers to machine tools, computers, lasers, robots and other production equipment as well as manufacturing processes." It will be useful for persons "who are in any way involved in the manufacturing process, in product design, or in converting of raw materials to finished products," but it does not reflect the many changes during the past 10 years. Contains some diagrams and tables.

INDUSTRIAL ROBOTICS AND AUTOMATED MANUFACTURING

Most of the material being published on automation and robotics seems to be aimed at the engineer or technician. Here are a few handbooks and books for managers, a trade journal, and several dictionaries, to use as a starting point.

Handbooks

Cleland, David I., and Bopaya Bidanda, eds. *The Automated Factory Handbook: Technology and Management.* Blue Ridge Summit, PA: TAB Professional and Reference Books, 1990. 812 pp.

This handbook is a practical guide for manufacturing planners, managers, and other professionals on the concepts, tools, and techniques of operating the automated factory. Its 38 chapters, each written by a leading specialist, are arranged within three parts covering: automated manufacturing, a managerial perspective (including chapters on such management considerations as quality, quality circles, project management, product design, worker incentives, and much more); planning and design issues in the automated factory; controlling and operating the automated factory (discussing such methods as manufacturing resources planning, reliability engineering, production schedules, the industrial robot). Each page has double columns. Diagrams are used throughout, and references are at end of chapters.

Nof, Shimon Y., ed. *Handbook of Industrial Robotics.* New York: Wiley, 1985. 1,358 pp.

A well-prepared, comprehensive (but now out of date) compilation of materials on the research, development, and application of industrial robotics, with an emphasis on the industrial aspects. Its 77 chapters by leading authorities are arranged in 13 major parts to cover: the development of industrial robotics; 3 parts on robots as computerized systems; 3 parts on robotics implementation; and one part each on 6 major industrial robotic application areas. Illustrations, diagrams, tables, bibliographies are used throughout; a glossary and 5 reference appendixes are at end.

Books

Hunt, V. Daniel. *Robotics Sourcebook.* New York: Elsevier, 1988. 321 pp.

An overview and reference source, with by far the longest of its four parts containing a dictionary of robotics terminology. The other parts cover: robot technology (an overview of the industry, a description of how robots work, and typical applications); industry competitiveness (discussing U.S. industry performance, international competitors and their markets, market trends); and reference material (lists of associations, companies, books, abbreviations, and robotic educational programs).

Maus, Rex, and Randall Allsup. *Robotics: A Manager's Guide.* New York: Wiley, 1986. 238 pp.

This is a nontechnical introduction for managers on the world of robotics and how it can impact the manufacturing workplace. The book's 11 chapters include an introduction discussing the manufacturing environment and automation in general, four chapters on actual uses and applications, and one chapter each on flexible manufacturing systems, economics, and the future. Suggested readings, a glossary, and lists of organizations and manufacturers are at end.

An earlier book written both for managers and engineers is *The Robotics Revolution: The Complete Guide for Managers and Engineers* by Peter B. Scott (Oxford, Eng.: B. Blackwell, 1984, 345 pp.).

Dictionaries

See also the dictionary section in V.D. Hunt's *Robotics Sourcebook* mentioned above.

Dorf, Richard C., ed. *Concise International Encyclopedia of Robotics: Applications and Automation.* Shimon Y. Nof, consulting ed. New York: Wiley, 1988. 1,190 pp.

A one-volume condensation and revision of a three-volume work designed as a ready-reference guide for scientists, engineers, and technologists seeking answers on subjects in the fields of robotics and automation. Signed articles, many of considerable length, for each term given, and most include one or more references for further reading.

Graham, Glenn A. *Automation Encyclopedia: A to Z in Advanced Manufacturing.* Robert E. King, ed. Dearborn, MI: Society of Manufacturing Engineers, 1988. 597 pp.

An encyclopedic dictionary often containing lengthy definitions of automation and related manufacturing terms. Useful diagrams are scattered throughout. It features material from the *Tool and Manufacturing Engineers Handbook* (4th ed., 1983–88, 5 volumes). "Resources/Reviewers" are listed at front. The U.K. edition has title *Encyclopedia of Industrial Automation* (Harlow, Essex, Eng.: Longman Scientific and Technical, 1988).

Periodicals

Robotics World. Atlanta, GA: Communications Channels (6/yr.).

Billed as "the end-user's magazine of flexible automation," this trade journal contains short articles on all aspects of robotics and the robotics industry, with regular columns about people, new products, coming events, etc. Its annual "Directory Issue" (September) is noted below. Indexed in PTS/PROMT.

Directories

Robotics World. "Directory Issue." Atlanta, GA: Communications Channels (annual, September issue).

A useful directory covering robot/robotic systems integrators, consultants, and component/conveyance suppliers. For each robotic company, the data usually given includes when the company was established, number of employees, contact person, fax number, types of robots sold or serviced, applications. An index of products and services is at end.

Associations

Robotic Industries Association, PO Box 3724, 900 Victors Way, Ann Arbor, MI 48106.

Robotics International of SME, PO Box 930, One SME Drive, Dearborn, MI 48121.

MOTION AND TIME STUDY

Niebel, Benjamin W. *Motion and Time Study.* 8th ed. Homewood, IL: Irwin, 1988. 799 pp. Ninth edition to be published in 1992.

A good, standard text on motion, time study, and wage payments programs. This most recently revised edition has much new and updated material to reflect technological changes and the effect of inflation, to note extensive use today of personal computers in establishing standards, and to broaden the application of motion and time study into service areas (government, hospital administration, etc.). Includes useful illustrations, forms, and diagrams. There are short bibliographies at end of chapters; a glossary, some helpful formulas, and special tables are at end of book.

Recently published but not seen for evaluation is a book by Fred E. Meyers called *Motion and Time Study: Improving Work Methods and Management* (Prentice-Hall, 1992, 319 pp.).

QUALITY CONTROL

Nowhere have the concerns of management and POM executives been more in evidence than in the area of product quality, reliability, safety. As Feigenbaum states in the preface to his book described below: "Quality has become the single most important force leading to organizational success and company growth in national and international markets." A growing number of books and many articles discuss this problem. Here are several of the more useful ones.

Handbooks

Juran, J. M., and Frank M. Gryna, eds. *Juran's Quality Control Handbook.* 4th ed. New York: McGraw-Hill, 1988. 1 volume (various pagings).

A comprehensive (about 1,800 pp.) extensively revised and updated reference work, in 42 chapters written by 31 experts. It examines all aspects of planning, producing, controlling, and improving quality for the 1990s. Included are: 12 chapters setting out the various managerial concepts and tools associated with quality; 10 chapters which follow the product through its life cycle; 4 on statistical tools; 6 focusing on applications of concepts, methods, and tools in important industries; and 9 chapters examining ways of managing quality in various national cultures. Charts, tables, and diagrams are found throughout. Bibliographical references are at end of each chapter and supplementary data are in appendixes. Two of Juran's books are noted below.

Walsh, Loren, Ralph Wurster and Raymond J. Kimber, eds. *Quality Management Handbook.* New York and Basel: M. Dekker and the ASQC Quality Press, 1986. 997 pp.

This handbook is intended as a handy desk reference for managers and other executives who must now have some simple understanding of the technology of quality. Each of its 49 chapters is written by a contributor, and the progression runs from chapters on more general topics such as organization and planning to specific topics in such areas as control, inspection, testing, measurement, design, technology. Several chapters at end discuss quality in specific industries such as the food industry. Useful diagrams and tables appear throughout the book. Short lists of references and/or recommended readings are with each chapter (but these are only books published prior to 1986).

Books

Feigenbaum, A. V. *Total Quality Control.* 3d ed., rev. New York: McGraw-Hill, 1991. 863 pp.

Almost of handbook length, this is a thorough, practical book directed to all persons responsible for the successful operation of an organization. It explains how to plan a quality program; how to set up an appropriate organizational structure for implementing it; how to engineer the required plans; and, through managerial leadership, how to involve all departments and the entire work force in the endeavor. The 24 chapters are in 7 parts: business quality management; the total quality system; management strategies for quality; engineering technology of quality; statistical technology of quality; applying total quality control in the company; the total imperative for the 1990s.

Garvin, David A. *Managing Quality: The Strategic and Competitive Edge.* New York: Free Press, 1988. 319 pp.

Professor Garvin's well-written 6-year study aims to provide a deeper understanding of successful quality management by blending theory and practice and by drawing on evidence from both the U.S. and Japan. In three parts: part 1 focuses on conceptual issues, including the history and meaning of quality in the U.S.; part 2 consists of a case study of quality in a single U.S. industry, the room air-conditioning industry; part 3 compares U.S. and Japanese approaches to quality management. A lengthy bibliographical "Notes" section is at the end.

Grant, Eugene L., and Richard S. Leavenworth. *Statistical Quality Control.* 6th ed. New York: McGraw-Hill, 1988. 714 pp.

This is the best known text on the title subject. It is designed as a practical working manual for production and inspection supervisors, engineers, and management to explain several techniques useful in improving product quality and in reducing costs. The majority of the book deals with various types of Shewhart control charts and also acceptance sampling systems and procedures. Includes descriptions of actual cases from a number of industries; there are statistical tables, a glossary of symbols, and a bibliography at end.

Harrington, J. James. *The Improvement Process: How America's Leading Companies Improve Quality.* New York: McGraw-Hill, 1987. 239 pp.

In his preface, Mr. Harrington says: "There is a direct relationship between quality and productivity—they complement each other; they do not detract from one another. Starting your company on its quest for quality will provide you with a process that improves productivity, decreases product cost, and increases your share of the market." His book is the result of a five-year study of the actions taken by 50 American companies to improve quality and services. It follows a step-by-step approach, is written in nontechnical language, and includes useful checklists and outlines of questionnaires. Harrington has had long experience as a quality manager, and his book is sponsored by the American Society for Quality Control.

Juran, J.M. *Juran on Planning for Quality.* New York: Free Press, 1988. 341 pp.

Dr. Juran is a pioneering expert on quality planning and control. His handbook, described above, is considered an essential reference work. This practical book includes the experience and ideas derived from his years of field testing and collaboration with many practicing managers (listed at the end). Much of it consists of a step-by-step "quality planning road map" outlining the sequence of basic activities for interdependent projects (chapter 2–10), and it is organized to show how the quality planning process applies to various levels of company activity. A glossary is at end.

Another of his recent books, *Juran on Leadership for Quality: An Executive Handbook* (Free Press, 1989, 376 pp.) was written for top management both to provide companies with the strategies needed to attain and hold quality leadership, and to define the roles of upper managers in leading their companies to that goal.

Messina, William S. *Statistical Quality Control for Manufacturing Managers.* New York: Wiley, 1987. 331 pp.

Designed as a sourcebook for the manufacturing manager, this book is based on the author's practical experience in quality control. "The main idea is to expose the basic statistical quality control techniques through examples set in a manufacturing environment." The first four chapters are an introduction to the foundations of statistics. There follow three chapters on statistical quality control (theory; control charts; acceptance sampling). The last two chapters describe manufacturing application and strategies. Statistical tables and a bibliography are at end of book.

An alternative and more recently revised text is *Introduction to Statistical Quality Control* by Douglas C. Montgomery (2d ed., Wiley, 1991, 674, [42] pp.).

Mohr, William L., and Harriet Mohr. *Quality Circles: Changing Images of People at Work.* Reading, MA: Addison-Wesley, 1983. 258 pp.

Because of recent interest in quality circles as a means of improving productivity and worker participation, it seems worth mentioning one title even though it is not recently published. This book is intended for both general and professional readers interested in learning about quality circles in an organization. The material is drawn from the lead author's experience in developing Hewlett Packard's quality circles, and also his related consulting. The authors begin with four chapters discussing the introduction, planning, and implementing of a quality circle program. This is followed by three chapters focusing on the problem-solving process and techniques for a quality circle (such as brainstorming, cause and effect analysis). The final four chapters cover the assessment and evaluation of QC programs, their long-term benefits, and their problems/pitfalls.

Still cited often is Philip B. Crosby's *Quality is Free: The Art of Making Quality Certain* (NY: McGraw-Hill, 1979, 309 pp.). It is a practical book for managers on "the art of making quality certain." A recent guide for managers is *Achieving Total Quality Management: A Program for Action* by Michel Périgord (Cambridge, MA: Productivity Press, 1990, 379 pp.). This latter book is a translation of a book published in Paris in 1987.

POM BIBLIOGRAPHIES

Zembicki, Christine. *Production and Factory Management: An Information Sourcebook.* (Oryx Series in Business and Management, No. 18). Phoenix, AZ: Oryx Press, 1988. 176 pp.

An annotated bibliography of reference sources in the following production management areas: factory management, site selection, plant layout, production operations, plant engineering, automation and robotics, quality control, human factors, purchasing and inventory control, budget and cost analysis, human resources, industrial safety. For each topic it usually cites dictionaries, handbooks, selected guides and texts, statistics, journals, associations, research centers. Since there are almost no more recent sources mentioned than a few in 1987, this bibliography will soon be outdated unless revised.

POM PERIODICALS

For a description of *Robotics World* see "Industrial Robotics and Automated Manufacturing" section of this chapter.

Automation. Cleveland: Penton Publishers, Inc. (monthly).

This trade journal returned to its original title in 1987 after having had the title *Production Engineering* from 1977 to 1986. It is useful for persons involved in manufacturing management and engineering, with the focus on automation technology. The January issue is an annual "Outlook" issue. Indexed in ABI/I, ASTI, TI; full text on BRS, DATA-STAR, DIALOG, DOW JONES, MEAD/NEXIS.

Industrial Engineering. Norcross, GA: Institute of Industrial Engineers (monthly).

Short articles of interest to industrial engineers, as well as regular departments such as a calendar of events, career opportunities. Subjects covered include automatic strategies, systems and controls, logistics, materials handling, quality management, new products and services. Indexed in ABI/I, ASTI, TI.

Among other IIE publications is a quarterly that is more quantitatively oriented, called *IIE Transactions.* This is a refereed journal devoted to the publication of new ideas in industrial engineering research and development. Of a more general nature is the IIE's bimonthly *Industrial Management,* with its short, practical articles for working managers and engineering managers on a broad range of management topics involving new techniques, improving quality and productivity, worker motivation, management/employee relations, etc. It is indexed in ABI/I, TI; full text on BRS, DATA-STAR, DIALOG, DOW JONES, MEAD/NEXIS.

Journal of Manufacturing and Operations Management. New York: Elsevier Science Publishing Co. (quarterly).

A new journal (1988) publishing two or three scholarly papers in each issue on operations management in manufacturing and service firms, with emphasis on empirical work, case studies, and applications. Most authors are academicians. This journal wants to represent OM as a functional area of business activity. It is published in collaboration with the Center for Manufacturing and Operations Management, University of Rochester.

Journal of Operations Management. Columbia, MO: American Production and Inventory Control Society and the University of Missouri–Columbia, College of Business and Public Administration (quarterly).

A research journal containing original articles and high quality research on a broad scope of operations management topics. The August 1989 issue included a four-part bibliography, "Manufacturing Strategy: A Selected Bibliography" by Paul M. Swamidass, one part of which covers books on business strategy. "Dissertations Abstracts" appear in the October issue each year. Indexed in ABI/I.

For persons interested in a monthly trade journal containing practical articles on improving manufacturing operations as well as news of interest to APICS members, see *P&IM Review* (Production and Inventory Management Review with APICS News). It is published by T.D.A. Publications, Hollywood, CA, and is sent free to APICS members.

Manufacturing Engineering. Dearborn, MI: Society of Manufacturing Engineers (monthly).

News about specific machinery, tools, automatic system, etc.; also regular departments such as new products, calendar of events, positions available. Indexed in ABI/I, ASTI.

Manufacturing Review. Fairfield, NJ: Published by the American Society of Mechanical Engineers and the Society for Integrated Manufacturing (quarterly).

This is a well-researched scholarly journal advancing the science, technology, and practice of production. It aims to publish "both archival articles and broader assessments of current trends across the whole spectrum of automation problems and the management and economic issues related to contemporary and future manufacturing practice." Includes book reviews.

National Productivity Review. New York: Executive Enterprises Publications (quarterly).

Thoughtful articles seeking to offer readers insights into and new approaches to productivity and quality. Aims to be informative, analytical, and practical but not highly technical. Includes books reviews and selected "Books and Articles in Brief." Indexed in ABI/I, BPI, PAIS.

Production. Cincinnati: Gardner Publications, Inc. (monthly).

Articles and news of interest to managers and engineers on such topics as manufacturing technologies, design, quality, materials handling, business strategies. Indexed in ABI/I, PTS/PROMT, TI; full text on BRS, DATA-STAR, DIALOG, DOW JONES.

Quality Progress. Milwaukee, WI: American Society for Quality Control (monthly).

A news magazine of the ASQC, with short articles on quality assurance/quality control. Special issues include: "QA/QC Software Directory" (March); "QA/QC Services Directory" (August); "QA/QC Salary Survey" (September). Includes book reviews in most issues and a list of books available from ASQC. Indexed in ABI/I, ASTI.

The ASQC also publishes a quarterly *Journal of Quality Technology* which contains technical papers on methods, applications, and related topics in the field of quality technology. Includes a few book reviews on statistical methods and quality control. Indexed in ABI/I, ASTI.

Plant is a Canadian industrial newspaper (Willowdale, Ont.: Maclean Hunter Ltd., 18 issues per year).

POM ASSOCIATIONS

American Production and Inventory Control Society, 500 West Annandale Road, Falls Church, VA 22046.

American Society for Quality Control, 310 W. Wisconsin Avenue, Milwaukee, WI 53203.

Institute of Industrial Engineers, 25 Technology Park/Atlanta, Norcross, GA 30092.

Institution of Production Engineers, 66 Little Ealing Lane, London W5 4XX, England.

Society of American Value Engineers, 60 Revere Drive, Suite 500, Northbrook, IL 60062.

Society of Manufacturing Engineers, PO Box 930, One SME Drive, Dearborn, MI 48121.

INDUSTRIAL RESEARCH

Books on new product development are described in Chapter 18.

Freedman, George. *The Pursuit of Innovation: Managing the People and Processes That Turn New Ideas into Profits.* New York: AMACOM, 1988. 346 pp.

Based on on-site visits and interviews at 18 innovative companies, this practical guide to "effective innovation" is written by an experienced manager of innovative product development. The four parts cover: organizing for innovation; implementing the creative process (including the 7 steps to innovation); company policies—company support; and the 8 varieties of autonomous innovation groups (including technical centers, new product centers, internal or external venture centers). An example of an innovation concept report is in an appendix.

Jain, Ravinder K., and Harry C. Triandis. *Management of Research and Development Organizations: Managing the Unmanageable.* New York: Wiley, 1990. 268 pp.

This book focuses on ways to improve R&D organization productivity and foster excellence in R&D enterprises. It is written for all managers of creative and somewhat autonomous personnel by an engineer/scientist and an organizational psychologist. Chapters examine such topics as job design, influencing people, motivation, leadership, managing conflict, performance appraisal. The authors also discuss creating a productive and effective R&D organization, technology transfer, and organizational change. Some discussion of R&D and society are in an appendix, including R&D expenditures. Further readings are listed with each chapter, and a bibliography is at end.

Miller, Donald B. *Managing Professionals in Research and Development.* San Francisco: Jossey-Bass, 1986. 403 pp.

Although this is an earlier book than the others in this section, it will still provide the reader with useful perspectives and some tools for managing professionals. Its half-title reads "A guide for improving productivity and organizational effectiveness," and it is arranged within three parts: special challenges of R&D management; getting the best from people; strategies and systems for long-term success. A bibliography is at end of book.

Roussel, Philip A., Kamal N. Saad and Tamara J. Erickson. *Third Generation R & D: Managing the Link to Corporate Strategy.* Boston: Harvard Business School Press, 1991. 191 pp.

Three senior executives at Arthur D. Little have designed this book "to give business leaders and their managers the concepts that will help them manage research and development as a strategic competitive weapon." These authors start by describing the first and second generation of R & D management. With this as background, they introduce the guiding principles of what they call the third generation R & D by using a fictitious company—describing the company and the experiences and challenges faced by its senior management in adapting these principles to the company's needs. This is followed by discussions of human and operational effectiveness in the carrying out of R & D.

Tushman, Michael L., and William L. Moore, eds. *Readings in the Management of Innovation.* 2d ed. Cambridge, MA: Ballinger, 1988. 769 pp. paper.

Here is an excellent selection of readings which should sensitize the reader to the range of issues that must be addressed by those interested in managing innovation within corporations over time. It provides a unified and comprehensive view of core issues in managing innovation with an emphasis on managerial problem solving. The selections are research-based articles from a wide range of disciplines, and many are new to this edition. Its 8 sections cover: innovation over time and in historical context; organization and innovation; technology and business strategy; managing functional areas; managing linkages; venturing and organization learning; governmental influence on innovation; executive leadership and the management of innovation and change. The selections are written by such respected authorities as Robert H. Hayes, James B. Quinn, James M. Utterback.

Twiss, Brian C. *Managing Technological Innovation.* 3d ed. London & New York: Longman, 1986. 238 pp. paper.

Designed for senior managers in all areas of the business and also for corporate planners, this book focuses "on those areas of management where the technology of a company relates to the firm as a whole." This new edition has been amended to incorporate the current state of knowledge as of the mid-1980s. The 8 chapter titles give a good idea of its scope: the process of technological innovation; strategies for R&D; creativity and problem solving; project selection and evaluation; financial evaluation of R&D projects; R&D program planning and control; organization for innovation; technological forecasting for decision making. Bibliographies are at end of chapters.

Statistics

National Science Foundation. *Research and Development in Industry. Detailed Statistical Tables.* Washington, DC: U.S. Government Printing Office (annual).

This contains statistics on: federal and company funds for R&D, by industry and size of company, for selected years from the 1950s; R&D funds related to employment and net sales; expenditures for energy and pollution abatement; funds for applied R&D by product field; geographic distribution of funds; employment of R&D scientists and engineers by industry and company size. This annual statistical survey is conducted by the Bureau of the Census for the NSF.

Three other NSF publications are: *Federal Funds for Research and Development:*

Detailed Statistical Tables (annual); *Federal R&D Funding by Budget Function* (annual, with statistics covering three years); *National Patterns of R&D Resources: Final Report* (annual, with data often covering 8 years).

The Battelle Memorial Institute publishes an interesting little annual report on *Probable Levels of R&D Expenditures in (year): Forecast and Analysis* (Columbus, OH). *Business Week* publishes an annual "R&D Scoreboard" in its special bonus issue each year (e.g. October 25, 1991). This gives R&D expenses statistics for over 900 U.S. companies arranged by about 40 industries. The statistics include, for each company, total R&D expenses, percent of sales and profits, number of dollars per employee, percent change from previous year. Another table ranks the top 200 foreign companies for R&D expenses.

Periodicals

R & D Management. Oxford, Eng.: B. Blackwell (quarterly).

Presents research papers on current problem areas in R&D management and on application of new methods of management in those areas. Includes book reviews. Indexed in ABI/I, TI.

R&D: Research & Development. Des Plaines, IL: Cahners Publishing Co. (monthly except semimonthly in February).

Calling itself an "international magazine of research and development," this contains short articles usually on technical processes or equipment; also news of science/technology, new products, innovative notebook, and so forth. An annual article on prospects for R&D funding is in January issue; the second February issue is a "Product Source," which includes a yellow pages section for companies in instrumentation, equipment, supplies, components, materials, and services. An annual "Salary Survey" is in May issue. Indexed in ABI/I, BPI, PTS/F&S; full text on BRS, DATA-STAR, DIALOG.

Research-Technology Management. Washington, DC: Industrial Research Institute (bimonthly).

Informative, pragmatic articles on all aspects of R&D management, usually written by practitioners. Includes descriptive reviews of books and articles on innovation and product development as well as on R&D. Indexed in ABI/I, BPI, PAIS, TI.

Research Policy. Amsterdam, The Netherlands: Elsevier Science Publishers (bimonthly).

An international journal written in English and devoted to authoritative papers on research policy, research management, and planning, including also innovation and technological change. Occasionally includes book reviews. Indexed in ABI/I.

Directories

American Council of Independent Laboratories. *Directory.* Washington, DC (biennial).

One-page profiles of the leading American independent testing, research, and inspection laboratories, including officers and scope of activities.

Directory of American Research and Technology. New York: Bowker (annual). Also on CD-ROM.

Subtitled "organizations active in production development for business," this is a useful directory of over 11,000 non-government facilities currently active in any commercially-applicable basic and applied research. Most are owned and operated by corporations. For each it lists the officers, number of professional staff, and fields of R&D activity. Indexes are by location, name of personnel, and subject of R&D activity. Formerly this was published as *Industrial Research Laboratories of the United States.*

Research Services Directory. 4th ed. Detroit: Gale Research, Inc., 1989. 841 pp. (Revised about every third year.)

This is a descriptive directory of U.S. for-profit organizations providing research services on a contract or fee-for-service basis to clients, and it includes laboratories, data collection centers, forecasting, and testing firms. Covers all major subjects such as advertising, communications systems, energy, industrial relations, marketing, social sciences, strategic planning, and much more. Information for each firm usually includes top officer, when founded, company description, principal fields of research, number of staff, principal clients, associated activities such as publications, libraries, memberships. Geographic, subject, and personal names indexes are at end. Companion volumes are: *Research Centers Directory* (annual) which covers university-related and independently operated nonprofit research facilities; *Government Research Directory* (4th ed., 1987); *International Research Centers Directory* (2 volumes, biennial).

Associations

Industrial Research Institute, 1550 M St, N.W., Washington, DC 20005.

Research & Development Society, 47 Belgrave Square, London, SW1X 8QX, England.

MATERIALS MANAGEMENT (INCLUDING PURCHASING)

Handbooks

Aljian's Purchasing Handbook. Paul V. Farrell, Coordinating Editor. 4th ed. New York: McGraw-Hill, 1982. 1 volume (various pagings). New edition scheduled for 1992.

A first-rate reference work (1,053 pages) on accepted policies, practices, and procedures as of 1982 in the many facets of purchasing and materials management, with each of its 32 sections written by two or three of its 90 expert contributors. Charts, tables, illustrations, and examples are used throughout. Section 30 contains a bibliography of books, periodicals, and reference tools needed in a purchasing library. Other useful features are a glossary, tables of weights and measures, conversion tables and equivalents, other miscellaneous tables, and general information. This comprehensive handbook is sponsored by the National Association of Purchasing Management; its previous editor was George W. Aljian.

Books

Dobler, Donald W., David N. Burt and Lamar Lee, Jr. *Purchasing and Materials Management: Text and Cases.* 5th ed. New York: McGraw-Hill, 1990. 843 pp.

This is considered by many to be the most comprehensive and the best basic text for both undergraduates and graduates. It focuses on the management of materials and the control of material costs in business and institutional enterprises. Of its 8 parts, four are over 100 pages in length. These cover: an introduction to the functions of purchasing and materials management; the fundamentals of purchasing; the fundamentals of materials management; and general management responsibilities. The other four shorter parts study: the generation of requirements; special purchases; contract administration; institutional and government purchasing. At end are about 100 pages containing cases, plus a useful selected bibliography arranged by broad topic. This is a well-written text with useful explanations, examples, and other illustrations used throughout.

Heinritz, Stuart et al. *Purchasing: Principles and Applications.* 8th ed. Englewood Cliffs, NJ: Prentice-Hall, 1991. 580 pp.

A popular, beginning text on purchasing principles and procedures. This latest edition is updated to meet the challenges and responsibilities of the 90s by its three coauthors: Paul V. Farrell, Larry C. Guinipero, and Michael G. Kolchin. The 6 basic parts cover: purchasing: a modern management function (including a chapter on ethical standards); purchasing strategies, organization, and systems; managing basic purchasing decisions (such as quality, price/cost, negotiation, legal aspects, managing in international markets); managing material flows; specialized purchasing techniques (planning and forecasting, value analysis/standardization, measuring performance, and so forth); retail, institutional, and government purchasing. Short case studies and a selected bibliography are at end.

Leenders, Michiel R., Harold E. Fearon and Wilbur B. England. *Purchasing and Materials Management.* 9th ed. Homewood, IL: Irwin, 1989. 672 pp.

Combining text with cases, this standard text for a first course studies the organization and operation of the procurement function. Increased emphasis in this latest revision is on the service context and on strategy in purchasing. There are also chapters covering legal aspects, foreign purchasing, public purchasing, and on quantity considerations such as material requirement and resource planning, and just-in-time production. The cases are at end of each chapter.

Magad, Eugene L., and John M. Amos. *Total Materials Management: The Frontier of Maximizing Profit in the 1990s.* New York: Van Nostrand Reinhold, 1989. 551 pp.

According to the preface, "this book covers the basic materials management function and provides valuable insights into various other functions related to it." It is written primarily for advanced undergraduate or graduate courses and is in four parts: materials management concept and organization; planning and control; procurement, materials flow, and distribution; implementation and control. Although it deals largely with concepts, there are many examples from various industries to clarify the concepts. Bibliographies are with chapters.

Zenz, Gary. *Purchasing and Management of Materials.* 6th ed. Edited by George H. Thompson. New York: Wiley, 1987. 542 pp.

Another standard text presenting the principles and procedures of purchasing and materials management in their modern multidimensional framework. Among its major additions and revisions are new chapters on international purchasing and value analysis, and an expanded treatment of computer applications. There is also a chapter focusing on purchasing in the public and nonprofit sectors. Some 80 pages at end contain short purchasing cases.

Periodicals

Journal of Purchasing and Materials Management. Tempe, AZ: National Association of Purchasing Management (quarterly).

Scholarly journal with short articles covering both the theory and practice of purchasing and materials management. Includes book reviews. Indexed in ABI/I, BPI.

Purchasing. Newton, MA: Cahners Publishing Co. (semimonthly except monthly for four months).

This is the principal purchasing trade journal for buying professionals. It contains articles and news on a wide range of topics, as well as many regular departments, several of which are on the outlook in Washington, job mart, "Purchasing's Forecasts" (consisting of charts and brief text for various economic indicators or machinery and equipment), "Purchasing Leadtimes" (tables for specific products). Special annual features include: "Steel Market Report" and "Specialty Steel Market Report" (first October issue); "Top 100" U.S. companies with largest purchasing departments (second November issue); "Salary Survey" (December). Indexed in ABI/I, BPI, TI; full text on BRS, DATA-STAR, DIALOG, DOW JONES.

Purchasing World. Cleveland, OH: Huebcore Communications (monthly).

A trade journal on "managing the business of buying," with articles and news on purchasing, materials, and related topics. Each issue contains a "Business Datatrak" section including a NAPM business barometer chart, and procurement trends; also spot market prices for specific raw materials, a section for "PW Predicts," news about new products, and more. Annual feature articles include an economic forecast in January and an update in July; an "Annual Salary Survey" (December). Indexed in ABI/I, PTS/F&S; full text on BRS, DATA-STAR, DIALOG.

Associations

International Material Management Society, 8720 Red Oak Blvd., Suite 224, Charlotte, NC 28217.

National Association of Purchasing Management, 2055 East Centennial Circle, PO Box 22160, Tempe, AZ 85285-2160.

BUSINESS LOGISTICS

The term "business logistics" (sometimes also called "physical distribution") is a concept which Professor Ballou defines as the process dealing "with all move-store activities that facilitate product flow from one point of raw-material acquisition to the point of final consumption, as well as the information flows that set the product in motion for the purpose of providing adequate levels of customer service at a reasonable cost" (see p.7 of his *Basic Business Logistics,* 1987). This encompases activities relating to transportation, inventory maintenance, order processing, purchasing, warehousing, materials handling, packaging, customer services standards, product scheduling.

GENERAL TEXTS

Handbooks

Ackerman, Kenneth B. *Practical Handbook of Warehousing.* 2d ed. Washington, DC: Traffic Service Corporation, 1986. 612 pp.

Focusing on one important logistics activity, this is a practical guide to warehousing, with particular emphasis on dry (not refrigerated) storage of packaged products. It is designed for both public and private warehouse operators, for users of public or contract warehouses as well as for executives, and it is written by an experienced warehouseman/author. There are 50 chapters arranged in the following 9 sections: background of the industry; elements of warehouse management; real estate aspects; planning warehouse operations; protecting the warehouse operation; the human element; productivity and quality control; handling of materials; handling of information.

The Distribution Handbook. Ed. by James F. Robeson and Robert G. House. New York: Free Press, 1985. 970 pp.

Sponsored by the National Council of Physical Distribution Management, this is a comprehensive professional guide to important distribution or distribution-related topics. Its 32 chapters, each by one of more of 40 expert contributors, are arranged within 14 sections, including: distribution planning and systems; financial analysis; the computer and quantitative analysis; demand forecasting; purchasing; transportation; facilities; inventory management; packaging; international distribution; organization; personnel. Useful checklists, tables, graphs, etc., are used throughout; appendixes include a descriptive directory of organizations, a list of publications, and a bibliography of other sources arranged by chapter (but only as of 1985).

The Warehouse Management Handbook. James A. Tompkins and Jerry D. Smith, eds.-in-chief. New York: McGraw-Hill, 1988. 702 pp.

A more recent handbook than Ackerman above, this one focuses on the science of the warehousing profession. Its 29 chapters, each by one or more of 36 contributors, are organized into four integrated parts: introduction and the context for warehousing; warehouse planning; equipment; functions of the warehouse operating systems. Bibliographies are included with most chapters.

Books

Allegri, Theodore H., Sr. *Materials Handling: Principles and Practice.* New York: Van Nostrand Reinhold, 1984. 516 pp. (Reprinted in 1992 by Krieger Publishing Co., in Malabar, FL).

Not since the early 1970s has there been a new book devoted just to the theory and practice of materials handling. Allegri covers many aspects of the movement and storage of materials and how they fit into an integrated systems network. He also discusses factory and warehouse layout, equipment selection and maintenance, safety and training, some mechanization concepts, and more. Illustrations, diagrams, and practical applications are found throughout; source material and data on organizations are included in an appendix at end.

Ballou, Ronald H. *Business Logistics Management.* 3d ed. Englewood Cliffs, NJ: Prentice-Hall, 1992. 688 pp.

The focus of this text is on the planning, organizing, and controlling of business logistics. It is arranged within the following 6 parts: introduction and strategy overview; initializing the logistics plan; logistics system fundamentals; configuring the network; planning logistics activities; organization and control. Increased attention in this latest edition is given to logistics in a worldwide setting, and also to the shift toward more service-oriented economies by industrialized nations. Practical examples are used throughout; a bibliography is at end.

Professor Ballou has also written an introductory book called *Basic Business Logistics* (2d ed., Prentice-Hall, 1987, 438 pp.).

Bowersox, Donald J., David J. Closs and Omar K. Helferich. *Logistics Management.* 3d ed. New York: Macmillan, 1986. 586 pp.

The subtitle of this introductory book pretty well describes its scope: "A Systems Integration of Physical Distribution Manufacturing Support, and Materials Procurement." Part 2 of its five parts covers the components of logistical systems (transportation, inventory, warehousing, and packaging). Part 3 considers logistics policy and control; part 4, logistical techniques and methodologies; part 5, future environments. Appendixes include an analysis and checklist on manufacturing location, and a logistical game.

More recently Professor Bowersox, with four colleagues at Michigan State University, published the results of a comprehensive research project in their book called *Leading Edge Logistics: Competitive Positioning for the 1990s* (Oak Brook, IL: Council of Logistics Management, 1989, 303, [197] pp.). This was based on close examination of 117 North American firms designated as leading edge companies.

Johnson, James C., and Donald F. Wood. *Contemporary Logistics.* 4th ed. New York: Macmillan, 1990. 579 pp.

This is one of the better introductory texts on the title subject, newly revised and including real-life examples throughout plus exhibits and other illustrations, which add to its interest and readability. Much of the book (section 2) is devoted to elements of logistics systems (including the traffic management function, inventory management, warehousing, distribution centers, international logistics, and so forth). The first section is an overview; the last examines methods of analyzing, designing, and implementing a logistics system. There are chapter references and case incidents; a glossary is at end.

Lambert, Douglas M., and James R. Stock, *Strategic Logistics Management.* 3d ed. Homewood, IL: Irwin, 1993. 862 pp.

As the title indicates, this is another good book that approaches the topic from a managerial perspective. There is a balance of theory and practical application, with the basic concepts and principles examined in light of how they interrelate and interface with other functions of the firm. The first three chapters provide an introduction; chapters 4–13 cover each fundamental area of logistics from a consumer service perspective, emphasizing financial implications throughout; the last five chapters focus on strategic aspects of logistics management from both the domestic and international perspectives. Diagrams, charts, and tables are used throughout. Suggested readings are with chapters; 12 cases and several "how-to" audits are at end of the book.

PHYSICAL DISTRIBUTION BIBLIOGRAPHIES

Council of Logistics Management. *Bibliography on Physical Distribution Management.* Oak Brook, IL. (annual).

A useful, continuing, loose-leaf, and annotated bibliography of management-oriented books and articles on logistics and physical distribution, arranged in topical sections. It was begun in 1967, with annual supplements each year to date, and it is compiled each year by Professor Bernard J. LaLonde, usually with varying co-compilers.

LOGISTICS DICTIONARIES

Cavinato, Joseph L., ed. *Transportation-Logistics Dictionary.* 2d ed. Washington, DC: International Thomson Transport Press, 1989. 312 pp. paper.
Concise definitions covering the whole area of transportation and logistics, revised and expanded to reflect changes as this field continues to grow and evolve. Supplementary data at end includes standard abbreviations, outline of transportation laws, metric conversion formulas, standard time differences in U.S. and foreign cities.

LOGISTICS PERIODICALS

Distribution. Radnor, PA: Chilton Co. (monthly).
A trade journal covering current developments in transportation and business logistics and published for traffic and transportation executives. The July issue is in two parts: part 1 contains a "Logistics Annual Report"; part 2 is a directory called "Warehouse Marketplace," described in next section of this chapter. An annual "Salary Survey" is in the September issue. Indexed in ABI/I, BPI, TI; full text on BRS, DATA-STAR, DIALOG, DOW JONES, MEAD/NEXIS.

Journal of Business Logistics. Oak Brook, IL: Council of Logistics Management, at Ohio State University (semiannual).
This journal is meant to serve as a forum for current research, opinion, and identification of trends in the transportation and distribution (logistics) area. Articles are scholarly and are usually written by academicians. A "Compendium of Doctoral Research in Logistics, 1970–1986" appears in vol.8, no.2 (1987) and vol.9, no.1 (1988), but no later lists have been published as of 1992. Indexed in ABI/I.

The Logistics and Transportation Review. Vancouver, Canada: Faculty of Commerce and Business Administration, University of British Columbia (quarterly).
An international journal for research papers on transportation and logistics, with an emphasis on the quantitative approach. Includes book reviews. Indexed in ABI/I.

Material Handling Engineering. Cleveland, OH: Penton Publishing (monthly).
A trade journal for articles and news on material handling products and systems. An extra issue in April is the "Handbook & Directory," described in the next section on directories. Indexed in ABI/I, ASTI, PTS/F&S; full text on BRS, DATA-STAR, DIALOG.

Modern Materials Handling. Newton, MA: Cahners Publishing Co. (monthly except semimonthly in September and October).
Short articles on materials handling; also equipment news. An extra issue in September is an annual "Casebook Reference Issue," with the directory part covering: manufacturers, equipment, consultants, distributors. The extra issue in March is a "Planning Guidebook." Indexed in ABI/I, ASTI, PTS/F&S; full text on BRS, DATA-STAR, DIALOG, DOW JONES.

Packaging. Newton, MA: Cahners Publishing Co. (monthly, with extra issues in March and June).

Incorporating the long-time trade journal *Modern Packaging,* this contains technically oriented articles on current developments in all phases of packaging. Two extra issues are: "Packaging Buyers Guide & Product Directory" (March) and "Packaging Line Guide" (June). A ranked list of "The Packaging 100" (July) includes news of each company. Indexed in ABI/I, ASTI, PTS/F&S, TI; full text on BRS, DATA-STAR, DIALOG, DOW JONES, MEAD/NEXIS.

Transportation & Distribution. Cleveland, OH: Penton Publishing, Inc. (monthly).

Billed as "the magazine for logistics professionals," this monthly contains several short articles and news about trends and people of interest to management personnel in the field of physical distribution. There are no longer any special issues. Former title was *Handling & Shipping Management.* Indexed in ABI/I, BPI, PTS/F&S; full text on BRS, DATA-STAR, DIALOG, DOW JONES, MEAD/NEXIS.

LOGISTICS DIRECTORIES

American Warehousemen's Association. *Membership Directory.* Chicago (annual).

Short geographic list of warehouses handling nonrefrigerated products, giving officers and size in square feet.

An annual *Directory of Public Refrigerated Warehouses* is published in Bethesda, MD, by the International Association of Refrigerated Warehouses.

Material Handling Engineering. "Handbook & Directory" (annual, second April issue).

The directory section of this special issue gives names and addresses for manufacturers of material handling equipment, with separate lists of services arranged by product, advertisers' sales locations, and local dealers and distributors; also a selection of manufacturers catalogs. The handbook portion consists of manufacturers advertising arranged into product categories, and articles providing solutions to material handling problems.

Modern Materials Handling. "Casebook Reference Issue" (annual, extra issue in September).

This directory issue lists major manufacturers of material handling equipment and systems; it also contains lists of products and equipment by type; consultants; a geographic list of distributors; a selection of manufacturers' catalogs; a list of associations. The casebook portion contains case histories, equipment selection guidelines, and equipment specification references, arranged by type of equipment.

LOGISTICS ASSOCIATIONS

American Warehousemen's Association, 1165 N. Clark Street, Chicago, IL 60610.

Council of Logistics Management, 2803 Butterfield Road, Suite 380, Oak Brook, IL 60521.

Institute of Packaging Professionals, Reston International Center, Suite 212, 1180 Sunrise Valley Drive, Reston, VA 22091.

International Material Management Society, 8720 Red Oak Blvd., Suite 224, Charlotte, NC 28217.

TRAFFIC AND TRANSPORTATION

Rapid changes have been occurring in the transport field in recent years. This trend is likely to continue, with more attention paid to the transportation function and the role of the transportation specialist. However these changes have not resulted in the publication of many newly revised books. The short list below makes no claim to being complete or to giving equal representation to each mode of transportation. Attention is called to the fact that most of these books are now more than five years old and that it will be important either to watch for more recent books or to supplement these with a monitoring of current periodicals in order to get a better picture of current industry changes and the latest regulations.

Except for two books below on traffic management, the reader is referred to the previous section on business logistics for books that discuss transportation and traffic management as an important component of the physical distribution function. Statistics on various modes of transportation are described in Chapter 6.

Frankel, Ernst G. *Management and Operations of American Shipping.* Boston: Auburn House Publishing Co., 1982. 260 pp.

This is a readable text that defines the concepts of the organization, management, and operations of American shipping, including cost analysis and finance. Frankel says, "While an attempt has been made to provide comprehensive coverage of the subject, equal attention is given to the discussion of novel and often provocative concepts, based on the belief that the problems facing American shipping, management and operations need new, imaginative, and possibly controversial solutions." A companion volume is *Regulation and Policies of American Shipping* (Auburn House Publishing Co., 1982, 347 pp.).

Harper, Donald V. *Transportation in America: Users, Carriers, Government.* 2d ed. Englewood Cliffs, NJ: Prentice-Hall, 1982. 645 pp.

A highly recommended (but now old) text on the U.S. intercity domestic freight and passenger transportation system presented "in the context of its being a decision-making problem and mainly from the transportation user's point of view." Thus it is organized around the three major decision-making segments: users of transportation service (shippers, receivers, and passengers); providers of transportation service (carriers); the government (federal, state, and local). Useful descriptive notes about added references are with each chapter.

Kendall, Lane C. *The Business of Shipping.* 5th ed. Centreville, MD: Cornell Maritime Press, 1986. 512 pp.

Kendall says his aim in preparing this analysis of the business of commercial shipping was to describe what transpires in the various divisions of ship owning and operating organization. His chapters thus discuss such topics as terminal management, the stevedore contract, ocean bill of lading, freight rates, schedules, bunkering, passenger cruises, and much more.

Lieb, Robert C. *Transportation.* 3d ed. Reston, VA: Reston Publishing Co., 1985. 486 pp.

A readable introduction to transportation topics with primary focus on intercity transportation. Four of its six sections examine: the five basic modes of intercity carriage; cost/demand/rate-making procedures; regulation and promotion; management problems and policy issues. A final section devotes attention to metropolitan transportation. Selected references are at end of chapters.

Locklin, D. Philip. *Economics of Transportation.* 7th ed. Homewood, IL: Irwin, 1972. 913 pp.

Although now very old, this has been the most widely used text on the economics of all modes of intercity transportation, well documented with bibliographies (now outdated) at end of each chapter. The coverage for rail transportation is in much greater depth than for other forms of transportation because Professor Locklin used the study of railroad rate theory and rate-making and the evolution of railroad regulations as background for his later discussions of variations found in other modes of transportation.

Morse, Leon W. *Practical Handbook of Industrial Traffic Management.* 7th ed. Washington, DC: Traffic Service Corporation, 1987. 642 pp.

Here is a good, practical introduction to industrial traffic management. Chapters cover all topics a traffic manager must be knowledgeable about, such as: freight classification, rates, routing; shipping documents, claims, expediting and tracing, shipping hazardous material; packaging, material handling, distribution, warehousing; government traffic, import-export traffic; managing the traffic department. Supplementary data in appendixes include a glossary, a list of publications and associations.

Richardson, J. D., and Julie F. Rodwell. *Essentials of Aviation Management.* 4th ed. Dubuque, IA: Kendall/Hunt, 1989. 528 pp.

Now revised entirely by Ms. Rodwell, this is a how-to book on how to run a successful small fixed-base operation in the national aviation system, with major emphasis on profit and positive cash flow. Chapters cover specific management functions as well as flight operations, aviation maintenance, safety, and more. Suggestions for further reading are with chapters; a glossary is at end.

Sampson, Roy J., Martin T. Farris and David L. Shrock. *Domestic Transportation: Practice, Theory, and Policy.* 6th ed. Boston: Houghton Mifflin, 1990. 747 pp.

As the subtitle indicates, this introductory text is a blend of theory and practice, meant for both business and economics students. It studies the various modes of domestic transportation as a whole rather than separately, and it brings together, rather than considering them separately, the traditional areas of transportation such as economics, physical distribution, and traffic management. This latest edition is substantially revised to incorporate significant recent changes, trends, and problems. Additional readings are at end of chapters. This note is based on examination of the 5th edition.

Taff, Charles A. *Commercial Motor Transportation.* 7th ed. Centreville, MD: Cornell Maritime Press, 1986. 434 pp.

A textbook on motor transportation and carrier management, with chapters on types of operations, equipment, financing, labor relations, insurance, pricing, regulations, and more. A selected bibliography is at end.

Tyworth, John E., Joseph L. Cavinato and C. John Langley, Jr. *Traffic Management: Planning, Operations, and Control.* Reading, MA: Addison-Wesley, 1987. 514 pp.

This introductory text emphasizes how to plan, organize, implement, and control traffic activities. The chapters are organized into three parts: the evolution, nature, and external environment; planning and operations; control. There is a practical orientation with frequent use of checklists, tables, forms, vignettes summarizing actual company experiences, and other practical examples. A useful bibliography, arranged by topic, is at end.

Wells, Alexander T. *Air Transportation: A Management Perspective.* 2d ed. Belmont, CA: Wadsworth Publishing Company, 1989. 556 pp.

Professor Wells' introductory, undergraduate text focuses primarily on providing a broad understanding of the management functions and organization of airlines. His material is arranged in four parts: an overview of aviation; structure and economics of the airlines; managerial aspects (including marketing, pricing, scheduling, fleet planning, labor relations, financing); the international scene. An appendix discusses career planning. Diagrams and tables are used throughout; suggested readings are with chapters.

Wood, Donald F., and James C. Johnson. *Contemporary Transportation.* 3d ed. New York: Macmillan, 1989. 547 pp.

A more recent introductory text than most described above, revised to reflect changes of the past decade in the nation's transportation system. Its four parts cover: introduction; the carrier modes; shipper issues (including physical distribution, inbound logistics, traffic management); carrier management (including managing transportation in the public sector, international transportation). Maps, diagrams, and other illustrations are used throughout; two case incidents and a bibliography are with each chapter.

Another recent introductory text, not seen for evaluation but written by three authoritative logistics professors, is *Transportation* by John J. Coyle, Edward J. Bardi and Joseph L. Cavinato (3d ed., St. Paul: West Publishing Co., 1990, 529 pp.).

TRAFFIC AND TRANSPORTATION BIBLIOGRAPHIES

Northwestern University. Transportation Center. *Current Literature in Traffic and Transportation.* Evanston, IL (monthly).

A subject listing of articles on the title subjects, compiled by the Center's Transportation Library. Useful primarily as a checklist because there is no cumulated issue. Publication is slow as of 1991.

Transportation Library (TLIB).

This is an online database covering published material on all modes of transportation (and on physical distribution and warehousing) that are in two transportation libraries which also prepare the periodic lists noted in this section: the Transportation Library at Northwestern University in Evanston, IL, and the Institute of Transportation Studies at the University of California, Berkeley. The database is part of the Transportation Research Information Services produced by the Transportation Research Board of the National Research Council, and it is available through DIALOG.

University of California. Institute of Transportation Studies. *Recent Transportation Literature for Planning and Engineering Librarians.* Compiled by Daniel Krummes and Michael Kleiber. Monticello, IL: Vance Bibliographies (monthly).

Based on a selection of the recent publications added to the ITS library, this monthly list is arranged by mode of transportation. It includes books, government documents, technical reports, conference proceedings, selected articles, with the emphasis on engineering aspects rather than on economics or business. Includes some foreign material. It is sold by Vance Bibliographies and issued as "Public Administration Series: Bibliography."

TRAFFIC AND TRANSPORTATION DICTIONARIES

For the *Transportation-Logistics Dictionary* see the section for "Logistics Dictionaries" in this chapter.

TRANSPORTATION FINANCIAL MANUALS

Carrier Reports. Lubec, ME (PO Box 39) (quarterly, with last issue an annual cumulation).

Tabular listing of financial data on the nation's leading carriers (truck and rail).

Moody's Transportation Manual. New York: Moody's Investors Service (annual, with weekly supplements).

This is the basic financial manual for all important modes of transportation, covering U.S. and larger Canadian companies. Information for companies having complete coverage usually includes: a brief corporate history; officers and directors; subsidiaries; material from annual report (CEO's letter to stockholders, independent auditor's report, management's discussion and analysis of financial conditions and results of operations); physical factors (statistics on mileage, freight tonnage, carloads and revenues, maintenance of ways and structures and equipment, employees and payroll); statistics from income statements, balance sheets, selected financial ratios; description of outstanding securities. Center blue pages contain a good selection of statistics for railroads and some data on other modes of transportation; also Moody's average of yields on railroad bonds and chronological list of maturing bonds and notes.

TRAFFIC AND TRANSPORTATION PERIODICALS

CCJ: Commercial Carrier Journal. Radnor, PA: Chilton Co. (monthly).

A trade journal for professional fleet management. The July issue each year contains a ranked list of "The Top 100" for-hire carriers; "the Second 100"; a section on "Industry Trends & Statistics"; a "Management Salary Survey." The April issue is a "Fleet Reference Annual," and the October issue is a "Buyers Guide," which is an alphabetical list of suppliers of products and services, with an index by product categories. Indexed in PTS/F&S.

Container News. Atlanta, GA: Communications Channels (monthly).

This is a trade journal for traffic managers and others involved in containerized and intermodal transportation and also for companies manufacturing equipment. An annual "World Container Ports Issue" (July) gives brief data on about 300 ports in the world including cargo volume.

Fairplay. Coulsdon, Surrey, Eng. and Germantown, NY (weekly).

Formerly titled *Fairplay International Shipping Weekly,* this contains recent developments and news about the commercial shipping industry, including shipbuilding, safety, port development, shipbrokering. In each issue are ship sales, prices (shipping company share prices, bunker prices in $, and prices of major foreign companies). "Newbuilding: A Quarterly Analysis of the World Shipbuilding Market" (see last issues in January, April, July, October) contains three lists: all world ships on order by 10 major vessel types; ships arranged by name of shipyard; completions reported during the past quarter.

Fairplay publishes separately a *World Ports Directory,* and an annual *Fairplay World Shipping Year Book.*

Traffic Management. Newton, MA: Cahners Publishing Co. (monthly).

Another trade journal, this one for buyers of transportation, services, and equipment. Usually contains about 6 feature articles plus news and regular departments. Each issue includes a page called "Economic Update" (charts and brief text) and a "Logistics Cost Index." Special annual features include: "Buyer's Guide" (March) which is described in the next section; "Annual Salary Survey" (April); "Annual World Commerce Issue" (September). Indexed in ABI/I, BPI, PTS/F&S, TI; full text in BRS, DATA-STAR, DIALOG, DOW JONES.

Traffic World. Washington, DC: Journal of Commerce (weekly).

A newsmagazine covering news of air, motor, rail, water, and freight (all kinds), as well as occasional sections dealing with computers, or international aspects. Each issue includes a digest of ICC orders and decisions as well as a "market report" (recent stock prices), and personal news. Indexed in BPI.

Transportation. Dordrecht, The Netherlands, and Norwell, MA: Kluwyer Academic Publishers (quarterly).

"An international journal devoted to the improvement of transportation planning and practice." Research papers are written in English and are concerned not only with policies and systems themselves, but also with their impacts on, and relationship with, other aspects of the environment. Includes book reviews. Indexed in ASTI.

Transportation Journal. Louisville, KY: American Society of Transportation and Logistics (quarterly).

A professional journal for scholarly papers on practices and techniques in a wide range of transportation and logistics topics, written principally by academic persons. Indexed in BPI, PAIS, TI.

Several other foreign or international periodicals are: *Canadian Transportation* (Don Mills, Ontario: Southam Business Information and Communications Group), a monthly with an annual "Transportation Guide" issue in July; *Intermodal Age International* (New York: Simmons-Boardman Publishing Corporation), a 6/yr. magazine of transport options; *Journal of Transport Economics and Policy* (Bath: London School of Economics and Political Science and University of Bath; 3/yr.), a professional journal; *Transport* (London; 10/yr.), official journal of the Chartered Institute of Transport; *Trans-*

port Reviews (London: Taylor & Francis Ltd.), a quarterly transnational, transdisciplinary journal, with each researched article including a bibliography and often an annotated list of suggestions for further reading.

TRAFFIC AND TRANSPORTATION DIRECTORIES

Official Directory of Industrial and Commercial Traffic Executives. New York: K-111 Press (annual).

A directory of U.S. and Canadian firms and their traffic executives. Includes also lists of transportation organizations; government departments, agencies, etc.; transportation and distribution consultants.

Thomas Register of American Manufacturers: Inbound Traffic Guide. New York: Thomas Publishing Company (annual).

The last volume of *Thomas Register* each year (vol.26 in 1992) contains an "Inbound Traffic Guide," which is a two-part directory of intermodal facilities and services. The "services" section lists the companies geographically under 18 classifications such as airlines, customs house brokers, insurance liability (where applicable), ocean carriers, ports, railroads. The "company profiles" section gives, for each firm when available, subsidiaries or divisions, names of company officials, number of employees, fax/telex/twx numbers, major areas served, other services, and special equipment. Asset ratings are given for companies in both parts.

Traffic Management. "Buyer's Guide" (annual, March issue).

A useful directory of transportation services for airfreight, motor carriers, railroads and intermodal, steamships and barges, including names of airlines, motor carriers, railroads, steamship lines, as well as lists of major North American ports, shippers' associations and agents, industry organizations, fleet equipment, and dock & warehousing equipment.

For the many directories covering specific modes of transportation consult the guides to directories listed in Chapter 7.

TRAFFIC AND TRANSPORTATION ASSOCIATIONS

These are just a few of many associations. For others relating to specific modes of transportation consult the *Encyclopedia of Associations* described in Chapter 3.

American Society of Transportation and Logistics, PO Box 33095, Louisville, KY 40232.

American Trucking Associations, 2200 Mill Road, Alexandria, VA 22314.

Association of American Railroads, American Railroads Building, 50 F Street, N.W., Washington, DC 20001.

Intermodal Transportation Association, 6410 Kenilworth Ave., Suite 108, Riverdale, MD 20737.

International Federation of Freight Forwarders Associations, 24 Baumackerstrasse, Postfach 8493, CH-8050, Zurich, Switzerland.

National Industrial Transportation League, 1090 Vermont Avenue, N.W., Washington, DC 20005.

21

A BASIC BOOKSHELF

In assembling a reference collection for a personal, business, or small public library one should start with a few essential works that are comprehensive in coverage and basic to almost any kind of business. This chapter suggests such a list and, although it is aimed more at a beginning collection for a company, it can easily be adapted for a small public library or to meet the more limited needs of a personal library.

It is assumed that all company collections will have the following: (1) a good dictionary and thesaurus (see Chapter 1); (2) an atlas—not necessarily an expensive one, but an up-to-date edition with print that is easy to read; (3) both a local newspaper and one for a major metropolitan area; (4) a weekly newsmagazine—either *Newsweek* or *Time;* (5) telephone directories for the immediate vicinity and perhaps for several large U.S. cities; (6) a zip code directory; (7) hotel and airline guides, if company personnel travel often; (8) a secretary's handbook (see chapter 13); (9) Reports 10-K and Annual Reports, at least, for competitor companies; (10) a small selection of trade journals, important books, and reference sources on the company's industry or business; and (11) a source for identifying articles in business journals, such as *ABI/INFORM* on CD-ROM. Each source below is described elsewhere in this book, where mention is made for those also available online or on CD-ROM. (Check the index for page references.)

In this chapter we are including prices so that you can estimate what such a basic reference bookshelf would cost. Don't forget to factor into your estimate the various items noted above, especially no. 10; also these are U.S. prices as of 1991 and are bound to change.

Almanacs and Information Yearbooks

The Business One Irwin Business and Investment Almanac. Homewood, IL: Business One Irwin (annual). $29.95, paper.

Statesman's Year-Book. New York: St. Martin's Press (annual). $69.95.

World Almanac & Book of Facts. New York: Newspaper Enterprise Association (annual). $16.95 ($7.95, paper).

Europa World Year Book. London: Europa Publications, Ltd. 2 volumes (annual). $495. More specialized but worth considering for its comprehensive coverage on all countries.

Bibliographies

Directories in Print. Detroit: Gale Research, Inc.; 2 volumes (annual). $250, and interim supplement, $155; or *Guide to American Directories.* Nyack, NY: Todd Publications; biennial). $75.

Encyclopedia of Business Information Sources. 8th ed. Detroit: Gale Research, Inc., 1990. 952 pp. $235. And Supplement, 1991. $90.

Harvard Business School Core Collection: Author, Title and Subject Guide. Boston (annual). $50.00 (plus postage); also their *Recent Additions to Baker Library* (monthly). $25.

Statistics Sources. Detroit: Gale Research, Inc. 2 volumes (annual). $325.

Biographical Dictionaries

Who's Who in America. Chicago: Marquis Who's Who. 2 volumes (biennial). $335.

Who's Who in Finance and Industry. Chicago: Marquis Who's Who (biennial). $210.

Some companies may feel they can do without the above volumes if they need only brief facts about executives. Those can be found either in *Standard & Poor's Register of Corporations, Directors and Executives, Vol. 2: Directors and Executives* (annual, listed below); or *Reference Book of Corporate Managements,* published annually in four volumes by Dun & Bradstreet Information Services ($725).

Dictionaries

Ammer, Christine, and Dean S. Ammer. *Dictionary of Business and Economics.* Rev. and expanded edition. New York: Free Press, 1984. 507 pp. $40.

Encyclopedia of Banking and Finance. 9th ed., rev. and exp. by Charles J. Woelfel. Rolling Meadows, IL: Bankers Publishing Co., 1991. 1,097 pp. $95.

Friedman, Jack P. *Dictionary of Business Terms.* New York: Barron's, 1987. 650 pp. $9.95, paper.

Johannsen, Hano, and G. Terry Page. *International Dictionary of Management.* 4th ed. East Brunswick, NJ: Nichols/GP Publishing, 1990. 359 pp. $42.50. Published also in London by Kogan Page.

McGraw-Hill Dictionary of Modern Economics. 3d ed. New York: McGraw-Hill, 1983. 632 pp. $59.95.

Directories of Companies

Every collection should have one of the following directories:

Dun & Bradstreet Information Services. *Top 50,000 Companies.* Parsippany, NJ (annual). $450. Some companies may want to consider instead the much more comprehensive *Million Dollar Directory* (5 volumes, annual; $1,250) which provides information on more than 160,000 U.S. companies, both public and private.

Standard & Poor's Register of Corporations, Directors and Executives. New York. 3 volumes and cumulated supplements. $498, lease basis.

Consideration should be given to purchasing a comprehensive directory of U.S. manufacturing firms, either *Thomas Register of American Manufacturers* (26 volumes, annual), $240, plus postage; or the *U.S. Industrial Directory* (3 volumes, annual), $160; also a directory of industrial companies for the state in which your company is located.

If your company has frequent inquiries about the names of leading foreign businesses, you may also want:

Dun & Bradstreet Information Services. *Principal International Businesses.* New York (annual). $610.

Directories of Associations

Select one of the following two depending upon whether your need is just for trade and professional associations or for a more extensive compilation of all kinds of associations:

Encyclopedia of Associations. Vol. 1 in 3 parts. Detroit: Gale Research, Inc. 3 volumes (annual). $320.

National Trade and Professional Associations of the United States. Washington, DC: Columbia Books, Inc. (annual). $55, paper.

Directories of Government Organizations

United States Government Manual. Washington, DC: Office of the Federal Register, General Services Administration (annual). $21, paper.

If your firm has frequent communication with Congressional staff you may prefer to have the annual *Congressional Staff Directory.* $64.

Directories of Periodicals

Select one of the following:

Gale Directory of Publications and Broadcast Media. Detroit: Gale Research, Inc. 3 volumes (annual, and interim supplement). $265.

Standard Periodical Directory. New York: Oxbridge Communications, Inc. (annual). $395.

Guide to Directories

Directories in Print. Detroit: Gale Research, Inc. 2 volumes (annual). $250.

Financial Manuals

Moody's Investors Service. *Moody's Industrial Manual.* New York: 2 volumes (annual). $1,150 (including semiweekly updates).

Statistical Compilations

United Nations. *Statistical Yearbook.* New York. $150; also their *Monthly Bulletin of Statistics.* $450.

U.S. Bureau of the Census. *Statistical Abstract of the United States.* Washington, DC: U.S. Printing Office (annual). $34 ($28, paper).

U.S. Bureau of Economic Analysis, Department of Commerce. *Business Statistics.* Washington, DC: U.S. Government Printing Office (biennial). $16, paper.

U.S. International Trade Administration. *U.S. Industrial Outlook.* Washington, DC: U.S. Government Printing Office (annual). $28, paper.

Current Statistical Monthlies

Board of Governors of the Federal Reserve System. *Federal Reserve Bulletin.* Washington, DC. $25.

U.S. Bureau of Economic Analysis, Department of Commerce. *Survey of Current Business.* Washington, DC: U.S. Government Printing Office. $23, or $52, if mailed first class.

U.S. Bureau of Labor Statistics. *Monthly Labor Review.* Washington, DC: U.S. Government Printing Office. $24.

U.S. Council of Economic Advisers. *Economic Indicators.* Washington, DC: U.S. Government Printing Office. $28.

Handbooks

Handbooks are such useful compilations of concise data on specific management functions that any (over 900 pages) in this book is worth considering for a small business collection. If you start by acquiring only those cited below, you may reduce the number purchased by choosing between the handbooks by Carmichael or Kay (in accounting), those by Altman or Logue (in finance), and the handbooks by Fallon or Mali (in management). These have somewhat similar coverage and you may need only one of the two. Check the annotations appearing elsewhere before making a choice.

Accounting

Carmichael, D.R., Steven B. Lilien and Martin Mellman, eds. *Accountants' Handbook.* 7th ed. New York: Wiley, 1991. 1 volume (various pagings). $115.

Kay, Robert S., and Gerald Searfoss, eds. *Handbook of Accounting and Auditing.* 2d ed. Boston: Warren, Gorham & Lamont, 1989. 1 volume (various pagings). $125. And periodic updates, $60.

Finance

Altman, Edward E., ed. *Handbook of Corporate Finance.* New York: Wiley, 1986. 1 volume (various pagings). $95. And a companion volume, *Handbook of Financial Markets and Institutions.* 6th ed., Wiley, 1987. 1 volume (various pagings). $95.

Levine, Sumner N., ed. *The Financial Analyst's Handbook.* Homewood, IL: Dow Jones Irwin, 1988. 1,870 pp. $80.

Logue, Dennis E., ed. *Handbook of Modern Finance.* Boston: Warren, Gorham & Lamont, 1990. 1 volume (various pagings). $110. And annual "Update," $44.50.

Human Resources

Famularo, Joseph J., ed. *Handbook of Human Resources Administration.* 2d ed. New York: McGraw-Hill, 1986. 1 volume (various pagings). $89.95.

Management

Fallon, William K., ed. *AMA Management Handbook.* 2d ed. New York: AMACOM, 1983. 1 volume (almost 1,600 pp.). $95.

Glass, Harold E., ed. *Handbook of Business Strategy.* 2d ed. Boston: Warren, Gorham & Lamont, 1991. 1 volume (various pagings). And a Supplementary Yearbook. $98.

Mali, Paul, ed. *Management Handbook: Operating Guidelines, Techniques, and Practices.* New York: Wiley, 1981. 1,522 pp. $95.

Walter, Ingo, and Tracy Murray, eds. *Handbook of International Management.* New York: Wiley, 1988. 1 volume (various pagings). $85. And a companion volume, *Handbook of International Business.* Wiley, 1988. 1 volume (various pagings). $90.

Marketing

Buell, Victor P., ed. *Handbook of Modern Marketing.* 2d ed. New York: McGraw-Hill, 1986. 1 volume (various pagings). $89.95.

Steinbrink, John P., ed. *The Dartnell Sales Manager's Handbook.* 14th ed. Chicago: Dartnell Corporation, 1989. 1,272 pp. $49.95.

Production

Aljian's Purchasing Handbook. P. V. Farrell, Coordinating Ed. 4th ed. New York: McGraw-Hill, 1982. 1 volume (various pagings). $74.95. New edition is scheduled for 1992.

White, John A. *Production Handbook.* 4th ed. New York: Wiley, 1987. 1 volume (various pagings). $95.

Public Relations

Lesley, Philip, ed. *Lesley's Handbook of Public Relations and Communications.* 4th ed., rev. and updated. Chicago: Probus Publishing, 1991. 874 pp. $39.95.

Periodicals and Newspapers

The starred (*) periodicals are of primary importance. Those designated with an (R) are included because their book review sections are of special interest. Prices are for an annual subscriptions in U.S.

Accounting Review (R). $90.
Bankers Magazine (Boston) (*). $85.
Barron's (*). $109.
Business and Society Review (R).
  $56.
Business Week (*). $44.95.
Economist (*). $110.
Euromoney. $285.
European Management Journal (R).
  $76.50 ($176.50 for institutions).
The Executive (Ada, OH) (R). $38.
Financial Executive. $40.
Financial Times newspaper (*).
  $420.
Forbes (*). $52.
Fortune (*). $49.95
Harvard Business Review (*). $75.

INC. $25.
Industrial and Labor Relations Review (R). $22. ($36 for institutions).
Institutional Investor (*). $265.
International Management. $65.
Journal of Business Strategy (*). $92.
Journal of Marketing (*R). $60.
Management Accounting. $115 to
  nonmembers.
Management Review (R). $45.
Personnel Journal. $50.
Personnel Psychology (R). $50.
Sales & Marketing Management (primarily for its special issues). $48.
Sloan Management Review (R). $50.
Wall Street Journal (*). $139.

A COMPANY LIBRARY

Once a firm has acquired this minimal collection it must make some arrangement to keep the periodicals and reference books up-to-date, since a "dead" collection is not useful for long. A small collection can be managed by almost any bright, imaginative employee with a flair for organizing material and an interest in helping people. If this arrangement proves successful, the company may consider increasing the growing collection to a full-fledged library. When this decision is made the services of a trained librarian become important.

Although a good company library is not an inexpensive proposition, experience has proved it can result in a significant saving for the firm. The following may be of interest to company managers considering such a library:

Christianson, Elin B., David E. King, and Janet L. Ahrensfeld. *Special Libraries: A Guide for Management.* 3d ed. Washington, DC: Special Libraries Association, 1991. 92 pp.

This is a useful pamphlet for management and for others who need information or counsel on establishing or evaluating special libraries and information services. It discusses what a special library is, how to start one, what resources are required (staff, space and equipment, budget). This new edition reflects recent developments in information management and increasing use of computer technology. Included is a list of suggested readings on planning and operating a special library.

Meant more for librarians and library students is *Special Libraries and Information Centers: An Introductory Text* on the organization and management of a special library by Ellis Mount (2d ed., Special Libraries Association, 1991, 230 pp.). Librarians just beginning to work in a corporate library may want to see *Special Libraries at Work* by Elizabeth Ferguson and Emily Mobley (Hamden, CT: Shoe String Press, 1984, 208 pp.). Yet another book, primarily for persons with no library training, is

Starting, Managing, and Promoting the Small Library by Robert Berk (Armonk, NY: M.E. Sharpe, 1989, 176 pp.).

Thus one comes full circle in this guide to business information sources by returning to the library as the basic source for information and to the librarian as a knowledgeable, interested individual who wants to help people make the fullest use of the vast and varied materials now available.

SUBJECT INDEX

This is somewhat of an analytical subject index because it cites not only all basic subjects covered but it also indexes many selected topics or data that are not whole books but rather are mentioned in annotations as being included in the reference source described. Several examples are: foreign exchange rates, gross domestic product (GDP), initial public offerings, money market rates, stock price indexes. These are identified in this index by use of the letter "n" after a page number. When you find such a citation, check the annotations on that page for the one or more books that include the topic indexed. If you want a list of all the databases mentioned in this book, check under headings "CD-ROMS" and "Computerized information services: specific." If you want reference to all of the ranked lists of largest companies, including the many appearing as annual issues of business periodicals, check under the heading "Corporations, ranked lists of largest."

When information on a specific subject or topic is cited as being found on more than just one page, the page number in boldface is the primary reference. See, for example, the entry for "Consumer price index, 60n, 71n, **129–131**, 543–544n."

AUTHOR/TITLE INDEX

In this index, the letter "n" after a page number indicates that the author or title does not appear as a separate entry on that page but rather is mentioned either in a general note or in an annotation to another book. An example is "Accounting and Business Research, 334n." When you find such a reference, check the annotations on that page for the entry mentioning the author or title you seek. Also in this index, when an author or title is mentioned on more than just one page, the page number in boldface is the primary reference. An example is "Journal of Marketing, 478, **487**, 587."